handbook of PEDIATRICS

ELEVENTH EDITION

handbook of
PEDIATRICS

HENRY K. SILVER, MD
Professor of Pediatrics
University of Colorado School of Medicine
Denver, Colorado

C. HENRY KEMPE, MD
Professor of Pediatrics and Microbiology
University of Colorado School of Medicine
Denver, Colorado

HENRY B. BRUYN, MD
Clinical Professor of Medicine and Pediatrics
University of California School of Medicine
San Francisco, California
Director of Child Health
and Disability Prevention
City and County of San Francisco

Lange Medical Publications
Los Altos, California

1975

A Concise Medical Library for Practitioner and Student

Handbook of Pediatrics, 11th ed. $7.50

Current Medical Diagnosis & Treatment 1975 (annual revision). Edited by M.A. Krupp and M.J. Chatton. 1044 pp.	1975
Current Pediatric Diagnosis & Treatment, 3rd ed. Edited by C.H. Kempe, H.K. Silver, and D. O'Brien. 1020 pp, *illus.*	1974
Current Surgical Diagnosis & Treatment, 2nd ed. Edited by J.E. Dunphy and L.W. Way. About 1140 pp, *illus.*	1975
Review of Physiological Chemistry, 14th ed. H.A. Harper. 545 pp, *illus.*	1973
Review of Medical Physiology, 6th ed. W.F. Ganong. 578 pp, *illus.*	1973
Review of Medical Microbiology, 11th ed. E. Jawetz, J.L. Melnick, and E.A. Adelberg. 528 pp, *illus.*	1974
Review of Medical Pharmacology, 4th ed. F.H. Meyers, E. Jawetz, and A. Goldfien. 721 pp, *illus.*	1974
General Urology, 7th ed. D.R. Smith. 436 pp, *illus.*	1972
General Ophthalmology, 7th ed. D. Vaughan and T. Asbury. 334 pp, *illus.*	1974
Correlative Neuroanatomy & Functional Neurology, 15th ed. J.G. Chusid. 429 pp, *illus.*	1973
Principles of Clinical Electrocardiography, 8th ed. M.J. Goldman. 400 pp, *illus.*	1973
Handbook of Psychiatry, 3rd ed. Edited by P. Solomon and V.D. Patch. 706 pp.	1974
Handbook of Surgery, 5th ed. Edited by J.L. Wilson. 877 pp, *illus.*	1973
Handbook of Obstetrics & Gynecology, 5th ed. R.C. Benson. 770 pp, *illus.*	1974
Physician's Handbook, 17th ed. M.A. Krupp, N.J. Sweet, E. Jawetz, E.G. Biglieri, and R.L. Roe. 728 pp, *illus.*	1973
Handbook of Medical Treatment, 14th ed. Edited by M.J. Chatton. 640 pp.	1974
Handbook of Poisoning: Diagnosis & Treatment, 8th ed. R.H. Dreisbach. 517 pp.	1974

Table of Contents

Preface

In the Eleventh Edition of this Handbook the authors have again made extensive revisions and additions, but the format and objectives have remained the same: to present to the practicing physician and medical student a concise and readily available digest of the material necessary for the diagnosis and management of pediatric disorders. We continue to stress the clinical aspects of the subjects covered - established concepts of pediatric diagnosis and treatment over the purely theoretical or experimental - but have included pertinent summaries of physiologic principles and recent advances as they apply to our knowledge of the various conditions that are discussed.

This Handbook is not intended to be used as a substitute for the more complete pediatric texts and reference works but as a supplement to them; however, recent advances have been included wherever they have seemed to the authors to deserve inclusion in a handbook of this type.

Because of the limitations of space, certain aspects of pediatrics have been severely condensed or omitted entirely. For the same reason, no attempt has been made to give complete source references. The authors realize that the concise format used tends toward oversimplification and dogmatism, but it was thought necessary to use this technic throughout most of the book for the sake of clarity and brevity.

We have been extremely pleased with the continued success this Handbook has enjoyed among medical students, members of house staffs, practicing physicians, and our colleagues in the Pediatrics Departments at medical schools both here and abroad. Spanish, Greek, Serbo-Croatian, Italian, Dutch, and Portuguese editions have been published, and Japanese and Turkish editions are now in preparation.

The authors wish to reaffirm their gratitude to all those who assisted in the preparation of the first ten editions of the Handbook. During the preparation of this edition we resubmitted many chapters to our colleagues for comment and criticism. Our thanks go to the following physicians for their generous contributions of time and talent: Charles August, Frederic W. Bruhn, Reuben Dubois, Donald Ferlic, William Frankenburg, Stephen Goodman, Ronald Gotlin, Charlene Holton, John Lilly, Rowle McIntosh, Frank Morriss, Gerhard Nellhaus, Donough O'Brien, David Pearlman, Arthur Robinson, Barry Rumack, Barton Schmitt, Michael Simmons, Morris Witkin, Robert Wolfe, and many others.

We wish also to take this opportunity to thank our readers throughout the world who have contributed useful suggestions.

Henry K. Silver
C. Henry Kempe
Henry B. Bruyn

Denver, Colorado
Berkeley, California
March, 1975

Metric System Prefixes
(Small Measurement)

In keeping with the decision of several scientific societies to
employ a uniform system of metric nomenclature, the following
prefixes have become standard in many medical texts and journals.

k	kilo	10^3
c	centi	10^{-2}
m	milli	10^{-3}
μ	micro	10^{-6}
n	nano	10^{-9}
	(formerly	
	millimicro, $m\mu$)	
p	pico	10^{-12}
	(formerly	
	micromicro, $\mu\mu$)	
f	femto	10^{-15}
a	atto	10^{-18}

Some Examples Used in This Handbook

Measurement	New Style	Formerly
10^{-6} meter	μm. (micrometer)	μ (micron)
10^{-9} gram	ng. (nanogram)	$m\mu$g. (millimicrogram)
10^{-12} gram	pg. (picogram)	$\mu\mu$g. (micromicrogram)
10^{-15} liter	fl. (femtoliter)	cu. μ (cubic micron)

1...
Pediatric History & Physical Examination

HISTORY

General Considerations in Taking the History.

For many pediatric problems, the history is the most important single factor in arriving at a correct diagnosis.

A. Interpretation of History: The presenting complaint as given by the informant may be a minor part of the problem. One should be prepared to go on, if necessary, to a more productive phase of the interview, which may have little or no apparent relationship to the complaint as originally presented.

B. Source of History: The history should be obtained from the mother or from whoever is responsible for the care of the child. Much valuable information can be obtained also from the child himself.

C. Direction of Questioning: Allow the informant to present the problem as she sees it; then fill in with necessary past and family history and other pertinent information. The record should also include whatever may be disclosed concerning the parents' temperaments, attitudes, and methods of rearing children.

Questions should not be prying, especially about subjects likely to be associated with feelings of guilt or shame; however, the informant should be allowed to volunteer information of this nature when she is prepared to do so. What worried parents most about child's illness? What did they expect would happen as a result of the illness? What do they expect will be done? What do they believe caused the illness? What are their basic worries? Hopes?

Is is useful for parents to have some idea of the doctor's diagnostic and therapeutic considerations and of the possible course of the child's illness.

D. Recorded History: The history should be a detailed, clear, and chronologic record of significant information. It should include the parents' interpretation of the present difficulty, and should indicate the results they expect from consultation.

E. Psychotherapeutic Effects: In many cases the interview and history-taking is the first stage in the psychotherapeutic management of the patient and his parents. The history-taker should introduce himself. Avoid being hurried or perfunctory. Avoid technical or ambiguous language. Recognize that socio-economic and cultural background, education, and knowledge influence the physician-patient communication.

HISTORY OUTLINE: GENERAL

The following outline should be modified and adapted as appropriate for the age of the child and the condition for which he is brought to the physician:

Name, address, home phone number, sex, date and place of birth, race, religion, nationality, referred by, father's and mother's names, father's and mother's occupations, business telephone numbers.

Date of this visit. Hospital or case number.

Previous entries: Dates, diagnoses, therapy, other data.

Summary of correspondence or other information from physicians, schools, etc.

Presenting Complaint (P. C.).

Patient's or parent's own brief account of the complaint and its duration.

Present Illness (P. I.) (or Interval History).

When was the patient last entirely well?

How and when did the disturbance start?

Health immediately before the illness.

Progress of disease; order and date of onset of new symptoms.

Specific symptoms and physical signs that may have developed.

Pertinent negative data obtained by direct questioning.

Aggravating and alleviating factors.

Significant medical attention and medications given and over what period.

In acute infections, statement of type and degree of exposure and interval since exposure.

For the well child, determine factors of significance and general condition since last visit.

Examiner's opinion about the reliability of the informant.

Previous Health.

A. Antenatal: Health of mother during pregnancy. Medical supervision, diet, infections such as rubella, etc., other illnesses, vomiting, bleeding, toxemia, other complications; Rh typing and serology, pelvimetry, medications, x-ray procedure.

B. Natal: Duration of pregnancy, birth weight, kind and duration of labor, type of delivery, sedation and anesthesia (if known), state of infant at birth, resuscitation required, onset of respiration, first cry.

C. Neonatal: Apgar score; color, cyanosis, pallor, jaundice, cry, twitchings, excessive mucus, paralysis, convulsions, fever, hemorrhage, congenital abnormalities, birth injury. Difficulty in sucking, rashes, excessive weight loss, feeding difficulties.

Development.

First raised head, rolled over, sat alone, pulled up, walked with help, walked alone, talked (meaningful words; sentences).

(1) Urinary continence during night; during day.

(2) Control of feces.

(3) Comparison of development with that of siblings and parents.

(4) Any period of failure to grow or unusual growth.

(5) School grade, quality of work.

Nutrition.
  A. Breast or Formula: Type, duration, major formula changes, time of weaning, difficulties.
  B. Supplements: Vitamins: type, amount, duration. Iron.
  C. "Solid" Foods: When introduced, how taken, types.
  D. Appetite: Food likes and dislikes, idiosyncrasies or allergies, reaction of child to eating.

Illnesses.
  A. Infections: Age, types, number, severity.
  B. Contagious Diseases: Age, complications following measles, rubella, chickenpox, mumps, pertussis, diphtheria, scarlet fever.
  C. Others.

Immunization and Tests.
  Indicate type, number, reactions, age of child.
  A. Inoculations: Diphtheria, tetanus, pertussis, measles, poliomyelitis, typhoid, mumps, others.
  B. Oral Immunizations: Poliomyelitis.
  C. Percutaneous Vaccination: Smallpox ("take" or not? Scar?).
  D. Recall immunizations ("boosters").
  E. Serum Injections: Passive immunizations.
  F. Tests: Tuberculin Schick serology others

Operations.
  Type, age, complications; reasons for operations; apparent response of child.

Accidents and Injuries.
  Nature, severity, sequelae.

Family History.
  (1) Father and mother (age and condition of health). What sort of people do the parents characterize themselves as being?
  (2) Marital relationships. Little information should be sought at first interview; most information will be obtained indirectly.
  (3) Siblings. Age, condition of health, significant previous illnesses and problems.
  (4) Stillbirths, miscarriages, abortions; age at death and cause of death of immediate members of family.
  (5) Tuberculosis, allergy, blood dyscrasias, mental or nervous diseases, diabetes, cardiovascular diseases, kidney disease, hypertension, rheumatic fever, neoplastic diseases, congenital abnormalities, cancer, convulsive disorders, others.
  (6) Health of contacts.

Personality History.
  A. Relations With Other Children: Independent or clinging to mother; negativistic, shy, submissive; separation from parents; hobbies; easy or difficult to get along with. How does child relate to others? Physical deformities affecting personality.
  B. School Progress: Class, grades, nursery school, special aptitudes, reaction to school.

Social History.
  A. Family: Income; home (size, number of rooms, living condi-

tions, sleeping facilities), type of neighborhood, access to playground. Localities in which patient has lived. Who cares for patient if mother works?
B. School: Public or private, overcrowded, type of students.
C. Insurance: Blue Cross, Blue Shield, or other health insurance?

Habits.

A. Eating: Appetite, food dislikes, how fed, attitudes of child and parents to eating.
B. Sleeping: Hours, disturbances, snoring, restlessness, dreaming, nightmares.
C. Exercise and play.
D. Urinary, bowel.
E. Disturbances: Excessive bedwetting, masturbation, thumb-sucking, nailbiting, breath-holding, temper tantrums, tics, nervousness, undue thirst, others. Similar disturbances among members of family. School problems (learning, perceptual).

System Review.

A. Ears, Nose and Throat: Frequent colds, sore throat, sneezing, stuffy nose, discharge, postnasal drip, mouth breathing, snoring, otitis, hearing, adenitis, allergies.
B. Teeth: Age of eruption of deciduous and permanent; number at one year; comparison with siblings.
C. Cardiorespiratory: Frequency and nature of disturbances. Dyspnea, chest pain, cough, sputum, wheeze, expectoration, cyanosis, edema, syncope, tachycardia.
D. Gastrointestinal: Vomiting, diarrhea, constipation, type of stools, abdominal pain or discomfort, jaundice.
E. Genitourinary: Enuresis, dysuria, frequency, polyuria, pyuria, hematuria, character of stream, vaginal discharge, menstrual history, bladder control, abnormalities of penis or testes.
F. Neuromuscular: Headache, nervousness, dizziness, tingling, convulsions, habit spasms, ataxia, muscle or joint pains, postural deformities, exercise tolerance, gait.
G. Endocrine: Disturbances of growth, excessive fluid intake, polyphagia, goiter, thyroid disease.
H. Special senses.
I. General: Unusual weight gain or loss, fatigue, skin color or texture, other abnormalities of skin, temperature sensitivity, mentality, bleeding tendency, pattern of growth (record previous heights and weights on appropriate graphs). Time and pattern of pubescence. Hyperactivity. Attention span.

The Health Record.

Every patient should have a comprehensive medical and health record containing all pertinent information. The parents should be given a summary of this record (including data regarding illnesses, operations, idiosyncrasies, sensitivities, heights, weights, special medications, and immunizations).

PHYSICAL EXAMINATION

A complete systematic examination should be performed at regular intervals in every child. One should not restrict the examination to those portions of the body considered to be involved on the basis of the presenting complaint.

Approaching the Child.

Adequate time should be spent in becoming acquainted with the child and allowing him to become acquainted with the examiner. The child should be treated as an individual whose feelings and sensibilities are well developed, and the examiner's conduct should be appropriate to the age of the child. A friendly manner, quiet voice, and a slow and easy approach will help to facilitate the examination. If the examiner is not able to establish a friendly relationship but feels that it is important to proceed with the examination, he should do so in an orderly, systematic manner in the hope that the child will then accept the inevitable.

The examiner should wash his hands in warm water before examining the child and should be certain that his hands are warm.

Observation of Patient.

Although the very young child may not be able to speak, one still may receive much information from him by being observant and receptive. The total evaluation of the child should include impressions obtained from the time the child first enters until he leaves; it should not be based solely on the period during which the patient is on the examining table.

In general, more information is obtained by careful inspection than from any of the other methods of examination.

Holding for Examination.
  A. Before Six Months: The examining table is usually well tolerated.
  B. Six Months to Three to Four Years: Most of the examination may be performed while the child is held in the mother's lap or over her shoulder. Certain parts of the examination can sometimes be done more easily with the child in the prone position or held against the mother so that he cannot see the examiner.

Removal of Clothing.

Clothes should be removed gradually to prevent chilling and to avoid the development of resistance in a shy child. In order to save time and to avoid creating unpleasant associations with the doctor in the child's mind, undressing the child and taking his temperature are best performed by the mother. The physician should respect the marked degree of modesty that may be exhibited by some children.

Sequence of Examination.

In most cases it is best to begin the examination of the young child with an area that is least likely to be associated with pain or discomfort. The ears and throat should usually be examined last. The examiner should develop a regular sequence of examination that can be adapted as required by special circumstances.

Painful Procedures.

Before performing a disagreeable, painful, or upsetting examination, the examiner should tell the child (1) what is likely to happen and how he can assist, (2) that the examination is necessary, and (3) that it will be performed as rapidly and as painlessly as possible.

GENERAL PHYSICAL EXAMINATION
(See also Chapter 8.)

Temperature, pulse rate, and respiratory rate (T. P. R.); blood pressure, weight, and height. The weight should be recorded at each visit; the height should be determined at monthly intervals during the first year, at three-month intervals in the second year, and twice a year thereafter. The height, weight, and head circumference of the child should be compared with standard charts and the approximate percentiles recorded. Multiple measurements at intervals are of much greater value than single ones since they give information regarding the pattern of growth that cannot be determined by single measurements.

Rectal Temperatures.

During the first years of life the temperature should be taken by rectum (except for routine temperatures of the premature infant, where axillary temperatures are sufficiently accurate). The child should be laid face down across the mother's lap and held firmly with her left forearm placed flat across his back; with the left thumb and index finger she can separate the buttocks and insert the lubricated thermometer with the right hand. Activity, apprehension, and fear may elevate the temperature.

Rectal temperature may be 1° F. higher than oral temperature. A rectal temperature up to 100° F. (37.8° C.) may be considered normal in a child.

General Appearance.

Does the child appear well or ill? Degree of prostration; degree of cooperation; state of comfort, nutrition, and consciousness; abnormalities; gait, posture, and coordination; estimate of intelligence; reaction to parents, physician, and examination; nature of cry and degree of activity; facies and facial expression.

Skin.

Color (cyanosis, jaundice, pallor, erythema), texture, eruptions, hydration, edema, hemorrhagic manifestations, scars, dilated vessels and direction of blood flow, hemangiomas, café-au-lait areas and nevi, Mongolian (blue-black) spots, pigmentation, turgor, elasticity, and subcutaneous nodules. Striae and wrinkling may indicate rapid weight gain or loss. Sensitivity, hair distribution, character, and desquamation.

Practical notes:
1. Loss of turgor, especially of the calf muscles and skin over the abdomen, is evidence of dehydration.
2. The soles and palms are often bluish and cold in early infancy; this is of no significance.

3. The degree of anemia cannot be determined reliably by inspection, since pallor (even in the newborn) may be normal and not due to anemia.
4. To demonstrate pitting edema in a child it may be necessary to exert prolonged pressure.
5. A few small pigmented nevi are commonly found, particularly in older children.
6. Spider nevi occur in about one-sixth of children under five years of age and almost half of older children.
7. "Mongolian spots" (large, flat black or blue-black areas) are frequently present over the lower back and buttocks; they have no pathologic significance.
8. Cyanosis will not be evident unless at least 5 Gm. of reduced hemoglobin are present; therefore, it develops less easily in an anemic child.
9. Carotenemia is usually most prominent over the palms and soles and around the nose, and spares the conjunctivas.

Lymph Nodes.

Location, size, sensitivity, mobility, consistency. One should routinely attempt to palpate suboccipital, preauricular, anterior cervical, posterior cervical, submaxillary, sublingual, axillary, epitrochlear, and inguinal lymph nodes.

Practical notes:

1. Enlargement of the lymph nodes occurs much more readily in children than in adults.
2. Small inguinal lymph nodes are palpable in almost all healthy young children. Small, mobile, nontender shotty nodes are commonly found as residua of previous infection.

Head.

Size, shape, circumference, asymmetry, cephalhematoma, bossae, craniotabes, control, molding, bruit, fontanel (size, tension, number, abnormally late or early closure), sutures, dilated veins, scalp, hair (texture, distribution, parasites), face, transillumination.

Practical notes:

1. The head is measured at its greatest circumference; this is usually at the midforehead anteriorly and around to the most prominent portion of the occiput posteriorly. The ratio of head circumference to circumference of the chest or abdomen is usually of little value.
2. Fontanel tension is best determined with the quiet child in the sitting position.
3. Slight pulsations over the anterior fontanel may occur in normal infants.
4. Although bruits may be heard over the temporal areas in normal children, the possibility of an existing abnormality should be excluded.
5. Craniotabes may be found in the normal newborn infant (especially the premature) and for the first two to four months.
6. A positive Macewen's sign ("cracked pot" sound when skull is percussed with one finger) may be present normally as long as the fontanel is open.

7. Transillumination of the skull can be performed by means of a flashlight with a sponge rubber collar so that it forms a tight fit when held against the head.

Face.

Symmetry, paralysis, distance between nose and mouth, depth of nasolabial folds, bridge of nose, distribution of hair, size of mandible, swellings, hypertelorism, Chvostek's sign, tenderness over sinuses.

Eyes.

Photophobia, visual acuity, muscular control, nystagmus, Mongolian slant, Brushfield spots, epicanthic folds, lacrimation, discharge, lids, exophthalmos or enophthalmos, conjunctivas; pupillary size, shape, and reaction to light and accommodation; media (corneal opacities, cataracts), fundi, visual fields (in older children).

Practical notes:

1. The newborn infant usually will open his eyes if he is placed in the prone position, supported with one hand on the abdomen, and lifted over the examiner's head.
2. Not infrequently, one pupil is normally larger than the other. This sometimes occurs only in bright or in subdued light.
3. Examination of the fundi should be part of every complete physical examination, regardless of the age of the child; dilatation of pupils may be necessary for adequate visualization.
4. A mild degree of strabismus may be present during the first six months of life but should be considered abnormal after that time.
5. To test for strabismus in the very young or uncooperative child, note where a distant source of light is reflected from the surface of the eyes; the reflection should be present on corresponding portions of the two eyes.
6. Small areas of capillary dilatation are commonly seen on the eyelids of normal newborn infants.
7. Most infants produce visible tears during the first few days of life.

Nose.

Exterior, shape, mucosa, patency, discharge, bleeding, pressure over sinuses, flaring of nostrils, septum.

Mouth.

Lips (thinness, downturning, fissures, color, cleft), teeth (number, position, caries, mottling, discoloration, notching, malocclusion or malalignment), mucosa (color, redness of Stensen's duct, enanthems, Bohn's nodules, Epstein's pearls), gums, palate, tongue, uvula, mouth breathing, geographic tongue (usually normal).

Practical note: If the tongue can be extended as far as the alveolar ridge, there will be no interference with nursing or speaking.

Throat.

Tonsils (size, inflammation, exudate, crypts, inflammation of the anterior pillars), mucosa, hypertrophic lymphoid tissue, postnasal drip, epiglottis, voice (hoarseness, stridor, grunting, type of cry, speech).

Practical notes:

1. Before examining a child's throat it is advisable to examine his mouth first. Permit the child to handle the tongue blade, nasal speculum, and flashlight so that he can overcome his fear of the instruments. Then ask the child to stick out his tongue and say "Ah," louder and louder. In some cases this may allow an adequate examination. In others, if the child is cooperative enough, he may be asked to "pant like a puppy"; while he is doing this, the tongue blade is applied firmly to the rear of the tongue. Gagging need not be elicited in order to obtain a satisfactory examination. In still other cases, it may be expedient to examine one side of the tongue at a time, pushing the base of the tongue to one side and then to the other. This may be less unpleasant and is less apt to cause gagging.

2. Young children may have to be restrained to obtain an adequate examination of the throat. Eliciting a gag reflex may be necessary if the oral pharynx is to be adequately seen.

3. The small child's head may be restrained satisfactorily by having the mother place her hands at the level of the child's elbows while the arms are held firmly against the sides of his head.

4. If the child can sit up, the mother is asked to hold him erect in her lap with his back against her chest. She then holds his left hand in her left hand and his right hand in her right hand, and places them against the child's groin or lower thighs to prevent him from slipping down from her lap. If the throat is to be examined in natural light, the mother faces the light. If artificial light and a head mirror are used, the mother sits with her back to the light. In either case, the physician uses one hand to hold the head in position and the other to manipulate the tongue blade.

5. Young children seldom complain of sore throat even in the presence of significant infection of the pharynx and tonsils.

Ears.

Pinnas (position, size), canals, tympanic membranes (landmarks, mobility, perforation, inflammation, discharge), mastoid tenderness and swelling, hearing.

Practical notes:

1. A test for hearing is an important part of the physical examination of every infant.

2. The ears of all sick children should be examined.

3. Before actually examining the ears, it is often helpful to place the speculum just within the canal, remove it and place it lightly in the other ear, remove it again, and proceed in this way from one ear to the other, gradually going farther and farther, until a satisfactory examination is completed.

4. In examining the ears, as large a speculum as possible should be used and should be inserted no farther than necessary, both to avoid discomfort and to avoid pushing wax in front of the speculum so that it obscures the field. The otoscope should be held balanced in the hand by holding the

handle at the end nearest the speculum. One finger should rest against the head to prevent injury resulting from sudden movement by the child.

5. The child may be restrained most easily if he is lying on his abdomen.

6. Low-set ears are present in a number of congenital syndromes, including several that are associated with mental retardation. The ears may be considered low-set if they are below a line drawn from the lateral angle of the eye and the external occipital protuberance.

7. Congenital anomalies of the urinary tract are frequently associated with abnormalities of the pinnas.

8. To examine the ears of an infant it is usually necessary to pull the auricle backward and downward; in the older child the external ear is pulled backward and upward.

Neck.

Position (torticollis, opisthotonos, inability to support head, mobility), swelling, thyroid (size, contour, bruit, isthmus, nodules, tenderness), lymph nodes, veins, position of trachea, sternocleidomastoid (swelling, shortening), webbing, edema, auscultation, movement, tonic neck reflex.

Practical note: In the older child, the size and shape of the thyroid gland may be more clearly defined if the gland is palpated from behind.

Thorax.

Shape and symmetry, veins, retractions and pulsations, beading, Harrison's groove, flaring of ribs, pigeon breast, funnel shape, size and position of nipples, breasts, length of sternum, intercostal and substernal retraction, asymmetry, scapulas, clavicles.

Practical note: At puberty, in normal children, one breast usually begins to develop before the other. In both sexes tenderness of the breasts is relatively common. Gynecomastia is not uncommon in the male.

Lungs.

Type of breathing, dyspnea, prolongation of expiration, cough, expansion, fremitus, flatness or dullness to percussion, resonance, breath and voice sounds, rales, wheezing.

Practical notes:

1. Breath sounds in infants and children normally are more intense and more bronchial, and expiration is more prolonged, than in adults.

2. Most of the young child's respiratory movement is produced by abdominal movement; there is very little intercostal motion.

3. If one places the stethoscope over the mouth and subtracts the sounds heard by this route from the sounds heard through the chest wall, the difference usually represents the amount produced intrathoracically.

Heart.

Location and intensity of apex beat, precordial bulging, pulsation of vessels, thrills, size, shape, auscultation (rate, rhythm, force, quality of sounds - compare with pulse as to rate and rhythm; friction rub - variation with pressure), murmurs (location, position in cycle, intensity, pitch, effect of change of position, transmission, effect of exercise).

Practical notes:

1. Many children normally have sinus arrhythmia. The child should be asked to take a deep breath to determine its effect on the rhythm.
2. Extrasystoles are not uncommon in childhood.
3. The heart should be examined with the child erect, recumbent, and turned to the left.

Abdomen.

Size and contour, visible peristalsis, respiratory movements, veins (distention, direction of flow), umbilicus, hernia, musculature, tenderness and rigidity, tympany, shifting dullness, tenderness, rebound tenderness, pulsation, palpable organs or masses (size, shape, position, mobility), fluid wave, reflexes, femoral pulsations, bowel sounds.

Practical notes:

1. The abdomen may be examined while the child is lying prone in the mother's lap or held over her shoulder, or seated on the examining table with his back to the doctor. These positions may be particularly helpful where tenderness, rigidity, or a mass must be palpated. In the infant the examination may be aided by having the child suck at a "sugar tip" or nurse at a bottle.
2. Light palpation, especially for the spleen, often will give more information than deep.
3. Umbilical hernias are common during the first two years of life. They usually disappear spontaneously.

Male Genitalia.

Circumcision, meatal opening, hypospadias, phimosis, adherent foreskin, size of testes, cryptorchism, scrotum, hydrocele, hernia, pubertal changes.

Practical notes:

1. In examining a suspected case of cryptorchism, palpation for the testicles should be done before the child has fully undressed or become chilled or had the cremasteric reflex stimulated. In some cases, examination while the child is in a hot bath may be helpful. The boy should also be examined while sitting in a chair holding his knees with his heels on the seat; the increased intra-abdominal pressure may push the testes into the scrotum.
2. To examine for cryptorchism, one should start above the inguinal canal and work downward to prevent pushing the testes up into the canal or abdomen.
3. In the obese boy, the penis may be so obscured by fat as to appear abnormally small. If this fat is pushed back, a penis of normal size is usually found.

Female Genitalia.

Vagina (imperforate, discharge, adhesions), hypertrophy of clitoris, pubertal changes.

Practical note: Digital or speculum examination is rarely done until after puberty.

Rectum and Anus.

Irritation, fissures, prolapse, imperforate anus. The rectal examination should be performed with the little finger (inserted slowly). Note muscle tone, character of stool, masses, tenderness, sensation. Examine stool on glove finger (gross, microscopic, culture, guaiac), as indicated.

Extremities.
A. General: Deformity, hemiatrophy, bowlegs (common in infancy), knock-knees (common after age two), paralysis, edema, coldness, posture, gait, stance, asymmetry.
B. Joints: Swelling, redness, pain, limitation, tenderness, motion, rheumatic nodules, carrying angle of elbows, tibial torsion.
C. Hands and Feet: Extra digits, clubbing, simian lines, curvature of little finger, deformity of nails, splinter hemorrhages, flat feet (feet commonly appear flat during first two years), abnormalities of feet, dermatoglyphics, width of thumbs and big toes, syndactyly, length of various segments, dimpling of dorsa, temperature.
D. Peripheral Vessels: Presence, absence, or diminution of arterial pulses.

Spine and Back.

Posture, curvatures, rigidity, webbed neck, spina bifida, pilonidal dimple or cyst, tufts of hair, mobility, Mongolian spot; tenderness over spine, pelvis, and kidneys.

Neurologic Examination. (After Vazuka.)
A. Cerebral Function: General behavior, level of consciousness, intelligence, emotional status, memory, orientation, illusions, hallucinations, cortical sensory interpretation, cortical motor integration, ability to understand and communicate, auditory-verbal and visual-verbal comprehension, recognition of visual object, speech, ability to write, performance of skilled motor acts.
B. Cranial Nerves:
  1. I (olfactory) - Identify odors; disorders of smell.
  2. II (optic) - Visual acuity, visual fields, ophthalmoscopic examination, retina.
  3. III (oculomotor), IV (trochlear), and VI (abducens) - Ocular movements, ptosis, dilatation of pupil, nystagmus, pupillary accommodation, and pupillary light reflexes.
  4. V (trigeminal) - Sensation of face, corneal reflex, masseter and temporal muscles, maxillary reflex (jaw jerk).
  5. VII (facial) - Wrinkle forehead, frown, smile, raise eyebrows, asymmetry of face, strength of eyelid muscles, taste on anterior portion of tongue.
  6. VIII (acoustic) -
    a. Cochlear portion - Hearing, lateralization, air and bone conduction, tinnitus.
    b. Vestibular - Caloric tests.

7. IX (glossopharyngeal), X (vagus) - Pharyngeal gag reflex, ability to swallow and speak clearly; sensation of mucosa of pharynx, soft palate, and tonsils; movement of pharynx, larynx, and soft palate; autonomic functions.
8. XI (accessory) - Strength of trapezius and sternocleido-mastoid muscles.
9. XII (hypoglossal) - Protrusion of tongue, tremor, strength of tongue.

C. Cerebellar Function: Finger to nose; finger to examiner's finger; rapidly alternating pronation and supination of hands; ability to run heel down other shin and to make a requested motion with foot; ability to stand with eyes closed; walk; heel to toe walk; tremor, ataxia; posture; arm swing when walking; nystagmus; abnormalities of muscle tone and speech.

D. Motor System: Muscle size, consistency, and tone; muscle contours and outlines; muscle strength; myotonic contraction; slow relaxation; symmetry of posture; fasciculations; tremor; resistance to passive movement; involuntary movement.

E. Reflexes:
1. Deep reflexes - Biceps, brachioradialis, triceps, patellar, Achilles; rapidity and strength of contraction and relaxation.
2. Superficial reflexes - Abdominals, cremasteric, plantar, gluteal.
3. Pathologic reflexes - Babinski, Chaddock, Oppenheim, Gordon.

2...

Pediatric Management During Illness

REST AND ACTIVITY DURING ILLNESS

During most acute illnesses the child may be allowed to establish his own limits of activity, since attempts to enforce bed rest often do more harm than good. When enforced bed rest results in a crying and resentful child, a compromise may be effected by permitting him to eat at least one meal with the family or by restricting his activities to quiet games in a single room.

The sick child requires a great deal of reassurance and should be spared the knowledge of the concern which others around him may feel. It is important to minimize the child's anxiety by discussion and explanation and to avoid the detrimental effects of restlessness and unhappiness which result from overzealous limitations.

In convalescence from a serious illness, provision must be made for a definite amount of rest. Occupational and play therapy are always useful if properly controlled. Most schools will provide a home teaching program if one is needed.

NUTRITION DURING ILLNESS

Infants.

In the severely ill infant, breast feeding may have to be temporarily discontinued. Regular emptying of the mother's breasts, manually or with a pump, may allow prompt reinstitution of breast feeding when the child can again nurse.

When the illness is not severe enough to warrant discontinuing breast feeding altogether, supplemental feedings of water with 5% carbohydrate added will provide the necessary increase in fluid and carbohydrate intake.

Acutely ill infants have a decreased ability to utilize fat and may have increased requirements for carbohydrates, water, and electrolytes to compensate increased losses. Dilute evaporated milk formulas, with added amounts of carbohydrate, are recommended for this purpose. When the acute phase has passed, the formula may be strengthened to overcome the deficits of calories, protein, and fat.

Children.

Acutely ill children, especially those with pain and fever, are generally anorexic and irritable. One should not attempt to supply optimal food requirements during the acute phase of the disease, but should provide the three items most needed: water, electrolytes, and sugar, especially to avoid ketosis. It is not unusual to give for several days a diet consisting only of such items as sweetened car-

bonated beverages, gelatin desserts, ice cream, sherbet, apple-
sauce, and fruit juices as well as an occasional glass of skimmed
milk.

Parents should be cautioned to avoid a struggle in feeding the
sick child. In general, free choice and frequent small feedings at
intervals of one or two hours are sufficient to maintain optimal water,
electrolyte, and sugar intake during the acute phase of the disease.
Requirements for protein should be met in the immediate convalescent period.

When the immediate acute phase has passed, solids may be introduced which are easily digestible and which the child enjoys.
Hamburger patty, buttered toast, strained fruits and vegetables,
and mashed potatoes with a small amount of butter are successful
foods during this period.

Vitamin intake in moderately increased amounts should be
continued throughout the convalescent period.

HOSPITALIZATION

Hospitalization nearly always involves some degree of psychic
trauma, especially in a young child; the need for hospital care must
therefore be balanced against the possible emotional consequences.
If the decision is made to hospitalize the child, then the physician,
the parents, and the hospital staff must try to minimize the psychological effect of the hospital stay and the procedures involved during
that time. Above all, the child must be made to understand the
parents' attitude. Candor and reassurance are never more important to the child than at this time, when it may seem to him that his
mother wants to "send him away" - because he is sick and too much
trouble. The physician can help by seeing to it that the practical
affairs of running a hospital interfere as little as possible with the
parents' visits.

Hospital personnel must be brought to a sympathetic awareness
of the sick child's emotional needs. The child should be given a
reasonable and candid explanation of what is likely to happen to him.
If surgery is to be performed, he should be told how anesthesia will
be administered and how he will feel and where he will be after
surgery. Explanation and forewarning can make significant modifications in the emotional sequelae of hospitalization, whereas failure
to prepare the child may have far-reaching psychological consequences.

The emotional state of the parents must also be considered. It
should be recognized that they may have a sense of guilt for the
child's illness and that this reaction may be aggravated when
hospitalization is necessary. Their defense mechanisms may be
manifested by an inclination to blame others, including the physician.

TREATMENT OF
CONSTITUTIONAL SYMPTOMS

FEVER

In children under eight years of age, the degree of fever does not always reflect the severity of the disease process. Extremes of temperature may occur without relation to the degree of infection. A small infant may have a very serious illness with normal or subnormal temperatures, whereas a child two to five years of age may have fever up to 104°F. (40°C.) with a minor respiratory infection. In children over eight years of age, temperature response is similar to that in adults.

Fever itself may cause convulsions in some children when the temperature goes very high very fast. Some of these children who have had "febrile convulsions" will later have epilepsy. Rapid elevation of temperature should therefore receive prompt care in the form of antipyretic measures and sedative drugs. The presence of C. N. S. infection as a possible cause of fever and convulsions must be considered and ruled out - if necessary, by examining the C.S.F. (see Appendix, Table 5).

Measures which are specifically directed toward depression of an elevated body temperature per se are usually not indicated except for high and prolonged fevers. The presence of a fever should not be obscured by the indiscriminate use of antipyretic measures.

Whenever possible, determine the cause of the fever (infection, dehydration, reaction to drug, C. N. S. disturbance, excessive clothing) and institute specific measures.

Reduction of Fever by Nonspecific Means: In addition to discomfort of the patient, prolonged elevation of fever above 104° F. (40° C.) may produce dehydration and harmful effects on the central nervous system. The following measures may be used:

1. Increased fluid intake.
2. Sponging with warm alcohol.
3. Bathing with warm or tepid water. Cold sponges provide a prompt cooling of the skin and may afford psychological relief; however, they produce a peripheral vasoconstriction which interferes with heat loss from the body.
4. Ice bags may be used for local comfort.
5. Antipyretic drugs are usually quite effective in reducing fever. However, they obscure the clinical picture and may cause numerous undesirable side effects such as diaphoresis, skin eruptions, hematologic changes, and nausea and vomiting. Therefore, they are to be employed cautiously.

SHOCK*

Shock is a clinical syndrome characterized by prostration and hypotension resulting from a profound depression of vital cell functions associated with or secondary to poor tissue perfusion. If cellular function is not improved, shock becomes irreversible and

---

*From Kempe, Silver, & O'Brien: Current Pediatric Diagnosis & Treatment, 3rd ed. Lange, 1974.

death will ensue even though the initiating cause of the shock is corrected.

Clinical Findings.

Early signs of shock are agitation, confusion, and thirst. As shock progresses, the patient will become less and less responsive and eventually comatose.

The skin is pale, wet, and cold. The nail beds are cyanotic, and local and peripheral edema may occur. Poor capillary filling and decreased skin turgor can be demonstrated. Tachycardia and tachypnea are present.

Newborns in shock appear pale and slightly gray. Poor capillary filling and decreased skin turgor are noted. Late shock may be manifested by a decrease in skin temperature, particularly of the extremities.

Immediate Treatment of Shock.

(1) Lay the patient flat. Elevation of the legs is helpful except in instances of respiratory distress, when it is contraindicated.

(2) Establish a patent upper airway and administer oxygen by mask or nasal catheter. If the clinical condition deteriorates, consider the use of an endotracheal tube and intermittent positive pressure breathing.

(3) Establish an intravenous site with a large bore catheter (No. 18 or larger). An emergency intravenous infusion can be established by inserting a one-and-one half inch No. 20 needle into the bone marrow cavity. The preferred site is the medial aspect of the upper one-third of the tibia.

(4) Initiate fluid therapy with lactated Ringer's injection or isotonic saline solution at a rate calculated for daily maintenance plus correction of existing dehydration.

(5) Establish a central venous pressure monitor in all cases of shock that are not easily reversible.

(6) Consider an arterial catheter as a useful guide to monitoring pressure and as a source of specimens for blood gases and arterial pH.

Evaluation of Emergency Therapy.

Constant observation of patient is imperative. The pulse and respiration rates, temperature (rectal), and blood pressure should be taken immediately and every 15 to 30 minutes or oftener thereafter until shock has been overcome. Perform Hgb., RBC, and hematocrit studies if there is any suspicion whatever that secondary shock exists and repeat as necessary to evaluate results of therapy. Remember that hemoconcentration usually precedes blood pressure and pulse changes. After potential or existing shock-producing factors have been eliminated, the patient should be observed carefully until it is reasonably certain that danger has passed.

If vital signs remain abnormal for even a brief period after initial measures have been taken, or if the patient shows evidence of further progression or peripheral circulatory failure, institute further vigorous anti-shock therapy.

Treatment of Specific Types of Shock.

A. Hypovolemic (Hemorrhagic) Shock: This is defined as a reduction in the size of the vascular compartment, with a falling blood pressure, poor capillary filling, and a low central venous pressure. Treatment consists of preventing further fluid loss and volume replacement of existing losses. Vasopressors should not be used. The choice of fluid used as a volume expander depends on the cause of the hypovolemia.

1. Blood loss - Whole blood is the replacement fluid of choice for shock due to hemorrhage. Type-specific blood is strongly recommended; however, unmatched type O Rh-negative blood has been used without causing serious transfusion reactions in emergency situations. The rate of blood replacement is judged by the rate of blood loss, the patient's response, and a rising central venous pressure.

2. Plasma loss - Dextran is a good temporary volume expander which is most useful when large amounts of plasma have been lost. Twenty ml./Kg. can be given in 30 minutes as a 6% w/v solution in normal saline. More may be administered according to the estimated amount and rate of blood loss. Burn cases respond well; however, the use of low molecular weight dextran in actively bleeding patients is not recommended since it has the property of coating and suspending platelets and thus inhibiting normal platelet agglutination.

3. Dehydration - Isotonic salt solutions are indicated in all instances of dehydration, including hypertonic dehydration, when there is an absolute depletion of body salt and fluid even though there is a relative hypertonicity. Lactated Ringer's injection or 0.5 N saline solution with added sodium bicarbonate (30 mEq. of $NaHCO_3$ per 500 ml. bottle) should be started at a rate of 25 to 35 ml./Kg./hour I.V. until skin turgor improves and electrolyte values can be obtained.

4. Burns and infection - Albumin and plasma are good volume expanders.

B. Cardiogenic Shock: This is defined as shock resulting from decreased cardiac output, e.g., due to cardiac tamponade, myocarditis, abnormal rates and rhythm, and biochemical abnormalities.

1. Cardiac tamponade secondary to fluid collection in the pericardial space or constrictive pericarditis is treated by evacuating the pericardial space or surgically excising the pericardium. Temporary treatment can be achieved by increasing the venous pressure with a transfusion of blood or blood substitutes. Vasodilators cause a drop in venous pressure and are contraindicated.

2. Abnormal heart rate and rhythm results in decreased cardiac output.

   a. Marked sinus bradycardia can occur during anesthesia, particularly when associated with surgery of the neck and thorax. Sinus bradycardia can be blocked with atropine, 0.01 mg./Kg. as a single I.M. dose. The minimum dose for newborns is 0.15 mg. regardless of weight. The maximum dose for older children is 0.6 mg.

   b. Atrioventricular block may occur secondary to inflammatory disease, surgical trauma, or ischemic injury to the conduction system. Prednisolone, 1 mg./Kg./day I.V. or I.M. in four equally divided doses, may be useful in such conditions. If slowing persists, the ventricu-

lar rate can often be increased with isoproterenol, 3 to
5 μg./Kg./minute by I.V. drip. The infusion is then
adjusted according to the pulse response.

c. Ventricular arrhythmias may be secondary to hypoxia,
acidosis, or myocarditis. Procainamide (Pronestyl®),
50 mg./Kg./day I.V., is useful in controlling premature
ventricular contractions.

3. Biochemical disturbances can result in decreased cardiac
output. These include acidosis, hypoxia, and hyperkalemia.

C. Bacteremic (Endotoxin, Septic) Shock: This type of shock occurs when overwhelming sepsis and circulating bacterial toxins
result in peripheral vascular collapse. Clinical recognition
depends on the toxic appearance of the patient, often in association with purpura, splinter hemorrhages, hepatosplenomegaly,
and jaundice. Adequate treatment of bacterial shock depends
on proper antibiotic therapy of the primary infection. In addition to anti infective agents, several other procedures are
useful in supporting the patient with bacterial shock.

1. Fluids should be replaced according to needs.

2. When bacteremic shock is due to gram-negative organisms,
corticosteroids should be used early. Give prednisolone,
2 to 4 mg./Kg./day I.V., or hydrocortisone, 10 to 40 mg./
Kg./day I.V.

3. Vasopressors should be used to maintain systolic blood
pressure at about 20 mm. Hg below the normal systolic
pressure. Levarterenol bitartrate (Levophed®), 0.1 mg./
Kg./minute by I.V. drip, can be increased (depending on the
blood pressure response) to a maximum dose of 1 mg./Kg./
minute. Levarterenol is supplied in ampules of 4 ml.;
each ml. contains 2 mg. of bitartrate (equivalent to 1 mg.
of base). A convenient initial dilution is 1 ml. in 250 ml. of
solution, which equals 4 μg./ml.

4 Heparin is of value when bacterial infections are complicated by intravascular coagulation.

D. Anaphylactic Shock: This is an extreme form of allergy or
hypersensitivity to a foreign substance. The diagnosis is
established by a history of exposure to an antigen and by clinical signs of respiratory distress and circulatory collapse.
Urticaria and angioneurotic edema are often present.

1. If shock is precipitated by a drug given intramuscularly,
apply a tourniquet proximal to the site of injection tight
enough to restrict venous return but not to interrupt arterial flow.

2. Give epinephrine, 1:1000 aqueous solution, I.M. stat. Follow with 0.1 ml./Kg. I.V. and repeat in 20 minutes if the
response is not satisfactory.

3. Give antihistamines, e.g., diphenhydramine (Benadryl®),
5 mg./Kg./day in four to six divided doses by I.V. push
over a five- to ten-minute interval.

4. Give prednisolone, 2 mg./Kg./day I.V. in four to six divided doses.

5. For treatment of respiratory distress or wheezing, give
aminophylline, 12 mg./Kg./day by I.V. drip in four divided
doses every six hours.

6. Secretions should be suctioned and may require repeated

bronchoscopy. Laryngeal edema may necessitate intubation followed by tracheostomy.

7. Hypovolemia should be treated vigorously with isotonic saline solution at rates of 25 ml./Kg./hour until the patient voids or the central venous pressure monitor indicates a rise to normal values.

8. Levarterenol (Levophed®), 0.1 mg./Kg./minute, can be infused to maintain a blood pressure 20 mm. Hg below the normal systolic level. This should be used only after adequate volume replacement.

E. Neurogenic Shock: There is usually a history of exposure to anesthetic agents, spinal cord injuries, or ingestion of barbiturates, narcotics, or tranquilizers. Examination reveals abnormal reflexes and muscle tone, tachycardia and tachypnea, and low blood pressure. The pathophysiologic mechanism is loss of vessel tone with subsequent expansion of the vascular compartment, resulting in relative hypovolemia. Many anesthetic agents have a direct effect on the myocardium which causes a decrease in cardiac ouptut.

1. Fluids - Neurogenic shock responds well to volume therapy. Give isotonic saline solution, 25 ml./Kg./hour I.V., until peripheral circulation and skin turgor improve.

2. Vasopressors - If fluid therapy is not successful, give either of the following:

   a. Methoxamine (Vasoxyl®), 0.25 mg./Kg. I.M. as a single dose, or 0.08 mg./Kg. I.V. given over a 10 to 15 minute interval.

   b. Phenylephrine (Neo-Synephrine®), 0.1 mg./Kg. I.M. as a single dose.

3. Levarterenol (Levophed®), 0.1 mg./Kg./minute by I.V. infusion, should be given if fluid therapy and vasopressors are unsuccessful.

F. Shock Due to Miscellaneous Causes:

1. Pulmonary embolism - May be present if there is a fracture or significant soft tissue injury followed by symptoms of chest pain, dyspnea, cyanosis, and signs of right heart failure. Treatment is supportive, with oxygen and analgesics. If hypotension occurs, isoproterenol (Isuprel®) is the drug of choice since it provides a bronchodilator effect. If right heart failure develops, a rapid-acting digitalis preparation such as digoxin should be given.

2. Respiratory disease - Respiratory disease due to any cause can result in sufficient hypoxia to cause shock. Shock of this nature is reversible only to the extent that the lung disease is reversible, and treatment should be directed toward the primary pulmonary disorder. Oxygen and alkali therapy will only temporarily improve the patient's condition.

3. Metabolic shock - Shock may be secondary to a number of metabolic conditions, such as adrenocortical insufficiency and diabetic acidosis.

Prognosis.

With prompt and effective emergency care for both the shock itself and the underlying condition, the immediate prognosis is excellent.

SUDDEN AND UNEXPECTED DEATH IN INFANCY

Sudden and unexpected death in infancy is relatively common, and may result from a number of causes. Infection of the respiratory tract is often noted, but its significance is not clear. There is usually a paucity and lack of uniformity of gross and microscopic observations in affected infants, although specific abnormalities may be observed in a few.

Infants who die suddenly are usually less than six months of age, with a peak incidence between one and four months. Most cases occur during the cold months. The incidence is higher in small infants and in the lower socio-economic groups. A number of etiologic mechanisms have been incriminated: (1) primary apnea secondary to moderate hypoxia; (2) suffocation: smothering due to nasal obstruction resulting from infection or by bedclothes or pillow (extremely unlikely), so-called "overlaying" by an adult, aspiration of gastric contents or a foreign body, laryngospasm; (3) infection (both bacterial and viral); (4) anomalies of the parathyroids; (5) anaphylactic shock from the aspiration of milk in children who have become hypersensitive to cow's milk protein; (6) ventricular fibrillation resulting from sudden fear and anxiety; and (7) vitamin E or selenium deficiency. None of these mechanisms have been conclusively shown to be the cause of the sudden death.

PREOPERATIVE AND POSTOPERATIVE CARE

GENERAL CONSIDERATIONS

Newborn infants withstand surgical procedures better than is usually recognized; this is especially true in the first 72 hours of life. Congenital defects requiring prompt surgery should be repaired as soon as possible after the diagnosis is made.

Psychological preparation of an older child for anesthesia and surgery is the combined responsibility of all physicians involved. The parents should also be encouraged to discuss surgery with the child, when possible, and must not deceive him under any circumstances. Simple and honest explanations the day before and on the day of surgery, with a fairly detailed description of what to expect, given in a way that the child can understand, will make for a smoother hospital stay and will significantly decrease untoward psychological reactions in the postoperative months and years.

Malignant hyperpyrexia may occur as a complication of anesthesia, especially in young boys with undescended testes, lordosis, kyphosis, and muscle disease.

PREOPERATIVE CARE

Preoperative Feeding.
  A. Routine stereotyped orders (e.g., "nothing by mouth after midnight") must be avoided. Fluid feeding should be administered as follows:

1. Infants - Regular formula feeding may be given up to four
   hours before operation, or a carbohydrate solution may be
   substituted.
2. Older children - Four to six hours before operation, give a
   large glass of strained, sweetened orange juice or carbonated
   drink. If surgery is scheduled for after 11 A.M., a liquid
   breakfast should be given four to six hours before surgery.

B. For correction of fluid and electrolyte imbalance, see Chapter
5. It is generally not necessary to correct minor degrees of
imbalance, but some attempt should be made to correct major
imbalances even if surgery must be delayed. The use of a
"cut-down" for intravenous drip expedites the administration
of whole blood and fluids to small children during a major
operative procedure and affords a route for the continuous administration of fluids postoperatively. However, the danger of
overhydration during surgery must be borne in mind constantly.

Preoperative Medication.

See Drug Dosages for Children in Appendix.

Vitamin Therapy.

A. Vitamin K, 1 to 3 mg., I.M., to all newborn babies and to
those who may have a vitamin K deficiency (e.g., liver disturbances, chronic gastrointestinal disease, infants in the
first three months of life).

B. Vitamin C, 25 to 1000 mg. orally or subcut. to the child with
possible nutritional disturbance.

Antibiotic Therapy.

Appropriate chemotherapeutic or antibiotic agents are given,
depending on the type and site of operation and possible infecting
agent (see Chapter 6).

Reduction of Fever.

Children with high fever withstand anesthesia and surgery
poorly; attempts should be made to reduce the temperature below
102° F. (38.9°C.) with aspirin, orally or rectally, alcohol or tepid
water sponges, adequate hydration, and antibiotics if necessary.

Enema.

Enemas are generally not necessary unless there is distention
or if the surgical procedure will involve the bowel.

Sedation.

The use of a sedative to allay apprehension and to help relax
the child should be considered even though the patient does not complain of these symptoms.

POSTOPERATIVE CARE

The child should be placed in a warm bed, usually on his side
or his abdomen (to insure a free airway). Inhalation anesthesia
easily produces edema of the upper respiratory tract in children.
If inhalation anesthesia has been used, the administration of oxygen

in an atmosphere of high humidity diminishes the danger of laryngeal edema and may be instrumental in reducing the need for postoperative tracheostomy. Vaporized detergents containing vasoconstricting agents may also materially aid in decreasing edema of the upper respiratory tract.

Blood and Fluid Replacements.

A. The estimated blood loss should be replaced either during or immediately after surgery.
B. Care should be taken to avoid the administration of excessive amounts of sodium chloride. In most instances reliance should be placed chiefly on the use of glucose in water.

Sedation.

Small doses of phenobarbital for the young child or small doses of morphine for the older child should be given to maintain adequate sedation.

Postoperative Feeding.

Oral feedings can usually be resumed six to 12 hours after most surgical procedures. Start with water or clear liquids and advance to the regular diet as rapidly as child tolerates.

Vitamins.

Vitamin C (100 to 200 mg. per day) and vitamin K (2 to 5 mg. per day) should be given to infants or young children for three to five days postoperatively.

Ambulation.

Early ambulation is advisable in the older child. In any case, the hospital stay should be as short as possible. An early return to the home will result in a general improvement in the child's emotional and physical well being.

3 . . .
Development & Growth

Development and growth are continuous dynamic processes occurring from conception to maturity and taking place in an orderly sequence which is approximately the same for all individuals. At any particular age, however, wide variations are to be found among normal children which reflect the active response of the growing individual to numberless hereditary and environmental factors.

The body as a whole and the various tissues and organs have characteristic growth patterns which are essentially the same in all individuals.

Development signifies maturation of organs and systems, acquisition of skills, ability to adapt more readily to stress, and ability to assume maximum responsibility and to achieve freedom in creative expression. Growth signifies increase in size.

DEVELOPMENT

The physician should know something about normal development at all ages if he hopes to give comprehensive pediatric care; he should be particularly familiar with development during the earliest years, since he occupies a unique position as family adviser during this period.

. There is no simple practical method of assaying the various behavioristic or emotional factors which determine a child's state of development. The following data should merely serve as a screening guide for recognition of marked variations from the average. Over-all developmental evaluation is indicated whenever an unexplained persistent retardation is found in any one area.

Various norms of development have been described. Those given below are relatively simple and do not demand specialized testing material.

DEVELOPMENTAL SCREENING*

The Denver Developmental Screening Test (DDST) is a device for detecting developmental delays in infancy and the preschool years. The test is administered with ease and speed and lends itself to serial evaluations on the same test sheet. (See Fig 3-1.)

Test Materials.
Skein of red wool, box of raisins, rattle with a narrow handle, small aspirin bottle, bell, tennis ball, test form, pencil, eight one-inch cubical counting blocks.

*From Frankenburg: Denver Developmental Screening Test. J. Ped. 71:181-91, 1967.

General Administration Instructions.

The mother should be told that this is a developmental screening device to obtain an estimate of the child's level of development and that it is not expected that the child be able to perform each of the test items. This test relies on observations of what the child can do and on report by a parent who knows the child. Direct observation should be used whenever possible. Since the test requires active participation by the child, every effort should be made to put the child at ease. The younger child may be tested while sitting on the mother's lap. This should be done in such a way that he can comfortably reach the test materials on the table. The test should be administered before any frightening or painful procedures. A child will often withdraw if the examiner rushes demands upon the child. One may start by laying out one or two test materials in front of the child while asking the mother whether he performs some of the personal-social items. It is best to administer the first few test items well below the child's age level in order to assure an initial successful experience. To avoid distractions, it is best to remove all test materials from the table except the one that is being administered.

Steps in Administering the Test.

(1) Draw a vertical line on the examination sheet through the four sectors (gross motor, fine motor—adaptive, language, and personal-social) to represent the child's chronological age. Place the date of the examination at the top of the age line. For premature children, subtract the months premature from the chronological age.

(2) The items to be administered are those through which the child's chronological age line passes unless there are obvious deviations. In each sector one should establish the area where the child passes all of the items and the point at which he fails all of the items.

(3) In the event that a child refuses to do some of the items requested by the examiner, it is suggested that the parent administer the item, provided she does so in the prescribed manner.

(4) If a child passes an item, a large letter "P" is written on the bar at the 50% passing point. "F" designates a failure, and "R" designates a refusal.

(5) Failure to perform an item passed by 90% of children of the same age should be considered significant, although not necessarily abnormal.

(6) Note date and pertinent observations of parent and child behavior (how child feels at time of the evaluation, relation to the examiner, attention span, verbal behavior, self-confidence, etc.).

(7) Ask the parent if the child's performance was typical of his performance at other times.

(8) To retest the child on the same form, use a different color pencil for the scoring and age line.

(9) Instructions for administering footnoted items are on p. 28.

Interpretations.

The test items are placed into four categories: Gross motor, fine motor—adaptive, language, and personal-social. Each of the

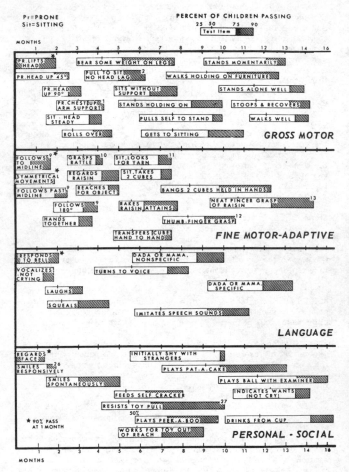

FIG 3-1. Denver Developmental Screening Test.

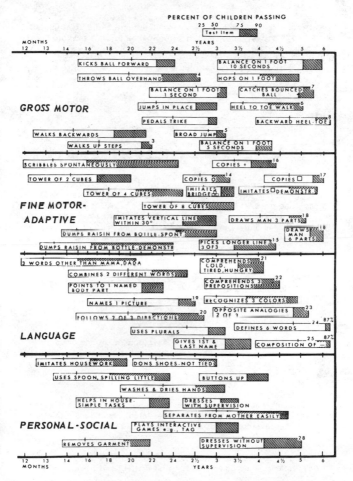

FIG 3-1 (cont'd). Denver Developmental Screening Test.

test items is designated by a bar which is so located under the age scale as to indicate clearly the ages at which 25%, 50%, 75%, and 90% of the standardization population could perform the particular test item. The left end of the bar designates the age at which 25% of the standardization population could perform the item; the point shown at the top of the bar 50%; the left end of the shaded area 75%; and the right end of the bar the age at which 90% of the standardization population could perform the item.

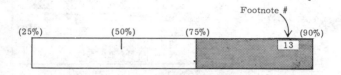

Failure to perform an item passed by 90% of children of the same age should be considered significant. Such a failure may be emphasized by coloring the right end of the bar of the failed item. Several failures in one sector are considered to be developmental delays. These delays may be due to:

(1) The unwillingness of the child to use his ability:
    (a) Due to temporary phenomena, such as fatigue, illness, hospitalization, separation from the parent, fear, etc.
    (b) General unwillingness to do most things that are asked of him; such a condition may be just as detrimental as an inability to perform.
(2) An inability to perform the item due to:
    (a) General retardation.
    (b) Pathologic factors such as deafness or neurologic impairment.
    (c) Familial pattern of slow development in one or more areas.

If unexplained developmental delays are noted and are a valid reflection of a child's abilities, he should be rescreened a month later. If the delays persist he should be further evaluated with more detailed diagnostic studies.

Caution: The DDST is not an intelligence test. It is intended as a screening instrument for use in clinical practice to note whether the development of a particular child is within the normal range.

Directions For Footnoted Items.

(1) Infant, when prone, lifts chest off table with support of forearms and/or hands.

(2) Examiner grasps child's hands, pulls him from supine to sitting position; child has no head lag.

(3) Child may use wall or rail only, not person; may not crawl.

(4) Child throws ball overhand three feet to within examiner's reach.

(5) Child performs standing broad jump over width of test sheet.

(6) Ask child to walk forward ⟳⟳ ⟳⟳ ⟳⟳ ➙, heel within one inch of toe.

(7) Examiner bounces ball to child; child must catch with hands (two or three trials).

(8) Ask child to walk backwards, , toe within one inch of heel.

(9) Examiner moves yarn in arc from side to side one foot above baby's head. Note if eyes follow 90° to midline (past midline, 180°).

(10) Infant grasps rattle when touched to his finger tips.

(11) Child looks after yarn dropped from sight over table's edge.

(12) Child grasps raisin between thumb and index finger.

(13) Child performs overhand grasp of raisin with tips of thumb and index finger.

(14) Copy. Pass any enclosed form. Do not demonstrate. Do not name form.

(15) "Which line is **longer**?" (Not **bigger**.) Turn paper upside down; repeat. (Pass three of three.)

(16) Pass crossing lines, any angle.

(17) Have child copy first. If he fails, demonstrate. Pass figure with four right angle corners.

(18) When scoring, symmetric parts count as one (two arms or two eyes count as one part only).

(19) Point to picture and have child name it.

FIG 3-2. Norm of development. (Adapted From Aldrich and Norval.)*

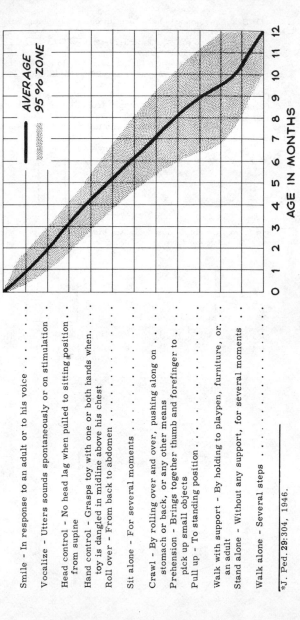

Smile - In response to an adult or to his voice . . . . . .

Vocalize - Utters sounds spontaneously or on stimulation .

Head control - No head lag when pulled to sitting position .
  from supine

Hand control - Grasps toy with one or both hands when. . . .
  toy is dangled in midline above his chest

Roll over - From back to abdomen . . . .

Sit alone - For several moments . . . .

Crawl - By rolling over and over, pushing along on . . . .
  stomach or back, or any other means

Prehension - Brings together thumb and forefinger to . . . .
  pick up small objects

Pull up - To standing position . . . .

Walk with support - By holding to playpen, furniture, or. .
  an adult

Stand alone - Without any support, for several moments .

Walk alone - Several steps . . . .

AVERAGE
95% ZONE

AGE IN MONTHS

0 1 2 3 4 5 6 7 8 9 10 11 12

*J. Ped. **29**:304, 1946.

(20) Examiner asks child to, "Give block to Mommie," "Put block on table," "Put block on floor." (Two of three.) **Caution**: Examiner not to gesture with head or eyes.

(21) Child answers two of three questions: "What do you do when you are cold?" "Hungry?" "Tired?"

(22) Examiner asks child to, "Put clock **on** table, **under** table, in **front** of chair, **behind** chair." **Caution**: Examiner not to gesture with head or eyes.

(23) Examiner asks child: "Fire is hot, ice is ____ ." "Mother is a woman, Dad is a ____ ." "A horse is big, a mouse is ____ ." (Pass if two of three are correct.)

(24) Ask child to define six: "Ball, lake, desk, house, banana, curtain, hedge, pavement." Any verbal indication of understanding is passed.

(25) Examiner asks, "What is a spoon made of?" "A shoe made of?" "A door made of?" (No other objects may be substituted.) Must pass all three.

(26) Examiner attempts to elicit a smile by smiling, talking, or waving to infant. **Do not touch.** Baby smiles responsively in two or three attempts.

(27) When child is playing with toy, pull it away from him. Pass if he resists.

(28) Child need not be able to tie shoes or button in the back.

PERSONALITY DEVELOPMENT

Personality development is a dynamic process, and no summary can give a complete picture of what takes place. The goal of the individual, both as a child and as an adult, is to be able to work, to play, to master personal problems, and to love and be loved in a manner that is creative, socially acceptable, and personally gratifying.

The development of personality is a complicated process involving all aspects of the individual and his environment. The process varies from one child to another, but on the whole all children pass through various phases of development of which details differ but of which the broad general outlines are essentially the same.

Each of these successive stages of development is characterized by definite problems which the child must solve if he is to proceed with confidence to the next. The highest degree of functional harmony will be achieved when the problems of each stage are met and solved at an orderly rate and in a normal sequence. On the other hand, it is well to remember that the successive personality gains which the child makes are not rigidly established once and for all but may be reinforced or threatened throughout the life of the individual. Even in adulthood a reasonably healthy personality may be achieved in spite of previous misfortunes and defects in the developmental sequence.

In considering psychologic development it is important to remember that it takes place within a cultural milieu. Not only the form of large social institutions but the framework of family life, the attitudes of parents, and their practices in child-rearing will be conditioned by the culture of the given period.

Psychologic development in childhood may be roughly divided into five stages: infancy (birth to 18 months), early childhood (18 months to five years), later childhood (five to 12 years), early adolescence (12 to 16 years), and late adolescence (16 years to maturity).

Infancy.

Perhaps the most striking features of the first year are the great physical development which takes place and the infant's growing awareness of himself as an entity separate from his environment.

Much of the psychologic development of the first year is interrelated with physical development, i. e., dependent upon the maturation of the body to the extent that the child can discriminate self and non-self. Knowledge of the environment comes with increasing sharpening of the senses (from indiscriminate mouthing to coordinated eye-hand movements). Beginning of mastery over the environment comes with increasingly adept coordination, the development of locomotion, and the beginnings of speech. The realization of himself as an individual in relation to an environment including other individuals is the basis upon which interpersonal relationships are founded.

The newborn infant is at first aware only of his bodily needs — of the presence or absence of discomfort (e.g., cold, wet). The pleasure of relief from discomfort gradually becomes associated with mothering and later (when perception is sufficient for recognition) with the mother. The child derives a feeling of security when his needs are satisfied and from contact with the mother. The feeding situation provides the first opportunity for development of this feeling of security, and it is therefore important for the physician to insure that this is a happy event.

The development of the first emotional relationship, then, comes through this close contact with the mother. It no longer will be just a meeting of the infant's physical needs but a sustained physical contact and emotional interaction with one person. Prolonged absence of this relationship, if no satisfactory substitute is provided, is damaging to the personality. If permanent, it leads to restriction of personality development, even to pseudoretardation in all areas. Such behavior may also occur in a home situation, but it is more striking and more common in infants who remain for long periods of time in the hospital or in other institutions where the nursing personnel is inadequate (either in number or ability) to give sufficient personalized and kindly attention to each child. If the infant is deprived of the security and affection necessary to produce a sense of trust, he may respond with listlessness, immobility, unresponsiveness, indifferent appetite, an appearance of unhappiness, and insomnia. In other cases the continued deprivation of consistent care in infancy may not become apparent until later life, when the individual may feel that he has no reason to trust people; this may result in his feeling no sense of responsibility toward his fellow men.

No particular technics are necessary to develop a baby's feeling of security. The infant is not easily discouraged by an inexperienced mother's mistakes; rather the child seems to respond to the warmth of her feeling and her eagerness to keep trying. The feeling of security derived from satisfactory relationships during the first year is probably the most important single element in the personality. It makes it possible for the child to accept restrictions without fearing that each restriction implies total loss of love.

Toward the end of the first year, other personal relationships also are developing, particularly with the father, who is now recognized as comparable in importance with the mother. Relationships perhaps are also forming with siblings.

Early Childhood.

In early childhood the child's horizon continues to widen. Increased body control makes possible the development of many physical skills. The very important development of speech permits extension of the social environment and increasing ability to understand and perfect social relationships.

Perhaps the central problem of early childhood is still, however, the development of control over the instinctive drives, particularly as they arise in relationship to the parents. The acceptance of limitations on the need for bodily love (the realization that complete infantile dependency is not permitted or desirable) and the control of aggressive feelings are prime examples. This control of primitive feelings is largely accomplished through the psychological process of "identification" with the parents - the desire in the child to be like the parents and to emulate them. With this desire comes the beginnings of conscience, the child's incorporation into his own personality of the moral values of the parents.

The child now begins to have a feeling of autonomy - of self-direction and initiative. The child 18 months to two-and-one-half years of age is actively learning to exercise the power of "yes" and "no." The difficulty the two-year-old has in making up his mind between the two often leads to parental misunderstanding; he may say "no" when he really means "yes," as if he were compelled to exercise this new "will" even against his better judgment.

At this period parental "discipline" becomes very important. Discipline is an educative means by which the parent teaches the child how to become a self-respecting, likeable, and socially responsible adult. Disciplinary measures have value chiefly as they serve this educative function; if used as an end in themselves, to establish the "authority" of the parent irrespective of the issues at hand, they usually lead only to warfare (open or surreptitious) between parent and child.

The goal is to allow the child to develop the feeling that he is a responsible human being, while at the same time he learns that he is able to use the help and guidance of others in important matters. The favorable result is self-control without loss of self-esteem. As adults, we should allow a child increasingly wide latitude in undergoing experiences which permit him to make the choices he is ready and able to make, and yet we must also teach him to accept restrictions when necessary.

Firmness and consistency in the parent are necessary, for the child must be protected against the potential anarchy of his poorly developed judgment. Perhaps the most constructive rule a parent can follow is to decide which kinds of conformity are really important and then to clearly and consistently require obedience in these areas. Then "discipline" will have the positive goal of making the

child socially compatible without making him feel guilty about his
basic drives or stifling his need for some expression of independence.

Later Childhood.

In this period, the child achieves a rapid intellectual growth
and actively begins to establish himself as a member of society.
Psychiatrists call this the latency period, because the force of the
primitive drives has been fairly successfully controlled, expressed
in a socially acceptable way, or repressed. The energy derived
from the instinctive drives of which society does not permit direct
expression is diverted into the great drive for knowledge - a process
of "sublimation." At no time in life does the individual learn more
avidly and quickly. Reading and writing (the intellectual skills) and
a vast body of information are quickly assimilated. The preoccupation with fantasy gradually subsides, and the child wants to be engaged in real tasks he can carry through to completion. Even in
play activities, the emphasis is on developing mental and bodily
skills through interest in sports and games.

Late childhood is also a period of conformity to the group. The
environment enlarges to include the school and, particularly, other
children. Much of the emotional satisfaction previously derived
from the parents is now derived from the child's relationships with
his peers. His desire to become a member of this larger group of
his equals tends to make the qualities of cooperation and obedience
to the will of the group (elements of democracy) important. It also
paves the way for questioning of the parental values where these
differ from those of the group: a direct impact of broader cultural
values upon the environment of the home.

Early Adolescence.

After the comparative calm of late childhood, early adolescence
is a period of upheaval. With the great changes in body size and
configuration comes a new confusion about the physical self (the
"body image"). Sexual maturation brings with it a resurgence of
the strong instinctual drives which have been successfully repressed
for several years. In our culture, in contrast to some primitive
cultures, the sexual drive is not permitted direct expression in
adolescence in spite of physical readiness.

The calm emotional adjustment is disrupted. Again the child
has to learn to control strong feelings: love, hate, and aggression.
Again the relationship to the parents is disturbed. The former doc-
ile acceptance of them as most important, most powerful, is replaced by rebellion. Yet as strongly as the adolescent rebels and
insists on independence from his parents, just as strongly does he
feel again the old dependence which, although not openly admitted,
is revealed in his unwillingness to accept personal responsibility
and his tendency to rely on parental care.

Again his position as an individual must be realigned, not in
relation to the family circle but in relation to society. Adolescents
are constantly preoccupied with how they appear in the eyes of
others as compared with their own conceptions of themselves. They
find comfort in conformity with their own age group, and fads in
clothing and manners reach a peak in early adolescence.

Perhaps most helpful to parents is the ability to "ride" with
each swing in adolescent behavior and not assume that each change

accurately presages the personality of the future adult. Adolescents are inexperienced in their new roles as potential adults, and their behavior tends to be erratic and extreme. Calm and stability provided by the parents can do much to keep them in equilibrium.

Late Adolescence.

By the sixteenth year most children have again reached comparative equilibrium. Body growth has slowed somewhat, and the adolescent has had time to adapt to his new physique. He has acquired comparative mastery over his biological drives, to the extent that they can now be channeled into more constructive patterns, the beginning of heterosexual social activity, which eventually leads to the choice of a marital partner.

The relationship to the parents is now more mature. With the discovery that responsible independence is neither frightening nor overwhelming but a position possible to maintain, the adolescent can cease to rebel and can accept his parents' help in planning constructively for his adulthood.

Again learning is rapid, particularly for the intelligent youth, who can absorb much more than a junior high school education.

Active preparation for adulthood characterizes late adolescence in our culture, although, as in more primitive cultures, some adolescents will have already taken on the responsibilities of job and marriage. Biologically, this is certainly feasible; it is the complexity and competition of our modern culture which so greatly prolongs the emergence into full adulthood.

GROWTH

General Considerations.

A. Fetal Growth: During fetal life the rate of growth is extremely rapid. During the early months the fetal rate of gain in length is greater than the rate of gain in weight when expressed as per cent of value at birth. By the eighth month the fetus has achieved 80% of his birth length and only 50% of his birth weight (Table 3-1).

B. Organs: At birth the proportion of the weight of the pancreas and of the musculature to that of the entire body is less than in the adult; the skeleton, lungs, and the stomach are the same; while the proportion of the weight of other organs is greater than in the adult.

C. Trunk-Leg Ratio: At birth, the ratio of the lower to the upper segment of the body (as measured from the pubis) is approximately 1:1.7. The legs grow more rapidly than the trunk; by the age of 10 to 12 years the segments are approximately equal.

D. Growth Rate: Rate of growth is generally more important than actual size, and height and weight data must be considered in relation to the variability within a certain age. For more accurate comparisons, data should be recorded both as absolute figures and as percentile for that particular age.

E. Weight Increase: The average infant weighs approximately 7 lb. 5 oz. (3333 Gm.) at birth. Birth weight doubles between

TABLE 3-1. Fetal and newborn dimensions and weights of the body and its organs.
(Adapted From Edith Boyd.) (See also Inside Front Cover.)

Age (Fetal) in Weeks*	Crown-heel (cm.)	Crown-rump (cm.)	Head circ. (cm.)	Body wt. (Gm.)	Adrenal (Gm.)	Brain (Gm.)	Heart (Gm.)	Kidney (Gm.)	Liver (Gm.)	Lungs (Gm.)	Pancreas (Gm.)	Pituitary (Gm.)	Spleen (Gm.)	Thymus (Gm.)	Thyroid (Gm.)
						PRENATAL AND NEWBORN									
12	9.0	7.5	7.4	18.6	.087	2.32	.098	.163	.097	.69	.013		.006	.010	.026
16	16.7	12.8	12.6	100	.417	14.4	.662	.962	5.94	3.23	.095	.011	.086	.122	.133
20	24.2	17.7	17.6	310	1.07	43.0	2.08	2.77	16.8	8.18	.314	.024	.410	.553	.352
24	31.1	21.9	22.3	670	2.02	91.0	4.47	5.69	34.5	15.2	.695	.040	1.16	1.53	.684
28	37.1	25.5	26.3	1150	3.16	153	7.70	9.43	57.4	23.7	1.22	.058	2.43	3.14	1.08
30	39.8	27.1	28.1	1400	3.78	189	9.78	11.5	70.3	28.2	1.53	.067	3.26	4.18	1.33
32	42.4	28.5	29.9	1700	4.44	228	11.6	13.8	84.3	33.0	1.88	.076	4.25	5.41	1.54
34	44.8	29.9	31.5	2000	5.11	268	13.7	16.2	100.0	37.8	2.24	.085	5.36	6.77	1.78
36	47.0	31.2	33.1	2450	5.77	309	15.9	18.6	113.0	42.7	2.61	.094	6.55	8.22	2.01
38	49.1	32.4	34.4	2900	6.45	352	18.2	21.0	129.0	47.5	3.01	.103	7.86	9.82	2.26
40	51.0	33.5	35.7	3150	7.10	394	20.6	23.5	143.5	52.5	3.40	.111	9.22	11.5	2.50
Age in Years						POSTNATAL									
1		See Inside Front Cover			4	875	43	62	350	160		0.15	30	23	
5					5	1250	90	110	575	305		0.23	55	28	
10					6	1325	145	150	825	450		0.33	77	31	
15					8	1340	245	220	1275	675		0.48	125	27	
Adult† Male					6	1375	300	320	1600	1000			165	14	
Female					6	1280	250	280	1500	750			150	14	

*Time from first day of last menstrual period.
†Adapted from several sources.

the fourth and fifth months and triples by the end of one year
(see inside front cover).

F. Water Content: The water content of the body is approximately
90% by weight in early fetal life; 70 to 75% at birth; and 55 to
60% at maturity.

G. Children destined to mature sexually at an early age tend to be
tall and have an advanced bone age; late maturing children are
short and show epiphyseal retardation.

H. Obese children are usually taller and exhibit an advanced bone
age.

Head and Skull.

A. Six fontanelles are usually present at birth.
   1. The anterior fontanel normally closes between ten and 14
      months but may be closed by three months or remain open
      until 18 months.
   2. The posterior fontanel usually closes by two months but in
      some children may not be palpable even at birth.

B. Cranial sutures do not ossify completely until later childhood.

C. While the averages of head and chest circumference in the first
   four years of life are approximately equal, during this period
   the head circumference may normally be from 5 cm. larger
   to 7 cm. smaller than the chest.

D. Growth of the skull as determined by increasing head circumference is a much more accurate index of brain growth than is
   the presence or size of the fontanel.

Sinuses.

A. Maxillary and ethmoid sinuses are present at birth, but are
   usually not aerated for approximately six months. The sphenoid
   sinuses are usually not pneumatized (or visible) until after the
   third year.

B. Frontal sinuses usually become visible by x-ray between seven
   and nine years of age, seldom before five.

C. Mastoid process at birth is relatively large and has a relatively wide communication with the middle ear. Its cellular structure appears gradually between birth and three years.

Eyes.

A. Eyes can follow, even at birth, and the ability to fixate is
   usually well developed by two or three months.

B. Strabismus normally may be present for the first six to eight
   months.

Abdomen.

The abdomen tends to be prominent in infants and toddlers. In
the infant the ascending and descending portions of the colon are
short compared with the transverse colon, and the sigmoid extends
higher into the abdomen than during later life.

Muscle.

At birth muscle constitutes 25% of total body weight as compared with 43% in the adult.

Ossification Centers.

A. At birth the average full-term infant has five ossification
   centers demonstrable by x-ray: distal end of femur, proximal

end of tibia, calcaneus, talus, and cuboid.
B. The clavicle is the first bone to calcify in utero, calcification beginning during the fifth fetal week.
C. Epiphysial development of girls is consistently ahead of that of boys during all of childhood.

TABLE 3-2. Primary or deciduous teeth.

	Calcification		Eruption*		Shedding	
	Begins at	Complete at	Maxillary	Mandibular	Maxillary	Mandibular
Central incisors	4th fetal mo.	18-24 mo.	6-10 mo. (2)	5-8 mo. (1)	7-8 yrs.	6-7 yrs.
Lateral incisors	5th fetal mo.	18-24 mo.	8-12 mo. (3)	7-10 mo. (2)	8-9 yrs.	7-8 yrs.
Cuspids	6th fetal mo.	30-39 mo.	16-20 mo. (6)	16-20 mo. (6a)	11-12 yrs.	9-11 yrs.
First molars	5th fetal mo.	24-30 mo.	11-18 mo. (5)	11-18 mo. (3)	9-11 yrs.	10-12 yrs.
Second molars	6th fetal mo.	36 mo.	20-30 mo. (7)	20-30 mo. (7a)	9-12 yrs.	11-13 yrs.

TABLE 3-3. Secondary or permanent teeth.

	Calcification		Eruption*	
	Begins at	Complete at	Maxillary	Mandibular
Central incisors	3-4 mo.	9-10 yrs.	7-8 yrs. (3)	6-7 yrs. (2)
Lateral incisors	Max. 10-12 mo. Mand. 3-4 mo.	10-11 yrs.	8-9 yrs. (5)	7-8 yrs. (4)
Cuspids	4-5 mo.	12-15 yrs.	11-12 yrs. (11)	9-11 yrs. (6)
First premolars	18-24 mo.	12-13 yrs.	10-11 yrs. (7)	10-12 yrs. (8)
Second premolars	24-30 mo.	12-14 yrs.	10-12 yrs. (9)	11-13 yrs. (10)
First molars	Birth	9-10 yrs.	5$\frac{1}{2}$-7 yrs. (1)	5$\frac{1}{2}$-7 yrs. (1a)
Second molars	30-36 mo.	14-16 yrs.	12-14 yrs. (12)	12-13 yrs. (12a)
Third molars	Max. 7-9 yrs. Mand. 8-10 yrs.	18-25 yrs.	17-30 yrs. (13)	17-30 yrs. (13a)

*Figures in parentheses indicate order of eruption. Many otherwise normal infants do not conform strictly to the stated schedule.

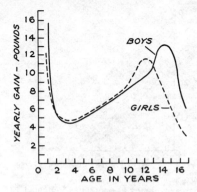

FIG 3-3. Yearly gain in weight. (Redrawn and reproduced, with permission, from Holt, McIntosh, & Barnett: Pediatrics, 13th ed. Appleton-Century-Crofts, 1962.)

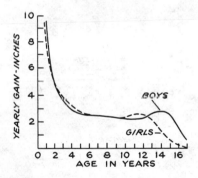

FIG 3-4. Yearly gain in height. (Redrawn and reproduced, with permission, from Holt, McIntosh, & Barnett: Ibid.)

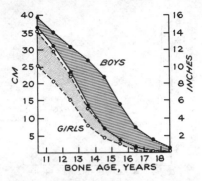

FIG 3-5. **Growth expectancy at bone ages indicated.** (Redrawn and reproduced, with permission, from Holt, McIntosh, & Barnett: Ibid.)

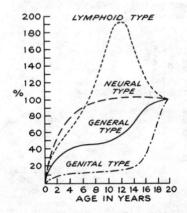

FIG 3-6. **Major types of postnatal growth of various parts and organs of the body. Lymphoid type:** Thymus, lymph nodes, intestinal lymphoid masses. **Neural type:** Brain and its parts, dura, spinal cord, optic apparatus, many head dimensions. **General type:** Body as a whole, external dimensions (with exception of head and neck), respiratory and digestive organs, kidneys, aorta and pulmonary trunks, spleen, musculature as a whole, skeleton as a whole, blood volume. **Genital type:** Testis, ovary, epididymis, uterine tube, prostate, prostatic urethra, seminal vesicles. (Redrawn and reproduced, with permission, from Holt, McIntosh, & Barnett: Ibid. [As redrawn from Scammon, in Harris et al.: Measurement of Man. University of Minnesota Press, 1930.])

4...
Nutrition & Feeding

The act of feeding is important to the young child not only because of the nutritive substances that are obtained from the food but also because of the emotional and psychological benefits that are derived. Drinking and eating are intense experiences to an infant and can and should be sources of great satisfaction. From these experiences, and from the persons who feed him, the baby obtains many of his early ideas about the nature of life and people.

Parents should be made to understand that there is much individual variation in the nutritional needs and desires of infants and that differences occur in the same child at various times.

The feeding of children is constantly being made more flexible and simple as the knowledge of their nutritional requirements increases; however, certain basic information and data are necessary for a practical understanding of the subject.

Neither strict adherence to a time schedule nor feeding when the infant cries is necessary for successful and satisfactory feeding. For most mothers and babies a flexible schedule with reasonable regularity is most satisfactory, but in some cases either a strict routine or complete "demand" feeding gives better results.

BREAST FEEDING

Advantages and Disadvantages.
  A. Advantages: Apart from considerations of economy and convenience (temperature, asepsis, automatic adjustment in most instances to infant's needs), breast feeding is superior to bottle feeding (with vitamin supplements) mainly for its psychologic advantages; because the composition of breast milk is ideal for most infants; because it may have specific antibacterial and antiviral activity and produces less infantile allergy; and for other reasons as yet unknown. Consideration must be given to the mother's attitude toward nursing, her emotional status, home conditions, breast anatomy, general health, the father's interest, and the baby's maturity, weight, vigor, appetite, and feeding characteristics.
  B. Disadvantages and Contraindications: Breast feeding is usually not possible for a weak, ill, or premature infant or one with a cleft palate or lip, although in such cases breast milk may be fed in some other way. Bottle feeding must be substituted for breast feeding if the mother's supply continues to be inadequate, as evidenced by poor weight gain, after three weeks of effort, if nipple or breast lesions are severe enough to prevent pumping, or if the mother is either pregnant or severely

(physically or mentally) ill. Menstruation is not a contraindication to breast feeding. Breast-fed infants probably should not be given oral poliomyelitis vaccine until several hours after nursing.

Breast milk may contain pregnane-3α, 20β-diol, which may be responsible for conjugated hyperbilirubinemia.

Colostrum.

Colostrum is an alkaline, yellow breast secretion which may be present in the last few months of pregnancy and for the first two to four days after delivery. It has a higher specific gravity (1.040-1.060), a higher protein, vitamin A, and mineral content, and a lower carbohydrate and fat content than breast milk.

Colostrum contains antibodies which may play a part in the immune mechanism of the newborn. Colostrum has a normal laxative action and is a natural and ideal starter food.

Transmission of Drugs and Toxins in Breast Milk.

A. Drugs Secreted in Small to Moderate Amounts: Alcohol, arsenic, barbiturates, salicylates, phenylbutazone (Butazolidin®), nicotine, caffeine, opiates, meperidine (Demerol®), quinine, hyoscine, atropine, antihistamines, vitamins, and laxatives (other than cascara). If the mother takes increased amounts of vitamin C it will be transmitted to her milk.

B. Drugs Secreted in Large Amounts or Presenting a Hazard to the Infant: Iodides, thiouracil derivatives, dicumarol, bromides, ergot, sulfonamides, tetracyclines, chloramphenicol and some other antibiotics, isoniazid, reserpine, opiates, and cascara.

Prelactation (Colostrum) Phase.

"True" milk will not come in until two to four days after delivery, and the infant may not nurse well for several days. Prelactation nursing tends to increase the milk supply, may lessen engorgement, and accustoms the mother and baby to each other. Initially, the infant should nurse no oftener than every two hours. Limit nursing at first to five minutes on each breast; after lactation begins, nursing should be limited to 20 minutes. Offer carbohydrate solution (but **not** a milk formula) to the baby if he seems hungry.

Lactation Phase.

Forty-eight to 96 hours postpartum, the breasts change from soft and empty to full and firm as milk secretion begins. The infant may be fed at each of his hungry periods, day and night. Nurse at one breast for five to ten minutes. Then put to other breast and allow to suckle as long as he seems to need it (not over 20 minutes). At next feeding, start at the breast previously nursed for the longer period. At the beginning of the lactation phase the milk supply seems to be more unstable and sensitive to stimuli such as fatigue, anxiety, and lack of suckling.

"Frequency days," when infants desire to feed oftener than they do before or afterward, occur for two or three days at the end of the first week. The infant may also have frequent, somewhat loose bowel movements (as many as 10 or 12 per day) during this same period.

The milk supply may decrease for a few days after the mother leaves the hospital. The mother should drink more fluid and have more rest during this time. Supplementary feedings should not be used during the first month. When the milk supply is adequate, the mother occasionally may limit nursing to one breast. The baby may be allowed to nurse up to 30 to 40 minutes in the absence of nipple tenderness.

After the first month, an occasional bottle should be offered in place of a feeding at the breast if the mother's milk supply is well established. When the mother leaves the baby for several hours, a milk formula and a bottle of sweetened water should be available. Solid food probably should not be added until the baby is at least three months old.

Weaning.

There is no "best time" for weaning, which depends on the needs and desires of both infant and mother. Gradual weaning is preferred. Cup or bottle feedings are increased progressively over a period of several days or weeks when the infant is to be weaned. Older infants may be weaned directly to the cup.

ARTIFICIAL FEEDING

Various formulas are in use; one consists of a standard formula for every baby (such as 13 oz. of evaporated milk, 19 oz. of water, and 1 or 1 1/2 oz. of added carbohydrate), allowing the appetite and digestive capacity of the child to determine the volume and number of feedings that will be taken. The physician should be acquainted with the basic requirements of artificial feeding and should be prepared to write an individual formula for each child which takes into account the infant's needs and desires. An evaporated milk-water-sugar formula has an advantage over proprietary preparations in that it can be more closely tailored to the infant's needs and is often less expensive.

If the formula is adequate in amount and composition and the infant is held while being fed, he will gain the physical or emotional satisfaction that accompanies breast feeding.

Recent studies have suggested that formulas containing elemental iron evoke more uniform hematologic values and are associated with a lower incidence of upper respiratory infections, but the value of such supplementation is doubtful.

Preparation of the Formula. (See Table 4-1.)

The exact ingredients should be determined by the physician.
A. An infant generally does not need more than one quart of whole milk or one large can (13 fl. oz.) of evaporated milk per day.
B. Sterilization of the formula is necessary only as long as some of the bottles must be stored before being used. Terminal sterilization is recommended.
C. Size of Nipple Holes: The holes are of the right caliber if a drop of milk forms on the end of the nipple and drops off with little shaking of the cool bottle when turned upside down.
D. One pint of whole milk per day is adequate for the child from one to five years of age who otherwise is receiving a reasonable diet.

TABLE 4-1. Satisfactory composition and schedule of milk feedings for infants up to one year of age.

Age (mo.)	0	1	2	3	4	5	6	7	8	9	10	11	12
Cal./day*	130-100/Kg. (60-45/lb.)					110-100/Kg. (50-45/lb.)				·100-90/Kg. (45-40/lb.)			
Fluid/day (ml.)	130-200/Kg. (2-3 oz./lb.)				130-165/Kg. (2-2½ oz./lb.)					130/Kg. (2 oz./lb.)			
No. feed./day†	6 or 7		4 or 5					3 or 4			3		
Oz./feeding	2.5-4	3.5-5	4-6	5-7	6-8	7-9							
Milk:‡													
Evaporated	65 ml./Kg. (1 oz./lb.) up to a total of 13 oz. (1 can) daily												
Whole	130 ml./Kg. (2 oz./lb.) up to a total of 28-32 oz. daily												
Sugar/day	1-1.5 oz. (30-45 Gm.)					§		None					

*The larger amount should be used for the younger infant.
†Will vary somewhat with individual babies.
‡Calories/oz.: Evaporated milk = 44; whole milk = 20; cane sugar = 120; Karo® = 120.
§Decrease sugar by ½ oz. (15 Gm.) every two weeks.

Whole milk: May be substituted for evaporated milk when sugar is no longer added to formula, but evaporated milk may be continued indefinitely.
Vitamins: Some prepared milk formulas may be deficient in vitamins C and D, and need to be supplemented with vitamins (25-50 mg. of C and 400 units of D daily).
Underweight or overweight infants generally have the same food requirements as do infants of the same age with a normal weight.
Undiluted whole milk or formulas of equal parts of evaporated milk and water should not be used for young infants, since their kidneys do not have a range of safety in the event of high environmental or body temperature.
Iron: Iron supplementation of formulas has been recommended, but its necessity and potential dangers have not been proved.

Feeding the Baby.

A. The bottle should be held, not propped.
B. More water may be added to formula if the infant consistently finishes each bottle and is receiving a liberal quantity of calories.
C. Infant need not take all of every bottle.
D. Baby should be burped during and at end of feeding.
E. After feeding, baby should be placed on side (preferably right) or prone.
F. Additional Fluids: A few ounces of water (with or without added sugar) should be offered between feedings once or twice every day, especially during excessively hot weather or when the baby is ill, regardless of whether it is ordinarily taken or not.

Vitamins.

Supplemental vitamins are usually unnecessary for the older child who is eating a relatively well balanced diet. The ingestion of more than the daily dietary requirement of vitamins is unnecessary and potentially harmful.

Vitamin C (or vitamin preparations containing vitamin C) may be placed directly into the infant's mouth. If it is put in the formula, it should be added just before feeding and after the bottle has been warmed. Orange juice may be started at any time during the first year; when orange juice is given in adequate amounts (3 oz. or more), supplemental vitamin C is no longer necessary.

TABLE 4-2.   Comparison of breast milk and cow's milk.
(Adapted from several sources.)

	Breast Milk	Whole Cow's Milk
Water	87-88%	83-88%
Protein	0.8-1.5%	3.2-4.1%
Lactalbumin	0.7-0.8%	0.5%
Casein	0.4-0.5%	3.0%
Sugar (lactose)	5.5-8.0%	4.5-5.0%
Fat	3.0-4.0%	3.5-5.2%
Minerals	0.15-0.25%	0.7-0.75%
Calcium	0.034-0.045%	0.122-0.179%
Phosphorus	0.015-0.040%	0.090-0.196%
Sodium	0.011-0.019%	0.051-0.060%
Potassium	0.048-0.065%	0.138-0.172%
Iron	0.0001-0.002%	0.00004-0.00015%
Copper	0.00003%	0.00002%
Vitamins (per 100 ml.)		
A	60-500 I.U.	80-220 I.U.*
C	1.2-10.8 mg.	0.9-1.8 mg.*
D	0.4-10.0 I.U.	0.3-4.4 I.U.*
Thiamine	0.002-0.036 mg.	0.03-0.04 mg.*
Riboflavin	0.015-0.080 mg.	0.10-0.26*
Niacin	0.10-0.20 mg.	0.10 mg.
Calories per fl. oz.	17-20	20

*Values are for pasteurized milk.

TABLE 4-3.   Approximate daily expenditure of
calories for first year.

Basal metabolism	55 Cal./Kg.
Specific dynamic action of foods	9 Cal./Kg.
Caloric loss in the excreta	8-11 Cal./Kg.
Allowance for bodily activity	22 Cal./Kg.
Growth	15-20 Cal./Kg.
Total:	110-120 Cal./Kg.

Night Feedings.

Infants will go eight hours between feedings at night at an average age of 1.25 months (range: newborn to 15 months). There is no correlation between the interval between feedings at night and such things as the age solids are added, type of milk offered, caloric intake, birth weight, or weight gain.

Weaning.

Small amounts of fluid may be offered from a cup at around four to six months; weaning from the bottle is best done gradually and may not be completed for several months.

Cost of Feedings for Young Infants.

The most economical feeding regimen consists of a formula containing vitamin D fortified evaporated milk, water, granulated sugar (or corn syrup), and ascorbic acid tablets.

TABLE 4-4. Composition of foods used for infant feeding.*

Name	Classification	Source	Normal Dilution†	Calories/Fl. Oz. Normal Dilution	Protein (Gm.)	Fat (Gm.)	CHO (Gm.)
Alacta®	Infant food modifier	Half skimmed milk powder	1:7	17	4.2	1.5	5.9
Baker's Infant Formula®	Routine infant food	Modified milk, sugars, fats	L=1:1, P=1:8	20	2.2	3.3	7.0
Bremil®	Routine infant food	Milk protein with oils, lactose	L=1:1, P=1:8	20	1.5	3.5	7.0
Carnalac®	Routine infant food	Milk with lactose	1:1	20	2.8	3.2	7.1
Casec®	Infant food modifier	Calcium caseanate	Varies	370‡	88	2	0
Dexin®	Infant food modifier	Dextrin, maltose	Varies	390	-	-	98‡
Dextri-Maltose® No. 1	Infant food modifier	Hydrolysis of starch	Varies		-	-	-
Dryco®	Low fat infant food	Whole and skimmed milk	1:8	16	4.0	1.5	5.7
Enfamil®	Routine infant food	Nonfat milk, lactose, oils	L=1:1, P=1:6	20	1.5	3.7	7.0
Evaporated milk	Routine infant food	Cow's milk	1:2	15	2.3	2.7	3.5
Gerber's Meat Base Formula®	Hypoallergenic infant food	Beef, fat, CHO	13:19.5	20	2.7	3.1	4.0
Isomil®	Hypoallergenic infant food	Soy, oils, corn sugar, sucrose	1:1	20	2.0	3.6	6.8
Lipomul®	Infant food modifier	Corn oil	-	180	-	-	-
Lofenalac®	Low phenylalanine	Casein hydrolysate, fat, CHO	1:6	20	2.2	2.7	8.5
Lonalac®	Low sodium infant formula	Casein, coconut oil, lactose	1:6	20	3.4	3.5	4.8
Lytren®	Oral electrolyte formula	-	80 Gm:1 qt.	8	-	-	-
Milk, cow	Routine infant food	-	-	20	3.3	3.7	4.8
Milk, human	Routine infant food	-	-	20	1.1-1.25	3.5-4.5	7.0
Modilac®	Routine infant food	Nonfat milk, corn syrup, corn oil	1:1	20	2.2	3.3	7.0
Mullsoy®‡§	Hypoallergenic infant food	Soy and sucrose	1 tbsp:2 oz.	20	3.1	4.0	4.5

Product	Description	Composition	Dilution†				
Nutramigen®	Modified infant food	Protein hydrolysate, sucrose, starch, corn oil	1:6	20	2.2	2.6	8.5
Olac®	Modified infant food	Nonfat milk, oil, CHO	L=1:1, P=1:6	20	3.4	2.7	7.5
Pedialyte Solution®	Oral electrolyte mixture		-	6	-	-	-
PM 60/40®	Low solute infant food	Nonfat milk, whey, oils	4:32	20	1.5	3.4	7.2
Portagen®	Modified infant food	Skimmed milk, sucrose, medium chain triglycerides, starch, oil	-				
Pregestimil†	Modified infant formula	Glucose, medium chain triglycerides, hydrolyzed casein	1:6	21	2.7	3.2	7.7
Probana®	Modified infant food	Casein hydrolysate, banana, lactic acid					-
ProSobee®	Hypoallergenic infant food		1:6	20	3.9	2.0	7.3
Protinal®	Protein product	Casein with CHO	1:1	20	2.5	3.4	6.8
SMA®			30 Gm.:1 oz.		61.25	<1.0	36.0
Similac®	Routine infant food		L=1:1, P=1:8	20	1.5	3.6	7.2
Somagen®	Routine infant food		L=1:1, P=1:8	20	1.7	3.4	6.6
Soyalac®‡§	Protein product	Milk, yeast, liver	Varies	-	70	-	22‡
Varamel®	Hypoallergenic infant food	Soy, oils, CHO	1:7	-	3.3	3.7	6.2
	Routine infant food	Modified milk, corn oil	1:1	16	2.5	2.9	4.2

*Adapted from data from the Department of Nutrition, University Hospital, University of Iowa.
†L = liquid; P = powder.
‡Composition per 100 Gm. powder.
§Also available in liquid form.

TABLE 4-5. Approximate daily dietary requirements of children at different ages under ordinary conditions. (Adapted from recommendations of the Committee on Growth and Development of the White House Conference on Child Health and Protection, the Food and Nutrition Board of the National Research Council, and other sources.)

	Water		Calories		Protein		Minerals*			Vitamins						
	ml./Kg.	oz./lb.	per Kg.	per lb.	Gm./Kg.	Gm./lb.	Ca (Gm.)	P (Gm.)	Fe (mg.)	A (I.U.)	B₁ (mg.)	B₂ (mg.)	Niacin (mg.)	C (mg.)	D (U.S.P.)	E (I.U.)
3 Days	80-100	1.2 -1.5														
10 Days	125-150	1.9 -2.3	100-130	45-60	3.5-4	1.8										
3 Months	140-165	2.1 -2.5			3.5-4		0.4	0.24	10	1400	0.3	0.4	5	35		5
6 Months	130-155	2 -2.3			3.5	1.6	0.5	0.4	15	2000	0.5	0.6	8	35	400	5
9 Months	125-145	1.9 -2.2			2.5				15	2000	0.7	0.8	9	35		5
1-3 Years	115-135	1.7 -2	90-100	41-45	2.5	1.4	0.8	0.8	15	2000	0.7	0.8	9	40	400	10
4-6 Years	90-110	1.3 -1.7	80-90	36-41	2.2	1.4	0.8	0.8	10	2500	0.9	1.1	13	40	400	20
7-9 Years	70-90	1.1 -1.3	70-80	32-36	2.2	1.1	0.8	0.8	10	3500	1.0	1.2	16	40	400	30
10-12 Years	60-85	0.9 -1.3	60-70	27-32	1.8	0.9	1.1	1.2	14	4500	1.0	1.4	18	50	400	30
13-15 Years	50-65	0.75-1	50-60	23-27	1.7	0.7	1.2	1.2	18	5000	1.5	1.8	20	50	400	30
15+	45-55	0.67-0.8	40-50	18-23	1.4	0.5+	1.2	1.2	18	5000	1.5	1.5	20	50	400	30
Adult	40-50	0.6 -0.75	40-45	18-21	1	0.5	0.8	0.8	10-18	5000	1.5	1.4	18	50	400	30

*Other minerals (all ages):

Magnesium	200-400 mg./day
Potassium	1-2 Gm./day
Sodium	1-2 Gm./day
Chloride	2-3 Gm./day
Iodine	45-150 μg./day

Other vitamins:

Folacin   Under 6 months, 0.05 mg.; 6 months to 10 years, 0.1-0.3 mg.; over 10 years, 0.4 mg.

B₆   Levels similar to thiamine up to 12 years; over 12 years, 1.6-2 mg.

B₁₂   Under 1 year, 1-2 μg.; 1 to 8 years, 2-4 μg.; over 8 years, 5 μg.

SOLID FOODS

Common Solid Foods and Time of Adding.

Solid foods may be added to the diet as follows: Single grain cereal (preferably rice), 2-4 months; puréed vegetables, 3-4 months; fruits and juices, 4-5 months; strained meat, egg yolk, 5-6 months; bacon, 8 months; finely chopped table foods, 9 months; egg white, 12 months.

A. Beginning Solid Foods: There is no exact time or order that is important in starting "solid" foods. The first physiologic requirement for foods other than milk occurs about the age of 4-6 months when a need for iron develops. Whenever solid foods are started, they should initially be given in small amounts for several consecutive days to determine the child's reaction and any adverse response. The amount given should be gradually increased if the food is well tolerated. If the baby continues to refuse it, another food may be tried; if that, too, is rejected, discontinue the attempt for a week or two before trying again. Commercially prepared baby foods have no nutritional advantage over those prepared by the mother.

B. Spoon Feeding: Many infants can learn to take semisolid food from a small spoon before the fourth month. If the infant cannot master spoon feeding, postpone the attempt for a few weeks; otherwise, undesirable behavior reactions can occur which may make spoon feeding difficult for months.

C. The transition from strained to chopped foods should be gradual and may be started when the infant begins to make chewing motions.

D. Egg and wheat should not be given to potentially allergic children (e.g., family predisposition) until the latter part of the first year.

E. Permit infant to feed himself with fingers or a spoon when he wishes to do so.

Digestion in Infancy.

Protein digestion and absorption are excellent in infancy. Amylase is present in only small quantities. The gastric glands are functionally active at birth and secrete hydrochloric acid (small quantities), pepsin, and rennin. Salivary digestion is relatively unimportant during early infancy.

Breast-fed babies usually empty the stomach by two to three hours; bottle-fed babies may require three to four hours or longer; newborn babies may empty the stomach even more slowly.

VITAMIN DEFICIENCIES AND HYPERVITAMINOSES

VITAMIN A DEFICIENCY AND EXCESS

Vitamin A deficiency is an uncommon condition which occurs only when children are given a deficient diet or when absorption or storage is impaired (chronic use of unfortified skimmed milk, chronic intestinal disorders, celiac syndrome, hepatic and pancreatic diseases, or prolonged use of mineral oil). It is characterized by failure to gain weight or to grow, xerophthalmia with loss of visual efficiency (night blindness, see p. 353) going on to keratomalacia, and dryness, scaliness, and follicular hyperkeratosis of the skin. Serum vitamin A levels are lowered, and dark adaptation is impaired.

Treatment consists of administration of oleovitamin A, 20,000 to 50,000 units daily for one to two weeks. The prognosis is excellent, but if necrosis and ulceration of the cornea have occurred some loss of vision may result.

Vitamin A toxicity in infancy is characterized by irritability, anorexia, tense fontanelles, craniotabes, and skin desquamation, especially of palms and soles. In older children, cortical hyperostosis may occur (see p. 361).

VITAMIN B₁ (THIAMINE CHLORIDE) DEFICIENCY
(Beriberi)

Thiamine deficiency results from inadequate intake, due usually (in developed countries) to idiosyncrasies of diet or excessive cooking or processing of foods. It is characterized by loss of appetite, listlessness, irritability, vomiting, constipation, and edema. Cardiac signs of deficiency include dyspnea, tachycardia, cyanosis, and signs of cardiac dilatation and failure. C. N. S. signs include apathy, drowsiness, peripheral neuritis (including cranial nerves), loss of deep tendon reflexes, paresthesias, convulsions, and coma.

In addition to correction of dietary abnormalities, treatment consists of giving thiamine hydrochloride, 10 to 50 mg. daily orally or parenterally for several weeks, or dried yeast tablets (brewer's yeast), 5 to 30 Gm. t. i. d.

VITAMIN B₂ (RIBOFLAVIN) DEFICIENCY

Riboflavin deficiency may occur in association with thiamine and niacin deficiencies and in galactosemia. It is characterized by thinness, maceration, and superficial fissuring of the skin at the angles of the mouth; smoothness, loss of papillary structure, and redness of the tongue; fissures and seborrheic dermatitis, especially in the nasolabial folds; and by vascularization and infiltration of the cornea and interstitial keratitis, with itching, photophobia, and excessive tearing.

In addition to correction of dietary deficiencies, treatment consists of administration of riboflavin, 3 to 10 mg. daily by mouth for several weeks, and dried yeast tablets (brewer's yeast), 5 to 30 Gm. t. i. d. If no response occurs within a few days, 2 mg. of riboflavin in saline solution may be given three times daily I.V.

NIACIN (NICOTINIC ACID, P.P. FACTOR) DEFICIENCY
(Pellagra)

Niacin deficiency is the principal but not the only dietary defect in pellagra. Early manifestations may include burning sensations, numbness, dizziness, anorexia, and weakness. Sharply demarcated, symmetrical areas of erythema appear on exposed portions of the body; these may become dark red, and are followed by scaling and residual pigmentation. Superficial vesicles may develop. Gastrointestinal symptoms include swelling and redness of the tongue, stomatitis, and vomiting and diarrhea. Effects upon the C.N.S. include depression, inability to sleep, and delirium.

Treatment is with nicotinamide (niacinamide), 50 to 300 mg. daily orally, or approximately half this amount I.M., I.V., or by hypodermoclysis. Nicotinic acid (niacin) is less frequently used because of its vasodilating effect. Dosage is similar.

Give also dried yeast tablets (brewer's yeast), 5 to 30 Gm., t.i.d., and a well-balanced diet when tolerated.

VITAMIN B$_6$ (PYRIDOXINE) DEFICIENCY

In young infants, vitamin B$_6$ deficiency has been reported to cause abnormal C.N.S. activity with increased irritability, gastrointestinal distress (abdominal distention, vomiting, diarrhea), aggravated startle responses, and convulsive seizures. The latter are of four types: (1) repeated and short, (2) limited to staring, (3) generalized shaking with transient cyanosis, or (4) very severe with status epilepticus. The spinal fluid protein is elevated. The deficiency has occurred chiefly where modified milk formulas were autoclaved in such a way that the pyridoxine was destroyed.

Occasionally infants are "pyridoxine dependent" and develop the manifestations of vitamin B$_6$ deficiency unless they are given large amounts of this vitamin.

Treatment is with pyridoxine (I.V. for active treatment of convulsions) and dietary correction. Clinical and EEG improvement is rapid, and recovery is usually complete.

VITAMIN C (ASCORBIC ACID) DEFICIENCY (SCURVY)

Avitaminosis C is usually due to inadequate intake. It may occur at any age but is most common between seven months and two years and is rare in the newborn infant. It is characterized by progressive irritability, especially when handled. The legs are held in the typical "frog position"; they are extremely tender when handled, are moved very little (pseudoparalysis), may be edematous, and may have palpable subperiosteal hemorrhages.

Hemorrhages may occur into the skin and into or from mucous membranes. Gums are bluish-purple and swollen, especially about erupted teeth. Marked angular mushrooming of the costochondral junction ("rosary") and depression of the sternum are also noted. Laboratory findings include reduction of capillary resistance and decrease of serum or white blood cell ascorbic acid levels. X-rays show thinning of bone cortices, loss of trabecular pattern ("ground glass" appearance), and thickening and irregularity at the epiphysial line, with a subepiphysial zone of rarefaction. Lateral spurring from the line of increased density and epiphysial separation may occur. Subperiosteal hemorrhages become visible during healing when the elevated periosteum becomes calcified.

Treatment is with ascorbic acid, 100 to 500 mg. per day orally (citrus juices sufficient to give an equivalent amount of ascorbic acid are also satisfactory), or sodium ascorbate injection, 0.2 to 0.5 Gm. I.V. or I.M. daily in divided doses for one week. With treatment, clinical improvement is rapid (within 48 hours), but x-ray evidence of healing may not appear for a week or more. Recovery is usually complete.

VITAMIN D DEFICIENCY (RICKETS)

Vitamin D deficiency may occur when there is inadequate intake of vitamin D and insufficient exposure to ultraviolet rays. It is more likely to occur, however, during periods of rapid growth, and produces the most marked changes in the bones that are growing most rapidly. It is uncommon in the first two or three months.

Clinical Findings.
A. Head: Craniotabes (early), asymmetry, bossing ("hot cross bun" skull), increased size of the fontanelles and skull, and delayed closure of the fontanelles.
B. Teeth: Delayed dentition, defects of the enamel, and a tendency to develop caries. The permanent teeth may be affected.
C. Thorax: Costochondral prominence ("rachitic rosary"), "pigeon-breast" deformity, flaring of the chest, and a depression along the insertion of the diaphragm (Harrison's groove).
D. Extremities: Widening of the epiphyses and bending of the shafts of the long bones. Green stick fractures may occur.
E. Other Bones: Scoliosis or kyphosis of the spine; deformity of the pelvis.
F. Other Findings: Relaxation of ligaments and poor development and tone of the muscles, with resultant deformities at the joints, protrusion of abdomen, weakness, and constipation. Shortness of stature may be an end result. Infantile tetany may occur.

Laboratory Findings.
Serum calcium is normal except with tetany. Serum phosphorus is decreased and alkaline phosphatase increased.

X-ray Findings.
Cupping, fraying, and flaring are seen at the ends of the bone. Shafts are denser than normal, and the trabeculae are prominent. The distance between calcified portion of shaft and the epiphysial center is increased. Periosteal reaction may occur.

Treatment and Prognosis.
Oleovitamin D, calciferol (D_2), or 7-dehydrocholesterol, activated (D_3), 10,000 to 50,000 units daily by mouth for one week, followed by 2000 to 5000 units daily for several months, plus adequate milk. Some cases of rickets are exceedingly resistant and require huge doses of vitamin D (25,000 to 150,000 I.U. per day). Healing may be complete, but in severe cases some deformity usually remains.

• • •

PROTEIN DEPRIVATION
(Kwashiorkor)

Kwashiorkor is caused by severe protein deficiency despite adequate calories, and is characterized by retarded growth and development, apathy, anorexia, edema, abdominal distention, skin and hair depigmentation and other skin lesions, diarrhea, and anemia. Duodenal and serum enzymes, serum cholesterol, and total lipids are decreased, and there is an absolute and relative decrease in serum albumin and an increase in the relative amounts of alpha and gamma globulins. Patients may not absorb disaccharides efficiently.

Treatment is with a gradually increasing high-protein, balanced diet and adequate vitamin supplements. Supplemental magnesium and potassium as well as routine broad-spectrum antibiotics may be of value.

5...
Fluid & Electrolyte Disorders

Robert W. Winters, M.D.*

FUNDAMENTAL CONSIDERATIONS

Fluid and electrolyte therapy should be divided into three phases: (1) repair of pre-existing deficits, (2) provision of maintenance requirements, and (3) correction of on-going losses.

Repair of Pre-existing Deficits.

Water, sodium, chloride, and potassium deficits occur through renal or extrarenal channels. It is the aim of deficit therapy to estimate and correct these deficits as soon and as safely as possible. These losses are best expressed in terms of body weight (ml. or mEq. per Kg. body weight).

Provision of Maintenance Requirements.

Maintenance requirements occur as a result of normal expenditures of water and electrolytes through the usual channels as the result of normal metabolism. These requirements bear a close relationship to metabolic rate and are ideally formulated in terms of caloric expenditure. However, it is easier to calculate maintenance requirements in terms of body weight, although factors which alter metabolic rate must be given consideration.

Correction of On-Going Losses.

Extrarenal losses may occur during therapy, usually via the gastrointestinal tract through loss (vomiting or diarrhea) or removal (suction) of secretions. Replacement of such losses should be made contemporaneously with losses and should be similar in type and amount to the fluid being lost. Hence such a replacement is best formulated as ml. of fluid and mEq. of electrolyte replaced per ml. of fluid and mEq. of electrolyte lost.

CALCULATION AND CORRECTION OF FLUID AND ELECTROLYTE LOSSES

DEFICIT THERAPY

History.

A detailed analysis of the history should be undertaken with the aim of determining (1) the magnitude of the deficit of water and

*Professor of Pediatrics, College of Physicians and Surgeons, Columbia University, and Attending Pediatrician, Babies Hospital and Vanderbilt Clinic, New York.

electrolyte; (2) whether or not an acid-base disturbance is present and, if so, what type; and (3) whether or not a significant potassium deficit is present.

The history should include information pertinent to the following: (1) type, severity, and duration of the loss; (2) an estimate of the weight loss (a recent pre-illness weight is often available, especially in infants); (3) estimates of the type and amount of the loss and of the intake (a balance sheet should be prepared); (4) frequency and approximate quantity of urine voided during illness; and (5) presence of fever or sweating.

Physical Examination.

A. Signs of Dehydration:
1. Skin and subcutaneous tissues - Dryness of the skin and mucous membranes, depression of the anterior fontanel, poor skin turgor (chronically malnourished infants may exhibit poor skin turgor without significant dehydration, whereas obese infants may become quite dehydrated without developing poor turgor). Sclerematous changes of skin suggest hypertonic dehydration.
2. Cardiovascular - Poor peripheral circulation, tachycardia, oliguria, and hypotension.
3. Fever, especially in the absence of infection.
4. In the average infant, when these signs are marked the total water deficit will be about 10 to 15% of body weight.
5. In children, the comparable figures are about 5 to 10% of body weight.

B. Signs Suggesting Specific Abnormalities: (For clinical signs of specific electrolyte disturbances, see pp. 70 ff.)
1. Hyperpnea is seen in metabolic acidosis, respiratory alkalosis, and sometimes in advanced pulmonary disease with respiratory acidosis.
2. Hypoventilation is present in respiratory acidosis due to central respiratory depression.
3. Cyanosis often occurs with respiratory acidosis.
4. Positive Chvostek and Trousseau signs and tetany may indicate respiratory or metabolic alkalosis.
5. Generalized seizures may be seen in alkalosis, water intoxication, and respiratory acidosis.

Laboratory Examination.

Laboratory examination gives information bearing upon abnormalities in (1) volume of body fluids and (2) concentration of specific components of the extracellular fluid.

A. Abnormalities in Volume of the Body Fluids:
1. An increase in the packed cell volume, hemoglobin, and serum proteins indicates hemoconcentration and (except in burns) diminished volume of the extracellular fluid. Intelligent interpretation of these indices requires an estimate of the pre-illness values.
2. Urine examination - The specific gravity of the urine in dehydration is usually higher than 1.010 unless diabetes insipidus or renal disease is present. However, a number of factors (solute excretion, potassium depletion) exert marked influences upon renal concentrating ability. There-

fore the specific gravity may not be very high in spite of severe dehydration. Significant glycosuria and proteinuria will elevate specific gravity.

Slight proteinuria, hyaline casts, and a few formed elements are often found in the urine of dehydrated patients and under these circumstances are not indicative of intrinsic renal disease. Ketonuria may be present. Nitroprusside and ferric chloride tests for ketones should be performed on the urine. Confirmation of the presence of ketones may be obtained by retesting the urine after volatilization of the ketones by acidification and boiling. A freshly voided urine specimen should be tested for pH, using indicator papers.

3. Elevation of the nonprotein nitrogen or blood urea nitrogen in the absence of pre-existing renal disease nearly always indicates a significant reduction of the functional extracellular volume. For this reason either of these determinations provides valuable information in the interpretation of serum electrolyte determinations and in the management of dehydrated patients.

B. Abnormalities in Concentrations of Specific Components: Abnormalities of serum sodium, potassium, and total CO_2 content are discussed in subsequent sections. Initial study of the serum electrolytes is highly desirable in any patient presenting with a serious disturbance of hydration or acid-base balance. In evaluating these determinations, it is important to exclude an obvious laboratory error by subtracting the sum of total CO_2 and chloride (both in mEq./L.) from the value for sodium (in mEq./L.). This difference is normally 10 mEq./L. and may be even greater, depending upon the normal values of any given laboratory; when the difference is less than 5 mEq./L., or when it is negative, a laboratory error has been made. This relationship can also be used to predict serum sodium from data on total CO_2 and chloride (serum Na^+ = total CO_2 + Cl^- + 10), but the result of this calculation is accurate only in the absence of excesses of other serum anions (phosphate, ketone acids, etc.).

Determination of the initial level of serum sodium is most important since it allows the classification of dehydration as isotonic (normal serum Na^+), hypotonic (low serum Na^+), or hypertonic (high serum Na^+). It is of particular importance to recognize the hypertonic state since specific therapeutic measures are called for in such cases (see p. 62). With hyperglycemia, the serum sodium may be low even though the dehydration is hypertonic or isotonic; this is because glucose contributes to the effective osmotic pressure of the extracellular fluid and draws water out of cells, thus diluting extracellular constituents. Hyperlipemia can produce an artifactual hyponatremia due to displacement of plasma water by lipids.

General Comments Concerning Deficits.

A. The Usual Magnitude of Deficits: The usual magnitude of deficits of sodium and water encountered in severe dehydration in infants is shown in Table 5-1.

TABLE 5-1. Magnitude of deficits of water and sodium.

	Water (ml./Kg.)	Sodium (mEq./Kg.)
Isotonic	100-120	8-10
Hypertonic	100-120	2-4
Hypotonic	100-120	10-12

Chloride deficits tend to parallel those for sodium but are also conditioned by the type of acid-base disturbance which develops. Potassium depletion usually complicates most instances of dehydration except those associated with adrenal cortical insufficiency or advanced renal insufficiency. These deficits are usually about 8-10 mEq./Kg. in a severe case; they may be higher in cases with alkalosis.

All of the above figures apply to severe dehydration in an infant. Less severe cases require proportionally less. In children with severe dehydration, the deficits are only about three-fourths of those encountered in infants.

B. General Outline of Treatment of Deficits:
1. Initial therapy should be aimed at restoring blood and extra-cellular fluid volume in order to relieve or to prevent shock and to restore renal function. This therapy should always be given intravenously. It is most convenient to initiate therapy with an isotonic sodium solution (10-20 ml./Kg.) either as sodium chloride or as a balanced sodium solution (Table 5-2) or Ringer's lactate, pending the results of the initial laboratory determinations. If the circulatory status is not improved following this infusion (1-2 hours), a colloid solution (10-20 ml./Kg.) should be given over the next hour or two.
2. The next phase of therapy should be devoted to repair of the remaining deficits of sodium, chloride, and water; this phase should be started as soon as circulatory status is improved. The formulation of this phase is dependent upon the relationship between the losses of water and sodium as these are reflected in the initial serum sodium.
   a. Isotonic dehydration - An additional 40-60 ml./Kg. of an isotonic sodium solution should be given over the next 12-18 hours for infants; 20-40 ml./Kg. is more appropriate for children.
   b. Hypotonic dehydration - In cases with severe hyponatremia, particularly when this is associated with symptoms suggesting cellular overhydration or persistently poor circulatory status, an infusion of hypertonic sodium solution calculated according to the formula given on p. 73 should be given. Lesser degrees of hypotonicity may be managed adequately by providing 10-20 ml./Kg. more of isotonic sodium solution than the amounts given above for isotonic dehydration.
   c. Hypertonic dehydration - In severe hypernatremic states, convulsions often accompany the rapid reduction of serum sodium to normal levels. Since circulatory collapse does not often accompany this type of dehydration, it is ad-

visable to follow a more leisurely program (48-72 hours) in reducing serum sodium to normal.

3. Repair of potassium deficits may be started after deficits of sodium, water, and chloride have been largely repaired (generally 18-24 hours after admission); since potassium must be administered slowly (see p. 71), significant deficits require several days for repletion.

4. Restoration of protein and caloric deficits may be started as soon as the patient can tolerate full oral feedings. Several weeks may be required for complete repair of these deficits.

In treating deficits, body weight and the serum electrolytes and BUN or NPN should be closely observed. Satisfactory therapy of the dehydration will be accompanied by an acute gain of body weight of about 10% and a prompt fall in the level of urea nitrogen.

Use of Solutions for Fluid Therapy.

Many fluids of highly complex composition have been recommended for treating dehydration. However, such specialized fluids are expensive and unnecessary. Virtually every problem encountered can be effectively managed with the use of combinations of the following simple, commonly available fluids: (1) 0.9% saline (155 mEq./L. of Na^+ and Cl^-), (2) 5% saline (855 mEq./L. of Na^+ and Cl^-), (3) 5 or 10% glucose in water. Appropriate additions may be made using the following additives (available in ampuls): 14.9% potassium chloride (2 mEq./ml. of K^+ and Cl^-), and 7.9% $NaHCO_3$ (45 mEq./50 ml. ampul of Na^+ and HCO_3^-). These additives should never be given undiluted.

An example of an isotonic "balanced" sodium solution (135 mEq./L. of Na^+, 105 mEq./L. of Cl^-, and 30 mEq./L. of HCO_3^-) is given in Table 5-2.

TABLE 5-2. Isotonic "balanced" sodium solution.

	Volume (ml.)	mEq.		
		Na^+	Cl^-	HCO_3^-
7.9% $NaHCO_3$*	33	30		30
0.9% NaCl	682	105	105	
Pyrogen-free H_2O	q.s. ad 1000			
Totals	1000	135	105	30

*180 ml. of M/6 sodium lactate may be used in place of $NaHCO_3$.

MAINTENANCE REQUIREMENTS FOR FLUID AND ELECTROLYTE

Maintenance therapy attempts to provide adequate water, sodium, chloride, and potassium to meet normal requirements. With presently available solutions it is virtually impossible to satisfy protein, carbohydrate, and fat requirements by peripheral vein, but fortunately this is seldom necessary. When it is necessary, a regimen of total parenteral nutrition should be provided by use of a central venous catheter. One should attempt to provide sufficient carbohydrate to prevent ketosis and to minimize protein breakdown without giving so much carbohydrate that severe glycosuria is produced. In general, the minimal amount of carbohydrate necessary to achieve these aims is that which provides about 25% of the total caloric expenditure (i.e., 25 Calories from carbohydrate or 6.5 Gm. of glucose per 100 Calories expended). For this amount to be effective it should be given either continuously over the entire 24-hour period for which it is intended or in multiple small doses during that period. It will not be effective and may produce glycosuria if given within a few hours. Average maintenance requirements are shown in Table 5-3.

As formulated, the maintenance requirements do not include allowances for such complicating factors as fever, excessive sweating, excessive insensible loss through hyperventilation, or impaired renal function. Appropriate adjustments of water and/or electrolyte requirements should be made under any of these circumstances. The amount of such adjustment is best determined by close observation of the patient and serial study of the serum electrolytes and serum nonprotein or urea nitrogen.

Composition of Maintenance Solutions.

For the requirements listed in Table 5-3, the solutions shown in Table 5-4 will be satisfactory. An alternative solution similar in composition with respect to sodium, potassium, and carbohydrate may be made by mixing 160 ml. of a balanced iso-

TABLE 5-3. Average maintenance requirements for fluid and electrolyte therapy.

	H_2O (ml./Kg.)	Na^+ (mEq./Kg.)	K^+ (mEq./Kg.)	Carbohydrate (Gm./Kg.)
Premature	50-70	1.5-2.0	1.5-2.0	2-3
Newborn	40-60	0.8-1.0	0.8-1.0	2-3
4-10 Kg.	120-100	2.5-2.0	2.5-2.0	5-6
10-20 Kg.	100-80	2.0-1.6	2.0-1.6	4-5
20-40 Kg.	80-60	1.6-1.2	1.6-1.2	3-4
Adult total	2500-3000	50	50	100-150

TABLE 5-4. Maintenance solutions.

	Volume (ml.)	mEq.				Carbohydrate (Gm.)
		Na^+	K^+	Cl^-	HCO_3^-	
7.9% $NaHCO_3$ *	16.7	20			20	
14.9% KCl	10		20	20		
5% glucose in water	q.s. ad 1000					43.5
Total	1000	20	20	20	20	43.5

*120 ml. of M/6 sodium lactate may be used in place of $NaHCO_3$.

tonic sodium solution (see p. 58) or Ringer's lactate with 840 ml. of 5% glucose in water and adding 10 ml. of 14.9% KCl to ensure a final concentration of 20 mM./L. of KCl.

Higher concentrations of glucose or other carbohydrates (invert sugar or fructose) may be used, but if the solution is hypertonic it must be given intravenously and not subcutaneously.

Maintenance Therapy in Newborns.

Maintenance requirements are not well understood in newborn and low-birth-weight infants. They are certainly more variable than in older infants and children. The figures in Table 5-4 represent rough but probably safe approximations for the first few days of life. In general, in this period of life the safest policy is to give too little rather than too much unless there are unexpectedly large extrarenal losses. Older prematures will require more liberal amounts of water and electrolytes.

Time Plan for Administration of Maintenance Requirements.

Each day's maintenance requirements should be administered intravenously throughout the 24 hours if possible. They should never be administered rapidly in a single continuous dose. Hypodermoclysis has little or no role in modern fluid therapy.

REPLACEMENT OF ON-GOING LOSSES OF FLUID AND ELECTROLYTE

Replacement of on-going losses from extrarenal channels should proceed as the losses are incurred; the composition of the solution being administered should approximate that of the fluid lost.

Determination of On-Going Losses.

A. Losses of Gastrointestinal Secretions (Vomiting or Suction):
The approximate composition of most gastrointestinal secretions is shown in Table 5-5. Although pure gastrointestinal juices are isotonic, in practice they are often hypotonic due to dilution from ingestion of water or ice, flushing of the suction tube with water, or to swallowing of saliva. Under these conditions, appropriate downward adjustments of the concentration of the various ions may be necessary.

Volumes of losses incurred must be accurately measured and their electrolyte composition ascertained either by direct measurement or by reference to Table 5-5.

TABLE 5-5. Composition of gastrointestinal secretions.

	mEq./L.				
	H^+	Na^+	K^+	Cl^-	HCO_3^-
Gastric	40-60	20-80	5-20	100-150	
Biliary		120-140	5-15	80-120	30-50
Pancreatic		120-140	5-15	40-80	70-110
Small bowel		100-140	5-15	90-130	20-40

TABLE 5-6. Composition of diarrheal stools.

	mEq./L. of stool water		
	Na$^+$	K$^+$	Cl$^-$
Average	50	35	45
Range	(40-65)	(25-50)	(25-55)

B. Losses Due to Diarrhea: The electrolyte composition of diarrheal stools is quite variable (Table 5-6). The estimation of
stool volume is difficult. When the infant is receiving full oral
feedings, stool volume in diarrhea may reach 50 or more ml./
Kg./day. When oral feedings are limited, 10-25 ml./Kg./day
is a more reasonable estimate. In a difficult case, measurement of both stool volume and electrolyte composition may be
necessary for accurate replacement.

Replacement Solutions for Major On-Going Losses.
   A. Losses of Gastric Juice: These may be replaced with a solution similar to that shown in Table 5-7, preferably by the
intravenous route.
   B. Losses of Small Bowel Juices: These may be replaced by a
balanced isotonic sodium solution (Table 5-2), to which is
added 7.5 ml. of 14.9% KCl per liter in order to give a final
concentration of 15 mM./L. of KCl.
   C. Losses Due to Diarrhea: See Table 5-8. An alternative fluid
consists of 2 parts isotonic balanced sodium solution (Table

TABLE 5-7. Replacement of gastric juice.

	Volume (ml.)	mEq.		
		Na$^+$	K$^+$	Cl$^-$
0.9% NaCl	580	90		90
14.9% KCl	20		40	40
Pyrogen-free water or 5% glucose	q.s. ad 1000			
Total	1000	90	40	130

TABLE 5-8. Replacement of losses caused by diarrhea.

	Volume (ml.)	mEq.			
		Na$^+$	K$^+$	Cl$^-$	HCO$_3^-$
14.9% KCl	20		40	40	
7.9% NaHCO$_3$*	67	60			60
5% glucose	300				
Pyrogen-free water or 5% glucose	q.s. ad 1000				
Total	1000	60	40	40	60

*361 ml. of M/6 sodium lactate may be used in place of
NaHCO$_3$.

5-2) or Ringer's lactate and 1 part 5% glucose in water to which is added 10-20 ml. of 14.9% KCl per liter to give a final concentration of 20-40 mM./L. of KCl. Equal parts of Darrow's K-lactate® and 5% glucose in water may also be used.

In any problem involving large contemporary losses, replacement therapy must be guided by serial blood chemistries and, if possible, direct analysis of the fluid being lost. The solutions recommended above represent only approximations and should be altered according to results of the laboratory tests and the response of the patient.

Method of Replacement of On-Going Losses.

It is especially important in small children with extensive contemporary losses that replacement not be allowed to fall behind contemporary losses. Contemporary losses should be estimated and replacement solutions given every six to eight hours in amounts sufficient to cover the previous six- to eight-hour period. Waiting for a period of 24 hours is not recommended. It is frequently possible and desirable to anticipate losses and replace them as they occur.

Solutions for replacement of any one day's contemporary losses should be given by a slow intravenous drip. Precautions outlined under potassium administration should be followed (see p. 71).

FLUID AND ELECTROLYTE MANAGEMENT IN COMMON PEDIATRIC DISORDERS

These programs include basic principles of supplying the total requirements for repair of deficits, replacement of contemporary losses, and maintenance of normal requirements.

INFANTILE DIARRHEA

Principal Clinical and Laboratory Manifestations.

The principal manifestations of infantile diarrhea are (1) dehydration and shock, (2) metabolic acidosis with compensatory hyperventilation, and (3) potassium depletion. Hypernatremia, when present, constitutes a special complicating factor which must be recognized on admission and handled with diligent laboratory control. A chronic nutritional problem frequently underlies diarrhea and requires continuing attention during convalescence.

Treatment.

A. Moderately Severe Cases Without Hypernatremia: The usual deficits derived from balance studies in diarrheal disease are H_2O, 100-150 ml./Kg.; Na^+, 8-12 mEq./Kg.; Cl^-, 7-10 mEq./Kg.; and K^+, 8-12 mEq./Kg.

Omit all oral feedings initially.

Rapid rehydration must be carried out intravenously. The first infusion should consist of 10-20 ml./Kg. of isotonic balanced sodium solution (see p. 58), or Ringer's lactate. In severe cases this may be followed by a transfusion of whole blood (10-20 ml. /Kg.). These phases of therapy should be completed by 2-4 hours after admission, by which time circulatory status and renal function should be improved.

Further hydration may be effected at a slower rate either by the methods outlined on p. 57 or by the use of 60-80 ml./Kg. of Darrow's K-lactate® * given intravenously. This phase of therapy should be completed by 12-24 hours after admission.

In cases with marked hyponatremia, it may be advisable to use hypertonic sodium solutions in lieu of isotonic solutions; if these are used, potassium in the amount of a total of 3 mEq./Kg. should be distributed throughout all subsequent fluids for the first day (see p. 71).

Maintenance requirements as well as replacement of losses from continuing diarrhea should be carried out as previously described by parenteral routes until oral fluids can be tolerated.

Oral fluids may be given only after the stools are no longer watery or voluminous, fever and/or dehydration is overcome, abdominal distention and anorexia have been relieved, and vomiting has stopped. When this has been achieved, oral feedings may be started as outlined in Chapter 16.

B. Milder cases without vomiting may be managed as outlined in Chapter 16.

C. Cases With Hypernatremia: Hypernatremia should be suspected in diarrheal disease in young infants with sclerematous changes, especially over the buttocks and thighs. Such infants often display prominent C. N. S. disturbances (lethargy, coma, muscular rigidity, exaggerated reflexes, convulsions, and elevation of C. S. F. protein). Intracranial bleeding and subdural effusions have been reported in such infants; permanent C. N. S. damage may occur.

Fluid therapy should avoid rapid return of serum sodium to normal levels, as this frequently is associated with a severe convulsive state. Careful laboratory control of therapy is essential. In general it is preferable to rehydrate these patients with a fluid containing 15-30 mEq./L. of sodium rather than to use completely sodium-free fluids. The exact amounts to be given are dictated by the individual case; generally no more than 200 ml. /Kg. (including maintenance requirements) should be given on the first day. Potassium deficits are variable in hypernatremia; no potassium need be added to the fluid therapy for the first day in most instances. It may be added subsequently if hypokalemia develops.

Even with a slower rate of reduction of serum sodium to normal, convulsions and twitchings may appear. In some instances definite hypocalcemia may be found; if present, it may be treated by the addition of 10-30 ml. of 10% calcium gluconate to the daily infusion. Symptomatic therapy of the convulsions may be necessary; for this purpose, phenobarbital (5 mg. /Kg., subcutaneously) or paraldehyde (2-4 ml. in oil, rectally) may be used.

---

*The composition of Darrow's solution is given in Table 5-9. It may be mixed by the method outlined on p. 58.

PYLORIC STENOSIS AND VOMITING

Principal Clinical and Laboratory Manifestations.

The principal problems encountered in pyloric stenosis are (1) dehydration, (2) metabolic alkalosis, and (3) potassium depletion. In older children vomitus is generally bile-stained, which reflects the loss of small bowel juices and is more likely to be associated with a hyperchloremic acidosis upon which a starvation ketosis is superimposed.

Treatment.

A. Replacement of Losses Due to Vomiting: After the diagnosis has been established, give nothing by mouth (see Chapter 16). Rehydration should then be carried out initially with 10-20 ml./Kg. of isotonic sodium solution. (Sodium chloride should be used when alkalosis is present; a balanced sodium solution [see p. 58] is more appropriate for cases with acidosis.) Following this, a transfusion of whole blood (10-20 ml./Kg.) may be necessary to combat shock.

After these measures, further hydration should be carried out according to the method outlined on p. 58. It is of particular importance in cases of pyloric stenosis to begin potassium repletion as soon as it is safe to do so; 3 mEq./Kg. of potassium should be provided per day for at least three days. This amount (3 mEq./Kg.) should be distributed throughout the daily fluids so that concentrations in excess of 40 mEq./L. can be avoided.

Maintenance fluid and electrolyte requirements (Table 5-3) should also be given parenterally.

In cases of vomiting not due to pyloric stenosis, the same general regimen should be followed. However, because the acid-base disturbance is usually a metabolic acidosis, balanced sodium solutions incorporating some bicarbonate or lactate are preferred over sodium chloride. Large amounts of bicarbonate, however, are not necessary. Ketosis is managed through the provision of adequate carbohydrate.

B. Pre- and Postoperative Replacement in Pyloric Stenosis: After the deficit has been completely restored and a start has been made on potassium repletion, operation may be performed (usually after 36 to 48 hours). After operation, no special precautions are needed with respect to electrolytes. Give full maintenance requirements of water and electrolyte.

   1. First day - Offer 50% of the maintenance fluid and electrolyte orally in multiple small feedings (15 to 30 ml.). Give the balance parenterally.

   2. On subsequent days, give full or partial maintenance requirements orally as tolerated. Start milk feedings with small amounts of half-skimmed milk, proceeding to dilute evaporated milk and then full formula as tolerated.

   3. Potassium - An additional 3 mEq./Kg./day should be provided from combined oral and parenteral intake for the first three postoperative days.

   4. If vomiting occurs, then ascertain cause; discontinue all oral feedings for eight to 12 hours and make up maintenance parenterally (see p. 58).

PREOPERATIVE PREPARATION FOR MAJOR SURGERY
(See also Chapter 2.)

Adequate preparation for surgery must include attention to the fluid, electrolyte, and nutritional status of the child.

Treatment.
A. Dehydrated infants and young children are poor surgical risks. The fluid, electrolyte, and blood losses during a long operation predispose to shock and its complications. Replacement of fluid and electrolyte deficits should therefore be completed prior to surgery, and at the time of surgery the volume and composition of the body fluids should, if possible, be normal. Even in emergencies, deficits of sodium and water should be repaired before surgery is undertaken.
B. Preoperative Fluids: If preoperative orders call for no oral intake after midnight, it is wise to give 50% of the calculated 24-hour maintenance fluid and electrolyte requirements from midnight to the time of operation intravenously.
C. During surgery, fluids should be administered I.V. This is best achieved by surgical cut-down in the small child and infant if an I.V. site is not secure. A slow drip of 5% glucose in water can be used to keep the I.V. route open until surgery, but care should be taken not to administer excessive amounts of this solution.
D. Whole blood should be immediately available during any surgical procedure. Blood should be administered as it is lost.

POSTOPERATIVE PERIOD (AFTER MAJOR SURGERY)

The principal problems encountered in the postoperative period differ depending on whether there has or has not been extrarenal loss of fluid and electrolytes. Little is known of the metabolic response to surgery in the infant, and the assistance of a consultant may be advisable in the unusual case.

Treatment.
A. Postoperative Patients Without Extrarenal Losses or Pre-existing Deficits:
1. Water - Same as for any maintenance program except in those few patients who, for incompletely understood reasons, show an acute (usually transient) oliguria postoperatively. This complication must be carefully watched for to avoid water intoxication.
2. Glucose - Same as for any maintenance program.
3. Sodium and chloride - Maintenance requirements of sodium (Table 5-3) may be given with safety, although some prefer moderate sodium restriction on the first day or two after surgery.
4. Potassium - Maintenance requirements of potassium may be given as soon as renal function and circulation are adequate. It must be emphasized again that a pre-existing deficit of great magnitude should be corrected prior to surgery. When this is not possible, potassium repletion should be instituted

on the first postoperative day. It is imperative, however, that precautions regarding potassium administration be applied (see p. 71). Potassium-containing juices and other fluids by mouth usually can meet the need during this period. If potassium intake remains inadequate after one or two days, potassium should be included in the parenteral fluids in amounts of 2 to 3 mEq./Kg./day and should be given with the precautions outlined. Postoperative alkalosis due to potassium depletion is a syndrome which usually appears after the second or third postoperative day unless there has been a previous uncorrected deficit. Preparations suitable for parenteral potassium administration are outlined in the section on hypokalemia.

5. Nitrogen - Nitrogen intake need not be encouraged during the immediate postoperative period. With minimal water intake, dehydration may actually be precipitated as a result of the large urinary losses of water necessary to clear the urea resulting from the catabolism of dietary protein. Parenteral administration of whole protein (plasma) is of little value to protein nutrition since considerable time is required for breakdown of plasma into amino acids.

B. Patients With Extrarenal Losses: In these patients replacement of contemporary losses must occur at the same time as the provision of maintenance requirements. Replacement should proceed as the loss is being incurred and with solutions of similar composition, usually by parenteral routes. Serial serum electrolyte determinations may be useful in complicated cases for checking adequacy of replacement.

C. Oral Feedings: Oral feedings of liquid or soft diets should be started as soon as tolerated.

D. Nutritional Deficits: Patients having severe nutritional deficits secondary to incompetent gastrointestinal function should be considered candidates for total parenteral nutrition delivered by central venous catheter.

INTESTINAL OBSTRUCTION
(See also Chapter 16.)

In intestinal obstruction there is continuing gastrointestinal secretory activity while absorptive function is depressed, resulting in either the accumulation or loss through vomiting of large quantities of gastrointestinal fluids. This produces abdominal distention, vomiting, dehydration, and shock; depletion of potassium, sodium, and chloride in varying combinations; and associated gross disturbances in acid-base balance.

Nothing should be given orally or by tube to the obstructed patient since food or fluid often stimulates the increase of secretions. If it is judged necessary to offer fluids orally, give only isotonic solutions.

Treatment.
A. Relieve distention by continuous suction from the small intestine and give nothing by mouth.

B. Deficit Therapy:
   1. Replacement of deficits should follow the principles already outlined. The anion composition of the sodium solutions used for rehydration should be adjusted in accordance with the prevailing disturbance of acid-base equilibrium - sodium chloride in cases with alkalosis and a balanced sodium solution in cases with acidosis.
   2. Significant deficits of potassium complicate virtually every case of intestinal obstruction; these should be managed according to the methods outlined on p. 71.
C. Maintenance fluid and electrolyte requirements must be met as needed.
D. On-going losses incurred through suction must be continuously replaced (volume for volume) with an appropriate solution.
E. Defer Surgery: If warranted, operative intervention should be deferred until the water, sodium, and chloride deficits have been corrected (in 36 to 48 hours) and some progress has been made on repair of the potassium deficit.
F. On the first postoperative day give the maintenance requirement of sodium and chloride. If there is evidence of hypokalemia, the full potassium requirements (2.5 to 3 mEq./Kg.) should be given. (Observe precautions in potassium therapy as noted on p. 71.)
G. Replace blood loss.
H. Oral feedings may be begun only in the absence of abdominal distention and nausea or vomiting, and when bowel sounds have returned.
   1. On the first day of oral feedings give 25% of the total water and electrolyte requirements in the form of clear fluids in small, frequent feedings. The balance of the requirements must be given parenterally.
   2. Increase oral feeding with clear fluids gradually until full maintenance requirements are tolerated.
   3. Dilute skimmed milk may be used in the first feedings. Follow this by a gradual transition to full formula or diet.

SALICYLISM

Salicylate intoxication occurs frequently and usually results from cumulative effects of prolonged administration of presumed safe doses of aspirin to ill infants and children, the accidental ingestion of large quantities of aspirin, or the accidental ingestion of methyl salicylate (oil of wintergreen). Severity of toxicity does not necessarily relate to dosage.

Pathologic Physiology and Clinical Findings.

Three basic effects of toxic amounts of salicylate account for the various metabolic disorders encountered in salicylism: (1) central respiratory stimulation; (2) abnormalities in the metabolism of carbohydrate and lipid, resulting in ketosis; and (3) increase in metabolic rate. The first effect leads to marked hyperventilation, which is the most prominent and important clinical sign in salicylism. When this is the only major disturbance, respiratory alkalosis results. In infants and young children, ketosis often occurs simultaneously with respiratory stimulation, and this leads to a mixed disturbance of acid-base equilibrium in which total CO_2 content is reduced but blood pH may be normal, acid, or alkaline.

In moderate or severe cases, hyperventilation may be accompanied by vomiting, sweating, flushed appearance, stupor, convulsions, and fever. A disturbance in blood coagulation (hypoprothrombinemia or thrombocytopenia) may lead to internal or external bleeding. Moderate degrees of dehydration occur as a result of polyuria, sweating, vomiting, and increased insensible water loss. The dehydration is usually isotonic, although it may be hypertonic in infants.

Exact diagnosis of the acid-base disturbance in any given patient is important in the design of therapy. Of greatest importance is the differentiation of patients with alkalosis from those with acidosis, since large amounts of bicarbonate administered to the former may precipitate tetany and convulsions.

A blood pH (arterial or arterialized venous) is the only absolute method for confident diagnosis. Lacking this, the following may be helpful:

A. Urinary pH: Alkalosis is likely when the urine is alkaline, but "paradoxical aciduria" may occur (see p. 75.)

B. Age: Younger children and infants are more apt to be acidotic, especially if there has been an interval of several hours since ingestion.

C. Dietary History: If the child's oral intake has been poor as a result of a febrile illness for which he has been receiving aspirin, acidosis is more likely.

D. Other Urinary Findings: Additional urinary findings may include the presence of 1+ to 2+ reducing substance, a 1+ to 2+ proteinuria, small numbers of formed elements, and a positive ferric chloride (Gerhardt) test after boiling the urine. The latter, however, does not necessarily indicate toxic levels of salicylates; such a test is also obtained when there are coal tar derivatives and phenols in the urine. In the presence of acidosis, a positive nitroprusside (Rothera) test for acetone may be obtained. (Salicylates per se do not give a positive reaction in this test.) Note that salicylism may mimic diabetic coma in producing not only acidosis but also reducing substances and acetone in the urine.

Treatment.

A. General Measures:

1. Provoke emesis if possible; otherwise, perform gastric lavage with a balanced sodium solution (Table 5-2).

2. Treat dehydration and peripheral vascular collapse, if present, as outlined on p. 58.

3. Vitamins K and C should be given, particularly if there is a disturbance of blood coagulation.

4. Reduce body temperature if hyperpyrexia is present by sponging with cool (not cold) water.

5. Maintenance fluids should be generous because of the increase in metabolic rate; in a moderately severe case, the maintenance requirements may be 50% above the usual range. Generous amounts of carbohydrate should be given; 10% glucose should be used.

6. Potassium depletion complicates nearly every case and should be managed as outlined on p. 71.

B. Treatment of Acid-base Disturbances:
  1. Patients with alkaline pH - All sodium and potassium should be in the form of chlorides. Respiratory depressants (e.g., morphine) should not be given; rebreathing or breathing CO_2-enriched mixtures is not advised.
  2. Patients with normal or acid pH values - Patients presenting with these types of disturbances show a marked tendency to recover through an alkalotic phase even when no large amounts of alkalinizing salts are given. Therefore, most of the sodium and potassium administered to such patients should be in the form of the chloride, with only moderate amounts in the form of bicarbonate.
C. Treatment of Severe Cases:
  1. Acute pulmonary edema may occur in severe salicylism. It should be treated vigorously with positive pressure oxygen, tourniquets, and aminophylline. Morphine should be avoided.
  2. Respiratory depression usually occurs as an accompaniment of acute pulmonary edema. It may be severe enough to warrant artificial ventilation.
  3. Severe cases may require one or more of the following measures designed to remove salicylate from the body at a rate faster than can usually be accomplished by conservative management alone.
    a. Measures designed to accelerate salicylate through the renal route - These all are designed to alkalinize the urine (preferably to a pH above 7.5), since with alkaline urines the rate of clearance of salicylate is markedly enhanced.
      (1) Large loads of sodium bicarbonate (up to 10 mM./Kg.) have been advocated, but these may produce severe systemic alkalosis.
      (2) Administration of acetazolamide (Diamox®) in doses of 5 mg./Kg. I. M. and repeated two times at four-hour intervals (if necessary) may produce an alkaline urine. One report states that unexpected death followed administration of acetazolamide, whereas other reports, generally discussing less severe cases, mention no such complications.
    b. Measures designed to remove salicylate via the extrarenal route -
      (1) Exchange transfusion has been used successfully and is probably particularly applicable to the small infant.
      (2) Intermittent peritoneal dialysis, using a fluid with the composition of normal extracellular fluid plus 5 Gm./100 ml. of human serum albumin (final concentration), has also been used successfully.
      (3) Hemodialysis is unquestionably the most efficient method for removal of salicylate, but it presents formidable technical difficulties in infants and small children.

SPECIFIC ELECTROLYTE DISTURBANCES

HYPOKALEMIA AND POTASSIUM DEPLETION

Predisposing Factors.
A. Extrarenal losses without commensurate intake, e.g., vomiting, diarrhea, intestinal suction.
B. Renal Losses:
    1. Acid-base disturbances - Metabolic acidosis, metabolic and respiratory alkalosis.
    2. Adrenal cortical factors - Excessive endogenous (stress) adrenal cortical secretion, exogenous adrenal steroid or corticotropin (ACTH) therapy (particularly in the presence of a large sodium intake), primary aldosteronism, or Bartter's syndrome.
    3. Use of diuretics.
    4. Polyuric phase of acute tubular necrosis or in primary renal or adrenal disease ("potassium-losing nephritis").
C. Recovery phase of diabetic acidosis.

Clinical Findings.
Potassium depletion of considerable proportions may exist with little clinical evidence.
A. Symptoms and Signs: Deep tendon reflexes are depressed. Muscle weakness and hypotonia are usually vague and not helpful in most pediatric patients. Frank paralysis is rare. Abdominal distention with diminished or absent peristalsis is sometimes seen. A fall in diastolic blood pressure may be seen where careful serial blood pressure records are available. Cardiac failure may occur.
B. Laboratory Findings:
    1. Serum potassium less than 3 mEq./L., particularly in the presence of alkalosis; the serum potassium may be normal in acidosis even though a significant deficit of total body potassium is present. Likewise in dehydration with prerenal azotemia, the initial serum potassium may be normal or even elevated but will drop sharply with rehydration.
    2. Ecg. - When the serum potassium concentrations drop to (or below) 3 mEq./L., the Ecg. changes described below may be observed. However, they are not specific for potassium depletion. The final diagnosis depends on knowing the serum potassium level. The reversal of an altered Ecg. pattern following the administration of potassium is also helpful.
        a. Frequently, an associated slight prolongation of the Q-T interval which is not due to a lengthening of the S-T segment as is the case in hypocalcemia.
        b. A decrease in height and inversion of the T waves. T waves are also influenced by the pH and the bicarbonate concentration of the blood and the sodium and calcium concentrations.
        c. Rounding and prolongation of the T waves so that they may run into the following P wave.
        d. Depression of the S-T segment.
        e. Possible inversion of the P waves; extrasystoles (especially ventricular) and A-V block.

Precautions and Treatment.

Because of the dangers of potassium intoxication, not over 3 mEq./Kg. of potassium can be given in 24 hours for the replacement of potassium deficits. This limiting factor makes potassium replacement a prolonged procedure. The total amount of potassium to be administered varies with the deficit present and the on-going losses. Estimate the deficit at the first observation as closely as possible and determine the maintenance needs (see p. 58) and keep accurate account of the on-going losses (see p. 60). On the basis of this information, recalculate the **total potassium needs** daily and give up to 5 mEq./Kg. of potassium per day as long as required. With good renal function, extra potassium will be excreted and will not be toxic as long as the rate of administration is slow (see precautions given in paragraph B2, below).

A. Oral Administration: If the patient has no gastrointestinal obstruction and can tolerate oral feedings without nausea or vomiting, adequate potassium is present in the ordinary full diet. With any dietary restriction the patient's potassium intake may be inadequate and should be checked. Potassium added to milk, orange juice, or ginger ale up to a level of 60 to 80 mEq./L. (total) may be offered. KCl is the preferred salt. However, potassium sometimes produces pylorospasm with nausea, vomiting, and anorexia; this is especially likely when levels exceed 80 mEq./L. A major danger exists in the common but false assumption that as soon as a patient is on oral feedings, his potassium troubles are over. Electrolyte composition of ingested fluids and foods should be determined by calculation.

B. Parenteral Administration: Potassium salts may be given I.V. if the following precautions are observed:

1. Solutions containing 20 to 40 mEq./L. of potassium are usually satisfactory. Avoid solutions containing more than 40 mEq./L.

2. Precautions - The following should be observed when potassium is given by parenteral routes:

   a. Do not start potassium administration until the patient is excreting urine in adequate amounts.

   b. Do not give potassium until the patient is definitely out of shock, to patients with oliguria or anuria, or to those suspected of having chronic nephritis with potassium retention.

   c. Do not give more than a **total** of 5 mEq./Kg. potassium per day; this amount should be given continuously over the entire 24-hour period for which it is intended. Ordinarily it takes several days to completely correct a marked potassium deficiency.

   d. If any of the symptoms of hyperkalemia appear during therapy, stop the infusion, again determine the serum potassium concentration, and take another Ecg.

   e. Prior to the administration of potassium -
      (1) Review and analyze the patient's history.
      (2) Calculate preceding intake and probable need.
      (3) Look for physical signs of hypokalemia.
      (4) Determine serum potassium levels.
      (5) Check the Ecg.

C. Control of Potassium Therapy:
1. Serial determinations of the serum potassium concentration and CO_2 content are desirable.
2. If analysis of serum is impossible, take serial Ecg.'s.
3. Potassium therapy is indicated as long as the serum level remains below 3.5 mEq./L.
D. Preparations Commonly Used in Parenteral Potassium Therapy:
1. 14.9% potassium chloride -
   a. 10 ml. ampul = 20 mEq. K^+ and 20 mEq. Cl^-.
   b. 20 ml. ampul = 40 mEq. K^+ and 40 mEq. Cl^-.
2. Potassium phosphate salts -
   a. KH_2PO_4 0.30 Gm.⎤ in 10 ml. water
      K_2HPO_4 1.55 Gm.⎦
      10 ml. vial = 20 mEq. K^+ and 10 mM. P.
   b. KH_2PO_4 1.00 Gm.⎤ in 20 ml. water
      K_2HPO_4 4.59 Gm.⎦
      20 ml. vial = 120 mEq. K^+ and 60 mM. P.
      These solutions should be added to other solutions and are of value in diabetic acidosis, where hypokalemia may be accompanied by hypophosphatemia.

HYPERKALEMIA AND POTASSIUM INTOXICATION

Predisposing Factors.
A. Shock and oliguria, particularly in the presence of continuing intake of potassium or the release of large amounts of potassium from the cells.
B. Chronic renal disease with nitrogen retention.

Clinical Findings.
A. Symptoms and Signs: Symptoms are frequently absent, but listlessness, mental confusion, and paresthesias may be present. Bradycardia, peripheral vascular collapse, and cardiac arrest may occur.
B. Laboratory Findings:
1. Serum potassium concentration above 6 mEq./L.
2. Ecg. - The following electrocardiographic findings correlate roughly with increasing potassium concentration.
   a. Peaked T-waves.   c. Increase in P-R interval.
   b. Increase in QRS duration.   d. A totally irregular rhythm and heart block.

Treatment.
Severe hyperkalemia should be considered a metabolic emergency, and its treatment should be carefully followed by serial estimation of the serum potassium and serial Ecg.'s.
A. Withhold potassium by all routes.
B. Calcium gluconate, 10%, 10 to 20 ml. cautiously I.V.; thereafter, calcium salts should be added to all intravenous infusions. (Amounts and rates of calcium should be controlled by Ecg. changes.)
C. Some authorities recommend digitalization.
D. Measures designed to rid the body of excess potassium -
1. Resins - Give potassium-free resin such as Kayexalate®
   (1 Gm./Kg.), either by retention enema or as multiple

divided doses by mouth. The oral route is preferred in
the absence of vomiting since results with oral usage are
more predictable. If an enema is used, it should be given
several times a day with a volume of 250 ml. each time.
2. Short-term peritoneal dialysis or hemodialysis.

HYPONATREMIA AND SODIUM DEPLETION

Hyponatremia may be classified as acute salt depletion, acute
dilutional hyponatremia, chronic dilutional hyponatremia, or inappropriate secretion of antidiuretic hormone (ADH).

Acute Salt Depletion.
A. Predisposing Factors:
  1. Untreated adrenal insufficiency (adrenal crisis).
  2. Repeated administration of mercurial diuretics to patients
     with restricted sodium intake.
  3. Removal of a large ascitic fluid collection, as in the cirrhotic
     patient (occasionally in the nephrotic) on a low salt intake.
  4. Excessive sweating without salt replacement, especially in
     children with mucoviscidosis.
  5. Administration of a large non–salt-containing clysis (iso-
     tonic glucose) to a salt-depleted individual.
  6. Chronic renal disease.
B. Symptoms and Signs: Essentially those of a combination of
   water intoxication and peripheral vascular collapse.
  1. Cool, clammy skin.
  2. Low blood pressure.
  3. Weakness.
  4. C.N.S. stimulation and sometimes convulsions.
  5. Thirst.
C. Treatment: Prompt I.V. administration of hypertonic salt
   solution (5% NaCl containing 855 mEq./L. of Na^+ and Cl^-).
   Dosage is calculated as follows:

$$\left[\begin{array}{c}\text{mEq. of} \\ Na^+ \\ \text{needed}\end{array}\right] = \left[\begin{array}{c}140 - \text{patient's} \\ \text{serum } Na^+ \text{ level} \\ \text{(in mEq.)}\end{array}\right] \times \left[\begin{array}{c}60\% \text{ Body Wt.} \\ \text{(Kg.)}\end{array}\right]$$

To avoid a large chloride excess, it may be desirable to
give some of the sodium as sodium HCO_3^- (usually one-third)
and the rest as sodium chloride.

Acute Dilutional Hyponatremia (Water Intoxication).
A. Predisposing Factors:
  1. Excessive administration of salt-free fluids.
  2. Failure to excrete water due to endogenous factors (exces-
     sive antidiuretic hormone secretion, as seen in some post-
     operative patients and secondary to morphine administration)
     or excessive administration of vasopressin (Pitressin®).
B. Symptoms and Signs: Gain in weight, vomiting, convulsions,
   oliguria (in severe instances). Urine osmolality (specific
   gravity) is significantly higher than plasma osmolality. Non-

protein nitrogen or blood urea nitrogen is nearly always normal.
C. Treatment: In the presence of severe symptoms, treatment should consist of rapid infusion of hypertonic salt solution calculated by the method described above.

Chronic Dilutional Hyponatremia.

Chronic dilutional hyponatremia is seen in chronic edematous states of various types. It is generally refractory to treatment with hypertonic salt solution unless a superimposed acute salt depletion has occurred. In general, chronic dilutional hyponatremia should not be treated although fluid restriction may be tried. Its occurrence indicates a poor prognosis. These patients often are prone to develop a superimposed acute depletion since they are frequently on a low-sodium intake because of their edema and are subjected to diuretic measures.

Inappropriate Secretion of ADH.

Inappropriate secretion of ADH occurs in tuberculous and other types of meningitis, bilateral far-advanced pulmonary disease, and in many other types of serious systemic disease. These patients are well hydrated and have normal nonprotein and urea nitrogen levels, but they produce small volumes of concentrated urine. They become hyponatremic when water intake continues at usual levels. (See Acute Dilutional Hyponatremia, above.) Treatment of hyponatremia requires water restriction.

HYPERNATREMIA

Since hypernatremia is a potent stimulus for thirst, its occurrence is limited to those patients (infants and unconscious persons) who do not have free access to water. It may be seen in any situation involving loss of water in excess of salt where special circumstances limiting water intake are present, e.g., infantile diarrhea, excessive administration of table salt to infants with mild diarrhea, and solute diuresis secondary to tube feeding of unconscious patients with large amounts of protein.

The treatment of infants with hypernatremia has been outlined earlier. In other instances, adequate water should be provided. In patients with diabetes insipidus, vasopressin (Pitressin®) should be given.

DISTURBANCES OF ACID-BASE EQUILIBRIUM

Disturbances of acid-base equilibrium may be classified in terms of the Henderson-Hasselbalch equation of the bicarbonate–carbonic acid system:

$$pH = 6.10 + \log \frac{(HCO_3^-)}{(H_2CO_3 + \text{dissolved } CO_2)}$$

In health (in adults), the ratio of HCO_3^- to $(H_2CO_3 + \text{dissolved } CO_2)$ is about $24/1.2$ or $20/1$, representing a normal pH of 7.40 with a total CO_2 content of 25.2 mM./L. (i.e., total CO_2 content =

24.0 + 1.2 = 25.2). In infants, the normal values for the ratio are 20/1 (pH = 7.40) and total CO_2 is 21 mM./L.

The denominator term is a function of the partial pressure of carbon dioxide (pCO_2) in the alveolar air, and can therefore be readily adjusted by change in pulmonary ventilation. The total CO_2 content measures both HCO_3^- and (H_2CO_3 + dissolved CO_2), and determination of the pH is necessary to ascertain the value of each. In practice this is desirable but not absolutely necessary, since an analysis of the clinical findings will nearly always clarify the diagnostic issue unless one is dealing with a complex acid-base problem.

Classification of Acid-Base Disturbances.

Disturbances of acid-base equilibrium can be classified as either metabolic or respiratory, depending upon whether the primary distortion affects the numerator (HCO_3^-) or the denominator (H_2CO_3) of the Henderson-Hasselbalch equation. Compensatory adjustments occur in the metabolic disorders by adjustment of the denominator, through alterations in the alveolar partial pressure of CO_2 as well as through renal adjustment, which tends to restore the numerator. Compensatory adjustments in respiratory disorders are principally renal and therefore affect the numerator in a direction which tends to restore the absolute value of the ratio towards normal (20:1).

A. Metabolic Acidosis: Metabolic acidosis results from an abnormal retention or production of fixed (nonvolatile) acids, as in diabetes, excessive ammonium chloride ingestion, diarrhea, starvation ketosis, salicylate intoxication, or renal insufficiency, which leads to a reduction in the numerator (HCO_3^-). Compensation occurs through hyperventilation, reducing the denominator. The kidney responds by increasing titratable acid and ammonium excretion. In addition, there may be some buffering of hydrogen ions by cellular or bone exchanges. Therapy should include attempts to control acid production as well as rehydration, providing adequate amounts of sodium and potassium. Large amounts of sodium bicarbonate should not be given acutely since they tend to produce an alkalosis during recovery phases. No sodium bicarbonate is necessary if the CO_2 content is greater than 15 mM./L. in acute acidosis.

B. Metabolic Alkalosis: A primary loss of hydrogen ions, as in vomiting of hydrochloric acid or the ingestion of excessive amounts of sodium bicarbonate, leads to an increase in the numerator of the ratio. Furthermore, any circumstances leading to chloride depletion coupled with sodium depletion tends to be associated with metabolic alkalosis. Respiratory compensation should theoretically be hypoventilation, but this is limited by demands of oxygen. Renal compensation initially leads to an alkaline urine with loss of potassium and sodium; but when chloride and/or potassium depletion supervenes the urine pH becomes acid ("paradoxical aciduria" with alkalosis). Some buffering occurs with a gain of hydrogen ions to the blood from cellular and bone sites in exchange for sodium and/or potassium. Therapy should attack the primary loss as well as provide adequate sodium, water, and potassium.

Recent work indicates that chloride depletion occupies a special role in states where bicarbonate concentration is ele-

TABLE 5-9. Composition of parenteral and oral solutions.
(All values per liter.)

Solution and Route	Na$^+$ (mEq.)	K$^+$ (mEq.)	Cl$^-$ (mEq.)	Others (mEq. or as noted)
5% and 10% glucose in water (I.V., subcut.)*				CHO 50 and 100 Gm.
Isotonic (0.9%) NaCl (I.V., subcut.)	154		154	
Hypertonic (3%) NaCl (I.V.)	515		515	
Hypertonic (5%) NaCl (I.V.)	855		855	
Normosol-R® (or Normosol-R in D5-W®) (I.V.)	140	5	98	Mg^{++} 3; Ac 27; Gluconate 23; (CHO 50 Gm.)
Polysal® (I.V., subcut.)	140	10	103	Ca^{++} 5; Mg^{++} 3; Ac 47; Citrate 8
Polysal® elixir (Oral)	5†	1.5†	4.3†	Ca^{++} 0.2; Mg^{++} 0.1; Lactate 2.4†
Lytren®‡ (Oral)	50	20	30	Ca^{++} 4; Mg^{++} 4; Citrate 35; P 10 mM.; Lactate 4
Ringer's injection (I.V., subcut.)	145	4	155	Ca^{++} 6
Lactated Ringer's injection (I.V.)	129	4	109.5	Ca^{++} 3.5; Lactate 27
1-Molar sodium lactate (11.2%) (For dilution)	1000			Lactate 1000
M/6 Sodium lactate (1.97%) (I.V., subcut.)	167			Lactate 167
Normosol-M in D5-W® (I.V.)	40	13	40	Mg^{++} 3; Ac 16; CHO 50 Gm.
Darrow's solution (K lactate) (I.V., subcut.)	123	35	105	Lactate 53
Gastric replacement with 10% dextrose (Baxter)§ (I.V., subcut.)	63	17	150	NH$_4^+$ 70
Intestinal replacement with 10% dextrose (Baxter)§ (I.V., subcut.)	138	12	100	Lactate 50
Potassium chloride (14.9%) (ampuls; to be added to other fluids)		2000	2000	
Sodium bicarbonate (7.9%) (ampuls; to be added to other fluids)	900			HCO$_3^-$ 900
Whole blood, citrated** (I.V.)				
Plasma (275 ml.)	40	1.4††	25	Protein 18 Gm.
Cells (225 ml.)		23		Protein 75 Gm.
A.C.D. diluting solution (125 ml.)	5			CHO 3.75 Gm.

*Contains 50 or 100 Gm. CHO and 200 or 400 Calories per liter.
†Per undiluted teaspoon (5 ml.) (see p. 273).
‡Normal dilution is 8 measures, as provided (80 Gm.), per liter of water (see p. 273).
§Contains 100 Gm. CHO and 400 Calories per liter.
**Values per unit of whole blood (625 ml.).
††Bank blood potassium levels may rise to as much as 30 mEq./L. of plasma.

vated. It is therefore necessary to provide an adequate chloride intake to correct metabolic alkalosis.

C. Respiratory Acidosis: Primary retention of CO_2 due to hypoventilation because of pulmonary disease or central factors raises the denominator. Compensation is renal; titratable acid and ammonium are excreted, while bicarbonate in the serum is increased. Buffering through extrarenal ion exchange is similar to that in metabolic acidosis. Therapy should be directed against the primary disease. High concentrations of oxygen should be avoided unless the patient can be artificially ventilated. If pCO_2 can be brought to normal by therapy the patient will become alkalotic unless he readjusts bicarbonate concentration to normal. An adequate chloride intake is necessary for this adjustment to occur.

D. Respiratory Alkalosis: A primary loss of CO_2 due to hyperventilation because of emotional factors, salicylate intoxication, or, rarely, in primary C.N.S. disease leads to a reduction in the denominator in the ratio. Compensation by the kidney and by extrarenal mechanisms is similar to that in metabolic alkalosis. Therapeutic measures should include rebreathing in emotional hyperventilation, rehydration with adequate potassium supplements, and calcium infusions for tetany.

6 . . .
Anti-infective Chemotherapeutic Agents & Antibiotic Drugs

Antimicrobial therapy is the use of chemotherapeutic agents (e.g., sulfonamides and antibiotics) for the treatment of an infectious disease by attack upon the etiologic agent. Maximum success in the use of these substances depends upon (1) identification of the pathogens to be eliminated, (2) selection of the therapeutic agent or agents most active against the pathogen, (3) administration of an adequate amount of drug to destroy the pathogen, and (4) selection of the appropriate route to achieve maximum contact of the agent with the pathogen.

Methicillin, oxacillin, and nafcillin are resistant to staphylococcal penicillinase and are used in the treatment of infections due to penicillin-resistant staphylococci. Cloxacillin and dicloxacillin are equally effective against penicillin-resistant staphylococci. Ampicillin, a "broad-spectrum" antibiotic, cephalexin, and trimethoprim are useful in the treatment of chronic urinary tract infections. Gentamicin is a useful agent for systemic and occasionally topical therapy of pseudomonas or mixed infection. Methacycline is a tetracycline with an antimicrobial spectrum identical with that of the other tetracycline antibiotics. Carbenicillin is a new antipseudomonas penicillin for intravenous use. Clindamycin is a semisynthetic antibiotic derived from lincomycin.

General Indications.

Antibiotic and chemotherapeutic agents are indicated (1) for diseases in which a specific microbial etiologic agent has been identified by culture or serology, (2) for diseases in which the clinical picture implies a definite etiologic diagnosis, and (3) as a possible lifesaving measure for a desperately ill patient when an exact or complete etiologic diagnosis has not yet been made.

Development of Resistance.

Resistance develops (1) if strains which are already genetically resistant to the agent being used gain dominance by selection, or (2) if "spontaneous" mutation to a state of resistance occurs.

Adequate dosage and combined therapy prevent or slow down the development of resistant strains. Topical therapy should often supplement systemic therapy in chronic infections.

Precautions in Newborns and Prematures.

Great caution is necessary in preventing overdosage in order to avoid serious and permanent damage (especially in premature infants, newborn infants, and in oliguric children). Comments on dosage for these infants are included in the text that follows.

TABLE 6-1. Antibacterial spectrum of antimicrobial agents.

Mode of Action	Activity Principally Against		
	Gram-Positives	Broad-Spectrum	Gram-Negatives
Bactericidal	Penicillins, bacitracin	Kanamycin, neomycin, cephalothin, ampicillin, penicillin*	Streptomycin, polymyxin B, colistin, gentamicin
Bacteriostatic	Erythromycin, oleandomycin, clindamycin	Tetracyclines, methacycline, sulfonamides, chloramphenicol	Nalidixic acid, cephaloglycin

*In very large doses, penicillin may be bactericidal against a number of gram-negatives.

Precautions in Oliguric Children.

Regular drug dosages are too high for children with reduced renal function. Dosage and time schedules must be adjusted to renal output in the case of the more toxic agents (streptomycin, chloramphenicol, neomycin, kanamycin, bacitracin, polymyxin, colistin, novobiocin, and gentamicin).

PEDIATRIC ANTIMICROBIAL THERAPEUTIC AGENTS

Aminosalicylic Acid (PAS).

Use: Tuberculosis.

Dosage: Oral: 250-300 mg./Kg./day in divided doses every 6 hours. Adolescent: 12 Gm./day.

Toxicity: Gastrointestinal symptoms, hypersensitivity (skin, fever, genital), renal irritation, goitrogenic, hematologic, hepatic.

Comment: Avoid or reduce dosage by half when renal function is impaired. Stop drug at first sign of skin rash.

Amphotericin B (Fungizone®).

Use: Active against a variety of fungi (candida, cryptococcus, blastomyces, sporotrichum, coccidioides, histoplasma).

Dosage:

I. V.: 0.5-1 mg./Kg./day or every other day, given over 4-6 hours.

Intrathecal: 0.5-1 mg. in 10 ml. spinal fluid every other day.

Incompatibility: Do not mix with penicillin G or tetracyclines.

Toxicity: Chills, fever, malaise. Significant renal, hepatic, and bone marrow damage. Thrombophlebitis, calcifications.

Comment: Indicated only in severe systemic fungal infections. Administration of corticosteroids before the daily dose is given may ameliorate side-effects. Blood levels should be followed.

Bacitracin.

Use: Effective against gram-positive organisms; ineffective against gram-negatives.

TABLE 6-2. Choice of anti-infective agents.

Organism (and Gram Reaction)	Drug(s) of First Choice	Drug(s) of Second Choice
Actinomyces (+)	Penicillin	Tetracycline, sulfonamides
Bacillus anthracis (+)	Penicillin	Tetracyclines, erythromycin
Bacteroides (−)*	Chloramphenicol, clindamycin	Tetracycline, penicillin
Bordetella pertussis (−)	Erythromycin + pertussis immune gamma globulin (for <1 year)	Tetracycline, ampicillin
Brucella (−)	Tetracyclines + streptomycin	Kanamycin
Candida albicans	Nystatin, amphotericin B	5-Flucytosine
Chlamydiae (agents of lymphogranuloma venereum, psittacosis, and trachoma)	Tetracyclines	Chloramphenicol, sulfonamides
Clostridia (+)	Antitoxin + penicillin	Erythromycin, kanamycin
Corynebacterium diphtheriae (+)	Antitoxin + penicillin	Erythromycin, clindamycin
Diplococcus pneumoniae (+)	Penicillin	Ampicillin, erythromycin, clindamycin
Enterobacter (Aerobacter) (−)*	Kanamycin, gentamicin	Polymyxin, colistin, cephalothin, tetracycline + streptomycin
Erysipelothrix (+)	Penicillin	Tetracyclines, erythromycin
Escherichia coli (−)*	Ampicillin, kanamycin, gentamicin	Tetracyclines, polymyxin, colistin, cephalothin, sulfonamides, cephalexin
Haemophilus influenzae (−)	Ampicillin	Chloramphenicol + streptomycin
Klebsiella pneumoniae (−)*	Kanamycin, cephalothin	Polymyxin, colistin, gentamicin, tetracycline + streptomycin
Leptospira icterohaemorrhagiae	Tetracyclines	Penicillin
Listeria monocytogenes	Ampicillin, tetracyclines	Penicillin, bacitracin
Mycobacterium leprae (+)	Sulfones	Solapsone, sulfonamides, diphenylthiourea, sulfoxone
Mycobacterium tuberculosis (+)*	Isoniazid + streptomycin + PAS or Isoniazid + streptomycin + ethambutol	Rifampin, viomycin, cycloserine, ethionamide, pyrazinamide
Mycoplasma pneumoniae	Tetracyclines, erythromycin	
Neisseria gonorrhoeae (−)	Penicillin + probenecid	Ampicillin + probenecid, spectinomycin
N. meningitidis (−)	Penicillin	Ampicillin, chloramphenicol
Nocardia (+)*	Sulfonamides + cycloserine	Sulfonamides + agent chosen by sensitivity tests
Pasteurella pestis or P. tularensis (−)	Streptomycin + tetracyclines	
Proteus mirabilis (−)*	Ampicillin, penicillin	Cephalothin, kanamycin

*Sensitivity tests usually indicated.

TABLE 6-2 (cont'd). Choice of anti-infective agents.

Organism (and Gram Reaction)	Drug(s) of First Choice	Drug(s) of Second Choice
Proteus vulgaris, P. morganii, * P. rettgeri (−)*	Kanamycin, gentamicin	Cephalothin, chloramphenicol
Pseudomonas aeruginosa (−)*	Gentamicin, carbenicillin	Polymyxin B, colistin, kanamycin, tetracyclines, neomycin
Rickettsiae (−)	Chloramphenicol (+ corticosteroids for Rocky Mountain spotted fever)	Tetracyclines
Salmonella (−)*	Ampicillin	Chloramphenicol, cephalothin, tetracyclines, kanamycin
S. typhi (−)*	Ampicillin	Chloramphenicol
Shigella (−)*	Ampicillin	Tetracyclines, cephalothin
Spirillum minus (−)	Penicillin	Tetracyclines
Staphylococcus (+)* if sensitive	Penicillin	Erythromycin, lincomycin, cephalothin
Staphylococcus (+)* if resistant	Methicillin, nafcillin, dicloxacillin, cloxacillin	Cephalothin, erythromycin, lincomycin-clindamycin, kanamycin
Streptococcus (+)	Penicillin	Erythromycin, cephalothin, ampicillin
Str. faecalis (+)*	Penicillin + streptomycin, ampicillin	Cephalothin
Treponema pallidum	Penicillin	Cephalothin, erythromycin

*Sensitivity tests usually indicated.

Dosage:
  Intrathecal, intraventricular: 500-5000 units/day (1000 units/ml.).
  Eye and skin: 500 units/ml.
Toxicity: Transient nephrotoxicity, nausea and vomiting. Topical or oral use harmless except for large denuded areas.
Comment: Largely superseded by penicillinase-resistant penicillins. Relatively safe for children under 1 year of age.

Carbenicillin.

Use: Covers pseudomonas, indole-positive proteus, and serratia. In general, its spectrum against gram-negative bacteria is comparable to that of ampicillin but is less active.
Dosage:
  I.M. and orally: Do not use.
  I.V.: 600 mg./Kg./day in divided doses every 2-4 hours (not well established). Newborn: 400 mg./Kg./day (not well established). Adolescent: Up to 30 Gm./day.
Comment: Relatively high doses of this drug are required. Its main use is in pseudomonas infections in patients with compromised renal function. SGOT rises have been reported. This may be due to muscle necrosis after intramuscular injection. Carbenicillin is probably synergistic with gentamicin.

Cephalexin (Keflex®).
  Use: See Cephalothin.
  Dosage: 50-100 mg./Kg./day orally (not well established).
    Adults: 1-2 Gm./day.
  Toxicity: Nausea, vomiting, diarrhea. Occasional SGOT
    rise, rash, pruritus.
  Comment: The same precautions apply to the use of this drug in
    persons who are sensitive to penicillin as apply to cephalothin,
    cephaloridine, and cephaloglycin. The peak blood and urine
    levels are delayed when the drug is administered with food,
    but the absorption is still good. Bactericidal activity against
    sensitive organisms is not as rapid as with cephalothin and
    cephaloridine. Unit for unit, this drug is not quite as active
    as the latter two drugs against sensitive organisms. Blood
    levels, in general, are adequate for sensitive gram-positive
    organisms and for many gram-negative organisms, but the
    peak blood level achieved on a standard dose varies consider-
    ably from individual to individual. The drug should not be re-
    lied on for initial therapy in seriously ill.persons. In the first
    6 hours following a single dose, 80-90% of the drug is excreted.
    Because of rapid excretion, frequent doses of probenecid may
    be necessary if high blood levels must be maintained.

Cephaloridine (Loridine®).
  Use: Generally the same as for cephalothin (see below) except
    that it is less resistant to staphylococcal penicillinase, its
    efficacy in Hemophilus influenzae infections is somewhat un-
    certain, and it may penetrate tissue fluids (including the
    C.S.F.) better.
  Dosage: I.V. or I.M.: 30-50 mg./Kg./day in divided doses
    every 4-6 hours given over 3-4 minutes or longer. Newborn:
    Do not use. Adolescent: Give no more than 4 Gm./day.
    Serious infections: May be used in doses up to 100 mg./Kg./
    day in divided doses every 4 hours, not to exceed 4 Gm. Use
    the lowest effective dosage.
  Toxicity: Definitely more toxic than cephalothin, with cases of
    oliguria and renal shutdown reported. Tends to build up after
    multiple injections, so that the 4-hour level is twice as high
    after multiple injections as after a single injection. Eosino-
    philia, leukopenia (rare). Impairment of free water clearance.
  Comment: Less painful than cephalothin following intramuscular
    injection. May be associated with a higher rate of superin-
    fections than cephalothin. Will probably be replaced by
    cefazolin (Ancef®), which achieves better levels of effective-
    ness and seems to be less toxic to the kidneys.

Cephalothin (Keflin®).
  Use: Equivalent to penicillin against gram-positive organisms
    except enterococcus (Streptococcus faecalis), which is rela-
    tively insensitive. Highly resistant to staphylococcal penicil-
    linase. Effective against most Escherichia coli, indole-
    negative proteus, most klebsiella, and many strains of
    Haemophilus influenzae. Ineffective against pseudomonas,
    most serratia, and most enterobacter. When used for gram-
    negative infections, individual sensitivities should be deter-

mined. This drug should definitely not be used in the treatment of meningitis.

Dosage:

Oral: Not absorbed.

I.M.: 60-150 mg./Kg./day in divided doses every 4-6 hours given in a large muscle.

I.V.: 60-150 mg./Kg./day in divided doses every 4-6 hours. Newborn: 50-150 mg./Kg./day in divided doses every 6 hours.

Adolescent: Up to 12 Gm./day in the usual case. Severe infections: May be used in doses of 150-200 mg./Kg./day in infections such as meningitis, with up to 24 Gm. being used in adults.

Incompatibility: Do not mix with polymyxin B, tetracyclines, erythromycin, calcium chloride, or calcium gluconate.

Toxicity: Pain at injection site; sterile abscesses, drug fever, positive direct Coombs test, anemia, thrombocytopenic purpura; brown-black precipitate in Benedict's test or Clinitest® for glucose (when glucose is normal).

Comment: Cephalothin is of special use as a penicillin substitute in penicillin-sensitive persons. Anaphylaxis has been reported but is rare clinically, although the incidence of "sensitivity" to cephalothin as demonstrated by in vitro tests in penicillin-sensitive persons is high. The reason for this discrepancy is not known at present. The drug is relatively nontoxic to the kidneys. It causes a positive direct Coombs response in normal persons and, because of difficulty in cross-matching blood, should be avoided in persons who may require transfusion. In combination with methicillin or kanamycin, it may be beneficial in the treatment of methicillin-resistant staphylococcal infections. In combination with kanamycin, it may be synergistic in the treatment of resistant Escherichia coli infection.

Chloramphenicol (Chloromycetin®).

Use: Bacteriostatic for a wide range of gram-positive and gram negative organisms, rickettsiae, and bedsoniae. Beginning in 1972, strains of Salmonella typhi isolated from Mexico and the southern U.S.A. were found to be resistant. Effective against most Bacteroides species and anaerobic streptococci.

Dosage:

Oral: 50-100 mg./Kg./day (crystalline) in divided doses every 6 hours. Palmitate is unpredictably absorbed.

I.M.: Should not be used since absorption is poor.

I.V.: 100-150 mg./Kg./day in divided doses every 12 hours (microcrystalline); 100 mg./Kg./day in divided doses every 6-8 hours (succinate). Full-term newborn: 25-50 mg./Kg./day in divided doses every 6-12 hours. Premature: 25 mg./Kg./day in divided doses every 6-12 hours. This drug should be avoided in premature infants. If used, serum levels should be followed to avoid toxicity initially and to avoid inadequate dosage as renal and liver function mature. An adequate blood level is 10-12 µg./100 ml. Adolescent: 100 mg./Kg./day.

Incompatibility: Do not mix with polymyxin B, tetracyclines, vancomycin, hydrocortisone, B complex vitamins.

Toxicity: In newborns up to 4 months of age, vasomotor collapse (gray syndrome). Aplastic anemia and other hematopoietic toxicity. Gastrointestinal symptoms, stomatitis, candidal infections. Allergy, hepatitis, and neurologic abnormalities occur rarely.

Comment: Should not be used when an equally effective drug is available. Mechanism of action is antagonistic to that of penicillin. Diffuses better than most penicillins (eye, C.S.F.).

Clindamycin (Cleocin®).

Use: Gram-positive organisms except Streptococcus faecalis; anaerobic organisms. Some activity against methicillin-resistant staphylococci.

Dosage: For mild to moderate infections, give 8-16 mg./Kg./ day; for severe infections, give 16-20 mg./Kg./day. Divide dosage into 3 or 4 equal doses. For adolescents, give 600-1200 mg./day in divided doses every 6 hours; for severe infections in adolescents, give 1200-1800 mg./day in divided doses every 6 hours. **Caution:** Do not use in infants under 1 month of age.

Incompatibility: Do not mix with erythromycin.

Toxicity: Generally well tolerated. Toxic reactions include nausea and vomiting and gastrointestinal disturbances in 6-9%; diarrhea or loose stools in 3%. No irreversible hematopoietic toxicity has been reported. Skin rash appears to be relatively common. Transient elevations in alkaline phosphatase and serum transaminases usually return to normal during therapy.

Comment: This drug is structurally similar to lincomycin, with somewhat better and more rapid absorption after oral dosage and greater activity in vitro against staphylococci and penumococci. It is active against α- and β-hemolytic streptococci, but is only slightly more effective than erythromycin. It is not indicated for infections due to enterococcus, gonococcus, meningococcus, or haemophilus and is inactive against gram-negative rods. Clinical studies to show its usefulness in difficult infections such as osteomyelitis are not available. It appears to be an effective drug against common anaerobic organisms, including anaerobic streptococci and various Bacteroides species.

Colistin (Coly-Mycin S® and Coly-Mycin C®).

Use: Pseudomonas aeruginosa; some other gram-negatives. Proteus and gram-positives are resistant.

Dosage:

Oral (colistin sulfate): Not absorbed. 15 mg./Kg./day in divided doses every 8 hours.

I.M. (sodium colistimethate): 5-10 mg./Kg./day in divided doses every 6-12 hours given deep into a muscle. Adult or adolescent dose: 2.5-5 mg./Kg./day. Newborn: 1.5-5 mg./Kg./day in divided doses every 12 hours (for the first week).

Toxicity: Proteinuria, cyclindruria, hematuria, increased BUN (reversible). Paresthesias, ataxia, drowsiness, confusion. Fever, rash, pain at injection site.

Comment: May be used orally for neomycin-resistant entero-pathogenic Escherichia coli infections. Use with care if renal function is abnormal. Gains access to C. S. F. only when used in doses greater than 10 mg./Kg./day, so that polymyxin or gentamicin should be used instead for C. S. F. infection. Do not use intrathecally.

Erythromycin.

Use: Gram-positive cocci, clostridia, Haemophilus influenzae, B. pertussis, Corynebacterium diphtheriae, rickettsiae, brucella, some bacteroides. Resistance of some group A streptococci and some pneumococci has been reported, although this is rare at present. May be of use in chronic bronchitis, cystic fibrosis, and some urinary tract infections because of action against L forms. Probably as effective as tetracycline for symptomatic relief of mycoplasmal infections, although the organisms continue to be shed.

Dosage:
  Oral: 30-50 mg./Kg./day in divided doses every 6 hours.
  I. M. : 10-20 mg./Kg./day in divided doses every 6 hours.
  I. V. : 40-70 mg./Kg./day in divided doses every 6 hours given over a 20-60 minute period.
  Full-term newborn and premature:
    Oral: 20-40 mg./Kg./day in divided doses every 6 hours.
    I.M., I.V.: 10 mg./Kg./day in divided doses every 12 hours.
  Adolescent: Up to 2 Gm./day. Higher doses could be used in severe infections.

Toxicity: Painful injection, gastrointestinal symptoms, candi-diasis, drug fever. Estolate (Ilosone®) is associated with intrahepatic cholestatic jaundice when treatment is for more than 10 days.

Comment: Troleandomycin is similar to erythromycin in spec-trum and activity. Do not use concomitantly with lincomycin.

Ethambutol (Myambutol®).

Use: Tuberculosis.

Dosage: 15 mg./Kg./day; retreatment, 25 mg./Kg./day for 60 days, then 15 mg./Kg./day.

Toxicity: Retrobulbar neuritis (3%). Patients should be routinely followed with monthly examination of visual acuity and color discrimination. Anaphylactoid reactions. Peripheral neuritis. May cause hyperuricemia.

Comment: Experience in the pediatric age range is limited.

Ethionamide (Trecator®).

Use: Alternative to aminosalicylic acid in the treatment of tuber-culosis and atypical mycobacterial infections.

Dosage: Give orally, 15-20 mg./Kg./day up to 0.75-1 Gm. daily.

Toxicity: Anorexia, nausea, vomiting, diarrhea, mental depres-sion, headache, asthenia, convulsions, peripheral neuropathy, acne, allergic skin reactions, purpura, sialorrhea, metallic taste, stomatitis, gynecomastia, impotence, menorrhagia, hepatitis, hair loss, goiter, and hypothyroidism.

Comment: To prevent serious hepatotoxicity, serum SGOT levels should be determined every month or more frequently and the drug stopped if the SGOT is $>$ 100 I. U./liter. Strongly encouraged patients must often endure unpleasant but non-serious side-effects.

Flucytosine (Ancobon®).

Use: Antifungal agent active against some strains of Candida, Cryptococcus neoformans, Torulopsis glabrata.

Dosage: Give orally, 150 mg./Kg./day in divided doses every 6 hours.

Comment: Ninety percent of the drug is excreted in the urine. Drug resistance has been reported during therapy. Sensitivity studies are indicated. Currently it is suggested that patients on therapy be followed with blood creatinine, BUN, SGOT, serum alkaline phosphatase, hematocrit, and white blood count determinations.

Gentamicin (Garamycin®).

Use: Most gram-negatives, including pseudomonas and proteus. Of particular use in Serratia marcescens infections. Some activity against gram-positives, including coagulase-positive staphylococci. Relatively inactive against pneumococci and streptococci.

Dosage:

Oral: 5-10 mg./Kg./day (about 6.2% of a single dose is absorbed). May be of use in nursery outbreak of diarrhea due to enteropathogenic Escherichia coli but is not recommended for routine use.

Topical: Cream, 0.1%, and ointment, 0.1%.

I.M. and I.V.: For newborn infants under 1 week of age, give 5 mg./Kg./day; for those over 1 week of age, give 7.5 mg./Kg./day. Intravenous administration should extend over a 30-minute period. In neonates and patients with renal failure, obtain serum levels during therapy since individual variations occur.

Intraventricular: In cases of neonatal meningitis, give 1 mg./day.

Toxicity: Irreversible vestibular damage has occurred, most often in uremic patients, and is related to excessive plasma levels. There is considerable variability in the serum level achieved at the same per Kg. dose in different patients. Serum levels should be measured in any patient requiring long-term therapy. Transient proteinuria, elevated BUN, oliguria, azotemia, macular skin eruption, and elevated SGOT have been reported. If used in uremic patients, dosage schedule should be modified. Should be used with caution in patients receiving ototoxic drugs. Overall toxicity is probably the same as or less than that of kanamycin.

Comment: Parenteral therapy with this drug should be reserved for serious Pseudomonas infections, hospital-acquired infections, and life-threatening infections of unknown but suspected gram-negative origin. If cultures later are positive for an organism sensitive to penicillin, methicillin, cephalothin, ampicillin, or kanamycin, therapy should be changed to one of these drugs. Every effort should be made to use this drug selectively so that drug resistance will not develop. Relative resistance has developed during therapy. Topical therapy with gentamicin for superficial infections of the skin or mucous membranes due to Pseudomonas has been effective.

Griseofulvin.

Use: Tinea species, Microsporum, Trichophyton. Ineffective against Candida, Cryptococcus, Blastomyces, Histoplasma, and Coccidioides.

Dosage (Griseofulvin®): 20 mg./Kg./day orally in divided doses every 6-12 hours. Microcrystalline (Grisactin®): 10 mg./Kg./day in divided doses every 6-12 hours. Adolescent: 1 Gm./day (Griseofulvin®); 0.5 Gm./day (Grisactin®).

Toxicity: Leukopenia and other blood dyscrasias, headache, incoordination and confusion, gastrointestinal disturbances, rash (allergic and photosensitity), renal damage, lupus-like syndrome.

Comment: Do not use in patients with hepatocellular failure or porphyria.

Isoniazid (INH, Nydrazid®).

Use: Tuberculosis.

Dosage:
Oral: 15-20 mg./Kg./day in divided doses every 6-12 hours. Give no more than 300 mg./day.

I. M. : 10 mg./Kg./day in divided doses every 12 hours. Newborn: Dosage is not well established. BCG vaccination is indicated for the child of a tuberculous mother along with INH prophylaxis.

Toxicity: Neurotoxic, due to pyridoxine deficiency (rare in children). Gastrointestinal symptoms, seizures, hypersensitivity. Reactions are rare, but more common in the elderly and the malnourished.

Kanamycin (Kantrex®).

Use: Bactericidal for staphylococci, coliforms, Proteus, some Pseudomonas, mycobacteria. Of use in special circumstances in some Vibrio, Salmonella, and Shigella infections.

Dosage:
Oral: Not absorbed.

I. M. : 15 mg./Kg./day in divided doses every 12 hours. Full-term newborn: 15 mg./Kg./day. Premature: 10 mg./Kg./day; avoid using I.V. Adolescent: 1 Gm./day in divided doses every 12 hours.

I.V.: 15-20 mg./Kg./day in divided doses every 6-8 hours. (For serious infections only.) Adolescent: In serious infections, 2 Gm./day I.V. for a short time.

Toxicity: Limit use to 10 days. Irreversible deafness occurs after prolonged administration of high doses. (Cumulative ototoxicity with other ototoxic drugs occurs.) Nephrotoxicity is transient unless prior renal impairment was present. The safe total dose is 0.5 Gm./Kg.

Comment: Modify dosage and use with caution in oliguric patients.

Lincomycin (Lincocin®): See Clindamycin.

Methacycline (Rondomycin®). See Tetracyclines.

Methenamine Mandelate (Mandelamine®).
  Use: Genitourinary infections. Not effective against Proteus.
  Dosage: 100 mg./Kg. orally immediately and then 50 mg./Kg./
    day in divided doses every 8 hours.
  Comment: Urine should be kept acid.

Metronidazole (Flagyl®).
  Use: Trichomonas, Giardia, Entamoeba histolytica.
  Dosage: The adult dosage is 250 mg. orally every 8 hours. Has
    been used in the therapy of Giardia infections and in the treat-
    ment of amebic dysentery in children in doses up to 50 mg./
    Kg./day.
  Toxicity: Nausea, anorexia, and other gastrointestinal intoler-
    ance. Glossitis and stomatitis. Leukopenia, dizziness,
    vertigo, ataxia, urticaria, and pruritus.

Nalidixic Acid (NegGram®).
  Use: Useful in gram-negative urinary tract infections with
    Escherichia coli, Enterobacter, Klebsiella, and Proteus.
    Pseudomonas is generally resistant.
  Dosage: 40-50 mg./Kg. orally in divided doses 4 times daily for
    initial therapy. For prolonged therapy, reduce dosage to 15
    mg./Kg./day. For adolescents, give 4 Gm./day; in prolonged
    therapy, reduce to 2 Gm./day.
  Toxicity: Gastrointestinal symptoms, hypersensitivity (pruritus,
    rash, urticaria, eosinophilia), seizures, pneumonitis.
  Comment: Toxicity is low, and the drug may be used for months.
    Resistance may develop. Use cautiously in patients with liver
    disease or impaired renal function. Do not use in children
    under 1 month of age. Use only for urinary tract infections.

Neomycin (Mycifradin®, Neobiotic®).
  Use: Bactericidal for gram-positive cocci, gram-negative
    bacilli, acid-fast bacilli, and actinomycetes.
  Dosage: Give orally (not absorbed), 100 mg./Kg./day in divided
    doses every 6 hours. Full-term newborn and premature: 50
    mg./Kg./day in divided doses every 6 hours.
  Toxicity: Nephrotoxic and ototoxic when used parenterally. Oral
    use causes diarrhea, reversible disaccharidase deficiency,
    malabsorption of carotene, glucose, and iron, and candidiasis.
    Topical use causes rashes and skin sensitization. Intrapleural
    or intraperitoneal use can lead to respiratory arrest (curare-
    like effect) which is potentiated by ether anesthesia and re-
    versible by neostigmine. **Note:** Use with caution by all routes
    in patients with renal and hepatic disease, including the rela-
    tively oliguric newborn.

Nitrofurantoin (Furadantin®).
  Use: Many gram-negative organisms are susceptible to concen-
    trations achieved in urine.
  Dosage: 5-7 mg./Kg./day orally. Reduce dosage after 10-14

days. Infant: 1.5 mg./Kg./day. Adolescent: 400 mg. every
day in divided doses every 6 hours.
Toxicity: Primaquine-sensitive hemolytic anemia, peripheral
neuropathy, rash, chills, fever, myalgia-like syndrome,
cholestatic jaundice.
Comment: Should only be used for urinary tract infections.

Nystatin (Mycostatin®).
Use: Candida albicans and other yeasts.
Dosage:
Oral: Not absorbed. < 2 years, 400-800 thousand units/day.
> 2 years, 1-2 million units/day in divided doses every
6-8 hours. Full-term newborn and premature: 200-400
thousand units/day.
Eye and skin: 100,000 units/Gm.
Toxicity: None.

Oleandomycin: See Erythromycin.

The Penicillins.
Because of protein binding, serum killing power is the pre-
ferred test of bacterial sensitivity and efficacy of therapy.
All penicillins are cross-allergenic.
The mechanism of action of tetracyclines and chloramphenicol
is antagonistic to that of the penicillins.
In serious infections, all penicillins should be given in divided
doses so that a dose is given every 4 hours.
A. Penicillins Rendered Ineffective by Staphylococcal Penicillinase:
(Ampicillin, penicillin G, procaine penicillin G, phenoxymethyl
penicillin.)
1. Ampicillin -
Use: 50-80% of Escherichia coli, some salmonellae, shigellae, Proteus. Enterobacter and Klebsiella are
usually resistant. Gram-positive cocci, nonpenicillinase-producing staphylococci, and Hemophilus in-
fluenzae are sensitive.
Dosage:
Oral: 50-150 mg./Kg./day in divided doses every 6
hours.
I.M., I.V.: 150-400 mg./Kg./day in divided doses
every 4 hours. Not stable in intravenous bottle.
For meningitis, begin with at least 200 mg./Kg./
day in divided doses every 4 hours. Newborn: 100
mg./Kg./day in divided doses every 6-8 hours.
(For meningitis, a higher dose may be required.)
Toxicity: Low toxicity. Diarrhea, skin rash, drug fever.
Superinfection.
Comment: Useful for genitourinary infections, chronic
Salmonella carriers, and Hemophilus influenzae meningitis. A loading dose of 50 mg./Kg. is desirable in
serious infections. Contains about 1.7 mEq. sodium
per 500 mg. of drug. Ampicillin levels in the C.S.F.
drop after the third day in meningitis as the pleocytosis
decreases. Although usually effective, cases of resistance of Haemophilus influenzae meningitis to intravenous therapy have been well documented. The drug

must be given parenterally for the entire course. Failure to improve, or increase in fever and irritability after initial improvement, indicates the need for repeat taps and a change to chloramphenicol therapy.

2. Hetacillin® -

Use: See Ampicillin.

Dosage: Give orally, I.M., or I.V., 25 mg./Kg./day.
The dosage for severe infections is not well established.

Toxicity: Probably similar to that of ampicillin.

Comment: Hetacillin is hydrolyzed in the body to ampicillin, which appears to be the active agent. Higher blood levels are achieved on oral administration if the drug is given in the fasting state. Peak blood levels following oral administration are in the range of 1 μg./ml., which is sufficient for sensitive gram-positive organisms but inadequate for systemic infections with common gram-negative organisms. Higher levels are achieved in urine, and (as with ampicillin) urinary tract infections due to sensitive gram-negative organisms may be treated with this drug. Hetacillin is more stable than ampicillin after reconstitution for intravenous use. Administration of hetacillin intravenously results in somewhat higher and more prolonged blood levels than the same dose of ampicillin.

3. Penicillin G, potassium or sodium salt -

Use: Gram-positive and gram-negative cocci, gram-positive bacilli. In high doses, some gram-negative organisms.

Dosage:

Oral: 100-400 thousand units/dose in 5 doses half hour before meals.

I.M.: 20-50 thousand units/Kg./day in divided doses every 4-6 hours.

I.V.: 20-500 thousand units/Kg./day in divided doses every 4 hours. Newborn: 50,000 units/Kg. in divided doses every 8-12 hours. Adolescent: 20-60 million units.

Aerosol: 2 ml. every 6 hours, 50,000 units/ml.

Intrapleural, intra-articular, intraperitoneal: 10-20 thousand units/ml.

Intrathecal, intraventricular: (Rare indications.) 5-10 ml./24 hours (1000 units/ml.).

Incompatibility: Do not mix with amphotericin B, metaraminol, phenylephrine, tetracyclines, vancomycin, vitamin C.

Toxicity: Hypersensitivity (anaphylaxis, urticaria, rash, drug fever). Change in bowel flora, candidiasis, diarrhea, hemolytic anemia. Neurotoxic in very large doses.

Comment: High concentration in the urine makes this agent useful in treatment of some urinary tract infections with gram-negative rods. One million units of potassium penicillin G contain 1.7 mEq. potassium. Avoid pushing large doses of potassium salt, as in initiating therapy for meningitis; use sodium salt instead.

4. **Procaine penicillin G -**
   Dosage: 100-600 thousand units I.M. every 12-24 hours.
   Newborn: Do not use. Causes sterile abscesses.
   Also contains 120 mg. procaine/300,000 units peni-
   cillin G, which may be toxic.

5. **Benzathine penicillin G -**
   Dosage: 0.6-1.2 million units I.M. every month.
   Comment: The preferred drug for rheumatic fever prophylaxis. Increasing the dose gives a more sustained
   rather than a higher blood level. In acute illness, the
   procaine penicillin in Bicillin C-R® may be desirable.

6. **Phenoxymethyl penicillin -**
   Dosage: Oral 50,000-400,000 units/Kg./day every 6
   hours (125 mg. = 200,000 units). Newborn: 90,000
   units/Kg. Adult (serious infections): >6 Gm./day in
   divided doses every 4-6 hours.

B. **Penicillins Resistant to Staphylococcal Penicillinase:** (Methicillin, nafcillin, oxacillin, cloxacillin, dicloxacillin.)

1. **Methicillin -**
   Use: Penicillinase- and nonpenicillinase-producing
   staphylococci. Is less effective than penicillin G
   for other gram-positive cocci.
   Dosage: I.V. or I.M.; 200-300 mg./Kg./day in divided
   doses every 4 hours. Not stable in intravenous bottle.
   Deterioration in dextrose in water or normal saline
   solution is rapid and is prevented by adding $NaHCO_3$,
   6 mEq./liter. Full-term newborn: 200-250 mg./
   Kg. in divided doses every 6-8 hours for the first
   10 days and then every 4-6 hours. Premature: 100
   mg./Kg. in divided doses every 6-8 hours for the
   first 10 days and then every 6 hours.
   Incompatibility: Do not mix with tetracyclines, kanamycin, neomycin.
   Toxicity: Hypersensitivity, kidney damage, hematuria
   (thought to be a hypersensitivity phenomenon). Reversible bone marrow depression. Painful when given
   intramuscularly.
   Comment: If therapy is initiated with methicillin because
   of suspected penicillin resistance, change to penicillin
   G when sensitivity to this agent is shown. One gram
   contains 2.5 mEq. sodium.

2. **Nafcillin -**
   Use: Staphylococci (penicillin-resistant and penicillin-
   sensitive), penumococcus, streptococcus.
   Dosage: I.M. or I.V.: 50-250 mg./Kg./day in divided
   doses every 4 hours. Adolescent: Up to 18 Gm./day.
   Oral doses are not recommended because absorption
   is unreliable.
   Incompatibility: Do not mix with B complex vitamins.
   Toxicity: Similar to that of methicillin, but hematuria
   has not been reported. Thrombophlebitis with intravenous use.
   Comment: Proper dose not well established. Good choice
   for coverage of gram-positive cocci before culture and
   sensitivity results are available.

3. **Oxacillin** - Nafcillin, cloxacillin, and dicloxacillin are preferred.

4. **Cloxacillin** -
   Use: Penicillinase-producing staphylococci.
   Dosage: 50-100 mg./Kg./day orally in divided doses every 6 hours given 1-2 hours before meals.
   Toxicity: Probably similar to that of other penicillins.
   Comment: Penicillinase-resistant. Dicloxacillin in equivalent dose is probably more active and better absorbed. For osteomyelitis, use a dosage of 100 mg./Kg./day.

5. **Dicloxacillin** -
   Use: Penicillinase-producing staphylococci.
   Dosage: 25-50 mg./Kg./day. In serious infections, begin with 50 mg./Kg./day and reduce dosage if serum killing power indicates this is possible.
   Toxicity: Gastrointestinal irritation, which appears to be dose-related.

Polymyxin B (Aerosporin®).

Use: Pseudonomas, some other gram-negative bacteria as determined by sensitivities on the specific organism.
Dosage:
   Oral: Not absorbed. 10-20 mg./Kg./day in divided doses every 4-6 hours.
   I.M.: 3.5-5 mg./Kg./day in divided doses every 4-6 hours (not to exceed 200 mg./day). Full-term newborn and premature: 3.5-4 mg./Kg./day in divided doses every 6 hours.
   I.V.: 3.5-5 mg./Kg./day in divided doses every 6-8 hours (not to exceed 200 mg./day). Full-term newborn and premature: 3.5-4 mg./Kg./day in divided doses every 6 hours.
   Intrathecal, intraventricular: 0.5-1 mg./ml. < 2 years: 2 mg./day or every other day. > 2 years: 5 mg./day or every other day.
   Intra-articular, intraperitoneal: (Rare indications.) 1 mg./ml.
Incompatibility: Do not mix with cephalothin, chloramphenicol, heparin, tetracyclines.
Toxicity: Pain at injection site; neurotoxicity (paresthesias, ataxia, drowsiness); nephrotoxicity (cylindruria, hematuria, proteinuria, increased BUN); fever, rash.

Rifampin.

Use: Neisseria, Mycobacterium; gram-positive cocci.
Dosage: Children - not well established. Adult - 600 mg./day.
Toxicity: Hepatotoxic in animals but does not appear to have additive hepatotoxicity when used in various drug regimens for the therapy of tuberculosis. Appears to be well tolerated and relatively nontoxic.
Comment: This drug's most striking contribution has been to the care of patients infected with multiple-resistant strains of Myco. tuberculosis. Although the results have been remarkably good, when used alone the development of resistance is rapid; therefore, the drug should always be used in combination with one or two drugs to which the organisms are sensitive. The drug should be reserved for patients who are treat-

ment failures on other drug regimens. Early work has shown that this drug may have a place in the therapy of the carrier of N. meningitidis who poses a hazard. The drug has also been used in the successful treatment of infections with N. gonorrhoeae and staphylococci, but offers no advantage over other drugs. Until more data are available, this drug should be reserved for therapy of patients with infections due to Myco. tuberculosis and Myco. leprae.

Spectinomycin (Trobicin®).

Use: Neisseria gonorrhoeae.

Dosage: Adult male, 2 Gm. I.M. as a single dose; adult female, 4 Gm. I.M. as a single dose.

Comment: Spectinomycin is in the same class of drugs as streptomycin and kanamycin. Toxicity reported after a single dose includes urticaria, dizziness, nausea, chills, fever, and insomnia. It is likely that the drug has some renal toxicity on prolonged use. Spectinomycin is not effective in eradicating concomitant incubating syphilis.

Streptomycin Sulfate.

Use: Mycobacterium tuberculosis, Hemophilus influenzae, some gram-negatives. Synergistic with penicillin against enterococci. Resistance develops quickly.

Dosage:

Oral: Not absorbed. 40 mg./Kg./day in divided doses every 6 hours.

I.M.: 20-40 mg./Kg./day in divided doses every 12-24 hours. Newborn: 10-20 mg./Kg./day. Use with caution.

Aerosol: 2 ml. every 6 hours (150 mg./ml.).

Toxicity: Damage to vestibular apparatus. Fatal C.N.S. and respiratory depression. Bone marrow depression, renal toxicity, hypersensitivity, superinfection.

Comment: Should never be used as the only drug. Dihydrostreptomycin is toxic to the eighth nerve and should not be used.

Sulfonamides: Sulfadiazine, Sulfisoxazole (Gantrisin®), Sulfamethoxazole (Gantanol®), Trisulfapyrimidines, Trimethoprim With Sulfamethoxazole (Bactrim®, Septra®)

Use: Bacteriostatic against gram-positive and gram-negative organisms. Approximately 80% of shigellae are resistant. Trimethoprim with sulfamethoxazole (co-trimoxazole) has a wide range of antibacterial activity but is primarily of value in the treatment of resistant Salmonella typhi and, perhaps, chronic urinary tract infections.

Dosage: (For sulfadiazine, triple sulfas, and sulfisoxazole.)

Oral: 120-150 mg./Kg./day in divided doses every 6 hours.

I.V.: 120 mg./Kg./day in divided doses every 6-12 hours; alkalinize urine. Newborn: Do not use (risk of kernicterus).

Dosage: (For sulfamethoxazole.) 50 mg./Kg./day orally in divided doses every 12 hours.

Dosage (oral): (For trimethoprim-sulfamethoxazole.) Capsule contains 80 mg. of trimethoprim and 400 mg. of sulfamethoxazole; pediatric suspension contains 20 or 40 mg. of trimethoprim and 100 or 200 mg. of sulfamethoxazole per 5 ml. Dosage is 150 mg./sq. M./day of trimethoprim and 750 mg./sq. M./day of sulfamethoxazole.

Toxicity: Crystalluria (mechanical urinary obstruction); keep fluid intake high. Hypersensitivity (fever, rash, hepatitis, lupus-like state, vasculitis). Neutropenia, agranulocytosis, aplastic anemia, thrombocytopenia. Hemolytic anemia in individuals deficient in glucose-6-phosphate dehydrogenase. (There is a high correlation between G6PD deficiency and sickle cell anemia, so do not use in these patients.) Trimethoprim-sulfamethoxazole may reduce rashes and gastrointestinal or hematologic symptoms.

Comment: Useful in infections of the urinary tract and for rheumatic fever prophylaxis. (Should not be relied upon for treatment of group A streptococcal infections.) Long-acting preparations (Kynex®, Madribon®, Sulfameter®) are occasionally associated with serious reactions. Sulfadiazine is preferred for C.N.S. infections since diffusion into the C.S.F. is better. Sulfamethoxazole is intermediate-acting and causes a slightly higher incidence of urinary sediment abnormalities. For trimethoprim-sulfamethoxazole, preliminary reports indicate some effectiveness against Pneumocystis carinii.

Tetracyclines.

Use: Gram-positive and gram-negative bacteria, rickettsiae, bedsoniae, Mycoplasma pneumoniae, brucella, some bacteroides.

Dosage: (For tetracycline, chlortetracycline, oxytetracycline.)
  Oral: 20-40 mg./Kg./day in divided doses every 6 hours. Do not give with milk.
  I.M.: 12 mg./Kg./day in divided doses every 12 hours; achieves poor levels; painful.
  I.V.: 12 mg./Kg./day in divided doses every 12 hours.
  Aerosol: 1 ml. every 12 hours (50 mg./ml. in 75% propylene glycol).

Dosage: (For demethylchlortetracycline [Declomycin®] and methacycline [Rondomycin®].)
  Oral: 12 mg./Kg./day in divided doses every 6 hours.
  Newborn: Do not use.

Incompatibility: Do not mix with amphotericin B, cephalothin, chloramphenicol, heparin, hydrocortisone, methicillin, penicillin G, polymyxin B.

Toxicity: In children under 10 years of age, tetracyclines cause damage to teeth and bone. Deposition in teeth and bone of premature and newborn infants can result in enamel dysplasia and growth retardation. Outdated tetracyclines can produce Fanconi's syndrome. Pseudotumor cerebri, bulging fontanels. Nausea, vomiting, diarrhea, stomatitis, glossitis, proctitis, candidiasis. Overgrowth of staphylococci in bowel. Disturbed hepatic and renal function. Drug fever, rash, photosensitivity.

Comment: Cross-resistance among the tetracyclines is complete.

Vancomycin (Vancocin®).

Use: Staphylococci, other gram-positive cocci, clostridia, corynebacteria. Main use is in treatment of staphylococcal enterocolitis and methicillin-resistant staphylococcal infection.

Dosage:
  Oral: Not absorbed. 2-4 Gm./day in divided doses every 6
    hours.
  I.V.: 40 mg./Kg./day. Adolescent: 2-3 Gm./day in divided
    doses every 4-6 hours.
Incompatibility: Do not mix with chloramphenicol, heparin,
  hydrocortisone, penicillin G.
Toxicity: Painful when given intramuscularly; do not use.
  Troublesome symptoms during intravenous administration
  include rash, chills, thrombophlebitis, and fever. Concomi-
  tant administration of corticosteroids may be necessary.
  Nephrotoxicity and irreversible ototoxicity have occurred.
  Does not interfere with the action of any known antibiotic.
Comment: Before the advent of the penicillinase-resistant antibiotics, vancomycin was used successfully in the treatment
  of subacute bacterial endocarditis, osteomyelitis, and serious
  soft tissue infections. High oral doses are exceedingly effective in staphylococcal enterocolitis.

MODIFICATIONS OF ANTIBIOTIC DOSES
FOR OLIGURIC PATIENTS

If creatinine clearance is less than 10 ml./minute, the patient
should receive a full loading dose and then half that dose at the
intervals recommended in Table 6-3.

If creatinine clearance is greater than 10 ml./minute but less
than 40 ml./minute, the intervals between doses should be twice as
frequent as those suggested below.

When possible, serum killing power or other means of measuring circulating antibiotic-like activity should be used, as the rec-

TABLE 6-3. Modifications of antibiotic doses
for oliguric patients. *

| Antibiotic | Modification of Dose Required in Uremia (Creatinine Clearance < 10 ml./Minute) | |
	Extent	Interval Between Doses
Ampicillin	Minor	8-10 hours
Cephalothin	Minor	24 hours
Chloramphenicol	None, except newborn and liver disease	8 hours
Erythromycin	None	8 hours
Isoniazid	Probably minor	Unknown
Lincomycin	Minor	12 hours
Methicillin	Minor	8-10 hours
Nafcillin	Minor	8-12 hours
Nitrofurantoin	Avoid	
Penicillin G	Minor	8-10 hours
Polymyxin B	Major	3-4 days
Streptomycin	Major	3-4 days
Tetracycline	Major	3-4 days
Vancomycin	Major	9 days

*Modified from Kunin: Ann. Int. Med. 67:151, 1967.

ommendations below are based on the serum half-life after a single injection, and accumulation of partially degraded active metabolites may occur with some drugs in the uremic individual.

Patients with lowered creatinine clearance but with normal BUN or serum creatinine concentrations should be given ordinary therapeutic doses unless severe liver disease is present.

ANTIVIRAL CHEMOTHERAPY

Few therapeutic agents are available for viral infections. The following drugs have limited usefulness.

Amantadine (Symmetrel®).

Use: Limited to prophylactic administration during identified A_2 influenza virus epidemics. Of no therapeutic value. Does not appear to interfere with immunity induced by vaccination.

Dosage:
1-9 years: 1-2 mg./Kg./day orally (do not exceed 150 mg./ day) in 2 or 3 doses.
9-12 years: 200 mg./day orally in 2 doses (total dose).
Adult: 200 mg./day orally in 1 or 2 doses.

Toxicity: C. N. S. irritability (nervousness, insomnia, dizziness, lightheadedness, drunken feelings, slurred speech, ataxia, inability to concentrate). Occasional depression and feelings of detachment; blurred vision (heightened with higher dosage, 300-400 mg./day, in elderly); less commonly, dry mouth, gastrointestinal upset, skin rash. Rarely, tremors, anorexia, pollakiuria, nocturia.

Idoxuridine.

Use: At present, limited to acute superficial herpes simplex or vaccinia virus keratitis. Should be administered under an ophthalmologist's supervision. Some prefer concomitant local corticosteroid administration.

Dosage: Solution should be used initially; place 1 drop in each infected eye every hour while awake and every 2 hours at night; with definite improvement, decrease to every 2 hours around the clock and continue treatment for 3-5 days after healing appears to be complete. Ointment: Instill 5 times a day (every 4 hours), with last dose at midnight.

Toxicity: Too frequent administration leads to small punctate defects in the cornea. Ingestion of 15 ml. of solution or 20 mg. of ointment is not known to be associated with poisoning.

Methisazone (Marboran®).

Use: In the prophylaxis of smallpox if given in the first 9 days after exposure; in the therapy of complications of vaccination, especially eczema vaccinatum.

Dosage: Give a loading dose of 250 mg./Kg./day orally followed by 50 mg./Kg. every 6 hours for 3 full days. An antiemetic should be given with the drug.

Toxicity: Vomiting, immediate gastric irritation, and late (5-6 hours) C. N. S. stimulation. Short courses of therapy are not associated with other effects, but patients should be observed for hematologic and hepatic toxicity.

7 . . .

Immunization Procedures, Vaccines, Antisera, Skin Tests, & Blood Products

Biologic products are used to test for susceptibility or sensitivity (e.g., Schick or tuberculin tests) or to immunize against infectious diseases. Active immunity may be conferred by the introduction of a specific antigen or vaccine which stimulates the production of antibodies. A relatively high degree of immunity can be conferred by serial parenteral injection of the antigen at specific intervals. The degree of immunity produced by each antigen is often greater when several antigens are given simultaneously than when each antigen is given separately (anamnestic response).

Passive immunity is conferred by the administration of serum from animal or human donors who have been actively immunized against the disease, or from human beings who have recovered from the disease. This immunity is transient and is used only when antibodies must be made available immediately and for a short time.

AGENTS CONFERRING ACTIVE IMMUNITY

PRECAUTIONS AND CONTRAINDICATIONS

Precautions.

(1) Before each injection sterilize needles by autoclaving, boiling, or by dry heat. The skin and the rubber stopper should be sterilized with 2% iodine tincture or other suitable antiseptic solution.

(2) Antigens containing alum or aluminum hydroxide should be given I.M. To prevent fat necrosis along the track of the needle, do not allow the outside of the needle to become coated with alum or aluminum hydroxide. Terminate injections with 0.1 to 0.2 ml. of air. A "sterile abscess" ("antigen cyst") is less likely to occur if the injection is given deep into the tissues and the area massaged after removal of the needle. Give fluid toxoids and saline-suspended vaccines subcut. except where intracutaneous injection is specified.

(3) Infants who have had febrile convulsions should be given fractional doses of antigen to test tolerance. Consider prophylactic use of phenobarbital elixir. At the time of second injection, question the parent about fever, somnolence, and local reactions. If these have occurred, decrease the volume of the second injection. If a convulsion or severe reaction is reported, withhold further injections for several months and then give single antigens only (omitting pertussis entirely), beginning with fractional doses (0.05 to 0.1 ml.) to test tolerance.

TABLE 7-1. Recommended combined immunization procedures for active immunization and tuberculin testing of normal infants and children. (1)

Age	Material
2 months	DTP; trivalent OPV (2)
4 months	DTP; trivalent OPV
6 months	DTP; trivalent OPV
12 months	Measles vaccine; tuberculin test
15-18 months	DTP; trivalent OPV
1-12 years	Rubella, mumps
4-6 years	DTP; tuberculin test; trivalent OPV (3)
14-16 years	TD; tuberculin test (4)

Abbreviations:

DTP: Diphtheria and tetanus toxoids and pertussis vaccine.
OPV: Oral poliovaccine.
TD: Tetanus and diphtheria toxoids, adult type.

(1) See separate disease sections for more detailed discussion of recommendations, contraindications, and precautions.

(2) Immunization may be started at any age. The immune response is limited in a proportion of young infants, and the recommended booster doses are designed to ensure or maintain immunity. Protection of infants against pertussis should start early. Newborn infants can best be protected through avoidance of household contacts by adequate immunization of older siblings. This schedule is intended as a flexible guide which may be modified within certain limits to fit individual situations.

(3) Frequency of repeated tuberculin tests is dependent on the risk of exposure of the children under care and the prevalence of tuberculosis in the population group.

(4) After age 14, follow procedures recommended for adults, i. e., tetanus toxoid booster every ten years as TD.

(4) Give aspirin, 65 mg. per year of age, within an hour or two of injection and repeat four hours later.

Contraindications.

Immunizations should be delayed in the following circumstances:

A. Respiratory or Other Acute Infections: Prolong the interval between injections (even up to six months); this rarely interferes with final immunity.

B. Cerebral Damage: Use fractional doses of single antigens (omitting pertussis entirely) rather than DTP.

C. Poliomyelitis Outbreaks: Exceptions include concurrent outbreaks of diphtheria, pertussis, typhoid, or smallpox.

D. Eczema or Other Skin Diseases: Withhold smallpox immunization (may produce generalized vaccinia); withhold from siblings also (danger of cross-infection) unless siblings can be effectively isolated for a period of 20 days.

E. Failure to Thrive: May be due to immunologic deficiency state.

Primary Immunization of Children Not Inoculated in Infancy.

In children six years of age and under, triple antigens (diphtheria and tetanus toxoids combined with pertussis vaccine) should be employed. In children over six years of age, many physicians prefer to use single antigens or a combination of diphtheria and tetanus toxoids without pertussis vaccine. This preference is based on the greater frequency of more severe febrile reactions following use of the triple antigens in this age group. Oral polio-vaccine may be used at any age.

In the routine immunization of children who have not received primary inoculations in infancy, bear in mind the following points:

A. Injections should be made into the midlateral thigh or deltoid muscles.

B. In children eight years of age and older, the "adult type" teta-nus-diphtheria toxoids may be given without performing a diphtheria toxoid sensitivity test. In younger children, it is advisable to perform a preliminary toxoid sensitivity test (see Moloney skin test).

Immunization of Institutionalized Children.

Antigens recommended are diphtheria, tetanus, pertussis, oral poliovaccine, live measles vaccine, influenza vaccine, and live mumps vaccine.

In institutions where infectious hepatitis is known to be endemic, immune serum globulin (human) is recommended for all patients on admission and for new employees (0.06 ml./Kg. repeated once in five months).

For children with cerebral damage, see above.

VACCINES AND TOXOIDS

Cholera Vaccine.

Contains eight billion killed cholera vibrios in each ml.
Dosage (initial series):

A. Three doses seven to ten days apart.

	6 Months-4 Years	5-9 Years	10 Years-Adult
1st	0.1 ml.	0.3 ml.	0.5 ml.
2nd	0.3 ml.	0.5 ml.	0.5 ml.
3rd	0.3 ml.	0.5 ml.	omit

B. Booster, every six months, 0.1 to 0.5 ml. according to age as above.

Diphtheria and Tetanus Toxoids, Adult Type, Adsorbed.

A. Indications: For primary immunization or recall of children eight years of age or older.

B. Dosage: Two doses of 0.5 ml. I.M., four weeks apart, and then a final dose of 0.5 ml. I.M. six to 12 months later.

Diphtheria and Tetanus Toxoids and Pertussis Vaccine, Adsorbed.

Purified diphtheria and tetanus toxoids combined with Phase I Bordetella pertussis organisms.

A. Dosage and Administration: See Table 7-1.

B. Advantages: More slowly absorbed and permits reduction in number of organisms necessary to produce adequate immunization. A higher degree of immunization is obtained by simultaneous use of several antigens which potentiate each other.

Influenza Virus Vaccine, Polyvalent.

The vaccine is prepared from the extra-embryonic fluids of chick embryos infected with influenza virus types A_1, A_2, and B. It is used for prophylaxis against epidemic influenza caused by any of the strains contained in the vaccine.

A. Dosage and Administration: Sensitivity to egg protein should be determined. An individual who can eat eggs is not unduly sensitive. Children (and pregnant women) receive two doses of 0.1 ml. each, intradermally, ten to 14 days apart. For those six to 12 years, 0.5 ml.

B. Advantages: The vaccine may be useful during epidemics; routine vaccination during October to December may be desirable in large institutions or in chronically ill children.

C. Disadvantages: Protection is temporary and incomplete.

Measles Virus Vaccine, Live, Attenuated.

A live attenuated chick embryo tissue culture measles virus vaccine for single dose active immunization. Inactivated measles virus vaccine, previously available, should no longer be used because of serious immunologic effects upon subsequent exposure to wild measles (atypical measles).

A. Dosage and Administration: 0.5 ml. of reconstituted measles virus vaccine is injected subcut. into the upper arm.

B. Advantages: Single dose administration of a vaccine, which produces an inapparent to mild noncommunicable infection, with persistence of antibody for an indeterminate period of time.

C. Contraindications: Pregnancy, leukemia, febrile illness, recent gamma globulin administration. Caution should be used in vaccination of children with brain damage or tuberculosis, those receiving steroid therapy, or those with neomycin, penicillin, or streptomycin sensitivity.

Mumps Vaccine, Live, Attenuated.

Chick embryo-adapted mumps strain (Jeryl-Lynn) to which neomycin has been added. Supplied as lyophilized powder. When reconstituted, use promptly and protect from sunlight.

Plague Vaccine.

A saline suspension of formalin-killed and detoxified Pasteurella pestis organisms. Each ml. usually contains two billion organisms. It is used for active immunization against plague in hyperendemic areas, or for persons entering such areas. Dosage:

A. Three doses subcut. seven to ten days apart:

	6 Months-4 Years	5-9 Years	10 Years and over
1st	0.1 ml.	0.3 ml.	0.5 ml.
2nd	0.3 ml.	0.5 ml.	0.5 ml.
3rd	0.3 ml.	0.5 ml.	omit

B. Booster every six months (give final dose as above).

Poliomyelitis Vaccine, Live, Oral, Types I, II, and III, or Triple Valent (Sabin).

Attenuated strains (Sabin) propagated in monkey kidney tissue for oral use only. Manufacturers employ different vehicles, but the dosage is uniform as 500,000 $TCID_{50}$ for each type. Four to six weeks should elapse between doses. The best sequence is to give type I first, then type III, and then type II; or to give three doses of trivalent vaccine six to eight weeks apart.

Q Fever Vaccine.

Prepared from membranes of chick embryos infected with Coxiella burnetii.

Dosage and Administration: Sensitivity to egg protein should be determined. In general, an individual who can eat eggs is not unduly sensitive. Adults and children over 12 years of age receive three subcut. injections of 1 ml. each at intervals of seven to ten days. Children under 12 years of age should be given three injections of 0.5 ml. each at the same intervals. A booster should be given annually, 1 ml. for adults and 0.5 ml. for children.

Rabies Vaccine (Duck Embryo).

A dried suspension of embryonic duck tissue infected with fixed virus killed with beta-propiolactone. This product circumvents the use of brain tissue, which is thought to contain the "paralytic factor"; it may reduce the danger of neurologic side-effects. Rabies antiserum is used in conjunction with vaccine (see p. 109).

Note: In certain cases the biting animal must be observed for 5 days to determine whether or not it has rabies. If exposure is severe, rabies antiserum (see p. 109) is given immediately; vaccine may or may not be given immediately depending upon the circumstances outlined in Chapter 24.

A. Dosage and Administration: 1 ml. subcut. daily for 21 days. Injection site is changed daily, using muscles of the abdominal wall, back, upper arm, thigh, and buttocks. Local pain is relieved by adding 1 ml. of 2% lidocaine (Xylocaine®) to the syringe.

B. Indications: See Chapter 24.

C. Disadvantages: Local reactions occur, chiefly during the second week of treatment. Most common are tenderness, erythema, and induration at all sites. A history of allergy, particularly to chicken egg albumin, should be noted. Nervousness, sleeplessness, or drowsiness may occur early; if symptoms of C.N.S. involvement occur after the seventh day, vaccine injections may have to be stopped unless urgency for continued treatment is great. The use of cortisone is under study in cases of postvaccinal encephalopathies.

Rocky Mountain Spotted Fever Vaccine.

Prepared from membranes of the embryonated chicken egg infected with Rickettsia rickettsii. It is used for the protection of all persons who are exposed to those ticks which transmit the disease (dog tick, common wood tick).

Dosage and Administration: Egg protein sensitivity should be determined. In general, an individual who can eat eggs is not unduly sensitive. Adults and children over 12: three subcut. injections of 1 ml. at intervals of seven to ten days. Under 12: three injections of 0.5 ml. at the same intervals. A booster should be given annually, 1 ml. for adults and 0.5 ml. for children. Vaccine is best given in late winter or early spring.

Rubella Virus Vaccine, Attenuated, Live.

Three attenuated strains are currently licensed in the United States. Of these, the "Cendehill R" strain causes the fewest cases of arthralgia.

Adverse reactions to rubella vaccine in children have been uncommon and are generally confined to very mild rubella-like symptoms, such as slight swelling of lymph nodes, low-grade fever, or rash. Adolescents and adults have experienced transient arthralgia (10-30%) and, more rarely, arthritis. Peripheral neuritis, resulting in prolonged and painful neuromuscular syndromes, has been observed in two forms: one affecting the upper extremities and the other affecting the lower extremities, resulting in a peculiar crouching posture ("catcher's crouch").

A. Indications:
1. Girls between one year of age and puberty - Vaccine should not be administered to girls less than one year old because of possible interference from persisting maternal rubella antibody. A family history of rheumatoid arthritis may contraindicate rubella vaccine.
2. Nonpregnant adolescent and adult females - Females of childbearing potential may be considered for vaccination only when the possibility of pregnancy in the following two months is essentially nil; each case must be considered individually. This cautious approach to vaccination of postpubertal females is indicated for two reasons: (1) because of the theoretical risk of vaccination in pregnancy and (2) because significant congenital anomalies occur regularly in approximately 3% of all births, and their chance appearance after administration of vaccine during pregnancy could lead to serious misinterpretation.
   If vaccination of a woman of childbearing potential is contemplated, the following steps are indicated:
   a. Optimally, the woman should be tested for susceptibility to rubella by the HI (hemagglutination inhibition) test.
   b. If immune, she can be assured that vaccination is unnecessary.
   c. If susceptible, she can be vaccinated only if she understands that it is imperative for her to avoid becoming pregnant during the following two months. To ensure this, a medically acceptable method for prevention of pregnancy should be followed. (This precaution also applies to women in the immediate postpartum period.)
3. Vaccination after exposure to natural rubella - While there is no evidence that live rubella virus vaccine given after exposure will prevent illness, there are no contraindications to vaccination of girls already exposed to natural rubella.
B. Contraindications: Pregnant women should not be given live rubella virus vaccine. It is not known to what extent infection of the fetus with attenuated virus might take place following

vaccination, or whether damage to the fetus could result. Therefore, **routine** immunization of adolescent girls and adult women should not be undertaken because of the danger of inadvertently administering vaccine before pregnancy becomes evident.

Attenuated rubella virus infection might be potentiated by severe underlying diseases (e. g. , leukemia, lymphoma, generalized malignancy) and when resistance has been lowered by therapy with steroids, alkylating drugs, antimetabolites, or irradiation. Vaccination of patients under these conditions is contraindicated. It is also contraindicated in persons with a family history of rheumatoid arthritis and known hypersensitivity to rabbits or to neomycin. In instances of febrile illness, vaccination should be postponed until the patient has recovered.

C. Precautions: Simultaneous administration of rubella vaccine in a combined product also containing rubeola (measles) and mumps vaccine is now possible. Vaccination should be delayed until at least six weeks after gamma globulin therapy or blood transfusion because of the possible suppressive effect of passive antibodies.

Excretion of live attenuated rubella virus from the throat has occurred in a majority of susceptible individuals to whom the vaccine was administered. There is no definitive evidence to indicate that such virus is contagious to susceptible persons who are in contact with the vaccinated individuals. Consequently, while transmission is accepted as a theoretical possibility, it has not been regarded as a significant risk by expert groups in their recommendations for use of the vaccine.

D. Dosage and Administration: **Note**: For subcutaneous injection only - not for intramuscular or intravenous use. Inject entire contents (0.5 ml.) of a single-dose vial subcut.

Smallpox Vaccine.

Active cowpox virus which has been passed through many generations of calves or has been produced from embryonated eggs.

A. Precautions: Because of the danger of the development of generalized vaccinia, children with generalized eczema should not be vaccinated and should be vigorously protected from contact with all newly vaccinated household members.

B. Dosage and Administration: Contents of one capillary tube administered by multiple puncture or the abrasion method for vaccination of those visiting one of the few remaining nations which harbor smallpox and for hospital health workers in the United States. Routine, universal smallpox vaccination is no longer indicated in the United States. Information for prospective travelers is obtained from each State Health Department or the Center for Disease Control, Atlanta 30333.

C. Technic of Administration: Skin needs no preparation or chemical cleansing. Alcohol should not be used. No bandage of any kind is advised following vaccination. "No take" always means technical failure in vaccination or presence of transplacental antibodies. Vaccination should be repeated, preferably at another site with fresh vaccine.

Tetanus Toxoid, Adsorbed.

Purified tetanus toxoid in a form designed to hold the antigen in the tissues for slow absorption.

Dosage and Administration: For primary immunization in older children and adults give two I.M. injections of 0.5 ml. at intervals of six to 12 weeks. A booster should be given every two years in areas heavily contaminated with tetanus; otherwise, every three to ten years. Fluid toxoid is preferable as a booster when rapid antibody response is required (see below).

There is an increased risk of significant toxoid reactions in children who have received repeated booster injections.

Tuberculosis Vaccine (BCG Vaccine).

A. Indications: See p. 269.

B. Dosage: 0.1 ml. intradermally (as superficially as possible). Check tuberculin skin test six to eight weeks later.

C. Contraindications: Premature or underweight infants, children with impetigo or other infectious skin diseases. Do not administer simultaneously with smallpox vaccination.

D. An INH-resistant strain of BCG is available, and INH therapy can be started for children who will continue to be exposed.

Typhoid Vaccine.

Dosage and Administration:

1. Three subcut. injections of 0.5 to 1 ml. each, at intervals of seven to 28 days.

2. Three intradermal injections of 0.1 ml. seven to 28 days apart may be equally acceptable for primary vaccination.

3. Booster injections consist of 0.1 ml. intradermally annually or 0.5 ml. subcut. every three years.

Typhus Vaccine.

Formaldehyde suspension of Rickettsia prowazeki grown on chick embryo.

Persons should be vaccinated who plan to travel through Asia, Africa, Continental Europe, and other areas where typhus fever in epidemic proportions may exist. Routine vaccination is not required in the United States.

A. Three doses subcut. seven to ten days apart: (The sensitivity of the patient to egg protein should be determined.)

	6 Months-4 Years	5-9 Years	10 Years and over
1st	0.2 ml.	0.5 ml.	1.0 ml.
2nd	0.2 ml.	0.5 ml.	1.0 ml.
3rd	0.2 ml.	0.5 ml.	1.0 ml.

B. A booster of 0.2 to 1 ml. (according to age, as above) may be given every 12 months while danger of infection exists.

Yellow Fever Vaccine.

Prepared from chick embryos which have been infected with yellow fever virus. It is used for vaccination of all persons who plan to travel in Central America, South America, or Africa.

A. Dosage and Administration: 0.5 ml. subcut. (reconstituted vaccine). Only one inoculation is necessary.
B. Booster: 0.5 ml. subcut. every six to eight years.
C. Disadvantages: Reactions following vaccinations may occur on or about the seventh day. They are usually mild. Sensitivity of the patient to egg protein should be determined.

AGENTS CONFERRING PASSIVE IMMUNITY

ADMINISTRATION OF ANIMAL SERA

Precautions.
A. History: Before the administration of animal sera to a patient, routine inquiry should be made regarding history of allergy in the patient or his family and whether such sera have been administered previously. Reactions due to horse serum sensitivity, while not frequent, may be severe, especially in an allergic patient who is known to be sensitive to horse dander.
B. Testing for Sensitivity: Intradermal and conjunctival sensitivity tests should be performed routinely. They must be done if the history suggests or indicates allergy.
   1. Procedure - Give 0.05 ml. of 1:10 dilution of serum in normal saline intradermally and two drops into the conjunctival sac of one eye. Readings are made at 20 minutes.
   2. Results - A positive eye reaction consists of a marked reddening of the conjunctiva. Local corticosteroid therapy is indicated. A positive skin reaction consists of pseudopod formation with erythema larger than 1.5 cm. If a reaction is positive, serum must be administered cautiously, or (preferably) the patient must first be desensitized (hyposensitized). In general, the conjunctival test is more sensitive than the skin test.

Desensitization (Hyposensitization).
   The salient feature in the production of desensitization (hyposensitization) is the administration of a series of divided doses of the serum. In the presence of sensitivity, proceed as follows:
A. Initially, give no more than 0.1 ml. of the serum subcut.
B. Double the dose every 20 minutes until a total of 1.6 ml. has been given. Absorption may be delayed by the use of a tourniquet if the local reaction is too severe. Twenty minutes after the last dose, give 0.1 ml. of serum diluted 1:20 in saline solution I.M. or very slowly I.V. Double the dose after 20 minutes and repeat procedure at 20-minute intervals until the full dose has been administered.
C. If a reaction occurs, the previous dosage is repeated, but not until all signs and symptoms have disappeared.
D. If untoward symptoms become severe, inject epinephrine hydrochloride, 1:1000, 0.2 to 0.5 ml. subcut. Desensitization should be discontinued altogether if severe reactions follow each successive dose. The temporary use of parenteral hydrocortisone should be considered in the presence of any sensitivity.

TABLE 7-2. Passive immunization (antiserum prophylaxis and therapy).

Disease	Product	Prophy-lactic Use	Thera-peutic Use	Dosage and Route	Indications	Hazards
Agamma-globulinemia	Human gamma globulin (165 mg./ml.)	X	X	0.3 ml./lb. I.M. each month.	Recurrent bacterial infections.	None
Botulism	Horse serum, bivalent (A and B)	X	X	Prevention: 5000 units I.M. Treatment: 10,000 units I.V. Give every 4 hours, 3 or 4 times.	Only if proved exposure to toxin. Suspected diagnosis (particularly in families).	Horse serum anaphylaxis, serum sickness.
Diphtheria	Horse serum		X	40,000-80,000 units I.V. or I.M. (or both). (Range: 20,000-200,000.)	Suspected diagnosis.	Horse serum anaphylaxis, serum sickness.
German measles (rubella)	Human gamma globulin (165 mg./ml.)	X		20-40 ml. I.M.	Susceptible women in first 4 months of pregnancy.	None
Infectious hepatitis	Human gamma globulin (165 mg./ml.)	X		0.01-0.05 ml./lb. I.M.	Epidemic or known exposure.	None
Measles (rubeola)	Human gamma globulin (165 mg./ml.)	X	X	Prevention: 0.1 ml./lb. I.M. Treatment: 0.3 ml./lb. I.M.	Any exposed and susceptible. Infants. Sick or institutional children. In pre-eruptive phase only of totally unprotected children.	None None None
Mumps	Mumps immune gamma globulin (human)	X		Children: 1.5 ml. total dose. Over 12 years: 3-4.5 ml. total dose.	Susceptible adults.	None
Pertussis	Pertussis immune gamma globulin (human)	X	X	Prevention: 1.25-2.5 ml.; repeat in 7 days. Treatment: 2.5 ml. I.M. daily or every other day for total dose of 7.5 ml.	Unvaccinated exposed infants. Affected children under 1 year of age.	None

Rabies*	Horse serum	X	1000 units/40 lb. to a maximum of 6000 units I.M.	Within 24 hours of bite by rabid animal.	Horse serum anaphylaxis, serum sickness.
	Human rabies immune globulin (HRIG)†	X	20 I.U./Kg.	Within 24 hours of bite by rabid animal.	None
Tetanus*	Human antiserum	X	Prevention: 2 units/lb. I.M. to maximum of 250 units (adult). Treatment: 65 units/lb. I.M. to maximum of 5000 units I.M.	Suspected diagnosis.	None
	Horse serum	X	15,000-30,000 units I.M. 50,000-100,000 units, 1/2 I.M., 1/2 I.V.	Nonimmunized child with injury. Suspected tetanus.	Horse serum anaphylaxis, serum sickness.
Vaccinia	Vaccinia immune gamma globulin (human)	X	Prevention: 0.15 ml./lb. I.M. Treatment: 0.3-0.6 ml./lb. I.M.	Exposed eczema, varicella, burn, etc. Generalized vaccinia, vaccinia necrosum.	None
Varicella-zoster (chickenpox)	Zoster immune gamma globulin (ZIG)	X	5 ml. I.M.	Susceptible children on long-term steroid therapy; susceptible adults.	None
	Zoster convalescent plasma	X	100-400 ml. I.V. (10-15 ml./Kg.).		
Variola (smallpox)	Vaccinia immune gamma globulin (human)	X	Prevention: 0.15 ml./lb. I.M.	Exposed, susceptible persons.	None

*Note: Human rabies immune globulin and human tetanus antiserum should speedily replace horse serum.

†HRIG is available by telephone (24-hour service): (214) 631-6240 (Cutter Laboratories).

Reduction of Serum Reactions.
A. Dilution: Unpleasant serum reactions may be reduced by diluting the serum ten to 20 times with 5 or 10% glucose in physiologic saline or by injecting the serum slowly into the tubing of the infusion apparatus during administration of I.V. fluids.
B. Retarding Absorption: The I.M. administration of animal serum is best made into the anterior thigh in order to allow tourniquet application to retard absorption if reaction occurs.
C. Antihistaminic substances may be given prophylactically one hour before administration and repeated as required. The following may also be given I.V. with antiserum when diluted: (I.M. or subcut. administration requires no dilution.) (1) Chlorpheniramine (Chlor-Trimeton®), 2 to 10 mg. I.V. (2) Diphenhydramine (Benadryl®), 2 to 10 mg. I.V. (3) Tripelennamine (Pyribenzamine®), 5 to 25 mg. I.V.

Treatment of Reactions.
A. Epinephrine hydrochloride, 1:1000, should always be on hand for immediate use. Give 0.2 to 0.5 ml. I.M.
B. Hydrocortisone orally or I.V. is of no immediate use but may minimize late reactions. (For children with a history of previous reactions, hydrocortisone may be given prophylactically at the time of administration.)

PREPARATIONS

Immune Serum Globulin (Human) (Placental).
Concentrated solution of the gamma globulin fraction of pooled normal human plasma obtained from venous blood, or from placental sources. This fraction contains most of the antibodies normally found in adult plasma, but antibody titer varies from lot to lot.
A. Indications: For prophylaxis and modification of measles and infectious hepatitis and for treatment of dysgammaglobulinemia.
B. Dosage:
  1. Prevention of measles -
    a. Six years or under - 0.2 ml./Kg. (0.1 ml./lb.) or 2 ml.
    b. Six to 12 years - 0.2 ml./Kg. (0.1 ml./lb.) or 5 ml.
    c. Over 12 years - 0.2 ml./Kg. (0.1 ml./lb.).
  2. Prevention or modification of infectious hepatitis - See Chapter 24.
  3. Treatment of hypogammaglobulinemia - See Chapter 17.
C. Administration: This material may be given I.M. deep into the upper outer quadrant of the buttocks but should never be given I.V. For measles prophylaxis globulin should be administered within the first six days after initial exposure, although some effect may be produced up to the tenth day if dosage is doubled.
D. Advantages: Prevention is desirable for children under three years, debilitated children such as asthmatics, pulmonary or cardiac cripples, and for inmates of institutions. The globulin may be of possible value in the treatment of measles when used in large doses in the pre-eruptive phase.
E. Disadvantages: Any febrile or catarrhal illness occurring within three weeks after exposure should be diagnosed as mild measles and the patient quarantined.

Mumps Immune Gamma Globulin (Human).

Gamma globulin concentrate of serum of high titer obtained from adult donors who have received mumps virus vaccine.

A. Indications: To confer temporary protection on susceptible exposed children or adults. At present, it is best limited to adults for the prevention of orchitis or oophoritis.

B. Dosage and Administration, for Prophylactic Use: Infants and children under ten years of age, 2.5 ml. I.M.; older children, 5 ml. I.M. Give within the first seven days after exposure.

Pertussis Immune Human Serum.

Gamma globulin fraction of serum from hyperimmunized donors.

A. Indications: For prevention and treatment of whooping cough.

B. Dosage and Administration: Give 2.5 ml. (vial contains equivalent of 25 ml. hyperimmune horse serum) on alternate days for three doses by deep I.M. injection into the buttocks.

Vaccinia Immune Gamma Globulin (Human).

(Available from Hyland Laboratories or from American National Red Cross Blood Centers.)

Concentrated from serum of recently vaccinated blood donors.

A. Indications: Eczema vaccinatum, generalized vaccinia, vaccinia necrosum, and in prophylaxis of smallpox and vaccinia.

B. Dosage and Administration: For treatment, 0.6 to 1 ml./Kg., I.M., repeated as necessary; for prophylaxis, 0.3 ml./Kg., I.M., once. Give in divided doses if necessary (large volumes).

Zoster Immune Gamma Globulin (ZIG).

(Available only from the Center for Disease Control, Atlanta 30333.) Obtained from zoster convalescent patients.

A. Indications: Progressive varicella in an immunosuppressed patient or as prophylaxis in such patients exposed to varicella.

B. Dosage and Administration: 5 ml. I.M., repeated as necessary.

Rabies Antiserum (Hyperimmune Serum) (Horse) (Lederle).

A concentrated serum derived from hyperimmunized horses.

A. Indications: See Rabies, Chapter 24.

B. Dosage: Each vial contains 1000 units. Up to 40 lbs., 1000 units are recommended; between 40 and 80 lbs., 2000 units; between 80 and 120 lbs., 3000 units.

C. Administration is into wound and proximal muscle, the rest into gluteal muscle. It may be administered in divided injections if the volume in one area is likely to cause discomfort. The entire recommended dose for treatment should be given as soon as possible after exposure has occurred, preferably within 24 hours (not after 72 hours). After 24 hours the efficacy of prophylactic serum administration rapidly diminishes. If the interval is greater than 24 hours or the wounds about the head and neck are particularly severe, two or three times as much serum as recommended above should be administered.

D. Precautions: In addition to skin and conjunctival tests for horse serum sensitivity, a careful history must be obtained to determine whether the child has an allergic susceptibility.

Diphtheria Antitoxin (Horse).

Concentrated globulin fraction obtained from the pooled serum of horses hyperimmunized against the toxin of Corynebacterium diphtheriae.

A. Indications: For immediate administration in all cases of suspected diphtheria. Early administration, prior to laboratory confirmation, is imperative since toxin cannot be neutralized after it becomes fixed in the tissues; damage once produced is irreversible by antitoxin therapy.

B. Dosage and Administration: Dosage depends on severity of infection rather than on age and body weight. Give I.V. or deep I.M. into the anterior thigh.

1. Moderate cases - 20,000 to 40,000 units.
2. Severe cases - 40,000 to 80,000 units.
3. Diphtheria gravis - 80,000 to 200,000 or more units.

C. Disadvantages: Antitoxin is not advised for the prophylaxis of exposed susceptibles, because of the danger of producing sensitization to horse serum. Susceptibility of all exposed individuals should promptly be determined with Schick test and a single injection of diphtheria toxoid (fluid) given at once. If Schick test is negative, the toxoid will act as an adequate booster. If positive, the patient should be examined at repeated short intervals and active immunization with diphtheria toxoid (fluid) continued. Active treatment with antitoxin is indicated if any suspicious clinical findings develop.

Tetanus Antitoxin (Equine, Bovine).

A concentrated globulin obtained from the serum of hyperimmunized horses and cows; no longer indicated if human globulin is available (see below).

Dosage and Administration: A previously immunized child should receive 0.5 ml. of fluid toxoid after each injury. Both toxoid and antitoxin should be given after massive contamination and after compound fractures or if severe blood loss has occurred. The non-immunized child or adult should receive prophylactic antitoxin alone and should not be given toxoid for two to three weeks. The patient should then be started on active immunization. At least 30,000 units of antitoxin I.M. are required for effective passive immunization, a large initial dose being preferable to several small doses.

1. Prophylactic - At least 5000 units should be given deep subcut., after tests for horse serum sensitivity and investigation of the patient's history for horse dander sensitivity.
2. Therapeutic - 50,000 to 100,000 units I.V. or I.M., following tests for sensitivity to horse serum and investigation of the family history for allergy.

Tetanus Immune Globulin (Human).

This gamma globulin is obtained from the sera of persons hyperimmunized against tetanus, and is used when passive prophylaxis against tetanus is indicated. It does not cause allergic manifestations and therefore does not require sensitivity testing prior to use nor observation following its administration.

Dosage and Administration: A lower dosage than is needed when equine or bovine antitoxin is used produces protective antibody levels which persist for three to four weeks. After severe exposure or delayed therapy, 500-1000 units of globulin may be required. The estimated dosage for children under five years of age is 75 units; for children five to ten years of age, 125 units. For children ten years of age or older, the adult dose (250 units) is used.

Tetanus toxoid should be administered at another site at the same time, since there is no apparent evidence of interference with the immune response by the previously administered immune globulin.

Gas Gangrene Antitoxin.

Usually trivalent, containing antitoxin against Clostridium welchii, Cl. septicum, and Cl. novyi.

Dosage and Administration: Single I.M. injections of 10,000 to 50,000 units of Cl. welchii and Cl. septicum antitoxin and 1500 to 7500 units of Cl. novyi antitoxin. Horse dander and serum sensitivity should be determined prior to injection.

Botulism Antitoxin.

Bivalent for botulism types A and B, containing 10,000 units of each antitoxin. Horse serum sensitivity should be determined.

Dosage and Administration: 10,000 units each of types A and B are given I.V. at four-hour intervals as the patient's condition warrants, usually for three or four doses. Prophylactic doses of 5000 units each are given I.M. upon definite indication only.

SKIN TESTS

Blastomycin Skin Test.

This test should be used in conjunction with the histoplasmin skin test and the tuberculin skin test.
  A. Test Material: Sterile filtrate from a culture of the mycelial phase of Blastomyces dermatitidis.
  B. Indications: For diagnosis of blastomycosis.
  C. Dosage and Administration: 0.1 ml. of diluted material intradermally. Tuberculin type syringe used for blastomycin skin testing should not have been used in other skin testing procedures, especially tuberculin tests.
  D. Results and Interpretation: Read after 24, 48, and 96 hours.
    1. Positive reaction - Induration of 5×5 mm. or more.
    2. Doubtful reaction - Induration of less than 5×5 mm., or erythema (without induration) greater than 5×5 mm.
    3. Negative reaction - No induration, or erythema of less than 5×5 mm.

Brucella Skin Test.

  A. Test Material: Suspension of brucella organisms.
  B. Indications: For diagnosis of brucellosis.
  C. Dosage and Administration: 0.1 ml. of 1:10 dilution of standard vaccine suspension intradermally.
  D. Contraindication: This test is contraindicated until serological testing has been performed, since it will provoke the appearance of a variety of specific antibodies. It requires careful interpretation.
  E. Results and Interpretation: Read after 24 hours. A positive reaction consists of an indurated reddish area, usually 3 to 4

cm. in diameter, which persists for several days. Hypersensitive individuals may have a systemic reaction and the induration may be extensive, persisting for several weeks. Positive reactions may be obtained two to three weeks after infection and remain positive for years.

Chancroid Skin Test (Ducrey Test).
A. Test Material: Saline suspension of killed Haemophilus ducreyi.
B. Indications: For diagnosis of chancroid.
C. Dosage and Administration: 0.05 ml. intradermally.
D. Results and Interpretation: The test is read after 48 hours. Induration over 2 cm. indicates a positive reaction. The test remains positive for many years after recovery from infection and so does not distinguish between past and present infections.

Coccidioidin Skin Test.
A. Test Material: A 1:100 dilution of the filtrate obtained from a culture of 10 selected strains of Coccidioides immitis grown in a synthetic medium.
B. Indications: For detecting sensitivity to Coccidioides immitis. The test does not evoke humoral antibodies.
C. Dosage and Administration: The 1:100 material is diluted ten times; 0.1 ml. of the resultant 1:1000 dilution is injected intradermally and read at 24 and 48 hours. If negative, repeat with 1:100 dilution. Patients with coccidioidal erythema nodosum are likely to be very sensitive; therefore, an initial testing with 1:10,000 dilution is advisable. If this is negative, 1:1000 should be tried, and only if that is negative should 1:100 be used. Tuberculin-type syringes used for coccidioidin testing should not have been used in other skin testing procedures, especially not for tuberculin tests.
D. Results and Interpretation: Induration over 0.5 cm. in diameter at either 24 or 48 hours is considered positive. Positive reactions may be obtained two to three weeks after infection and remain positive for many years.

Dick Test.
Because of the danger of sensitization to an antigen of the beta-hemolytic streptococcus and the ready use of penicillin in the therapy of streptococcal infection, this test is no longer indicated and is of historical importance only.

Echinococcus Skin Test.
A. Test Material: Antigens obtained from dog tapeworm or from hydatid fluid.
B. Indications: For diagnosis of echinococcus disease. Does not evoke humoral antibodies. Obtained from N.I.H., Bethesda, Md.
C. Dosage and Administration: 0.25 ml. given intradermally into the skin of the outer upper arm. This usually results in a blanched, infiltrated area 1 cm. in diameter. A control injection of normal saline is made nearby.
D. Results and Interpretation: Blanching and infiltration of the test area increases and may show pseudopods. The initial reading is made one-half hour after injection. A delayed reaction is read between 18 and 24 hours.

1. Positive immediate (half-hour) reaction should have wheal measuring at least 2.4 cm. in one diameter, or 2.2 cm. in both diameters. Positive reaction indicates antigenic experience with echinococcus and that sensitivity has resulted.
2. A negative immediate reaction is recorded when the wheal is smaller than 2.3 cm.
3. Positive delayed response has infiltration and edema at least 4 cm. in diameter. A positive reaction indicates present or past infestation. It remains positive throughout life.

Histoplasmin Skin Test.
A. Test Material: Culture filtrate of Histoplasma capsulatum.
B. Indications: For diagnosis of histoplasmosis.
C. Dosage and Administration: 0.1 ml. intradermally of a 1:1000 dilution. Read in 48 and 72 hours.
D. Results and Interpretation: The reaction is positive if at either reading the area of induration is more than 0.5 cm. in diameter. The test is of little diagnostic value at present because its exact specificity has not been established. Cross-reactions may occur if the individual has become sensitized to other fungi (B. dermatitidis, C. immitis, or C. albicans).

Lymphogranuloma Venereum Skin Test (Frei Test).
A. Test Material: Antigen prepared from chick embryo-grown LGV agent.
B. Indications: For diagnosis of lymphogranuloma venereum.
C. Dosage and Administration: 0.1 ml. intradermally.
D. Results and Interpretation: Read in 48 to 72 hours. A reddish papule 6 mm. or more in diameter surrounded by a faint erythematous area of varying size indicates a positive reaction. A control is used to rule out hypersensitivity to chick protein. The reaction remains positive for several years after infection has subsided and so fails to distinguish between past or present infection. Positive reaction may occur following infection with psittacosis agent.

Moloney Test for Diphtheria Toxoid Sensitivity (Modified).
A. Test Material: A 1:100 dilution of fluid diphtheria toxoid.
B. Indications: To determine degree of sensitivity to diphtheria toxoid prior to its use in active immunization of older children (over eight years) or adults.
C. Dosage and Administration: 0.1 ml. intradermally.
D. Results and Interpretation: Read in 48 hours. Reaction is positive if erythema is more than 1 cm. in diameter. With such a reaction, perform a Schick test. If Schick is also positive, further immunization is necessary; **only fluid toxoid should be used.** Start with small doses (0.05 ml. subcut.).

Mumps Skin Test.
A. Test Material: Killed virus suspension prepared from extra-embryonic fluid of infected chick embryos.
B. Indications: To determine susceptibility to mumps during or after adolescence. Often positive in absence of history of infection. May evoke humoral antibodies.

    C. Dosage and Administration: 0.1 ml. intradermally.
    D. Results and Interpretation: The test should be read in 24 to
        36 hours. Immunity is indicated by induration and erythema
        1.5 cm. or more in diameter.

Schick Test (Diphtheria Toxin, Diagnostic).

    A. Test Material: A sterile solution of the toxic products of
        growth of Corynebacterium diphtheriae.
    B. Indications: A test for detecting susceptibility to diphtheria.
    C. Dosage and Administration: 0.1 ml. of the Schick test material
        (representing $1/50$ M.L.D. of diphtheria toxin) intradermally
        into the flexor surface of the forearm.
    D. Results and Interpretation: A positive reaction (a circumscribed
        area of redness and infiltration 1 to 2 cm. in diameter) occurs
        in 24 to 48 hours and is at its height in 48 to 72 hours. Read in
        three to four days. It remains positive for six to 12 days, is
        followed by slight scaling, and leaves a brownish spot. A dif-
        fuse pseudoreaction may occur, differentiated by earlier appear-
        ance and disappearance and by lack of subsequent pigmentation.
        A persistently positive reaction after apparently adequate im-
        munization should suggest dysgammaglobulinemia.

Toxoplasma Skin Test.

    A. Test Material: Extract of killed toxoplasma organisms.
    B. Indications: For detecting past or present toxoplasma infection.
    C. Dosage and Administration: 0.1 ml. (1:500) intradermally.
    D. Results and Interpretation: Read in 24 to 48 hours. Present or
        past infection is indicated by redness and swelling more than
        0.5 cm. in diameter. Occasional false positives do occur.

Trichinella Skin Test.

    A. Test Material: Extract of dried, ground trichinellae.
    B. Indications: For diagnosis of trichinosis.
    C. Dosage and Administration: 0.01 to 0.02 ml. of trichinella
        extract is injected intradermally. A control injection of saline
        is made in the same manner on the other arm.
    D. Results and Interpretation: The area should be observed for
        24 hours. A positive reaction is of the immediate type and
        appears usually within 15 to 20 minutes after the injection. In
        rare instances, the reaction may be delayed, reaching its
        height at 24 hours. A positive reaction consists of 5 to 30 mm.
        of induration or 10 to 50 mm. of erythema. The control rarely
        shows induration of over 3 mm. and erythema over 5 mm.
        1. The test is not positive until the second week of infection.
        2. Normal individuals may give positive skin tests from pre-
           viously unrecognized trichinosis or infestation with other
           parasites, such as Trichuris trichiura.

Tuberculin Skin Test (Mantoux Test).

    A. Test Material: Either Purified Protein Derivative of Tubercu-
        lin, U.S.P. (PPD), or Old Tuberculin, U.S.P. (OT), may be
        used. PPD is a highly purified protein fraction isolated from
        culture filtrates of human type strains of Mycobacterium tuber-
        culosis. It is supplied as sterile tablets of three strengths:
        First, Intermediate, and Second Test Strengths. OT is a fil-

trate of a concentrated broth culture of tubercle bacilli, dispensed in solutions of 1:10,000 (0.1 ml. = 0.01 mg.); 1:1000 (0.1 ml. = 0.1 mg.), the usual test dose; and 1:100 (0.1 ml. = 1 mg.). Intermediate Test Strength PPD is comparable in strength to 1:1000 OT.

B. Indications: For determination of tuberculin sensitivity.

C. Dosage and Administration: Injections should be made intradermally on the flexor surface of the forearm so as to raise a small bleb. Care should be taken to avoid injecting tuberculin subcut. If this occurs, no local reaction develops and a general febrile reaction may result.

The recommended methods for performing the tuberculin test utilizing PPD are as follows:

1. Inject 0.1 ml. PPD First Test Strength (0.00002 mg.) intradermally. If negative, a second test is made with 0.1 ml. PPD Second Test Strength (0.005 mg.).

or 2. One injection of 0.1 ml. PPD Intermediate Test Strength (0.0001 mg.) intradermally. This dose represents five times the concentration of the First Test Strength and one-fiftieth that of the Second Test Strength. First Test Strength PPD should be used in cases of suspected tuberculosis.

If OT is used, 1:1000 should be employed first, followed by 1:100 if negative. In suspected cases of tuberculosis (pulmonary, meningeal, or skin), start with 1:10,000.

D. Results and Interpretation: A positive reaction shows a definite palpable induration greater than 6 to 8 mm. in diameter. Redness is to be disregarded. Readings are made after 48 to 72 hours, preferably 72 hours. A positive reaction indicates a past or present infection. A large or hemorrhagic response suggests active disease which should be treated promptly. If active tuberculosis is suspected, only dilute solutions should be used for testing (especially with eye tuberculosis). Known positive reactors should not be retested. A negative reaction excludes the possibility of tuberculosis in most cases. False-positive reaction can occur as a result of infection with anonymous mycobacteria.

Tuberculin Skin Test (Tine Test).

Useful as a screen, but PPD should be used when the diagnosis is suspected.

A. Test Material: Disposable disk which administers 0.05 mg. U.S. Standard OT (5 I.U.) or 0.0001 mg. U.S. Standard PPD (5 I.U.) by the Mantoux technic.

B. Administration: The site is the volar surface of the mid-forearm. The skin must be clean and dry. Grasp the patient's arm firmly with one hand, stretching the skin of the forearm tight; apply the disk with the other hand, hold for 1 sec., and withdraw.

C. Results and Interpretation: The reaction should be read in 48 to 72 hours. Induration is the only criterion of response. Two mm. or more of palpable induration around one or more puncture sites is equivalent to 5 mm. or more by the Mantoux technic. With positive reactions, areas of induration around the puncture sites tend to coalesce.

Tularemia Skin Test.
  A. Test Material: A detoxified suspension of killed Pasteurella
     tularensis organisms.
  B. Indications: To detect past or present infection with tularemia.
  C. Dosage and Administration: 0.05 ml. intradermally.
  D. Results and Interpretation: The test should be read after 48
     hours. An erythematous area 1 cm. in diameter is considered
     a positive reaction. Even as early as the first week of the
     disease this reaction is almost always positive. Positive re-
     actions persist for many years after recovery and cannot be
     used to differentiate previous or active tularemia.

THERAPEUTIC BLOOD FRACTION PRODUCTS

It should be borne in mind that whenever therapeutic blood fractions are given there is a risk of transmitting the virus of serum
hepatitis. This risk is greater when pooled blood fraction products
are given than when whole blood is used.

Antihemophilic Human Plasma.
  Plasma from freshly drawn blood processed for retention of
antihemophilic activity.
  A. Indications: For use in hemophilic subjects who are bleeding.
     Antihemophilic plasma returns the clotting time of hemophilic
     blood to normal limits for six to 24 hours.
  B. Dosage and Administration: Inject I.V. Restoration of dry
     material to half the original volume is recommended. 50 ml.
     of diluent is added to dried plasma, representing 100 ml. of
     original plasma. Dosage varies from patient to patient.

Fibrinogen (Parenogen®).
  Fibrinogen is a protein essential for blood coagulation.
  A. Indications: Hypofibrinogenemia leading to hemorrhagic epi-
     sodes. Plasma fibrinogen levels of less than 50 mg./100
     ml. are considered critically low.
  B. Dosage: Determined by following plasma fibrinogen levels.
     One Gm. of dried fibrinogen is dissolved in 50 ml. of water for
     injection. Give 25 to 200 ml. I.V.

AHF or Factor VIII Concentrates.
  A. Indications: Therapy of hemophilia A.
  B. Dosage and Administration: Reconstitute lyophilized material
     (stored at $4°$C.) and inject by I.V. push. Dose is calculated
     as follows:

Units VIII = Desired in vivo level in per cent × 0.5 × wt. in Kg.

Usual level desired is 40%; however, 20% is minimal hemostatic level.
  Cryoprecipitates are a blood bank product made from fresh
frozen plasma used for therapy of factor VIII deficient hemophilia or von Willebrand's disease. A dosage of 1 pack/5 Kg.
usually gives an VIII level of 40%.

Normal Human Plasma.

Five per cent solution of heat-treated human plasma protein fraction (Plasmanate®). For treatment of shock due to dehydration and infection. Give 15 ml./lb. I. V. no faster than 5-10 ml./minute.

Normal Human Serum Albumin.

Five Gm. of normal serum albumin (salt-poor) and 20 ml. of buffer diluent, or 5% (12.5 Gm. in 250 ml. or 25 Gm. in 500 ml., Albumisol®).

A. Indications: For treatment of hypoproteinemia, as replacement therapy for deficiency diseases, for treatment of shock due to hemorrhage if no whole blood is available, for peripheral vasomotor collapse from other causes, or for treatment of hyperbilirubinemia.

B. Dosage and Administration: 5 Gm. of albumin are therapeutically equivalent to 100 ml. of citrated plasma. It is given I. V.

Thrombin (Bovine).

Thrombin is a plasma protein of human or bovine origin applied topically to produce hemostasis.

A. Indications: As hemostatic agent in the treatment of hemorrhage.

B. Dosage and Administration: Thrombin solution in strengths of 1000 units per ml. applied to a bleeding area produces a clot within three seconds and usually controls bleeding. Oral administration of the powder in small amounts of isotonic saline may control gastric hemorrhage in some instances. Bleeding from bone may be controlled by applying thrombin powder directly. Thrombin is usually packaged in 1000 units, 5000 units, and 10,000 units, with diluent. It should only be applied topically.

Factor IX (Konyne®).

A. Indications: For therapy of congenital factor IX deficiency (Christmas disease) or severe liver disease. This lyophylized product contains factors IX, II, VII, and X in vials of 500 units. *

B. Dosage and Administration: Dosage is calculated as factor VIII (see above) except that twice the calculated dose is given initially (for tissue diffusion).

---

*A unit of a clotting factor is that contained in the equivalent of 1 ml. of fresh plasma with 100% clotting activity.

8 ...
The Newborn Infant: Assessment & General Care*

CLINICAL ASSESSMENT

Clinical evaluation of a newborn infant should include consideration of (1) aspects of the maternal and obstetric history, including labor, delivery, and medications; (2) the need for resuscitation and its effectiveness; (3) the physical examination, including gestational age assessment and search for possible birth injuries and congenital anomalies; and (4) assessment of the level of care required by the neonate.

High-Risk Factors in Obstetric History.
The risk of neonatal mortality or morbidity is increased in pregnancies associated with previous neonatal death or complications, multiple gestation, incompetent cervix, antepartum hemorrhage (placenta previa, abruptio placentae), premature rupture of membranes, Rh sensitization, maternal infection (especially rubella, cytomegalovirus, Herpesvirus hominis infection, and amnionitis), chronic maternal disease (cardiac; renal; endocrine, especially diabetes), toxemia, failure to obtain prenatal care, maternal age < 15 years or > 40 years, antepartum trauma, or major surgery. Complications during labor or delivery (prolapsed cord, abnormal presentation [face, brow, breech; shoulder dystocia], cesarean section, fetal distress, prolonged labor, high forceps delivery, complications of analgesia and anesthesia [hypotension, delivery of infant during peak drug levels] and prolonged rupture of membranes) are also responsible for increased neonatal mortality.

In recognized high-risk pregnancies, the condition of the fetus during labor should be determined by continuous fetal heart rate monitoring or by observing scalp blood pH. Fetal distress is often accompanied by meconium passage and is diagnosed by abnormal fetal heart rate pattern (bradycardia, late decelerations) or fetal acidosis (pH < 7.25).

IMMEDIATE CARE OF THE NEWBORN

In the Delivery Room.
A. Aspirate mucus gently from nose and throat with a rubber-bulbed syringe (preferable) or a catheter attached to a glass trap. This should be done, if possible, with head down before the infant's first breath is taken and is conveniently carried out before delivering the infant's shoulders.

*Revised by Michael A. Simmons, MD, and Frank H. Morriss, Jr., MD.

B. Neither immediate nor delayed clamping of the cord appears to be clearly superior in the healthy full-term infant.

C. After toweling off thoroughly, keep infant warm (preferably under a radiant heater). Wrap in warm blankets for transfer to nursery.

D. Administer nalorphine (Nalline®) or levallorphan (Lorfan®) to reverse respiratory depression due to morphine, codeine, or other opiates.

E. Assign Apgar score at 1 and 5 minutes (Table 8-1).

F. Carry out brief initial screening examination, checking for gross abnormalities, adequate chest expansion and air exchange, abdominal masses, torsion of testes, signs of adequate perfusion, and number of umbilical arteries.

G. Gastric lavage should be performed on all sick infants or those delivered by cesarean section.

H. Instill 1% silver nitrate or suitable antibiotic into the eyes. A mild chemical conjunctivitis should result.

I. Identify infant with bracelet and footprinting or necklace.

J. Very small preterm infants should not be stimulated to cry and should not be laryngoscoped except upon specific indications. Avoid vigorous chest pressing, alternate hot and cold baths, jack-knifing, holding the infant upside down for more than a few seconds, spanking, and rubbing the spine. The infant should not be weighed or bathed until its condition is stabilized.

K. Encourage parental contact if the infant's condition permits.

In the Nursery.

A. Place in heated crib. Prevent contamination. Assess gestational age. Administer vitamin K$_1$ (phytonadione [AquaMephyton®, Konakion®]), 1 mg. I. M. Perform eye care if not done in delivery room. Do not weigh or bathe until infant is stabilized and temperature is normal.

B. Keep under close observation for at least four to eight hours. If there is a great deal of mucus, elevate the foot of the crib and aspirate with a suction tube. Examine the umbilical cord at frequent intervals for bleeding. Check temperature every hour until stabilized and above 98.6°F. (36°C.). Check to see that voiding of urine and passage of meconium stools occur.

C. Routine rubs with chemotherapeutic or antibiotic ointments are not needed and are not recommended because of the danger of sensitization. Talcum and oils generally are not necessary and (especially if perfumed) may lead to sensitization. Bathing with triple dye (brilliant green, proflavine, and crystal violet) significantly reduces colonization with staphylococci.

D. For prevention of infections, see discussion in Chapter 9.

RESUSCITATION

During Delivery of the Potentially Asphyxiated Child.

A. Give mother 100% oxygen continuously by mask.

B. Deliver infant slowly, keeping the head down.

Immediately After Delivery.

A. Place in 30 degree Trendelenburg position. Permit adequate

delivery of placental blood to the child except for suspected hemolytic disease of the newborn (erythroblastosis fetalis).
B. Clear airways again with gentle bulb suction.
C. Stimulate by flicking soles of feet, rubbing back, or gently flexing and extending extremities. (**Caution:** Do not spank or swing the baby or immerse him alternately in cold and hot water.)
D. Dry infant to reduce heat loss and keep warm. An overhead radiant warmer may be of value.

After Clamping and Cutting the Cord.

A. Place in 15 to 30 degree Trendelenburg position and keep warm.
B. Administer oxygen by means of a funnel or mask or in an incubator, if required.
C. Check Apgar score. (Table 8-1.)
   1. Resuscitation of the vigorous infant (one-minute Apgar score > 7) -
      a. Infant who is breathing well - Briefly and gently suction mouth, nose, and pharynx with bulb syringe or soft rubber catheter; pass catheter through mouth into stomach to check patency of esophagus and aspirate stomach contents, noting volume.
      b. Infant who is dusky, but whose respiratory effort is adequate - Gently suction mouth, nose, and pharynx, and administer oxygen by face mask. Keep warm. Stimulate gently.
   2. Resuscitation of the moderately depressed newborn (one-minute Apgar score 4-7) - Suck out nose and throat briefly while administering oxygen by face mask.
      a. If initial heart rate of < 100 accelerates promptly and good muscle tone is developing, infant may not need more than face mask oxygen.
      b. If bradycardia or weak respiratory efforts persist, administer intermittent positive pressure ventilation (IPPV) with Ambu® bag and mask and 100% oxygen at 30-40 breaths/minute and 30-40 cm. water pressure. Listen to both sides of chest for adequate ventilation, and for heart rate. If heart rate does not accelerate after one minute, proceed to intubation.*
   3. Resuscitation of severely depressed newborn (one-minute Apgar score 0-3) -
      a. Suction briefly, intubate, and administer IPPV with 100% oxygen via Ambu® bag to tube at the rate of 30-40 respirations per minute and a pressure of 30-40 cm. water. Auscultate over both lungs and withdraw endotracheal tube slightly if breath sounds on left are poor.
      b. If heart rate is < 50 or decelerating after 60 seconds of IPPV, begin external cardiac massage at 60/minute. Obtain umbilical artery pH and pCO_2, and determine base excess. Correct acidosis, if present, by adequate ventilation. Consider administration of diluted sodium bicarbonate, based on observed base deficit. In the presence of hypotension or known blood loss, administer whole blood (which may be obtained from placenta) or plasma

---

*Intubation should be performed by experienced persons.

TABLE 8-1. Apgar score of newborn infant.

Sign	Score		
	0	1	2
A Appearance (color)	Blue; pale.	Body pink; extremities blue.	Completely pink.
P Pulse (heart rate)	Absent.	Below 100.	Over 100.
G Grimace (reflex irritability in response to stimulation of sole of foot)	No response.	Grimace.	Cry.
A Activity (muscle tone)	Limp.	Some flexion of extremities.	Active motion.
R Respiration (respiratory effort)	Absent.	Slow; irregular.	Good strong cry.

        volume expander.

    c. If there is no sustained heart rate response after five minutes of cardiac massage, give **IPPV** and therapy for acidosis, obtain chest x-ray to look for diaphragmatic hernia, pneumothorax, etc., and consider needle and syringe aspiration of pleural spaces as indicated. Consider intracardiac epinephrine, 1 ml. of 1:10,000 solution.

GENERAL CARE

The infant should be wrapped in a blanket or placed in an incubator in a recovery area of the nursery and carefully observed for abnormal appearance, vital signs, or symptoms. If the newborn infant is in satisfactory condition after the recovery period, he should be evaluated (taking into account the gestational age and possible factors of risk), weighed, and bathed with a bland soap and plain water. Bathing with a solution of 1% hexachlorophene **followed by thorough rinsing** should be reserved for infants with a significantly increased risk of skin infections. (Avoid excessive use.)

Routine Care of the Term Appropriate-for-Gestational-Age (AGA) Newborn. (See Fig 8-1.)

Feeding can be started as early as two to six hours of age in vigorous term babies. Sterile water or 5% glucose in water should be offered initially. When the infant has demonstrated that he can suck and swallow adequately and has taken one of these liquids well, he can be offered breast milk or full-strength milk formula (20 Cal. /oz.) 2 to 4 oz./feeding every four hours or more often on demand. Avoid high-protein formulas.

Urination and passage of meconium stools should be documented in the first 24 hours. Circumcision has not been proved to be necessary or beneficial; however, if performed, it should be delayed to at least the second or third day of life.

In most states, screening for phenylketonuria is mandatory. Samples of blood or urine for screening tests should be taken only after adequate intake of milk for 24 hours.

Routine Care of the Preterm Newborn.

A. The prematurely born neonate should be cared for in an incubator designed to keep him warm, to protect him from infection, to provide an atmosphere with increased humidity and
   oxygen if required, and still to allow him to be carefully observed with minimal handling.

   The infant may be placed in a neutral thermal environment
   (that environmental temperature at which heat production and
   oxygen consumption are minimal) appropriate for his weight
   and postnatal age, or he may be servocontrolled to maintain
   a skin temperature of 96.8 to 98.6°F. (36 to 37°C.). Humidity
   is maintained at about 50%. When a preterm infant weighs
   1800 to 2000 Gm. or more, he can often maintain his body
   temperature out of an incubator.

B. Infants of less than 36 weeks' gestational age have an increased
   risk of apnea and bradycardia. When available, the use of apnea (or heart rate) monitors is advised with these infants.

C. Preterm newborns weighing 1500 to 1700 Gm. or less should be
   given intravenous 10% dextrose solutions to supplement the inadequate oral intake which occurs during the first few days
   after birth. If glycosuria occurs in a markedly preterm infant,
   the concentration of dextrose should be reduced. I.V. supplementation should be continued until the infant is receiving a
   combined I.V. and oral intake of at least 100 ml./Kg./day.

   Infants of less than 34 to 36 weeks' postconceptual age usually do not suck and swallow well enough to take nipple feedings.
   These infants can be gavage-fed via intermittent (or in some
   cases continuous) nasogastric polyethylene feeding tubes, beginning with 2 to 5 ml. sterile water. Subsequent feedings with
   full-strength formula may be increased 1 to 5 ml. in volume
   every three hours. Residual gastric contents should be aspirated
   before each feeding to assess delayed gastric emptying and the
   ability to tolerate an increased volume of formula.

   When gavage-fed infants are about 34 to 36 weeks old post-
   conceptually and demonstrate a good sucking ability, nipple
   feedings may be attempted. In premature infants in whom
   conventional feedings have been poorly tolerated, nasogastric
   or nasojejunal feedings may be of value.

   Preterm infants should be given iron supplementation, either
   in the form of commercial formulas containing iron or oral iron
   preparations. Recommended intake from two months of age is
   2 mg./Kg./day of elemental iron. Vitamin A, C, and D supplementation is also indicated unless adequate amounts are provided in the formula.

   Peripheral intravenous hyperalimentation with amino acid
   and glucose solutions has been used in very premature infants;
   however, the safety of this method of providing nutrients to
   preterm infants has not been established.

D. Oxygen: Preterm infants should not be placed routinely in oxy-
   gen-supplemented environments. Hypoxemia is the only indication for augmented oxygen therapy. Infants who are cyanotic
   may be placed in oxygen-rich environments sufficient to relieve
   the cyanosis, but determination of arterial pO_2 from temporal
   or right radial artery punctures or from umbilical artery catheters is essential for adequate management of infants who con-

tinue in oxygen-rich environments. Therapy should be aimed at maintaining the arterial pO_2 between 50 and 80 mm. Hg to avoid retrolental fibroplasia.

E. In general, infants with an 8% or greater chance of dying (see Fig 8-1) and those with significant morbidity factors should be cared for in a special nursery for high-risk newborns.

F. The transportation of ill or high-risk infants to a referral nursery should be done swiftly, utilizing air transport for long distances, with a nurse or physician accompanying the infant if possible. Portable incubators with adequate means for temperature and oxygen support are essential.

G. Catheterization of the umbilical vein should be done sparingly because of the risk of subsequent portal hypertension and other complications.

H. Avoid excessive hyperglycemia when administering glucose solutions intravenously; it appears to be associated with an increased incidence of subsequent intracranial hemorrhage.

Special Care of the Small-for-Gestational-Age (SGA) Newborn. (See Fig 8-1.)

Approximately two-thirds of preterm SGA infants and one-third of term SGA infants develop neonatal hypoglycemia (blood glucose < 20 mg /100 ml). These infants are optimally managed by the prophylactic administration of intravenous dextrose solutions and frequent blood glucose determinations during the first four days of life.

Special Care of the Large-for-Gestational-Age (LGA) Newborn.

Particular attention must be given to these newborns because their large size may fail to stimulate an adequate level of concern by those caring for them even though they actually have a much higher risk of morbidity for a given gestational age than do AGA infants.

LGA infants should be observed carefully for hypoglycemia, transient tachypnea, and birth injuries (intracranial hemorrhage, phrenic nerve paralysis, Erb's palsy).

PHYSICAL EXAMINATION

Current management of the newborn infant is based in part on his gestational age and the adequacy of his intrauterine growth for that gestational age. A clinical assessment of gestational age made within the first six hours is based on historical data and the presence or absence of certain physical features.

A complete physical examination of the newborn who is vigorous at birth may be postponed until he has been observed to progress uneventfully through the recovery and transitional period of the first six to 12 hours of life. An infant who is obviously ill at birth deserves a thorough examination as soon as he has reached a relatively stable state following any required resuscitative measures.

Characteristics of Term Infant.

A term newborn has the following characteristics at birth and shortly thereafter:

A. Resting Posture: Extremities flexed and somewhat hypertonic (determined to some extent by intrauterine position [e. g., following frank breech presentation the neonate's thighs may be flexed onto abdomen]). Fists clenched. Asymmetries of skull, face, jaw, or extremities may result from intrauterine pressures.

B. Skin: Usually ruddy and often mottled. Localized cyanosis of hands and feet (acrocyanosis) normally disappears after several days except when infant is cool. Subcutaneous tissues may feel full and slightly edematous in term newborn; skin dry and peeling in post-term.

1. Lanugo (fine downy growth of hair) may be present over shoulders and back.
2. Vernix caseosa (whitish or clay-colored, cheesy, greasy material) may cover body but is usually on back and scalp and in creases of term baby.
3. Milia of face (distended sebaceous glands producing tiny whitish papules) are especially prominent over nose, chin, or cheeks.
4. Mongolian spots (benign bluish pigmentation over lower back, buttocks, or extensor surfaces) may be found in infants of dark-skinned races.
5. Capillary hemangiomas ("flame nevi") are common on eyelids, forehead, and neck.
6. Petechiae are sometimes present over the head, neck, and back, especially in association with nuchal cord; if generalized, thrombocytopenia should be suspected.
7. Newborns of 32 weeks' or more gestational age may perspire when too warm. The forehead is usually the first site noted.

C. Head: Head is large in relation to the rest of the body; may exhibit considerable molding with overriding of the cranial bones, except in cesarean and breech deliveries.

1. Caput succedaneum (localized or fairly extensive ill-defined soft tissue swelling) may be present over scalp or other presenting parts. It usually extends over a suture line.
2. Cephalhematoma (see Chapter 9).
3. Anterior and posterior fontanelles may measure 0.6-3.6 cm. in any direction and are soft. They may be small initially. A third fontanel between these two is present in approximately 6% of infants and is more likely to occur in children with various abnormalities.
4. Transillumination normally produces a circle of light no greater than 1.5 cm. beyond the light source in term infants.
5. Craniotabes (slight indentation and recoil of parietal bones elicited by lightly pressing with thumb) is normal in newborns.

D. Face:

1. Eyes - The irises are slate-gray except in dark-skinned races. Tears may or may not be present. Most term infants look toward a light source and transiently focus on a face. Subconjunctival, scleral, and retinal hemorrhages are abnormal. The pupillary light reflex is present. Lens opacities are abnormal. A red reflex can be seen on ophthalmoscopic examination.
2. Mouth - Small, pearl-like retention cysts at the gum margins and the midline of the palate (Bohn's and Epstein's pearls)

are common and insignificant. The tonsils are usually quite small.

3. Nose - The newborn, a preferential nose-breather, experiences respiratory distress in bilateral choanal atresia. Patency should be confirmed by passage of a nasogastric tube if obstruction is suspected.

4. Ears - Eardrums may be difficult to visualize but have a characteristic opaque appearance and decreased mobility. Severe malformation of pinnas may be associated with abnormalities of the genitourinary tract. Normal newborns respond to sounds with a startle, blink, head turning, or cry.

5. Cheeks are full because of the sucking pads.

E. Chest:

1. Breasts - Palpable in more mature males and females; size is determined by gestational age and adequacy of nutrition.

2. Lungs - Breathing is abdominal and may be shallow and irregular; rate is usually 30 to 60/minute, with a range of 20 to 100/minute. Breath sounds are harsh and bronchial. Faint rales may be heard immediately following birth and normally clear in several hours.

3. Heart - Rate averages 130/minute, but rates from 90 to 180 may be present for brief periods in normal babies. Sinus arrhythmia may be present. The apex of the heart is usually lateral to the midclavicular line in the third or fourth interspace. Transient murmurs are common. During the first day, systolic blood pressure taken in the arm by the flush, palpation, or auscultation method is 45 to 55 mm. Hg. and by the Doppler method is 55 to 65 mm. Hg.

F. Abdomen: The abdomen is normally flat at birth but soon becomes more protuberant; a markedly scaphoid abdomen suggests diaphragmatic hernia. Two arteries and one vein are present in the umbilical cord. The liver is palpable; the tip of the spleen can be felt in 10% of newborns. Both kidneys can and should be palpated. Bowel sounds are audible shortly after birth. Between 5 and 25 ml. of cloudy white gastric fluid can be aspirated from the stomach.

G. Genitalia: Appearance in both sexes is gestational age-dependent. Edema is common, particularly after breech delivery.

1. Females - The labia minora and clitoris are covered by labia majora in term neonates. A mucoid secretion exudes from the vaginal orifice.

2. Males - Testes are in the scrotum; rugae cover the scrotum. The prepuce is adherent to the glans of the penis. White epithelial pearls 1-2 mm. in diameter may be present at the tip of the prepuce.

H. Anus: Patency should be checked. Anteriorly displaced anus may be associated with stenosis.

I. Hips: Dislocation is suspected if abduction of the thighs is limited. Test for dislocation as follows: (1) Place the middle fingers over the greater trochanters and the thumbs over the region of the lesser trochanters. Apply pressure against the greater trochanters and bring the thighs into abduction. A snap felt in abduction (Ortolani's sign) is suggestive of dislocation, although a faint click is not uncommon during the first 24 hours after birth or even longer in breech presentations. (2)

Fix the pelvis with one hand with the thighs abducted, apply pressure with the thumb against the inner thigh, and feel for a snap as the head of the femur slips over the acetabular rim.
(3) Attempt to telescope the femur by pulling forward and pushing backward. Reexamine at one week and periodically thereafter.

J. Feet: Many apparent abnormalities may be only the transient result of intrauterine position. Clubfoot requires prompt orthopedic attention.

K. Neurologic Examination:
1. Neurologic development is gestational age-dependent.
2. Reflexes - Most reflexes, including the Moro, tonic neck, grasp, sucking, rooting, stepping, Babinski, deep tendon, abdominal, cremasteric, and Chvostek reflexes, are normally present at birth.

L. Weight: As a rule, males weigh more than females; white infants more than nonwhite; and second-born more than first-born.

Characteristics of the Preterm Infant.

The preterm or premature infant is comparatively inactive, with a feeble cry and irregular respirations (periodic breathing). He has a relatively large head, prominent eyes, and a protruding abdomen. The skin is relatively translucent, often wrinkled, red, and deficient in subcutaneous fat. The nails are soft, lanugo is prominent, and vernix is thick. The musculature is poorly developed, the thorax less rigid, and breast engorgement usually absent. Testes may be undescended.

In general, preterm infants weigh less than 2500 Gm., have a crown-heel length less than 47 cm., a head circumference less than 33 cm., and a thoracic circumference less than 30 cm.

The preterm infant has physiologic handicaps due to functional and anatomic immaturity of various organs.

A. His body temperature is more difficult to maintain due to decreased insulation by subcutaneous fat and large surface area/body weight ratio. Consequently, his body temperature falls unless his environment is thermally supported.

B. Respiratory difficulties are common because of weak gag and cough reflexes (increased risk of aspiration); pliable thorax and weak respiratory musculature (results in less efficient ventilation); deficiency of surfactant (allowing alveoli to collapse on exhaling and contributing to the respiratory distress syndrome); and defects in C.N.S. control (apnea).

C. Because of immature renal function, iatrogenic disturbances of water or electrolyte balance may occur. Large solute loads may not be adequately excreted, and organic acids may accumulate, leading to metabolic acidosis.

D. Ability to combat infection is decreased due to inadequate placental transmission of 19-S immunoglobulins, relative inability to produce antibodies, and impaired phagocytosis, leukocyte bactericidal capacity, and inflammatory response. Epidermal and mucosal barriers are not as effective as in term infants.

E. Because of impaired conjugation and excretion of bilirubin, hyperbilirubinemia is more common and more severe in preterm infants.

F. Hemorrhagic diathesis is more common due to clotting factor deficiencies and increased permeability of vessels.

G. Deficient antenatal accumulation of iron and vitamin E and rapid body growth and blood volume expansion contribute to a more pronounced anemia in the first months of life.

H. Disturbances of nutrition may be a consequence of the faulty absorption of fat, fat-soluble vitamins, and certain minerals as well as reduced stores of calcium, phosphorus, proteins, ascorbic acid, and vitamin A.

Characteristics of the Small-for-Gestational-Age (SGA) Infants.

Regardless of his gestational age, the SGA infant's weight is less than the 10th percentile for that age, and he often appears malnourished. With increasingly severe intrauterine growth retardation, the infant's length as well as weight are compromised. In severe SGA neonates, weight, length, and head circumference are all below the 10th percentile for gestational age.

SGA infants have a higher morbidity and mortality than infants who are appropriate-for-gestational-age (AGA). SGA infants should be carefully examined for congenital anomalies, evaluated for intrauterine infection, and watched for the possible development of hypoglycemia, pulmonary hemorrhage, hyperviscosity, and feeding difficulties.

SGA infants do not require as warm an incubator as do preterm AGA infants of the same weight.

Characteristics of the Large-for-Gestational-Age (LGA) Infant.

An LGA neonate is one whose birthweight is greater than the 90th percentile for his gestational age. Only a portion of LGA neonates are infants of diabetic mothers (IDM), but all LGA infants have higher morbidity and mortality rates than AGA infants of the same gestational age. Birth injuries - especially brachial plexus injuries and fractures of the clavicle - and hypoglycemia are more common in LGA babies. Transient tachypnea (not progressing to respiratory distress syndrome) and developmental retardation subsequent to the neonatal period are also more common.

Infants of diabetic mothers have a characteristic macrosomic appearance. They are obese and plethoric, and have round, full faces. In addition to the above problems they share with other LGA infants, they have an increased incidence of renal vein thrombosis (manifested by flank mass and hematuria) and congenital anomalies (especially skeletal and frequently below the waist) as well as an increased incidence of respiratory distress syndrome, hypocalcemia, and hyperbilirubinemia.

LABORATORY DATA IN THE NEWBORN INFANT

Blood. (See also Normal Blood Chemistry Values in Appendix.)

Red cell counts and hemoglobin may be as much as 20% higher in capillary blood than in venous blood at birth. Nucleated red blood cells up to 500/cu. mm. may be found normally. Pyknocytes ("burr cells") may be present (< 2% in full-term and up to 5.6% in premature infants). Sedimentation rate is greatly accelerated. Plasma proteins and blood sugar are reduced. Reticulocyte count is elevated (2 to 6%). Fetal hemoglobin is 44 to 95% of total. The glucuronide conjugating mechanism is not fully developed at birth. Extracellular water content and total body water are high. Deficiency of glutathione stability system of red cells is present, and there is increased instability of reduced glutathione. Asymptomatic hypertyrosinemia, especially in low birth weight infants, often occurs; its significance is not yet clear.

Prothrombin, plasma thromboplastin component, proconvertin, and Stuart factor are reduced. Proaccelerin may be normal or elevated. Plasminogen level is reduced.

Gastrointestinal Tract.

Gastrointestinal enzymes are adequate except for digestion of starches. Pancreatic amylase remains deficient for months. Liver glycogen is low.

Electrocardiography.

Right ventricular preponderance may continue for a few months. Ectopic beats are relatively common during the first week.

Cerebrospinal Fluid.

Spinal fluid is xanthochromic and frequently contains increased numbers of leukocytes and elevated protein (mean > 100 mg./100 ml.). Red blood cells may be present. Permeability of blood-brain barrier is increased.

ASSESSMENT OF RISK AND LEVEL OF CARE REQUIRED

A newborn's risk of dying in the neonatal period can be estimated by referring to the accompanying chart based on his birth weight and gestational age. The mortality risk increases with decreasing gestational age and with inappropriately grown neonates.

Factors that affect the mortality rate include the following: (1) gestational age, (2) weight, (3) high-risk obstetric history, (4) low Apgar score at 5 minutes, (5) difficult or prolonged resuscitation, (6) severe birth injury, and (7) abnormal physical findings at birth (e. g., congenital anomalies).

NORMAL PHYSIOLOGIC EVENTS
DURING THE NEONATAL PERIOD

Transition From Fetus to Newborn.

A. Cardiovascular System:

1. A remarkable transition from the fetal parallel pulmonary and systemic circulations to the adult arrangement of these circulations in series occurs at birth. This transition is not complete, however, for several days to weeks, when the ductus arteriosus and foramen ovale are closed and the pulmonary vascular resistance has diminished. The accompanying chart describes the changes that occur during this transition.

2. The fetus pumps almost half of his cardiac output to the placenta, and only a small percentage to the lungs and kidneys. After the umbilical cord is clamped, the cardiac out-

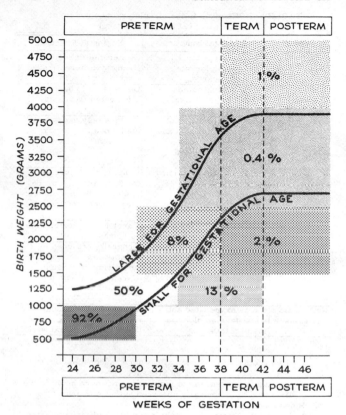

FIG 8-1. Neonatal mortality risk based on weight and gestational
age. (Colorado data.)

put is redistributed so that the lungs and kidneys receive a
much greater proportion.
    3. The mean systemic arterial blood pressure is about the
same in both the fetus and the newborn but increases during
the neonatal period and subsequently.
B. Respiratory System:
    1. The factors causing the infant to take the first breath are
thought to be (1) low paO_2, (2) high $paCO_2$, (3) low pH, (4)
evaporative cooling, and (5) gasp reflex due to recoil of
thorax after delivery.
    2. Intrathoracic negative pressures as great as 60 to 70 cm.
water are required to expand the lungs during the first

TABLE 8-2. Changes in the circulatory mechanism at birth. (Adapted from Scammon.)

Structure	Prenatal Function	Postnatal Function
Umbilical vein	Carries oxygenated blood from placenta to liver and heart.	Obliterated to become ligamentum teres (round ligament of liver).
Ductus venosus	Carries oxygenated blood from umbilical vein to inferior vena cava.	Obliterated to become ligamentum venosum.
Inferior vena cava	Carries oxygenated blood from umbilical vein and ductus venosus and mixed blood from body and liver.	Carries only unoxygenated blood from body.
Foramen ovale	Connects right and left atria.	Functional closure by 3 months, although probe patency without symptoms may be retained by some adults.
Pulmonary arteries	Carry some mixed blood to the lungs.	Carry unoxygenated blood to lungs.
Ductus arteriosus	Shunts mixed blood from pulmonary artery to aorta.	Generally occluded by 4 months and becomes ligamentum arteriosum.
Aorta	Receives mixed blood from heart and pulmonary arteries.	Carries oxygenated blood from left ventricle.
Umbilical arteries	Carry oxygenated and unoxygenated blood to the placenta.	Obliterated to become the vesical ligaments on the anterior abdominal wall.

few breaths. In the normal newborn, succeeding breaths require 5 to 10 cm. water pressure.

3. The liquid present in the lungs of the newborn prior to the first breath is normally absorbed within minutes.

C. Blood Gases and pH:
1. The fetal pH is only slightly lower (0.05 pH unit) than the adult value. During labor, the pH falls slightly, and the vigorous newborn attains a relatively normal acid-base state within one to three hours of birth. By 24 hours of age, the healthy neonate has a pH of 7.4.
2. Fetal pCO_2 is slightly higher than the maternal pCO_2. During labor, pCO_2 rises somewhat, but following recovery from birth the normal neonate has a lower pCO_2 (approximately 32 mm. Hg) than the adult.
3. The fetal hemoglobin oxygen saturation is relatively high, but the fetal paO_2 (about 30 to 40 mm. Hg) is much lower than adult values. During the first 24 hours of neonatal life, the paO_2 increases from about 55 mm. Hg shortly after birth to about 90 mm. Hg.

Changes Occurring After Birth.

A. Metabolic:

1. The principal metabolic substrate for the human fetus is glucose. Following birth, the neonate develops the metabolic capacity to utilize fats and amino acids absorbed from his diet.

2. The metabolic rate increases gradually during the neonatal period. At birth, term infants have a higher metabolic rate than do preterm infants.

3. One-third of healthy, term infants and about one-half of preterm neonates develop clinically apparent "physiologic jaundice" during the first week of life. Clinical jaundice is not manifest until the second or third day of life, with peak bilirubin levels on days 5 to 7. Term infants rarely exceed indirect bilirubin levels of 12 mg./100 ml., and preterm infants rarely exceed 15 mg./100 ml. The etiologic factors are not completely understood, but an important cause is the delayed maturation of hepatic glucuronyl transferase, which is necessary for bilirubin conjugation.

B. Renal: In late gestation, the fetal urine flow rate is high and the urine osmolality low. The newborn initially also excretes a dilute urine (between 100 and 400 mOsm./L.) which varies inversely with the urine flow rate (5 to 0.5 ml./Kg./hour for well-hydrated neonates). With increasing age, the neonatal kidney excretes a more concentrated urine, with a greater urea content. The ability to excrete many drugs is altered.

C. Immunologic: Passive immunity against diphtheria, tetanus, pneumococcal infection, the rash-producing toxin of the streptococcus that causes scarlet fever, and the viruses of measles, rubella, herpes simplex, infectious hepatitis, mumps, and poliomyelitis is present in most infants at birth if the mother is immune.

At birth, the term infant has a normal adult serum concentration of IgG (derived from the mother), and low or undetectable amounts of IgA, IgM, IgD, and IgE. The greater the gestational age, the higher the IgG level. The lack of IgM antibodies, which are especially effective in killing gram-negative bacteria, predisposes neonates to gram-negative infections. However, in fetal infections with syphilis, toxoplasmosis, rubella, cytomegalovirus, and Herpesvirus hominis, IgM levels may be increased in serum from cord blood and venous blood.

IgG concentrations decrease to about age two or three months, then rise again as the neonate responds to antigenic stimuli in his environment. Infants begin to synthesize IgM globulins in the first days of life. Breast-fed neonates receive secretory IgA antibodies in colostrum and human milk.

D. Clinical:

1. For about 30 minutes, the infant is active and alert, heart rate is rapid, and there may be nasal flaring, mild grunting and retracting, auscultatory rales, irregular respiratory movements, and mucus present in the mouth. Bowel sounds are absent. Body temperature falls. During the subsequent one-half to two hours, the infant falls asleep, has decreased heart and respiratory rates, and bowel sounds are present. Then the neonate arouses and again is active, with labile

heart rate and swift color changes due to vasomotor instability and a period of hemoconcentration at about six hours
of age that contributes to his plethoric appearance. Meconium is usually passed during this period but may be delayed
(in about 6% of newborns) for over 24 hours.

Urination usually occurs soon after birth but may be delayed until the second day in about 8% of newborns. Body
temperature returns to normal.

2. Weight - Both term and preterm newborns lose weight initially. Term infants lose 5 to 8% of their birth weight by
the third to fifth day (over 10% is excessive) and regain
their birth weight by the second week of life. Preterm neonates may experience a greater relative weight loss and require longer to regain their birth weight, primarily because
of the difficulty in providing them with an adequate caloric
intake. Healthy term neonates subsequently gain about 30
Gm./day.

3. Position - Relaxation from intrauterine to infantile. May
lift head from prone position. Asymmetries diminish.

4. Skin - Change from ruddy to paler pink. Desquamation of
trunk and extremities usually mild but may be extensive,
especially in postmature infants. Fissures may develop
at ankles and wrists. Lanugo begins to fall out. Petechiae
disappear. Rashes (erythema neonatorum toxicum) common
during first few days. Harlequin color change (midline de-
marcation of body into pale and plethoric halves) may occur.

5. Head and face - Molding and caput disappear. Eyes may
show muscular imbalance.

6. Chest - Breast engorgement may increase and secretion
may be present. (Not likely to occur in premature infants.)

7. Abdomen - Vomiting is common, usually caused by irritation of gastric mucosa by foreign material (e.g., blood,
amniotic fluid) ingested at or after birth. The umbilical
cord dries up and falls off during the first or second week.

8. Genitals - Pseudomenstruation may occur in females.

9. Hemoglogin and erythrocytes increase during first day and
then both fetal and adult fractions of hemoglobin fall. The
urine is pale, acid, of low specific gravity, and may contain reducing substance, acetone, and casts, but less than
10 red and 10 white cells per cu. mm. Rarely, ingested
sugars may be present in urine. Galactosuria with a peak
at three days may be present. Urates may cause pink staining of the diaper and a false-positive reaction for protein.

10. Stools may contain blood that was previously swallowed.
Eighty percent of infants pass their first stools within 24
hours.

11. Gas is visible by x-ray in the gastrointestinal tract within
a few minutes after birth. Swallowed air reaches the cecum
in three to five hours and the descending colon in ten hours.

12. Meconium stools may be passed for about three days; these
are followed by rather frequent transitional stools (loose,
slimy, brown to green) for three or four days and subsequently by milk stools (curdy, yellowish-white).

13. A relative hypoglycemia often develops; infants may remain
asymptomatic in spite of blood glucose levels which are below 30 mg./100 ml.

14. Exudates, nasal secretions, and stools frequently contain many eosinophils.
15. T_4, PBI, and uptake of tagged triiodothyronine by red blood cells are elevated, with highest levels being reached on the second to fifth day of life. Less elevation occurs in infants who are kept warm.
16. Plasma 17-hydroxycorticosteroid levels are maintained at near-adult levels. Urinary 17-ketosteroid excretion is elevated for first week of life.
17. Hydrolysis of lactose in the intestines may be relatively impaired during the first few days of life.

DISTURBANCES DUE TO ANTENATAL FACTORS

Maternal Factors Affecting the Infant.

A. Infection: Infants born of mothers who have had rubella during pregnancy may be small for gestational age and may have brain lesions (microcephaly, hydrocephalus, meningoencephalitis), eye lesions (cataracts, glaucoma, microphthalmia, retinitis), deafness, cardiac defects (especially pulmonary valve or artery stenosis or both, patent ductus arteriosus, and ventricular septal defect), pulmonary complications, thrombocytopenic purpura ("blueberry muffin" lesions), hepatosplenomegaly, hepatitis, jaundice, bone lesions, peculiar dimples of the skin, areas of skin pigmentation, retardation of somatic growth, chromosomal abnormalities, abnormal fingerprints and palmar creases, and may shed virus for many months (with or without clinical abnormalities) and have psychomotor retardation. Cord IgM may be elevated.

Syphilis may produce abortions, stillbirths, or congenital syphilis. Influenza during the first trimester may cause congenital anomalies. Maternal urinary tract disease increases the incidence of prematurity. Toxoplasmosis, cytomegalic inclusion disease, and live virus vaccines may produce disease in the infant. A number of other viruses (mumps, varicella, Herpesvirus hominis, rubeola, coxsackieviruses, and other picornaviruses, poxvirus, serum and infectious hepatitis virus, and arboviruses), bacteria, and other infectious agents (malaria parasites, Histoplasma, Mycobacterium tuberculosis) may be transplacentally transmitted to the fetus and produce disease.

B. Noninfectious Maternal Factors:
1. Diabetes mellitus.
2. Congenital thrombocytopenic purpura may occur if the mother has had thrombocytopenia, platelet iso-immunization, or received quinine.
3. Iodine deficiency or an enzymatic defect of thyroid metabolism may result in cretinism in the child.
4. Severe iron deficiency predisposes to anemia in the infant.
5. Roentgen irradiation of the mother may produce bony defects and mental deficiency in the child.
6. Rh and ABO factor sensitization.
7. Severe anoxia during pregnancy may predispose to congenital abnormalities.

8. Acetonuria during pregnancy, possibly due to dysnutrition, may be associated with lowered intelligence quotient in the offspring.

9. Drugs - **Progestins, testosterone,** and other hormones may cause virilization and advanced bone age of the female fetus. **Thalidomide** may cause phocomelia. **Nitrofurantoin** may cause hemolysis; **sulfonamides, novobiocin, oxacillin, cephalothin, sodium benzoate,** and **salicylates** may cause competitive binding with albumin in serum with resultant hyperbilirubinemia due to displacement of bilirubin; and **chloramphenicol** can lead to cardiovascular collapse and the "gray syndrome." **Aminopterin,** methotrexate, and chlorambucil may cause anomalies and abortions. **Dicumarol** may cause hemorrhage and fetal death. **Heroin, morphine,** and other narcotics may cause convulsions, tremors, neonatal death, and neonatal withdrawal symptoms in maternal addiction. Smoking may cause small-for-gestational age infants. **Streptomycin** may cause deafness. Certain **cancer chemotherapeutic agents** and **phenothiazines** may cause a parkinsonism-like syndrome. **Mepivacaine** and **lidocaine** may cause C.N.S. depression or seizures and irritability. **Thiazides** may cause electrolyte imbalance, thrombocytopenia, and leukopenia. **Inorganic mercury** may cause brain damage with cerebral palsy. **Reserpine** may cause nasal congestion, bradycardia, hypothermia, and drowsiness in the newborn. **Tetracyclines** may produce retarded bone growth and mottled and stained teeth. **Magnesium sulfate** may cause depression or convulsions in the newborn. **General anesthetics** may cause respiratory depression; **spinal anesthetics,** maternal hypotension with fetal distress; **paracervical block,** fetal bradycardia. **Oxytocin** induction may lead to water intoxication in the mother and hyponatremia, hypotension, and hypotonia in the infant. Vitamin K_3 may cause hyperbilirubinemia; **salicylates,** coagulation defects with neonatal bleeding; **quinine,** thrombocytopenia and deafness; **ganglionic blocking agents,** paralytic ileus. **Phenobarbital** may increase the rate of neonatal drug metabolism; a large dose may depress the infant. **Hexamethonium** may produce ileus; **atropine,** tachycardia, **prochlorperazine,** depression; **chloroquine,** retinal damage; **adrenocortical steroids,** adrenal insufficiency; and **oral hypoglycemic agents,** hypoglycemia. **Radioactive iodine** may produce fetal thyroid destruction. **Thiouracil derivatives, potassium iodide,** and **potassium perchlorate** may produce congenital goiter.

10. Certain iodine-containing dyes for cholecystograms cause prolonged increased PBI in offspring.

11. Myasthenia gravis.

12. Advanced maternal age is associated with increased perinatal mortality, increased fetal distress in post-term pregnancies, increased incidence of hydrocephalus and congenital heart disease, C, D, and E trisomies, and Klinefelter's syndrome.

Heredity.

Heredity is the most important factor in certain congenital defects (see Appendix).

MULTIPLE BIRTHS

Twins may be monozygotic (identical) or dizygotic (fraternal). The intrauterine growth of each twin parallels that of a singleton until about 34 weeks of gestation. Thereafter, the fetal growth rate is less than that for a singleton. As a consequence, many twins (and triplets) are small for gestational age as well as preterm.

If the birth weights of twins are discrepant by 200 Gm. or more, the twins are regarded as discordant twins. If monozygotic twins are discordant, placental vascular anastomosis may have allowed one twin to chronically transfuse the other, resulting in a small, anemic donor and a large, plethoric recipient twin who may develop congestive failure.

PROGNOSIS

For Neonatal Survival.

The prognosis for survival for a given newborn depends upon several factors:

A. Gestational Age: Mortality risk is approximately halved for every two weeks added to gestational age after 28 weeks.

B. Birth Weight: Small-for-gestational-age and large-for-gestational-age infants have increased mortality risks.

C. Multiple Birth: Mortality is greater than for singletons; the second-born twin has a greater mortality risk than the first-born.

D. Maternal Age: Neonatal mortality risk increases with very young and very elderly mothers.

E. Presence of Life-Threatening Condition Apparent at Birth: Severe congenital anomalies, erythroblastosis fetalis, hemorrhage, congenitally acquired infections, etc.

For Neonatal Morbidity.

Neonatal morbidity risk is increased by all of those factors which raise the mortality risk as well as by low Apgar scores at five minutes, and high-risk obstetric factors (antepartum hemorrhage, diabetes, toxemia, etc.).

For Long-Term Development.

In general, the more preterm the neonate, the greater chance he has of having some developmental handicap in later childhood (cerebral palsy, hearing, seeing, and learning disabilities). Twins have a higher risk of long-term disabilities than singletons; small-for-gestational-age and large-for-gestational-age infants have a greater risk than appropriate-for-gestational-age infants.

In long-term follow-up studies of infants born prior to 1953 weighing less than 1500 Gm. at birth, two-thirds had some developmental handicap. For infants weighing less than 1000 Gm. at birth who were 28 to 31 weeks' gestational age, the incidence of handicaps was about 75%. However, the advent of intensive care nurseries has resulted in an improved outlook for survivors of preterm births, so that among survivors born more recently who weighed 1000 Gm. or less and who were cared for in an intensive care nursery, many fewer now have definitely abnormal developmental quotients on follow-up.

9 . . .
The Newborn Infant:
Diseases & Disorders*

The newborn infant is susceptible to a large number of diseases and abnormal conditions affecting older children, but he also may develop a number of problems peculiar to the neonatal period.

DISEASES OF THE RESPIRATORY SYSTEM

RESPIRATORY DISTRESS OF THE NEWBORN

Respiratory distress is more common with maternal illnesses (maternal hypoxia, hemorrhage, shock, cardiorespiratory disease, toxemia, severe anemia, low blood pressure); abnormal uterine contractions; obstruction of the newborn's respiratory passages (aspirated material; congenital abnormalities, including choanal atresia, diaphragmatic hernia, lobar emphysema, lung cysts, tracheo-esophageal fistula, macroglossia, glossoptosis, agenesis or hypoplasia of the lungs, laryngeal or tracheal web, tracheomalacia, vascular ring, pressure on the trachea from without); injury to phrenic nerve, epiglottis, or larynx; depression of the respiratory center (anesthetics or analgesics to the mother, cerebral hemorrhage); drugs; fetal shock; and various diseases and congenital defects involving the infant including intracranial hemorrhage, muscular weakness, cardiac disease, and pulmonary disorders such as idiopathic respiratory distress syndrome of the newborn, pneumomediastinum, pneumothorax, pneumonia, pneumonitis, pulmonary hemorrhage, and a transient tachypnea of the newborn.† Immaturity of the respiratory system may be an important factor in premature infants.

Treatment is directed toward adequate oxygenation and elimination of the underlying causes, if possible. Complete supportive care should include temperature, fluids, glucose, etc. The use of an artificial respirator to administer intermittent positive pres-

---

*Revised by Michael A. Simmons, MD, and Frank H. Morriss, Jr., MD.

†Transient tachypnea with respiratory distress in the newborn has been described. It lasts two to four days and is more common in males than females. It is characterized by tachypnea, costal or sternal retractions, grunting, and sometimes cyanosis. X-ray shows a pattern of symmetric, parahilar, pulmonary congestion. Possible cause is impaired lymphatic clearing of alveolar fluid.

sure breathing or continuous distending pressure (continuous positive airway pressure [CPAP] or continuous negative pressure
[CNP]) may be of value, especially for the small infant.

Apnea of greater than 30 seconds' duration occurs in about 25%
of low birth weight infants. In most instances, cutaneous stimulation results in resumption of breathing; in the remainder, resuscitation with bag and mask is usually effective.

IDIOPATHIC RESPIRATORY DISTRESS SYNDROME (RDS); HYALINE MEMBRANE DISEASE (HMD) OF THE LUNGS*

Hyaline membranes are found principally in lungs of newborn
infants who have died between one hour and a few days after birth
(especially premature infants, those delivered by cesarean section
or from mothers with bleeding or diabetes, or infants who experienced intrauterine distress).

The hyaline membrane is composed principally of fibrin derived from the pulmonary capillaries of the newborn infant and not
from the inspiration of aspirated amniotic fluid. A deficiency of a
surfactant (dipalmityl lecithin?) which is deficient in human fetuses
until about the 34th to 35th week of gestation has been described in
these infants. A test has been devised to estimate the adequacy of
effective surfactant production. When the lecithin:sphingomyelin
ratio of amniotic fluid is 2:1 or greater, the likelihood of RDS is
small. Infants who have died have low concentrations of pulmonary
phospholipids and reduced concentrations of saturated fatty acids
of lung phosphatidyl choline. Hypotension, diminished pulmonary
blood flow, pulmonary artery vasoconstriction, vascular shunts,
and ventilation-perfusion imbalance, acidosis, and hypoxia may
all result from primary alveolar collapse. Pulmonary lymphatics
are larger in affected lungs than in normal controls.

Clinical Findings.

The manifestations consist of dyspnea, tachypnea, nasal flaring, retractions of costal margins and lower sternum, grunting
respirations, and cyanosis. Symptoms are usually present immediately after birth but may be delayed for two to four hours. During this time hypotension may be present. In the early stages
x-ray reveals a reticulogranular pattern throughout the lungs, with
prominence of bronchial air shadows; generalized atelectases may
occur later. Blood pH is low, blood gases reveal hypoxemia (right-
to-left shunting) and, later, hypercapnia. Systemic hypotension
and hypothermia may be present. Cerebral, pulmonary, and visceral hemorrhages may develop in fatal cases. Marked coagulation
defects and laboratory or pathologic evidence (or both) of disseminated intravascular coagulation are frequently found in sick infants.
There is no evidence of postnatal adrenal hypofunction in RDS or
that steroid treatment of the newborn infant is beneficial.

Prevention and Treatment.

Administration of an adrenal corticosteroid (dexamethazone
or betamethasone) to a pregnant woman without hypertension or

---

*See second footnote on p. 136.

edema between the twenty-sixth to thirty-second week of gestation and at least 48 hours before the birth of the infant decreases the risk of HMD developing. RDS is less common after prolonged rupture of the membranes, maternal heroin addiction, and antenatal bacterial infection.

Adequate and prompt resuscitation of all high-risk and premature infants is the most important preventive step. Regulate ambient oxygen concentration so that arterial pO_2 is 70 to 90 mm. Hg (at sea level) and maintain humidity (at 60 to 80%) in environment. (See Bronchopulmonary Dysplasia, below.) Maintain thermal balance. Give antibiotics if infection is suspected. Frequent blood pressure measurements and monitoring of urine output (> 2 ml./Kg. /hour) can enable one to predict inadequate perfusion, which should be treated with whole blood transfusion (up to 10 ml./Kg.), plasma, or 5% albumin infusion (up to 10 ml./Kg.). Infants with respiratory distress should have intravenous fluid support (65-100 ml./Kg./24 hours of 10% dextrose in water with 3 mEq. of sodium, 2 mEq. of potassium, and 3 mEq. of bicarbonate per 100 ml.). Continuous positive airway pressure (CPAP) by means of a respirator or face mask or constant negative pressure (CNP) should be used. Avoid rapid infusion of alkali solutions. Documented metabolic acidosis may be corrected slowly with diluted $NaHCO_3$. Chronic umbilical vein catheterization may be associated with portal vein occlusion, embolization, sepsis, and local necrosis and thrombosis. Indwelling umbilical artery catheterization also has potential hazards. Wrapping the newborn infant in its intrauterine position has been suggested, but its effectiveness has not been proved. Frequent arterial blood gas determinations are necessary to maintain and adjust the inspired oxygen concentration. The use of assisted ventilation with continuous or intermittent positive pressure or continuous distending pressure without controlled ventilation by experienced personnel is of value in small premature infants with severe disease. In some cases bronchopulmonary dysplasia and other serious complications have been reported after respirator therapy. Avoid laryngoscopy and excessive handling. Do not give oral feedings while the infant has respiratory distress.

Course and Prognosis.

Death may occur or the condition may persist for two to four days and then improve rather rapidly. Infants with severe disease may have a prolonged recovery period (more than a week). Occasionally, residual pulmonary and neurologic sequelae may occur, perhaps related to the severity of disease or the use of continuous high concentrations of oxygen, usually by prolonged positive pressure ventilation.

PNEUMOTHORAX, PNEUMOMEDIASTINUM, SUBCUTANEOUS EMPHYSEMA, PNEUMOPERICARDIUM, AND PULMONARY INTERSTITIAL EMPHYSEMA
(Air Block)

Air block occurs in 1% of newborn infants but is asymptomatic in many. It is caused by the migration of air from a ruptured alveolus along perivascular sheaths into the mediastinum and thence to the pleural space, thoracic cavity, or pericardium.

Onset is abrupt. Sudden collapse is common. Signs include increased activity, dyspnea, tachypnea, grunting, flaring, shift in apical impulse, hyperpnea, and cyanosis. There may be minimal movement of the chest in spite of marked suprasternal and infrasternal retractions. Increase in chest size may be more prominent on one side. Other signs include tympany and hyperresonance to percussion, shift of mediastinum, and diminution in heart sounds, depending on the type and degree of involvement.

A chest x-ray is helpful for diagnosis, but if sudden collapse occurs an attempt to remove pleural air by needle aspiration may be justified.

The majority of cases of pneumothorax (and almost all cases of pneumomediastinum) involve only small amounts of air and require no specific treatment. These conditions may be complications of assisted ventilation.

Treatment.

Give oxygen. Aspiration of air from pleural or pericardial space or thoracotomy is usually necessary only in severe or long-standing cases.

Course and Prognosis.

Absorption of air from abnormal locations occurs spontaneously in most cases, but removal of air may be necessary.

WILSON-MIKITY SYNDROME

Respiratory distress, primarily in low birth weight infants, may develop insidiously days or weeks after birth and is characterized by cyanosis, tachypnea, wheezing, coughing, apnea, a progressively greater need for oxygen, and radiologic changes. The condition may continue for months; clinical improvement may occur months before resolution of the radiologic changes. The cause is obscure; exposure to excessive oxygen may be a factor. Treatment is supportive.

BRONCHOPULMONARY DYSPLASIA

Bronchopulmonary dysplasia resembling the Wilson-Mikity syndrome is a chronic lung disease occurring in infancy. It appears to be associated with oxygen toxicity in small, severely ill infants who have received continuous high concentrations of oxygen over long periods of time, usually by prolonged positive pressure ventilation. Pulmonary problems may persist for many months.

Patent ductus arteriosus may also develop and death may result, since infants with this condition often have cardiac enlargement, cor pulmonale, and pulmonary dysplasia with fibrosis, overexpanded lung, and infiltrates.

DISEASES DUE TO PERINATAL FACTORS

FRACTURES

Fractures of Clavicle.

This is the most commonly occurring fracture at birth and generally involves the middle third of the bone. Examination reveals limitation of motion on the affected side and absence of the Moro reflex on the side with fracture; crepitus may be elicited.

With immobilization of arm and shoulder, healing is spontaneous and complete. Even when not recognized and without specific treatment, good callus formation and healing usually occur.

Fractures of Extremities.

These usually are caused by a difficult delivery. Signs of fracture are generally present, and the Moro reflex is absent on affected side.

Treatment consists of immobilization for fractures of upper extremity; immobilization and traction for fractures of lower extremity.

Fracture of Skull.

Fractures of the skull may be entirely asymptomatic. Only depressed fractures require surgical treatment; 10% of cephalhematomas are associated with linear fractures.

HEMORRHAGES

Cephalhematoma.

An accumulation of blood between the periosteum and a skull bone. The blood does not cross a suture line. The mass is soft, fluctuating, and irreducible, and does not pulsate or increase in size with crying. During the first days of life it may be obscured by superimposed caput succedaneum. (See Fracture of Skull, above.) Absorption of a large quantity of blood may cause hyperbilirubinemia. No treatment is required (blood should not be aspirated). The condition generally clears within a few weeks or months.

During the healing process a firm ring often can be palpated at the periphery of the hematoma and may simulate a skull defect.

Sternocleidomastoid Hemorrhage.

This hemorrhage may not appear until the third week of life and generally produces a mass in the midportion of the muscle, resulting in a torticollis to the affected side. It is more common after breech presentations and is often associated with a fibroma-like mass; the etiology in many cases remains obscure.

Passive hyperextension of the neck should be started early and in most cases is all that is necessary. Surgical intervention may be indicated for those cases that do not resolve with conservative therapy.

Intracranial Hemorrhage.

This condition can result from obstetric trauma, hypoxia, coagulation disorders, infections, circulatory disturbances, erythroblastosis fetalis, or hypernatremia; it occurs more commonly in premature than in full-term infants. The hemorrhage may be subdural or subarachnoid but occurs commonly in the subependymal region and may rupture into the ventricles or extend into the brain substance. It may arise from a tear of the tentorium. Symptoms and signs may be present at birth or may appear later and include somnolence, restlessness, irritability, opisthotonos, disturbed respiratory and cardiac function with cyanosis, high-pitched, shrill cry, failure to nurse well, muscular twitchings, and convulsions. The fontanel may be bulging. Hemorrhage of the retina and abnormalities of the pupils may occur. Temperature regulation often is disturbed. The Moro reflex may be exaggerated at birth, disappearing later, or may be absent throughout. Paralyses generally do not appear for several days. Anemia may occur. Symptoms may be present at birth, clear for a day or so, and reappear.

An increase in the pressure of the C. S. F. may be of diagnostic significance, but the presence of bloody fluid in the cerebrospinal spaces is not of particular help in the newborn since a small amount of bleeding may occur in the normal child who has not had a particularly difficult delivery and is asymptomatic.

Rest, warmth, sedation, elevation of the head, minimal handling, and vitamin K may be helpful. There is disagreement as to the value of performing repeated spinal punctures. When a subdural hematoma is present it should be evacuated.

Most infants survive and make a complete recovery, but cerebral palsy, mental deficiency, convulsive susceptibility, or hydrocephalus may result. With extensive or severe involvement, death may occur (usually within the first three days).

Liver and Spleen Hemorrhage.
Hemorrhage of the liver and spleen may result in formation of a palpable subcapsular hematoma which may not rupture for some time (> 48 hours) after birth and then produce signs of rapidly progressive collapse. It is occasionally the result of vigorous attempts at resuscitation with flexion of the legs upon the abdomen. Treatment is with whole blood transfusions and surgical exploration, if necessary.

Adrenal Hemorrhage: See Chapter 22.

PERIPHERAL NERVE INJURIES

Brachial Plexus Palsy.
In Erb-Duchenne (upper arm; C5 and C6 or their trunks) paralysis, simultaneous involvement of the phrenic nerve may occur. The arm is adducted, extended, and internally rotated with pronation of the forearm. The Moro reflex is absent on the affected side, and there is sensory loss on the lateral portion of the arm. The forearm and hand are not affected. In Klumpke's paralysis the trauma involves nerves from C7, C8, and T1, or their trunks. There is loss of normal function of the small muscles of the hand. Sympathetic fibers of T1 may also be damaged with resultant ptosis and miosis. Erb-Duchenne and Klumpke's paralyses may occur together.

Physical therapy and splinting to prevent deformity of the involved portions of the extremity are indicated in all cases.

Neuroplasty should be considered in persistent cases.

A period of several months may elapse before a definite prognosis can be given. In the majority of cases the paralysis is due to edema and hemorrhage about the nerve fibers or to nerve injury without laceration; in these instances the outcome may be excellent. If laceration has occurred, return of function is not to be expected.

Phrenic Nerve Palsy.

Often associated with brachial plexus paralysis. There may be cyanosis and rapid, labored, irregular respirations with thoracic breathing. Fluoroscopy shows elevation of the diaphragm and paradoxic respirations on the affected side.

Recovery is possible if neither laceration nor avulsion of the nerve has occurred. If there is no spontaneous recovery from paralysis, good results can be obtained with diaphragm plication.

Facial Palsy.

Generally due to injury to the peripheral portion of the facial nerve by pressure of forceps or of the shoulder or a foot during labor or delivery. When the infant cries there is movement only on one side of the face and pulling to the unaffected side. The paralyzed side is smooth and may appear to be swollen. The forehead does not wrinkle. The eye on the affected side may not close.

Treatment is symptomatic.

The condition usually clears within a few weeks if nerve fibers have not been torn; in some cases with persistent paralysis, neuroplasty may be indicated. Permanent paralysis is more likely to occur when damage is due to pressure from the shoulder than when it is due to trauma from forceps.

INFECTIONS OF THE NEWBORN*

SEPSIS OF THE NEWBORN

Sepsis should be suspected in neonates born to mothers who have fever, prolonged ruptured membranes, frank amnionitis, or any suspected or treated infectious disease, and all cases of obscure illness in the infant. Appropriate bacterial and viral cultures (blood, nasopharyngeal, urine, stool, C.S.F.) should be taken.†

Infection may enter the blood stream from a variety of sites. It may begin prenatally, perinatally, or in the newborn period, and may be caused by any pathogenic organism. Localization may occur in any part of the body.

---

*Conjunctivitis of the newborn is discussed in Chapter 19.
†Deliberate colonization of newborn infants with a coagulase-positive staphylococcus of relatively low pathogenicity (502A) is now seldom employed as a means of controlling nursery outbreaks of pathogenic staphylococci.

Elevated levels of IgM at birth are associated with an increased incidence of congenital infections, particularly subclinical infections with "silent" C. N. S. involvement. However, the absence of IgM does not rule out congenital infection.

Clinical Findings.
A. Symptoms: Onset is frequently insidious. Symptoms may be present at birth.
   1. Anorexia, poor weight gain, lethargy, or restlessness may be the only findings.
   2. Temperature instability is a common manifestation, with hypothermia more common than fever.
   3. Gastrointestinal (vomiting, diarrhea, abdominal distention), C. N. S. (restlessness, convulsions), or respiratory tract manifestations may be prominent.
B. Signs: (Both bacterial and viral infections.)
   1. Hepatomegaly, splenomegaly, pallor, cyanosis, and jaundice (especially in the first 24 hours) often occur.
   2. Hemorrhage, with a petechial rash, is frequent.
   3. An associated meningitis or other focal infection is not uncommon.

Treatment.
A. Specific Measures: Cultures should be obtained, and antibacterial therapy in full dosage with appropriate antibiotics (see Chapter 6) should be instituted immediately.
B. General Measures: Isolate the patient and give supportive therapy as indicated.
C. Prophylactic Treatment: Pregnant women near term who have known group B streptococci in the vagina may need prophylaxis.

Course and Prognosis.
With early treatment, the majority of infants recover. Mortality increases with delay in therapy. Careful observation should be made for localization of the infection.

DISTURBANCES OF THE BLOOD AND BLOOD GROUP INCOMPATIBILITIES

Thrombocytopenia may be a manifestation of intrauterine infection, disseminated or focal intravascular coagulation, and platelet isoimmunization with or without maternal thrombocytopenia.

Polycythemia shortly after birth with a central venous hematocrit greater than 65% (or peripheral hematocrit greater than 70%) may be due to placental-fetal transfusion, to twin-twin transfusion in utero, or to intrauterine growth retardation.

Anemia in newborn infants may be due to blood loss from fetoplacental transfusion at delivery, fetofetal transfusion in twins, chronic fetomaternal transfusion, ruptured liver or spleen, fracture; C.N.S., gastrointestinal, or pulmonary hemorrhage; hematoma, cord bleeding, hemolysis (erythroblastosis fetalis, red cell defects, hemoglobinopathies), and congenital aplastic or hypoplastic anemia.

TABLE 9-1. Special features of infection in newborns.
(Adapted from Morriss.)

Infection	Common Organisms	Manifestations and Treatment
Meningitis	Escherichia coli, pseudomonas, klebsiella-enterobacter, salmonella, Staphylococcus aureus, streptococcus (esp. group B), pneumococcus, Listeria monocytogenes, Haemophilus influenzae, enterovirus	May be present at birth; may occur at any time as an isolated infection; or may be a manifestation of sepsis of the newborn. Symptoms of sepsis plus irritability, bulging anterior fontanel, opisthotonos, seizures, abnormal Moro reflex. Watch for rapidly increasing head circumference as sign of hydrocephalus. **Treatment:** Give ampicillin and kanamycin until organism is identified.
Pneumonia	Esch. coli, klebsiella-enterobacter, pseudomonas, staphylococcus, streptococcus (esp. group B), cytomegalovirus, Herpesvirus hominis, coxsackievirus B, rubella virus	Symptoms of sepsis plus tachypnea, nasal flaring, irregular respirations, and rales. May be present at birth. Chest x-ray essential. Suspect pseudomonas in infants who have been mechanically ventilated. **Treatment:** Give specific therapy when known.
Urinary tract	Esch. coli, klebsiella-enterobacter, proteus, pseudomonas	Occasionally presents as sepsis but more often by abnormal weight loss in first few days, failure to gain weight, feeding difficulty, lethargy, fever, unexplained jaundice, vomiting, cyanosis or pallor. More common in males and preterm infants. Urinalysis and culture of urine obtained by suprapubic aspiration are necessary. Pyuria is not a frequent finding. **Treatment:** Give specific therapy when indicated.
Diarrhea	Esch. coli (enteropathogenic types), klebsiella-enterobacter, salmonella, shigella, staphylococcus, many viruses	Frequent explosive, water-loss stools with or without blood; poor feeding, vomiting, fever, weight loss, dehydration, acidosis. May progress to cardiovascular collapse. "Epidemic diarrhea of newborn," usually caused by Esch. coli, spreads rapidly in nurseries and can be fatal. Illness varies in severity. Mortality rate may be high. Obstetric services and newborn nurseries may have to be closed. **Treatment:** Isolate infant. Correct fluid and electrolyte imbalance. Give specific therapy when known.

Skin infections		
Impetigo of newborn	Staphylococcus, streptococcus, pseudomonas, viruses	Papules, pustules, or vesicles in moist areas or in skin creases. Vesicles often thin-walled, initially with clear fluid. Pseudomonas may produce punched-out necrotic ulcers. Infection may spread to other areas. **Treatment:** Give topical or systemic antibiotics (or both) as indicated.
Cutaneous candidiasis	Candida albicans	Erythematous maceration of skin in groin and perianal areas. May have oral lesions (thrush). **Treatment:** See Chapter 12.
Ritter's disease*	Staphylococcus (phage type II)	Rapidly progressing cellulitis with loosening and sloughing of epidermal layers. May have positive Nikolsky sign. **Treatment:** Specific antibiotic therapy.
Umbilical cord (omphalitis)	Esch. coli, streptococcus, staphylococcus, klebsiella-enterobacter	Erythema and edema of skin around umbilicus. Serous or purulent discharge from cord. **Treatment:** Ampicillin and kanamycin pending cultures.
Intrauterine infections†		
Herpes simplex	Herpesvirus hominis	If acquired in utero, illness may be manifested at birth by skin vesicles. If acquired intrapartum, onset of illness is usually at four to seven days, with lethargy and poor feeding. A few vesicles may appear. The infant then suddenly becomes quite ill, with jaundice, purpura, bleeding, pneumonia, seizures, and death. Cultures of vesicular fluid may grow virus in 48 hours. Complement fixation titers peak at about 14 days. **Treatment:** Isolate the infant. Idoxuridine or cytarabine may be tried, though neither has proved to be uniformly effective.

*Scalded skin syndrome; toxic epidermal necrolysis
†The following intrauterine infections are discussed elsewhere in this book: cytomegalic inclusion disease (cytomegalovirus) and rubella, Chapter 24; syphilis, Chapter 25; toxoplasmosis, Chapter 26.

HEMORRHAGIC DISEASE OF THE NEWBORN

This is a somewhat obscure disorder which may be due to a combination of etiologic factors. The essential feature is the accentuation of the coagulation defects which are found in all newborn infants. The major defect seems to be a deficiency of available prothrombin. The condition is more common in breast-fed infants who did not receive vitamin K.

Diarrhea, treatment with antimicrobial agents, and a diet low in vitamin K may produce hypoprothrombinemic bleeding in infants beyond the newborn period.

Clinical Findings.
A. Signs: Bleeding of the skin, umbilical cord, mucous membranes, or viscera may occur spontaneously or following mild trauma, usually between the second and fifth days of life, when the available prothrombin is at its lowest level.
B. Laboratory Data: The activity of prothrombin, plasma thromboplastin component, proconvertin, and Stuart factor may be decreased. Prothrombin time (one-stage) is usually prolonged. Coagulation time may be normal or prolonged.

Treatment.
A. Vitamin K_1, 1 to 5 mg. I.V., to raise the prothrombin level. Repeat once if necessary. Avoid overdosage. (May be given I.M., but the effect will be slower.)
B. Transfusion of fresh, matched whole blood, 15 to 20 ml./Kg., or fresh frozen plasma, 10 ml./Kg.
C. Pressure dressings and topical application of coagulants (thrombin, fibrin foam) to accessible bleeding sites.

Prophylaxis.
At birth the intestine is sterile and it may take several days before the normal intestinal flora produces sufficient vitamin K for the infant. The administration of vitamin K to the mother will elevate the prothrombin level of the newborn infant, but it must be used with caution. Avoid overdosage. Vitamin K_1 (AquaMephyton®, Konakion®), 1 mg. I.M., should be given prophylactically to the newborn infant.

Prognosis.
With adequate and early therapy, death is rare and complete recovery occurs.

ERYTHROBLASTOSIS FETALIS
(Hemolytic Disease of the Newborn)

1. DUE TO Rh INCOMPATIBILITY

Eleven per cent of pregnancies among the white population occur as a result of the mating of an Rh-negative woman with an Rh-positive man. However, the incidence of this disease is much lower than this because not all women are capable of producing anti-Rh agglutinins and because immunization occurs slowly; one or more pregnancies with an Rh-positive fetus or previous transfusion with Rh-positive blood generally are necessary before a harmful degree of sensitization can develop. Severe Rh sensitization is more likely to occur when mother and infant have ABO compatibility.

Clinical Findings.

A. Symptoms and Signs:
1. Placenta may be enlarged; vernix is often yellow.
2. Marked edema (hydrops fetalis) and other signs of cardiac failure (pleural and pericardial effusions, ascites, etc.) may occur in severe cases. The infant may be stillborn.
3. Jaundice appears during the first 24 hours.
4. Progressive anemia.
5. Hepatosplenomegaly is common.
6. C.N.S. signs — See Kernicterus, below.
7. Bleeding tendency is occasionally seen.

B. Laboratory Findings:
1. Mother is Rh-negative; infant is Rh-positive.
2. Anti-Rh titer of mother is increased.
3. Sensitized Rh-positive infants may occasionally type as Rh-negative due to ''blocking antibodies.''
4. Direct Coombs (anti-human globulin) test on infant red cells is positive.
5. Reticulocytes and nucleated red blood cells in peripheral blood are increased.
6. Anemia may be present at birth or may appear within first few hours or days. Other manifestations of erythroblastosis fetalis may occur in the absence of anemia.
7. Serum indirect (and, occasionally, direct) bilirubin increased (see Appendix).
8. Anti-Rh agglutinins may be present in serum of infant.
9. Significant reduction of PSP binding capacity, a measure of reserve albumin binding capacity.
10. Hypoglycemia (often asymptomatic) may occur.
11. After the 24th week of gestation there may be an elevated peak at 450 nm in spectrophotometric reading of optical density of fluid obtained by amniocentesis.

Complications.

Kernicterus may occur after any condition causing cerebral anoxia (even without severe hyperbilirubinemia) but generally follows erythroblastosis fetalis with marked elevation of unconjugated bilirubin (over 20 mg./100 ml.). It is characterized by destructive and degenerative changes of the brain associated with yellow staining with bile pigment in the nuclear areas of the midbrain and medulla. Initially it is manifested by hypotonia, lethargy, and poor sucking in some cases. Later, spasticity, abnormal Moro reflex, deafness, mental retardation, opisthotonos, and fever may develop. These findings may subside, but in many children there will be reappearance of permanent signs of extrapyramidal involvement. Death may occur in the early stages of the disease.

Premature infants appear to be more susceptible than mature neonates to the development of kernicterus at any given bilirubin concentration; they frequently are free of clinical signs and may not respond favorably to exchange transfusion. A decrease in the quantity or capability of albumin to bind bilirubin - or lowering of the blood-brain barrier to bilirubin - may be an important pathogenetic mechanism. Acidosis, drugs, hypoxia, hypothermia, hypoglycemia, or cold stress may facilitate the development of kernicterus at lower bilirubin levels.

Any Rh-negative mother with an Rh antibody titer of 1:32 or greater in the fourth or fifth month of pregnancy should have two amniocenteses at one-week intervals and the optical density of amniotic fluid (Δ O. D.) at 450 nm measured. (Some investigators recommend that serum titers greater than 1:32 should be present before performing amniocentesis.) If the Δ O. D. 450 is falling, the fetus may be left in utero safely. If the Δ O. D. 450 is found to be rising or staying the same, and the levels are in arbitrarily defined upper zone II or lower zone III, the fetus should receive one or more intraperitoneal transfusions before the thirty-second or thirty-third week of gestational age.

Prenatal Care.

The mother's Rh type should be determined in all pregnancies. The antibody titer (Rh or ABO) should be monitored throughout the pregnancy in all Rh-negative women or those with a possible history of disease in previous pregnancies. Minimum sedation should be used in sensitized women.

Prevention.

Rh sensitization may be prevented in almost 100% of cases by the administration of 1 ml. of high potency Rh_o (D) immune human globulin (RhoGAM®) I. M. within 36 to 72 hours after delivery to an Rh_o-negative woman previously unimmunized to the Rh_o antigen as determined by the absence of an anti-Rh_o in her sera prior to and at the time of delivery. The infant must be Rh_o-positive and the Coombs reaction on cord blood specimen must be negative.

Treatment.

A. Early induction of labor may be indicated if previous pregnancies have resulted in stillbirths, neonatal deaths, or hydrops due to erythroblastosis, or if serial evaluations of amniotic fluid indicate significant sensitization, or if hydrops is suspected from ultrasound or x-ray examination. Excessive prematurity should, however, be avoided.

B. Specific Measures:

1. Exchange transfusion with fresh type O, Rh-negative blood cross-matched with maternal serum. In the presence of frank hydrops and anemia (hematocrit < 30%), an initial partial packed red cell exchange transfusion should be done to raise hematocrit to > 40% prior to the two-volume whole blood exchange.

   Indications for exchange transfusion are as follows:
   (1) Clinical illness at birth on significant jaundice within the first 12 hours. (2) Cord bilirubin over 4.5 mg./100 ml. (3) Cord hemoglobin under 14 Gm./100 ml. (4) Rise in unconjugated serum bilirubin greater than 0.5 mg./100 ml./ hour within the first 48 hours. (5) Unconjugated bilirubin greater than 20 mg./100 ml. (6) Early signs of kernicterus.

(7) Significant reduction of reserve albumin binding capacity in association with rapidly rising total serum bilirubin (Waters).

2. Extensive edema, effusions, and ascites; may require paracentesis and thoracentesis. Positive pressure ventilation, digitalization, and the use of diuretics may be necessary.

C. Supportive Measures:
1. Determine hemoglobin daily until stabilized and then every two weeks until hematopoiesis develops.
2. Breast feeding may be allowed, depending on child's state.
3. Albumin may be administered to the severely hyperbilirubinemic infant to increase the amount of bilirubin removed with the exchange. Dosage: 1 Gm./Kg. of salt-poor albumin (25 Gm./100 ml.) one hour before exchange. Do not use for edematous infant or one in cardiac failure.

D. Prevention and Treatment of Complications (Kernicterus): Exchange blood transfusions shortly after birth are said to lessen the incidence of kernicterus; these may be repeated as a therapeutic measure even after kernicterus has become established.

E. It would appear that phenobarbital administration to mothers prenatally may produce a lowered peak level of bilirubin in the full-term newborn, but the efficacy and safety of such therapy is as yet unproved. Treatment of the newborn infant has been reported to be effective by most but not all investigators.

F. Phototherapy is not indicated in hemolytic disease.

Course and Prognosis.

The affected infant may be born dead or may die within the first few days of life. In other instances, complete recovery may occur without clinical evidence of the disease or after mild or severe manifestations. Sensorineural hearing impairment may develop. Residual damage of the C. N. S. (kernicterus) may occur, particularly if the jaundice was prolonged and the serum was saturated with bilirubin.

After the sixth day the prognosis is good, although some increase in anemia usually occurs.

The disease is quite variable and in any single instance no definite prognosis can be given. The over-all mortality rate of exchange transfusion is approximately 1 to 3% but is considerably less in vigorous infants.

Multiple exchange transfusions are effective in preventing long-term sequelae due to hyperbilirubinemia.

Some patients become anemic from slow, persistent hemolysis even if their neonatal course was benign. Anemia following phototherapy is not uncommon. Simple transfusion is indicated if hemoglobin falls below 7 Gm./100 ml.

Intrauterine transfusions are associated with approximately 50% successful results. The risk to the fetus from a single intrauterine transfusion is between 5 and 20%. Even with fetal transfusion, the mortality in hydrops fetalis is still quite high.

No significant correlations have been found between the presence or absence of brain damage and the maximum bilirubin concentration, birth weight, sex, presence or absence of hemolytic disease, or the use of exchange transfusion.

2. DUE TO ABO INCOMPATIBILITY

ABO incompatibility is the commonest type of fetal-maternal blood group incompatibility.

The mechanism is the same as in hemolytic disease of the newborn due to Rh incompatibility except that the immunization is caused by the group A or B substance instead of the Rh substance. The disease commonly affects first-born infants. Most cases are subclinical and are due to incompatibility of A substance, but incompatibility of B substance may produce a more severe illness.

Clinical Findings.
A. Symptoms and Signs: Jaundice may appear during the first 24 hours but is often delayed until 48 to 72 hours. Hepatosplenomegaly may be present. C.N.S. signs are uncommon.
B. Laboratory Data:
   1. Mother is generally type O.
   2. High anti-A or anti-B titer in the mother. Titer may not rise until several days after delivery. Correlation of severity of fetal sensitization with maternal titers is generally poor.
   3. Elevated serum bilirubin (see Appendix).
   4. The indirect Coombs test is positive in most cases.
   5. Anti-A or anti-B agglutinins may be present in infant's serum.
   6. Reticulocyte count increased.
   7. Spherocytosis and microcytosis often present. Increased osmotic and mechanical fragility of red cells often present.
   8. Hemoglobin usually normal.
   9. Erythrocyte acetylcholinesterase reduced.
   10. Increased in vitro hemolysis.

Treatment and Prognosis.
Most cases do not need treatment, but exchange transfusion is indicated for those infants whose indirect serum bilirubin rises **significantly** above 20 mg./100 ml. Although similar in pathogenesis to the disorder caused by Rh incompatibility, it is much milder.

JAUNDICE IN THE NEWBORN

"PHYSIOLOGIC" JAUNDICE OF THE NEWBORN
(Jaundice of Undetermined Etiology)

This is a normal phenomenon, since almost all infants show some elevation of serum bilirubin during the first week of life. Many factors unique to the neonatal period may be causative. They include relative deficiency of hepatic glucuronyl transferase activity, absence of bacterial flora to convert conjugated bilirubin to urobilinogen, increased enterohepatic circulation of bilirubin, inhibitory effect of maternal serum on bilirubin conjugation, and persistent patency of the ductus venosus. The jaundice appears after the first day of life (generally between the second and fifth days) and clears within one to two weeks. Jaundice is the only sign, although some infants are lethargic and eat poorly at the height of jaundice. Dehydration and starvation may aggravate the condition; lower serum bilirubin levels during the first week of life have been noted in low birth weight infants who are fed in the first two hours of birth rather than after 24 to 36 hours. Infants small for gestational age have lower average mean serum bilirubin concentrations than those with appropriate weight for age. Stools are normal in color. Jaundice is more severe in premature infants. The course is uneventful, and there are no sequelae. No treatment is usually necessary. Recent reports indicate that continuous exposure of an infant with a bilirubin level greater than 10 mg./100 ml. to artificial visible light will decrease the degree of hyperbilirubinemia, particularly in premature infants, but the danger and long-term value of such therapy have not been determined. There have been conflicting reports about the value of administration to women of small doses of phenobarbital during the last weeks of pregnancy - or ethanol prior to delivery - in lowering bilirubin levels in their offspring during the first days of life. The administration of phenobarbital may reduce the level of hyperbilirubinemia in the neonate, but the safety of this procedure is unproved.

Neonatal hyperbilirubinemia may be more severe in certain races (e. g., Oriental) than others (e. g., Caucasian) living in the same area, possibly due to an increased incidence of red cell enzyme deficiencies.

There is no convincing evidence that nonhemolytic jaundice significantly affects ultimate intelligence and neurologic status.

PATHOLOGIC JAUNDICE OF THE NEWBORN

Abnormal jaundice may occur in a number of conditions, including: (1) abnormalities of the blood (erythroblastosis fetalis due to Rh or ABO incompatibility, hemoglobinopathies [Bart's, Zurich], congenital leukemia, other hemolytic anemias); (2) defects involving enzyme activity (persistent deficiency of glycuronyl transferase [Crigler-Najjar disease], inhibition of enzyme activity [novobiocin], glucose-6-phosphate dehydrogenase deficiency [especially in premature black infants], deficiency of uridine diphosphopyridine glucose dehydrogenase, erythrocyte glutathione peroxidase deficiency); (3) infections (urinary tract infection, sepsis, syphilis, congenital hepatitis, toxoplasmosis); (4) anatomic abnormalities (atresia of the bile ducts, choledochal cysts and bile plugs, high small bowel obstruction, congenital malformation of the intestine, cystic fibrosis); and (5) other disorders including those with unknown mechanisms (cytomegalic inclusion disease, cretinism, internal hemorrhage, hypoxia).

Certain drugs may increase jaundice by competing for albumin binding (sulfonamides, salicylates, heme pigments, intravenous fat, sodium benzoate), by competing for the conjugating mechanism (salicylates, chloramphenicol, water-soluble analogues of vitamin K, sulfisoxazole, sulfamethoxypyridazine, sulfadimethoxine, steroids, caffeine with sodium benzoate), by increasing hemolysis (synthetic vitamin K), or by unknown mechanisms.

In a few infants breast feeding may be associated with hyper-bilirubinemia that persists for 2 to 6 weeks; the milk contains pregnane-3(alpha), 20(beta)-diol and there is abnormal inhibition of hepatic glucuronyl transferase activity.

GASTROINTESTINAL DISEASES OF THE NEWBORN

MECONIUM PLUG SYNDROME

Abdominal distention and lack of meconium passage with or without bilious vomiting may occur in infants who otherwise do not appear very ill but are obstructed by a meconium plug in the colon.

Expulsion of the plug may occur after digital examination or the use of enemas. Occasionally Hirschsprung's disease may develop subsequently.

CONGENITAL BILIARY ATRESIA

Congenital biliary atresia may be associated with absence or obstruction of either intrahepatic or extrahepatic biliary passages. Biliary atresia and neonatal hepatitis may be different forms of the same basic disease process.

Clinical Findings.
A. Symptoms and Signs: Jaundice (appearing shortly after birth or delayed for days or weeks) may be mild at first, then progresses and becomes severe. The skin eventually takes on a bronze, olive-green color. Stools are clay-colored or white and of putty-like consistency, although stools during the first days of life may have the appearance of normal meconium. Other symptoms include splenomegaly and progressive enlargement of the liver, hemorrhages due to deficiency of vitamin K, deficiencies of other fat-soluble vitamins, and dwarfing in long-standing cases.

Any or all of the clinical findings of congenital biliary atresia may be present also in **neonatal (congenital) hepatitis;** even liver biopsy may also give identical results. Juvenile cirrhosis may follow. Some infants with neonatal hepatitis may have α_1- antitrypsin deficiency.

B. Laboratory Findings: Stools occasionally contain small amounts of bile pigments or derivatives of bile pigments. The urine contains large amounts of bile pigments. Urine urobilinogen is generally absent. Bilirubin and icterus index increase progressively (may be variable in first weeks). Prothrombin concentration is reduced. The radioactive rose bengal test is of value in determining complete obstruction to the outflow of bile.

In neonatal hepatitis there may be fluctuating bilirubin levels. Alkaline phosphatase activity is a good indicator of disturbed parenchymal function in the follow-up period.

Treatment.

A. General Measures: Give a diet low in fat and high in fat-soluble vitamins, and with medium chain triglycerides as the source of fat. Treatment with choleretics is sometimes of value in differentiating those cases with blockage of the biliary system from those with atresia. Phenobarbital may reduce blood lipid, bile acid, and bilirubin levels.

B. Surgical Exploration and Repair: Exploration is indicated if congenital biliary atresia is suspected. Hepatic portoenterostomy appears to improve markedly the prognosis of patients with biliary atresia (especially of the nonfamilial type) if it is performed before the age of 2 months. Differentiation from neonatal hepatitis (using operative cholangiograms) should be carried out before that time.

Course and Prognosis.

The general condition may remain good for many months without surgery. Some cases apparently clear spontaneously. Improvement appears to be enhanced by surgical correction.

NECROTIZING ENTEROCOLITIS

This idiopathic disease occurs predominantly in low birth weight preterm neonates, who often have a history of maternal fever or amnionitis, postnatal respiratory difficulty (apnea, mild RDS), infection, high osmolar oral feedings, or exchange transfusion. Despite the history, they do well for two to five days before developing lethargy, vomiting, abdominal distention, hypothermia, recurrence of apnea, bloody stools, and finally cardiovascular collapse. Early abdominal x-rays show air-fluid levels, dilated loops of bowel, and separation of loops of bowel secondary to edema in the bowel walls. Linear streaks of intraluminal air (pneumotosis intestinalis) develop and are pathognomonic. If the disease continues to progress, pneumoperitoneum and gas in the portal vein may be seen. Cultures may reveal gram-negative bacteremia, but no specific organism is etiologic.

Therapy consists of antibiotic administration (ampicillin and gentamicin) and fluid (including colloid or whole blood), electrolyte, temperature, and circulatory support. Indications for laparotomy include perforation, persistent localized tenderness for over 12 hours, and abdominal wall cellulitis. Laparotomy for resection of necrotic intestine or for pneumoperitonitis may be necessary.

The disease has a high mortality rate. A spotty epidemiologic distribution has been noted.

Infants managed conservatively may develop late intestinal (usually colonic) stenosis, which requires resection.

PHYSIOLOGIC VOMITING

During the first day or two of life, vomiting of mucus or blood-streaked material occurs in many babies. It clears spontaneously, but improvement may be speeded if the stomach is lavaged.

For other causes of vomiting, see Table 16-1.

CONVULSIONS OF THE NEWBORN

Convulsions in the first few weeks of life are most commonly due to hypocalcemia, intracranial birth injury, C. N. S. infection, congenital cerebral malformation, maternal addiction, perinatal anoxia, pyridoxine deficiency, bilirubin toxicity, hypernatremia, mepivacaine toxicity, cerebral edema, hypomagnesemia, hypoglycemia, or unknown causes. The peak incidence of convulsions occurs on the first day of life when perinatal anoxia is the most common cause and on the second day of life when intracranial hemorrhage and cerebral contusions are the most common causes. The seizures may vary in pattern and be clonic, myoclonic, focal, or generalized, or they may merely produce transient stiffening of the body. Momentary changes in respiratory rate, brief periods of apnea, slight posturing, chewing and sucking motions, abnormal cry, paroxysmal blinking, or localized twitching may also occur.

Treatment is directed toward correcting any deficiency or eliminating possible causes of the convulsive state. Until the cause is determined, intravenous therapy with pyridoxine, calcium, magnesium, and glucose should be tried, followed by anticonvulsant drugs (diazepam, phenobarbital, diphenylhydantoin, paraldehyde) as necessary.

Approximately half of neonates with convulsions will eventually be normal. The best prognosis is for those with hypocalcemia, intracranial birth injury, convulsions due to unknown causes, and normal electroencephalograms. Approximately one-fifth will die and one-quarter will show neurologic deficits.

METABOLIC AND ENDOCRINE DISEASES OF THE NEWBORN

NEONATAL HYPOCALCEMIA

The newborn may demonstrate functional hypoparathyroidism. This is particularly true of infants born prematurely or after complicated pregnancies or intrapartum periods. Hypocalcemia in the first 36 hours of life is associated with prematurity, asphyxia, infants of diabetic mothers, infants born to mothers with hyperparathyroidism (symptomatic or asymptomatic), difficult intrapartum periods, DiGeorge's syndrome, stress (infection, respiratory distress syndrome, exchange transfusion), and infants treated with sodium bicarbonate for acidosis.

Adaptation toward calcium homeostasis begins soon after birth in healthy infants and progresses without incident in breast-fed infants. In infants fed with cow's milk formulas, relatively high concentrations of phosphate may exceed the renal phosphate secretion capacity, and accumulation may produce disturbances in calcium homeostasis, resulting in tetany. Late-onset hypocalcemia of this type (neonatal tetany) usually occurs near the end of the first week of life but may occur any time during the first 2 months.

Hypocalcemia in the neonate may be associated with hypomagnesemia and may fail to respond to calcium until the hypomagnesemia is corrected.

Clinical Findings.

A. Symptoms and Signs: Increased irritability, localized twitchings, periods of apnea, convulsions, vomiting, hypertonicity, high-pitched cry, and respiratory distress are the principal findings. Periods of immobility may occur. Laryngeal signs are uncommon. Chvostek's sign is of no value, since it is present in many normal infants. Carpopedal spasm is uncommon. The Moro reflex is not depressed. In premature infants with early onset hypocalcemia, there are usually no symptoms or abnormal signs.

B. Laboratory Findings: Total serum calcium is low (< 7.5 mg./100 ml.). Ionized calcium is also depressed (< 3.5 mg./100 ml.). Serum phosphorus is generally elevated.

Treatment.

A. Immediate treatment in severe cases consists of giving calcium gluconate, 0.1 to 0.2 Gm./Kg./dose as a 10% solution **slowly** I. V. Subsequently add calcium lactate or gluconate, 0.5 to 1 Gm./Kg./day to the infant's formula. This regimen can usually be discontinued after one week. **Do not** give concentrated calcium solutions by mouth.

B. A modified cow's milk formula with a more favorable Ca/P ratio - such as Similac PM 60/40® - may be beneficial.

Prognosis.

Excellent in late onset tetany, unless anoxia, with resultant permanent brain damage, has occurred during episodes of convulsions; variable with early onset depending on severity of predisposing factors. There is no evidence that hypocalcemia alone has an adverse effect in the early-onset disease.

NEONATAL HYPOGLYCEMIA
(See also Chapter 22.)

Asymptomatic physiologic hypoglycemia with blood glucose levels under 50 mg./100 ml. occur commonly in the neonatal period; blood glucose levels are higher if the infant is fed in the first hours after birth. Significant hypoglycemia (blood glucose < 20 mg./100 ml. in low birth weight infants or < 30 mg./100 ml. in full-term infants) may occur and be associated with irritability, lethargy, limpness, high-pitched cry, difficulty in feeding, sweating, apnea, cyanosis, tremors, and convulsions. Hypoglycemia is especially likely to occur in infants with low or increased birth weight or period of gestation, erythroblastosis fetalis, infection (especially with gram-negative bacilli), polycythemia, C.N.S. injury or anomaly, galactosemia, leucine sensitivity, Beckwith's syndrome, neonatal cold injury, or trisomy 13-15, and in infants born to mothers with toxemia or diabetes. It may also occur in an idiopathic form. The smaller of twins is more likely to be hypoglycemic. The condition appears to be more common in males. Low levels may occur within a few hours after birth and again on the third day. There may be associated hypocalcemia and polycythemia.

Prompt improvement usually occurs after the administration of glucose I.V. Rarely is more than 15% glucose at a rate of 125 ml./

Kg./24 hours required, and rapid administration of hypertonic glucose should be avoided. In refractory cases the administration of hydrocortisone (5 mg./Kg./24 hours) may be necessary. Do not discontinue glucose infusions abruptly.

The prognosis in patients with both symptomatic and asymptomatic hypoglycemia, except in newborn infants of diabetic mothers, tends to be poor, probably because of underlying brain damage; some children remain normal despite repeated severe episodes of hypoglycemia.

INFANTS OF DIABETIC MOTHERS

These infants often present serious problems and have increased morbidity and mortality rates, an increased incidence of congenital anomalies, and sudden intrauterine death. The exact mechanism is not known.

Clinical Findings.
A. Symptoms and Signs: Infant is usually larger than the average for the expected stage of maturity, with lethargy, round red face, cardiomegaly, hepatomegaly, splenomegaly, and a tendency to cyanosis, edema, and tetany. Large amounts of fluid are present in the trachea and bronchi and in the stomach. There may be an increased incidence of congenital anomalies. Symptoms of hypoglycemia are sometimes but not always present. Infants of diabetic mothers have an increased incidence of hyaline membrane disease, tetany of the newborn, impaired metabolism of bilirubin, and clotting abnormalities (renal vein thrombosis).
B. Laboratory Findings: Hypoglycemia often develops. In most infants it may be no more marked than the physiologic hypoglycemia of the normal newborn. Hypoglycemia, prolonged for several days, has been reported in association with maternal chlorpropamide (Diabinese®) therapy.

Additional findings can include erythroblastosis of peripheral blood or extramedullary hematopoiesis. There may be an increased incidence of hyperbilirubinemia. Also, there may be abnormal placenta, increased insulin levels, reduced free fatty acids, disturbed adrenocortical and thyroid function, hypocalcemia, and reduced serum growth hormone levels.

Prevention.
Good control of the mother's diabetes and close observation of the infant are most important.

Treatment.
Restrict maternal sedation. Aspirate upper respiratory tract and gastric contents as often as necessary. Dilute carbohydrate solutions orally or parenterally may be indicated. Glucagon, 200 μg./Kg. I.V., may be of value for hypoglycemia. Administer calcium if tetany develops. Correct serum electrolyte imbalance if present. Cortisone or hydrocortisone should be tried only in severe cases. Early delivery may be of value if falling maternal estriol levels indicate that the fetus is at rest. See p. 137 for

treatment of hyaline membrane disease of the lungs. If gestational age is short, treat as a premature infant regardless of actual birth weight.

DISTURBANCES OF THE SKIN IN THE NEWBORN

TRAUMATIC SUBCUTANEOUS FAT NECROSIS

Cheeks and neck are most often involved as a result of trauma from forceps blades, but other parts of the body may also be involved. Lesions are isolated areas of induration which are firm, have sharply defined margins, and are not attached to deeper tissues.

The condition generally clears spontaneously.

ERYTHEMA TOXICUM NEONATORUM

An extremely common eruption of unknown cause which is found in the newborn period only and occurs around two to four days of age. The lesions are scattered and not numerous and consist of irregular, poorly circumscribed, erythematous spots with pale central zones ("flea-bite" dermatitis). They contain many eosinophils. No treatment is indicated.

SCLEREMA
(Sclerema Adiposum)

Sclerema is characterized by diffuse hardening of the subcutaneous tissues which does not pit on pressure and begins in the lower extremities and rapidly spreads upward to involve almost the entire body. The skin is tense and cool. Sclerema may appear at any time during the first weeks of life and occurs most often in premature infants or those who are undernourished, dehydrated, and debilitated. The condition usually terminates fatally within a few days, although in some cases the administration of cortisone has been accompanied by recovery.

DISEASES OF THE UMBILICUS

The contents of the umbilicus include the umbilical vein, two umbilical arteries, the rudimentary allantois, the residual omphalomesenteric duct, and the gelatinous Wharton's jelly.

CONGENITAL ABNORMALITIES

Persistence of the allantois causes patent urachus. Persistence of a portion of the omphalomesenteric duct may produce a Meckel's diverticulum. Omphalocele with variable defects of the abdominal wall may occur. Increased quantity of Wharton's jelly is manifested by the persistence of a granuloma when the umbilical cord sloughs. Healing may be speeded by cauterization of the granuloma with a silver nitrate stick.

In approximately 1% of infants, only one umbilical artery is present; there is an increased incidence of congenital abnormalities in this group, especially of the gastrointestinal and urinary tracts in live-born infants.

UMBILICAL HERNIA

This is a common finding, especially in Negro infants, and is due to weakness or faulty closure of the umbilical ring. It rarely causes incarceration or strangulation. Most cases clear spontaneously during the first 18 months of life.

• • •

INTRAUTERINE GROWTH RETARDATION
(Dysmaturity, Small for Dates, Small for Gestational Age)

These infants are characterized by birth weights that are disproportionately low for their gestational ages. A number of conditions may be associated with impaired intrauterine growth: (1) Intrauterine undernutrition: Placental insufficiency, multiple pregnancies, cardiovascular disease in the mother, toxemia, high altitude, arteriovenous anastomoses in identical twins. (2) Infants with congenital abnormalities: Chromosomal trisomies, Turner's syndrome, Silver's syndrome, de Lange's syndrome, etc. (3) Intrauterine infection: Rubella, cytomegalovirus, toxoplasmosis, syphilis.

Small birth weight may be suspected prior to delivery if the uterus is disproportionately small on palpation or if a small fetus is shown by ultrasound or x-ray. Intrauterine undernutrition may occur in infants who are post-term. The infant's neurologic examination will reflect his age, not his size. Infants have a much higher incidence of asphyxia during labor, meconium aspiration, and transient symptomatic hypoglycemia as well as major congenital anomalies, massive pulmonary hemorrhage, polycythemia, and electrolyte imbalance.

"Postmaturity syndrome" may occur in those who are fullterm or post-term and show signs of intrauterine growth retardation. Growth in length and head circumference are usually not significantly affected unless involvement was prolonged. Mild involvement results in relatively thin, long infants with loose, flabby, dry, parchment-like skin and deficient subcutaneous tissue. There is increased susceptibility to skin infections. The infant often has an excellent appetite and gains at an excessive rate. More severe disturbance is frequently associated with intrauterine hypoxia, including passage of meconium into the amniotic fluid, green staining of membranes and skin, hypoglycemia, and hypocalcemia.

Infants exhibiting intrauterine growth retardation have a poorer long-term prognosis for general development than infants appropriate in size for gestational age.

10 . . .

Emotional Problems

Ruth S. Kempe, M.D.

Emotional conflict is reflected fairly openly in the behavior of most children. This is fortunate, because the child is seldom sufficiently aware of the nature of his emotional difficulties to seek help directly. Only when his behavior becomes disturbing to adults does the existence of emotional difficulties become recognized. For this reason the problems of the passive or withdrawn child are often overlooked.

However - and this is most important in considering the specific problems mentioned below - a given type of stress does not necessarily produce a given type of behavior response. Emotional difficulties in children are manifested by symptoms which are often nonspecific but which represent attempts on the part of the child to deal with the anxiety resulting from a conflict which is either internalized or in the environment. The cause of the difficulty must be sought in the child's total emotional environment, past and present. The symptom ''chosen'' is apt to depend on the individual child's stage of development and to reflect those facets of his personality which are already weak or poorly integrated. Often the developmental skill most recently acquired - or acquired with difficulty and thus still poorly integrated - is lost at times of stress. For example, the two-year-old may suck his thumb after the birth of a sibling; the five-year-old may become enuretic in the same situation. Frequently there will be behavioral disturbances in several areas at once.

The most helpful approach is to bear in mind that the disturbed child is an individual whose past experiences have helped to shape his present personality and that he is now reacting with disturbed behavior to some conflict or stress the nature of which may not be immediately apparent. Obviously, then, we cannot examine the child alone in order to help him; we must examine also those factors in his environment with which he may be in conflict. Conflict may center around a developmental problem, i.e., the child may be unwilling or unable to progress to a more mature state of development, especially if his relationship with his parents seems to him to be threatened by a new step he is required to take away from the shelter of infancy. Conflict may also be narrowly confined to one significant person, e.g., a parent or sibling.

In order to define areas of stress it is worthwhile to learn as much as possible about the child in four areas: (1) The child himself (e.g., mental and physical capabilities or handicaps; strengths and weaknesses in social relationships). (2) Developmental history, with particular attention to past or present difficulties. (3) His total emotional environment. (4) Particular crises or events of probable importance to the child.

The emotional environment of the very young child consists almost entirely of his relationship with his parents. All children are dependent upon their parents for the love, security, and guidance they so much need. To a child this relationship is the most important of all; it is the earliest, the closest, and the most enduring. It is within the family circle that the child undergoes most of his early experiences, and by the time he begins to meet outsiders (at two or three years of age) he will already have developed many attitudes and learned ways of reacting to others. For the parent, too, this relationship is unique, invested as it is with opportunities for fulfillment of some of his own needs. Parents frequently have difficulty in dealing with those problems which they themselves have poorly resolved or with which they had particular difficulty as children. The mature parent, on the other hand, can help his child develop freely without using him as a "second chance" to gratify his own unfulfilled wishes.

Because of the pervasive influence of the relationship between a child and his parents, it is virtually impossible to deal with difficulties manifested in the child's behavior without knowing the parents and understanding their role in the conflict. Nor is it enough to know only one parent, since both parents influence the child's behavior not only by their direct relationship with him but also by their influence on one another. A child often learns repetitive patterns of behavior that are ineffective for him or not available to him. For example, in a family that never allows open expression of anger, the parents may develop such covert ways of dealing with these feelings as leaving home, drinking, or retreating into such physical symptoms as headaches. Since he can't drink or run away, the child may develop tics or other unsatisfactory ways of discharging anger and tension.

There are other relationships of importance, particularly to the older child, which may produce stresses. Although siblings usually have real affection for each other, they may also become rivals for the parent's attention if not for his affection. Once the parent accepts this as inevitable and the negative feelings accompanying it as natural, much of the problem of sibling rivalry can be turned into constructive channels. Parental acceptance of negative feelings, with control of the hostile behavior which accompanies them, can assist the child in developing emotional control. Learning to accept the necessity for sharing the attention of the parents, without feeling guilty about the natural desires for exclusive attention and negative feelings toward siblings, can prepare children for inevitable competition in later life. The sibling rivalry is also ameliorated when parents give some individual and undivided time to each child. Here the quality of undivided attention and responsiveness to the child is more important than the length of time spent.

Relationships with peers among the child's playmates involve some of the same feelings the child has toward siblings - especially in areas of competition. These relationships are particularly apt to reveal immature social adjustment, because children are not very lenient with one another's weaknesses.

Finally, school and society also make specific demands on the growing child. Inability of the child to meet these requirements may bring about disturbances of behavior both in school and at home.

ROLE OF THE PHYSICIAN

The physician is often the first person to whom parents turn for help with the emotional problems of their children. If he is interested he can be very helpful. If not interested, he should be wary of giving casual or superficial advice.

Most psychologic problems do not need or cannot get the attention of a specialist in child psychiatry. Every physician who sees many children in his practice must deal with the common dilemmas that arise within a family as a natural and important part of his work. No doctor can afford to look at his patient only as an aggregation of physical symptoms, for he knows that emotional ill health is often responsible for physical symptoms or can affect the extent and speed of recovery from physical illness. In actual practice the pediatrician or general practitioner probably concerns himself with many more emotional difficulties than he realizes. Because he sees the family often and knows its members well, he is aware of them as people and has opportunities to observe changes in attitudes and responses which may represent emotional difficulties or provide a favorable background for their later development. In following a young mother through pregnancy and delivery, for example, he may observe that she is anxious about her ability to care for her baby. Therefore, he listens more attentively to her questions and offers her more frequent appointments. He will realize that sensitivity to her anxieties and support for her in her new role as a mother will help her more than any specific recommendations about the baby. In all this he will not consider himself to be practicing psychiatry, although what he is doing is in fact excellent preventive psychiatry.

For the same reasons he will not give the obese fourteen-year-old girl just a physical examination and a diet sheet. He will discuss her general activities with her and her mother and will attempt to ascertain how effectively she functions in her home, school, and social environments. He may suggest to the mother that she encourage her daughter to undertake a new grooming program and new activities which would make her a more attractive and interesting person. He does this because he knows a young girl's anxiety about her unattractiveness or the fear that she is not loved may only increase her desire for oral gratification; his immediate objective in this instance is to offer her an adequate temporary substitute, i.e., the prospect of making herself more attractive and likeable.

It will be obvious in this chapter that little attempt has been made to present a formal discussion of psychiatric diagnosis or make careful distinctions - important as these may be in specialized practice - between conduct disturbance, neurosis, and psychosis. Attempts to determine whether symptoms indicate neurosis or some "less serious" degree of disturbance, and detailed reconstruction of the psychodynamics of emotional maladjustments in children, are part of psychiatric practice but may not be possible or necessary elsewhere. Arriving at a formal psychiatric diagnosis does clarify the physician's thinking about the nature of the problem. However, finding a name for the child's illness may give the physician an unwarranted feeling of understanding the situation thoroughly and of having completed his job. It is equally important for the pediatrician or general practitioner to try to understand the total situation as thoroughly as possible and to concern himself with evolving a plan for dealing with the difficulty.

One of the first concerns of the physician will be to evaluate the severity of the problem. Should he attempt to deal with it himself or should he refer it to a specialist? Very severe emotional problems are usually easy to recognize, and the physician's aim in these cases will be to make a successful referral to a psychiatrist. But the less obvious problems can be considerably more difficult to evaluate, and here a detailed examination is worthwhile. Certain points in the outline on p. 163 are particularly pertinent: (1) Duration of symptoms. Transitory symptoms are usually more easily treated than those which have remained unchanged for months or years. (2) The over-all adjustment of the child. Generalized difficulties, with several symptoms which affect performance in school, home, and with peers, indicate a more severe problem. (3) Concern of the parent and child about the symptoms. If the symptom itself produces little discomfort and is effective in dealing with the child's underlying anxiety (as is true of some phobias), the patient may have little incentive to change without considerable pressure from the environment and the therapist.

If a detailed evaluation does not clarify treatment potentialities, discussion with a psychiatrist may be of help. Or if the physician finds that little progress has been made after seeing the patient for several interviews, he can at any point discuss with the parent the question of referral. Since most children will have transitory psychologic symptoms during periods of stress, the physician may wish to follow his patient for a time to see if the problem resolves spontaneously rather than to refer immediately.

In order to deal effectively with the psychologic illnesses of children, the physician must understand the wide variations compatible with normal behavior development. This can and should be one of his most valuable contributions. Reassurance about normal behavior variants can prevent more serious problems from occurring. Treatment in such instances becomes primarily a matter of education of the parents by the physician.

Perhaps the role of the physician should also be considered from a more personal viewpoint. His attitudes toward other people and toward himself as a doctor and as a person will influence his reaction to any given problem brought to him by a patient. We have already said that parents have difficulty helping their children with problems they themselves have not solved. This is also true of doctors, and a physician must always be conscious of the part his own personal attitudes play in his professional thinking. This does not mean, of course, that a doctor cannot help a patient because he has difficulties of his own; but it does mean that he must measure the influence of his personal concerns on his professional attitudes and minimize that influence as much as possible.

The Initial Interview.

Not only will the physician need to evaluate the parents' specific attitudes toward their child; he must also have some kind of impression of the parents as individuals - of the problems they face apart from those related to their roles as parents. The physician must be cautious, however, in assuming that only the parents are at fault; this can defeat any therapeutic attempt. Some understanding of the parents' own individual needs and some recognition and

confidence in their parental ability and responsibility can do much
to support a parent-child relationship and put it on a more positive
footing. Most people genuinely wish to be good parents, and this
desire can be strengthened by encouragement. The anxiety and
frustration aroused in parents by a child's difficult behavior need
alleviation through discussion and management planning. Since
much of the physician's work will be with the parents, it is important
that he establish a good relationship with them.

The case history of an emotional problem is best taken in an
unhurried, informal manner, allowing the mother to place stress
on areas with which she is most concerned. Evolution of the presenting problem in relation to coincident family events might be
a clue to diagnosis. At any rate, a brief family history places the
problem in its appropriate historical setting.

We wish in particular to stress the value to the parent of the
opportunity to talk freely to the physician. It is essential for the
physician to have sufficient time available to listen calmly and
without hurry. For this reason it is often wise to schedule a special
time for such an interview. Most parents appreciate the opportunity
and are perfectly willing to pay for the extra time needed. The
greatest error doctors without psychiatric training make in dealing
with emotional problems is to underestimate the value to the patient
of their own ability to listen calmly, attentively, and with understanding. Frequently this is the only situation in which the parents
will be able to arrive at with the physician at the source of the problem. Physicians sometimes tend to assume the traditional authoritative role expected of them and to feel uncomfortable if they do not
give the patient something definite and concrete, even if it is only
a diagnosis. Mutual exploration of the problem by doctor and parent and a mutual decision about what is to be done are more constructive than an authoritative unilateral dispensation of advice.

When the physician feels the problem is such as to warrant
special help from a psychiatrist or child psychologist, he can do
much to make referral easier for the parent. The apprehension
many people have about psychiatry can be partially relieved before
referral by explaining the simple mechanics of the problem and by
outlining a general picture of psychotherapy. In making a referral
for psychotherapy it is important to recognize that every parent
in these circumstances will have some aversion to such a referral.
His unrealistic feelings of failure as a parent, of worry about being
"analyzed," of having a child who is "crazy" or "psycho" should
all be recognized. It is usually helpful to the parent to let him know
that most people share these feelings before accepting a referral
and to help the parent to express them. The realization that his
own physician knows how he feels can increase the patient's confidence in his doctor's recommendations. Of course the physician's
own attitudes about psychiatry will very much influence the parents'
feelings about the referral.

Evaluation of Emotional Problems in Children (Sample Outline).

A. Presenting Symptoms: Time of onset and accompanying circumstances in detail. History of previous attempts to deal
with the problem and attitudes toward it.
B. Other symptoms, past and present.

C. Total present adjustment of child in family, school, peer situations. Include descriptions of patient's abilities, personality
traits, activities.

D. Developmental History: Pregnancy and mother's attitude toward it. Feeding history, toilet training, sleep problems,
motor development, disciplinary difficulties, sex curiosity and
information.

E. Family History: Include major events such as births of siblings, moves, illnesses, accidents, deaths, separations,
parental discord. Is child's symptom a reaction to serious
problems in a parent?

F. Parent-Child Relationships: Past difficulties. Parents' areas
of special concern with the child. Differences of opinion between parents about the child.

G. Observation of the Patient: Observe reactions to the physician,
medical examination, and to the parents with and without the
doctor present. Attempt by direct conversation with the patient
to become acquainted and to learn about his general interests.
May also include discussion of his feelings about the problem
if he is old enough and verbal enough to confide and has a sufficiently good relationship with the doctor. Some statement by
the physician about his wish to help and an opportunity for the
child to ask questions (with an explicit understanding about
confidentiality) is certainly indicated in these circumstances.

H. Special examinations may be indicated, such as a screening
developmental examination, testing of vision or hearing, psychological testing, etc.

I. Outside opinions may sometimes be obtained, e. g. , from the
school.

Principles of Treatment.

Because treatment for nonspecific symptoms can hardly be
definitive, little will be said of specific remedies for the problems
discussed below. After a thorough understanding of the situation
has been reached by the family, a further course of action often becomes self-evident. With his unbiased viewpoint and understanding
of the importance of feelings, the doctor can help the family to see
more clearly, perhaps for the first time, the real nature of their
difficulties. The therapeutic problem is to isolate those factors in
the child's external and internal emotional environment (physical
handicaps, unreasonable parental expectations, unconscious fantasies, etc.) which arouse intense anxiety. Coping with the presence
of the anxiety and, if possible, removing its cause tend to make the
symptom unnecessary. The degree to which the anxiety is due to
deeply unconscious conflict will greatly affect the desirability of
attempting treatment in pediatric practice. Sometimes the physician's use of his professional knowledge and authority will help to
give weight to his recommendations, and often a ''common sense''
view of the situation combined with a new understanding will be all
that is needed. Parent and child can then go on - with continued
help, if desired - to consolidate their gains with time. Education
of the parent is also part of this process, if parents are unaware
of normal behavior variations or emotional needs.

Example: An eight-year-old boy referred for correction of a
patent ductus arteriosus may be found to have emotional difficulties
directly related to his physical problem. The physician can use the

authority of his knowledge of the boy's excellent prognosis to help the mother be less overprotective and the father to be less disappointed in his son's potential as an athlete. He can show understanding of the boy's feelings of inadequacy and defeat and correct his unjustified apprehensions about the future.

PROBLEMS ASSOCIATED WITH PHYSICAL HANDICAPS

Nature of Handicaps.

Emotional maladjustment frequently accompanies physical disability. The worst offenders are the obvious physical defects such as crippling (e.g., cerebral palsy, paralysis following poliomyelitis), blemishes, cleft palate, and harelip. Chronic illness (e.g., epilepsy, diabetes, cardiac disease, tuberculosis, orthopedic conditions like osteochondritis) also imposes an additional burden of adjustment. Even in acute illness, if hospitalization is necessary, the young child may be considerably disturbed. In the very young hospitalized child, separation from parents is the crucial problem; in the older child, fantasies about illness and procedures become important.

The less obvious physical defects, such as impaired hearing and eyesight, place the child at a considerable disadvantage in both the social and educational spheres. If they are unrecognized, the child's difficulties may be blamed on other causes.

Attitudes Toward Illness

The psychopathology of emotional illnesses of this sort is in most instances based not only upon the real limitations resulting from the defect itself but also upon the patient's adjustment to it. Children seldom understand the reason for their handicap and so may come to feel inferior or even guilty (assuming it to be a punishment). Competition with playmates actually becomes more difficult. If the disorder requires restriction of activity, children may rebel against what seems to be unfair discrimination and blame the parents rather than the illness.

The attitude of the parents is often the single crucial factor, since it usually conditions the child's response to his illness. Irrational guilt on the part of the parents, who may feel somehow responsible for the defect, underlies much of the distortion in their attitudes. They may be ashamed of the defect and may resent having the child, or may be over-critical and over-demanding of the child in an attempt to force him to overcome his disability by the sheer strength of their desire that he do so. Or they may be over-protective, encouraging his impulse to self-pity and to withdrawal from valid competition. They may treat him differently from his siblings, causing resentment among them and further problems for the child.

Treatment.

Treatment should in all cases begin with correction of the disability as far as possible. Corrective measures should then be followed by a carefully planned therapeutic regimen (including physiotherapy and occupational therapy), emphasizing as much normal activity as possible. Adequate explanation of this regimen to parents and child will produce better cooperation.

Psychologic management consists primarily of allowing the parents to discuss their problems freely and evaluation and redirection of parental and patient attitudes. In making the initial diagnosis of illness or handicap, the same kind of management will often prevent the development of unhealthy attitudes.

PSYCHOLOGIC PROBLEMS ASSOCIATED WITH MENTAL DEFICIENCY

The problems which arise when a pediatrician finds that he is dealing with a mentally retarded patient are often less directly concerned with the child than with the adjustment of the family to the situation. The diagnosis of mental deficiency is one of the most difficult for the physician to present to a parent, and yet it provides an opportunity for him to do a great service in the prevention of later family disruption. Diagnosis is often uncertain for many months, and during this period the physician bears the burden of deciding how much information he can safely and accurately impart to the parent. Differential diagnosis includes ruling out severe psychologic disturbance or psychosis and pseudo-retardation on the basis of severe disturbance in the mother-child relationship (see p. 32). Even when the diagnosis is certain, the physician has only begun his task, for he is often in the best position to help parents deal with the problem. Their consternation, guilt, hopelessness, and resentment all must be recognized. Unwillingness to accept his evaluation is not unusual. Genetic counseling and careful explanation of etiology, incidence, and prognosis provide a more realistic foundation for their attitudes. Detailed guidance in the development and management of the retarded child over the course of the years is very valuable. Referral to local parents' groups (such as Aid to Retarded Children) may give those parents who wish to keep their retarded child at home moral support as well as practical help in dealing with the home care of the retarded child. In the older retarded child, low mental capacity may help precipitate conduct disturbances, which must then be evaluated as in other children, bearing in mind the additional handicap.

The advice to institutionalize the child depends not upon the I. Q. alone. Primary consideration should be given to the wishes of the parents, who alone can make this decision. Frequently physicians urge placement because they know of no other solution, even though crowded institutions and prohibitive costs in private nursing homes may make it utterly impossible. Parents are then left floundering, without any positive approach to the problem.

EDUCATIONAL PROBLEMS ASSOCIATED WITH MILD MENTAL RETARDATION

The education of the severely retarded child (I. Q. far below 70) depends upon special school facilities. However, there is a large group of children whose I. Q. 's range from 70 to 90 in whom a diagnosis of mental deficiency should not be made but who do have a real intellectual handicap. Often this "slowness" is not recognized until the child is in the primary grades. Prognosis is excellent for

successful social participation and unskilled job placement if
emotional adjustment is good. However, these children are apt to
be aware of their intellectual inadequacy, and this feeling of inferiority may make for resentful asocial behavior, particularly if the
cause goes unrecognized and the child is considered lazy. A less
demanding academic program for these children allows them the
satisfaction of performing adequately what is asked of them in
school. Help in developing nonacademic skills and interests will
make such a child a more effective adult.

EDUCATIONAL UNDERACHIEVEMENT WITH NORMAL
OR SUPERIOR INTELLIGENCE

This problem is extremely common in the early school years
and may be due to various causes. The parents may assume that
the child is lazy and demand greater school achievement. The child
may feel utterly inadequate in school and resent the pressure put
upon him to learn. The diagnosis usually depends on careful neurologic examination, individual testing by an experienced psychologist, and evaluation of the child's emotional status.

Educational underachievement may be generalized or specific,
as in reading difficulty (dyslexia) with secondary generalized retardation. Neurologic examination may show mild neurologic dysfunction manifested by poor posture, poor reflexes, or other deviant
motor responses. Motor coordination and behavior may be poorly
modulated. Hyperactivity and short attention span are important
symptoms. Children with specific learning problems appear to
have a developmental delay or defect which is revealed during
psychologic testing of temporal and spatial perception, e.g., in
visual-motor and auditory sequencing.

Learning difficulties may be secondary to emotional problems
resulting in generalized inhibition of active or aggressive behavior,
so that the learning process itself subsequently becomes inhibited.
Cultural or social deprivation may interfere with learning, e.g.,
if verbal communication is inadequate. Difficulties of interpersonal
relationships and high levels of anxiety may make it impossible for
a child to perceive and integrate new knowledge or may make him
unwilling or unable to reproduce what he has absorbed.

Treatment depends on accurate assessment of the cause of
underachievement. Vision and hearing problems and neurologic
defects should be ruled out or corrected if possible. In children
with "minimal brain dysfunction" as described above, drugs such
as dextroamphetamine (Dexedrine®) or methylphenidate (Ritalin®)
may be helpful in controlling hyperactivity.

Relief from parental pressure is of great benefit to the child;
if the parents have a realistic understanding of the nature of his
difficulties, they can be helpful rather than critical. Special
classes or tutoring may be available for children with perceptual
handicaps.

Evaluation of the child's emotional adjustment often reveals
other difficulties, such as exaggerated sibling rivalry, enuresis,
and disciplinary problems at home. Again, exploration of the
parent-child relationship is usually the most productive course, and
disturbances in this relationship must be dealt with independently
of the educational problem. Tutoring or remedial reading instruc-

tion (by someone other than the parent) may be very helpful, for even when the etiology is primarily emotional, the child needs individual educational help to show him he can learn and to help him make up lost ground.

PSYCHOLOGIC PROBLEMS IN THE BRIGHT CHILD

If the environment lacks sufficient stimulation, the bright child may become bored and seek unacceptable outlets for imagination and energy. Punishment merely aggravates the difficulty by causing resentment and further misbehavior. Instead there should be recognition of the child's needs.

Extra training in art, music, and science helps such children by supplementing the school routine with creative activities. It is important to recognize that superior intelligence may give a false impression of maturity, and the bright child may have unmet needs for dependency or social protection.

SPEECH DEFECTS

Among the common speech defects of children are delayed, indistinct, or babyish speech, and stuttering or stammering, all of which are more common in boys.

Evaluation of mental and hearing capacity is important where speech is delayed or indistinct. Rarely, neurologic disease, usually associated with mental deficiency, causes poor speech development. Occasionally the parent is so over-protective of the child that the effort to speak distinctly is not necessary and the child relies largely on non-verbal communication. Babyish speech or jargon (when mental ability is normal) frequently announces its own etiology: either the child has unsatisfied dependent needs or these needs are overindulged by a doting parent.

Stuttering (compulsive repetition of certain syllables or words) and stammering (complete blocking of some speech) are now almost universally considered to be psychogenic. Incomplete brain dominance is rarely considered responsible. Most case histories indicate that stuttering occurs first with emotional tension in the child three to six years of age, at which time speech is still a recently acquired skill. Indeed, it is frequently seen as a transient "normal" phenomenon in young children. When emotional tension is relieved by some change in the environment, the stuttering disappears spontaneously.

Stuttering or stammering in the older child, especially if severe, is difficult to treat. Evaluation of adjustment is indicated, often with referral to a child psychologist or psychiatrist for prolonged help. The child's attention should be turned from the act of speech to the specific technics of breathing and enunciation used (by a speech therapist), and his inadequate confidence should be bolstered if possible.

DEVELOPMENTAL PROBLEMS

Developmental problems are those difficulties encountered by parents in understanding and dealing with the individual variations in behavior of the young child (thumb-sucking at one year of age, temper tantrums at two, occasional toilet accidents). These diffi- culties have been considerably aggravated during the past decade by the flood of "child care" literature, representing many conflicting viewpoints. Confusion in the parent's mind leads to inconsistency in bringing up children. The physician, by reassuring the parents as to the normality of the child's behavior and the efficacy of their child-rearing methods, can frequently prevent serious problems from arising. Distortions in the parent-child relationship, brought on by early misunderstanding of normal behavior, may lay the foundation for disorganizing mental illness.

FEEDING

Feeding problems usually arise between one and two years of age when the normal decrease in appetite due to lowered growth gradient arouses anxiety in the parent. Urging the child to eat produces resistance, which further decreases the appetite.

Therapy often consists only of explanation of this cycle to the parent and reassurance concerning the nutritional needs (perhaps including a prescription for vitamins). In severe feeding problems, the mother's anxiety about the feeding situation is based on severe unconscious conflict concerning nurture or mothering and may well require psychiatric help.

SLEEP

Sleeping problems are most marked between the ages of two and six but may also occur in the first year (especially when parents are very permissive). The young child who refuses to sleep alone usually reflects the parents' over-protectiveness; their unwilling- ness to impose this normal and desirable restriction on the child gives firmer ground to his fears of being alone. Disturbances from three to six years of age may be due to nightmares (dreams from which the child awakes to full consciousness and which can be re- membered) or to night terrors (from which the child does not spon- taneously awake and which are not remembered). Nightmares can frequently be traced to some exciting or frightening event of the preceding day. Sleepwalking seems to be an accompaniment of a frightening dream and is roughly equivalent to a night terror. Pin- worm infection should sometimes be considered in sleep disturbances.

Treatment aims at a happy, quiet bedtime and soothing when sleep is interrupted. Severe night terrors need evaluation since these usually indicate fairly severe anxiety. Encouraging the child to discuss nightmares is often of aid. However much the child may desire to sleep in the parent's bed, this is not the answer to sleep- ing problems. Sleeping with one or both parents tends to encourage unconscious sexual fantasies and eventually increases anxiety.

BLADDER CONTROL

Enuresis is involuntary urination at night after three to four years of age. It is more frequent (up to 65% of cases) in boys.

The optimal time for beginning bladder training in most children is between 15 months and two years of age. Training should be non-coercive and gradual, with tolerance of accidents. The average bladder capacities of normal children are larger (382-975 ml./sq. M.) than in enuretics (198-355 ml./sq. M.). Enuretics also have daytime urinary frequency.

Causes of Enuresis.
A. Training:
1. Insufficient training - Usually the mother is over-protective, or physical circumstances have not permitted training.
2. Too early training - Especially if coercive, this may produce confusion and resentment rather than compliance. *
B. Emotional Disturbance: This is the most common cause of enuresis. Enuresis as a symptom of emotional illness has justifiably been likened to headache as a symptom of physical illness. Often there are other behavior difficulties (such as marked shyness, sibling rivalry, temper tantrums) or school problems (especially educational disability).
C. Physical Disease (relatively infrequent):
1. Spina bifida or other lower spinal cord lesions, if significant, are usually accompanied by neurologic sensory changes which may be noted on physical examination.
2. Congenital anomalies of the genitourinary tract, especially the urethral valve. Test for residual urine is diagnostic. Urethral dilatations are psychologically very traumatic as a treatment procedure.
3. Cystitis, tuberculosis, or other infections of the urinary tract usually produce dribbling during day as well as night.
4. Diabetes - Enuresis may be an early symptom of diabetes; a urinary examination is diagnostic.
5. Nocturnal epilepsy may be accompanied by enuresis.

Treatment.
A. Encourage the child to be dry but avoid shaming tactics.
B. Physical Measures: Limit excessive fluids at bedtime and awaken for toilet two to four hours after bedtime.
C. Evaluation of child's total adjustment, particularly the parent-child relationship and the chronology of family events, initiates the most important phase of treatment, which aims at improving the child's emotional relationships. Except for some of those cases where enuresis represents regression linked to a specific traumatic event (e. g., birth of a sibling or the move to a new neighborhood), therapy of enuresis is apt to be rather time-consuming for the physician and may require the help of a psychologist or psychiatrist.
D. Imipramine hydrochloride (Tofranil®) has been empirically useful in treating enuresis, but it appears to be associated with a high relapse rate and its safety is still to be determined.

*Approximately one-third of children continue bedwetting at age three and one-half years, and at least one-fifth do so at five years.

BOWEL CONTROL

Permanent bowel control is usually more easily achieved than bladder control, probably in part because of the individual differences in neurologic maturation involved. If movements are regular, training for bowel movement control may be begun after the age of one year, somewhat earlier than for bladder control. A considerable percentage of children, however, are not ready to start bowel training until close to two years.

Constipation occurs frequently between two and three years and seems to be part of the "negative phase" of this period. The child's withholding of bowel movements seems to represent an attempt on his part to exercise some individual autonomy against demanding, controlling parents. Treatment is aimed at withdrawing parental interest from the gastrointestinal tract; usually the child's interest will gradually decline as well.

Encopresis (involuntary defecation) in an older child may be a transient response to family stress; if persistent, it is best dealt with by a psychiatrist. It may be associated with severe constipation of long duration.

THUMBSUCKING

In the very young child, thumbsucking is related to the need for satisfaction of the oral drive, which is primary at this age. Thumbsucking occurs in both breast-fed and bottle-fed infants who have had sufficient to eat but insufficient sucking. This may reach maximum intensity in the second half of the first year or not until about 18 months. Continued sucking in children beyond two years of age seems to occur particularly at times of boredom or anxiety, when a feeling of security is desired (as at bedtime). Here sucking seems to express a desire for the feelings of security and satisfaction which in infancy were associated with feeding. It is often found when parents are either over-protective or over-demanding or give the child insufficient attention.

Up to the age of five, thumbsucking is not usually considered permanently detrimental to the jaw structure. Malocclusion resulting from late thumbsucking may require some orthodontic repair, but this is usually minor.

Treatment.
  A. Younger Children: Treatment may require only explanation and reassurance to the parents concerning the child's oral needs and some satisfaction of those needs by more prolonged eating and mouthable toys. The use of physical restraints and scolding only serve to aggravate the condition.
  B. Older Children: Thumbsucking in older children again requires some reassurance of the parent. Usually the child has some unrecognized cause for insecurity (e.g., difficulty with school work) or demands more attention and indulgence than the parent is willing to give. Satisfaction of the child's dependent needs may be helpful if it is accompanied by gradual encouragement of independence in activities more consistent with his age.

NAILBITING

Nailbiting is usually overt evidence of anxiety in the older child. Unless associated with other symptoms, it does not usually indicate severe pathology.

MASTURBATION AND SEX INTERESTS

Interest in his genitals and in physical sex differences and pleasure in genital manipulation are normal in the prepubertal child. Awareness of physical sexual differences is present in small children just as is the awareness of social differences between the sexes in dress, games, and mannerisms.

Masturbation is damaging chiefly because of the guilt and shame aroused by adult criticism. Parental anxiety about manifestations of sexuality in children is based upon the unwarranted presumption that these are equivalent to adult sexuality and are abnormal. Aside from occasional slight irritation, there are no physical sequelae. Mental deficiency or psychosis is never caused by masturbation.

If understood by parents, occasional masturbation is usually a transient habit and will disappear if the child is provided with sufficient diverting occupation.

Continued or excessive masturbation in the prepubertal child has usually limited or indirect sexual significance and should rather be viewed as a symptom of insecurity or anxiety indicative of other emotional conflict. In the child after puberty, masturbation would undoubtedly be universal if adult prohibitions were not so strong. Here the conflict is more severe because of genital maturing and accounts for much of the "nonspecific" guilt found in adolescents. Treatment should be focused on the child's emotional relationships and not on the act itself. Reasonable restriction should be placed on the activity for social reasons.

TICS

Tics occur most often between five and ten years of age. They are sometimes attributable to or initiated by some physical cause such as local irritation but usually represent emotional maladjustment, particularly in relation to school or social pressures. Evaluation of adjustment and relief from pressure, when possible, are indicated. For example, the only child who grows up in a family atmosphere where control of aggression is rigid and conformity is expected in all areas may find no acceptable outlet for angry and worried feelings. The facial tic allows some limited and distorted expression of tension, but it provides little or no relief.

Gilles de la Tourette's disease is a form of tic characterized by extensive and varied bodily movements accompanied by vocal grunts which may represent choked-off obscenities.

FEARS AND PHOBIAS

Transient fears are very common in small children, particularly between the ages of two and four, and in part represent a phase of learning about what is strange or potentially dangerous. Fear of animals, loud noises, and strangers is especially common. Attempts to ridicule fears or to force a child into fearsome situations usually aggravate the response. Very gradual exposure to the feared situation, accompanied by explanation and reassurance, are usually most helpful.

A phobia might be considered the displacement of anxiety or fear from an internal unconscious conflict to an external object or situation which can be avoided. Attempts to remove the phobia by rational arguments seldom succeed, but encouraging the child to control the expression of the phobic symptoms may help avoid extension of the symptoms. If the cause of the underlying anxiety can be dealt with, the phobia itself may disappear. One parent or the other will often be found to share the fears or phobias of the child, who has perhaps responded to nonverbal evidences of the parent's anxiety.

School phobia, for example, often represents anxiety at separation from the mother and results from the ambivalent, mutually dependent relationship between mother and child. Efforts should be made to deal with this problem promptly. Consultation with the school will often make possible some compromise on a temporary basis for encouraging the child to attend school. Being accompanied to school by friends, or some flexibility of schedule, may help until the child's and the mother's underlying anxiety can be relieved. Psychosomatic symptoms, such as stomach ache, vomiting, or headache, are often a disguise for school phobia.

TEMPER TANTRUMS

Temper tantrums occur in most children in the latter half of the second year (see Personality Development in Chapter 3). From this point on, there is a gradual decrease in the frequency and severity of tantrums, with perhaps a second peak at about six years of age. Early temper tantrums are uninhibited expressions of frustration and rage. Frustration is frequently due to unsuccessful attempts to perform complicated physical feats or to make oneself understood with inadequate linguistic resources. Treatment consists of relief of these frustrations whenever possible.

Gradual education by the parent toward more acceptable expressions of rage (usually verbal) is the second step. Isolation during the tantrum as an aid to the child in achieving control of feelings is usually helpful. Attempts to retaliate or to appease do not work and are poor education.

DISTURBING PERSONALITY TRAITS

Often a child presents no specific conduct disturbances but social adjustment is poor. Instead of considering the traits mentioned below as inherited and immutable personality characteristics, parents and teachers are now beginning to realize that such traits, if pronounced, are of psychologic significance and that professional advice should be sought.

Aggressiveness or Withdrawal.

These seemingly opposite characteristics are grouped together because they are alike in etiology; both represent an attempt on the part of the child to compensate for a serious lack of satisfaction in some of his relationships. Frequently such characteristic relationships involve the vacillating indulgent-punitive attitudes of some parents, intense rivalry with a sibling, or a feeling of mental or social inferiority.

Evaluation of the child's home, social, and school adjustments is necessary before the significance of the behavior becomes clear.

Fear and Timidity.

Excessive fear or timidity usually occurs when parents are over-protective (thus encouraging fear) or demand too much independence (making the child feel unsupported). Fears usually are overcome not by denial of danger or by refusing to accept the fear itself, but by gradual reassurance and by encouragement of independence. Helping the child to become realistically more competent (e.g., learning how to play baseball, how to ride the bus) increases self confidence.

Dependency.

Parents and teachers frequently complain of a child's "babyishness," his being "immature" for his age. Dependency here implies excessive demands for attention and evasion of a normal amount of responsibility; it usually results from a distorted parent-child relationship. The parent may encourage dependency in order to obtain emotional satisfaction from continued closeness with the child. Conversely, he may thrust the child away before he is ready for the degree of independence demanded. Such parental confusion usually reflects the parent's own unresolved dependency conflicts.

Compulsions and Obsessive Acts.

These occur often in normal children, especially during the primary school years. They may be formally organized by a group of children into a game or as rules for membership in the group. They might, in the individual child, be an attempt to reinforce a rigid (and therefore weak) conscience by rigid compliance with an essentially meaningless ritual, using the ritual as a means of shutting out the feelings and impulses which are feared because they are not socially acceptable.

If obsessive thoughts, fears, and acts become so marked as to interfere seriously with ordinary activity, they can be viewed as neurotic symptoms requiring psychotherapeutic help.

Delinquency.

Much of the delinquency in the U.S.A. may be looked upon as a social illness expressed in the form of a gang whose collective conscience considers society an enemy and therefore fair game. Such delinquency is fostered by the disadvantages of being an underprivileged member of society when these disadvantages are not counteracted by strongly satisfying relationships within the family.

Of more direct concern to the pediatrician is the individual delinquent, particularly the early or first offender who comes from a relatively stable social background. Since a delinquent act implies inadequate prohibition by the conscience, it is worthwhile to assess the degree of guilt over wrongdoing as opposed to the fear of being caught and punished. One should assess not only the strength of the child's conscience but also his relationships to authority figures (parents, teachers) who might provide support and guidance in a conflict over right and wrong.

Many parents of delinquent children admonish strictly but demonstrate by their behavior that they have unrecognized conflicts in the same area as the child. On the other hand, many first offenders who come from a privileged background never reach the courts and never repeat the offense because the forces of authority in the family and community are quickly mobilized to understand and block further delinquent expression.

In occasional cases a repeatedly delinquent child is acting out a need for punishment based on neurotic guilt. Psychotherapy should help. More often, however, repeated delinquency represents a truly defective conscience deriving from the poor quality of early relationships. These children are often depressed, deprived of affection, and have no feeling of self worth. The feeling that someone is on their side is most helpful to them. This does not mean condoning their antisocial behavior but making such behavior less desirable by offering more satisfying ways of coping with underlying problems.

With delinquents, the focus of treatment is not punishment but the development of control over behavior. An environment must be provided in which consistent external control helps to strengthen the child's own inadequate controls. If parents are unable to offer these controls in a way the child can accept (especially in adolescence), placement away from home in a school or foster home may ease the conflict and give the child a less personal but more acceptable aid to self control.

PSYCHOSOMATIC PROBLEMS

The intimate relationship between emotional state and physiologic function (normal and abnormal) is striking from early infancy throughout life. From the mild physiologic deviations such as urinary frequency accompanying examination apprehension to the life-threatening conditions such as anorexia nervosa or duodenal ulcer, it is necessary to recognize the physical components of emotional states. A close working relationship between psychiatrist and pediatrician can make possible the simultaneous treatment of an underlying emotional conflict and of its expression in physical symptoms. There have been many efforts to categorize the personality types that are especially prone to certain illnesses. Dependency conflicts are often seen in patients with ulcers; conflicts involving expression of anger in patients with ulcerative colitis; and problems associated with the acceptance of sexual maturation and femininity may often be present in girls with anorexia nervosa. However, treatment does not consist simply of making conscious the patient's underlying conflicts. It is often difficult to help a patient find a solution to the conflict which will prove to be healthier than the somatic malfunction. Prolonged and combined psychiatric and pediatric treatment may be needed.

Hysterical conversion symptoms are physical complaints without apparent bodily change on physical examination. They represent a neurotic use of physical subjective complaints (pain, anesthesias, paralyses, blindness, etc.) as a substitute expression of unconscious impulses. It is important to definitively rule out physical illness so as to place the focus of treatment in the psychiatrist's office. For example, hysterical partial blindness or tunnel vision in a prepubertal girl may be related to conflicts about "seeing" sexual phenomena; when this diagnosis is made, physical methods of treatment can be bypassed in favor of psychiatric management.

PSYCHOSES

Psychoses are rare before adolescence, although probably not as rare as previous diagnostic figures indicate.

Except for very rare severe depressions, most childhood and adolescent psychoses are schizophrenic in nature. (Mild depression is common as a chronic condition in childhood but is often masked by denial, apathy, or anxious hyperactivity.) The most reliable evidence is probably the persistent withdrawal from any meaningful human relationships, since disorganization of thought systems is difficult to evaluate in the fantasy-rich and inexperienced minds of children. Schizophrenic children often have disturbances in motility (which are not, however, pathognomonic) such as twirling, toe walking, and excessive clinging in a very immature manner. Diagnosis should be tentative until adequate psychiatric evaluation is made and treatment carried out by a psychiatrist. Prognosis for recovery from the psychotic episode is often good, but the ultimate prognosis is not so favorable, since many of these patients have recurrences.

During the earliest years, psychosis may be difficult to differentiate from severe mental retardation; indeed, in many instances, neurologic abnormalities of varying severity may be present along with an otherwise characteristic picture of infantile autism. Neurologic defect may eventually be considered as only one of the handicaps which contribute to the cause of autism.

Early infantile autism is an entity (presumably without neurologic defect) in which the child has never formed an attachment relationship, even with the mother, and in which people are invested with no more emotional interest than physical objects. Symptoms include absent or poorly communicative speech and stereotyped motor behavior with marked anxiety in response to changes in routine.

Symbiotic psychosis is an early interactional psychosis that usually involves a history of a "normal" mother-child relationship during the first year. In symbiotic psychosis, difficulty in separation from the mother is severe and is followed by intense anxiety and regression. Gradual withdrawal and loss of speech may lead to a state similar to infantile autism.

Treatment of psychoses in children requires skillful and prolonged psychotherapy. Prognosis is poor if speech development is absent.

PSYCHOACTIVE DRUGS

Tranquilizers and antidepressants have limited use in pediatrics, chiefly because children are much more prone to act out their conflicts than to suffer from anxiety. In acute anxiety states tranquilizers may be justified, but not on a continuous basis since this usually delays the diagnosis and management of the underlying conflict.

Hyperactive children with brain damage may benefit from a therapeutic trial of medication. The kind of medication depends upon the neurologic status of the child. Anticonvulsant drugs such as mephobarbital (Mebaral®), phenobarbital, and diphenylhydantoin (Dilantin®) may be used if the electroencephalogram indicates a convulsive potential. The use of dextroamphetamine sulfate (Dexedrine®) can be helpful in hyperactive, neurologically impaired children. Methylphenidate (Ritalin®) is felt by many investigators to be superior to dextroamphetamine in the management of hyperactive behavior (again in the absence of a convulsive potential). Both drugs should be given adequate trial in gradually increasing morning and noon doses (see Appendix) over a period of weeks unless such side-effects as irritability, anorexia, and insomnia interfere.

HYPERACTIVITY SYNDROME

The "hyperactivity syndrome" is a well recognized but poorly defined syndrome affecting predominantly boys from the preschool years up through the age of puberty. The major symptoms are hyperactivity, excitability, impulsiveness, and distractibility in the absence of structural neurologic disease and psychosis. When symptoms are severe, the child is brought to the pediatrician in preschool years, often with complaints of uncontrollable behavior. Later, the consultation is usually initiated by the school, where inability to adjust to classroom needs for control and concentration have led to disruptive or aggressive behavior and to academic failure.

The correlation of neurologic and behavioral findings is not consistent, and one must not equate hyperactivity with "minimal brain damage." Hyperactive children may show "soft" neurologic signs on physical examination or may have some increase in diffuse slow activity (plus perhaps transient abnormal discharges) in the EEG. There may be an absence of these findings, or they may occur in children without hyperactivity with other behavior problems. Children with hyperactivity tend as a group to score lower on all psychometric tests of intelligence and perceptual parameters (especially achievement tests), but variations occur from one individual to another.

Response to medication is also variable. There is some indication that the hyperactive children who do not respond to medication often come from families with more serious mental illness.

Anxiety can cause behavior which must be differentiated from the hyperactivity here described. In the group responsive to medication, dextroamphetamine or methylphenidate given in morning and noontime doses can lead to remarkable quieting of activity and increased attention span. Adequate trial requires gradually increasing dosage and several weeks of medication. Special teaching technics to alleviate distractibility or perceptual difficulties are often needed.

11 . . .
Adolescence

PSYCHOLOGIC ASPECTS OF ADOLESCENCE

Concurrently with growth acceleration during adolescence, there occurs an acceleration in ego development. Although the early adolescent generally is socially competent and is able to assume increasing responsibility, he may make unrealistic demands for the privileges that to him represent being "grown up." Many areas of conflict through which the child has passed at an earlier stage of emotional development are reawakened and intensified in late adolescence. Concerns about parental love, sibling rivalry, and about the adolescent's own real or imagined physical or intellectual shortcomings make adolescence a time of great doubt and insecurity.

Characteristically, the adolescent swings quickly from the desire to be more mature to the desire to resort to a childlike state and again become protected by those who love him. While he seeks greater responsibilities at one moment, at the next he may want to be freed of the responsibilities and the demands that are made upon him because he is "growing up." These lightning changes from childish to more mature behavior are frequently puzzling and frightening both to the adolescent and to his parents. The adolescent's constant posing in a great variety of different roles must be regarded as experimentation rather than taken seriously by physicians, parents, and teachers. In general, problems of this nature will be minimized if the adolescent's associates can maintain a consistent, realistic, and supportive attitude.

The rapid acceleration of growth of the child's body during this period may give rise to a variety of carefully hidden fantasies and fears. These physical changes introduce a degree of strangeness into the child's previously comfortable knowledge of his body. This, as well as the fears which may accompany the awakening of sexual drives, concern about masturbation, and the increasing social and school demands may make adolescence a time of intense emotional experience.

Concern with bodily changes may be expressed as a fear of being physically imperfect, and an understanding of this fear of imperfection is of great importance to the physician in the management of adolescent patients. Fears of real or imagined physical imperfections may not be verbalized by the adolescent patient, but they can be brought out into the open by the understanding physician. For example, expressed concerns about being too tall, too short, too fat, too thin, or about acne or dysmenorrhea may symbolize more than concern about the specific complaint; they may instead represent a general intense concern with being physically perfect.

Known imperfections or chronic disease such as diabetes, epilepsy, asthma, or rheumatic fever may present a tremendous emotional problem to the adolescent desiring to be physically perfect. He often rebels against previously well accepted medical advice from a physician whose relationship to the patient has always been good.

Concern with physical perfection may result in various degrees of hypochondriasis. However, suspicion of hypochondriasis should not prevent the physician from carrying out a complete and careful examination to determine the presence of any specific disease. Undue anxiety about minor symptoms should alert the physician to the possibility of underlying hypochondriasis; without minimizing the presenting symptom to the patient, the physician should be prepared to give sympathetic and careful attention to the underlying psychologic problem.

In middle and late adolescence some degree of conflict with authority will probably occur no matter how satisfactory the parent-child relationship has been. A certain degree of limiting authority is essential in spite of the stresses which result, in order to assist the adolescent in defining the boundaries of his own individuality at a time when he is striving for greater maturity and independence. Parents, physicians, and teachers must be aware of the child's need for well defined limits so that they may be sympathetic with unreasonable demands without at the same time giving in to them, especially when these demands conflict with the parents' own values or household or community rules. Parents should realize that an overly compliant adolescent may simply be postponing a process that is essential to maturation.

The Physician's Attitude Toward the Adolescent Patient.

It is impossible to deal adequately with adolescent patients in a hurried manner. The difficulty of providing sufficient time makes the medical care of adolescents extremely difficult. In general, it is desirable for the physician to assume a friendly and supportive attitude, to avoid prying, and to take the adolescent patient and his complaints seriously. In performing the physical examination he should take into consideration the marked shyness that frequently exists in both boys and girls. Adolescent girls should be draped by nurses and should be chaperoned throughout the examination. Vaginal examination should be avoided unless it is specifically indicated.

In initiating the conversation with the adolescent, the physician may use the approach suggested by Bird* and say: "I don't know quite how to talk to people of your age. It doesn't seem fair to talk to you as if you are a child, because in many ways you are no longer a child. But if I treat you completely like an adult, that hardly seems fair, either, because there are still many things about adult life that you do not know and cannot be expected to know."

The Physician and the Parent of the Adolescent Patient.

Counselling of parents is an indispensable part of the management of the adolescent's problem. Parents can often be helped to make a more realistic evaluation of their child's behavior if they understand the normal physical and psychologic changes that occur during adolescence. The physician should not "take sides" in conflicts relating to discipline and behavior; but by showing parents

---

*Bird, B.: Talking With Patients. Lippincott, 1955.

that their child's behavior is common during adolescence, he may
be able to help them to assert authority if they otherwise have been
unable to do so. The teen-ager, in spite of his demands for freedom from control and in spite of his natural desire for independence,
is in actuality afraid that he may not be able to maintain adequate
control over himself. Parents can help by providing realistic standards and good examples of behavior and by insisting upon his co-
operation in matters of discipline and conduct in the home and community. Firm but fair parental authority is of tremendous therapeutic value; even though the adolescent may complain about it at
length, he finds it a reassuring demonstration of his parents' interest in his future welfare and development.

Medical Problems of Adolescence.

A. Hypochondriasis: Once a careful medical examination has
   ruled out physical causes as the basis of headache, dizziness,
   palpitations, insomnia, vague abdominal pains, or other complaints that the adolescent may have, the physician should
   attempt to determine whether they might have a psychosomatic
   basis. Anxiety about these complaints may represent a more
   basic variety of fears, or it may represent the adolescent's
   uneasiness about his own worth. It has been pointed out that
   physical complaints are easier to face and easier to verbalize
   than are psychologic sources of anxiety.

   The adolescent may also use a minor symptom as a means
   of demanding the attention and services of a physician he ad-
   mires as compensation for the attention he feels he deserves
   but does not receive from other adults. The trivial nature of
   the complaint should never cause the physician to reject the
   patient. Interviews with an understanding and kindly physician
   can serve as valuable therapeutic tools in improving hypochon-
   driacal symptoms.

B. Acne: Acne is a serious problem to the adolescent even in its
   mildest form. It may cause him to feel unclean in the emotional as well as the physical sense of the word, and the physician's insistence on skin cleanliness may enhance this fear.
   Some teen-agers regard acne as related to masturbation;
   others may ascribe the condition to some real or imagined sin
   on their part.

C. Dysmenorrhea: Menstrual pain severe enough to cause frequent
   absences from school is a common problem in the teen-age
   period. Unless properly managed it can develop into a fixed
   pattern of disability. The therapeutic approach of greatest
   value consists of a detailed, frank, and simple explanation of
   the menstrual process. This should be done regardless of the
   degree of sophistication the patient assumes, and will frequently alleviate a variety of fears which are based on misunderstanding or misinformation. It is most helpful to point out to
   the teen-ager suffering from dysmenorrhea that, besides the
   disagreeable aspects, this complaint does fully prove the patient's ability to ovulate and therefore ensures the prospect of
   normal motherhood. This frequently places a positive value
   upon an otherwise merely disagreeable physical complaint.

   The use of a drug containing an analgesic agent and a stimulant may be helpful. This may be more effective if given two

to three days prior to the expected onset of menstrual flow; the last daily dose of stimulant-containing drugs should be given no later than 4:00 p.m. to avoid sleeplessness. The adolescent should be encouraged to regard some menstrual discomfort philosophically in order to avoid periodic invalidism.

D. Obesity: The diagnosis of obesity in adolescence should not be based simply upon a variation in weight from that indicated on standard charts. Attention should be paid to the total body configuration, pattern of growth, and weight in the preceding years. Rapid increase in weight during the adolescent period may be related to emotional stress if the child resorts to food as a source of immediate satisfaction and comfort. Obesity on this basis may be helped by repeated interviews with a sympathetic physician; the objective of these conferences should be to allay underlying anxieties and to seek more constructive sources of satisfaction. In families where obesity is common, "good food" may be considered to be important as a source of health and satisfaction or as part of a cultural pattern. Therapy in these cases may be extremely difficult unless the adolescent has a strong desire to lose weight and possesses sufficient intelligence to carry through a program of dietary restriction. The caloric intake of very active adolescents may be extremely large without excessive gain in weight (3500 to 4000 Calories and 100 to 125 Gm. of protein per day for boys; 2500 to 3000 Calories and 75 to 95 Gm. of protein per day for girls). On the other hand, if the child markedly reduces his activity, obesity may occur even though the caloric intake is only average. In these cases increased physical activity must be encouraged.

Care must be taken to provide an adequate intake of protein, calcium, and vitamins with all dietary regimens.

In general, the results of attempting to correct obesity in adolescents have been disappointing.

PHYSICAL ASPECTS OF ADOLESCENCE

During adolescence various physical, psychologic, and endocrine changes occur that have a profound influence on the individual. These changes follow an orderly sequence, but wide individual variations in the time of their appearance may occur. The first signs of adolescent sexual maturation appear between eight and 14 years of age (Table 11-1). They seem to be initiated by neural or neurohumoral stimuli from the hypothalamus; these stimuli cause secretion of gonadotropic hormones by the anterior pituitary, with resultant growth of genital organs and appearance of secondary sex characteristics.

General Biologic Considerations.

Growth during adolescence is a function of biologic rather than of chronologic age.

Growth of different parts of the body may be uneven, and the adolescent may be living on various levels of maturity in different organ systems and functional processes.

A. Variations in Both Sexes: Broadly built children tend to grow faster and mature earlier than slender ones.

B. Variations Between Boys and Girls: Girls mature earlier than boys. They have their adolescent height and weight spurts earlier than boys, and until they are 18 years old their skeletal development exceeds that of boys of the same age.

C. Variations in Male Children: Early in adolescence, some boys (about 10%) have an increase in subcutaneous fat which is commonly lost with the onset of the eventual height spurt; they normally may have swelling and tenderness of either one or both breasts at about the time pubic hair first appears.

D. Variations in Female Children: The menarche occurs between ten and 17 years of age (average: 13 years). It generally takes place within two years of the time when the sesamoid at the distal end of the first metacarpal appears.) Irregularities of menstruation are very common during adolescence, and cycles are anovulatory for the first year or two; consequently,

TABLE 11-1.   Normal pattern of sexual maturation.

Approx. Age (yr.)	Sexual Characteristics		Status of Hormone Production
	Boys	Girls	
3 to 7	Infantile	Infantile. Vaginal pH alkaline.	Very small amounts of 17-K's (both sexes) and estrogens (females) in urine.
7 to 9		Uterus begins to grow.	Estrogens and 17-K's begin to increase.
9 to 10		Growth of bony pelvis. Budding of nipples.	
10 to 11	Increased vascularity of penis and scrotum.	Budding of breasts. May be unilateral at first. Pubic hair appears.	Estrogen excretion greatly increased in the female.
11 to 12	Prostatic activity. Pubic hair appears.	Cornification of vaginal epithelium. Vaginal pH acid. Growth of genitalia.	Gonadotropins demonstrable in urine (both sexes). Estrogen excretion cyclic (female).
12 to 13	Rapid growth of testes and penis.	Axillary hair. Menarche (average $12\frac{1}{2}$ yrs.). Anovulatory menstruation.	
13 to 15	Axillary hair. Down on upper lip. Voice change.	Earliest normal pregnancies can occur.	Pregnanediol in urine during luteal phase (female).
15 to 16	Mature spermatozoa (average, 15 yrs.; range, 11 to 17 yrs.)	Acne.	
16 to 17	Acne.	End of skeletal growth.	
17 to 21	End of skeletal growth.		

pregnancy during this period is very unlikely. Periods of amenorrhea are more likely to occur during the summer than winter.

Girls who menstruate late eventually become taller than those with early onset of menses. The menarcheal ages of mothers and daughters are positively correlated.

Physiologic Considerations of Adolescence.

In both sexes there is an increased need for vitamins (especially vitamin D), calcium, and protein during adolescence. There is an increased incidence of thyroid disturbances (enlargement of the thyroid as well as hypothyroidism and hyperthyroidism), tuberculosis, disturbances of epiphyses, anemia, dental caries, and circulatory instability.

Preceding the onset of menstruation, basal metabolism rises and nitrogen and calcium retentions increase; this is followed by a postmenarche decrease in retention of these minerals and a fall in metabolism.

Striae are common during adolescence even in the non-obese child. They appear to be associated with increased adrenocortical function, although obesity may also play a part.

In females, estrogens are responsible for changes in labia minora, vagina, uterus, and tubes as well as for changes of the nipple and duct structures. Androgens are responsible for pubic and axillary hair and enlargement of clitoris.

TABLE 11-2. Differentiation of complete
and pseudoprecocious development.

Manifestations	True Precocious Puberty	Pseudoprecocious Puberty
Secondary sexual characteristics	Present.	Present.
Penis and testes	Enlarge simultaneously.	Penis enlarges. Testes infantile (except with unilateral tumor).
Spermatogenesis or ovulation	Occurs.	Absent.
Bone age	Moderately incr.	Markedly or moderately incr.
Urinary 17-ketosteroids	Incr. to adolescent levels.	Markedly incr. in males. Normal for age in females.
Urinary gonadotropins	Incr. to adolescent levels.	Not incr. (except with chorionepithelioma).
Familial tendency	Sometimes present.	Absent.

MENSTRUATION
(See also Chapter 22.)

During early adolescence menstrual cycles are anovulatory and painless. The interval between the first few periods may be several months. As time passes the menstrual interval tends to regulate itself, but periodic oligomenorrhea (especially in times of emotional stress) may persist for several years.

DISTURBANCES OF MENSTRUATION

ANOVULATORY BLEEDING OF ADOLESCENCE

Irregular, acyclic anovulatory bleeding (metropathia hemorrhagica) is most frequently functional in nature and may merely represent a variation from normal.

This entity occurs frequently and, in exceptional cases, may be associated with serious acute and chronic blood loss. Endometrial hyperplasia is the only pathologic finding, but the possibility of entities such as incomplete abortion may necessitate pelvic examination. Clotting abnormalities must also be considered.

Estrogen production approximates that in ovulatory cycles, although cyclic variation is not usually obvious.

Treatment.
A. Correct bleeding with a progestin (e.g., medroxyprogesterone acetate [Provera®], 10 mg. orally for the last five days of the month). Bleeding occurs three to six days after discontinuance and is usually limited to five days. Monthly treatment is continued until the patient establishes her own cycles. Normal sexual maturation will not be altered by these doses of hormone.
B. A few patients may continue to complain of spotting and will require additional oral estrogens (e.g., conjugated estrogenic substances [Premarin®], 5 mg. orally daily for 20 days for several cycles - or 10 mg. for young or rapidly bleeding girls); monthly progestin therapy may then be instituted. Preparations with a lower estrogen content often manifest bleeding as a side-effect.
C. If the patient presents with severe hemorrhage and anemia, a rapid cessation of bleeding may be obtained with conjugated estrogenic substances (Premarin®), 20 mg. I.V. immediately and repeated as needed every two to three hours. Oral Premarin®, 5 mg., is also given and repeated daily for 20 days. Medroxyprogesterone acetate (Provera®), 10 mg./day orally, is added the last five days of the period. Iron replacement therapy is also indicated to compensate for the blood loss. Treatment as in A is then initiated one month after withdrawal.
D. Curettage and transfusion may be required in an occasional case, but the need to repeat these measures suggests that ideal replacement therapy has not been achieved.

DYSMENORRHEA
(See also p. 180.)

Dysmenorrhea is one of the commonest menstrual abnormalities of adolescence. In most instances it is manifested by pain alone, but it may be accompanied by vomiting, diarrhea, and dizziness. It is usually a primary condition which occurs in girls who are ovulating and may be an expression of a combination of psychic and physiologic factors which may include: a low pain threshold, ignorance regarding menstruation, inability to accept the feminine role, relative ischemia of the myometrium, hypertonic uterine contractions, and an imbalance in the production of progesterone and estrogen. Secondary dysmenorrhea due to inflammatory disease, cysts of the ovary, endometriosis, and stenosis of the cervix is uncommon in adolescence.

Treatment of primary dysmenorrhea consists of correcting misconceptions about menstruation, reducing tensions, encouraging a regular program of exercise, and administering mild analgesics and antispasmodics. Reversion to anovulatory cycles using cyclic estrogen therapy for a few months may be of value.

DELAYED MENARCHE AND AMENORRHEA

Delayed menarche may be a reflection of complete absence of sexual development (e. g. , in cases of sexual infantilism and gonadal dysgenesis); a congenital malformation (imperforate hymen, absence of uterus, some types of hermaphroditic syndrome); or it may be found in cases which appear to have normal sexual development except for the failure to menstruate.

During the first two years following the first menstrual period the diagnosis of postmenarcheal amenorrhea should be limited to those cases with an interval of 12 months or more between periods. Postmenarcheal amenorrhea may arise from lesions directly impairing some link in the hypothalamic-pituitary-ovarian mechanism which sustains sexual function or from a variety of disorders whose mode of interference with this mechanism is not clear. Cases of amenorrhea may be due to pregnancy; destructive lesions or functional disturbances (emotional disorders) involving the hypothalamus; destructive lesions of the pituitary; certain conditions inducing functional hypopituitarism, hyperthyroidism, hypothyroidism, diabetes mellitus, diseases of the adrenal cortex, chronic infections, debilitating diseases, obesity, and undernutrition; and certain disturbances of the ovaries (menopause praecox, fibrocystic disease, pregnancy).

Rational therapy is dependent upon precise diagnosis. If a patient shows normal feminine secondary sexual development, there is nothing to be gained by hormonal treatment. False amenorrhea due to an imperforate hymen is readily relieved by incision and drainage.

A trial of the progestin may be indicated in the girl suspected of having anovulatory bleeding. In patients without normal female sexual characteristics, a buccal smear or karyotype should be performed to rule out intersex abnormalities (e. g. , Turner's syndrome).

12 . . .
Skin

PRINCIPLES OF TREATMENT

Sensitivity of Skin.
   The child's skin is more sensitive than the adult's, and areas treated with topical medications must be carefully observed for evidence of irritation from too great concentration of drug.

Choice of Topical Medications.
   A. Choice of medication is determined as much by the presenting morphology of a lesion as by the diagnosis. Treat the stage as well as the type of dermatitis.
   B. Familiarity with a limited number of types of medication will prove more useful than attempting to try the immense variety of skin remedies endorsed by others.

Application of Medications.
   A. Under-treatment is sometimes more effective than over-treatment. Improvement in a skin disease sometimes occurs with discontinuance of all therapy.
   B. Treatment Dermatitis: The medication itself may produce a skin lesion, and frequent observation is necessary when a new therapy is tried. Especially when treating allergic conditions such as eczema, the physician should know the antigenic potentialities of the medication in use.
   C. Adequate and complete instructions should be given. The anxious mother must be cautioned against over-enthusiastic application of medication.

Special Diagnostic Procedures.
   A. Microscopic Examination:
      1. Types of specimens -
         a. Scrapings from the edge of an active lesion in suspected fungous infection of skin.
         b. Hair shafts in suspected tinea of scalp.
      2. Preparation of specimen - Put scrapings from possible fungous lesions on a glass slide and add a few drops of 20% potassium or sodium hydroxide solution. Allow to stand for 20 minutes and then examine under the "high-dry" lens of the microscope by diffuse light. In a properly cleared specimen, fungous elements, if present, will be seen as fragments of mycelium and spores of various types.
   B. Examination With Hand Lens: In suspected scabies, examine a non-excoriated burrow with a hand lens and look for the female mite at the end of the burrow or for small black dots of feces

along the burrow. The mite may be demonstrated under the
microscope by teasing it out of the burrow with a delicate
needle or by slicing off the top of the burrow and placing the
whole specimen on a slide.

C. Wood's Light: (Ultraviolet irradiation passed through Wood's
filter.) For diagnosis of Microsporum infections only.
Examine in a darkened room for fluorescence.

D. Patch Tests and Scratch Tests: These are sometimes useful in
determining the possible source of an allergic skin reaction.

1. In the patch test, a piece of gauze containing a solution or
suspension of the suspected allergen is applied to the skin
of the forearm, thigh, or lower back. The gauze is covered
with a piece of plastic material. The test is read after 48
hours, and erythema with or without vesicular reaction is
significant. The test may become positive as late as seven
days after removal of test material.

2. In the scratch test, solutions of substances potentially allergenic are applied to the skin of the same areas of the body
as in the patch test. The test solutions are best obtained
from commercial sources. A drop of solution is placed on
the skin, and the tip of a pin or scalpel is drawn through it
without causing bleeding. The test is read after 15 minutes.
Significant reactions are erythema and edema.

CONGENITAL DISEASES OF THE SKIN

PIGMENTED NEVI

Freckles (Ephelides).

The simplest form of nevus and almost a "normal" condition.
However, freckles may constitute a cosmetic problem when confluent or especially numerous. Freckles are small, brown, pigmented macules more commonly located in areas exposed to sunlight. They may disappear in seasons when there is little sunlight.

Avoid excessive exposure to sunlight to prevent excessive
freckling.

True Pigmented Nevi (Moles).

These very common lesions vary from light brown to almost
black in color. They may be present at birth (2 to 3% of white infants) or may appear during the first five years of life.

A. Types:
1. Nevus spilus - Smooth, flat, no hair.
2. Nevus pilosus - With a growth of downy or stiff hair.
3. Nevus verrucosus - Hyperkeratotic, raised, sometimes
wart-like areas.

B. Treatment:
1. Nevus spilus - May be excised for cosmetic reasons or if
subject to trauma or repeated irritation. Electrodesiccation
and cryotherapy are contraindicated. Tissue removed
should be submitted to pathological examination to rule out
malignant melanoma.

2. Nevus verrucosus - May be removed surgically for cosmetic reasons.
3. Any pigmented nevus that is subjected to repeated irritation from clothing or infection should be surgically removed.

C. Prognosis: Good for all types except when there is microscopic evidence of nevus cell invasion of the epidermis.

VASCULAR NEVI

These nevi consist of an abnormal mass of blood vessels of the skin which may be discolored or tumor-like.

Nevus Flammeus ("Port Wine Mark").

This is a smooth, flat, superficial angioma which varies in color from red to dark purple. It is located most often on the face or neck, and varies in size from a few mm. to an area which covers most of the face and neck.

A. Treatment: Surgery, irradiation, or tattooing may be carried out but only by an expert. Cosmetic creams may mask lesions of small size.

B. Prognosis: The less intensely colored types often disappear spontaneously in infancy or early childhood.

Capillary Hemangioma ("Strawberry Mark").

A slightly raised, sharply demarcated, bright red spot varying from several mm. to 2 to 3 cm. in diameter which does not blanch completely on pressure. It usually appears during the first six weeks of life (occasionally is present at birth). Commonly there is an increase in size for a few months, but few such nevi will continue to increase after 12 months of age.

A. Treatment: Treatment is rarely indicated and only for those lesions of face, scalp, and other areas where trauma or infection may produce bleeding, ulceration, and scarring, or where the lesions are of such size and location as to cause psychological trauma during early childhood before natural regression of the condition has occurred. Carbon dioxide freezing is the treatment of choice, but x-ray irradiation or surgery, undertaken by a physician trained in these types of therapy, also produces satisfactory results if carried out before the age of 18 months. After that time, removal by these means is difficult.

B. Prognosis: Most such hemangiomas will spontaneously regress and disappear by ten years of age.

Cavernous Hemangioma.

These tumors are formed from large, sinus-like blood vessels in the skin and often have a capillary component. They are raised, poorly circumscribed, blue to purple and are readily blanched by pressure. Distribution and behavior are similar to the capillary type. Although most cavernous hemangiomas regress spontaneously, serious hemorrhage may result from trauma, and indications for therapy are therefore more liberal than for capillary hemangiomas.

A. Treatment: Radium or x-ray irradiation (and sometimes also injection of sclerosing material) or surgical excision (large, deep tumors) when treatment is indicated.

B. Prognosis: Most lesions will involute spontaneously. However, some persist, and some may become arteriovenous fistulas. They occasionally accompany retrolental fibroplasia or internal hemangiomas in vital organs.

ICHTHYOSIS

Abnormal cornification of the skin, characterized by generalized thickening, scaling, and marked dryness. It is usually present at birth. With increase in age, as cracks appear in the folds and there is continued exfoliation of the epidermis in irregular patches, the skin may resemble fish skin or alligator hide. Mild cases, often passing for "dry skin," are relatively common.

The patient should bathe infrequently with synthetic, non-fat soap and lubricate the skin with mineral oil each day. Vitamin A, 10,000 to 20,000 units per day during the winter months, may be of some value. Topical administration of vitamin A, 0.05% in polyethylene glycol (Retin A®), has been most promising.

Improvement may occur with simple treatment measures, but the prognosis for recovery is hopeless for some cases and very poor for moderate cases.

UNCOMMON CONGENITAL SKIN DISORDERS

Anhidrotic Ectodermal Dysplasia.

A rare familial syndrome characterized by marked inhibition of sweating, sparse hair, alteration of the nails; dry, white, smooth, glossy skin; saddle nose, prominent supraorbital ridges, and faulty dentition. Convulsions with fever occur due to decreased ability to dissipate heat through evaporation. A hearing defect may also be present. There is increased sodium chloride content in the sweat (see Appendix).

Epidermolysis Bullosa.

This sometimes familial disorder appears at any age but most commonly in early infancy. Vesicles and large bullae develop following trauma to the skin. The prognosis is variable depending on the form of the disease.

Keratosis Pilaris.

A fairly common condition characterized by a fine papular eruption limited to the pilosebaceous orifices, giving the skin a rough, granular texture. Some cases are associated with a deficiency of vitamin A, but in others no etiology can be determined. Treatment with vitamin A, 10,000 to 20,000 units daily, may be tried, and mild, emollient keratolytic agents also may be helpful. Bathing should be restricted and only synthetic nonfat soap used.

Cutis Hyperelastica.

A condition characterized by extreme elasticity of the skin. The skin may appear normal but can be extended by pinching and pulling. When released it snaps back as though it were a sheet of rubber. No treatment is necessary.

Ehlers-Danlos Syndrome.
This consists of skin hyperelasticity and friability, fragility of blood vessels, hyperextensibility of the joints, and at times multiple, freely movable subcutaneous fatty nodules. Prophylaxis against injury is most important. No specific therapy is available.

Adenoma Sebaceum.
Pinhead-sized to pea-sized, rounded, elevated papules or nodules situated particularly upon the nose, cheeks, and chin. The color may be that of normal skin, waxy, or reddish, and there may be an associated telangiectasia. Adenoma sebaceum may occur in association with tuberous sclerosis. Mental deficiency and convulsions may be associated with either condition in a familial pattern.

Treatment consists of applying carbon dioxide snow to the lesions. Surgical planing is the treatment of choice. Larger adenomas may require electrodesiccation. Recurrence of lesions is common.

Ritter's Disease (Dermatitis Exfoliativa Neonatorum).
See Table 9-1.

INCONTINENTIA PIGMENTI

Incontinentia pigmenti is a rare hereditary disorder, most common in females, characterized by developmental defects of the skin, anomalies of dentition (pointed, wide teeth), concomitant neurologic symptoms, osseous deformities, and alopecia. In the neonatal period skin lesions are erythematous and vesicular; these become verrucous and then pigmented, and eventually fade.

DEPIGMENTATION
(Albinism, Vitiligo)

Generalized depigmentation (albinism) is rare. Localized depigmentation (vitiligo) may occur on any part of the body, and the hair of the affected area is white. The cause is not known, but these disorders may be associated with endocrine abnormalities. Treatment is unsatisfactory.

DISEASES DUE TO BACTERIA

IMPETIGO

Clinical Findings.
A. Impetigo of the newborn.
B. Impetigo Contagiosa: In older children, due to group A streptococcus or staphylococcus. Multiple lesions of varying sizes and shapes, with vesicles, blebs, and crusts on an erythematous base. With healing at the center of the lesion, circinate lesions may be mistaken for ringworm.

C. Ecthyma: Differs from impetigo only in that the lesions are
   more deep-seated and are therefore likely to leave pigmentation
   and slight scarring.

Treatment.
A. Impetigo of the newborn.
B. Impetigo Contagiosa and Ecthyma:
   1. Local measures -
      a. Rupture all intact vesicles or mature pustules, and re-
         move crusts and other debris by washing with antiseptic
         detergent (pHisoHex®) and water. Wet dressings to soak
         the crusts may be necessary before crusts can be removed.
      b. Apply antibiotic ointment (not penicillin) in water-soluble
         base at lease three times a day for five days.
         (1) Bacitracin ointment.
         (2) Neomycin ointment.
         (3) Bacitracin-polymyxin combination.
   2. General Measures - Many cases are resistant to local ther-
      apy and will require systemic antibiotics. Erythromycin
      is the drug of first choice.

Prognosis.
   Impetigo generally responds well to therapy, but skin lesions
may act as primary sites for metastatic infections.
   Observe for nephritis and other complications of staphylococcus
or streptococcus infections.

FOLLICULITIS

   Follicle infections may be superficial or deep. The lesion
consists of pinhead-sized or slightly larger pustules surrounded by
a narrow area of erythema. Many pustules are usually present in
the same area. The commonest cause is a staphylococcus.
   Folliculitis is most often secondary to intertrigo and chronic
irritation of the skin (e. g., from diapers), but it may be secondary
to drainage of chronic otitis media or similar source of purulent
material.

Treatment.
   Essentially the same as for impetigo, with rupture of all
localized pustules and application of antibiotic ointment. The
systemic use of antibiotics is reserved for cases with fever and
complicating cellulitis. For prophylaxis, see under furunculosis
below.

FURUNCULOSIS

   Furuncles usually start as painful, deep-seated infections of a
sebaceous gland or hair follicle which gradually approach the surface and appear red and elevated. After several days, the skin in
the center becomes thin and a pustule may form. With rupture or
after careful incision, a "core" of necrotic material, together with
liquid pus, is discharged.

The fusion of several furuncles produces a carbuncle.

Multiple, recurrent furuncles may occur in certain children (usually over the age of five years). The cause is unknown. Bouts may continue to recur over several years and usually cease after adolescence.

Treatment.
A. Local Measures:
   1. Immobilization of affected part if an extremity is involved.
   2. Heat (in the form of warm moist saline dressings frequently renewed; see Table 12-1.) and drainage after the lesions become localized and fluctuant. Deep incisions are not necessary; a small incision with a needle or scalpel is sufficient. A furuncle must never be squeezed. During drainage, an antibiotic ointment dressing may be applied.
B. General Measures:
   1. Prophylaxis of folliculitis and furunculosis -
      a. Rule out diabetes in recurrent cases.
      b. Treat possible contributory skin disease -
         (1) Seborrhea or excessive oil on skin.
         (2) Excessively dry skin.
         (3) Acne.
   2. Control of nasal carrier state is most effective in preventing recurrent furunculosis. Instill as ointment 5 mg. neomycin per Gm. water-soluble base, twice daily for one month.
   3. Daily bathing and cleansing of the entire body with pHiso-Hex® is most important. This should be vigorously carried out for at least one month.
C. Specific Measures: Systemic antibiotics are sometimes necessary in cases of recurrent furunculosis. Erythromycin (see p. 85) is the drug of first choice. Vaccines and toxoids have not proved to be effective.

DISEASES DUE TO FUNGI

Principles of Treatment and Prophylaxis.
A. Treat acute active fungous infections initially as for any acute dermatitis; it may be necessary to treat the dermatitis before using fungicidal medication.
B. Most fungicidal agents are strong skin irritants. Undertreat rather than overtreat.
C. Keep skin dry. Moist skin favors the growth of fungi.
D. Group or community showers or bathing places, if not strictly supervised, should be avoided.

TINEA CIRCINATA OR TINEA CORPORIS
(Body Ringworm)

Lesions begin as one or more irregular, erythematous, slightly raised, scaly patches which are soon covered with small vesicles. The lesions tend to spread, but central clearing occurs and results in the typical ring-shaped lesion with the active lesions around the healed center. Itching may be present but is usually mild. The usual location is on face, neck, hands, and forearms, but any part of the body may be affected.

Most common cause is animal-born Microsporum lanosum from a cat or dog.

Treatment.
A. Local Measures: If intense inflammation is present, first use soothing measures and then apply either of the following preparations three times per day for at least two weeks.
   1. Benzoic and salicylic acid ointment (Whitfield's ointment), $1/4$ strength (see Table 12-1).
   2. Ointment of zincundecate (undecylenic acid and zinc undecylenate) may be used in the less chronic and thickened lesions.
B. Fungicidal Measures:
   1. Tolnaftate (Tinactin®), 1% cream applied to lesions twice a day for two to four weeks, depending on response.
   2. Griseofulvin (Fulvicin®, Grifulvin®) or griseofulvin microsized (Grisactin®), for four to eight weeks, depending upon response.
C. General Measures:
   1. Avoid contact with infected household pets.
   2. Avoid exchange of clothes without adequate laundering.

TINEA CRURIS
(Eczema Marginatum, "Jock Itch")

Lesions are sharply circumscribed, red plaques with a tendency to heal in the center, but the clinical appearance may be modified by perspiration and bacterial contamination. They are commonly found in the inguinal region during adolescence and may become acutely inflamed and macerated.

Treatment.
See Principles of Treatment and Prophylaxis, above.
A. Local Measures:
   1. Secondarily infected or inflamed lesions are treated with potassium permanganate, 1:10,000 (or 1:20 aluminum acetate solution), wet compresses; perineal areas should be treated with local soaks by sitz baths (see Table 12-1).
   2. Fungicidal medicaments -
      a. Sulfur (3 to 4%) and resorcinol (2%) lotion, b.i.d.
      b. Weak solution of iodine (not more than 1% tincture), b.i.d.
      c. Ointment of zincundecate (undecylenic acid and zinc undecylenate), b.i.d.
      d. Salicylic acid (1%) and sulfur (3%) ointment.
      e. If the above measures are not successful, give griseofulvin (Fulvicin®, Grifulvin®) as for tinea corporis.
B. General Measures:
   1. Dusting powder should be used on involved area two or three times a day, especially when perspiring excessively.
   2. Bathing - Keep area clean and dry, but avoid overbathing.
   3. Avoid rough-textured clothing.

EPIDERMOPHYTOSIS; DERMATOPHYTOSIS
("Athlete's Foot," Tinea of Palms and Soles)

Fungous infection in the interdigital areas is probably very widespread in older children and adults and does not always produce clinical manifestations. The causative organisms are Trichophyton and Epidermophyton. Three basic types of lesions are found.
A. Red, dry, scaly, and fissured eruptions between the toes.
B. Acute, tense, papulovesicular, and bullous eruptions on the soles or on the sides of the feet.
C. Dry, scaly, thickened areas between the toes or on palms.

Treatment.
A. Local Measures: **Do not overtreat.**
    1. Acute stage (one to ten days) - Treat as for any acute dermatosis, using soaks (see Table 12-1) for 20 minutes b.i.d. or t.i.d. If mild secondary infection is present, use 1:10,000 potassium permanganate soaks.
    2. Subacute stage - Any of the following may be used:
        a. Ointment of zincundecate (undecylenic acid and zinc undecylenate), b.i.d.
        b. Whitfield's ointment, $1/4$ to $1/2$ strength.
    3. Chronic stage - Use any of the following:
        a. Iodine as 0.1 to 1% tincture; paint on areas daily.
        b. Benzoic and salicylic acid (Whitfield's ointment), $1/4$ to $1/2$ strength.
        c. Ointment of zincundecate b.i.d.
        d. Tolnaftate (Tinactin®) solution twice daily.
B. General Measures: Put special emphasis on personal hygiene.
    1. Wear rubber or wooden sandals in community showers and bathing places.
    2. Wear well-ventilated shoes, if possible.
    3. Dry carefully between toes after bathing.
    4. Change socks frequently.
    5. Use dusting and drying powders on affected areas p.r.n.
    6. 1% sodium hypochlorite solution foot-soaks before and after bathing in community showers are of questionable value.

FUNGOUS INFECTIONS OF THE SCALP
(Tinea Capitis, Tinea Tonsurans)

Fungous infections of the scalp are common in children and rare in adults. Specific etiology must be determined because it guides treatment. The most common cause is Microsporum lanosum, which is transmitted from an animal source (cat or dog). It is not infectious from child to child, and spores are not easily seen microscopically. Microsporum Audouini infections are rare; they are transmitted from a human source and are highly infectious from child to child (epidemics occur in schools). Spores are easily seen microscopically. Achorion (Trichophyton) schoenleini infection (favus) is extremely rare in the U.S.A. Trichophyton tonsurans infection is relatively common in Southwest U.S.A.

Clinical Findings.

Clinical appearance is consistent and usually easily recognized, beginning as small, rounded, reddened, scaly patches on any part of the scalp. Lesions consist of rounded, hairless, slightly reddened areas covered with grayish scales and broken stumps of hair.

A. Fluorescence of the active lesions can be seen under Wood's light in Microsporum infections; trichophyta do not fluoresce.

B. Microscopic examination of hair treated with potassium hydroxide shows round spores along a shaft.

Treatment.

A. Clip hair closely in vicinity of lesions. Scrub scalp with synthetic nonfat soap each night. Apply one of the following medications for a trial period of at least one week:
  1. Mild tincture of iodine (2%) each night after scrubbing.
  2. Ointment salicylanilide (5%) in Carbowax® twice each day.
  3. Half-strength Whitfield's ointment twice each day.
  4. Undecylenic acid ointment each morning and night for scalp has been washed.

B. Antifungal Medications:
  1. The treatment of choice is with griseofulvin (Fulvicin®, Grifulvin®), 20 mg./Kg./day in three doses, or griseofulvin micro sized (Grisactin®), 10 mg./Kg./day in three doses. Continue for four to eight weeks, depending on response. Leukopenia may be indication to stop drug.
  2. Tolnaftate (Tinactin®), 1% solution or 1% cream locally three times daily for one to six weeks.

C. Epilation of the entire scalp may be necessary. This should be done only by a radiologist or dermatologist.

D. Follow-up Care: Check results for several months by observing clinical appearance and by examining with Wood's light.

Prophylaxis.

Treatment of infected individuals or household pets, with re-examination to determine cure, is essential. Avoid exchange of headgear. In epidemics, examine all potential cases with Wood's light and treat infected individuals.

Prognosis.

Chief complication is formation of kerions (abscess-like swellings). Trichophyton tonsurans infections, which are now extending over the U.S.A. from West to East, are resistant to simple forms of treatment and usually require griseofulvin (Fulvicin®, Grifulvin®) treatment.

TINEA VERSICOLOR

Tinea versicolor is an uncommon childhood disease caused by Microsporum furfur and characterized by small yellowish-brown macules which slowly spread and coalesce to form large brownish patches covered with a fine, furfuraceous, mealy scaling, usually over the chest and back. Treatment with sodium thiosulfate, 10% aqueous solution, b. i. d.; Whitfield's ointment, 1/4 to 1/2 strength;

zincundecate ointment or other mild fungicidal agents, b.i.d.; or tolnaftate (Tinactin®), 1% solution or 1% cream locally, is usually effective.

CANDIDIASIS
(Moniliasis)

Common in early infancy and usually the result of monilial infection (Candida albicans) in the mother's vagina. The eruption may resemble eczema and may be scaly, papulovesicular, and erythematous, with a sharp border. It usually occurs in moist areas of the body which are subject to rubbing, most often in the diaper area, axillae, and the inguinal regions. However, it may cause a generalized skin eruption or become invasive and produce a variety of visceral lesions. It is often associated with monilial infection of the mouth ("thrush") and may be a complication of hypoparathyroidism, diabetes mellitus, or prolonged antibiotic therapy.

Treatment.
  A. Local Measures:
    1. Moist soaks (aluminum acetate solution) if lesions are acutely inflamed and wet.
    2. Iodochlorhydroxyquin (Vioform®), 3% in cream or hydrophilic ointment, applied three times daily. Some infants may react with marked rash, necessitating discontinuation of this preparation.
    3. Nystatin (Mycostatin®) cream, 100,000 U./Gm. applied to the lesions three times daily.
    4. Keep area dry.
  B. Thrush: Any of the following may be used.
    1. Suspension of nystatin (Mycostatin®), 100,000 U./ml., 10 drops applied to mouth four times daily after ingestion of food or milk.
    2. Gentian violet, 1:10,000 in 10% alcohol (or 1% aqueous solution), applied locally to lesions in mouth twice daily for three or four days. Avoid prolonged use.
    3. Sodium borate (25%) in glycerin applied locally twice daily.

DISEASES DUE TO VIRUSES

VERRUCAE

While not all types of "warts" have definitely been shown to be infectious or to be caused by viruses, the evidence of apparent autoinoculation and person-to-person spread in the various types of "warts" is most suggestive.

Clinical Findings.
  A. Verruca Vulgaris (the common wart): A sharply circumscribed, firm, round elevation of the skin which may have a

roughened, thick surface or papillary protuberances. It is
common in childhood and usually appears in multiple distribution on hands or feet.
B. Verruca Plana Juvenilis (flat or plane wart): A small, round,
slightly elevated, flat lesion, usually the color of the surrounding skin. It is common in children and usually occurs in linear
distribution on the face, neck, or on the backs of the hands.
C. Verruca Plantaris (plantar wart): Represents a common wart
(verruca vulgaris) modified by pressure, which forces the
hypertrophied epithelium into the skin and by irritation stimulates further cornification. It is located on the soles of the feet
and appears either singly or in groups.

Treatment.
   Treatment of all warts is not entirely satisfactory. Cases have
been reported of spontaneous disappearance after psychotherapy
("suggestion" therapy), but this corresponds to the rate of spontaneous disappearance without psychotherapy.
A. Verruca vulgaris is best removed by curettage followed by
cauterization of the base with 50% trichloroacetic acid (except
on face, where scarring may result). Chemical cauterization
with 60% salicylic acid ointment is also effective. Apply the
ointment for two days, scoop out the macerated tissue, and re-
apply the ointment.
B. Verruca plana juvenilis should rarely be surgically excised.
Cryotherapy with liquid nitrogen is most successful for this
type of verruca as well as for verruca vulgaris.
C. Verruca Plantaris:
   1. Surgical removal by scalpel or electrodesiccation is the
   only consistently successful treatment procedure. Patient
   is usually incapacitated for about one week after each operation.
   2. Application of liquid nitrogen or chemical cauterization may
   be attempted and has a better than 50% chance of at least
   partial success.
      a. Trichloroacetic acid applied carefully to the center of
      the wart, protecting surrounding skin with vaseline.
      Several applications may be required, with removal of
      the desiccated area before each procedure.
      b. 40% salicylic acid plaster for 24 hours, followed by re-
      moval of macerated material and reapplication of plaster.

HERPES SIMPLEX CUTANEOUS
INFECTION: See Chapter 24.

ECZEMA HERPETICUM
(Kaposi's Varicelliform Eruption)

   A syndrome in children which results from a primary infection
with herpes simplex virus or secondary infection with vaccinia and
is characterized by a vesicular eruption and a febrile reaction complicating a preexisting atopic dermatitis or eczema. The lesions
go through the same stages as those of herpes simplex (vesiculation,
umbilication, and crusting). Death may result.

Dye-light procedures may be most useful in treatment (see p. 473).

MOLLUSCUM CONTAGIOSUM

Molluscum contagiosum is an uncommon contagious virus infection characterized by scattered pinhead-sized to pea-sized, waxy, white or pale pink, centrally umbilicated papules which contain a white, cheesy material. They occur mainly on the face and trunk but may occur on the extremities as well. They have a characteristic histologic picture (molluscum bodies).

Treatment.
The individual lesions may be excised with a sharp curet and cauterized with tincture of iodine or phenol solution, or treated by electrodesiccation. The patient should be examined subsequently to make certain that autoinoculation has not recurred.

DISEASES DUE TO PARASITES

PAPULAR URTICARIA

A very common skin eruption of infancy and early childhood which is associated with the bite of common dog or cat fleas, bedbugs, or human fleas, and is the result of sensitivity to these types of insects. It is commonly seen during the warmer months and usually disappears if the child is removed from exposure to the insect source. Lesions are distributed mostly on arms, legs, and exposed areas of the face and neck. The initial lesion is a small papule which itches and is soon excoriated. Secondary infection is very common.

Differentiate from varicella, scabies, and pediculosis.

Treatment.
Removal or at least partial control of insect sources in and around the house by means of spray of 5% DDT or use of 5% DDT powder dusted on dogs, cats, cushions, rugs, and around baseboards. Powder may be dusted on bedclothes and mattress.

Local treatment of itching lesions with phenolated calamine lotion is rarely necessary.

SCABIES

An infestation of the skin with Sarcoptes scabiei, an insect mite which is rarely visible with the naked eye.

Clinical Findings.
A. The Initial Lesion: This consists of a small vesicle at the point of entrance of the parasite into the skin and a linear elevation of the skin caused by the burrowing of the insect through the superficial layers. The subsequent reaction con-

sists of vesicles, papules, scaling, and excoriations in linear distribution. These "runs" are found most frequently on the interdigital surfaces, the axillary, cubital, and popliteal folds, and the inguinal region. Facial lesions are rarely observed except in nursing infants whose mothers have scabetic lesions on the breasts. Itching is intense, especially at night and when warm, and excoriation from scratching is commonly seen. Secondary infection is common.

B. Diagnosis: The diagnosis is confirmed by dissection of burrow and microscopic examination of the scrapings for the mite.

Treatment.
A. Local Measures: Any of the following may be used.
1. Gamma benzene hexachloride (Gexane® or Kwell®), 1% in cream base, applied each night for three nights is the treatment of choice.
2. Application of 10% crotamiton cream (Eurax®) once daily for two days to the entire body.
3. Benzyl benzoate - Give preliminary and follow-up shower, and instruction for changes of linens. Apply benzyl benzoate emulsion (see Table 12-1) morning and evening for two days, using a paint brush or an ordinary hand insecticide spray.
4. Sulfur (if above measures are not available) - After preliminary bath or shower, sulfur ointment, 4 to 5%, is rubbed in from neck to toes each night for three to five nights. Do not change clothing or bed linen or bathe during this period. On the day after final application of sulfur, repeat bath and shower, change clothing and linen. Soothing baths or shake lotion (see Table 12-1) may be necessary during treatment in patients with sensitive skins.

B. Check all contacts and treat as indicated. Dogs may be a source of infestation.

PEDICULOSIS
(Louse Infestation)

Clinical Findings.
A. Pediculus capitis: Severe itching of the scalp with excoriation, secondary infection, and enlargement of occipital and cervical nodes. Ova are attached to hairs as small, round, gray lumps (called "nits").
B. Pediculus corporis: Produces intense itching and multiple scratch marks and excoriations. Close examination will reveal hemorrhage points or spots where the lice have extracted blood. Lesions are most common on the upper back, sides of the trunk, and the upper outer arms. The insect lives in the folds of clothing and is present on the skin only when foraging.
C. Pediculus pubis: Extremely rare in children. May affect eyebrows or axillary areas.

Treatment.
All forms of louse infestation can be eradicated by dusting with DDT powder (10% in talc or pyrophyllite). Special technics are given below.
For head and pubic lice, other synthetic pediculocides are also

effective, quick in action, and relatively non-irritating. These include Topocide® (a mixture of DDT, benzyl benzoate, and benzo-
caine in water plus a wetting agent), and Kwell® (gamma benzene
hexachloride in a greaseless base). Topocide® is applied twice at
12-hour intervals, while Kwell® need be applied only once.

A. Pediculus capitis: Dust hair thoroughly each day for five days
   with DDT powder and then shampoo vigorously. Repeat treatment at end of two weeks and recheck for "nits." Launder all
   clothes. A simple measure for the removal of the ova is to
   comb the scalp daily with a fine comb dipped in hot vinegar
   (dilute acetic acid).
B. Pediculus corporis: Dust 10% DDT powder over body and in all
   folds of clothing. Treat extra clothing by dry-cleaning, steam-
   ing, or with DDT powder.
C. Pediculus pubis: 10% DDT powder dusted along eyelids or in
   axillary or pubic area daily for five days.

DISEASES DUE TO PHYSICAL
AND CHEMICAL AGENTS

DIAPER DERMATITIS
(Intertrigo, Diaper Rash)

A condition which is to be expected in at least a mild form at
some time during the diaper-wearing stage of infancy.

Clinical Findings.
A. Mild Form: Essentially a chafing reaction which occurs where
   two moist skin surfaces are in apposition or where normal skin
   is subjected to the prolonged irritation of a wet diaper. The
   lesion consists of a patch or a diffuse erythematous reaction
   covering the perineal area, the buttocks, and the genitals. If
   the region about the external urethra is involved there may be
   pain on urination.
B. Ammoniacal Diaper Dermatitis: Produces papulovesicular
   lesions which become umbilicated, leaving ulcer-like craters.
   The dermatitis is caused by the ammonia which is formed in
   the voided urine by the action of urea-splitting bacteria in the
   diaper or on the skin. There may also be an associated ulceration about the external urethral meatus in circumcised male
   infants.
C. Infection of Diaper Dermatitis: May occur as -
   1. Monilial infection.
   2. Folliculitis - Due to skin and intestinal bacteria. Most
      common. May be confirmed by microscopic examination
      of smear or culture. Marked erythema with sharp border.
   3. Vaccinia of diaper area - Associated with primary vacci-
      nation against smallpox; resembles very severe ammoniacal
      dermatitis.

Treatment.
A. Mild Form:
   1. Exposure of diaper area during day to warm, dry air. This

is best accomplished during sleep and with infant lying on folded diapers. An incandescent lamp may be placed at a safe distance over the exposed buttocks.

2. Application of a paste made from corn starch and water.
3. Application of zinc oxide ointment or starch lotion at night. (See Table 12-1.)

B. Ammoniacal Type: More extensive exposure to mild heat.
C. Infection: Treat as for impetigo or moniliasis. Vaccinia should be treated as for severe ammoniacal diaper rash.

Prophylaxis.

Preventive measures are more important than treatment and should be a part of any treatment regimen.

A. Local Measures:
1. Change diapers as frequently as feasible.
2. Wipe diaper area two or three times daily with 1:1000 quaternary ammonium chloride solution.
3. After fecal soiling, cleanse diaper area with cottonseed oil or mineral oil instead of with water.
4. Avoid tight-fitting water-proof pants. These confine and concentrate ammonia in the diaper area.
5. Apply protective ointment such as zinc oxide paste (see Table 12-1) or petrolatum at the earliest sign of erythema.

B. Washing of Diapers: Use mild detergent soap and rinse thoroughly. After washing, rinse in ammonium chloride solution (1:10,000 to 1:25,000 concentration) and allow to dry.

MILIARIA RUBRA
("Prickly Heat," "Heat Rash")

This disorder is extremely common in infancy and early childhood. It is caused by heat from external environment or excessive clothing. Miliaria sometimes occurs during febrile disease and must be differentiated from exanthemata, such as varicella.

Clinical Findings.

Lesion consists of pinhead-sized erythematous papules situated at the openings of sweat glands and is thus distributed where sweat glands are concentrated (i.e., face, neck, shoulders and chest).

The lesions may become inflamed and pruritic (miliaria rubra) or appear as small pearl-colored papules (sudamina).

Treatment.

A. Starch lotion (see Table 12-1) may be useful.
B. Miliaria disappears rapidly if excessive clothing is removed and child is kept cool and dry.

DERMATITIS VENENATA
("Poison Ivy" or "Poison Oak")

A contact type of dermatitis due to a vegetable antigen found in Rhus toxicodendron (ivy) and Rhus diversiloba (oak). Dermatitis venenata may also result from contact with contaminated clothes or the fur of a dog or cat.

Clinical Findings.
    Eruption appears from several hours to a few days after contact with the plant. The lesion consists of multiple vesicles, papules, and blebs on an erythematous base and is accompanied by intense itching and burning. There may be swelling of the involved area. Vesicles often appear in linear streaks from brushing against twigs or leaves. In the severe forms, the nephrotic syndrome may occur.

Treatment.
    The objective of treatment is to counteract the poison in severe cases and simply to relieve itching in the milder cases.
    A. Local Measures:
        1. Small areas - Symptomatic relief is obtained with a soothing antihistaminic lotion or calamine lotion with phenol.
        2. Larger areas - Exudation and swelling may be present.
            a. Warm, moist compresses of Burow's solution.
          or b. A bath in tub with lukewarm potassium permanganate solution (see Table 12-1).
    B. General Measures:
        1. One of the barbiturates or chlorpromazine, as a sedative, and an antihistaminic drug as an antipruritic may be useful.
        2. In severe forms - Local application of hydrocortisone cream, 1 to 2.5%, two to four times a day. Orally administered hydrocortisone or prednisone may be indicated (see Chapter 22).

Prophylaxis.
    A. Destruction of plants may be carried out by manual removal or by chemical means (2, 4-D or 2, 4, 5-T) near dwellings and in areas frequented by people.
    B. Avoid Rhus-infested areas or wear adequate protective clothing.
    C. Thorough washing of the skin with detergent soap and water within a few minutes of exposure may be of value in preventing the development of lesions.
    D. Desensitization procedures may be dangerous due to occurrence of anaphylactic reaction or other type of serious generalized allergic reaction.

DISEASES OF UNKNOWN ETIOLOGY

ACNE

    This disease represents, in part, an overactivity of the sebaceous glands and is characteristic of adolescence (see Chapter 11), but the etiology is unknown. Endocrine and nutritional factors have been implicated. Mild forms should be considered a "normal" finding in adolescence.

Clinical Findings.
The primary lesion is the comedo, a plug of sebum filling the pilosebaceous orifice, which produces a "blackhead" or "whitehead." The other common clinical characteristics of acne are due to modifications of the comedo by inflammation, pustulation, cyst formation, and scarring. There may also be an associated seborrheic scaling and greasy skin. The openings of the pores are prominent.

Sites of predilection are the face (forehead, nose, cheeks) and the torso (over shoulders, especially on the back and occasionally over the buttocks). Frequently acne is complicated by bacterial infection with resultant folliculitis or furunculosis. Scarring results from infection as well as from cystic changes in larger glands.

Treatment.
Almost any therapeutic measure used in treating acne results in improvement in about 80% of cases. These include hormones, antibiotics, restrictive dietary regimens, autogenous vaccines, and a great variety of local therapeutic agents. In general, very simple measures such as the following are sufficient: (1) Teach the adolescent to leave his skin alone and to avoid squeezing or rubbing his face. (2) Apply drying and slightly irritating preparations (see below). (3) Restrict those foods which are known to cause flare-ups. In general, these include chocolate, nuts, fried foods, and some carbonated drinks. (4) Expose the skin to ultraviolet rays, either from sunshine or by careful use of sunlamps sufficient to produce the mildest erythema level. (5) Assure the patient that healing ultimately occurs if further insults, e.g., squeezing blackheads, are avoided.

Comedones should be extracted only if they are large, with surrounding induration. This should never be done with the fingers. Use a "comedo extractor," which produces equal pressure around the circumference of the plug. Preliminary treatment with hot water compresses will facilitate removal. Fluctuant cystic lesions should be incised with a small, sharp scalpel. Hot compresses for one-half hour t. i. d. facilitate drainage.

Keratolytic Ointments:
(1) Resorcinol and sulfur cream -

℞ Resorcinol	0.3-2.0
Sulfur, ppt.	0.3-3.0
Hydrophilic ointment, q. s. ad	30.0

Sig.: Apply after cleansing at night and remove in the morning.

(2) Apply salicylic acid—sulfur ointment during day (see Table 12-1); or apply Fostex Cream® twice a day for five minutes, until reddening and drying occur, and use the same agent as a soap as long as the condition persists.

Skin-colored cosmetics may help the patient to feel a little less conscious of the blemishes.

Topical administration of vitamin A, 0.05% solution in polyethylene glycol (Retin A®), may be most effective.

Prophylaxis.
> This should be a part of routine care in adolescence.
A. Skin Hygiene: Child should be taught to scrub face vigorously with washcloth and soap and water twice a day. Avoid greasy cleansing creams and other cosmetics. Shampoo scalp one or two times a week.
B. Nutritional Guidance: Diet should be adequate and well-balanced. Avoid excess of carbohydrates, chocolate, nuts, and fatty, fried, and spicy foods.

SEBORRHEA;
SEBORRHEIC DERMATITIS

A relatively common skin eruption in infancy and childhood; it may also occur during adolescence.

Clinical Findings.
A. "Dandruff" and "Cradle Cap": Scaling, erythematous, poorly circumscribed rash, covered with oily, yellowish scales, especially prominent over scalp. In young infants this is called "cradle cap"; in children and adults, "dandruff." The lesion may spread downward over the forehead, ears, eyebrows, nose, and the back of the neck.
B. Erythematous, moist, scaly areas in flexural zones such as elbows, axillae, and, particularly in infancy, behind the ears.
C. Papular, erythematous, scaly and moist lesions may also occur on forehead and face.

Treatment.
> Usually produces relief in less than one week.
A. Scalp: Treatment depends on age group.
   1. Infancy ("cradle cap") -
     a. Scrub scalp vigorously each day with fingers or with soft brush and soap and water.
     b. Coal tar lotion (see Table 12-1) may be applied twice daily to more severe cases but is generally unnecessary with mild forms.
   2. Childhood ("dandruff") -
     a. Shampoo carefully one or two times a week with green soap or soapless detergent shampoos. Selenium sulfide suspension (Selsun®) may be most effective when used twice a week for two weeks.
     b. Apply salicylic acid and sulfur ointment (see Table 12-1) once daily for not more than seven days, or coal tar, 1 to 5% one or two times a week. Follow by shampoo.
B. Face and Flexural Areas: Avoid greasy ointments.

>   ℞ Coal tar
>   Sulfur, ppt.
>   Salicylic acid, aa   3.0
>   Emulsion base, q.s. ad 100.0
>   Sig.: Apply b.i.d.

TABLE 12-1. Medications useful in the treatment of skin diseases in childhood.

NAME	ACTION	PRESCRIPTION	INSTRUCTIONS AND REMARKS
BATHS:			
Starch and soda	Cleansing and soothing.	1/4 cup each of cornstarch and soda in bathinette or 1/2 cup starch and 1 cup soda to tub. Use tepid water.	Do not use soap. Bathe child for 15 minutes and then dab (do not rub) dry.
WET DRESSINGS:			
Normal saline sol. (0.9%)	Cleansing and soothing.	2 tsp. (9 Gm.) salt to 1 qt. water.	Wring out a washcloth or turkish towel and lay it on the affected areas 15 minutes twice a day or continuously. Use no waterproof covering, as the usefulness of these agents is due to the cooling effect of evaporation.
Sodium bicarbonate solution (3%)	Cooling, soothing, anti-pruritic.	2 Tbsp. (30 Gm.) to 1 qt. water.	
Potassium per-manganate sol. (1:10,000)	Antipruritic, antiseptic, astringent, deodorizing.	Dissolve one 0.3 Gm. (5 gr.) tablet in 3 qt. warm water. For bath, 15 tablets in 1 qt. water and add to full tub.	Permanganate is poisonous and should not be used internally or on large denuded areas. Keep solution away from children.
Aluminum subacetate solution (Burow's solution)	Mildly astringent and cleansing.	Use 4 Domeboro® tablets, or 1 tsp Domeboro powder, or 50 ml. Burow's Solution to 1 qt. water.	
Magnesium sulfate	Promotes blood flow. Localizes infections and aids phagocytosis.	2 Tbsp. (30 Gr.) to 1 qt. hot water.	Wring out a washcloth or turkish towel and lay on the affected areas 15 minutes twice a day or continuously. Cover with plastic material and keep warm with hot water bottle. Do not use electric heating pad.
PAINTS:			
Gentian violet	Antiseptic (monilla, gram-positive cocci), astringent.	1% aqueous solution.	Apply to affected areas with swab of cotton once daily. May be used in the mouth. Will stain clothing.

TABLE 12-1 (cont'd.). Medications useful in the treatment of skin diseases in childhood.

NAME	ACTION	PRESCRIPTION		INSTRUCTIONS AND REMARKS
PAINTS (Cont'd.):				
Castellani's paint	Fungicidal and anti-septic.	Basic fuchsin, saturated alcoholic sol.	10	Apply to affected part as a paint b.i.d. or t.i.d. Solution does not keep over one month. Will stain clothing. Begin with a 1:3 dilution, then progress to a 1:2 dilution and finally to full strength if necessary.
		Phenol, 5% aqueous sol.	100	
		(Filter, add:) Boric acid	1	
		(After 2 hrs.:) Acetone	5	
		(After 2 hrs.:) Resorcinol	10	
Neomycin sol.	For pyodermas.	0.1% aqueous solution		Apply locally b.i.d. to q.i.d. with cotton.
LOTIONS:				
Basic lotion (Sulzberger)	Soothing and as vehicle for other agents.	Zinc oxide	20	May add active medication: phenol, 1/4%; benzocaine, 3-10%; coal tar sol., 3-20%; ichthammol, 2-10%. May add color. Apply b.i.d. or t.i.d.
		Talcum	20	
		Glycerine	15	
		Water, q.s. ad	120	
Calamine lotion	Soothing, antipruritic, and drying.	Prescribed with or without 1/4% phenol.		Apply as a lotion 3 to 6 times per day. **Caution:** If phenol is added, frequent application may cause serious burn.
Starch lotion	Soothing, antipruritic, and drying.	Corn starch	24	Apply as lotion 3 to 6 times per day.
		Zinc oxide	24	
		Glycerine	12	
		Lime water, q.s. ad	120	
Coal tar solution	Keratoplastic, healing.	Add to starch lotion, 0.5 to 4%.		Apply with cotton b.i.d.
Olive oil lotion	Soothing and protective.	Zinc oxide	10	Apply 4 to 6 times per day.
		Olive oil		
		Lime water āā, q.s. ad	120	
Benzyl benzoate	Scabicide.	Benzyl benzoate	40	After thorough bathing, apply over whole body from neck to toes b.i.d. for 2 days.
		Soft soap liniment	40	
		Alcohol, 95%, q.s. ad	120	

OINTMENTS:

Hydrophilic ointment as base for:	Vehicle for water-soluble medications.		Apply sparingly with fingertips twice a day.
Ammon. mercury	Psoriasis, seborrhea.	5%	
Sulfur, salicylic ac.	As a fungicide.	1% salicylic acid, 3% sulfur.	
Coal tar sol.	For eczemas.	5% coal tar solution.	
Zinc oxide paste	Protective and soothing.	Prescribe as such.	Apply locally b. i. d.
Ammoniated mercury ointment	Keratoplastic, bactericidal.	Prescribed as 2 or 5%.	Apply 3-5 times per day. Hg sensitivity may be induced by too frequent use.
Coal tar ointment	Keratoplastic and keratolytic.	Prescribe as such.	Apply to not more than 1/4 body surface often enough to keep area covered. Remove at least once a day with mineral oil. Avoid exposure to direct sun.
Ichthammol ointment	Keratoplastic and keratolytic.	Prescribe as such.	Apply t. i. d. as a paste. Same precautions as with coal tar ointment.
Salicylanilide, 5%, in Carbowax 1500®	For tinea capitis.	Dispense 60 Gm.	Apply locally b. i. d. to entire scalp. (It is not necessary to clip the hair.)
Whitfield's ointment	Fungicidal.	Use 1/4 strength for children.	Apply t. i. d. Watch for signs of increased irritation.
Salicylic acid-sulfur ointment	Keratolytic, fungicidal.	Sulfur, 1%, and salicylic acid, 5% in anhydrous wool fat.	Apply b. i. d. or t. i. d.
Gamma benzene hexachloride	For scabies and pediculosis.	Dispense 60 Gm.	Apply locally b. i. d. for 1 to 3 days.
Sunscreen ointment	Protects from actinic burn.	Methyl salicylate 5 / Hydrophilic ointment, q.s. ad 100	Good protective cream for small babies and blond children exposed to sunlight. Apply every 3 to 4 hrs., remove with water.

POWDERS:

Zincundecate	Fungicidal.	Prescribe as such.	Apply b. i. d. to affected area.

ERYTHEMA MULTIFORME

Erythema multiforme is commonly a manifestation of sensitivity to some drug acting as the antigenic stimulus, but in many cases the cause is undetermined. It is rare in infancy and uncommon before the fourth year.

Clinical Findings.
A. Skin Eruption: Appears suddenly; in its earliest form it is usually macular and erythematous, with irregular distribution over any area of the body. This progresses rapidly to papular and vesicular phases, with polymorphous lesions. Some lesions may appear as concentric rings of variegated tints or as concentric rings of vesicles. Sites of predilection are the backs of the hands, the forearms, and the sides of the neck. Eruption may appear in "crops" and persist over two to four weeks, and may recur. Itching is slight.
B. Systemic Symptoms: Fever, joint pains, malaise, or nausea may accompany or precede the skin manifestation.
C. Severe Form: Erythema multiforme bullosum (Stevens-Johnson syndrome) may include the following additional findings:
   1. Marked inflammation of one or more mucous membrane—lined cavities (mouth, nose, urethra, vagina) or eyes.
   2. Pneumonitis - Apparent by x-ray and manifested by cough.
   3. Necrotic changes in bullous lesions of the skin which may slough out.

Treatment.
Eliminate causative stimuli, if identified. Soothing lotions (see Table 12-1) or antihistaminic drugs may be of some value.

In the bullous type, prescribe peroxide rinses after eating, broad-spectrum antibiotics for prophylaxis of infection in necrotic areas of skin or mucous membranes (see Chapter 6), and corticosteroids (see Chapter 22).

PITYRIASIS ROSEA

An acute self-limited disease of unknown cause which must be differentiated from other erythematous eruptions; it is not common in childhood.

A primary lesion or "herald patch" may precede the generalized rash by three to ten days; it is usually larger and has a more intensely red border than subsequent lesions, which consist of pink to red erythematous oval patches which may be flat or slightly raised and have a pale, wrinkled central area. Patches show wide variation in size and shape and are often covered with thin scales which are adherent at the center but tend to separate at the edges. There may be some itching. The rash is usually confined to clothed areas of the body. The lesions tend to be parallel to the ribs.

Treatment.
Rarely necessary; complete healing generally occurs in two to eight weeks. Itching may be relieved with starch lotion (see Table 12-1).

LEINER'S DISEASE
(Erythroderma Desquamativum)

This disease of early infancy is presently considered to be an exfoliative dermatitis due to staphylococcal infection. It is often accompanied by diarrhea due to the same organism. Treatment is as for serious staphylococcal infection and as for staphylococcal enterocolitis.

PSORIASIS

Psoriasis is characterized by bright red, tiny, circumscribed spots which become covered with dry, silvery scales shortly after onset. With increase in size, the central area becomes less red and more thickly covered with scales. Eruption is common on extensor surfaces of the extremities, trunk, and scalp. Recurrence and remission are the rule.

Psoriasis is extremely rare before the age of three and uncommon before the age of ten.

Treatment is symptomatic and guided by the local condition of the eruption. Soothing wet dressings (see Table 12-1) and bland ointments are useful during the acute stage. In the chronic stage, chrysarobin ointment, 0.1 to 5%, with salicylic acid, and ultraviolet radiation, combined with crude coal tar ointment, are sometimes effective.

Prognosis.
Prognosis is for persistence and recurrence of skin lesions, sometimes over several decades. Most treatment measures available at the present time have limited value.

13 . . .

Heart

PHYSICAL EXAMINATION OF THE HEART

Point of Maximum Cardiac Impulse Varies Considerably.
A. Infant: Third or fourth interspace, just outside the nipple line.
B. Two to Five Years: Fourth interspace at the nipple line.
C. Over Five Years: Fifth interspace, at or within the nipple line.

Percussion.
May be difficult during early childhood.

Auscultation.
A. First and second sounds are of equal intensity during the first
   year. The second sound is usually split; it is best heard in the
   left second interspace.
B. Innocent ("Functional") Murmurs: These are heard in more
   than 50% of children, may persist for many years, and have no
   pathologic significance. The etiology of most of these murmurs
   is obscure.
   Innocent murmurs usually change in character with changes
   in position, exercise, phases of respiration, and the location
   of the stethoscope.
   There are four main types, which may be coexistent or
   occur separately:
   1. Systolic, musical, vibrant murmur - Best heard in the
      fourth left interspace but may also be heard toward the apex.
   2. Venous hum - A continuous, variable humming sound or roar
      heard best in the second left or right interspace. It is usu-
      ally present in the sitting position and disappears with change
      in position of head, if pressure is applied to the jugular vein,
      or if the child lies down.
   3. Systolic, blowing murmur - Heard best in the second and
      third left interspaces.
   4. Carotid bruit - Early to midsystolic murmur heard over
      supraclavicular fossa or carotid artery, accentuated by
      exercise and unaffected by posture.

Cardiac Rate and Rhythm.
In infants and children, the cardiac rhythm and rate vary
widely, and multiple determinations must be made.
In infants, the rate may vary from 70 in sleep to 180 when crying. In older children, emotional factors (including the medical
examination) may affect the pulse. Any rate over 150 requires investigation.

Blood Pressure.

The cuff must cover two-thirds of the length of the upper arm or leg. A cuff that is too narrow will produce an apparent increase in blood pressure; one that is too wide will produce an apparent decrease.

For infants the "flush" method may be used. Apply a cuff above the wrist or ankle. Wrap a piece of rubber sheeting or rubber glove snugly around the foot or hand, starting distally, so that the blood is pressed from the extremity. Inflate the cuff to a pressure slightly above the suspected systolic pressure. Remove the rubber bandage. Reduce the pressure in the cuff slowly and note the pressure at which blood reenters the foot or hand, causing a sudden flush. This is the approximate mean pressure.

Comparison of the blood pressures in the upper and lower extremities simultaneously is of great importance in the diagnosis of coarctation of the aorta. Systolic pressure in the lower extremities is normally higher than that found in the upper extremity by about 20 mm. Hg; in coarctation of the aorta, blood pressure is lower in the legs than in the arms. The cuff must cover the same relative area of the arm and leg.

Excitement and struggling will increase the systolic pressure as much as 50 mm. Hg above the usual level.

X-RAYS

X-ray examination of the chest for cardiac evaluation should include posteroanterior, oblique, and lateral films. Films following barium swallow or fluoroscopy may be necessary in determining the configuration of the heart. The cardiorespiratory ratio is of little value, especially in infants and young children.

For technic of positioning infants, see Chapter 32.

TABLE 13-1. Normal blood pressures at various ages.*

Ages	Mean Systolic ± 2 SD	Mean Diastolic ± 2 SD
Newborn	80 ± 16	46 ± 16
6-12 months	89 ± 29	60 ± 10
1 year	96 ± 30	66 ± 25
2 years	99 ± 25	64 ± 25
3 years	100 ± 25	67 ± 23
4 years	99 ± 20	65 ± 20
5-6 years	94 ± 14	55 ± 9
6-7 years	100 ± 15	56 ± 9
7-8 years	102 ± 15	56 ± 8
8-9 years	105 ± 16	57 ± 9
9-10 years	107 ± 16	57 ± 9
10-11 years	111 ± 17	58 ± 10
11-12 years	113 ± 18	59 ± 10
12-13 years	115 ± 19	59 ± 10
13-14 years	118 ± 19	60 ± 10

*Reproduced, with permission, from Haggerty, R.J., Maroney, M.W., A.S. Nadas: Essential hypertension in infancy and childhood. Am J Dis Child 92:535, 1956.

Angiocardiography is a special technic by which the chambers of the heart and the major vessels are outlined roentgenographically following the injection of a radiopaque material. This material may be injected directly into a vein, through an intracardiac catheter, by retrograde injection through an artery, or through an arterial catheter. It is now routine procedure done at most cardiac catheterizations and is an extremely valuable diagnostic tool.

ELECTROCARDIOGRAPHY

TABLE 13-2. Upper limits of the normal P-R interval in children. *

Pulse Rate	Below 70	71 to 90	91 to 110	110 to 130	Above 130
Birth to 18 mos.	0.16	0.15	0.145	0.135	0.125
18 mos. to 6 yrs.	0.17	0.165	0.155	0.145	0.135
6 to 13 yrs.	0.18	0.17	0.16	0.15	0.14
13 to 17 yrs.	0.19	0.18	0.17	0.16	0.15

*Reproduced, with permission, from Ashman and Hull: Essentials of Electrocardiography. Macmillan, 1941.

Normal Configurations.
 A. P Wave: Upright in lead I, inverted in aVR when sinus rhythm is present.
 B. QRS Complex: In children the height may vary greatly. Prominent Q waves in lead III are not unusual.
 C. T Wave: Inverted in V_{4R}-V_2 in all children from 48 hours to approximately eight years of age. Upright in all other leads.

Axis Deviation Patterns.
 A. Right Axis Deviation: Deep S wave in lead I; tall R wave in lead III. Right axis deviation is a common finding in young infants.
 B. Left Axis Deviation: R wave high in lead I; S wave deep in lead III. LAD is associated with various congenital lesions, e.g., ostium primum defect, tricuspid atresia, and with left ventricular hypertrophy.

SPECIAL STUDIES

Circulation Time.
 In infants and children, the measurement is difficult to make by any method which requires cooperative effort on the part of the patient. Measurement is rarely useful except in following the progress of congestive failure, especially in rheumatic heart disease.

 The fluorescein method depends upon the fluorescence of this drug under ultraviolet light. Five per cent fluorescein solution, 0.07 ml./lb., is injected in an antecubital vein and the time measured to the appearance of fluorescence on the mucous membranes of the lips. This measures the time taken from the arm vein, through the heart and pulmonary system, and thence to the lip. Seven seconds is normal for infants; 11 seconds for older children.

For older children inject 3 to 5 ml. of 20% sodium dehydrocholate (Decholin Sodium®) rapidly I.V. Normal is eight to 15 seconds before the appearance of a sour taste in the mouth.

Venous Pressure.

This is of little diagnostic aid in infants because of technical difficulties and because normal values have not been established. Above four years of age, normal is 40 to 120 mm. water.

Phonocardiography.

This is a device for making recordings of heart sounds and murmurs and is frequently an aid to diagnosis.

Respiratory Function and Exercise Tolerance Tests.

These studies are useful in determining the degree of functional impairment which has been caused by the heart lesion.

Catheterization of the Heart. (See Table 13-3.)

This consists of the passage of an opaque catheter of small caliber through the vein into the right side of the heart or through an artery to the left side of the heart. It is useful in the diagnosis of congenital heart lesions in the following ways:

A. X-ray localization of the catheter may demonstrate defects in the heart and relative size of the right antrium and right ventricle.
B. Determination of pressures in the atria, ventricles, and pulmonary vessels.
C. Determination of oxygen content of blood withdrawn from the various chambers.
D. Special technics using dyes or catheters sensitive to special substances, e.g., hydrogen, may be used for the detection of small communications between heart chambers and great vessels.
E. Risks associated with this procedure include thrombosis of great vessels and irreversible renal damage.

CONGENITAL HEART DISEASE

The incidence of congenital heart disease is estimated to be six to eight cases per 1000 live births. With the development of technics for the surgical repair of many types of congenital heart defects, it has become extremely important to determine whether or not a congenital lesion is correctible by surgery, and an accurate clinical diagnosis is necessary before surgery may be undertaken.

The history often gives a clue to the existence of congenital heart disease. The following are suggestive: (1) Poor weight gain and a history of a feeding problem. (2) Attacks of fainting or "blackouts," which in a small infant may be manifested as "sighing attacks" accompanied by pallor. (3) Difficulty in swallowing, with frequent regurgitation of uncurdled milk. (4) Respiratory difficulties, including stridor, and the mother's description of the infant's deriving comfort from a position of hyperextension when having difficulty breathing. (5) Intolerance of exercise. The child may be described

TABLE 13-3. Relative pressures and oxygen content as obtained during cardiac catheterization. (Modified after Marple.)*

	PRESSURE			OXYGEN CONTENT			
	Right Atrium	Right Ventricle	Pulmonary Artery	Right Atrium	Right Ventricle	Pulmonary Artery	Systemic Artery
Normal heart	5/0	25/2	25/8	Equals vena cava	Equals right atrium	Equals right ventricle	95-100% saturated
Atrial septal defect	Normal or slightly increased	Normal or increased	Normal or increased	Greater than vena cava	Equals right atrium	Equals right ventricle	Normal†
Ventricular septal defect	Normal	Normal or increased	Normal or increased	Equals vena cava	Greater than right atrium	Equals right ventricle	Normal†
Patent ductus arteriosus	Normal	Normal or increased	Normal or increased	Equals vena cava	Equals right atrium	Greater than right ventricle	Normal†
Tetralogy of Fallot	Normal	Increased	Decreased; lower than right ventricle	Equals vena cava	Equals or is greater than right atrium	Equals right ventricle	Decreased
Eisenmenger complex	Normal	Increased	Increased	Equals vena cava	Greater than right atrium	Equals right ventricle	Decreased
Valvular pulmonary stenosis	Normal	Increased	Decreased	Equals vena cava	Equals right atrium	Equals right ventricle	Normal
Valvular pulmonary stenosis with patent foramen ovale	Increased	Increased	Decreased	Equals vena cava	Equals right atrium	Equals right ventricle	Decreased

*Postgraduate Medicine 9:239, 1951.
†May be decreased if there is associated pulmonary hypertension.

as frequently assuming a squatting position when tired in play. (6) Cyanosis, either intermittent or continuous. Cyanosis in the newborn period, when due to congenital heart disease, is most commonly caused by transposition of great vessels, tricuspid atresia, tetralogy of Fallot, and truncus arteriosus. (7) The history of the mother's pregnancy, with emphasis on illness during the first trimester, should be part of every complete examination of a child. Ask specifically about bleeding, rubella, excessive vomiting, severe anemia, and excessive sweating.

In addition to the specific treatment measures outlined in the following discussions, attention must be paid to the following: (1) The diet must be carefully controlled to assure a high-protein, high-vitamin intake, but excessive weight gain must be avoided. (2) Hydration must be rigidly maintained. (3) Prevent common infections by avoiding exposure to known infectious disease, active immunization, and passive immunization when exposure is known to have occurred. (4) Personality development should also be considered. Frank discussion with the parents should include prognosis and symptoms which the doctor should be informed about. Within the limits imposed by the disease, the child should be allowed to live as normal a life as possible.

ACYANOTIC TYPES

Positional Defects.

A. Dextrocardia: This lesion consists of right-sided heart, with or without reversal of position of other organs. If there is no reversal of other organs, the heart usually has other severe defects. With complete situs inversus, the heart is usually normal.

   1. Clinical features - Apical pulse and sounds are heard on the right side of the chest. Reversal of position of other organs, i. e., situs inversus, may be present. X-ray shows the cardiac silhouette on the right side. On Ecg. the P waves are usually inverted in lead I; QRS is predominantly down in lead I; lead II resembles normal lead III and vice versa.

   2. Treatment and prognosis - With situs inversus and no heart defects, the prognosis is excellent. If severe heart defects are present, definitive diagnosis is imperative since corrective surgery is frequently beneficial.

B. Coronary Artery Anomalies: A left coronary artery arising from the pulmonary artery is symptomatic. A right coronary artery arising from the pulmonary artery or a single coronary arising from the aorta usually presents no problems or symptoms.

   1. Clinical features - Symptoms appear within a few days or weeks after birth: recurrent dyspnea, pallor, sweating, vomiting, coughing, tachycardia, hepatomegaly. X-ray shows progressive enlargement of the heart. Ecg. shows inversion of T waves over the left precordium, especially just after feeding, and infarct patterns may be present.

   2. Treatment and prognosis - If only one coronary artery arises from the pulmonary artery, ligation occasionally results in improvement. Otherwise, death usually occurs before one year of age.

Coarctation of Aorta.

Blood pressure is high in the head and upper extremities, low in the lower part of the body and in the legs. In the "infantile" ("preductal") type, there is a constriction between the subclavian artery and the ductus arteriosus (incompatible with life if the ductus closes). In the "adult" ("postductal") type, there is a constriction at or distal to the ductus arteriosus.

A. Clinical Features: There may be minimal findings in early childhood. The older child may have numbness of the legs, headaches, and epistaxis. Femoral or dorsalis pedis pulsation is absent, weak, or delayed. Systolic murmurs may be present over the sternum and left back. Cardiac enlargement may or may not be present on routine x-ray examination. The site of coarctation and dilatation may be seen on a PA film. Coarctation is the commonest cause of heart failure from the first week through the first month of life. Older children may show notching of the ribs by collateral vessels. Ecg. may be normal or show left ventricular hypertrophy. Symptomatic infants show combined ventricular hypertrophy.

B. Treatment and Prognosis: Surgical correction is ideally postponed until eight to 15 years. Onset of cardiac failure requires vigorous treatment, including digitalis, diuretics, and oxygen. Response to such medical treatment allows further postponing surgery to a more ideal age. The prognosis is excellent with successful surgery.

Vascular Rings.

A. Double aortic arch, right aortic with right brachial arch, anomalous right subclavian artery, anomalous innominate artery, anomalous left carotid artery.

1. Clinical features - There are usually no symptoms. Constriction of the esophagus and trachea may cause vomiting, dysphagia, and stridor, and predispose to recurrent respiratory infections. The child may hold his head in hyperextension. X-ray of the heart with barium in the esophagus will establish the diagnosis. Outlined trachea with contrast material will add to diagnostic detail. Ecg. examination is noncontributory.

2. Treatment and prognosis - Surgical correction is indicated if the trachea or esophagus is constricted. The prognosis is excellent.

B. Persistent Patent Ductus Arteriosus: High aortic pressure shunts blood through ductus into pulmonary artery in systole and diastole. Left ventricular output, blood volume, and pulse pressure are increased.

1. Clinical features - A murmur in the 2nd or 3rd interspace to the left of the sternum appears in infancy. At first it may be systolic alone, but by two years of age most patients will show a diastolic component with a "machinery" sound and thrill. Pulse pressure is wide. X-ray shows enlargement of the left atrium and ventricle, increased pulmonary vascular markings, and expansile pulsation of the pulmonary arteries. Ecg. may be normal or may show left ventricular or combined hypertrophy.

2. Treatment and prognosis - Surgical division and ligation of the ductus. Operative mortality is so low that the procedure

should be undertaken as soon as possible after diagnosis.
With surgical repair, the prognosis is excellent. Without
repair, SBE or cardiac failure may develop.

Septal Defects.

A. Interatrial Septal Defect: This type of anomaly is very common,
particularly in girls. There are three types: (1) foramen secundum defect (high in the atrial septum); (2) foramen primum
defect (low in the septum, often with deformity of the mitral or
tricuspid valve and with persistent atrioventricular canal); and
(3) Lutembacher's syndrome, which consists of atrial septal
defect in association with congenital or acquired mitral stenosis.
In foramen secundum and foramen primum defects, oxygenated
blood shunts from the left to the right atrium.

1. Clinical features - Linear growth may be retarded and the
chest may bulge in time due to the enlarged right ventricle.
Murmur is systolic. Primum defect is common in Down's
syndrome. Secundum defect causes a grade III, blowing,
systolic murmur. Primum defect causes a grade IV, harsh
murmur. Murmurs are loudest near the second left interspace in secundum defect and transmitted to the apex or back
in primum defect. The second heart sound is widely split
and fixed. X-ray shows slight cardiac enlargement in secundum type and globular enlargement in primum type. Pulmonary vessels are enlarged and may show pulsation on fluoroscopy. The aortic shadow is small. Ecg. shows right
ventricular hypertrophy with an incomplete right bundle
branch block in secundum defects and right ventricular
hypertrophy with left axis deviation in primum defects.

2. Treatment and prognosis - Surgical closure is recommended
for secundum defect. Primum defect is more difficult to repair. With pulmonary vascular obstruction, surgery is not
recommended.

With repair, life expectancy is prolonged beyond the 35
years expected without repair.

B. Interventricular Septal Defect: The defect may be very small
and produce no symptoms, or very large and cause congestive
heart failure in infancy. Oxygenated blood passes from the left
to the right ventricle. (Large defect may lead to Eisenmenger's
complex, which is discussed below under cyanotic types.)

1. Clinical features - A systolic, harsh, loud murmur, often
with thrill, in the third left interspace. There may be a
diastolic inflow murmur at the apex. The x-ray may be
normal or show cardiac enlargement with increased pulmonary vascular markings. The Ecg. may show left or combined ventricular hypertrophy.

2. Treatment and prognosis - With moderate to large defects,
surgical closure should be done at four to five years of age.
The prognosis following surgery is good. Surgery is not indicated if obstructive pulmonary vascular disease is present.
Some ventricular septal defects may close spontaneously or
reduce in size.

Aortic Stenosis.

In this outflow tract lesion of the left heart constriction of the
aortic valve causes the left ventricle to hypertrophy. Systolic blood

pressure is lower than normal, and pulse pressure is low unless
there is associated aortic insufficiency.
- A. Clinical Features: A loud, harsh murmur is heard in the
  second or third right interspace, with transmission to neck and
  prominent thrill. The second heart sound is normal or weak.
  Pulse pressure is narrow. X-ray may show slight left ventricular enlargement. Ecg. is frequently normal but may show left
  ventricular preponderance.
- B. Treatment and Prognosis: Surgical valvulotomy is indicated in
  the severe case with a high-pressure gradient across the valve
  (as determined by catheterization of the left ventricle).   Operative mortality is less than 10%. Restriction of activity will
  postpone failure. The prognosis is guarded. Sudden death
  may occur, and life expectancy is only about 30 years.

Valvular Pulmonic Stenosis.

This outflow tract lesion of the right heart may occur with other
anomalies, but commonly occurs with an otherwise normal heart.
If this is the sole lesion, right ventricular pressure is increased.
Pulmonary blood flow is normal. With failure, cyanosis may result from stagnant blood flow.
- A. Clinical Features: Symptoms are rare in infancy. Many children are asymptomatic. Dyspnea, fatigue, and, rarely, cyanosis develop after age two. A loud, harsh, systolic murmur,
  often with thrill, is heard in the second to fourth left interspaces. X-ray shows right ventricular enlargement with a
  dilated main pulmonary artery. Pulmonary vascular markings
  are normal in the absence of cyanosis. Ecg. shows right ventricular hypertrophy.
- B. Treatment and Prognosis: Pulmonary valvulotomy should be
  undertaken between the ages of five and ten in all severe cases.
  The operative mortality is about 10%. Treat cardiac failure
  with digitalis (see p. 231) and other measures (see p. 225).
  The prognosis is poor without surgical repair. Death occurs
  within two to four years after the first attack of failure. The
  long-term prognosis with repair is not known at present.

CYANOTIC TYPES

Intertract Lesions.
- A. Valvular Pulmonic Stenosis With Interatrial Septal Defect
  (Patent Foramen Ovale): Venous blood from the right atrium
  is shunted into the left atrium before oxygenation, causing
  cyanosis. The right atrium and ventricle are enlarged.
  1. Clinical features - May simulate tetralogy of Fallot (see
     below). Differentiation is often possible only by cardiac
     catheterization (see Table 13-3). Ecg. shows right ven-
     tricular hypertrophy.
  2. Treatment and prognosis - Surgical repair of the stenotic
     valve is possible, and the prognosis is good after repair.
- B. Cor Triloculare Biatriatum: Failure of development of the right
  ventricle. Cyanosis at birth. Soft, systolic murmur over the
  precordial area. Dyspnea, x-ray, and Ecg. demonstrate large
  left ventricle. Life expectancy is limited. Treat as cardiac
  failure.

C. Cor Biloculare: Interatrial septal defect with small right ventricle or a large interventricular septal defect. Marked cyanosis, dyspnea, and cardiac failure early in life. Death usually occurs within a few months.

Outflow Tract Lesions of the Right Heart (Usually Combined Lesions.)

A. Tetralogy of Fallot: (Pulmonary stenosis with interventricular septal defect.) This is the most common cyanotic type of congenital heart disease. It may include overriding dextraposition of the aorta. Right to left shunt is fundamental to the lesion. A small amount of blood flows through the pulmonary artery, and the blood is poorly oxygenated.

1. Clinical features - Cyanosis occurs early as the ductus closes ("blue baby"). Lips and nail beds may be blue. Dyspnea is apparent early. The older child may squat or lie down during play. "Spells" may occur due to cerebral anoxia. Clubbing of the digits usually appears after two years. Congestive heart failure rarely occurs. A loud, harsh systolic murmur is heard at left base, frequently with thrill. Blood findings consist of polycythemia and increased hematocrit and RBC. The circulation time is short as a result of overriding aorta. X-ray usually shows a typical "wooden shoe" contour of the heart. The heart is not enlarged. The apex is blunt and elevated above the diaphragm. The pulmonary artery segment is concave. The right ventricle is enlarged. Pulmonary vessels appear to be scarce, and the lung fields are unusually clear. Ecg. shows marked predominance of the right ventricle and peaked P waves.

2. Treatment and prognosis - Surgery is usually indicated. Procedures available are anastomosis of the subclavian artery (Blalock-Taussig) and side-to-side anastomosis of the pulmonary artery to the aorta (Potts). Open heart surgery with repair of the ventricular septum and pulmonary stenosis is being attempted at present. If the pulmonary artery is absent or too small, no surgery is possible. Without surgery, death occurs within 20 years. With surgery, the prognosis is probably markedly improved toward a normal life.

B. Eisenmenger's Complex: This lesion consists of ventricular septal defect without pulmonary stenosis but with increased pulmonary vascular resistance and resultant right to left shunt.

1. Clinical features - Severe symptoms develop early with congestive failure, sometimes first in infancy. Dyspnea, repeated infection, and cyanosis are all common. Hemoptysis may occur in older children. The systolic murmur is not so loud as with smaller ventricular septal defects. No thrill is noted. The 2nd pulmonic sound is accentuated. X-ray shows cardiac enlargement, apparently involving both ventricles and the left atrium. Pulmonary vessels are engorged, with pulsation on fluoroscopy. Ecg. shows right ventricular hypertrophy, occasionally right bundle branch block.

2. Treatment and prognosis - No specific treatment is indicated and surgery is not possible. Restrict activity and treat cardiac failure. The prognosis is good with restricted life. Long-term prognosis is poor.

Transposition of Great Vessels.

The aorta arises from the right ventricle; the pulmonary artery arises from the left ventricle. Blood from the right heart goes through the systemic vessels and returns to the right side. Blood from the left heart goes through the lungs to return to the left side. This anomaly is incompatible with life unless patent foramen ovale, ductus arteriosus, or interventricular septal defect is also present. The coronary arteries arise from the aorta and carry anoxic blood.

A. Clinical Features: Marked cyanosis is apparent at birth or shortly thereafter. Dyspnea, engorged neck vessels, and an enlarged liver become apparent in the neonatal period. Murmurs are not typical nor always present. The heart enlarges rapidly in the first few weeks of life. X-ray shows enlargement of ventricles with a narrow base on PA view; a wide base on lateral or oblique views. Pulmonary vascular markings are increased. Ecg. may show myocardial damage due to ischemia, and right ventricular hypertrophy.

B. Treatment and Prognosis: Palliative surgery for the creation of an atrial septal defect by balloon catheter or by the Blalock-Hanlon procedure is sometimes carried out. Corrective surgery by the Mustard procedure is recommended at about two years of age. If a ventricular septal defect and pulmonic stenosis are present, the prognosis is poor, although the patient may survive to early adulthood.

Tricuspid Atresia.

This lesion consists of marked stenosis of the tricuspid valve and a small right ventricle, with or without pulmonary stenosis. Blood from the right atrium goes through the septal defect to the left atrium and into the systemic arteries. The pulmonary circulation goes through a patent ductus arteriosus or interventricular septal defect. Collateral circulation through bronchial arteries must develop to sustain life.

A. Clinical Features: Cyanosis is apparent shortly after birth. The neck vessels and the liver are engorged and pulsating. Murmurs are not typical nor always present. If the blood supply to the lungs is by way of an open ductus or large bronchial arteries, a continuous murmur is present. X-ray shows enlargement of the left ventricle, a concave left border, and small pulmonary vessels. The aorta is continuous with the cardiac shadow in left anterior oblique views. Ecg. shows left ventricular hypertrophy and left axis deviation (the only cyanotic type of congenital heart disease with this finding).

B. Treatment and Prognosis: Pulmonary anastomosis, as in tetralogy of Fallot, has been attempted and slight improvement has been noted. In older infants, anastomosis of the superior vena cava to the right pulmonary artery may be carried out. The prognosis is poor. Patients rarely survive for one to three months.

DISEASES OF ENDOCARDIUM
AND MYOCARDIUM

ACUTE RHEUMATIC HEART DISEASE

Acute rheumatic heart disease may involve all parts of the heart and accompanies an attack of active rheumatic fever. For discussion of diagnosis and treatment of acute rheumatic fever and heart disease, see Chapter 29.

CHRONIC RHEUMATIC HEART DISEASE

The chronic rheumatic heart is the residuum of rheumatic fever with persistent damage to the valves.

Clinical Findings.
The mitral and aortic valves are the most commonly involved.
A. Mitral Valve Involvement: Occurs early in the course of almost every case of rheumatic carditis. The appearance of an apical murmur in the course of an obscure febrile illness may be the first sign of the rheumatic cause of the disease.
   1. Mitral regurgitation usually occurs first.
      a. A moderate, blowing, pan-systolic murmur is present at the apex or slightly to the right and may merge with the first heart sound.
      b. A soft, low-pitched murmur in mid-diastole, loudest at the apex, may be present; it does not indicate organic stenosis.
   2. Stenosis of the mitral valve is a late change appearing with the passage of years.
      a. A rumbling, moderate, mid- or late-diastolic murmur is present, sometimes with a palpable thrill.
      b. The first heart sound usually is sharp, preceded by the crescendo presystolic murmur.
      c. A visible bulge of the chest wall may be apparent in long-standing cases.
B. Aortic Valve Involvement: May occur with mitral involvement. Regurgitation is the only change observed in childhood.
   1. A soft or moderate, blowing, diastolic murmur is present, occurring immediately after the second sound and heard best just to the left of the sternum in the second to fourth intercostal interspaces. It may be transmitted to the neck and to the apex.
   2. "Corrigan" pulse, with wide pulse pressure, capillary pulsation, and loud systolic impact in the femoral area.
   3. Systolic blood pressure may be elevated and diastolic pressure lowered, giving a wide pulse pressure.

Complications.
A. Cardiac Failure:
   1. Hepatomegaly may be the earliest indication.
   2. Edema, manifested by puffiness of face or unexpected weight gain, occurs later.

       3. Pulmonary rales are rarely found early in failure.
       4. Sedimentation rate may be normal in presence of decompen-
         sation.
  B. Atrial fibrillation in mitral stenosis due to dilatation of the
     left atrium may occur in the older child.
  C. Subacute bacterial endocarditis.

Treatment.
     The treatment of chronic rheumatic heart disease consists of
preventing progress of the disease and treating the complications.
  A. Specific Measures: None available.
  B. General Measures:
     1. Prevent recurrences of acute rheumatic fever by treating
       upper respiratory infections promptly with appropriate anti-
       biotic agents (see Chapter 6) and maintaining a prophylactic
       antibiotic program (see Chapter 29).
     2. Attempt to prevent further valvular damage during a recur-
       rent bout of rheumatic fever by adequate and careful treat-
       ment of the rheumatic fever (see Chapter 29).
     3. Established routine -
       a. Avoid fatigue and overexertion by restricting play activ-
         ities to sedentary games and exercise within the individ-
         ual's tolerance.
       b. Rest - Nine to ten hours of bed rest every night, and a
         rest period after lunch.
  C. Surgical Measures: Valvulotomy of the stenosed mitral valve
     is rarely indicated in children.
  D. Treatment of Complications:
     1. Congestive heart failure.
     2. Atrial fibrillation.
     3. Bacterial endocarditis.

Prognosis.
     Depends upon the presence and extent of valvular damage.
  A. If the heart is greatly enlarged or cardiac failure occurs early
     in the disease: about 70% mortality within ten years.
  B. Enlarged heart after adolescence has passed: survival to 30
     years of age is rare.
  C. Little or no enlargement early in disease and maximum care in
     follow-up: prognosis excellent.
  D. In the absence of recurrences, the murmur may decrease and
     the heart size return to normal limits.

SUBACUTE BACTERIAL ENDOCARDITIS (SBE)

     Subacute bacterial endocarditis is rare under the age of three
years. It generally develops in the heart or great vessel which already is diseased. The two common predisposing diseases are
rheumatic heart disease and congenital heart disease.
     SBE may develop in children with rheumatic valvular damage
or congenital heart disease and in children with surgical repair of
congenital defects.

Clinical Findings.
A. Symptoms:
1. History of predisposing heart disease.
2. Usually insidious onset of chronic, low-grade fever, anorexia, or malaise, but fever may be spiking.
3. There may be a history of preceding infection (respiratory, skin, dental abscess, etc.), dental extraction, or tonsillectomy.

B. Signs:
1. Of associated heart disease. New murmurs may appear or existing ones be altered.
2. Petechiae on skin, under nail-beds, or in conjunctivae.
3. Spleen may be palpably enlarged.

C. Laboratory Findings:
1. Blood culture should be repeated several times. If the clinical picture is suggestive of SBE, it is extremely important that the causative organism be identified if possible.
2. Leukocytosis may not be marked, but sedimentation rate is elevated.
3. Progressive anemia.
4. Hematuria.

Treatment.
A. Specific Measures: These depend upon the causative organism and, where possible, the results of the determination of this organism's sensitivity to various antibiotics or combinations of antibiotics.
1. Streptococcus viridans - Give penicillin daily for at least four weeks. If sensitivity is known to be less than 0.1 units/ml., use procaine penicillin G, 600,000 units two to three times daily. If sensitivity is not known or is known to be greater than 0.1 units/ml., give penicillin G, 2,000,000 to 10,000,000 units I. M. daily in four to six doses, depending upon body weight and organism resistance. If fever persists, the initial dosage should be doubled and, if necessary, redoubled.
2. Hemolytic streptococcus, Group D (Str. faecalis, or enterococcus) - Combined therapy.
   a. Penicillin G as above for at least four weeks.
   b. Streptomycin - 60 mg./Kg. body weight per day given in three to four doses for duration of penicillin therapy.
3. Hemolytic Staphylococcus aureus - Initial therapy is with methicillin continued for at least ten days. Continue therapy for two months with methicillin, oxacillin, nafcillin, or cloxacillin orally. If there is failure of response to initial therapy, shift to cephalothin (Keflin®). In some cases treatment with a combination of bacitracin plus vancomycin or ristocetin may be necessary. (See Chapter 6.)
4. If organism is unknown, all cultures negative, and clinical evidence strong, treat as for Group D streptococcus or with a combination of vancomycin or ristocetin plus kanamycin or neomycin, or with bacitracin plus kanamycin or neomycin (see Chapter 6). If patient is very ill and clinical evidence is strong, treatment should not be unduly delayed pending positive blood culture.

    5. In children allergic to penicillin, cephalothin (Keflin®) should be given.

B. Surgical correction of congenital heart lesion, if present.

C. General Measures:
    1. Transfusion of fresh whole blood, especially if anemia is severe.
    2. Oral or parenteral iron therapy (see Chapter 17).
    3. Adequate treatment of infections of skin, teeth, tonsils, etc.
    4. High-protein, high-vitamin diet.

D. Follow-up Measures:
    1. Sedimentation rate should be determined at periodic intervals. If elevated initially it should decrease toward normal.
    2. Blood culture should be repeated at intervals over the course of the following three months.
    3. Leukocytosis should be absent before stopping antibiotic therapy.

Prognosis.

Depends upon the organism producing the disease, the presence of congenital heart disease which cannot be corrected surgically, damage to other organs by emboli, the presence and results of treatment of cardiac failure, and the rapidity with which diagnosis is made and treatment started. In the absence of specific factors preventing a favorable outcome, the prognosis for the single occurrence is excellent. Prognosis for recurrence should be guarded.

CARDIAC ENLARGEMENT IN NEWBORN INFANTS

Cardiac enlargement unassociated with any other malformation of the heart has been observed in newborn infants. It is most commonly associated with erythroblastosis fetalis and diabetes mellitus in the mother, and may also occur in newborns with high hematocrit.

Cardiac failure should be treated if present. The prognosis depends on the associated diseases. With survival, the heart will return to normal size.

ENDOCARDIAL FIBROELASTOSIS
(Endocardial Sclerosis)

Endocardial sclerosis may occur as a pathologic finding with any congenital heart defect. It may occur without such defect in infants entirely normal at birth.

The onset is between birth and six months of age, with episodes of vomiting, paroxysmal dyspnea, and slight cough. Cardiomegaly and cardiac failure become apparent. Ecg. reveals left ventricular hypertrophy.

Treatment for cardiac failure consists of maintenance of digitalis for at least two years or until the heart returns to normal size. The prognosis is poor in fulminating cases. Survival is extended, but complete recovery is rare.

MYOCARDITIS

Myocarditis is an inflammation or degeneration of the heart muscle, usually secondary to systemic infections. It may occur in conjunction with a severe infection, but certain infections are more prone to cause myocardial injury. The most common causes of myocarditis are rheumatic fever, Coxsackie virus infection, and diphtheria. It also occurs in some viral diseases (e.g., rubeola, poliomyelitis, influenza), rickettsial diseases (typhus), and in other severe bacterial infections. Collagen diseases and endocardial fibroelastosis may have an associated myocarditis.

Clinical Findings.
Diagnosis is difficult because the myocarditis may be masked by the primary disease. There may be no cardiac symptoms or there may be precordial oppression, pain or tenderness, tachycardia out of proportion to fever, and abnormalities of rhythm. In severe cases, evidence of congestive failure is present (see below). The pulse is usually weak and rapid, the blood pressure low, and the heart frequently enlarged. The Ecg. findings are variable or may be normal. If the patient survives, there is usually no permanent myocardial damage.

Complications.
A. Congestive failure.
B. Arrhythmias.

Treatment.
A. Specific Measures. No specific measures are known, and treatment is aimed at the primary disease. In nonspecific acute myocarditis where other measures have failed, corticotropin (ACTH) or cortisone should be considered.
B. General Measures: Patient should be kept at bed rest until all evidence of active myocarditis has disappeared and the Ecg. has returned to normal or is no longer changing. Oxygen, digitalis, and other supportive treatment should be given as indicated.
C. Treatment of Complications:
1. Congestive failure. (See below.)
2. Arrhythmias - Treat specific arrhythmia, if indicated.

MYOCARDIAL FAILURE

Myocardial function may be impaired by a variety of disorders; if this impairment is great enough, myocardial failure results.
The most common of these disorders are viral myocarditis, rheumatic heart disease, congenital heart disease, hypertension (e.g., of renal origin), and pulmonary heart disease (following chronic respiratory disease). Contributing factors in myocardial failure include severe anemia and certain acute and chronic diseases.

Clinical Findings.
The symptoms and signs of myocardial failure in children will vary with the age of the child and with the nature of the associated conditions.

A. Symptoms:
   1. Dyspnea and weakness, which may be manifested in infancy as episodes of gasping or sighing.
   2. Loss of appetite.
   3. Nausea and vomiting, especially in infancy.
   4. Chronic nonproductive cough.
B. Signs:
   1. Pallor or cyanosis (first perioral).
   2. Distention of the veins of the neck.
   3. Heart is usually enlarged; arrhythmias may occur.
   4. Heart sounds are of poor quality, with the normal sharp difference between the two sounds becoming less distinct.
   5. Increase in the pulse rate above that expected for the age group and the associated disease.
   6. Rales of pulmonary edema may be heard.
   7. Enlargement of the liver is one of the earliest and most accurate signs; the degree of enlargement reflects the severity of cardiac failure. Failure may be relatively rapid in onset in infants and may be heralded by fever, tachycardia, and minimal increase in respiratory rate.
   8. Slight generalized edema may occur.
   9. Previously heard heart murmurs may become weaker or disappear due to low output.
C. Electrocardiogram: Not specific nor diagnostic, but may show the following:
   1. Tachycardia.
   2. Low amplitude of QRS and T waves.
   3. Abnormal shape of RS-T segment.
D. X-ray usually demonstrates enlargement of the cardiac silhouette and congestion of pulmonary vessels.

Treatment.
A. Specific Measures: If possible, treatment of myocardial failure should start with the underlying cause. However, treatment of failure very often represents the only contribution the physician may make to the comfort of the severe case.
B. General Measures:
   1. Bed rest is essential in all types of heart failure.
      a. In many children this may only be accomplished with the aid of sedatives, especially the longer-acting types such as phenobarbital (see Appendix).
      b. Narcotics may be necessary.
   2. **Oxygen is extremely important and should be used even when dyspnea and cyanosis are absent.**
   3. Digitalis is of great assistance, but should be used with caution in the presence of diphtheritic myocarditis or acute rheumatic fever with severe myocarditis. For dosage and preparations, see Table 13-4.
   4. Diuretics may be used to accelerate the removal of edema, especially following digitalization. Meralluride (Mercuhydrin®), 0.1 to 0.5 ml. I.M. or I.V., may be used.
   5. Morphine may be of value for paroxysmal dyspnea or any restless infant with failure.
   6. Low-sodium diet may be of some value in older children with edema but is rarely indicated in infancy.

DISORDERS OF RATE AND RHYTHM

Certain changes in the rate and rhythm of the heart occur as part of a specific heart disease or congenital defect. Many of these changes will be corrected with successful treatment of the underlying disease state.

Sinus arrhythmia, with accelerated pulse on inspiration, is common in childhood. Marked arrhythmia may require electrocardiographic study to rule out other causes.

Gallop rhythm, with three heart sounds heard in each cycle, usually occurs as an ominous sign in the course of heart disease and failure. This should not be confused with the normal, physiological third heart sound, which is heard best at the apex.

PAROXYSMAL TACHYCARDIA

Paroxysmal tachycardia may occur at any age. Etiology is unknown in most cases. There are two types: supraventricular (PST) and ventricular (PVC). Most are idiopathic and occur in males. The disease may be secondary to infections or associated with various congenital heart lesions. Some cases have a short P-R interval and prolonged QRS complex (Wolff-Parkinson-White syndrome).

Clinical Findings.
A. Symptoms:
1. Onset is sudden, usually in the first four months of life. It is a frightening experience in older children.
2. Pallor, sweating, vomiting, restlessness, labored respirations, fever, and sometimes, in infancy, cyanosis.
B. Signs:
1. High pulse rate (may be 180 to 400) may be too rapid to count, requiring Ecg. for accurate determination.
2. Rate in supraventricular type is steady; in ventricular type the rate may show variations.
3. Heart often enlarged, with murmurs in one-third of patients.
4. Cardiac failure, with dyspnea and orthopnea, may develop if serious heart disease is present or if the arrhythmia is particularly rapid and long in duration. The liver may become enlarged with the onset of cardiac failure.
C. Electrocardiogram:
1. Supraventricular type shows abnormal P waves which at times may be difficult to identify because of the rapid rate. The QRS complex is usually normal. In ventricular tachycardia, P waves show no relation to QRS complexes which are wide and bizarre.
2. P-R interval is shortened and QRS duration prolonged in Wolff-Parkinson-White syndrome.

Treatment.
Spontaneous return to normal rhythm is common. If symptoms persist, the need for treatment is urgent. Give oxygen.
A. Mechanical Measures:
1. Vagal stimulation by pressure on the eyeballs or on the carotid sinus (of particular value in supraventricular tachy-

cardia). **Caution:** Bilateral simultaneous carotid sinus
pressure is dangerous and should not be used.
2. Induce child to gag or vomit as a means of vagal stimulation.
B. Drugs:
1. Supraventricular tachycardia - Digitalis in full digitalizing
doses (see Table 13-4).
2. Ventricular tachycardia - Quinidine sulfate has rapid action.
First give 15 to 30 mg. orally. If this is tolerated, give
6 mg./Kg. orally every two hours. Procainamide hydrochloride (Pronestyl®) may be used. Continuous Ecg. monitoring is essential.

Prognosis.
This depends upon success of treatment and duration of attack.
Death is due to cardiac failure. Attacks usually disappear as the
child grows older. Prophylactic digitalis may be given over several
months' time and then withdrawn under observation for recurrence.
Wolff-Parkinson-White syndrome is generally not harmful.

ATRIAL FIBRILLATION

Rare in childhood. Usually occurs as a complication of rheumatic heart disease.

Clinical Findings.
There are no symptoms. The rhythm is irregular, and sounds
vary in intensity. A variable pulse deficit is present.

Treatment.
A. Give digitalis in full digitalizing dose, preferably parenterally
(see Table 13-4), to slow the rate and assist the ventricle.
B. Give quinidine to convert to regular atrial sinus rhythm. Drug
may be discontinued in 24 hours (see Appendix).

HEART BLOCK

First Degree Block.
P-R interval is prolonged. First degree block may be the
result of a myocarditis, as in rheumatic fever. It should be suspected if, in the course of observing such a case, the first heart
sound at the apex suddenly is noted to diminish in intensity. Diagnosis is established by repeated electrocardiograms.

Complete Heart Block.
In this form, the atria and ventricles beat independently. Complete block occurs as a congenital lesion associated with other types
of congenital heart disease, usually a septal defect, and, at times,
after surgical repair of septal defects.
Symptoms are minimal, consisting only of occasional mild syncope. Signs include a slow but regular ventricular rate, 40 to 60
per minute. The diagnosis is established by Ecg., which shows
dissociation of the P wave and the QRS complex.

Treatment.

Treat underlying heart disease. An electrical pacemaker may be necessary. The prognosis depends on the underlying disease.

DISEASES OF THE PERICARDIUM

PERICARDITIS AND PERICARDIAL EFFUSION

Etiology.
- A. Secondary to other disease processes.
    1. Acute rheumatic fever and other collagen diseases. Effusion usually is non-suppurative.
    2. Septicemia, with purulent pericardial effusion.
    3. Uremic state.
- B. Acute benign pericarditis of unknown etiology.
- C. Coxsackievirus pericarditis.

Clinical Findings.
- A. Symptoms:
    1. There may be pain, which the older child will describe as being less severe in the upright position.
    2. Symptoms of cardiac failure, as a result either of the primary disease process or of the constrictive effect on the heart of the pericardial fluid.
- B. Signs: (Most often encountered with effusion.)
    1. Pulse may be paradoxical due to fall in systolic blood pressure during inspiration.
    2. High diastolic blood pressure, with low pulse pressure.
    3. Distended, non-pulsating neck veins.
    4. Area of cardiac dullness may be enlarged to percussion.
    5. Apical pulsation may be absent.
    6. On auscultation, heart sounds are distant.
- C. X-ray shows enlarged mediastinal shadow. Pulmonary vessels may appear normal despite apparent presence of marked cardiac failure. Fluoroscopy reveals absent or diminished marginal pulsations.
- D. Electrocardiogram: Decreased amplitude of all waves, especially of the QRS complex. T waves may be exaggerated at first but later are rounded, lower in voltage, and occasionally inverted.

Complications.

Chronic adhesive pericarditis may result from pericardial inflammation. The bands of scar tissue that are produced may result in stress on the myocardium during systole.

Treatment.
- A. Paracentesis should be performed if the volume of fluid accumulated in the pericardium is producing tamponade, or if the nature of the infecting organism is unknown.
    1. Determine by percussion or x-ray the location of the left cardiac border.

TABLE 13-4. Digitalis preparations and dosages
for pediatric use.

	Age	Total Digitalizing Dose (TDD)	Division of TDD	Maintenance
Digoxin*†	Prem.	0.04 mg./Kg. orally	1st dose, half of TDD; 2nd dose, ¼ of TDD after 6-8 hours; 3rd dose, ¼ of TDD after 6-8 hours.	¼ to ⅓ of TDD in 2 divided doses in 24 hours.
	Newborn	0.05 mg./Kg. orally		
	1-12 mo.	0.08 mg./Kg. orally		
	1-5 years	0.06-0.07 mg. /Kg. orally		
	5-15 years	0.05-0.06 mg. /Kg. orally		
Digitoxin	< 2 years	0.035 mg./ Kg. orally	Same as digoxin	⅕ to ¹⁄₁₀ of TDD given every 12 hours.
	> 2 years	0.025 mg./Kg. orally or 0.02 mg./Kg. I. V. or I. M.		
Deslanoside‡	< 2 years	0.03 mg./Kg. orally	Give ¾ of TDD I. V. or I. M.: ¼ in 3-4 hours and repeat every 3 hours until effect is obtained.	Initial digitalization only. Maintain with digoxin or digitoxin.
	> 2 years	0.01-0.02 mg. /Kg. orally		

*Use ⅔ of calculated dose when administering I. M. or I. V.
†Purified digitalis preparations have ver⸱ narrow margins of safety. Give
too little rather than too much. The entire dose may be given stat., parenterally or orally, or may be divided in half and given 4 hours apart. For
slower digitalization, distribute over a 24-hour period.
‡The margin of safety for lanatoside products is **very narrow** in children.

    2. Site for introduction of needle is one to two cm. within the
       area of cardiac dullness in the fourth or fifth interspace
       (depending upon the size of the child).

    3. Other sites, more difficult to utilize, are to the right of the
       sternum in the fourth or fifth intercostal interspace and
       through the diaphragm cephalad under the xiphoid process.

    4. Insert a 20-gauge needle on a sterile 10 ml. syringe, with
       suction as the needle passes through the chest wall. Fluid,
       if present in the pericardium in abnormal quantities, will
       readily flow into the syringe. Withdraw as much as can be
       obtained with ease. This amount may total 250 ml. in a
       child six or more years of age with acute pericarditis with
       effusion such as that caused in rheumatic fever.

B. General Measures:

    1. Treatment of the underlying condition.

    2. Same as those used for cardiac failure.

    3. Corticotropin (ACTH) and cortisone have been used in the
       treatment of severe cases of acute benign pericarditis of
       unknown etiology with apparently good results.

C. Surgery: Surgery may be indicated to cut fibrous bands of
    chronic adhesive pericarditis.

•   •   •

USE OF DIGITALIS

Action.
A. Cardiac Failure: Digitalis increases the force of the contraction of the myocardium, therefore increasing the cardiac output and decreasing venous pressure.
B. Arrhythmias: Digitalis slows the conduction time between
atrium and ventricle and depresses the A-V and S-A nodes.
C. Prolongs the refractory period of the A-V node and therefore
slows ventricular rate in atrial fibrillation.

Digitalization.
Digitalis must be administered in large initial doses in order
to achieve tissue saturation. When this has been accomplished,
smaller doses will maintain saturation by replacing that part of the
drug which is utilized and excreted.

Criteria of Adequate Digitalization.
The dose of digitalis preparations in childhood must be determined individually. In general, children require more digitalis in
proportion to weight than do adults. Premature infants require
relatively less than full-term infants. Changes in the dose may be
necessary in the course of digitalization on the basis of signs either
of toxicity, inadequate digitalization, or gain in weight.
Decreasing signs of cardiac failure, especially slowing of the
heart rate, are criteria for adequate digitalization. However, even
in the absence of such changes, if Ecg. changes due to digitalis
(e. g., S-T depression) are present it can be assumed that digitalization has been accomplished and increase in dosage is not indicated.

Toxic Effects.
These are difficult to evaluate in small children.
A. Slight. Anorexia, nausea and vomiting, headache.
B. Moderate: Diarrhea, excitement, and disorientation.
C. Marked: Abdominal pain, conduction defects as noted on Ecg.
(coupling of rhythm and slowing of heart rate), atrial or ven-
tricular fibrillation.

Relationship of Digitalis to Potassium Ion.
Potassium and digitalis have antagonistic pharmacologic properties. Digitalis toxicity is more likely to occur in any clinical
disorder in which decreased potassium is present. In these circumstances the dose of digitalis should be reduced or potassium
given.

14 . . .
Ear, Nose, & Throat

Examination of the ear (including visualization of both ear drums) and a test of hearing are essential parts of the pediatric examination.

HEARING LOSS AND DEAFNESS

Hearing is as important to speech as sight to reading. Hearing is the means by which the individual controls the articulation and sound quality of his own voice. Deafness ranks with mental retardation as one of the main causes of delay in normal speech development.

Hearing loss of any degree over 20 db in the speech range (500-2000 c/s) can interfere with both education and speech development. Any child with symptoms indicative of brain injury, mental retardation, speech problems, or autism should have his hearing checked, because hearing loss may simulate any of these disorders.

It is of the utmost importance that severe hearing loss or deafness be detected as early as possible so that habilitative procedures may be instituted immediately. It is now routine in audiology clinics to test infants as young as three months old. Referral to an audiology facility is essential whether the suspected loss is mild or severe.

Etiology.
As in adults, there are three types of hearing loss. They are directly related to etiology, and can be classified as follows:
  A. Sensorineural Hearing Losses: Involve the organ of Corti, the 8th nerve system, the midbrain area, or a combination of these.
  B. Conductive Hearing Loss: Involves only the middle ear structures (tympanum, ossicles, eustachian tube) or the external auditory canal.
  C. Mixed Losses: Involve both the sensorineural and the conductive apparatus.

''Psychogenic'' hearing loss (apparent hearing loss on audiometry, but with no organic basis or real difficulty in hearing speech) often is a symptom of underlying emotional disturbance.

Clinical Findings.
  A. Symptoms: Hearing defects are often noticed by the child's family, and sometimes very early; if there is any question, the child should be referred to an audiology center.

B. Signs:
  1. Otologic examination -
     a. Abnormalities of the external ear canal and ear drum;
        presence of middle ear fluid (retraction, decreased
        mobility of the ear drum); or evidence of diseased or
        obstructive adenoids or sinus infection.
     b. Tuning fork tests -
        (1) Weber test - Lateralization to one ear indicates either
            a conductive loss in that ear or a sensorineural loss
            in the other ear.
        (2) Rinne test - If fork is heard louder behind the ear than
            in front, a conductive loss is certain.
  2. Observed behavior -
     a. Sensorineural losses (mild to profound) -
        (1) Up to four months - Failure to stir or to be aroused
            by a voice or noises when sleeping; failure to become
            quiet when spoken to; failure to startle to loud noise.
        (2) Four months to one year - Failure to orient (localize)
            to soft, interesting sounds on both sides; failure to
            respond to his name when called softly out of his
            vision.
        (3) One to two years - Failure to have varied vocaliza-
            tions of consonants and vowels, or to have some
            sounds stand for certain things; strident, loud voice
            quality (begins only after nine months), with only
            simple vowel sounds being voiced (a harsh "ah" is
            typical); often, the use of "a-mah," "a-mah," sound-
            ing like "mama," at about one year, which later is
            lost. (This develops from vibrations felt when being
            held closely; but after walking starts, it is lost.)
        (4) Two years and over - Speech development retarded or
            faulty for age group (speech may sound like "jargon";
            the only problem may be continued substitutions for
            consonant sounds); language development retarded for
            age group; educational problems (slow learning, be-
            havior problems in school, restlessness, nervous-
            ness).
     b. Conductive losses (mild to moderate) -
        (1) Up to one year - Failure to respond to softer sounds,
            but good awareness of louder sounds; soft voice qual-
            ity.
        (2) One to two years - Soft voice quality; failure to re-
            spond to very soft voice when name is called; subtle
            retardation in speech and language development, but
            normal speech articulation.
        (3) Two years and over - Measurable retardation in
            language development and use of speech; failure to
            respond to name when whispered very softly or from
            far away.

Treatment.
  A. Medical correction of defects.
  B. Audiologic Correction: A significant hearing loss as mild as
     20 db may be considered for amplification via wearable hearing
     aids. Proper audiologic habilitation should always be secured

TABLE 14-1. Causes and types of hearing loss.

	Cause	Type	Degree of Loss
Congenital			
Endogenous	Hereditary (recessive, X-linked, or dominant)	Sensorineural (organ of Corti)	Usually severe to profound
Exogenous	Asphyxia	Sensorineural (organ of Corti)	Moderate (usually ski-slide audiogram)
	Maternal rubella and other viruses	Sensorineural (organ of Corti)	Moderate to severe
	Erythroblastosis	Sensorineural (brain stem)	Mild to severe (falling audiogram)
	Ototoxic drugs (quinine, kanamycin, dihydrostreptomycin)	Sensorineural (usually organ of Corti)	Moderate to profound
Either endogenous or exogenous			
	Congenital atresia or stenosis, or congenital ossicular deformity	Conductive (may be unilateral)	Moderate
Acquired	Mumps	Sensorineural (usually cochlear and unilateral)	Profound
	Measles	Sensorineural (usually cochlear)	Moderate to profound
	Meningitis	Sensorineural (cochlear and 8th nerve)	Moderate to profound
	Ototoxic drugs (kanamycin, dihydrostreptomycin)	Sensorineural (usually cochlear)	Moderate to profound
	Labyrinthitis	Sensorineural (cochlear)	Slight to profound
	Tumors	Sensorineural (8th nerve)	Moderate to profound
	Trauma	Conductive, sensorineural, or mixed	Moderate to profound
	Cerumen		
	Foreign bodies		
	Perf. tympanum		
	Serous otitis media	Conductive	Slight to moderate
	Otosclerosis		
	Acute otitis media		
	Cholesteatoma		
	Chronic otitis media		

when a hearing aid is applied. Children as young as one month may be fitted with a hearing aid. Referral to a competent audiology center should be made.

C. Educational Treatment:

1. The hard-of-hearing child (20 to 65 db average loss) may, if trained early enough, succeed in regular school situations with supplementary help. (Tutoring, curriculum help, and speech and hearing therapy are indicated for the more severe cases.)

2. The very severe losses (65 to 100 db average) may do best in oral schools for the deaf and hard-of-hearing, where the residual hearing is used in combination with other approaches.

3. Profoundly deaf children, such as those with postmeningitis deafness or total congenital deafness, may not benefit from acoustic treatment of any sort and may benefit most from manual language technics in schools for the deaf. Occasionally a hard-of-hearing child is also found who has central agnosic disorders that make him a candidate only for such schools.

CONGENITAL MALFORMATIONS OF
THE EXTERNAL EAR

Congenital malformation of the auricle is a cosmetic problem; an associated deformity of the inner ear usually exists, and associated abnormalities of the urogenital system may be present.

A small skin tag, fistula, or cystic mass in front of the tragus is a characteristic remnant of the first branchial cleft. These are best treated surgically.

Protruding auricles are a dominant hereditary characteristic. Otoplasty may be done to place the ears in a position more parallel to the head. This should be done before six years of age if the child's life is made socially difficult by the malformation.

Bilateral agenesis of the external auditory canals or ears can be corrected surgically. A hearing aid is fitted at two to four weeks of age so that children are not deprived of auditory stimulation during early development. Surgery is performed before school age in patients with bilateral agenesis and after childhood in patients with unilateral agenesis.

OTITIS EXTERNA
(Inflammation of the External Ear Canal)

The most common cause of otitis externa is maceration of the ear canal lining due to frequent swimming or shower bathing. Trauma, reactions to foreign bodies, and eczema are other contributing factors. Pyogenic (especially pseudomonas or staphylococcus) or mycotic superinfections are common.

Treatment.

A. Pyogenic Infections: Treatment is aimed at keeping the external ear canal clean and dry and protecting it from trauma. Debris should be gently removed from the ear canal with a cotton applicator or irrigation. Insert a wick soaked with 1:17 Burow's solution to reduce edema and permit visualization. Give systemic antibiotics (usually penicillin) in full doses for ten days if there is evidence of extension of the infection beyond the skin of the ear canal (fever or adenopathy). Topical antibiotics combined with a corticosteroid applied on a wick or as ear drops are often helpful. During the acute phase, swimming should be avoided if possible.

B. Removal of Foreign Bodies: Removal should always be under direct vision and never done blindly. A stream of lukewarm saline directed past the foreign body into the external canal may float it out. Vegetable matter, such as peas and beans, swells in the presence of water and should instead be removed with a wire loop; care should be taken not to push the object farther into the canal. If the object is large or is wedged in place, the patient should be referred to an otolaryngologist.

C. Removal of Impacted Cerumen: Cerumen in the external ear must be removed before the examination can continue. It may be removed with a wire loop or with cotton on the end of a thin wire applicator. Cerumen may be softened, if necessary, by instilling mineral oil or Cerumenex®. It may also be washed out with warm water or saline, using a syringe. Irrigation is contraindicated if any possibility of a perforated eardrum exists.

Prognosis.

Resistant chronic infection, especially in the presence of eczema, usually requires prolonged therapy. After removal of a foreign body, rapid improvement occurs.

OTITIS MEDIA
(Inflammation of the Middle Ear)

Some degree of involvement of the middle ear occurs with most upper respiratory infections in infancy and early childhood. Specific signs and symptoms are often absent. No treatment is necessary for this mild inflammation.

ACUTE SUPPURATIVE OTITIS MEDIA

Acute otitis media is common in infancy and childhood. Intelligent use of antibiotic therapy has diminished the frequency of progression to severe illness and perforation. Inadequate therapy is responsible for most of the present-day complications.

The most common bacterial pathogens are pneumococci, H. influenzae (especially in children under four years of age), and the beta-hemolytic streptococci. In newborn infants, Escherichia coli, Staphylococcus aureus, and Klebsiella pneumoniae may be predominant. In two-thirds of cases, no pathogen can be found and viral etiology is likely. Nasopharyngeal cultures frequently fail to recover the organism found in the middle ear. Acute otitis media in infants may be related to feeding the bottle to the infant in the horizontal position. Sudden altitude changes may force organisms into the middle ear.

Clinical Findings.

A. Symptoms: Irritability and restless sleep may be the only signs in an infant or the infant may also rub or pull at his ear. Older children will complain of pain, dizziness, and headache. Fever in infants may be very high, sometimes with convulsions, or it may be absent. Symptoms of an upper respiratory tract infection are usually present.

B. Signs (Examination of the Ear):

1. Distortion or absence of light reflex; impaired mobility of the drum.

2. The drum is usually flaming and diffusely red rather than the normal pearl-gray; it may be bulging.

3. If the tympanic membrane has ruptured, an opening may be seen discharging pus or serous fluid.

4. A conductive type hearing loss is always present. If it persists over four weeks, consider myringotomy.

   Note: Mild redness of the drum in the presence of high fever often is entirely nonspecific and related only to the fever. Hyperemia of the drum may also occur with crying.

Treatment.

A. Specific Measures: Full doses of systemic antibiotics for ten days. (See Table 6-2 for drugs of choice.) Penicillin is the drug of choice for streptococcal or pneumococcal otitis. Penicillin with triple sulfonamide or ampicillin alone is preferred in children under the age of four or for those proved by ear culture to be infected with H. influenzae.

B. Local Measures:

1. Analgesic ear drops are generally contraindicated because they obscure physical findings, and in any case their efficacy is unproved.

2. Vasoconstrictor nose drops are also of questionable efficacy, since they cannot be delivered to the eustachian tube.

C. General Measures:

1. Aspirin or other analgesics should be given to reduce the discomfort and fever.

2. Combinations of syrup of ephedrine or pseudo-ephedrine, elixir of phenylephrine (Neo-Synephrine®), or syrup of phenylpropanolamine hydrochloride (Propadrine®) and syrup of an antihistaminic, in equal parts, may be of value. The dose is $1/2$ to 1 tsp. (2 to 4 ml.) every four hours.

D. Surgery: Myringotomy during the early, acute stage is usually not necessary when full doses of antibiotics and vasoconstrictors are used, but it may provide immediate relief if pain is severe and there is pronounced bulging of the eardrum. Later, myringotomy may be indicated if there is no response to antibiotics within 48 hours or when mastoiditis is present.

   Tonsillectomy and adenoidectomy do not significantly affect the later occurrence of otitis media.

Complications.

Perforation of drum, resulting in chronic otitis media; mastoiditis; occasionally, meningitis or brain abscess; chronic serous otitis ("glue ear").

Course and Prognosis.
Untreated, the disease is self-limited unless complications occur. Spontaneous perforation leads to prompt systemic improvement, but infection may become chronic. Prompt and prolonged (ten days) antibiotic therapy usually prevents perforation and complications.

Continuing drainage in spite of adequate antibiotic therapy usually indicates that the infection has become chronic or that mastoiditis has developed. Mastoid x-rays showing clouding of the air cells or demineralization of the bony trabeculae may indicate the need for mastoidectomy. External otitis may be treated as described above.

The incidence of deafness in children does not have a significant relationship to otitis media.

SECRETORY (SEROUS) OTITIS MEDIA

This is a common cause of mild hearing loss in children, most often between the ages of two and seven. The middle ear contains sterile fluid which varies from a thin transudate to a very thick consistency ("glue ear"). Eustachian tube obstruction is usually due to primary congenital tube dysfunction. Other possible contributing factors are allergic rhinitis, adenoidal hyperplasia, supine feeding position, or a submucous cleft.

Onset is usually sudden, with a slight conductive hearing loss. Symptoms may include slight earache, a feeling of watery bubbles in the ear, or a sensation that the head is full. If the ear is not completely filled with fluid, there may be air bubbles or a meniscus visible through the tympanic membrane. The eardrum shows a loss of translucency, diminished movement, and a change in color from the normal gray to a more pale or even bluish hue.

Initial treatment is with oral antihistamine decongestants. If the duration has been over eight weeks, the child should be referred for myringotomy, suctioning, and the insertion of plastic ventilation tubes. Unilateral serous otitis media can be treated conservatively for a longer period of time. Anti-allergic management may be of value in the allergic child.

CHRONIC PERFORATION OF THE EARDRUM

Pyogenic organisms are usually the causative agents. Excessive adenoidal tissue may predispose to chronic infection.

Clinical Findings.
A. Symptoms: Recurrent or persistent ear drainage. Chronic otitis media may be painless and free of fever in the intervals between acute exacerbations.
B. Signs: The eardrum is perforated. Peripheral perforations provide a greater risk of cholesteatoma formation. Marked scarring of the drum signifies previous perforations. Mastoid tenderness may be present.
C. X-ray studies for evidence of mastoid involvement.
D. Laboratory Findings: Bacteriologic study is imperative. Specific etiologic diagnosis must be made by culture of drainage

fluid. Secondary invaders following perforations are frequent causes of chronic drainage and are much more resistant to therapy. These include pseudomonas, Escherichia coli, Klebsiella pneumoniae, and staphylococcus.

E. A conductive type hearing loss will be present.

Treatment.

Keep water out of the ear by plugging the ear with cotton soaked in mineral oil or impregnated with petrolatum when washing or bathing. Swimming should be forbidden. Instill appropriate antibiotic drops; systemic antibiotics are indicated for purulent drainage or systemic signs.

Myringoplasty or tympanoplasty is done at about age 10 or older. Cholesteatoma is a pocket of skin which invades the middle ear and mastoid spaces from the edge of a perforation. This type of chronic otitis should be treated surgically when diagnosed.

Complications.

Hearing loss, mastoiditis, brain abscess, meningitis, and labyrinthitis (with dizziness).

Course and Prognosis.

With massive and prolonged antibiotic treatment and surgical drainage of mastoid bone when indicated, the prognosis is good. If no treatment is given, hearing loss is certain.

ACUTE BULLOUS MYRINGITIS

In this condition, bullae form between the outer and middle layers of the tympanic membrane. Though this condition was previously thought to be viral, recent studies demonstrate that 50 to 75% of patients with acute bullous myringitis have underlying suppurative acute otitis media. The organisms are very similar to those found in isolated suppurative acute otitis media, with the exception that Mycoplasma pneumoniae is occasionally involved. The patient complains of ear pain on the involved side. Examination reveals one to three bullae containing straw-colored fluid. Antibiotics are prescribed as for acute suppurative otitis media. The bullae do not have to be opened unless they cause severe pain.

MASTOIDITIS

Inflammation of the mastoid antrum and air cells with bone necrosis. Pyogenic bacteria, chiefly streptococci, staphylococci, and Pseudomonas species, are the causative agents.

Clinical Findings.

A. Symptoms: Pain behind the ear, irritability, fever.
B. Signs: Tenderness over the mastoid bone, reddening and swelling over the mastoid area. The eardrum usually shows the changes of acute suppurative otitis media.
C. X-ray Findings: In the acute phase there is diffuse inflammatory clouding of the mastoid cells; there is no evidence of bone

destruction. With accumulation of the exudate there is resorption of the calcium of the mastoid cells so that they are no longer visible. Subsequently there is destruction of the cells, and areas of radiolucency representing abscesses.

With chronic mastoiditis there is an increase in thickness of the mastoid cells and sclerosis of the bone. This is associated with a reduction in size of the cells. Small abscess cavities may persist in the sclerotic bone.

D. Laboratory Findings: In the acute phase, WBC and sedimentation rate are elevated. Myringotomy is indicated to define the offending organism.

Treatment.

A. Specific Measures: Intravenous administration of an antibiotic likely to affect the beta-hemolytic streptococci and pneumococci, the most common causative organisms.

B. Surgical Measures: In the presence of increasing toxicity and extension of the disease process, surgical intervention and drainage may be necessary. Mastoidectomy is seldom necessary when adequate amounts of antibiotics are employed early in the course of the disease.

Complications.

Bacterial meningitis and brain abscess.

Course and Prognosis.

If appropriate antibiotics are given in sufficient dosages over an adequate period, complete cures can be expected. Chronic infections usually require surgical intervention to eradicate the infectious focus. Prognosis is generally good.

DISEASES OF THE NOSE AND SINUSES

COMMON COLD

Nonbacterial upper respiratory infections are exceedingly common in the pediatric age group; about two to four such infections per year are considered usual in the United States.

A number of viruses are specific agents. Secondary bacterial invaders (beta-hemolytic streptococcus, pneumococcus, H. influenzae) frequently contribute to prolongation of illness (beyond four days).

Clinical Findings.

A. Symptoms: Malaise, sneezing, "stuffiness" of head, sore throat, and cough.

B. Signs: Serous nasal discharge and moist and boggy nasal mucous membranes. Fever is generally slight but may be high in an infant.

C. Laboratory Findings: Normal or low WBC.

Treatment.

A. General Measures: Give aspirin for pain or fever. Oral antihistamines, e.g., chlorpheniramine, diphenhydramine, or phenylephrine, reduce nasal congestion and rhinorrhea.

Humidifying the air (vaporizer or bathroom shower water) is helpful in relieving nasal and pharyngeal discomfort and cough.
B. Local Measures: Topical vasoconstrictors, e.g., phenylephrine (Neo-Synephrine®), $1/4\%$, or ephedrine sulfate, 1%, in saline provide prompt symptomatic relief of nasal congestion but should not be used for more than one week. Over-use of any topical medication may result in irritation and "rebound" congestion.

Course and Prognosis.

The usual course is of four days' duration. Continuation of rhinitis, regardless of whether it is serous or purulent, considerably beyond this period suggests bacterial complications which would respond to antibiotic therapy. A culture should confirm the superinfection. Prognosis is excellent, but reinfections occur throughout life.

RECURRENT RHINITIS

A child with a chief complaint of "constant colds" is not uncommon in office practice.

Differential Diagnosis and Treatment.
A. Common Cold: The most common cause of recurrent runny nose is repeated viral upper respiratory tract infection. The onset is usually after six months of age. The bouts of rhinorrhea are usually accompanied by fever. Cultures are negative for bacteria. There is usually some evidence of contagion within the family.

Serum immunoelectrophoresis is an excessively ordered test. Children with immune defects do not have an increased number of colds.

Treatment consists of specific reassurance. The parents can be told that their child's general health is good; that he will not have a great number of colds for more than a few years; that his exposure to colds is building up his body's supply of antibodies; and that the child's problem is not the parents' fault.
B. Allergic Rhinitis: The onset of "hay fever" usually occurs after two years of age, i.e., after the child has had adequate exposure to allergens. There is no fever or contagion among close contacts. The attacks include frequent sneezing, rubbing of the nose, and a profuse clear discharge. The nasal mucosa is pale and boggy. Smear of nasal secretions demonstrates over 20% of the cells to be eosinophils. Oral decongestants and antihistamines should be prescribed.
C. Chemical Rhinitis: Prolonged use of vasoconstrictor nose drops beyond seven days results in a rebound reaction and secondary nasal congestion. The nose drops should be discontinued.
D. Vasomotor Rhinitis: Some children react to sudden changes in environmental temperature by manifesting prolonged conges-

tion and rhinorrhea. Oral decongestants can be used periodically to give symptomatic relief.

Unwarranted Therapy.
Administration of human gamma globulin injections is the most
common error made in treatment of recurrent rhinitis. The injections may be initiated without determining the serum IgG level
or as a consequence of misinterpreting the results by comparing
them with adult levels rather than with norms for age. Many
studies show that human gamma globulin injections do not benefit
patients with frequent upper respiratory tract infections. In addition to being painful and expensive, they may cause anaphylaxis or
iso-immunization. Other worthless approaches to this problem include administration of bacterial vaccines or prophylactic antibiotics and tonsillectomy and adenoidectomy.

PURULENT RHINITIS

Purulent rhinitis caused by pathogenic bacteria is an occasional
aftermath of nonbacterial upper respiratory infections, particularly
in allergic children. In infants with persistent rhinitis, consider
congenital syphilis.

Etiology and Clinical Findings.
A. Pyogenic Infection: Usually due to hemolytic Staphylococcus
   aureus, H. influenzae, or pneumococcus. Infection with these
   organisms is characterized by purulent nasal discharge, dried
   pus about the nares, and inflamed nasal mucous membranes.
B. Nasal diphtheria is characterized by chronic serosanguineous
   nasal discharge.
C. Foreign bodies usually cause mucopurulent discharge from one
   nostril only, and that discharge often has a foul odor.

Treatment.
A. Local use of nose drops and systemic vasoconstrictors followed
   by repeated nasal suction.
B. Infection: Appropriate antibiotic in adequate dosage (see
   Chapter 6).
C. Diphtheria: See Chapter 25.
D. Foreign Body: Usually requires the services of a specialist.

Prognosis.
Excellent. Improvement is prompt with specific therapy.

SINUSITIS

Inflammation of the mucous membrane lining of the paranasal
sinuses. In early infancy, the ethmoid and maxillary sinuses are
most frequently inflamed. The frontal sinuses rarely become infected until six years of age. The most common bacterial pathogens
are hemolytic Staphylococcus aureus, beta-hemolytic streptococcus,
and the pneumococcus. Most sinus obstruction occurs without
superinfection.

Sinuses are involved in most cases of upper respiratory tract infection, but sinus infection usually does not persist after the nasal infection has subsided. Predisposing factors to persistent sinus infection include obstruction to normal sinus drainage and physical irritation of the mucous membranes, such as occurs in diving or swimming. Obstruction may be caused by allergy with edema of the mucous membranes, deformity of the nasal septum, hypertrophied adenoids, previous accumulation of pus and cellular debris, and edema of mucous membranes from nasal infection.

ACUTE SINUSITIS

Clinical Findings.
  A. Symptoms: Mucopurulent discharge from nose and persistent postnasal drip; fever, headache, and malaise.
  B. Signs: Tenderness over involved sinus; pain upon percussion; cellulitis in area overlying the affected sinus; periorbital cellulitis, edema, and proptosis (especially with acute ethmoiditis); failure to transilluminate; nasal voice.
  C. X-ray Findings: Clouding of the affected sinus region is often present, or a fluid level may be observed.
  D. Laboratory Findings: Culture of nasal discharge to determine etiologic agent. Eosinophils in nasal secretion suggest allergy.

Treatment.
  A. Specific Measures: Systemic use of dicloxacillin for ten days in full doses is indicated for signs of superinfection (fever, purulent discharge, or overlying cellulitis).
  B. General Measures:
    1. Combination of syrup of ephedrine or elixir of phenylephrine and syrup of an antihistamine in equal parts serves the dual purpose of sedation and vasoconstriction. The dose is 2 to 4 ml. every four hours.
    2. Vasoconstrictor nose drops followed by repeated high nasal suction.
    3. Aspirin to decrease discomfort.

Course and Prognosis.
    A single attack of sinusitis does not predispose to recurrences unless contributing underlying abnormalities (nasal allergy, deflected septum, obstructing adenoid, etc.) remain uncorrected. The immediate prognosis is good.

CHRONIC SINUSITIS

Repeated episodes of sinusitis may be due to allergic causes, cystic fibrosis, anatomic deformity resulting in poor sinus drainage, or recurrent irritating factors (such as repeated diving).

Clinical Findings.
  A. Symptoms: May be minimal.
    1. Stuffy nose, especially in the morning or late afternoon.
    2. Nasal discharge of variable amount and character.

       3. Headache.
- B. Signs: May be minimal.
  1. Moderate or mild tenderness over infected area. Pain on
     percussion of affected part.
  2. Intermittent low-grade fever.
- C. X-ray Findings: The most common finding is membrane thick-
     ening, which may be associated with fluid and cysts or polyps.
     The bone surrounding the sinus may be thickened.
- D. Laboratory Findings:
  1. WBC elevated or normal.
  2. Sedimentation rate elevated or normal.
  3. Culture for bacterial pathogens should be made.
  4. Numerous eosinophils in the nasal smear suggest an allergy.

Treatment.
- A. Specific Measures: Chronic infection may be primary or
     secondary; in either case it should be treated with full doses
     of a suitable antibiotic (see Chapter 6).
- B. General Measures:
  1. Establishment of good drainage -
     a. Nasal vasoconstrictors (see p. 243) and frequent nasal
        suction.
     b. Removal of anatomic deformity.
     c. Combinations of syrup of ephedrine or elixir of phenyl-
        ephrine (Neo-Synephrine®) and syrup of an antihistamine,
        in equal parts, serve the dual purpose of sedation and
        vasoconstriction. The dose is 2 to 4 ml. every four
        hours.
  2. Allergic irritants must be removed.
  3. Humidification may be beneficial.

Complications.
    In persistent sinusitis, bronchitis may occur from the bronchial
aspiration of infected material from the draining sinuses. This
clinical combination is known as the sinobronchitis syndrome; it is
frequently associated with a chronic cough, and chronic bronchitis
may develop.

Course and Prognosis.
    The course is usually protracted, especially in those children
who suffer from a combination of an allergy and an infection. When
the therapeutic approach encompasses all possible etiologic factors,
the ultimate prognosis is good. Recurrences in adulthood are frequent, however. Sinus surgery for correction of chronic sinusitis
is uncommon in children, but if complications of extension of the
infection into the orbit (orbital cellulitis or abscess) or intracranial
cavity (meningitis or brain abscess) occur, prompt surgical treatment is essential.

EPISTAXIS

Etiology.
- A. Trauma to Nose: The most common cause of epistaxis in child-
     hood is nose picking or nose rubbing, which results in abrasion

of the anterior inferior part of the nasal septum (Kiesselbach's area); other causes are falls or blows.
B. Bleeding diseases (e. g., hemophilia, leukemia, purpura, hereditary telangiectasia of Weber-Osler-Rendu).
C. Infections: A bloody, purulent nasal discharge is found in syphilis and diphtheria.
D. Foreign body.
E. Tumor: Severe epistaxis may occur with many tumors (e.g., angiofibroma, lymphoma, sarcoma).
F. Allergic rhinitis.

Clinical Findings.
In addition to the bleeding from the nose, blood may be swallowed and produce nausea and vomiting of coffee-ground vomitus and tarry stools. Blood may be found under the fingernails.

Treatment.
A. Mild Bleeding: Any of the following are usually successful.
   1. Compress nose between fingers for at least ten minutes. Have child in sitting position. Do not release intermittently to see if bleeding has stopped.
   2. Cotton plug with petrolatum inserted into nose and allowed to remain four hours.
B. Persistent Bleeding: A pledget of cotton with phenylephrine, 1/4%, or epinephrine, 1:1000 solution, or cocaine, 1%, placed in the nose for five minutes will stop most bleeding from Kiesselbach's area. Cauterization with silver nitrate sticks, chromic acid bead, trichloroacetic acid, or the electrocautery should be limited to selected cases.

Prophylaxis.
Petrolatum ointment to irritated and crusted regions of the nasal septum and discouragement of nosepicking will prevent recurrences in cases due to such local trauma.

Prognosis.
Epistaxis may recur but rarely leads to serious difficulties.

DISEASES OF THE THROAT

ACUTE TONSILLITIS AND PHARYNGITIS
(See Table 14-2.)

Acute tonsillitis and pharyngitis are usually recurrent and are almost invariably associated with systemic manifestations. They are most prevalent during winter and may occur at the onset of scarlet fever.

Etiology.
A. Bacterial: Mainly due to beta-hemolytic streptococcus. Note: Diphtheritic membranes may simulate tonsillar exudate but differ from it in being more firmly adherent, grayish in ap-

TABLE 14-2. Differential diagnosis of
exudative tonsillitis and acute pharyngitis.

Etiology	Fever	Exudate	Adenopathy	WBC	Splenomegaly	Heterophil Titer
β-Hemolytic streptococcus	High	Can be wiped off	Cervicals only	15,000 +	Occasionally	No change
Adenoviruses	Moderate	Can be wiped off	Minimal or none	10,000 or less	Never	No change
Infectious mononucleosis virus	Moderate	Resists wiping	Generalized	Abnormal lymphocytes	Frequently	Elevated
Corynebacterium diphtheriae	Moderate	Resists wiping, extends beyond tonsil	Cervicals only	15,000 +	Never	No change

Note: Mouth lesions are also seen in agranulocytosis, thrush,
herpes simplex, coxsackievirus, and syphilis infections.

pearance, and usually extending across the tonsillar pillars.
Tonsillar membranes are also seen in infectious mononucleosis.
B. Viral: The adenovirus group of viruses may cause exudative
tonsillitis.

Clinical Findings.
A. Symptoms: Fever, malaise, and pain on swallowing.
B. Signs:
   1. A flushed, febrile child, usually appearing moderately toxic.
   2. Enlarged, injected tonsils, frequently covered with a whitish
      exudate.
   3. Enlarged, tender cervical lymph nodes.
   Note: Look for deformity of the tonsillar pillars, suggesting
   peritonsillar abscess (very uncommon in early childhood); and
   for swelling in the midline of the pharynx, suggesting retropharyngeal abscess. (This usually occurs before two years of
   age.)
C. Laboratory Findings:
   1. Bacterial - Leukocytosis with a shift to the left. WBC may
      be as high as 20,000/cu. mm.
   2. Viral - With viral tonsillitis and pharyngitis, the WBC is
      normal or low.
   3. Throat culture to identify significant bacterial pathogens.

Complications.
A. Otitis media, cervical adenitis, sinusitis, peritonsillar abscess, pneumonia.
B. Delayed sensitivity-type reaction (rheumatic fever, glomerulonephritis).
C. Spread to distant structures (septic joints, osteomyelitis).

Treatment.
  A. Analgesics: Aspirin is usually adequate. Do not overdose.
  B. Local Measures: Gargles or throat irrigations with hot, non-irritating solutions (saline or 30% glucose) often relieve pain. Hard candy usually reduces symptoms also.
  C. Antibiotic Treatment: Procaine penicillin G, I. M. daily, or penicillin V orally four times daily, should be given for ten days only if beta-hemolytic streptococci are cultured.

TONSILLECTOMY AND ADENOIDECTOMY

Very few children require tonsillectomy and adenoidectomy. If possible, surgery should be deferred for two to three weeks after an acute attack has subsided.
  A. Indications for Surgery: Persistent nasal obstruction, persistent oral obstruction, cor pulmonale, recurrent peritonsillar abscess, recurrent pyogenic cervical adenitis, suspected tonsillar tumor, and some cases of recurrent serous otitis media.
  B. Contraindications to Surgery: Acute phase of tonsillitis; uncontrolled systemic disease (diabetes mellitus, tuberculosis, heart disease); hemorrhagic disease, polio epidemics. Great care must be taken in evaluating the child with cleft palate, submucous cleft palate, or bifid uvula for adenoid and tonsil surgery because of the risk of aggravating the defect of the short palate. Tonsillectomy and adenoidectomy do not significantly affect the later occurrence of otitis media.
  C. Invalid Reasons for Surgery: "Large" tonsils, recurrent colds and sore throats, recurrent streptococcal pharyngitis, parental pressure, school absence, and "chronic" tonsillitis. Over 95% of tonsillectomies and adenoidectomies are performed for these unjustified reasons.

ACUTE CERVICAL ADENITIS

The classic case of acute cervical adenitis involves a large, unilateral, isolated tender node. About 50% of such cases are due to beta-hemolytic streptococci, 30% to staphylococci, and the remainder perhaps to viruses.

The most common site of invasion is from pharyngitis or tonsillitis. Other entry sites for pyogenic adenitis are periapical dental abscess (usually producing a submandibular adenitis), impetigo of the face, infected acne, or otitis externa (usually producing pre-auricular adenitis). The problem is most prevalent among preschool children.

Clinical Findings.
  A. Symptoms and Signs: The chief complaints are a swollen neck and high fever. The mass is often the size of a walnut or even an egg; it is taut, firm, and exquisitely tender. If left untreated, it may develop an overlying erythema. Each tooth should be examined for a periapical abscess and percussed for tenderness.
  B. Laboratory Findings: The white count is usually about 20,000/-

cu. mm. with a shift to the left. A tuberculin skin test should
be given and a throat culture obtained.

Differential Diagnosis.
Four general categories can be distinguished on the basis of the
clinical findings. (Acute unilateral adenitis has been described
above.)
A. Acute Bilateral Cervical Adenitis: Painful and tender nodes
   are present on both sides, and the patient usually has fever.
   1. Infectious mononucleosis - This diagnosis can be aided by
      the finding of over 20% atypical cells on the white blood cell
      smear and a positive mononucleosis spot test.
   2. Tularemia - There is a history of wild rabbit or deerfly
      exposure.
   3. Diphtheria - This only occurs in nonimmunized children.
B. Subacute Unilateral Adenitis: An isolated node usually exists,
   but it is smaller and less tender than that in acute pyogenic
   adenitis.
   1. Nonspecific viral pharyngitis - This accounts for about 80%
      of subacute cases.
   2. Beta-hemolytic streptococci - The streptococcus can occa-
      sionally cause a low-grade cervical adenitis; the staphylo-
      coccus never does.
   3. Cat scratch fever - The diagnosis is aided by the finding of
      a primary papule in approximately 60% of cases. Cat
      scratches are present in over 90% of cases.
   4. Atypical mycobacteria - The node is generally nontender and
      submandibular. A false-positive PPD test is diagnostic. A
      PPD-S test gives 5 mm. of induration, whereas the PPD-
      Battey test gives greater than 10 mm. of induration.
C. Cervical Node Cancers: These tumors usually are not suspected until the adenopathy persists despite treatment. Classically, the nodes are painless, nontender, and firm to hard in
   consistency. Cancers which may appear in the neck are reticulum cell sarcoma, leukemia, Hodgkin's disease, lymphosarcoma, and cancers which have an occult primary in the
   nasopharynx (e.g., rhabdomyosarcoma). The patient with a
   cervical node that has been enlarging for more than two weeks
   despite treatment or is still large and unchanged for more than
   two months should be referred to a surgeon for biopsy.
D. Imitators of Adenitis: Several structures in the neck can be
   infected and resemble a node.
   1. Mumps - The most common pitfall in diagnosis is mistaking
      mumps for adenitis.
   2. Thyroglossal duct cyst - When superinfected, this congenital
      malformation can become acutely swollen. Helpful findings
      are the fact that it is in the midline and that it moves up-
      ward with tongue protrusion.
   3. Brachial cleft cyst - Aids to diagnosis are its location along
      the anterior border of the sternocleidomastoid muscle and
      its smooth and fluctuant consistency. Occasionally, it is
      attached to the overlying skin by a small dimple.

Complications.
The most common complication in the untreated case is sup-

puration of the node. In the preantibiotic era, extension sometimes occurred internally, resulting in jugular vein thrombosis, carotid artery rupture, septicemia, and compression of the esophagus or larynx. Poststreptococcal acute glomerulonephritis has also been reported.

Treatment.

Penicillin for ten days is the drug of choice unless Staphylococcus aureus is suspected. The patient should be referred to a dentist if a periapical abscess is suspected. Analgesics (even codeine) are necessary during the first few days of treatment.

Early treatment with antibiotics prevents most cases of pyogenic adenitis from progressing to suppuration. However, once fluctuation occurs, antibiotic therapy alone is insufficient. When fluctuation or pointing is present, the physician should incise and drain the abscess.

A good response includes resolution of the fever and improvement in the tenderness after 48 hours of treatment. Reduction in size of the nodes may take several more days. If there is no improvement within 48 hours and the PPD test is negative, it can be safely assumed that the infecting organism is penicillin-resistant S. aureus; dicloxacillin, 50 mg./Kg./day orally, should then be added to the treatment regimen. Aspiration of the node with an 18-gauge needle and 0.5 ml. of normal saline in the syringe to obtain material for Gram's stain and culture may be helpful at this stage.

Prognosis.

After the infection clears, the node may remain palpable for several months but will gradually decrease in size unless it is scarred. Recurrent pyogenic adenitis is rare. When it occurs, it is usually due to diseases such as granulomatous disease of childhood or to an immunologic disorder.

15...
Respiratory Tract

By far the most common respiratory illnesses of children are caused by specific viruses. Among these are the adenovirus group, influenza A and B, parainfluenza 1, 2, and 3, and RS virus. Mycoplasma pneumoniae is also a common offender. These agents do not restrict themselves to causing specific syndromes, although their frequency as the etiologic agent in a number of syndromes varies. Thus, a given agent may cause pharyngitis in one child, croup in another, and bronchiolitis or pneumonia in still others.

DISEASES OF THE LARYNX, TRACHEA, AND BRONCHI

LARYNGEAL STRIDOR

The most common causes of stridor are laryngeal infections, tetany, foreign body, neurologic disorders, or anatomic abnormalities (macroglossia, anomalous aortic arch, micrognathia, Pierre Robin syndrome, and some types of congenital heart disease).

Other causes are congenital deformity or flabbiness of the epiglottis and supraglottic aperture, epiglottal redundancy, relaxation of the laryngeal wall, congenital absence of tracheal rings, aortic rings, or other vascular rings, malformation of the vocal cords, a partially occluding laryngeal web, and cysts.

Clinical Findings.
A. Inspiratory stridor, especially pronounced with crying, is present from birth. Congenital laryngeal stridor usually persists for six to 18 months and the child is entirely asymptomatic and without cyanosis.
B. Noisy breathing (usually inspiratory) and mild intercostal and supraclavicular retraction. Hoarseness, dyspnea, and a laryngeal "crow" may be present.
C. Laryngoscopic examination reveals anatomic cause.
D. Stridor often disappears when the neck is extended.

Treatment.
Treatment is directed at the underlying cause. Congenital stridor requires no therapy, but special care in feeding the child must be exercised in some cases. Severe stridor due to other causes requires specific etiologic diagnosis and therapy.

Course and Prognosis.

Congenital stridor is a self-limited disease with an excellent prognosis. The prognosis of severe stridor due to other causes is that of the specific disease.

FOREIGN BODIES IN THE LARYNX AND BRONCHIAL TREE

Pins, peanuts, feathers, pebbles, chicken bones, sunflower seeds, and beads are inhaled most often, but any small object may act as a foreign body.

Clinical Findings.
A. Symptoms: History of playing with a foreign body. Often starts with choking, gagging, and coughing. Considerable subjective distress with inspiratory stridor, followed by "silent period."
B. Signs:
  1. Laryngeal or tracheal - Hoarseness and marked inspiratory stridor, without cyanosis, or with cyanosis if foreign body is large enough to cause obstruction. Wheezing may be localized.
  2. Bronchial obstruction - If obstruction is complete, atelectasis follows. If partial, a fluid medium develops which results in local purulent infection and finally an abscess. Often, a ball valve effect occurs early, accompanied by distal hyperaeration. Major physical findings are little or no air entry, asymmetric chest motion, dullness, and tracheal shift.
C. X-ray Findings:
  1. Opaque foreign bodies can be identified readily by the shadow they cast on a roentgenogram.
  2. Non-opaque foreign bodies can be identified by an inspiratory-expiratory film. If the age of the patient precludes his co-operation for such films, fluoroscopy should be done. Partial obstruction of the trachea results in hyperaeration of both lungs and a decrease in the size of the mediastinum with expiration. (Normally, the mediastinum increases in relative size with expiration.) Nonopaque foreign bodies in the bronchi cause hyperaeration if the obstruction is incomplete, or atelectasis if the obstruction of the involved lung is complete.

Treatment.
A. Attempt to produce cough by placing patient in head-down position and hitting over the involved chest area with the cupped hand.
B. When the foreign body is lodged in the trachea, an emergency tracheostomy to keep the airway open may be necessary to sustain life until definitive treatment can be undertaken.
C. Laryngoscopy or bronchoscopy will permit removal of the foreign body, although postural drainage and physical therapy combined with bronchodilator aerosol (isoproterenol) have markedly reduced the need for bronchoscopy.

Prophylaxis.
A. Keep small objects such as beads, buttons, or certain foods (e.g., nuts, popcorn) out of the reach of small children.

B. Prevent child from running with food or objects in his mouth.

C. Discourage siblings from force-feeding infants in play.

Prognosis.

Prompt diagnosis and removal of the entire foreign body usually results in complete recovery. Prolonged presence of foreign body results in pulmonary abscess formation and bronchiectasis which may not be reversible.

CROUP

Croup may be of viral (myxovirus, respiratory syncytial, etc.), bacterial (Hemophilus influenzae, Corynebacterium diphtheriae), spasmodic, allergic, or foreign body origin. The sequence and the time at which symptoms appear may aid in determining the etiology (Table 15-1).

Clinical Findings.

A. Viral Croup: Most common form; usually characterized by a gradual onset of respiratory symptoms, including cough, inspiratory stridor, and dyspnea, and low-grade or moderate fever. Systemic involvement is not marked. Children under three years are most frequently affected. WBC is not elevated.

B. Spasmodic Croup: Onset of night cough with loud stridor is usually sudden, frequently associated with a preceding mild upper respiratory tract infection or external irritant such as smoke or cold air.

TABLE 15-1. Differential diagnosis and treatment of croup.

	"Viral"	H. influenzae	Diphtheritic	Foreign Body	Spasmodic or Tetanic
Dysphagia	–	+++	±	+ to +++	–
Hoarseness	+ to +++	++ to +++ Voice normal in quality but decreased in quantity	±	+ to ++	±
Nasopharynx	Sl. hyperemia, mild edema	"Cherry-red" epiglottis	Membrane	Foreign body may be seen	Normal
Fever	Variable	High (103° F. or more)	Moderate or high	Normal	Normal
WBC	Normal or low*	Very high (18,000+)	Moderately high	Normal	Normal
Specific antibiotic	None	Ampicillin I.V. with loading dose	Antitoxin and erythromycin	Antibiotics for prophylaxis only	None
Other treatment	Steam, tracheostomy as necessary. (Oxygen is contraindicated.)			Removal of foreign body	Vomiting, steam, calcium, sedation

*High with secondary invaders.

C. Hemophilus influenzae Croup: Rapid onset of high fever, early dysphagia (either expressed or implied by refusal of food), salivation, marked toxicity and prostration (out of proportion to duration of illness), rapid respiration with increasing dyspnea, and inspiratory stridor. Hoarseness is an early symptom, suggesting serious involvement. Children between three and seven years are most frequently affected. WBC is markedly elevated. Swelling of the epiglottis is evidence on x-ray.

D. Foreign Body Croup: See p. 251.

E. Diphtheritic Croup: Inspiratory stridor and a nasopharyngeal membrane or a history of exposure to diphtheria. Insidious onset and relentless progression of symptoms.

F. Angioneurotic edema of the larynx.

G. Other: Space-occupying lesions of the larynx, compression by vascular anomalies, ingestion of drugs.

Treatment. (See Table 15-1.)

A. Specific Measures: Presumptive etiology determines the treatment. Forceful depression of the tongue for children suspected of having viral or H. influenzae croup should be avoided unless one is prepared to pass an endotracheal tube immediately.

In many children (particularly those under three years of age), nasotracheal intubation for two to three days is often less hazardous than tracheostomy, and ventilatory assistance is easier.

1. Viral croup -

   a. Endotracheal tube - An open airway is best created by passage of an endotracheal tube. The endotracheal tube should be placed by a physician promptly on indication; if tracheostomy is necessary, it should be performed by an experienced operator. No anesthesia is required and none should be given. Objective indications for tracheostomy are increase in restlessness, variations in heart rate (particularly a marked increase), fatigue, and dilation of pupils. Cyanosis is an extremely late sign and may only be present as pallor.

      Intermittent positive-pressure breathing may obviate the need for tracheostomy.

   b. Antibiotics to prevent or treat secondary infection (see Chapter 6).

   c. A solution of racemic epinephrine given either by inhalation or by IPPB may be of value.

2. Spasmodic croup - The etiology is unknown, and no specific therapy exists.

   a. Calcium - If tetany is considered to be a possibility, a trial of calcium therapy is indicated (see p. 416).

   b. Emesis - The production of vomiting by gagging with a tongue blade or by the use of an emetic agent (mustard, ipecac) may be tried in order to terminate an attack.

3. Haemophilus influenzae croup -

   a. Antibiotics - Ampicillin (Polycillin®, Penbritin®, Omnipen®) or combined streptomycin and chloramphenicol in full doses will quickly eliminate the severe toxemia of this infection.

(1) Ampicillin, 150 mg./Kg. immediately, followed by 200/mg./Kg./day in four doses, I.V. until oral route is possible, for seven days.

(2) Streptomycin, 50 mg./Kg. I.M. per 24 hours divided into four doses. Discontinue after three days.

(3) Chloramphenicol, 60 to 150 mg./Kg./day orally in four doses per day for two to four days. Reduce to lower dose and continue for a total of seven days.

    b. Nasotracheal tube is preferred over tracheostomy. Either is usually necessary even within a few hours of the apparent onset of the illness. The method is the same as for viral croup.

4. Diphtheritic croup -

    a. Diphtheria antitoxin given I.V. at once, after testing for serum sensitivity (see Chapter 7).

    b. Penicillin G, 20,000 to 50,000 units/Kg./day I.M. or I V. in four to six doses, may hasten disappearance of organisms.

    c. Tracheostomy is necessary.

5. Foreign body croup (see p. 251).

6. Angioneurotic edema.

B. General Measures (regardless of etiology):

1. Mist and steam -

    a. Hospital care - In the hospital, continuous cold air humidifiers are of particular value in avoiding excessive heat of steam and thus tend to decrease the discomfort of the patient and his attendant. Mist also diminishes the need for fluid in the presence of fever. Oxygen may obscure signs of obstruction and is generally contraindicated.

    b. Home care - In the home, steam provided by a hot shower gives the most effective moisture therapy and is preferable to commercially available humidifiers, which may result in scalding. The child's crib may be placed in the bathroom overnight or during the day.

2. Supportive measures - Children with croup are exceedingly anxious and should receive the most permissive individual care while they have respiratory distress. Increasing anxiety is a sign of progressive anoxia.

    a. Children should be allowed to assume a position of comfort or should be held if they so desire.

    b. Dysphagia is marked; the foods of choice are ice cream, gelatin desserts, cold water, or cool skimmed milk. Prevent dehydration.

    c. It has not been proved that corticosteroids are of value in treatment.

Course and Prognosis.

A. Viral Croup: Often has a protracted course of five to seven days with gradual improvement or, infrequently, gradual tiring of the patient necessitating elective tracheostomy. Prognosis is generally good.

B. Hemophilus influenzae Croup: Overwhelming and fatal sepsis may occur when antibiotic therapy is not promptly instituted. The course is stormy initially, but with specific antibiotic therapy the prognosis is good.

C. Diphtheritic Croup: Increasingly rare in this country. Without early antitoxin therapy the chances of toxic complications of diphtheria are considerable, as is the danger of anoxia from obstruction also.

D. Spasmodic Croup: The disease is self-limited and never fatal. It has a short course. May be clear during the day but show progressively milder exacerbations for a few nights.

E. Foreign Body Croup: Prompt removal of the foreign body brings complete recovery.

BRONCHITIS

TABLE 15-2. Differential diagnosis of bronchitis.

Type*	Symptoms	Signs	Laboratory	X-ray
ACUTE				
Viral	Paroxysmal dry cough, most severe at night; productive after 4-6 days.	Fever mild or absent. Coarse rales and rhonchi after a few days. Respiratory rate accel.	Relative neutropenia.	Usually negative. May show increased bronchial markings.
Bacterial			Leukocytosis	
CHRONIC				
Bacterial	Productive cough most severe after awakening	N or transient fever. Scattered coarse rales and harsh expiration.	Leukocytosis sometimes.	Increased bronchial markings.
Allergic			Eosinophilia of nasal sm.	
Mechanical drying	Dry, non-productive cough, most severe after awakening. Mild hoarseness; feeling of dryness in nasopharynx.			

*Foreign body aspiration: see p. 251.

Complications.

Permanent changes in the bronchial tree and subsequent bronchiectasis.

Treatment.

General treatment measures for all types include warm, moist air, expectorants, and sedatives.

A. Acute:
  1. Viral - None.
  2. Bacterial - Antibiotics.

B. Chronic:
  1. Bacterial - Antibiotics, bronchodilators; postural drainage.
  2. Allergic - Elimination of allergens.
  3. Mechanical drying - Proper humidification of room air.

ACUTE BRONCHIOLITIS
(Acute Obstructive Bronchitis, Capillary Bronchitis, Generalized Obstructive Emphysema)

Acute bronchiolitis in infants is a serious, widespread inflammation of bronchioles believed to be of infectious or allergic origin. It is generally seen in the winter months and affects children under two years of age. It is frequently recurrent and often confused with asthma.

Acute bronchiolitis is caused by viruses (agents of primary atypical pneumonia; influenza types A, B, C; adenovirus group, respiratory syncytial virus, parainfluenza, etc.), bacteria (H. influenzae, pneumococci, hemolytic streptococci), or allergy.

Clinical Findings.

The infant's bronchioles are easily obstructed by inflammatory exudate and edema as well as by constriction of the circular musculature. This produces many small areas of atelectasis.

A. Symptoms:
  1. Dyspnea, with rapid, shallow respirations.
  2. Prostration.
  3. Cough may be totally absent.
B. Signs:
  1. Fine crackling and sibilant rales, with marked diminution of breath sounds due to decreased air exchange. Wheezing is often present as well.
  2. Fever may be moderate or high. Fever due to dehydration is likely in the face of decreased fluid intake in a child struggling for breath.
  3. Intermittent cyanosis.
  4. Intermittent prostration.
  5. Inspiratory retraction of intercostal and suprasternal spaces.
  6. Emphysematous chest - Marked overinflation of the chest, resulting in:
     a. Hyperresonant percussion note.
     b. Depression of the diaphragm and easy palpation of the liver border. **Note:** This should not be confused with cardiac failure, which may or may not be present.
C. Laboratory Findings: WBC is of little help in differentiating between viral and bacterial etiology in this condition. Antibiotic therapy should not be withheld because WBC is low.
D. X-ray Findings: Chest x-ray may reveal emphysema and increased bronchovascular markings. Small areas of atelectasis may be seen. On fluoroscopic examination, the diaphragm is low and shows limited respiratory excursion. The intercostal spaces are wide and the lungs characteristically overinflated.

Complications.

The chief danger to life in acute bronchiolitis lies in rapidly progressing exhaustion and anoxia. The degree and duration of bronchiole obstruction determine the severity of the condition.

Treatment.

A. Emergency Measures:
  1. The child should be placed in a warmed atmosphere which is high in oxygen and well saturated with water vapor.
  2. Determination of pH and immediate correction of acidosis, if present.
  3. Bronchodilator aerosol (isoproterenol) is of questionable value.
B. Specific Measures:
  1. Antibiotics are of value in bronchiolitis caused by bacteria.

Since an immediate etiologic diagnosis is usually impossible and since the condition is serious, antibiotics are indicated. In order to cover the three most common bacteria named above, one of the following courses is suggested:

a. A single broad-spectrum antibiotic such as ampicillin. **Caution:** See Chapter 6.

b. Parenteral penicillin and streptomycin. **Caution:** See Chapter 6.

2. Prednisone and hydrocortisone - There is no convincing evidence that corticosteroids alter the course of the disease.

C. General Measures:

1. Parenteral fluid therapy should be given initially to decrease the effort required in taking fluids by mouth.

2. Sedation - Small doses of phenobarbital, by suppository, may be used to calm the child while treatment with high humidity and oxygen is instituted. Heavy sedation with opiates or other drugs is dangerous since sedatives tend to further depress the cough reflex and respiratory centers. Postural drainage should be vigorously pursued.

Course and Prognosis.

With prompt therapy the death rate is markedly lowered. With recovery, there are usually no sequelae; but in the case of asthmatic bronchiolitis repeated recurrences of the acute episode (two to five times per year) are often seen. Infants and young children who have had two or more episodes of acute bronchiolitis are almost certain to have asthma later.

With adequate therapy, marked improvement usually occurs within 24 to 36 hours. The overall prognosis is good, but in a few instances death may occur in spite of all therapy. Because of the recurrent nature of acute bronchiolitis in the allergic child, control of the allergic condition should be carried out.

LOBAR EMPHYSEMA

Lobar emphysema in the newborn infant or young child is an uncommon disorder frequently associated with malformation of the cartilage rings of the bronchus or other abnormality. It causes valvular obstruction which allows entry of air on inspiration but does not permit air to escape on expiration. Manifestations are tachypnea and other signs of severe respiratory difficulty, localized hyperaeration, shift of the heart to the opposite side, and poor breath sounds over the involved area. X-ray shows marked radiolucency of a lobe or an entire lung field; lung markings traverse this area. Treatment is initially medical (i. e., bronchial dilation followed by postural drainage). If clinical deterioration occurs in spite of medical therapy, surgical removal of the involved area is warranted.

DISEASES OF THE LUNGS AND PLEURA

PNEUMONIA

Anatomic differentiation of pneumonia is of no value in child-hood. For successful treatment an educated guess as to the etiologic agent is of greatest therapeutic importance.

Etiology.
   A. Bacteria: Especially pneumococci, staphylococci, streptococci, H. influenzae, klebsiella, Mycobacterium tuberculosis, Mycoplasma pneumoniae, psittacosis-lymphogranuloma group.
   B. Fungi: Candidiasis, histoplasmosis, coccidioidomycosis.
   C. Viruses: Respiratory syncytial, adenovirus, influenza, parainfluenza viruses.
   D. Rickettsiae: Coxiella burnetii.
   E. Protozoa: Pneumocystis carinii, especially in transplant patients, prematures, and those with deficient immune response.
   F. Chemicals and Food: Inhalation of kerosene, lipid materials, zinc stearate; food aspiration.

Clinical Findings.
   A. Symptoms: Fairly sudden onset; rapidly rising fever; chills in older children; rapid respiration, cough; vomiting and diarrhea may occur; meningismus may be present, especially with right upper lobe involvement; convulsions may occur at onset; pleural pain in older children (may be referred to abdomen); abdominal distention common.
   B. Signs: Dyspnea with frequent expiratory grunts; dilated nostrils during respiration; flushed cheeks; cyanosis (occasionally); dullness, diminished breath sounds, rales, prolonged expiration phase; stiff neck or abdominal pain occasionally.
   C. Laboratory Findings: These vary with etiology.
      1. Bacterial - High WBC (18,000 to 30,000), positive nasopharyngeal cultures, and, frequently, positive blood culture.
      2. Tuberculosis - See p. 265.
      3. Viral and rickettsial - Normal or slightly elevated WBC early in the disease which drops later. Cold hemagglutinins and streptococcus-MG agglutinins may be demonstrated during convalescence in cases of primary atypical pneumonia. Complement-fixing antibodies show specific rise in pneumonias due to influenza virus, adenovirus, and the agent of psittacosis-LGV.

Complications.
   A. Bacterial: Empyema, lung abscess, pneumatocele, atelectasis, local hyperaeration, bronchiectasis, meningitis, peritonitis, and septic arthritis. (Tuberculosis: see p. 265.)
   B. Viral or Rickettsial: Atelectasis, bronchiectasis.
   C. Chemical: Atelectasis, lung abscess, and bronchiectasis.

Treatment.
   A. Specific Measures:
      1. Bacterial - Combined medical and surgical treatment is usually necessary for staphylococcal pneumonia in infants.

2. Tuberculosis - See p. 265.
3. Mycoplasmal - Tetracyclines.
4. Rickettsial - See Table 6-2.
5. Chemical - Prophylactic antibiotic therapy in the acute phase.
B. General Measures: Oxygen to relieve respiratory distress.

Prognosis.
Antibiotics have revolutionized the therapy of pneumonitis.
Prognosis of children treated promptly is excellent. Complications,
however, present considerable therapeutic difficulties, and in the
case of bronchiectasis changes may be irreversible.

LÖFFLER'S SYNDROME
(Eosinophilic Pneumonia)

Löffler's syndrome is a clinical syndrome which may be an unusual allergic reaction to visceral larva migrans, ascariasis,
toxocariasis, or some other infestation or infection. It is characterized by mild fever, dyspnea, and cough with minimal physical
signs in the chest. Hepatosplenomegaly may be present. There is
striking eosinophilia (60% or more). Hyperglobulinemia and positive
heterophil titer may be present. X-ray reveals transitory and mi-
grant localized infiltration of the lung fields or diffuse involvement
with miliary or nodular lesions or lobar consolidation which may involve one or more lobes.
Use specific therapy when available. Antihistaminic substances
may be of value. Spontaneous clearing occurs in two to six weeks.
See also Visceral Larva Migrans in Chapter 26.

INTERSTITIAL PLASMA CELL PNEUMONIA
(Pneumocystis carinii Pneumonia)

Interstitial plasma cell pneumonia has a predilection
for premature or immature debilitated infants six weeks to six
months of age. In the U.S.A., older children, particularly those
with hypogammaglobulinemia or with severe systemic disease, are
affected. It has an insidious onset. The fully developed disease is
characterized by little or no fever, respiratory distress, cyanosis,
extreme tachypnea, and a bluish-white facial pallor. Chest findings
may be minimal. X-rays reveal widespread bilateral involvement
of both lungs with patchy peribronchial infiltration, interstitial involvement, and widespread irregular areas of consolidation. Treatment with pentamidine isethionate (Lomidine®), 500 mg. total dose
divided into ten daily I.M. injections, and trimethoprim-sulfamethoxazole (Bactrim®, Septra®), 25 mg./Kg./day orally q.i.d.

CHRONIC RESPIRATORY DISEASES

Chronic respiratory diseases which most frequently come to
the attention of the pediatrician include allergic disorders, cystic
fibrosis (mucoviscidosis), congenital cystic disease of the lungs,
sinobronchitis, Hamman-Rich syndrome (progressive diffuse fibrosis of the lungs of unknown etiology, characterized by cough, dyspnea,

and cyanosis, and associated with minimal physical findings), tuberculosis, mycotic infections, sarcoidosis, parasitic infections, tumors,
and idiopathic pulmonary hemosiderosis.

PNEUMOTHORAX

Pneumothorax is not common in the pediatric age group except
in premature infants. It may occur in newborn infants following
instrumentation of the respiratory tract or due to spontaneous rupture of the alveoli with the first breath; in infants as a complication
of pertussis or staphylococcal pneumonia; in older children as a result of trauma to the chest wall or spontaneous rupture of an emphysematous bleb; or at any age as a complication of pneumonia or lung
abscess, as a result of perforation by a migrating aspirated foreign
body, and as a complication of tracheostomy. In the newborn infant
the age at onset of pneumothorax varies inversely with age; abnormal findings do not develop for days or weeks after birth in small
premature infants. Consider diaphragmatic hernia, lobar emphysema, or solitary cyst of the lung in the differential diagnosis.

Clinical Findings.
A. Symptoms: Dyspnea, if the vital capacity has suddenly been
   reduced; chest pain in older children; and cyanosis in severe
   cases, especially in tension pneumothorax.
B. Signs: Hyperresonance on the affected side; breath sounds
   and tactile or vocal fremitus are decreased or absent. Cardiac
   dullness may be obliterated, and mediastinal shift may occur.
C. X-ray Findings: Air in the pleural space; may be associated
   with mediastinal emphysema and pneumothorax of other side.

Treatment.
A. Newborn Infants: **This is an emergency.** Tension pneumothorax with increasing cyanosis requires relief of tension by
   prompt aspiration of air to reduce the intrapleural pressure.
B. Older Children: Spontaneous resorption almost invariably occurs, and no treatment is usually required.

Course and Prognosis.
In the newborn infant, tension pneumothorax will produce increasing cyanosis. Unless the diagnosis is promptly made, the
condition relieved, and the lung reexpanded by treatment, the
prognosis is poor. Spontaneous recovery from pneumothorax in
other conditions is excellent.

PLEURISY

A complication of acute or chronic pulmonary infection, usually
due to pyogenic bacteria, tuberculosis, or coxsackievirus (pleurodynia). Occasionally it is a complication of rheumatic fever or
associated with pericarditis.

Clinical Findings.
A. Symptoms: Pain, chiefly with coughing, on the affected side of

chest (may also occur in shoulders or abdomen), and recurrence of previously resolved fever.
B. Signs (variable and may be absent): Guarded and grunting respirations, diminished respiratory excursion on the affected side, and friction rub on auscultation over the affected area. Dullness and decreased breath sounds may be present.
C. X-ray Findings: Thickening of pleural shadow along thoracic wall or between lobes of lung. Blunting of costophrenic sulci with small amounts of fluid. Occasionally, nothing is seen on x-ray.

Treatment.
A. Specific Measures: Treat the acute or chronic disease.
B. General Measures:
1. Analgesics, including codeine, may be necessary.
2. Strapping the involved side with adhesive tape will reduce pain. Strapping should probably not be used in the presence of acute bacterial pneumonia, since it decreases chest expansion and favors extension of the infection.

PLEURISY WITH EFFUSION

Pleurisy with effusion may complicate chronic and acute pulmonary infections or may be associated with a generalized disease.

Clinical Findings.
A. Symptoms: There may be none if pleural effusion is slight. A secondary rise in temperature in the course of an acute pulmonary infection is characteristic of the development of pleural effusion, which may then develop into empyema. Respiratory distress is present, occasionally with cyanosis.
B. Signs: Dyspnea and orthopnea, occasionally with cyanosis; lag of chest motion on the involved side, mediastinal shift to the opposite side, flat percussion note over the affected side, and absent breath sounds on auscultation.
C. Laboratory Findings: Fluid obtained by thoracentesis should be carefully examined and the fluid cultured. The fluid may consist of an exudate, transudate, blood, or chyle. Note cell type.
1. Exudates -
a. Infected - As in the early phases of empyema complicating acute or chronic pulmonary infections.
b. Sterile - As part of the inflammatory reaction associated with pneumonia. Sterile exudate may be seen in polyserositis, rheumatic fever, and in abdominal or thoracic neuroblastoma or other tumors. Rule out tuberculosis.
2. Transudates - Clear, sterile, yellow fluid of low specific gravity containing no fibrin and few, if any, endothelial cells. Transudates are found in the pleural spaces in congestive heart failure, nephrosis or malnutrition, vascular anomalies, and acute glomerulonephritis.
3. Blood - As a result of trauma to the chest, disturbances of the clotting mechanism, and tumors, especially neuroblastoma.
4. Chyle - As a consequence of trauma or obstruction of thoracic duct or as a complication of cystic hygroma of the neck.

D. X-ray Findings: Chest x-ray shows uniform density obscuring underlying lung, commonly associated with shift of mediastinal contents and at times depression of the hemidiaphragm.

Treatment.
A. Specific Measures: Check Mantoux and treat underlying cause.
B. General Measures: Analgesics may be necessary. Adhesive strapping of the affected side is indicated if pain is severe.
C. Thoracentesis, unless required for relief of respiratory distress, is indicated chiefly for diagnostic purposes.

Prognosis.
Prognosis is good for spontaneous recovery.

EMPYEMA

Empyema is almost always a complication of acute or chronic pulmonary disease. Empyema due to staphylococci, streptococci, or influenza bacilli may occur early in the course of pneumonia in children under four years of age. Empyema due to pneumococci or the Klebsiella-Enterobacter group occurs in older children.

Clinical Findings.
A. Symptoms: All the symptoms of uncomplicated pneumonia in children may be seen in empyema. A secondary rise in fever or its undue persistence in the course of pneumonia suggests the diagnosis.
B. Signs: Dyspnea, occasionally with cyanosis, lag of chest motion on the affected side, dullness to percussion, decrease or suppression of chest sounds, and decreased or absent fremitus. Intercostal spaces may be widened, and there may be a shift of the mediastinum. Toxicity is marked.
C. X-ray Findings: X-ray of the chest reveals a diffuse density indicating pleural fluid or thickening. Purulent pleural exudates are usually loculated, except in the early states of infection. Exudate may occupy any dependent portion of the pleural space and is commonly located in the inter-lobar spaces.
D. Laboratory Findings: WBC is usually high; counts of 30,000 or more are frequent. Blood culture is usually positive. Pus obtained by thoracentesis should permit specific diagnosis.

Treatment.
A. Specific Measures:
1. Specific antibiotic therapy should be instituted after etiologic diagnosis has been established by thoracentesis and culture. (For choice of drugs, see Table 6-2.)
2. In addition to systemic use of antibiotics, local instillation of antibiotic solutions may be required in order to sterilize the pleural cavity. (See Chapter 6 for dosages and drug concentrations for intrapleural instillation of antibiotics.)
B. Local Measures: Repeated aspiration of pus and instillation of specific antibiotics into the pleural cavity are necessary (see above). Fibrin solvents (streptokinase and streptodornase) are not indicated in chronic empyema and may cause marked systemic reactions.

C. General Measures: When dyspnea is a prominent complaint, oxygen will tend to overcome the respiratory embarrassment and compensate for the reduced vital capacity.

D. Surgical Measures: Closed-suction drainage without rib resection usually suffices. Thoracotomy with surgical drainage may be required early in the course in infants and when improvement does not occur after the third week of the disease in older children, or with severe respiratory distress, loculated pus, or marked mediastinal shift. Decortication is no longer necessary; it should only be considered after one year of therapy and evidence, by pulmonary function studies, that the procedure is indicated.

Prognosis.

Empyema is a serious disease, especially in small children. Prompt diagnosis is essential for the prevention of loculation and subsequent chronicity. When local and systemic antibiotic therapy are promptly instituted and thoracentesis and/or thoracotomy are performed, the prognosis is generally good.

BRONCHIECTASIS

Bronchiectasis is a chronic, progressive disorder of the lungs characterized by infected cavities consisting of saccular or tubular enlargement of the bronchi. It may follow aspiration of a foreign body but usually is a complication of a preceding respiratory infection such as pneumonia, pertussis, measles, influenza, or sinobronchitis. Bronchiectasis in infancy often is associated with fibrocystic disease. The bacterial flora usually contains staphylococci, but other organisms, such as klebsiella, haemophilus influenzae, pseudomonas, and proteus may be found. Congenital bronchiectasis is considered by many to be a clinical entity.

Clinical Findings.

A. Symptoms: The child's general health may be good initially. Later, there is chronic cough, usually "loose," which may be noted only at night or in the morning, and dyspnea on exertion. Eventually, anorexia and weight loss may be noted. The older child may expectorate moderate or large amounts of foul-smelling sputum.

B. Signs: Low-grade fever. Moist rales, which persist after coughing, may be heard over the involved area. Clubbing of the fingers occurs when the pulmonary involvement is marked and of long standing.

C. Laboratory Findings: Anemia is present in long-standing cases. Pathogenic bacteria may be found in the sputum.

D. X-ray Findings: X-rays of the chest may show only increased bronchovascular markings extending toward the base of the involved lung. Eventually the lung proper may appear to contain many small air-filled cavities. Bronchography may differentiate between diffuse or localized involvement.

Treatment.

Once the presence of a foreign body or tuberculosis has been ruled out, the medical and surgical management of bronchiectasis does not vary significantly regardless of the original cause.

A. Specific Measures:
1. Antibiotics - Systemic antibiotics are preferable. In the early stage, the intravenous route is necessary in order to obtain adequate lung tissue levels.
2. Aerosol therapy with antibiotics have no value. Use of systemic antibiotics is to be emphasized.
3. Bronchodilator aerosol (isoproterenol), five to ten breaths, followed in ten to 15 minutes by vigorous postural drainage every four to six hours.
4. Regular postural drainage breathing exercises three times daily.

B. General Measures: An adequate diet is necessary. Pancrelipase (Cotazym®) should be used in cases of fibrocystic disease, although it has no value in therapy of pulmonary complications of the disease.

C. Surgical Measures:
1. When infected postnasal secretions from adenoidal tissue and tonsils contribute to the disease, tonsillectomy and adenoidectomy may be indicated.
2. Drainage of paranasal sinuses may also facilitate local therapy of infected paranasal sinuses.
3. Bronchial washout under anesthesia with a mucolytic agent is sometimes useful.
4. When saccular bronchiectasis is limited to one or two lobes and is severe and progressive, surgical removal of the involved lobes may be lifesaving. Postural drainage should be given a 12-month trial before surgery.

Prophylaxis.

Most bronchiectases can be prevented through the proper prophylaxis and prompt treatment of the antecedent influenza, pneumonia, sinusitis, pertussis, measles, or foreign body.

Prognosis.

A. Saccular Bronchiectasis: With adequate postural drainage, some children have shown striking improvement. Operation is usually necessary.

B. Mild to Moderate Bronchiectasis: Medical treatment is often successful; milder cases may be entirely reversible.

C. Fibrocystic Disease: The management of pulmonary disease and bronchiectasis requires long-term therapy, including postural drainage and antibiotics when indicated. In general, the course in this group is less satisfactory than in those with simple post-infectious bronchiectasis.

D. Sinobronchitis: The prognosis is best in children suffering from sinobronchitis or bronchiectasis due to chronic drainage from infected adenoids, tonsils, and sinuses.

POSTOPERATIVE ATELECTASIS

Following prolonged general anesthesia, parts of the lung occasionally fail to expand. Infection commonly develops in the collapsed areas. Postoperative atelectasis develops most commonly following thoracic surgery, but it may follow any prolonged surgical procedure, particularly when paralytic agents have been given and assisted ventilation used to maintain gas exchange.

Atelectasis develops regularly during anesthesia in experimental animals and man. It can be minimized by intermittent hyperinflation of the lungs. In the nonanesthetized state, this is achieved by periodic sighing. Following surgery, many patients hypoventilate, do not sigh, and thus permit the collapse of the lung to progress.

Clinically, postoperative atelectasis is manifested by sudden development of fever, cyanosis, and varying degrees of respiratory distress. Cough, if present at all, is not marked. A chest x-ray reveals collapse of the lung in the involved areas.

Prevention consists of breathing exercises and postural drainage to induce coughing. Intermittent hyperinflation during surgery and proper hyperinflation with air prior to extubation will help to prevent atelectasis. Antibiotics frequently are indicated.

POSTPERFUSION SYNDROME

When pump oxygenators are used to perfuse the systemic circulation during cardiac surgery, there is little perfusion of the lung (except through the bronchial circulation). The lack of blood flow through the lung occasionally leads to gradual depletion of pulmonary surfactant. When significant amounts of pulmonary surfactant have been lost during prolonged pump perfusion of the systemic circulation, the lungs tend to become atelectatic. While simple atelectasis is usually easily reversed by hyperinflation, it is extremely difficult to open up the alveoli of patients who lack pulmonary surfactant. The clinical syndrome, therefore, presents itself as atelectasis, severe cyanosis, and systemic arterial oxygen desaturation, respiratory distress, fever, and secondary hypoxic acidosis. The chest x-ray shows diffuse atelectasis.

Postperfusion syndrome is particularly apt to develop in patients who have pulmonary hypertension. The high pulmonary vascular resistance probably lessens perfusion of the pulmonary parenchyma by bronchial vessels and predisposes such patients to the development of postperfusion syndrome.

PULMONARY TUBERCULOSIS

Tuberculous lesions are described as either active or inactive and as being of either the primary or reinfection (secondary) type.

Primary pulmonary tuberculosis usually is asymptomatic but is occasionally manifested as a mild pneumonitis which resolves more slowly than an acute bacterial pneumonitis. The diagnosis is often made in retrospect, after the reaction to the tuberculin skin test has changed from negative to positive, and sometimes not until the x-ray shows slow resolution and calcification of the pulmonary lesion. A diligent search for contacts is imperative to prevent infection of others and superinfection of the patient.

Tuberculosis is transmitted by droplet or dust from an infected adult with an open lesion. Contacts may be parents or others living in the same household who are suffering from chronic cough which may be falsely attributed to other causes (e. g., cigarette smoking).

Domestic servants and grandparents are a frequent source of infection for children below the age of five years. The organism is rarely transmitted from the childhood type of the disease or from casual contact with a single open case.

Reinfection tuberculosis is rare in children under ten but may occur in adolescence. Lesions are usually in the apex of the lung.

Atypical (unclassified or anonymous) mycobacteria have been shown to cause drug-resistant cervical adenitis and skin lesions (swimming pool granuloma), and children with Mycobacterium balnei infection may have a positive tuberculin skin test.

Types.
A. The Primary (Ghon) Complex: Consists of a lesion in the periphery of the lung (most commonly at the base of the upper lobes or in the lower lobes) with involvement of the lymphatics draining the area, and enlargement of the regional lymph nodes.
B. Progression may be in one of three directions if the lesion does not heal spontaneously:
   1. Pneumonitis as a result of direct extension to nearby areas.
   2. Endobronchial - Extrinsic pressure on bronchus or erosion of bronchus with occasional massive seeding of distal lung.
   3. Lymphohematogenous spread to both lungs (miliary pulmonary tuberculosis), bone, kidney, or brain - the latter leading to tuberculous meningitis and tuberculoma formation.
C. Adult Type: Slowly progressive apical lesion with fibrous reaction and repair by encapsulation and calcification.

Clinical Findings.
The majority of cases of primary tuberculosis are found by noting a change in reactivity from negative to positive of routine periodic tuberculin tests, or by investigation of children with a history of possible contact with an adult who has open tuberculosis.
A. Symptoms: In children, evidence of pulmonary involvement may be absent or expressed only as fatigue and malaise, low-grade fever, and weight loss. Appetite is poor. Cough, with or without expectoration, is not common in either primary or reinfection tuberculosis except in infants.
B. Signs:
   1. Primary lesion - No signs are found if the primary focus is small, even if mediastinal lymphadenopathy is marked.
   2. Tuberculous pneumonitis may be a segmental lesion of the collapse-consolidation type following breakthrough of caseous nodes into the bronchial tree or progressive primary pneumonitis with cavitation. Both show dullness on percussion and alteration in breath sounds. Eventually, fine rales are heard, usually after characteristic x-ray findings appear. Minimal physical findings may go hand in hand with x-ray evidence of extensive pulmonary disease.
   3. Miliary infections of the lung - The pulmonary examination is usually negative; manifestations include irregular spiking fevers, extreme toxemia and malaise, and splenomegaly.
   4. Skin test - Tuberculin reaction is positive (see Chapter 7).
   5. Tuberculin skin testing is always indicated in pneumonitis.
C. Laboratory Findings:
   1. WBC - Not distinctive during the acute illness. In miliary tuberculosis, leukopenia or leukocytosis occurs.

2. Sedimentation rate is occasionally elevated during the period of tuberculous activity.

3. Bacteriologic studies - It is usually necessary to isolate the acid-fast organism from gastric washings, since small infants and children swallow rather than expectorate sputum. Gastric washings should be collected each morning before arising for three days, concentrated, and cultured; a portion is stained for acid-fast bacilli.

D. X-ray Findings: Serial chest x-rays are the most important single method for following the course of the disease.

The presence of a positive tuberculin skin test and the demonstration of the tubercle bacilli in gastric washings confirm the etiologic impression obtained by x-ray examination.

1. Primary tuberculous pneumonitis, the early x-ray manifestation of pulmonary tuberculosis, may involve all or part of a lobe. It is always accompanied by lymphadenopathy, and sometimes by pleural thickening and pleural effusion. There is a diffuse infiltrative lesion which is indistinguishable from pneumonitis due to bacteria or other causes except for striking lymphadenopathy. Constitutional symptoms may be present when no x-ray findings exist, or x-ray findings may be striking in the absence of symptoms.

2. Healing - There may either be complete resorption of the exudate and disappearance of the lymphadenopathy without residual scarring, or fibrosis and calcification of the primary lesion and lymph nodes, as well as pleural thickening.

3. Miliary tuberculosis cannot be seen on x-ray in its earliest stages. As the disease progresses, small, nodular densities throughout the lungs appear as a faint stippling. Later, the small nodules coalesce, producing larger nodular densities scattered throughout the lung fields and giving the characteristic "rice grain" or "snowflake" appearance. (This may be indistinguishable from the picture produced by pertussis pneumonitis, Löffler's pneumonia, coccidioidomycosis, histoplasmosis, metastatic tumor, hemosiderosis, berylliosis, or pulmonary alveolar microlithiasis.)

4. Reinfection (secondary) tuberculosis is found most often in girls and during and after adolescence. Apical lesions usually occur with this type but are quite uncommon with primary tuberculosis. Hilar lymphadenopathy may not be demonstrable. Cavitation is infrequent in the pediatric age group.

Complications of Primary Tuberculosis.

Pleural effusion, disseminated (miliary) tuberculosis, tuberculous meningitis; tuberculosis of the bones and joints, kidneys; tuberculous cervical lymphadenitis.

Treatment.

A. General Treatment:

1. Bed rest is not enforced. As a rule, children are better off in their own homes than in sanatoriums.

2. Nutrition - A diet appropriate and adequate for the child's age is all that is necessary.

3. Fresh air and sun therapy - Formerly this was thought to be the most important tool in clinical management. While

fresh air has a general tonic effect on the body and increases appetite, intensive sun exposure may be harmful in pulmonary tuberculosis.

4. Clinical aids in following the course of the disease include daily temperature, the child's general condition (including the presence or absence of malaise, weight gain or weight loss), sedimentation rate, and serial chest x-rays.

B. Specific Treatment*: Routine pretreatment work-up should include three gastric examinations for smear and culture, an early morning urine specimen for smear and culture, x-rays of chest (posteroanterior and lateral).

1. Under three years of age - Any child under three years of age with a positive tuberculin skin test, with or without roentgenographic evidence of pulmonary disease, should be considered to have active tuberculosis.

   a. Isoniazid (INH), 16 mg./Kg./day orally in two divided doses for 12 to 18 months. If possible, INH blood levels should be determined. (Satisfactory levels are those over 0.4 mcg./ml. six hours after a standard dose.)

   b. Streptomycin sulfate, 20 mg./Kg./day in a single daily dose for one to three months.

   c. Sodium or potassium aminosalicylate (NaPAS or KPAS), 200 mg./Kg./day divided into four doses for 12 to 18 months.

   d. Ethambutol - Experience with ethambutol in the pediatric age group is limited. The usual dose is 20 mg./Kg./day for four to six weeks and 15 mg./Kg./day thereafter. The drug should not be used in a child whose visual acuity cannot be tested. Retrobulbar neuritis has been reported.

2. Three to ten years of age - Indications for treatment include (1) evidence of recent infection, e. g., recent tuberculin conversion or strongly positive tuberculin test; (2) positive x-ray findings consistent with active tuberculosis with a positive tuberculin test; (3) history of recent primary infection and development of measles; and (4) steroid therapy used for some other reason in a tuberculin-positive child.

   a. Isoniazid as above.

   b. PAS - Three to six years, 200 mg./Kg./day; six to eight years, 6 Gm./day; eight to ten years, 8 Gm./day.

   c. Streptomycin as above.

3. Ten years and older - Indications in this age group are essentially the same as in para. 2. However, serious consideration should be given to prophylaxis at the anticipated onset of the adolescent growth spurt, the development of secondary sex characteristics, and, in particular, the proximity of the menarche. INH prophylaxis during adolescence is indicated where primary infection caused known illness.

   a. Isoniazid and streptomycin as above.

   b. PAS, 19 Gm./day in four or five doses.

   c. Pyridoxine hydrochloride, 25 mg./day.

4. The simultaneous use of cycloserine and ethionamide in all cases of tuberculous meningitis, miliary tuberculosis, and progressive primary disease has been recommended until

---

*Regimen used at the National Jewish Hospital, Denver, Colorado.

the drug susceptibility pattern of the infecting strain is determined.

C. Treatment of Complications: Triple drug therapy is mandatory in miliary tuberculosis, tuberculous meningitis, bone and joint tuberculosis, and renal tuberculosis. The treatment regimen should follow that outlined in para. B2 with the recommendation that streptomycin be continued for three months and INH and PAS for 18 months. Drug-resistant cases should be treated with rifampin (see Chapter 6).

Prophylaxis and Public Health Measures.

A. Contacts: Identification of contacts is the imperative responsibility of the physician caring for the child. Complete separation of the patient from his contact should occur promptly. Report to the local health department. Case-finding includes a tuberculin test on all immediate household contacts, servants, relatives, teachers, babysitters, school bus drivers, etc. X-rays of the chest should be repeated in two months on all positive reactors. Routine tuberculin testing of all tuberculin-negative children should be repeated every six to 12 months throughout childhood. If a child has no reaction to 0.001 mg. of PPD (or its equivalent), there is little possibility that he has tuberculosis. It is important to recognize that there is considerable skin test cross-reactivity between Myco. tuberculosis and members of the atypical group.

B. BCG Vaccination (see Chapter 7): This is an attempt to artificially stimulate immunity against tuberculosis. It may be administered by the intradermal route and usually results in the gradual appearance of a positive tuberculin test. The use of BCG (multiple puncture method) in pediatric practice is limited to tuberculin-negative children living in areas where there is a high incidence of tuberculosis or in households with patients known to have had tuberculosis.

C. Pasteurization of all milk for human consumption.

Prognosis.

A. Subclinical Infection: Primary infection frequently is unrecognized. The vast majority of children recover spontaneously.

B. Under the age of three years and during adolescence, the disease is more serious than at any other time during childhood.

C. Miliary tuberculosis and its complication, tuberculous meningitis, occur most frequently in small children but are not limited to this age group. While specific therapy is now available, these conditions still have a moderately serious prognosis and, in any case, require prolonged therapy extending from one to three years even in the presence of good clinical response.

D. Reinfection tuberculosis in adolescence may be prevented by INH prophylaxis. It has a good immediate prognosis with proper specific and general therapy. However, future reactivation may occur in stress situations such as pregnancy.

16...
Gastrointestinal Tract

SYMPTOMS

There are, in pediatrics, many diseases which do not specifically involve the gastrointestinal tract but which may have presenting manifestations referable to the digestive system. These symptoms frequently require the immediate attention of the physician. The underlying cause may not be immediately apparent.

ANOREXIA

Anorexia may occur as a passing phase of normal development (Spock's "anorexia of runabouts") or may be a presenting manifestation of almost any acute febrile illness and of some chronic illnesses. Most frequently, and especially when protracted, it is of psychogenic origin.

Treatment.
  A. Physiologic Anorexia Accompanying an Acute or Chronic Illness: Avoid overenthusiastic forcing of fluids, especially in the acute phase of illness. Give the usual minimum daily requirements of vitamins for the age group.
  B. Psychologic Anorexia:
    1. Both physician and parent should have a clear understanding of psychologic mechanisms. The parents' definition of "lack of appetite" must be determined and clarified, and parents should be encouraged to discuss their interpretation of the symptom.
    2. Careful history and physical examination should allow the physician to assure the parent that no organic disease exists. Reassure with regard to weight gain.
    3. Parents should offer a normal diet at regular mealtimes and depend upon the child's nutritional needs to "dictate" his appetite. There should be no coaxing, bribing, or threatening, and no insistence on a special diet or special foods.
    4. Excess intake of milk should be avoided; one pint per day is adequate for most children over one year of age.
    5. Small feedings of fruit or crackers may be given between meals without comment or discussion.
    6. Psychiatric consultation is indicated only for persistent or severe cases.

RECURRENT ABDOMINAL PAIN

Recurrent abdominal pain is frequent in children. It may result from a number of conditions but is most commonly a manifestation of functional gastrointestinal illness with a varied and erratic history. Pain seems to be precipitated by emotional stress. The pain may be of varied intensity and duration and is frequently associated with headache, pallor, nausea, vomiting, constipation, dizziness, and anorexia. There may be tenderness on deep palpation over varying sections of the abdomen. Laboratory and x-ray examinations are usually negative. Proctoscopic examination may reveal mucosal pallor, prominent vascular markings, dilated rectal lumen, and lymphoid hyperplasia. Various behavioral disturbances may occur.

The child is often described as being "very good," sensitive, insecure, and very close to other members of the family. Treatment is primarily directed toward a clearer understanding of the psychologic factors involved in producing the symptoms. The multiple diagnostic studies often required must be carefully managed to minimize the development of preoccupation with illness by both parents and child. Restriction of lactose ingestion should be tried.

VOMITING
(See Table 16-1.)

Vomiting is a common symptom throughout childhood and may be associated with a wide variety of diseases of all degrees of severity. A serious disease must always be considered if vomiting is protracted or severe.

The presence of other cases of vomiting and/or diarrhea in the family and community may have diagnostic significance.

Physical examination should emphasize the ears, throat, and chest in a search for infectious processes. Examination of the abdomen should include auscultation, which may show the high-pitched, tinkling diastolic sounds associated with intestinal obstruction. Central nervous system infection (see Chapter 25) may first manifest itself by vomiting.

Treatment is discussed below.

RECURRENT (CYCLIC) VOMITING

Recurrent cyclic vomiting is a syndrome characterized by recurrent attacks of violent vomiting without apparent cause, sometimes associated with headache and abdominal pain. A family history of migraine is frequently obtained. The onset is sudden, and all types of food, including water, will be vomited over a period of several hours to several days. Dehydration and electrolyte depletion, together with starvation ketosis, must be treated with intravenous fluids. Sedation may be of value.

Differential diagnosis must exclude other causes of vomiting (see Table 16-1).

TABLE 16-1. Causes, characteristics, and treatment of vomiting.

Cause	Age	Appears Ill	Relation to Intake	Fever	Diarrhea	Treatment (For details see p. 273)
Physiologic ("spitting up")	Infancy	No	Varies	No	No	None
Feeding Faults: Over-feeding	Infancy	No	Immediate	No	Occasional	Formula management (see Chapter 4).
Poor feeding technic	Infancy	No	Immediate	No	Rare	Instruct mother (see Chapter 4).
Obstruction of G.I. Tract						
Appendicitis or Meckel's diverticulitis	All ages	Moderately	None	Yes	Occasional	Surgery (see p. 305).
Ileus with peritonitis	All ages	Severely	None	Yes	Yes	Chemotherapy and/or surgery.
Congenital anomalies	Infancy	No	Varies	No	None	Surgery (see p. 285).
Pyloric stenosis	2-3 wks	No	Varies	No	No	Surgery (see p. 292).
Acute Infectious Diseases ("Parenteral Vomiting"): Almost any disease with fever at onset. Also pertussis	<10 yrs.	Moderately to severely	Immediate	Yes	Occasional in younger ages	Treat specific disease. Nothing by mouth, then liquid diet and finally soft diet.
Epidemic vomiting (viral)*	All ages	Mild	Varies	Yes	Occasional	Restrict intake. Liquid diet, then soft.†
Specific enteric inf.*: epidemic vomiting and diarrhea, salmonellae or shigellae	All ages	Moderately	Immediate	Usual	Usual	Nothing by mouth, then liquid, then soft diet. Chemotherapy in salmonellae and shigellae.
Central Nervous System: Expansile lesions, tumor, hematoma, or edema	All ages	Moderately	None	No	None	Surgery and parenteral fluids.
Acute meningitis	All ages	Severely	None	Yes	Occasional in younger ages	Treat specific disease. Parenteral fluids.
Motion sickness	All ages	Mildly	Immediate	No	None	Meclizine sedation (see dosage in Appendix).†
Toxic Vomiting: Poisoning	All ages	Moderately	None	No	Occasional	See Chapter 31.
Food poisoning*	All ages	Moderately	Within 6 hours	No	Occasional	Gastric lavage, sedation, parenteral fluids; later, liquid diet.
Diabetic acidosis	All ages	Severely	None	No	None	Treat diabetes (see Chapter 22).
Psychogenic or Emotional: Rumination	Infancy	No	30 min. later	No	None	Thicken formula with cereal. Sedation.
"Cyclic vomiting"	>2 yrs.	Occasionally	Immediate and late	Occ.	None	Parenteral fluids, sedation; later, soft diet.†
Simple excitement	All ages	No	None	No	None	Sedation and soft diet.†
Cardiac Disease: May be congestive failure or digitalis intoxication	All ages	Perhaps severely	None	No	Rare	Digitalis in failure or stop digitalis if intoxication. Sedation and soft diet.
Cardiospasm and esophageal stricture	All ages	No	Immediate	No	None	Parenteral fluids, sedation; later, liquid diet and soft diet. Dilatation procedures.
Chalasia	Infancy	No	Immediate	No	No	Put in upright position after feeding.

*Check for other cases in family or community. †Chlorpromazine suppository.

DIARRHEA
(See Table 16-2.)

Diarrhea is a common symptom throughout childhood, becoming less common as a nonspecific symptom in the older age groups. The physician should always consider the symptom serious and must begin general treatment measures as soon as diagnostic findings are obtained. A simple, mild diarrhea may gradually become severe, and the patient should be under careful observation.

In addition to the findings presented in Table 16-2, the following information should be obtained: (1) Duration, frequency, and description (consistency and color) of diarrheal stools. The mother may interpret watery stool as urine. (2) Presence of vomiting. (3) Presence of other cases of diarrhea or vomiting in the family or community. (4) Estimate of weight loss. Recent routine weighing may be compared.

Examine the abdomen for tenderness, either localized or generalized, and abnormal masses. Examine rectally for further localization. Diarrhea may accompany certain systemic infections.

For treatment, see Table 16-2.

GENERAL SYMPTOMATIC TREATMENT MEASURES
FOR VOMITING AND DIARRHEA
(See Tables 16-1 and 16-2.)

General Considerations.
   A. The young child loses more weight through vomiting and diarrhea than from a marked reduction in caloric intake when on a controlled diet.
   B. For purposes of treatment, all cases of vomiting or diarrhea should be assumed to require strict control of diet.
   C. Fats and cereal starches aggravate early cases of diarrhea or vomiting and should not be given for at least 24 hours. Lactose intolerance is common.
   D. Symptomatic medications (see below) are secondary to diet control in therapy.
   E. Avoid overuse of fluids or foods containing salt; hypernatremia may result. Exclusive intake of water may produce hyponatremia.
   F. The electrolyte status of infants and small children with diarrhea or vomiting should always be followed carefully in the laboratory when these facilities are available (see Chapter 5).

Treatment Methods.
   A. Parenteral Fluid Therapy Is Indicated:
      1. If vomiting or diarrhea produces or threatens dehydration and acidosis.
      2. If surgery is contemplated.
   B. Nothing by mouth for six to eight hours in infants and for 24 hours in older children. Liquid, such as ice chips, may be given in amounts sufficient to dampen mucous membranes.
   C. Liquid Diet: Small amounts of clear fluids (as tolerated).
      1. Infants - Give 1 to 4 oz. every two to four hours by mouth. The following mixtures are useful: (1) Glucose-saline solution: 4 tsp. cane sugar, 1/2 tsp. table salt, 1 quart boiled

TABLE 16-2. Causes, characteristics, and treatment of diarrhea.

Cause	Age	Appears Ill	Fever	Stool Examination Gross	Stool Examination Microscopic	Treatment (See also p. 273)
Nutritional Variations						
Excess carbohydrate in formula	Infancy	No	None	Thin, frothy, yellow	Excess starch	Formula management (see p. 43).
Excess fat in formula	Infancy	No	None	Soft, greasy, bulky, yellow	Excess fat	Formula management (see p. 43).
Breast feeding ("physiologic" diarrhea)	Infancy	No	None	Green, mucous, scanty	Nonspecific	None necessary.
Starvation	All ages	Moderately	None	Rare, scanty, green-brown	Nonspecific	Oral feeding (gradually).
Acute Infectious Diseases: "Parenteral Diarrhea"	<5 yrs.	Moderately	Yes	Nonspecific	No pus	Treat disease, usually respiratory. Liquid diet, then soft diet.
Specific Enteric Infections*						
Viral: Epidemic vomiting and diarrhea	All ages	Mildly	Slight	Nonspecific	No pus	Nothing by mouth; liquid diet, followed by soft diet.
Bacterial: Salmonellae (see p. 498)	All ages	Moderately	Moderate	Nonspecific, may have pus	Blood and pus	Specific antibiotics. Parenteral fluids as necessary. Liquid diet
Shigellae (see p. 499)	All ages	Severely	Moderate	May have blood	Blood and pus	followed by soft diet.
Staphylococcal enterocolitis (p. 490)	<5 yrs.	Severely	High	Mucoid, watery, purulent	Pus	
Enteropathogenic Escherichia coli (EPEC)	<2 yrs.	Moderately to severely	Usually absent	Watery mucus	No blood or pus	Parenteral blood or fluids; liquid diet. Neomycin, 100 ml./Kg./day orally in 3 doses for 5 days; or colistin, 10-15 ml./Kg./day orally.
Amebic dysentery	All ages	Mildly	Slight	May have blood	Blood and pus	See Chapter 26.
Surgical Conditions: Appendicitis and Meckel's diverticulitis	<5 yrs.	Moderately to severely	Slight	Nonspecific	Nonspecific	Surgical (see pp. 297 and 305).
Intussusception	<5 yrs.	Severely	Slight	Bloody with mucus	Blood	Surgical (see p. 299).
Food Poisoning*: Usually staphylococcal; 1 to 6 hours after meal	All ages	Moderately to severely	None	Mucous; may have blood	Blood, rare w.b.c.	Parenteral fluids may be necessary; nothing by mouth, then liquid diet, then soft diet.
Allergic Diarrhea: Cow's milk	Infancy	No	None	Yellow, bulky, mucous	Eosinophils	Use non-cow's milk formula.
Other allergens	All ages	No	None	Soft, mucous, bulky	Eosinophils	Elimination diet.
Celiac Syndrome	Usually <2 yrs.	No	None	Foul, greasy, bulky, frothy	Fat and/or excess starch	See p. 281.
Chronic Ulcerative Colitis	>4 yrs.	Mildly to severely	None	Small, brown, mucous	Pus and blood	See p. 279.

*Check for other cases in family and community.

TABLE 16-3. Differential diagnosis of rectal bleeding in infants and children.

Etiology	Usual Age Group	Additional Chief Complaints	Amount of Blood	Type of Blood	Blood With Movement	Treatment
Allergy	Infants	Colicky abdominal pain	Mod. to large	Dark or bright	Yes	Eliminate allergen
Anal fissure or proctitis	< 2 yrs.	Pain	Small	Bright	No	Soften stool; anal dilatation; habit training
Bacterial enteritis	Any age	Diarrhea, cramps	Small	Usually bright	Yes	See Chapter 25.
Duplication of bowel	Any age	Variable	Usually small	Usually dark	Yes	Surgery
Esophageal varices	> 4 yrs.	Signs of portal hypertension	Variable	Usually dark	Yes	Acute: medical. Portal hypertension: surgery.
Hemangioma or telangiectasia	Any age	Usually none	Variable	Dark or bright	Yes or no	None
Hemorrhagic dis. of the newborn	Newborn	Other evidences of blood	Variable	Dark or bright	Yes or no	Vit. K, transfusion
Idiopathic	Any age	Variable	Variable	Dark or bright	Yes or no	Surgery for diagnosis; vit. K, transfusion
Inserted foreign body	Child	Pain	Small	Bright	No	Removal
Intussusception	< 18 mo.	Abdominal pain; mass	Small to large	Dark or bright	Yes	Barium enema or surgery
Meckel's diverticulum	Young child	None or anemia	Small to large	Dark or bright	Yes or no	Surgery
Peptic ulcer	Any age	Abdominal pain	Usually small	Dark	Yes	Bland diet
Swallowed f. b.	Any age	Usually none	Small	Dark	Yes	None
Swal. maternal blood	Newborn	None	Variable	Dark	Yes	None
Systemic bl. dis.	Any age	Other evidences of blood	Variable	Dark or bright	Yes or no	As indicated
Volvulus	Infant or young child	Abdominal pain, intestinal obstruction	Small to large	Dark or bright	Yes or no	Surgery

water. (2) Polysal® elixir - 1/2 tsp. in at least 30 ml. of water for each 10 lb. body weight (composition given on p. 76). (3) Lytren® - one measure, as provided, in 120 ml. of water (composition given on p. 76). (4) Grape or apple juice, 500 ml., water 500 ml., and table salt, 1/2 tsp. (5) Table salt, 1/2 tsp., corn syrup, 1 to 2 oz., orange juice, 8 oz., water to make 1 quart. **Caution:** Unless diarrhea or vomiting continues, give no more than 150 ml./Kg./day (75 ml./lb./day) of above fluids.

2. One to five years -
   a. Any of above mixtures, 4 to 8 oz., given every two to four hours while awake.
   b. Gelatin dessert, 1 to 3 tablespoons every two hours.
   c. Frozen, fruit-flavored ice sticks.
   d. Segments of fresh orange.
3. Five years and over - Any items under 2, plus:
   a. Carbonated beverages as tolerated.
   b. Clear soups, bouillon, or clear chicken broth.

D. Soft Diet as Desired:
   1. Infants -
      a. Apple purée, 2 to 4 tablespoons as desired (not oftener than every two hours), is an excellent way of providing pectin, which is often effective in relieving diarrhea. Other sources of pectin include bananas, pears, cranberries, lemon, grapefruit, and various jellies.
      b. Crushed ripe banana or prepared banana flakes, 2 to 4 tablespoons every four hours.
      c. Boiled skimmed milk in quantity equal to that of regular formula may be tried. **Note:** Temporary lactose intolerance is common following severe diarrhea.
   2. Age one and over - Any item mentioned above, plus boiled egg, toast or soda crackers, whole ripe bananas, puréed vegetables and fruits, lean meats, and custards and puddings.

E. Specific Symptomatic Medication:
   1. Suspension of kaolin - Best used as diarrhea subsides. Give 30 to 60 Gm. per day in four to six doses.
   2. Camphorated tincture of opium (paregoric) - Not tolerated in young child with vomiting; sometimes useful in older child with diarrhea and tenesmus. Because of the danger of "masking" a surgical condition, paregoric should never be used if this possibility exists.
      a. Infants - 0.2 ml. per month of age every six hours (no more than 2 ml. in any 24-hour period).
      b. One to five years - 2 ml. every six hours.
      c. Five years and over - 4 ml. every six hours.

F. Sedation: Especially valuable in older child with vomiting, when it is best given by rectal route. Do not overlook the possibility of a surgical condition.

G. Gastric Lavage: In toxic vomiting give sodium bicarbonate, 1 tsp. in 4 oz. of warm water. If lavage is not available, encourage emesis by pharyngeal stimulation after giving sodium bicarbonate solution to drink.

H. Rectal Fluid Therapy: Give 5% glucose in saline, as for parenteral route; at home, prepare glucose-saline solution. Dose: 2 to 4 oz. every two to four hours. Use rubber bulb type of syringe (ear syringe). Do not give plain water.

I. Infants with prolonged severe diarrhea may require supplemental vitamin K.

CONSTIPATION

Constipation refers to the character of the stool rather than to the frequency of defecation. Constipated stools are hard, dry, and small. In infancy they may occur one to three times per day. The normal breast-fed infant may go as long as seven days without a bowel movement and not be constipated. Older children, especially boys, are loath to report failure of evacuation each day and may become severely constipated without the parent's knowledge.

Etiology.
A. Dietary: In infants, constipation may result from too little carbohydrate or fat in formula, inadequate bulk from fruits and vegetables, or insufficient fluid intake or, more rarely, exclusive milk intake. In older children, daily water intake may be too low.
B. Toilet-training Faults:
   1. Too early stress on toilet training; usually little training is necessary.
   2. Too frequent use of suppositories, enemas, and cathartics.
   3. In older children, failure to develop a regular toilet habit, failure to heed the desire to defecate while engaged in play, or embarrassment in presence of strangers. Many healthy children produce a normal bowel movement at two-to-four-day intervals.
C. Disease States: Hypothyroidism, marked anemia, congenital megacolon, and any disease causing fever and dehydration.
D. Mechanical obstruction.
E. Rectal Conditions:
   1. Anal fissure, causing pain on attempted evacuation.
   2. Anal or rectal stenosis, especially in infancy, requiring excess effort for evacuation.
F. Drugs: Calcium salts, narcotics, and aluminum hydroxide gels tend to produce constipation in children.

Treatment.
A. Acute Constipation: Where evacuation is desired immediately.
   1. Mineral oil, tap water or normal saline solution, 2 to 4 oz. as retention enema; await spontaneous evacuation. (Avoid repeated use.)
   2. Suppositories of glycerin or soap are valuable in infants but are emotionally traumatic in some children.
B. Chronic Constipation: Where dietary measures are necessary.
   1. In young infants -
      a. Fluids - Offer plain water or water with approximately 5% carbohydrate one to three times daily between feedings.
      b. Sugar - Increase sugar content of formula.
      c. Molasses - Replace 1 tbsp. of the usual carbohydrate in the formula with 1 tbsp. of molasses.
      d. Prune juice - Give 15 ml. daily.

      e. Proprietary solutions of dioctyl sodium sulfosuccinate (Colace®) may be employed to keep the stools more soft. Dosage - 10 to 20 mg./day.

  2. In older infants -
    a. Fruits - Increase amounts of puréed fruits in diet, especially prunes and plums. The amount needed will vary with individual infants.
    b. Fluids - Attempt to increase fluid intake.
    c. Stool-softening solutions as in 1e above.

  3. In older children -
    a. Fluids - Attempt to increase fluid intake.
    b. Fruits - Add prunes, apricots, and figs to daily diet.
    c. Bulk - High-residue substances such as bran, whole wheat, oatmeal, and green leafy vegetables should be a major part of the daily diet.
    d. Neo-cultol®, 4 ml. at bedtime for a few nights.
    e. Methylcellulose, 0.5 Gm. at bedtime for a few nights, may be helpful.

C. Rectal Conditions:
  1. Anal or rectal stenosis in infancy may be stretched by the physician by means of daily insertion of well-lubricated rubber-sheathed finger. One such treatment usually suffices.
  2. Anal fissure - Diagnostic rectal examination usually produces temporary relaxation of the anal sphincter sufficient to permit healing. Rarely, silver nitrate cauterization and local anesthetic ointments may be necessary.

COLIC

Colic is a syndrome in small infants characterized by recurrent abdominal pain and paroxysms of crying. It usually occurs in the first-born, starting at around ten days of age and lasting through the third month. It is a source of great anxiety for the parents.

Etiology.

The causes of colic are probably multiple. The following may be of varying importance in each case:

A. Air: The passage of large bubbles of swallowed air through the intestines of the infant is associated with discomfort. Excess amounts of air may be swallowed -
  1. If nipple holes are too small (with leakage of air around nipple during sucking), or too big (with gulping of milk and air).
  2. When infant cries, a cyclical pattern may be established: Cry ──→Swallowed air ──→Colic──→Cry, etc.
  3. When the hungry infant sucks on hands and fingers.

B. Food: Over-distention of the bowel with ingested food will cause pain. This may occur through over-feeding with large volumes of formula as a result of efforts to quiet infant by giving him something to eat. Paradoxically, genuine hunger may initiate this cycle of events.

C. Emotional Factors: Colic occurs most often in a first-born infant during the first week at home. The hyperactive, tense infant is likely to have colic. Family tension and parental anxiety may be aggravating factors.

D. Intestinal allergy to cow's milk, especially in families with a history of clinical allergy in other members. (See symptoms under Allergic Diarrhea in Table 16-2.)

Treatment.

In treating colic, the physician must first deal with the acute attack; steps should then be taken to prevent recurrences.

A. Treatment of the Acute Attack:
1. "Burping" - Remove swallowed air from stomach by "burping" the baby over the shoulder with gentle pats on the back and pressure on the lower abdomen.
2. Soothe the baby to prevent crying and further air-swallowing:
   a. "Burp" child (as above).
   b. Try rhythmic movement of baby (rocking, walking, etc.).
   c. Apply warmth to abdomen, using rubber hot water bottle wrapped in soft cloth.
   d. Sedative - Elixir of phenobarbital, 1/2 tsp (8 mg.), every eight hours in formula.
3. Reassure the parents, by examination of the infant, that no serious condition exists.
4. Facilitate passage of air through the bowel -
   a. Suppository - A small suppository will stimulate bowel movement and expulsion of air.
   b. Enema - An enema of 1 to 2 oz. of warm water to produce the same result may be indicated if suppository fails.

B. Prevention of Further Attacks.
1. Examine bottle nipples and enlarge any holes that are too small and discard any with holes that are too large.
2. Evaluate food intake in the light of the infant's needs, to avoid hunger periods. If the child is not being overfed, more foods may be introduced, such as solids.
3. Adjustment of the formula seldom is successful, and repeated unsuccessful changes of the ingredients usually do not reassure anxious parents.
   a. Elimination of cow's milk may be necessary.
   b. Reduction of fat content through use of half skimmed milk may be of help. In the breast-fed infant the mother's supply may not be adequate for the moment and should be supplemented.
4. A pacifier may be of value in some children.
5. Environmental factors should be examined, especially parental attitudes and anxieties, and psychologic assistance for the parents given, if necessary.
   a. Reduce excitement to a minimum.
   b. Prevent chilling or overheating.
   c. Place near repetitive noise (vacuum cleaner, running water, radio, etc.).
6. Sedation - Elixir of phenobarbital (see above).

ULCERATIVE COLITIS

Clinical Findings.

A. Symptoms and Signs: Onset is usually between ages eight to ten years, but may occur even under the age of two years.

There is a history of insidious onset of recurrent bouts of diarrhea, often bloody and accompanied by cramping abdominal pain. Low-grade fever, anemia, weakness, and weight loss are present. A distinctive perirectal ulcerated skin lesion or arthritis may be associated. Proctoscopic examination shows mucosa to be diffusely inflamed, edematous, and often bleeding.
B. Laboratory Findings: Stools show mucus and blood.
C. X-ray Findings: Barium enema demonstrates loss of normal haustral markings, together with narrowing of the colon. Twenty per cent of patients may show normal x-ray.

Treatment.
A. High-protein, high-carbohydrate, normal fat, low-residue diet.
B. Salicylazosulfapyridine (Azulfidine®), 0.5-1 Gm. 4 times daily. Continue for two weeks, withhold for one week, and then give a second course for two weeks.
C. Surgery: Ileostomy or colectomy is indicated in protracted or severe cases.
D. Psychiatric evaluation of emotional factors.
E. Corticotropin and the cortisones may be of temporary value. Rectal instillation of hydrocortisone, 50 mg. in 100 ml. of saline, may also produce relief.

Prognosis.
Over half of the reported patients have shown either great improvement or eventual cure of the disease. Carcinoma of the colon may occur after many years.

DISEASES OF THE LIVER

Some of the more important causes of liver disease of childhood are outlined here; reference will be made to other chapters for more detailed discussions.

HEPATOMEGALY
(Enlargement of Liver)
(See Appendix.)

JAUNDICE
(See also Chapter 9 for Jaundice of the Newborn.)

Etiology.
A. Regurgitation Types:
1. Bile duct obstruction, congenital biliary atresia, parasitic infestation, cirrhosis resulting from late effects of erythroblastosis, liver abscess (pressure on bile duct).
2. Obstruction due to diseases in liver parenchyma - Poisons (including carbon tetrachloride, chloroform, mushrooms, and phosphorus) and infections (viral hepatitis, infectious mononucleosis).

B. Retention Types:
   1. Hemolytic - Congenital hemolytic anemia, erythroblastosis, Mediterranean anemias, sickle cell anemia, transfusion reaction following use of incompatible blood.
   2. Septicemia - Especially in the newborn period.
   3. Hepatocellular disease - Viral hepatitis.
   4. Hepatic immaturity - Physiologic jaundice of the newborn.

Laboratory Findings.

A. Regurgitation Types (Obstruction): Urine shows absent or normal urobilinogen and increased bilirubin (bile foam test). Stool shows decreased or absent urobilinogen. Blood shows increased direct bilirubin.
B. Retention Types: Urine shows increased urobilinogen or absent bilirubin (bile). Stool shows increased urobilinogen. Blood shows increased indirect bilirubin.

PLASMA CELL HEPATITIS

A syndrome occurring mostly in young girls and characterized by severe, prolonged hepatitis, obesity, amenorrhea, generalized vascular disease, and arthralgia. Serum gamma globulin is usually elevated. Cortisone may be effective.

MALABSORPTION DISEASES - "CELIAC SYNDROME"

A number of specific disease entities and some unknown causes can result in the syndrome once referred to as "celiac disease." The principal symptoms are (1) acute crises with severe diarrhea, (2) frequent pale, bulky, foul-smelling stools, (3) failure to gain weight, along with wasting and stunting of growth, and (4) abdominal distention.

The principal malabsorption syndromes are (1) cystic fibrosis, (2) gluten-induced enteropathy, (3) disaccharidase deficiencies, and (4) idiopathic steatorrhea.

1. CYSTIC FIBROSIS

Clinical Findings.

A. Symptoms and Signs:
   1. Meconium ileus may be the initial manifestation in the newborn period, with signs of intestinal obstruction due to thick, clay-like meconium.
   2. Chronic respiratory disease leading to bronchiectasis and pulmonary fibrosis, with few, if any, gastrointestinal symptoms.
   3. Marked increase in chloride content of sweat is a striking and diagnostic feature of cystic fibrosis and may occur in the absence of any other elements of this disease.
   4. Additional symptoms of cystic fibrosis include prolapse of rectum, a peculiar form of hepatic fibrosis, heat shock due to sodium loss with excessive sweating, and retarded growth.

B. Laboratory Findings:
1. Concentration of chloride in sweat, above 60 mEq./L., is a specific diagnostic finding in cystic fibrosis (see Appendix).
2. Assay for pancreatic enzyme in duodenal juice as obtained by intubation. In cystic fibrosis only small amounts may be obtained, and amylase, lipase, and trypsin content is decreased. Stool may be examined for tryptic activity by diluting a specimen, free of urine, 1:10 and 1:100 with 5% sodium bicarbonate solution in distilled water. A drop of each dilution is then placed upon the gelatin surface of an unexposed piece of x-ray film and incubated for one hour at 98.6°F. (37°C.). Rinse in cold water and observe for clearing of the film. Consistently negative tests showing no clearing in either dilution are suggestive of congenital fibrocystic disease.
3. Stool fat content may be estimated by staining with 1% scarlet red in absolute alcohol.
C. X-ray Findings: Chest x-ray is normal early but later may show scattered areas of obstructive emphysema, increased density, lung abscesses, bronchiectasis, and bronchial pneumonia. GI series may show delayed emptying time of the stomach and clumping of barium in the ileum and colon. Cor pulmonale may produce characteristic cardiac changes.

Treatment.

A long-term treatment regimen must be contemplated, and follow-up is extremely important. Treatment consists of three parts:

A. Treatment and Prophylaxis of Pulmonary Infections: The morbidity and mortality due to cystic fibrosis are essentially the result of the pulmonary defect, i.e., the excessive, abnormally viscid mucus which impairs the patient's defenses against bacterial infection and causes bronchial obstruction, emphysema, and atelectasis. Initial treatment −
1. Antibiotics in full therapeutic dosage (see Chapter 6) for at least four weeks. The specific drug is preferably chosen on the basis of sputum culture and sensitivity tests.
2. Aerosol therapy by mask three or four times a day, using a Mistogette® mask with air compressor, may be of some value. Use 2 ml. of the following solution per treatment:

$$\text{R}\!\!\!/ \quad \text{Propylene glycol}$$

Propylene glycol		
Phenylephrine hydrochloride		
(Neo-Synephrine®), 1%	aa	60 ml.
Distilled water, q.s.ad		500 ml.

Add appropriate antibiotic: Neomycin, 100 mg./ml.; polymyxin, 10 mg./ml.; bacitracin, 10,000 units/ml.; or streptomycin, 50 mg./ml.

B. Treatment of Dietary Deficiencies:
1. Give pancreatin, powder or granules, 5 to 10 Gm. 3 times daily with meals; Viokase®, 1.5 Gm. 3 times daily with meals; or Cotazym®, 2000 to 4000 units with each meal. These agents may be mixed with some form of solid food (bananas for small infants). Dose varies with age and with the child's need as established by trial.

2. Diet - Stress proteins and give a minimum of fat. Skimmed milk may be used in place of whole milk. Otherwise, with the use of pancreatin, no special diet is needed.

3. Intestinal crisis - As for severe diarrhea; give liquid diet, then soft diet. Supplemental salt should be added to diet during periods when salt loss may occur.

C. Continuous Prophylaxis:

1. Aerosol therapy - With or without pulmonary symptoms, a mist tent is used at night and during naps with a solution containing 10% propylene glycol and 90% half-molar sodium chloride. Salt mist will more effectively dissolve viscid mucus.

2. Add antibiotics systemically and by aerosol when infection becomes more severe, as indicated by increased coughing, fever, weight loss, and dyspnea, or decreased appetite. Antibiotics should be chosen on the basis of sputum culture and sensitivity studies.

3. Protect from infection involving the respiratory tract when possible; provide immunization and booster inoculations against pertussis, influenza, and rubeola.

4. For excessive loss of sodium chloride in sweat in hot weather, with fever, and in patients with hyponatremia, add 1 Gm. of salt to the daily diet up to two years of age, 2 Gm. per day over two years of age.

Prognosis.

Owing to the present stage of development of technics in treatment, the prognosis is unknown. It is at best guarded. Adult cases are increasingly recognized. Recovery, if it takes place, occurs at some time during adolescence. Parents of a child with congenital fibrocystic disease should be informed of the genetic etiology of the disease; they have approximately one chance in four, with each pregnancy, of giving birth to another child with the disease.

2. GLUTEN-INDUCED ENTEROPATHY
("Celiac Disease")

A defect in enzyme activity or metabolism is apparently precipitated by an allergic reaction to gluten. Antibodies may be found in the serum and in the bowel. Onset of the disease can occur from infancy to five years of age.

Symptoms are those of the "celiac syndrome." There may be no diarrhea.

Treatment.

If dehydration and electrolyte depletion crisis occurs, stop all oral intake and treat as outlined in Chapter 5.

With the resumption of oral feedings give a high-protein, low-fat, no starch diet, with vitamin supplements and iron. Maintain a restricted diet for three to four months.

Wheat and rye gluten-free diet may be necessary for many years, together with a low-fat intake. Fats should be introduced with care and close observation. Parents must be instructed in regard to the wide variety of commercial products containing wheat.

Examples include ice cream, frankfurters, some types of candy bars, and commercially produced fried chicken or fish.

Dietary control should be dependent upon the over-all appearance and change in the child rather than the character of the stools. Growth and weight gain are the primary measures of success.

3. DISACCHARIDASE DEFICIENCIES

The basic defect appears to be congenital absence or deficiency in one or more of the disaccharidase enzymes in the small bowel. Absence or deficiency of invertase, maltase, isomaltase, and lactase has been reported.

Intestinal biopsy is becoming more available and contributes to the diagnosis. More often, however, the response to dietary restriction of a specific type of sugar is the basis for diagnosis.

Although the basic condition may persist, the symptoms often become less severe in later years.

4. IDIOPATHIC STEATORRHEA

This entity is differentiated from gluten-induced enteropathy by failure of response to the withdrawal of gluten from the diet and from disaccharidase deficiency by failure of response to manipulation of the sugar intake. Treatment includes elimination of all starches and reduction in the fat intake. Since this syndrome is of such obscure origin, it is impossible to state how long a treatment regimen should continue. Each case is a very special challenge.

SURGICAL DISORDERS OF THE DIGESTIVE SYSTEM

The accurate diagnosis and efficient management of surgical disorders of the gastrointestinal tract require awareness of the most common conditions which may be encountered as well as recognition of the relative emergency nature of each. (See Chapter 5 for preoperative and postoperative fluid and electrolyte therapy and the fluid management of intestinal obstruction.)

ESOPHAGEAL ATRESIA WITH OR WITHOUT TRACHEO-ESOPHAGEAL FISTULA

Pathology.

In 88% of cases, the upper esophageal pouch ends blindly and the lower pouch communicates directly with the back of the trachea. About 10% of cases have esophageal atresia without an associated tracheal fistula.

Over 30% of children with this condition have associated anomalies; the most common of these are congenital heart disease and malformations of other portions of the intestinal tract, chiefly imperforate anus.

Clinical Findings.

A. Symptoms: This disorder can be diagnosed in the nursery, usually within two days after birth. Characteristic findings are:
1. Excess salivation ("blowing bubbles").
2. Coughing and gagging if feedings are attempted.
3. Respiratory distress which may lead to cyanosis.

B. Signs:
1. Aspiration pneumonia - Depending on the amount of feeding which has been attempted, this may not develop until two or three days after feeding was begun.
2. Pneumonitis from reflux of gastric juice through the lower esophageal segment.
3. Passing of stomach tube - As soon as the diagnosis is suspected, attempt to pass a radiopaque catheter into the stomach so that position can be checked on x-ray. It should be at least No. 10 F. so that it will not coil up in the pouch. Esophageal atresia can be ruled out if the nasal catheter is passed into the stomach without difficulty.

C. X-ray Findings:
1. Plain x-ray - Demonstration of the large, air-filled esophageal pouch, extending down to the level of the T2 vertebral body, is sometimes possible on anteroposterior and lateral chest x-rays. A radiopaque catheter will pass only to the T2 level. Aspiration pneumonitis is usually present in the right upper lobe. Air in the stomach and intestine, in association with a blind upper pouch, indicates connection between the tracheal and lower segment of the esophagus.
2. Contrast examination - Instill only 0.5 ml. of a water-soluble contrast material directly into the upper pouch through a catheter under fluoroscopic control with the infant held upright. All contrast material must then be aspirated from the upper pouch. Overfilling of the upper pouch leads to aspiration of contrast material into the lungs, aggravating the pneumonitis.

Treatment.

A. Preoperative Preparation:
1. A sump (Replogle) catheter is placed in the upper pouch and attached to suction.
2. Place infant with the head elevated at least 30 degrees to minimize aspiration of gastric juice through the distal fistula.
3. Give antibiotics if pneumonitis is present.
4. Give oxygen as necessary to prevent cyanosis.
5. Maintenance fluids should be administered intravenously. Give no fluids by mouth.

B. Surgical Repair:
1. If the infant has moderate or severe pneumonitis, gastrostomy should be performed - under local anesthesia if necessary.
2. Primary repair of the esophagus should be performed when the infant is clinically stable. A premature infant or an infant with pneumonitis may tolerate only division of the fistula from the trachea, with esophageal repair postponed until the lungs clear.
3. Maintain body temperature during transport and operation.

   4. Monitor blood gases and correct acidosis or hypoxia if detected.
 C. Postoperative Care:
   1. Return the baby to an incubator, where oxygen can be given and nebulized water added to the atmosphere, for several days.
   2. Fluid therapy - Intravenous maintenance therapy plus gastric losses.
   3. Feedings through the gastrostomy - At first the stomach is kept deflated; feedings should not be started until the third postoperative day and then should be given with caution. As a rule, 15 ml. of 10% glucose and water are given at two-hour intervals. After one day, a milk formula can be given in small frequent feedings.
   4. Oral feedings - Begin oral feedings when the general condition of the child is good and after an esophagogram shows good healing (usually on about the tenth postoperative day). The oral feedings are gradually increased, and the gastrostomy tube is elevated. The gastrostomy tube is usually withdrawn after six weeks and the gastric opening allowed to close spontaneously.

Course and Prognosis.
   In general, the earlier the diagnosis is made and the less the insult to the lung, the better the child's chances are of surviving the surgical procedure. Prematurity is an added risk, as is the presence of other anomalies such as congenital heart disease. Postoperative esophageal dilatations for strictures are necessary in most patients.

TRACHEO-ESOPHAGEAL FISTULA
WITHOUT ESOPHAGEAL ATRESIA (H TYPE)

   Diagnosis of this anomaly is often difficult and is made late. The connection between the esophagus and the trachea is usually small and situated in the lower cervical esophagus. Because of aspiration through the fistula, most babies have had repeated pneumonia when the diagnosis is made. Most infants have intermittent, marked abdominal distention because of air forced through the fistula by crying.

Clinical Findings.
 A. Symptoms:
   1. Choking, coughing, or cyanosis with feedings.
   2. Persistent or recurrent pneumonitis.
   3. Abdominal distention with gas.
 B. Signs:
   1. Observed difficulty with feedings.
   2. Signs of pneumonitis.
   3. Endoscopy is usually necessary to reveal fistula. Barium studies are often normal.

Treatment.
 A. Preoperative Care: Give appropriate antibiotics for pneumonia and fluid replacement as necessary.

B. Surgical Measures: Division of the fistula can be accomplished through a cervical incision.

C. Postoperative Care: Oral feedings may be initiated several days after the operation, depending on the infant's condition.

Course and Prognosis.
In most cases, the prognosis is extremely favorable.

ESOPHAGEAL STRICTURE OR STENOSIS

Partial obstructions of the esophagus cause a variety of feeding problems in infancy or childhood. They may be caused by vascular ring or other congenital malformations; of postsurgical origin following correction of tracheo-esophageal fistula; may result from ingestion of corrosive chemicals (e.g., lye); or may follow peptic erosion of the lower esophagus (e.g., from reflux of gastric acids through a relaxed cardia, hiatus hernia, or aberrant gastric mucosa in the lower esophagus).

The principal complications are malnutrition and aspiration pneumonia.

Clinical Findings.
A. Symptoms.
1. Regurgitation of food is the most common symptom. With vascular ring there is usually some dysphagia in the neonatal period, but there may be no significant symptoms until the infant starts on solid food. Vomiting is not forceful; regurgitated material is usually undigested, contains saliva, and does not smell sour.
2. Respiratory distress is suggestive of compression of the trachea by a bolus of food lodged in the esophagus or of tracheal aspiration.
3. Dysphagia may be the presenting symptom.
4. Bleeding from the gastrointestinal tract is not frequent.

B. Signs: Often there are no signs, or there may be varying degrees of malnutrition, depending on the duration of symptoms. After repair of tracheo-esophageal fistula, there may be esophageal dyskinesia without significant stricture.

C. X-ray Findings: The obstruction can be seen with the fluoroscope when the esophagus is outlined with swallowed barium. Ciné studies should include the pharynx to evaluate the swallowing mechanism and rule out dyskinesia.

The length of the obstruction varies with the disease process causing the stenosis.
1. Congenital lesions may involve only a short segment.
2. Hiatus hernia with reflux of gastric secretion - The stenosis may involve a short segment adjacent to the herniated stomach or may be rather extensive, involving a large portion of the lower esophagus. In these cases the herniation can be demonstrated.
3. Strictures due to caustic chemicals - Ingestion of caustic chemicals usually causes extensive involvement of the esophagus.

D. Esophagoscopy: Details of the nature of the obstruction are determined by esophagoscopy.

Treatment.
A. Reflux Esophagitis With or Without Hiatus Hernia:
  1. Give small, frequent, thickened feedings and keep the baby upright (60 degrees) after feedings.
  2. Dilatations are of no value if reflux is not controlled.
  3. Surgical control of reflux is often required to control stricture formation.
B. Postoperative Stricture:
  1. Dilate as necessary.
  2. Obtain esophagograms to rule out reflux.
  3. Correct reflux if present.
C. Ingestion of Corrosives: Ammonia rarely causes esophageal burns. Lye solutions usually cause burns and stricture.
  1. Esophagoscopic examination is indicated if the history reveals the possibility of a burn. Visualize the burn but do not pass the instrument through it.
  2. Give systemic antibiotics to control mediastinitis, which often complicates esophageal damage.
  3. Systemic corticosteroids may or may not minimize stricture formation.
  4. Gastrostomy is often necessary for nutrition and to facilitate dilatation.
  5. Dilate if the esophagogram demonstrates a stricture. Dilatation may be accomplished by passing a string at esophagoscopy or by having the child swallow a string, which is then attached to rubber dilators of increasing sizes. These are drawn upward through a gastrostomy opening and then through the stenosed area.
  6. Resection or esophageal replacement is usually not considered until at least one year of dilatation has proved unsuccessful.

INGUINAL HERNIA AND HYDROCELE

The testis forms cephalad to the kidney and descends into the scrotum during the last trimester. As it descends, the peritoneum descends with it to form the tunica vaginalis. The peritoneal connection between the abdominal cavity and the scrotum (the processus vaginalis) is normally obliterated. All hernias, hydroceles, and ectopic testes relate to abnormalities in this process.

Hernia.
An intermittent bulge lateral to the pubic tubercle comes out when the child is crying, straining, or standing, and reduces spontaneously when he is relaxed or supine.

Treatment consists of elective surgery when the child is in good health. If there is a visible hernia on the left, there is a 50% chance that a hernia sac will be present on the right also; if the hernia is on the right, there is only a 10% chance of a sac on the left. In females, hernias are more often bilateral.

Incarcerated hernias do not reduce when the child is relaxed. Incarceration occurs most often in children under one year of age. Strangulation follows incarceration, and the hernia becomes tender and erythematous. The abdomen becomes distended, with vomiting and signs of bowel obstruction. Pressure on testicular vessels in the inguinal canal by an incarcerated hernia can cause testicular infarction.

Incarcerated hernia can often be reduced by gently squeezing the bowel back into the abdomen along the axis of the inguinal canal. Sedation (pentobarbital, 4 mg./Kg., and meperidine, 1 mg./Kg.) is necessary in most cases.

Strangulation is managed by nasogastric suction, rehydration, correction of electrolyte deficiencies, and surgery when the patient's condition is stable. (Stabilization should not take more than two to three hours.) Attempted reduction may rupture ischemic bowel or return necrotic bowel into the abdomen.

The ovary is often incarcerated in females. Strangulation is rare, and hernias may usually be repaired electively.

Hydrocele.

Hydrocele is very common in newborns. Spontaneous regression by age six months is the rule. Frequent and rapid change in size indicates a patent processus vaginalis with communication to the peritoneal cavity. Hernia often develops, and communicating hydroceles should be repaired.

Acute hydrocele may develop about the testis or in the spermatic cord and may be difficult to differentiate from incarcerated hernia. Acute hydrocele in the canal of Nuck presents as an oblong, firm swelling in the groin of a female infant and may be confused with a groin node. Exploration is required in doubtful cases.

ACHALASIA
(Cardiospasm)

Achalasia results from failure of the normal relaxation of the cardio-esophageal junction. The resulting functional obstruction causes intermittent dysphagia and frequent regurgitation of undigested food. It is encountered more often in older children presenting with poor feeding, with failure to grow normally, and, occasionally, with respiratory infections resulting from aspiration of regurgitated food. Barium swallow demonstrates the widened esophagus, with a gradual narrowing at the cardio-esophageal junction.

Surgical division of muscle layers over the narrowed cardio-esophageal junction (Heller procedure) is almost always necessary eventually.

CHALASIA
(Cardio-esophageal Relaxation)

This condition of unknown cause occurs in young infants (usually about one week old). Vomiting, usually not bile-stained and occasionally projectile, occurs when the infant is supine. Dehydration and malnutrition may result. Aspiration pneumonia may occur.

Barium examination shows free reflux from the stomach into the esophagus with absent or uncoordinated esophageal peristalsis.

Treatment consists of keeping the child upright in a small padded chair during feedings and for at least an hour afterward.

Small, frequent, thickened feedings are administered. Most infants will stop vomiting within several months.

HIATAL HERNIA AND REFLUX

Esophageal hiatal hernia is a congenital defect permitting reflux of gastric contents with vomiting (sometimes projectile), aspiration, and failure to thrive. In many cases the esophagitis leads to stricture formation and occult bleeding. Most cases of "congenital short esophagus" are not congenital but the result of prolonged, undetected esophageal reflux with esophagitis and scarring.

An infant with reflux may have only aspiration pneumonitis, poor weight gain, or iron deficiency anemia as the presenting symptom. Symptomatic reflux often occurs in infants after tracheoesophageal fistula repair, in children with severe scoliosis, and in brain-damaged infants.

Treatment consists of maintaining the child upright (60 degree angle or more) as much as possible for several months and giving small frequent feedings of a thickened formula. If the condition does not improve with treatment or if there is esophagitis or frequent aspiration, the hernia should be repaired.

CONGENITAL HERNIA OF THE DIAPHRAGM

The most common area of herniation is in the left postero-lateral portion, the foramen of Bochdalek. Foramen of Morgagni hernias rarely present in the newborn period and rarely cause significant respiratory symptoms.

Clinical Findings.
  A. Symptoms: Cyanosis and dyspnea in a newborn infant should suggest the diagnosis. Respiratory distress is usually constant and severe.
  B. Signs: Cyanosis is usually present. Chest movements are asymmetric, and dullness is noted on the affected side. Breath sounds may be absent. The abdomen is strikingly scaphoid and may feel less full on palpation than usual. The mediastinum (trachea) shifts away from the affected side.
  C. X-ray Findings: Chest x-ray (required for all infants with respiratory distress) usually shows a portion of the gastrointestinal tract in the thorax and marked displacement of the mediastinum. Avoid introducing contrast media into the gastrointestinal tract.

Treatment.
  A. Preoperative Care: All infants who are symptomatic in the first few hours of life have severe respiratory and metabolic acidosis requiring immediate treatment with bicarbonate. As soon as the diagnosis is suspected, a nasogastric tube should be passed and attached to suction. This prevents further distention of the gastrointestinal tract with air or fluid and makes aspiration less likely. Endotracheal intubation should be performed early. This facilitates oxygenation and lowering pCO_2.

If pCO_2 rises above 85 mm. Hg, the infant becomes severely obtunded. Ventilation pressures must be less than 30 mm. Hg to prevent alveolar rupture and pneumothorax.

B. Surgical Measures: **Diaphragmatic hernia is a surgical emergency.** The viscera are reduced from the thorax through a subcostal incision. The diaphragm is closed and a chest tube left in place to water-seal drainage. The infant must be kept warm. If abdominal closure requires tension, close only the skin to prevent undue pressure on the diaphragm or inferior vena cava.

C. Postoperative Care: An endotracheal tube is left in place and attached to a T-piece, CPAP (continuous positive airway pressure), or respirator as indicated. Maintain a fluid intake of 100 ml./Kg./day of 10% dextrose in 0.25 N saline solution. Add potassium, 2-3 mEq./Kg./day, beginning on the second day. Albumin or plasma should be added to the I.V. fluid to replace chest tube losses. Give antibiotics as indicated.

Course and Prognosis.

Survival depends on the degree of pulmonary hypoplasia. Lung weights of infants who do not survive are about half those of normal infants of the same gestational age and birth weight. The morphology of the lung on the side of the hernia is that of a 28- to 30-week-old fetus. In survivors, the lungs develop normally.

PYLORIC STENOSIS
(Congenital Hypertrophic Pyloric Stenosis)

Pyloric stenosis is more apt to occur in first-born infants and is more common in males than in females. In most cases the diagnosis is made between three and four weeks of age. It is important to differentiate this condition from adrenal insufficiency and subdural hematoma because all three conditions can produce projectile vomiting and poor weight gain.

There is a marked increase in the size of the circular musculature of the pylorus, causing obstruction of the lumen. In the average case the enlargement is the size and shape of an olive.

Clinical Findings.

A. Symptoms:

1. Vomiting begins in most cases after the fourteenth day of life. It is usually mild at first and becomes progressively more forceful and eventually projectile. Vomiting occurs within one-half hour of feeding and does not contain bile. The infant is hungry and will refeed immediately.

2. Hunger - The child is always hungry because very little food can pass into the duodenum. Appetite may be lost in the later stages when metabolic derangements are marked.

3. Bowel movements - The infant may develop loose green "starvation" stools.

4. Weight - Failure to gain weight or loss of weight with decrease in subcutaneous fat are signs of progressive disease.

5. Gastrointestinal bleeding - Gastritis in the obstructed stomach will occasionally result in bleeding.

     6. Jaundice - 2 to 5% of infants with pyloric stenosis develop jaundice. Bilirubin is mainly unconjugated and clears promptly when stenosis is relieved.

B. Signs:
    1. Dehydration, with decrease in skin turgor.
    2. Distention of the epigastrium - Frequently the outline of the distended stomach can be seen.
    3. Gastric waves passing from left to right may be evident during and after feeding.
    4. Mass - Palpation of the upper right quadrant during feeding frequently reveals the olive-shaped mass. Practical Note: If the tumor cannot be palpated during feeding it is best to aspirate the stomach. Palpation is usually successful when the stomach is empty.

C. Laboratory Findings:
    1. Metabolic alkalosis, hypokalemia, and variable hyponatremia.
    2. Urinalysis usually reveals a markedly alkaline urine of high specific gravity. If salt depletion is present, the infant may have an acid urine but still suffer from alkalosis.
    3. Hemoconcentration may be manifested by increased hemoglobin and hematocrit values.

D. X-ray Findings: If the typical mass in the right upper quadrant is not palpable, a barium study will demonstrate an enlarged stomach with increased intensity of peristaltic waves, marked narrowing and elongation of the pylorus with abnormal retention of the barium in the stomach. Relatively little food passes beyond the pylorus even after six or seven hours. **Caution:** All barium should be aspirated from the stomach at the conclusion of the examination.

Complications.
    Tetanic seizures due to metabolic alkalosis and a reduction of free serum calcium.

Treatment.
A. General Measures:
    1. Rehydration - Give the following I.V. in the first 8 hours: 100 ml. 0.66 N saline solution/Kg. body weight with 1 mEq. KCl/Kg. body weight. Then give maintenance fluids with sufficient NaCl and KCl to correct alkalosis. Specific therapy with amino acids, ammonium chloride, or other sources of H^+ are **never** indicated.
    2. Give plasma and blood if indicated by severe cachexia or anemia.
    3. Gastric decompression - A No. 8-10 F. plastic tube placed to suction will partially decompress the stomach. Often, a large-bore tube must be placed for gastric lavage before induction of anesthesia in order to remove retained milk curds.

B. Surgical Measures: Ramstedt pyloromyotomy divides the hypertrophied muscle bundles that obstruct the pylorus. The operation should not be performed until rehydration and correction of alkalosis are complete.

C. Medical Treatment: Some prefer to treat with methscopolamine, 0.1 mg. orally or subcut. every 4 hours before feeding. The head should be elevated at least 30 degrees for 1-2 hours after feeding. This therapy is desirable only when adequate surgical and anesthetic facilities and nursing care are not available.

D. Postoperative Care:
1. Feedings - Four to six hours after surgery, begin 15 ml. of 5% glucose and water orally every two hours; gradually increase to 30 ml. every two hours. When this volume is tolerated, substitute 30 ml. of formula every two hours. Increase gradually by 30 ml. every day until a normal quantity is taken, usually on the fourth postoperative day. **Note:** Occasional attacks of vomiting may occur after the operation. If so, a more gradual increase in volume or a temporary reduction in oral intake is indicated.
2. I.V. fluids may be necessary on the first few postoperative days to supplement the oral intake (see Chapter 5).

Prognosis.
Complete relief is to be expected following adequate surgical repair. Mortality rate is quite low.

MECONIUM ILEUS
(Obstruction of the Intestines)

This condition represents the earliest known manifestation of fibrocystic disease, which affects all the mucus-secreting glands of the respiratory and alimentary tracts (see p. 201). It is characterized by marked reduction in the production of trypsin by the pancreatic glands. It is this latter disability, operating in utero, which leads to the presence of inspissated meconium, causing intestinal obstruction in the newborn period. About 10 to 20 cm. of intestine in the region of the lower ileum are obstructed. The ileocecal valves and the entire colon are normal, but there may be associated atresia of small bowel.

Clinical Findings.
A. Symptoms: The symptom is that of intestinal obstruction in the newborn: progressively more severe vomiting, beginning within the first day or two of life. The vomitus contains bile. The family history may reveal a relative with known fibrocystic disease.
B. Signs: Abdomen is markedly distended, and distended loops of bowel may be seen through the abdominal wall. Firm masses within the loops strongly suggest meconium ileus. In most cases, no meconium will have been passed.
C. Laboratory Findings: If meconium appears in stools, it can be shown to contain no trypsin. The sweat test shows high chlorides (see p. 282).
D. X-ray Findings:
1. Marked intestinal dilatation with air-fluid levels throughout the abdominal cavity on upright x-ray. Practical Note: Despite the fact that their location and appearance may suggest colon, these loops are dilated small bowel. A granular, mottled appearance within a loop, due to bubbles of gas and meconium, should suggest the presence of meconium ileus.
2. Microcolon on barium enema.

3. Free air seen in the peritoneal cavity, or fluid between loops of bowel, indicates perforation.
4. Calcification of the peritoneum, when present, represents antenatal perforation and meconium peritonitis.

Treatment.
A. Preoperative Care: It is essential that the child receive adequate fluid and electrolyte preparation for surgery.
   1. Provide continuous gastric suction through nasogastric tube.
   2. Some centers have reduced obstruction by diatrizoate methylglucamine (Gastrografin®) enemas. The hypertonic contrast medium draws water into the bowel and "floats out" the inspissated meconium. This procedure, which is often successful, must be done under fluoroscopy by a radiologist familiar with newborn infants. It will not relieve associated atresia, volvulus, or peritonitis.
B. Surgical Measures: Several choices are available in the operative approach to this problem. The method of approach depends on the general condition of the child.
   1. Resection of the portion of the distal ileum which contains the greatest amount of meconium. The loop is brought out and sutured to the skin. Postoperatively, the terminal ileum and colon are cleansed with pancreatic enzyme suspension. Closure of the enterostomy is performed two to three weeks later.
   2. Excision of the portion of the dilated distal ileum and end-to-side anastomosis, with creation of an exteriorized "chimney." The chimney is used for instillation of pancreatic enzyme, acetylcysteine (Mucomyst®), and mineral oil; subsequently, it is closed electively in six to nine months.
C. Postoperative Care:
   1. At operation many surgeons prefer inserting a gastrostomy tube, as this is associated with fewer pulmonary complications in the postoperative period than when a nasogastric tube is used.
   2. After the immediate obstruction is relieved, therapy for the prevention of pulmonary and nutritional disturbance of fibrocystic disease becomes necessary (see p. 282).

Course and Prognosis.
Pancreatic enzyme should be given orally. There is no definite relationship between meconium ileus and the severity of the symptoms of cystic fibrosis.

CONGENITAL ATRESIA OR STENOSIS
OF INTESTINE AND COLON

These disorders are thought to result from vascular obstruction in the mesenteric vessels in the fetal period of development. Atresia designates a complete block, while stenosis indicates narrowing of the intestinal lumen. Atresia or stenosis of the duodenum is frequently associated with Down's syndrome.

Meconium ileus must be considered in any child with intestinal atresia (see p. 293).

Clinical Findings.
A. Symptoms: Atresia of the intestinal tract or colon causes
   vomiting on the first day of life. Intestinal stenosis may not
   come to the physician's attention for weeks or months. The
   vomitus contains bile.
B. Signs: Depending on the level of involvement, abdominal distention is often present and becomes progressively worse. Peristaltic waves are often seen. Intestinal loops may be outlined
   on the abdominal wall. Dehydration is common because of
   persistent vomiting. Meconium may be dry and gray-green
   rather than black and viscous.
C. Laboratory Findings (Farber Test): The absence in the meconium of cornified epithelial cells from the skin and amniotic
   fluid suggests atresia, but the test is frequently misleading
   and should be discarded.
D. X-ray Findings:
   1. Upright abdominal x-ray shows air and fluid levels and re-
      veals marked dilatation of the duodenum and distention of the
      proximal loops of small bowel which may contain fluid levels.
      The distal loops will be free of gas if the obstruction is com-
      plete. In partial obstruction there may be gas without disten-
      tion distal to the point of obstruction.
   2. Presence of free air in the abdominal cavity means that
      perforation has already occurred.
   3. A granular, mottled appearance in small bowel due to gas
      and meconium suggests meconium ileus.
   4. Barium enema is an important part of the preoperative x-ray
      study. In low intestinal atresia, it will often demonstrate the
      markedly decreased caliber characteristic of the unused por-
      tion of the gastrointestinal tract - the so-called "microcolon."
      The chief indication for barium enema is to rule out Hirsch-
      sprung's disease and malrotation with volvulus, which can
      present with symptoms identical with those of intestinal
      atresia.

Treatment.
A. Preoperative Care:
   1. Decompression - Institute constant gastric suction.
   2. Parenteral fluids and electrolytes.
   3. Prophylactic antibiotic therapy is indicated.
B. Surgical Measures: End-to-end anastomosis, where possible,
   is usually preferred for the surgical correction of atresia or
   stenosis. In all cases of atresia and marked stenosis, early
   intervention is essential to prevent perforation. If the infant
   is debilitated or if perforation has occurred, ileostomy is
   safest for lower atresias. Duodenal and jejunal atresias must
   be corrected by anastomosis because of severe fluid losses
   from a jejunostomy.
C. Postoperative Care: Provide fluids and antibiotics as required.
   Gastrostomy, if done during surgery, will simplify care in the
   immediate postoperative period and will prevent many pulmonary complications.

Course and Prognosis.
   The mortality rate in infants with atresia or marked stenosis
is greatly increased by delay in diagnosis.

When the diagnosis is made and surgical treatment instituted early, mortality rates should be less than 10%.

MALROTATION OF INTESTINES AND COLON

This congenital condition is due to incomplete rotation of the gut and lack of attachment of the mesentery of the small intestines. Malrotation may result in a volvulus of the midgut or obstruction of the third part of the duodenum by peritoneal bands.

Clinical Findings.
  A. Symptoms:
    1. Younger children - Vomiting is the outstanding complaint. Most children with malrotation of the intestines have symptoms of obstruction at some time during the first year of life, most frequently during the first month.
    2. Older children - Recurring attacks of vomiting, nausea, and abdominal pain.
  B. Signs: Abdominal distention, occurring first in the epigastric area and then becoming generalized, and dehydration. Bile is usually present in the vomitus. Blood may be present in the stools if there is associated midgut volvulus. When present in the stool, blood indicates a true **surgical emergency** since the entire midgut may become necrotic within hours of the onset of symptoms.
  C. Laboratory Findings:
    1. Hematocrit and RBC are elevated due to dehydration.
    2. Slight leukocytosis is usually present. Marked leukocytosis suggests impending or actual gangrene of the bowel.
  D. X-ray Findings:
    1. Plain films of the abdomen may or may not show dilatation of the stomach and duodenum.
    2. Barium examination - The cecum and ascending colon are displaced to the left.

Treatment.
  A. Surgical Measures: Surgical correction aims at relieving duodenal compression by dividing bands near the duodenojejunal junction. If volvulus has occurred in the small intestine, it is reduced by unwinding the mass of small bowel loops, transferring the cecum and ascending colon from the right to the left upper quadrant, and freeing the duodenum.
  B. General Measures:
    1. Gastric suction with aspiration of fluid and gas should be instituted before and maintained during and after surgery. A gastrostomy is helpful in the pre- and postoperative period.
    2. Fluid and electrolyte therapy should be rapid and adequate before early surgery is attempted.
    3. Postoperative fluid therapy is discussed in Chapter 5.

Course and Prognosis.
  Recurrences after surgical correction are uncommon.

MECKEL'S DIVERTICULUM

Meckel's diverticulum may be asymptomatic throughout life or may be associated with any of the following: (1) Hemorrhage. (2) Meckel's diverticulitis, with symptoms identical with those of acute appendicitis. (3) Perforation. (4) Intussusception, with the diverticulum as the leading point. (5) Patent omphalomesenteric duct, with a diverticulum opening at the umbilicus. (6) Intestinal obstruction from a vestigial band connecting the diverticulum to the umbilicus.

Clinical Findings.

Symptoms and signs depend upon the nature of the complication caused by Meckel's diverticulum. X-ray examinations are generally of no value in attempting to demonstrate Meckel's diverticulum. Recently, radioactive technetium perchlorate has been used to demonstrate ectopic gastric mucosa in the diverticulum.

Bleeding is usually massive, and the child passes bright-red blood per rectum. The bleeding is from ulceration in the diverticulum or from the normal ileum adjacent to it. Bleeding, perforation, and diverticulitis occur only in the diverticuli that contain ectopic gastric mucosa and therefore secrete acid. Foreign bodies lodged in the diverticulum can cause any of these symptoms.

Treatment.

Treatment consists of operation as soon as the patient can be made ready. In cases of gastrointestinal hemorrhage in which Meckel's diverticulum is suspected but unproved, operation may be deferred until the diagnosis is established or until bleeding occurs a second time.

Course and Prognosis.

The prognosis is excellent following surgery. If perforation through a gangrenous diverticulum has occurred, massive peritonitis may follow and is a serious threat to life.

DUPLICATIONS OF THE GASTROINTESTINAL TRACT

These are cysts of enteric origin associated with and often communicating with various levels of the gastrointestinal tract. They may occur anywhere from the upper esophagus to the anus and are often intimately associated with the adjacent area of the gastrointestinal tract, usually sharing a common muscular wall. The nature of the mucosal lining varies considerably and may not necessarily correspond to the level of the gastrointestinal tract to which the cyst is adacent. There is considerable variation in the size and shape of these cysts.

A duplication may present as an asymptomatic mass with gastrointestinal bleeding, intestinal obstruction resulting from volvulus or intussusception, or with evidence of localized peritonitis. Special types of duplications include (1) neurenteric cysts which usually arise from the proximal small bowel and extend toward the vertebral column, and are associated with a bony defect in the vertebral column and extension through the diaphragm and into the chest; and

(2) hindgut duplications, which actually represent a double colon and are often associated with doubling of the anus and the perineal structures.

Diagnosis may often be made by radioactive technetium perchlorate to demonstrate ectopic gastric mucosa in the duplication.

Treatment consists of resection of the duplication and, in most cases, of the adjacent bowel also. The prognosis is good.

BILIARY ATRESIA

A diagnosis of biliary atresia should be considered in any infant who develops jaundice after the seventh day of life. The jaundice may be variable, with yellow scleras. The stools are white or clay-colored. Pruritus is rare in the first few months, and weight gain is normal early. The liver is enlarged and firm. The spleen becomes palpable after several months. The serum bilirubin fluctuates in the range of 10 to 14 mg./100 ml. The ^{131}I rose bengal test shows less than 5% radioactivity in the stools after 24 hours.

If the cause of the jaundice is unknown even after laboratory tests, early operation is mandatory, before irreversible cirrhosis occurs. Ten per cent of infants with biliary atresia have extrahepatic obstructions that are amenable to surgical repair. Approximately one-fourth of the remainder may benefit from the Kusui procedure, in which the bile ducts are anastomosed to the intestine. These procedures are most successful when carried out before the infants involved are two months old.

CHOLEDOCHAL CYST

Choledochal cyst is less common than biliary atresia. In most cases the "cyst" is a blind common duct, but it may represent a duplication that communicates with the common duct. The manifestations consist of intermittent jaundice, fever and chills (when infected), and a mass in the right upper quadrant. X-ray examination shows a mass on a plain film and indentation of the duodenum on an upper gastrointestinal series.

The cyst may be excised or it may be drained into the gastrointestinal tract by means of a Roux-en-Y procedure.

The overall prognosis is excellent, but some patients develop cholangitis or biliary tract stones.

INTUSSUSCEPTION

This condition is potentially one of the most dangerous surgical emergencies in early childhood. It is characterized by the telescoping of one portion of the intestine into a more distal position, resulting in impairment of the blood supply and leading to necrosis of the involved segment of bowel.

In 95% of cases, no specific cause of intussusception can be found, but viral infections (adenovirus) have recently been implicated as the cause of some cases. The condition is most frequent between the ages of five months and one year. Telescoping occasionally occurs around a Meckel's diverticulum.

Pathology.
  A. Intussusception most commonly involves the telescoping of the ileum into the colon (ileocolic type).
  B. Gangrene of the intussusception occurs if the incarcerated bowel loses its blood supply for a period of about three hours. Necrosis may not occur for 12 to 36 hours.

Clinical Findings.
  A. Symptoms: A sudden onset of recurrent, paroxysmal, sharp abdominal pain in a well-nourished, healthy child suggests intussusception. The child perspires and draws up his legs to ease the pain. During the first two hours the child appears well in the pain-free intervals. Vomiting frequently occurs after the onset of the abdominal pain but is not universally present. It usually becomes progressively more severe.
  B. Signs: The extent and severity of abnormal physical findings will depend on the duration of the symptoms.
    1. Shock, dehydration, and fever - After one or two hours of recurrent pain, evidence of shock occurs with each episode and frequently persists into the intervals between attacks. It is characterized by pallor, sweating, and lassitude. After five or more hours, dehydration and listlessness are noted and the eyes are sunken and soft. A low-grade fever is usually found as a result of dehydration and obstruction.
    2. Mass - Careful palpation usually reveals a mass in the abdomen. It is sausage shaped or ovoid and in most cases is quite firm and not tender. Its location varies, but it frequently is in the upper mid-abdomen. The right lower quadrant is characteristically less full than usual. If the leading point of the intussusception has reached the rectum, it may be possible to palpate a mass of the shape and consistency of the cervix of the uterus by rectal examination. Blood frequently is found on the examining finger after examination, and this confirms the diagnosis.
    3. Evacuation of a "currant jelly" blood clot in a bowel movement.
  C. Laboratory Findings: Depending on the duration of symptoms, concentration of blood and urine may be found. These findings are partial guides for replacement fluid and electrolyte therapy.
  D. X-ray Findings:
    1. Plain film of abdomen - There is frequently an absence of bowel gas in the right lower quadrant. Dilated loops of small bowel, when present, suggest obstruction of the small intestine.
    2. When barium enema examination is performed, the intussusception is outlined as an inverted cap and an obstruction to the further progression of the barium is noted. There is frequently a "coiled spring" appearance to the barium column in the region of the intussusception. Barium enema may also be used to reduce the intussusception (see Treatment, below).

Treatment.
  A. Specific Measures:
    1. Nonoperative reduction by barium enema administered by a skilled radiologist under fluoroscopic control will reduce

intussusception safely in two-thirds of cases. The enema must reach above the ileocecal valve, and unless the ileum is filled it may be impossible to tell if complete reduction has occurred. Subsequent laparotomy may be necessary when reduction actually has not been accomplished.

Perforation can occur from the pressure of the enema if the bowel wall has been weakened due to impairment of its vascular supply.

Hydrostatic reduction (barium enema) should **not** be attempted if there are physical findings of peritonitis.

2. Surgical reduction is the method of choice if enema is not successful, and in patients over four years of age. The bowel is usually found to be viable.

B. General Measures:
  1. Preoperative care -
     a. Fluids and electrolytes - One to two hours of intensive fluid and electrolyte therapy are usually necessary before the child can be considered a good risk for surgery. Parenteral fluids should be started before the patient is sent to x-ray for hydrostatic reduction.
     b. Deflation of the stomach by constant gastric suction is essential before, during, and after surgery.
  2. Postoperative care - Parenteral feedings and nasogastric suction should be continued until the infant passes feces normally since postoperative ileus may be more prolonged than after other types of intestinal obstruction. Fever may persist for two or three days, especially if the patient had symptoms of viral gastroenteritis preceding his intussusception. Antibiotics are rarely indicated unless the bowel has perforated preoperatively.

Course and Prognosis.

With early diagnosis and treatment, the mortality rate is extremely low. The longer the delay before treatment, the higher the mortality rate.

With adequate early treatment, the prognosis is excellent and recurrences are uncommon. For this reason, no attempt is made to do anything more than reduce the intussusception unless some condition which caused the obstruction, such as a polyp or Meckel's diverticulum, is discovered at surgery.

Children over four years of age who have intussusception frequently have a small bowel lymphosarcoma, polyp, or other leading point for the intussusception and should be explored.

POLYPS OF THE INTESTINAL TRACT

Most polyps are located in the rectum, but they may be found anywhere in the intestine. They may be single or multiple. As a rule they are soft, and they may show ulceration of the surface. Intussusception may occur when the polyp acts as the initiating focus.

Clinical Findings.
  A. Symptoms:
     1. Rectal bleeding - This depends on the degree and severity of surface erosion of the polyp. Bleeding may be severe for a

brief period if the polyp sloughs. The blood is bright red
when the polyp is in the rectum or sigmoid, whereas blood
from other areas may be dark or occult.
2. Abdominal cramps occasionally occur, or the sharp pain
typical of intussusception may be present.
B. Signs: Pallor of anemia may be present due to chronic bleeding
from a polyp. Prolapse of the rectum occasionally occurs.
The polyp may be palpable on rectal examination.
C. Proctoscopy: The polyp may be visualized if within reach of
the proctoscope.
D. Laboratory Findings: Anemia.
E. X-ray Findings: A barium enema should be performed to determine the presence of polyps in the colon, particularly those
beyond the reach of the proctoscope; filling defects should be
looked for by enema and double contrast enemas. It is difficult
to demonstrate rectal polyps by barium enema.

Treatment.
A. Specific Measures: In most cases removal of the polyp from
the lower intestine is possible through a proctoscope or sigmoid-
oscope. General anesthesia is usually employed. Be prepared
to fulgurate the base since bleeding may be brisk.
B. General Measures: Blood transfusion preoperatively to correct
anemia.

Course and Prognosis.
Polyps found in children under ten years of age are invariably
juvenile polyps and have no malignant potential. Laparotomy is
never indicated in this age group unless bleeding causes persistent
anemia or intussusception develops. Juvenile polyps will slough in
time.
Multiple polyps in the older child raise the question of Peutz-
Jeghers syndrome, Gardner's syndrome, or multiple polyposis.
Family history, excisional biopsy of the lowest polyp, and examination for cutaneous manifestations will rule out these rare causes of
polyps. All children with Gardner's syndrome and multiple polyposis
should have total or subtotal colectomy with ileoproctostomy.

CONGENITAL MEGACOLON
(Hirschsprung's Disease)

Infants with Hirschsprung's disease lack normal development
of Meissner's and Auerbach's plexuses in the distal bowel. The
defect always begins at the anus and may involve all or most of the
large bowel. In most cases, only the rectosigmoid is involved.
The disease is five times more common in males and usually causes
symptoms soon after birth.

Clinical Findings.
A. Symptoms: Obstipation, abdominal distention, and vomiting
may begin in the first few days of life. Obstipation may alternate with watery diarrhea. Complete obstruction, perforation,
or acute enterocolitis may develop at any time. Poor weight
gain and specific nutritional deficiencies are common.

B. Signs: The abdomen is distended, often with palpable loops of bowel and wasted extremities. Rectal examination shows no stool in the ampulla. There may be an explosive release of feces and flatus when the examining finger is withdrawn.

C. X-ray Findings: An upright abdominal x-ray may show massive distention of the colon with gas and feces. In advanced cases, there may be air-fluid levels. Look carefully for air in the wall of the bowel which indicates enterocolitis.

Barium enema should be performed **without** the usual bowel preparation. Use only sufficient barium to study the colon up to the junction of the collapsed bowel and that distended with stool. In a positive examination, involved segment is spastic, with an irregular, saw-toothed outline. This may be best seen on a lateral view. In the newborn, this may not be striking, and the only positive finding may be retention of barium in the proximal bowel for more than 24 hours after the examination.

D. Rectal Biopsy: This should be performed after the barium enema has been completed. A biopsy specimen taken at least 4 cm. above the mucocutaneous junction shows absence of ganglion cells in both Meissner's and Auerbach's plexuses. (A normal newborn may have no ganglion cells up to 2 cm. from the mucocutaneous junction.) In Hirschsprung's disease, there is often marked hypertrophy of nerve fibers in Meissner's plexus but no ganglion cells.

Treatment.

A. General Measures:
1. Rehydration, correction of electrolyte depletion, and albumin or blood as necessary.
2. Give antibiotics if there is evidence of enterocolitis or perforation.

B. Surgical Measures:
1. Colostomy is usually necessary and must be done as an emergency procedure if perforation or enterocolitis is suspected.
2. Resection of the aganglionic segment with reestablishment of continuity (Swenson, Duhamel, or Soave procedures) at 6 months or older. Waiting allows the patient to resume normal growth and allows the distended proximal colon to resume its normal size.
3. Anal myomectomy may be all that is required for a patient with very short involved segment.

C. Medical Treatment: Only in rare cases should the patient be managed without operation. Symptoms may be controlled with stool softeners and enemas, but enterocolitis is constant threat of life.

Course and Prognosis.

At least 90% of patients are symptom-free after surgical treatment. Fecal incontinence or damage to the sacral nerves is rare if the procedures are properly performed.

IMPERFORATE ANUS

Most males with an imperforate anus have a fistula to the membranous urethra and no connection between the hindgut and the perineal skin. Most females have a fistula to the perineum at the posterior junction of the labia (posterior fourchette). In the female, communication between the rectum and the urinary tract is extremely rare.

Clinical Findings.

A. Males: There is no opening where the anus should be. The intergluteal fold may be well developed, with good sphincter response to perineal stimulation. Look for a fistula along the median raphe. Watch for meconium in urine. There is a significant incidence of associated atresias in the gastrointestinal tract, especially tracheo-esophageal fistula. Absence of a perineal fistula means that the patient probably has a communication to the urethra and requires a colostomy. In doubtful cases, injection of contrast medium is occasionally of value.

B. Females: Look for a fistula in the posterior fourchette and perineum. Gentle dilatation of the fistula with a sound will often relieve obstipation temporarily. A high vaginal fistula cannot be handled by dilatation; the patient should have a colostomy.

C. General Findings: Since there is a high incidence of absence of kidneys and strictures of the ureteropelvic and ureterovesical structures, all infants with imperforate anus require intravenous urograms.

Treatment.

A. Conservative Measures: Pass a nasogastric tube if no fistula is found or if the abdomen is distended. Perforation can occur if the bowel is allowed to become massively distended. Time should not be wasted waiting for air to distend the rectum for x-ray confirmation.

B. Surgical Measures: Perineal fistulas in males or females require only dilatation during the newborn period; anoplasty can be done later.

Pull-through operations for patients with a high imperforate anus should be done after the age of six months. The best results are reported following a transcoccygeal approach. The results are poor if the child has myelomeningocele or a significant malformation of the lumbosacral spine.

Prognosis.

All infants with perineal fistulas should be continent because bowel passes normally through the levators. Infants with a high pouch have about a 60% chance for complete rectal continence. Fecal impaction is a frequent problem, and infants may require stool softeners, suppositories, or anal dilatation.

APPENDICITIS

Appendicitis is the most common pathologic lesion of the intestinal tract requiring surgery in childhood. Most cases are seen in children between the ages of four and 12 years and may be associated with other illnesses, especially measles. The cause is not clear, although some cases seem to result from impaction of a fecalith in the lumen of the appendix with resultant congestion of the distal appendix and bacterial invasion by organisms residing in the intestinal tract. Pinworms may occasionally cause appendicitis.

Clinical Findings

A. Symptoms:
1. Pain - Acute periumbilical or generalized abdominal pain, usually constant, which, after one to five hours, becomes localized in right lower quadrant. Urinary pain or frequency may be present if the appendix lies near the bladder or ureters.
2. Vomiting, usually only after prolonged pain.
3. Constipation frequently, but diarrhea occasionally.

B. Signs:
1. Fever - This is low grade, varying from 100 to 101.6° F. (37.8 to 38.7° C.), or may be absent early in the course. Very high fevers are suggestive of appendiceal perforation, with peritonitis; or of the simultaneous presence of bacterial enteritis, especially if accompanied by diarrhea. **Note:** Appendicitis may complicate enteritis.
2. Appearance - The child usually is anxious and may be ''doubled up,'' with his hips flexed. He walks bent over and often holds his right side.
3. Palpation may reveal a difference in muscular tension between the two sides of the abdomen. The hand should be warm and palpation gentle. Localization of tenderness may be difficult, but an opinion about whether the pain is greatest on the right or left side may be formed by observing the child's expression while palpating each area and noting the involuntary spasm of the abdominal musculature.
4. Psoas sign - Most children tend to flex the right thigh in an effort to decrease the spasm of the psoas muscle. However, the elicitation of a positive psoas sign on hyperextension of the leg, revealing spasm and pain, is generally of doubtful value in small children.
5. Rectal tenderness, or a mass consisting of peritoneal fluid or an indurated omentum wrapped around an inflamed appendix.

C. Laboratory Findings:
1. WBC - Two or three consecutive determinations frequently will show a rise in the total WBC with an accompanying shift to the left in the neutrophilic series.
2. Urine - It is imperative that a careful urinalysis be made in order to rule out inflammation of the kidney or bladder. **Note:** Irritation of the ureter may occur, and a few white or red cells may appear in the urine. A neglected abscess behind the bladder may lead to hematuria and urgency.

D. X-ray Findings:
1. In uncomplicated appendicitis, plain films of the abdomen (rarely necessary) may show a fecalith, scoliosis, or an abnormal gas pattern.
2. When exudate has formed, evidence of peritoneal inflammation may be established by noting disappearance of the peritoneal line and preperitoneal fat line along the right wall of the abdomen, or obliteration of the psoas shadow.
3. Perforation - In the presence of perforation, fluid may accumulate between loops of bowel. However, free intra-abdominal air is rare except in children less than two years of age.

4. With abscess formation, there may be evidence of a soft tissue mass in the region of the perforation. Barium enema may show extensive pressure deforming the cecum and ascending colon.

5. In atypical cases, a plain film of the chest is of value to rule out reflex pain and abdominal spasm of an undiagnosed pneumonitis.

Differential Diagnosis.

A. Mesenteric Lymphadenitis: Abdominal rigidity is generalized, and pain in the right lower quadrant results from swelling of mesenteric nodes. A respiratory infection or streptococcal sore throat generally precedes the abdominal pain. Tenderness is minimal, vomiting absent, and WBC normal or elevated. Fever tends to be higher than with appendicitis.

B. Pyelitis.

C. Pneumonia: Cough and increased respiratory rate usually are present. The fever commonly is very high, 104 to 105° F. (40 to 40.6° C.), and the WBC may be over 20,000. Rales frequently are heard, and abdominal spasms are likely to be temporary and to decrease gradually during gentle palpation.

D. Gastroenteritis of Viral or Bacterial Etiology: Diarrhea frequently accompanies the vomiting and abdominal pain. Localizing tenderness is absent. A history of similar illness in other members of the family is helpful in making the diagnosis.

E. Pneumococcal Peritonitis: (Most frequently seen in children with nephrosis.) Tenderness is general and fever is quite high, 104 to 105° F. (40 to 40.6° C.). WBC is markedly elevated.

F. Constipation: Abdominal pain without fever. Feces can usually be felt through the abdominal wall and by rectal examination. Gentle enema may bring prompt relief of symptoms.

G. Pinworms.

H. Meckel's Diverticulitis.

Complications.

Appendiceal perforation and abscess formation, paralytic ileus, and obstruction (if adhesions are formed following surgery or perforation).

Treatment.

A. Surgical Measures: Appendectomy should be done as soon as the child has been prepared by adequate fluid and electrolyte administration. If there is doubt as to diagnosis, an exploratory laparotomy with removal of the appendix and culture of peritoneal fluid should be performed. Intravenous antibiotic therapy may be indicated if peritoneal contamination has occurred.

B. General Measures:
  1. Preoperative care -
     a. Preoperative Wangensteen gastric suction through a nasal tube to deflate the stomach and prevent vomiting.
     b. Rehydrate with 0.5 N saline solution. Add KCl as necessary after the child has voided. Defer surgery until the urine specific gravity is 1.020 or less.
     c. Administration of plasma depends on the degree of toxicity but is usually indicated in cases of peritonitis.

        d. Temperature must be brought below 102°F. (38.9°C.) with hydration and rectal aspirin.

    2. Postoperative care in simple appendectomy does not require a nasogastric tube. Intravenous fluids are usually required for 24 hours.

    3. Postoperative care with ruptured appendix -
        a. Nothing by mouth until ileus is terminated.
        b. Gastric suction - Continuous gastric suction should be employed until intestinal peristalsis is normal.
        c. Fowler's position (semi-sitting) should be maintained in order to permit drainage into the pelvic region.
        d. Morphine is the analgesic of choice.
        e. Parenteral fluid therapy is administered as indicated (see Chapter 5).
        f. Antibiotics as needed (see Chapter 6).

C. Treatment of Complications:
    1. Appendiceal perforation requires antibiotic therapy. Begin therapy prior to surgery. Perforation is relatively uncommon (10%) in the first 24 hours of the disease, but increases to about 80% during the second to fourth days.
    2. Paralytic ileus - This results from peritoneal infection or electrolyte imbalance. When peritonitis causes paralytic ileus, drugs to increase intestinal tone and to stimulate peristalsis are contraindicated. Gastric suction should be continued.
    3. Obstruction - This results from the formation of adhesions. It is best treated conservatively by passage of a Miller-Abbott or Harris tube until the obstruction is relieved. If intestinal obstruction occurs late, reexploration may be required to remove obstructing adhesions and bands.

Prognosis.
    Excellent with early diagnosis and surgical removal.

FOREIGN BODIES IN THE GASTROINTESTINAL TRACT

    The incidence is highest in children one to three years of age. Coins, toys, and marbles may lodge in the esophagus. If passed into the stomach, they usually pass through the entire gastrointestinal tract without incident. If x-rays are taken for presumed ingestion, be sure to include the esophagus and pharynx if the foreign body is not in the abdomen.

    A blunt foreign body in the esophagus may be removed by passing a Foley catheter under fluoroscopy. The balloon is inflated and the catheter withdrawn. Have a laryngoscope and forceps available in case the foreign body comes to rest near the larynx. This procedure may be unsuccessful; if this is the case, the foreign body should be removed under general anesthesia by esophagoscopy.

    Pointed foreign bodies such as pins, nails, screws, etc. usually pass without incident. Explore only for pain, fever, vomiting, or local tenderness. Only 2 to 4% of such cases require surgery. X-ray examination is required only if the foreign body has not passed in four or five days. If a pin or other sharp object remains in the same location for four or five days, the point may have penetrated the bowel and surgery is then indicated.

17...
Blood

BLEEDING DISEASES IN CHILDHOOD

GENERAL CONSIDERATIONS

Family History.
A family history of easy bruising and excessive bleeding is valuable in the following disorders: (1) Hemophilia (males only). (2) Where the clinical picture is similar to that of hemophilia, but either sex may be affected. (3) Congenital thrombocytopenia or platelet dysfunction syndromes. (4) Hereditary hemorrhagic telangiectasia. (5) PTA, Ac-globulin, proconvertin, and Stuart factor deficiencies, which may be hereditary and **not** X-linked.

Physical Examination.
A. Bruises on the extremities are found in many normal children and usually have no clinical significance.
B. Generalized lymphadenopathy and petechiae are not produced by any of the diseases resulting from a defect of the clotting mechanism.
C. Petechiae are present where there is an abnormality in number or function of the platelets, or a defect of the blood vessels.
D. Hemarthrosis is typical of the hemophilias.

Laboratory Examination.
"Routine" preoperative bleeding and clotting time determinations are essentially valueless without an adequate history and careful physical examination.

HEMOPHILIA

At least nine types of congenital disorders of the clotting mechanism have been differentiated, including hemophilia "A," "B," and "C." AHF deficiency (hemophilia "A") and PTC deficiency (hemophilia "B") are hereditary, are transmitted by females, and appear usually in males. Hemophilia "A" (75%) and "B" (15%) comprise over 90% of all congenital hemorrhagic diseases due to defective formation of a fibrin clot.

Clinical Findings.
A. Symptoms and Signs:
1. May vary greatly in severity; many cases are mild.
2. All affected members of a family generally have equally severe disease.

TABLE 17-1. Differentiation of coagulation defects.

KEY: N = Normal V = Variable ↑ = Increased ↓ = Decreased

Variable	Coagulation Time	Bleeding Time	Clot Retraction	Platelet Count	One-Stage Prothrombin Time	Prothrombin Consumption	Partial Thromboplastin Time	Thrombin Time
Hemophilia "A," AHF deficiency*	↑	N	N	N	N	↓	↑	N
Hemophilia "B," Christmas disease†	↑	N	N	N	N	↓	↑	N
Plasma thromboplastin antecedent (PTA) deficiency, hemophilia "C," factor XI deficiency	N or ↑	N	N	N	N	↓	↑	N
Prothrombin deficiency, factor II deficiency	N or ↑	V	V	N	↑	↓	N	N
Proaccelerin deficiency‡	N	N	N	N	↑	N	↑	N
Proconvertin deficiency, serum prothrombin conversion accelerator (SPCA) deficiency§	N	N	N	N	↑	N	N	N
Stuart-Prower factor (factor X) deficiency disease	N or ↑	N	N	N	↑	N or ↓	↑	N
Afibrinogenemia, factor I deficiency	No clot	N	No clot	N	↑	N or ↓	N	↑
Thrombasthenia (Glanzmann's syndrome)	N	↑	↓	N	N	N or ↓	N	↑
Von Willebrand's disease**	N or ↑	↑	N	N	N	N or ↓	↑	N
Thrombocytopenia	N	↑	↓	↓	N	N or ↓	↓	N
Fibrin stabilizing factor, factor XIII deficiency	N	N	N or ↓	N	N	N	N††	N

*Also known as factor VIII deficiency disease.

†Also known as plasma thromboplastin component deficiency (PTC) disease and factor IX deficiency disease.

‡Also known as plasma and serum accelerator globulin (Ac-globulin) deficiency disease and factor V deficiency disease.

§Also known as stable factor deficiency disease, co-thromboplastin deficiency disease, and factor VII deficiency disease.

Other blood clotting factors: factor III = thromboplastin; factor IV = calcium; factor XII = Hageman factor.

**Associated with factor VIII deficiency.

††Diagnosis should be suspected in a congenital bleeding state when all screening tests are normal. The thromboelastograph may be abnormal; diagnosis is confirmed by showing instability of fibrin clot in urea.

3. Bleeding is common from the nasal or oral mucous membranes or from lacerated or contused tissues.
4. Bleeding occurs into the joints (where it may rupture through the capsule and spread widely), into the genitourinary tract, and into the skin and muscles (but petechiae do not occur).

B. Laboratory Findings: (See Table 17-1.) Routine bleeding and clotting tests are often normal in mild hemophilias. The kaolin partial thromboplastin test, prothrombin consumption test, and thromboplastin generation test should be performed in any suspected case of hemophilia. A specific-factor assay should be carried out to confirm the diagnosis. Also, the carrier state may be detectable by appropriate specific-factor assays.

Treatment.

A. Specific Measures: The specific treatment of hemophilia consists of replacing missing clotting factors. In hemophilia "A," only fresh frozen plasma, lyophilized fresh plasma, factor VIII concentrates, or cryoprecipitates of fresh plasma should be used. Stored or fresh blood, plasma, or a concentrate of factor IX is effective in hemophilia "B." Because of the danger of hepatitis, whole blood or frozen plasma should be used instead of pooled plasma except for emergency treatment. Dosage is determined by the severity of the bleeding to be treated. (Initial dose of plasma should be 10 ml./Kg.) For severe bleeding, give 5 ml./Kg. every five hours subsequently. Hypervolemia may be avoided by the use of AHF or factor VIII concentrates in smaller doses. Cryoprecipitated (one 20 to 30 ml. pack containing 75 to 200 units AHF globulin/5 Kg.), glycine-precipitated, and lyophilized antihemophilic globulin are of value. Therapy in some patients may be complicated by the development of platelet dysfunction, probably related to the relatively large amounts of fibrin degradation products contained in the AHF concentrates or in stored plasma.

B. Treatment of Hemarthrosis: **In addition to above** -
1. Early - Bed rest, temporary immobilization, pressure and cold over area of bleeding, and sedatives and analgesics. Avoid aspirin. A short course of adrenocortical steroids may shorten the convalescent period.
2. Late - Measures listed above, as indicated, plus diathermy, passive and then active exercises, and prevention of ankylosis in unphysiologic position. Repeated episodes of joint effusion as well as hematuria may be treated by adrenocortical steroids.

C. Local Measures for Bleeding From Open Wound (Skin, Tooth Socket, etc.): (Above measures as indicated.)
1. **Do not cauterize.**
2. Avoid suturing if possible. If sutures are required, give replacement therapy until 24 to 36 hours after sutures have been removed.
3. Pressure bandage and application of cold to accessible area.
4. Thrombin is the hemostatic agent of choice. Gelatin foam or fibrin may be used as a vehicle for the thrombin.

D. Other Measures: Many patients with bleeding can be cared for at home.

Prognosis.

The outlook for life is good unless extensive injury results in uncontrollable bleeding. There is some increase in the frequency of bleeding in late winter and spring, but bleeding may occur at any time of the year. An antibody (IgG) to factor VIII or IX may develop following repeated transfusions.

OTHER BLEEDING DISEASES

DISSEMINATED INTRAVASCULAR COAGULATION

Disseminated intravascular coagulation (DIC) is characterized by intravascular consumption of plasma clotting factors (factors II, V, and VIII) and platelets; fibrinolysis, with production of fibrin split products; widespread deposition of fibrin thrombi which produce tissue ischemia and necrosis in various organs (principally the lungs, kidneys, gastrointestinal tract, adrenals, brain, liver, pancreas, and skin); a generalized hemorrhagic diathesis; a micro-angiopathic hemolytic anemia, with fragmented, burred, and helmet-shaped erythrocytes; and shock and death. The disorder has been found with infections, surgical procedures, burns, neonatal conditions (especially sepsis and RDS), malignancies, severe hypoxia and acidosis, other metabolic disorders, and a variety of miscellaneous causes (e.g., hemangioma, transfusion reactions, drugs, hemolytic-uremic syndrome). The clinical manifestations depend on the systems involved.

Treatment is with heparin, replacement of depleted coagulation factors or platelets, supportive therapy, and removal of the causative agent or triggering event.

PURPURAS

Purpuras are bleeding diseases which may be due to a reduced number or abnormal function of platelets, or a defect in or abnormality of the vascular system.

CLASSIFICATION OF PURPURAS

Purpuras are differentiated by the clinical picture, the number and type of platelets in the peripheral blood, and the number and type of megakaryocytes in the bone marrow.

Purpuras With Low Platelet Counts and Normal or Increased Numbers of Megakaryocytes.

1. Immunologic - (a) Postinfectious; (b) drug-induced; (c) certain collagen diseases (e. g., lupus erythematosus); (d) congenital, due to iso-immunization resulting from maternal sensitization to some drugs, with passive transfer of maternal anti-platelet antibody.

2. Infectious mononucleosis.
3. Hypersplenic states (e.g., Banti's syndrome, Gaucher's disease, postinfectious, cirrhosis).
4. Thrombotic thrombocytopenia.
5. Hemolytic-uremic syndrome.
6. Associated with large hemangiomas.
7. Wiskott-Aldrich syndrome.
8. Congenital deficiency of megakaryocytes (may be associated with absence of the radius).

Purpuras With Normal Platelet Counts but With Abnormalities of the Vascular System.
1. Anaphylactoid or "vascular" (Henoch-Schönlein) purpura (see below).
2. Scurvy.
3. Non-thrombocytopenic purpura associated with infection (meningococcemia, subacute bacterial endocarditis, etc.) or chemical and animal agents (penicillin, snake venoms, etc.).
4. Hereditary hemorrhagic telangiectasia.
5. Traumatic or mechanical purpuras, including those associated with certain skin diseases (Ehlers-Danlos syndrome, telangiectatic purpura, etc.).
6. Associated with chronic disease (hypertension, cardiac disease, Cushing's syndrome, etc.).
7. Psychogenic purpura.
8. Toxic.

Purpuras With Normal Platelet Counts, Normal Megakaryocytes, and Defective Function of Platelets.
1. Thrombasthenia.
2. Thrombocytopathy, congenital.
3. Uremia.
4. Cirrhosis of the liver.
5. Von Willebrand's disease.
6. Following aspirin ingestion.

Purpuras With Low Platelet Counts and Decreased Numbers of Megakaryocytes.
1. Toxic, following exposure to various poisons and drugs.
2. Due to severe infections.
3. Uremia.
4. In hypoplastic and aplastic anemias.
5. Leukemia and other malignancies.
6. As a result of ionizing irradiation.
7. With megaloblastic anemia.
8. Congenital form which may be associated with absence of the radius.

IMMUNOLOGIC THROMBOCYTOPENIC PURPURA
(Purpura Hemorrhagica, Idiopathic Thrombocytopenic Purpura)

Etiology.
Many cases occur two or three weeks after an infection (usually viral, but occasionally urinary or dental) and seem to be causally

related to such infections. These cases are presumed to be associated with anti-platelet antibodies. In a few patients, no association with any agent or condition can be found.

In the neonatal period, thrombocytopenic purpura may follow infection or exchange transfusion or may be due to maternal iso-antibodies to the infant's platelets.

Clinical Findings.

Thrombocytopenic purpura is common before the age of six years, and a previous history of easy bruisability can be obtained in many.

A. Symptoms and Signs:
   1. Bleeding into the skin or from the nose, gums, and urinary tract is the most common symptom. Bleeding into joints or from the bowel is uncommon. C. N. S. bleeding occurs rarely but may be fatal.
   2. Petechiae usually are present.
   3. Fever, pallor, lymphadenopathy, and hepatosplenomegaly are usually absent.

B. Laboratory Findings: The platelet count is low and the bleeding time is prolonged. RBC and WBC are normal unless severe hemorrhage has occurred, in which case there will be a drop in RBC and an elevation in reticulocytes and WBC. Megakaryocytes in the bone marrow are normal or increased in number. Anti-platelet antibodies may be demonstrated. Other hematologic tests are normal.

   In the congenital form, the mother may also exhibit thrombocytopenia at the time; or she may have specific platelet antibodies.

Treatment.

A. Specific Measures: Transfusion of platelet concentrates may be carried out when there is C. N. S. bleeding. Usually the effect is short-lived (< 24 hours).

B. General Measures:
   1. Eradicate infection, if present. In the presence of active infection, antibiotics and chemotherapeutic agents are not contraindicated unless the thrombocytopenia is the result of the administration of these drugs. In this case the medication should be stopped and therapy with other agents instituted. All medications should be given either orally or intravenously.
   2. Data are conflicting about the value of adrenocortical steroids.
   3. Transfusions to maintain hemoglobin levels.
   4. Prevent trauma. Regular diet and vitamins. Avoid aspirin.
   5. Watchful waiting for six to eight months.
   6. Infusion of compatible platelets from the mother or exchange transfusion has been recommended for neonatal isoimmune thrombocytopenia.

C. Surgical Treatment:
   1. Splenectomy is indicated -
      a. If conservative therapy has been carried out for six to 12 months without improvement.
      b. If the disease process is very severe and the patient is becoming steadily worse in spite of other therapy.

   c. If the patient is having recurrent bouts of severe thrombo-
      cytopenic purpura for which no definite etiology can be
      determined.
   d. In an adolescent girl with severe menorrhagia.
2. Splenectomy is contraindicated if the number of megakaryocytes in the bone marrow is decreased.
D. Azathioprine (Imuran®) may be of value in the treatment of
   chronic idiopathic thrombocytopenic purpura not responding
   to conventional therapy.

Course and Prognosis.
   At least 75% of children with thrombocytopenic purpura with
normal or elevated numbers of megakaryocytes in the bone marrow
will have a spontaneous and complete recovery within six months
even without therapy, but spontaneous recovery may occur after a
period of as long as $3\frac{1}{2}$ years. A few will need splenectomy, and
very occasionally a child will go on to die in spite of all forms of
therapy.
   Evidence of clinical activity may continue for from two weeks
to several months, but significant improvement usually occurs
within three to four weeks.

ANAPHYLACTOID OR "VASCULAR" PURPURA
(Henoch-Schönlein Purpura)

   Anaphylactoid purpura is a disease of unknown cause. Many
patients have a history of allergic manifestations. Some cases of
anaphylactoid purpura follow infections; a causal relationship with
group A streptococcal infections has not been proved. The disease
tends to recur, and it may persist over a span of many years.

Clinical Findings.
A. Symptoms and Signs:
   1. Abdominal and joint pains are present in most children,
      but the pain may occur only in the abdomen (Henoch type)
      or only at the joints (Schönlein type). The pain may pre-
      cede the development of skin lesions.
   2. Either small or large joints may be involved. The joints
      are painful and swollen.
   3. Ecchymoses, petechiae, and/or bullous hematomas may be
      present. The initial lesions may resemble urticaria, but
      these soon become hemorrhagic. They often appear first
      around the elbows and ankles and over the buttocks.
   4. Gastrointestinal hemorrhage is common in children.
   5. Nephritis may occur in over one-third of cases.
   6. Intussusception may develop.
   7. Associated group A beta-hemolytic streptococcal infections
      are frequent.
B. Laboratory Findings:
   1. Platelet count and other hematologic tests are normal.
   2. Eosinophilia may be present in some cases.
   3. Serum IgA may be elevated.

Treatment.
   In many cases, treatment is either unnecessary or ineffective.

A. Specific Measures:
   1. Eradicate infection, using appropriate antibiotics.
   2. Eliminate allergens, if known.
   3. Antihistamines, if allergy is suspected.
B. General Measures: Adrenocortical steroids may relieve joint and abdominal symptoms. They do not appear to benefit renal complications.
C. Prevention of Recurrences:
   1. Prophylactic penicillin if a streptococcic etiology can be established.
   2. Remove other known allergens.

Course and Prognosis.
   The disease may vary in degree from mild to quite severe. Complete recovery eventually occurs in most cases, but recurrences are not infrequent and nephritis occasionally persists and may become chronic. Death during the acute phase of the disease is rare.

CHILDHOOD ANEMIAS

   Anemias in children differ from those in adults in that they may be more pronounced and develop much more rapidly. This is due in part to the fact that in childhood growth is associated with an increased need for blood-building substances. Furthermore, infections, which are so common in childhood, have a more profound effect on blood formation in early life than later.
   Nucleated red cells appear more readily in the peripheral blood of children, and enlargement of the spleen, liver, and lymph nodes occurs more readily in children than in adults.

Etiologic Classification of Anemias.
   On basis of relationship of hemoglobin and RBC.
A. Hypochromic Microcytic Anemia:
   1. Iron deficiency due to -
      a. Inadequate storage (prematurity).
      b. Deficient intake (dietary deficiency).
      c. Poor absorption.
      d. Chronic blood loss.
      e. Poor utilization (infections and inflammation).
      f. Milk sensitivity with intestinal dysfunction and blood loss.
   2. Mediterranean anemia (thalassemia).
   3. Copper deficiency or transient dysproteinemia (may be secondary to iron deficiency).
   4. Pyridoxine deficiency.
   5. Lead poisoning.
B. Normochromic Normocytic Anemias: Sudden hemorrhage, decreased blood formation (e.g., leukemia, hypothyroidism), inflammation (e.g., juvenile rheumatoid arthritis), infections, and certain hypersplenic states.
C. Macrocytic Anemias: Rare pernicious anemia of childhood, megaloblastic anemia of infancy, malabsorption syndrome (occasionally), hypothyroidism (rare), early anemia of pre-

maturity, and with some conditions with very active bone marrow.

PHYSIOLOGIC "ANEMIA" OF THE NEWBORN

A gradual drop in red cells and hemoglobin occurs normally during the first ten to 12 weeks of life. The RBC is reduced to 3.5 to 4.5 million/cu. mm., and the hemoglobin reaches a low of 10 to 12 Gm./100 ml. in full-term infants and may fall as low as 7 Gm./100 ml. in the premature infant. This is followed by a gradual increase in the number of red cells, with a correspondingly slower rise in hemoglobin level (which results in a relative hypochromic microcytic blood picture). These early changes occur even if the nutritional status of the mother during pregnancy was adequate.

Initial drop is not altered by early treatment with iron, but administration of iron after the second or third month in the full-term infant prevents a further reduction and results in a gradual rise of hemoglobin.

ANEMIA OF PREMATURITY

Although at birth the red cell count and hemoglobin of a premature infant are only slightly lower than those of a full-term one, the subsequent reduction that occurs is greater in prematures. The magnitude of the drop of red cells and hemoglobin is inversely proportional to the size of the infant. In very small infants (2 lb. at birth), a reduction of hemoglobin to 7 to 8 Gm./100 ml. and a reduction of red cells to 2.5 to 3 million/cu. mm. may occur. Lowest levels are reached at about the end of the second month of life. More severe anemia occurs in prematures than in full-term infants because there is a greater growth in body size and a correspondingly greater increase in blood volume in premature infants. Furthermore, the total stores of blood-building substances which may be utilized for hemoglobin production are smaller in the premature infant, and the hemopoietic system may be less active.

Clinical Findings.

Pallor is the principal manifestation. The anemia generally is normochromic and poikilocytic early in the course of disease and hypochromic and microcytic late in the course.

Treatment.

The initial drop in hemoglobin or RBC cannot be prevented by early treatment with iron. Supplemental vitamin E may be beneficial. After the second month of life, some source of iron should be made available, but transfusions seldom are necessary.

Course and Prognosis.

The course is self-limited. In most cases, recovery is complete by the eighth month.

IRON DEFICIENCY ANEMIA

Because expansion of blood volume is part of the growth process, children have more need for iron than do adults. In the average full-term infant, the stores of iron available at birth are adequate for three to six months. In the premature infant, twin, or child born of a mother with a deficiency of iron, the iron reserves will be used up earlier, and these children are more likely to develop an iron deficiency anemia.

Iron deficiency anemia (see above) may result from inadequate storage, deficient intake, chronic blood loss, poor utilization of iron, or milk protein sensitivity. The latter may be associated with chronic respiratory disease and diarrhea. It has been suggested that factors in the diet other than the amount of iron are important in the etiology of iron deficiency.

Clinical Findings.
  A. Symptoms and Signs:
    1. Pallor may be the only early finding.
    2. Easy fatigability, weakness, listlessness, and irritability appear later.
    3. Interference with growth may occur in long-standing cases.
    4. Spoon-shaped nails and slow growth of nails.
    5. In more marked cases, heart murmurs, splenomegaly, and hepatomegaly may also be found. Congestive heart failure occasionally occurs.
    6. Pica, especially of ice, occasionally occurs.
  B. Laboratory Findings:
    1. Hypochromic microcytic anemia with moderate or no reduction in red cells; hematocrit low.
    2. Anisocytosis, poikilocytosis, and polychromatophilia may be marked.
    3. Reticulocyte count is low, normal, or slightly elevated.
    4. Marrow usually but not always hyperplastic.
    5. Serum iron low; iron-binding capacity increased; transferrin saturation reduced.
    6. Blood may be present in stools.
    7. Precipitins to milk are found in some cases.
    8. Histologic abnormalities of the bowel may be present.
    9. In severe iron deficiency, there may be associated copper deficiency and a decreased serum albumin level.

Treatment.
  A. Specific Measures: Iron is specific therapy. Other blood-building elements are not necessary.
    1. Medicinal iron - Iron should be given as the ferrous salt. The daily dose should give 4.5 to 6 mg./Kg. of elemental iron in 3 divided doses. Adequate vitamin C should be given to ensure optimal iron absorption. Therapy should be continued for several months after the concentration of hemoglobin returns to normal in order to build up some reserve of iron.

      Iron choline citrate complex appears to be at least as effective and causes less gastrointestinal upset. It may be given with meals.

      Intramuscular iron (iron dextran injection [Imferon®], 50 mg./ml.) should be used only when treatment with oral iron is not feasible. The dosage should be determined according to the package insert. The first injection should consist of a test dose with subsequent injections being given daily until the total dose is administered.

2. Dietary iron - Food contains insufficient iron for effective therapy of iron deficiency anemia. Absorption of iron from most foods (including milk) is generally good; phytates (oatmeal, brown bread) may inhibit absorption.
   a. Good sources of iron include liver (5 mg./100 Gm.); dried fruits such as apricots, prunes, and raisins; and pinto beans.
   b. Fair food sources of iron (1 to 3 mg./100 Gm.) include beef, veal, carrots, beans, spinach, peas, sweet potatoes, and peaches.
3. Transfusions of packed red cells are reserved for patients with severe symptomatic anemia for whom rapid rise in hemoglobin is desired.
4. If evidence of heart failure is present, transfuse very slowly. Parenteral diuretics and partial exchange transfusion may be of value.
5. It has been suggested that ingestion of whole cow's milk aggravates and prevents correction of the anemia.

B. General Measures: Elimination of underlying defects generally is necessary before medicinal iron produces improvement.

Course and Prognosis.

Progressive anemia will result unless medicinal or dietary therapy is instituted and the underlying abnormality, if any, removed. Improvement is then prompt, with a rise in the reticulocyte count appearing in four to seven days and a rise in hemoglobin of approximately 0.1 to 0.2 Gm./100 ml./day. Simple iron deficiency anemia due to a low intake of iron should clear rapidly, but the presence of other deficiencies, congenital malformation, or infection may alter this favorable outcome.

HYPOPLASTIC ANEMIA*

Congenital hypoplastic anemia (Blackfan-Diamond syndrome, aregenerative pure red blood cell anemia) is associated with decreased hemoglobin, reticulocytes, and, rarely, white blood cells. Erythroid precursors are decreased or absent from the marrow. It usually responds well to adrenocortical steroids and transfusions, if necessary. Splenectomy may be helpful for children with hypersplenism. There are no skeletal anomalies.

Hypoplastic anemia, often with pancytopenia, developing after the age of two years may occur as an autosomal recessive disorder in association with abnormal pigmentation, skeletal anomalies (absent, hypoplastic, or supernumerary thumb, hypoplastic or absent radius, etc.), retarded growth, hypogonadism, small head, renal anomalies, microphthalmos, strabismus, and abnormalities of the reproductive tract (Fanconi's syndrome). The condition may

---

*Most children given large doses of chloramphenicol temporarily develop some degree of bone marrow depression; in some instances, permanent and potentially fatal aplastic anemia may occur even after small doses. A rise in serum iron and a decrease in reticulocytes may be premonitory findings.

respond to testosterone; some reports suggest also using adrenocortical steroids.*

HEMOLYTIC ANEMIAS

General Considerations.

The hemolytic anemias of childhood may be due to (1) congenital
defects in the production of red cells or hemoglobin or both (hereditary spherocytosis, congenital nonspherocytic hemolytic anemia,
congenital elliptocytosis, thalassemia, congenital hemoglobinopathies, and congenital defects in erythrocyte enzyme synthesis [e. g.,
glucose-6-phosphate dehydrogenase]); or to (2) acquired defects in
the red cells or their environment (hemolytic anemia due to toxic
substances, infections, radiation, thermal injury, specific antigen-
antibody reactions, idiosyncrasy to certain organic substances,
hypersplenism, and incompatible blood transfusions). The principal
feature of the hemolytic anemias is a reduction of the life span of
the erythrocytes.

Symptoms and signs may include easy fatigability, anemia,
jaundice, and splenomegaly. Gallstones may develop after many
attacks of hemolysis.

The peripheral blood usually shows reticulocytosis, nucleated
red blood cells, hyperbilirubinemia, and markedly diminished
levels of haptoglobin. The urine and feces contain increased
amounts of urobilinogen. Erythroid hyperplasia of the bone marrow often results in widening of the marrow spaces. In long-
standing cases hemosiderosis may occur.

CONGENITAL (HEREDITARY) SPHEROCYTOSIS
(Congenital Hemolytic Anemia, Hereditary Hemolytic Jaundice)

A hereditary (dominant) disease due to excessive destruction
of abnormally shaped cells (spherocytes). The disease may be discovered during a "hypoplastic" crisis, during which the reticulocyte count may be very low and the degree of anemia more profound
than usual. These may occur at periodic intervals.

Other members of the family may have overt or subclinical
disease with slight spherocytosis and increased fragility of red
blood cells in hypotonic saline solution. A small percentage of
cases will occur in the absence of other affected family members.

There is spherocytosis, increased osmotic fragility, and reticulocytosis; the osmotic fragility test will be abnormal if the blood
is incubated (at 37° C. for 24 hours) prior to testing. The auto-
hemolysin test is also abnormal. Maturation arrest of all elements
in the marrow may be present at times of crises. Neonates may
show early and exaggerated jaundice. Cholelithiasis may develop
in the second or third decade.

---

*Hepatocellular carcinoma has been noted in association with C-17
alkylated anabolic androgen therapy for the treatment of aplastic
and hypoplastic anemias.

Treatment is by splenectomy, ideally performed after three to four years. Because of the increased risk of sepsis in splenectomized individuals, prophylactic penicillin should be given until at least four or five years of age. Until the time of splenectomy, folic acid, 1 mg./day, should be given.

Following removal of the spleen, the underlying defect of the red cells persists, but most patients will have a complete remission from the hemolysis and anemia.

NONSPHEROCYTIC HEMOLYTIC ANEMIA ASSOCIATED WITH DEFICIENCIES OF VARIOUS ENZYMES

See also General Considerations, above.

Approximately 10% of black males, a small percentage of whites, and varying percentages of Orientals have a deficiency of erythrocyte glucose-6-phosphate dehydrogenase (G6PD) which may predispose them to increased hemolysis upon exposure to primaquine, naphthalene, sulfonamides, synthetic vitamin K, fava beans, aspirin, acetanilid, phenacetin, or acetaminophen, or occasionally with certain infections. The disorder is inherited as an X-linked recessive or intermediate dominant defect.

In addition, other patients may have other intrinsic defects of the red blood cells with clinical manifestations that appear during the neonatal period. They may have a deficiency of pyruvate kinase or an unstable hemoglobin.

There is macrocytosis, increased mean corpuscular volume, reticulocytosis, and basophilic stippling of the red cells. Serum iron may be normal or low. Osmotic fragility is normal or increased. The autohemolysis test, when done with and without glucose and ATP, is useful in classifying this group of anemias.

Transfusions should be given for severe anemia. Splenectomy benefits a few patients.

HEMOLYTIC-UREMIC SYNDROME
(Syndrome of Hemolytic Anemia, Thrombocytopenic Purpura, and Nephropathy; Thrombotic Microangiopathy)

This disorder, occurring mainly in children between the ages of six months and two years, is characterized by (1) a sudden onset of hemolytic anemia (with pallor, mild jaundice in some cases, and, usually, a negative Coombs test); (2) thrombocytopenic purpura (with petechiae, ecchymoses, and adequate megakaryocytes in the bone marrow); (3) nephropathy (with renal insufficiency, azotemia, and acute renal necrosis); and (4) central nervous system involvement (with drowsiness and convulsions). Clinical manifestations of the syndrome are frequently preceded by diarrhea (commonly due to enterovirus infection) or, less often, by an upper respiratory infection, with an intervening symptom-free period of one to ten days. Other findings which may be present include hepatosplenomegaly, hypertension, and cardiac failure. The red blood cells may be fragmented and helmet-shaped or burr-shaped. The mortality rate is high (> 25%). Disseminated intravascular coagulation

or pathologic consumption of platelets may be factors in the progressive pathologic changes.

Packed red blood cell transfusions and peritoneal dialysis are
often required as supportive measures. The benefit of heparin or
streptokinase is not proved. Complete recovery of hematologic
manifestations usually occurs, but permanent impairment of renal
function is not uncommon.

Partial forms of the disease may also occur.

HEREDITARY ELLIPTOCYTOSIS
(Ovalocytosis)

See also General Considerations, above.

This is a congenital disease characterized by numerous elongated or oval cells. It is usually asymptomatic, but some patients
may have mild to severe hemolysis. In the latter, splenectomy
may be of value.

. . .

HEREDITARY HEMOGLOBINOPATHIES

MEDITERRANEAN ANEMIA
(Cooley's Anemia, Thalassemia)

Mediterranean anemia is a relatively common anemia which is
due to an inherited defect in the synthesis of the beta chains of
hemoglobin. It may occur in a severe homozygous form, characterized by pronounced changes in the blood and in various organ
systems; or it may occur as the "trait," with little or no anemia
and no systemic changes. It is most common in Italians and Greeks
but occurs occasionally in persons of non-Mediterranean background.

Major (Homozygous) Form.

Severe hypochromic microcytic anemia which starts in the
first year of life. Both parents will be carriers of the "trait."

A. Symptoms and Signs: Symptoms secondary to the anemia;
jaundice of varying degrees; enlargement of liver and spleen;
"mongoloid" appearance; pathologic fractures.

B. Laboratory Findings: Hypochromic microcytic anemia, anisocytosis, poikilocytosis, basophilic stippling, and decreased
fragility of the red cells with the presence of target cells,
nucleated erythrocytes, and increased number of reticulocytes
in the peripheral blood. (Reticulocyte count may fall in association with drop in hematocrit.) Elevated levels of "fetal"
hemoglobin.

C. X-ray Findings: Changes in the bones (widening of the medulla,
thinning of the cortex, and coarsening of trabeculation) due to
extreme marrow hyperplasia. "Hair-on-end" appearance.

Minor (Heterozygous) Form. (Thalassemia trait.)

Evidence of mild anemia and splenomegaly may be present. Blood smear shows hypochromic microcytosis, target cells, anisocytosis, and poikilocytosis. The diagnosis may be confirmed by finding elevated levels of fetal or A_2 hemoglobin on hemoglobin electrophoresis.

Treatment.

Transfusions are the only effective means of temporarily overcoming the anemia in severe cases but do not alter the underlying disease. Other hemopoietic agents are entirely ineffective and should not be used. Recent reports suggest that iron chelation combined with hypertransfusion (maintaining hemoglobin at high levels [> 11 Gm./100 ml.]) may be beneficial; chronic hypoxia rather than iron loading may be the significant factor in the production of myocardial and hepatic damage.

Splenectomy may be of value when the spleen is so large as to produce discomfort or if an acquired hemolytic component is superimposed on the primary disease.

Course and Prognosis.

In spite of repeated transfusions, children with thalassemia major generally succumb within the first two decades of life from intercurrent infections or from progressive hepatic and cardiac failure due to deposition of iron. Gallbladder stones frequently develop in patients surviving to the early teens. Thalassemia trait is associated with a normal life span.

The more severe the anemia and the earlier its onset, the more rapidly the disease progresses to a fatal outcome. Maintaining the hemoglobin above 10 Gm./100 ml. may be effective in improving the condition of children with abnormal cardiac symptoms.

SICKLE CELL ANEMIA
(Sicklemia)

Sickle cell anemia is an inherited abnormality of hemoglobin (hemoglobin "S") limited almost exclusively to blacks. In hemoglobin S, the amino acid valine replaces the normally occurring glutamic acid in the beta chain. Although the sickle trait occurs in about 8% of the black population, the disease with anemia occurs only in homozygotes.

Clinical Findings.

Onset of clinical manifestations may be at any time in the first decade. They include -

A. Symptoms and Signs:
  1. Fever, headache, joint involvement (pain and swelling), osteopathy (particularly of metacarpals and phalanges), abdominal pain and tenderness, pallor, jaundice, splenomegaly (in the very young), hepatomegaly, cardiomegaly, and hemic heart murmurs. Ulceration of the skin over the lower extremities is most unusual during childhood. Splenomegaly is usually absent in older individuals because "autosplenectomy" occurs as the result of repeated throm-

TABLE 17-2. Summary of findings in abnormal
hemoglobin diseases and thalassemia.*

	Hemoglobin Types	Anemia	Splenomegaly	Arthralgie	Evidence of Incr. Blood Destruction	Target Cells	Sickling	Microcytosis	Hypochromia
Normal adult	A, A (F†)	0	0	0	No	0	0	0	0
Normal newborn	A, F	0	0	0	No	0	0	0	0
Iron deficiency anemia	A, A (F†)	+ to ++++	±	0	No	±	0	+ to ++++	+ to ++++
Some acquired anemias	A, F	+ to ++++	+ to ++++	±		±	0	0	0
Sickle cell trait	A, S	0	0	0	No	+	+	0	0
Sickle cell anemia	S, S (F†)	+++	±	++	Yes	++	+++	0	0 to +
Thalassemia minor	A, A (F†)	±	0 to +	0	±	+	0	0 to +	0 to +
Thalassemia major	A, F	++++	++++	0	Yes	++	0	++++	++++
Sickle cell—thalassemia dis.	S, F, A	++	+++	++	Yes	++	++	++	++
Sickle cell—Hgb. C dis.	S, C (F†)	+	++	±	Yes	+++	++	±	+
Sickle cell—Hgb. D dis.	S, D (F†)	+	++		Yes	±	+	+	+
Sickle cell—Hgb. G dis.	S, G	0	0		No	0	+	0	0
Thalassemia—Hgb. C dis.	C, A	+	0		Yes	+++	0	+	±
Thalassemia—Hgb. E dis.	E, F	+++	++		Yes	++	0	+	+
Thalassemia—Hgb. G dis. (?)	G, F		++			++	+	+	0
Sickle cell—hereditary spherocytosis	S, A	++	++			++	+	+	0
Hgb. C trait	A, C	0	0	0	No	0 to +++	0	0	+
Homologous Hgb. C dis.	C, C	+	+++	+	Yes	++++	0	±	+
Hgb. D dis.	A, D	0	0		No	?	0	0	0
Hgb. E trait	A, E	0	0	0	No	±	0	0	0
Homologous Hgb. E dis.	E, E (F†)	++	±		Yes	+++	0	++	0
Hgb. G trait	A, G	0	0	0	No	0	0	0	0
Homologous Hgb. G dis.	G, G	0	0		No	0	0	0	0
Hgb. H trait (?)	A, H	+	++		Yes	+	0	+	+
Hgb. I trait	A, I	0	0		No	0	0	0	0

*Adapted from Alway, Wintrobe, and other sources.
†Sometimes present.

boses. There may be episodes of vascular occlusion and
infarction. Enuresis and nocturia may be present. Patients with sickle cell anemia have an increased resistance
to malarial infection; an increased susceptibility to salmonella sepsis, osteomyelitis, and pneumococcal sepsis,
pneumonia, and meningitis; and an increased risk of anesthetic complications.

2. In the severe form the general picture is of poor health,
development, and nutrition.

3. During a painful "crisis," the picture may be that of acute
rheumatic fever, acute surgical abdomen, or infection of
the C. N. S. "Aplastic" crises may occur with diminished
red cell production superimposed on rapid destruction.

B. Laboratory Findings: Sickle-shaped red blood cells in the
peripheral blood smear. Normochromic anemia, reticulocyto-

sis, nucleated red blood cells in the peripheral blood, leukocytosis, hyperbilirubinemia, increased excretion of urobilinogen, increased LDH, increased resistance of red blood cells to
osmotic lysis, and an abnormal electrophoretic pattern, with
50-100% hemoglobin S and increased amounts of fetal hemoglobin. There is excretion of excessive quantities of urine of
low specific gravity.

Heterozygotes (carriers of sickle trait) may be identified by
a screening test (Sickledex®, sodium metabisulfite test) followed
by hemoglobin electrophoresis. Characteristically, 35 to 45%
hemoglobin S is found. Heterozygotes are not anemic and -
except for conditions with extreme hypoxia - are asymptomatic.

Treatment.

Parenteral fluid therapy, analgesics, and transfusion for severe anemia and crises are the only consistently effective methods
of treatment. Placing the patient in oxygen during the crisis and
giving bicarbonate has been recommended.

Adequate hydration of the patient at the onset of a crisis sometimes obviates the need for transfusions. Because infection exacer-
bates sickling of the patient's red blood cells, all infections should
be treated promptly and vigorously.

The use of urea and cyanate for the prevention and treatment of
crises has been recommended, but the benefits have not been proved.

Course and Prognosis.

The course is determined by the severity of the sickling tendency and resulting hemolysis, the frequency and duration of crises,
and the age of the patient. Interference with growth, nutrition, and
general activity is common, although many patients lead active
lives with persistent hemoglobin levels of 7 to 9 Gm./100 ml.

The prognosis for survival is less favorable for younger patients than for those who develop severe manifestations of the disease late in the first decade. Some children with sickle cell anemia
live for years. Death is from intercurrent infection or the occurrence of sickle thrombi in vital organs.

OTHER HEMOGLOBINOPATHIES

More than 20 different hemoglobins have been reported; certain
of these may be further subdivided chemically (e.g., there are at
least three different types of hemoglobin D) even though they behave
in the same way electrophoretically. Table 17-2 summarizes some
of the more frequently seen hemoglobinopathies.

CHRONIC CONGESTIVE SPLENOMEGALY
(Banti's Syndrome)

Banti's syndrome is produced by congestion and stasis in the
spleen and characterized by splenomegaly, moderate hepatic enlargement in early cases, moderate anemia, leukopenia, thrombocytopenia, and varices and hemorrhages of the upper gastrointestinal tract. It may result from a congenital abnormality of the

splenic vessels or may follow hepatic disease with obstruction of the splenoportal circulation, thrombophlebitis of splenic vessels, or pressure of enlarged lymph nodes on the veins. In some instances the underlying pathology may lie in the spleen itself.

Treatment is with transfusions when necessary and treatment of the underlying disease whenever possible. Splenectomy and bypass operations to improve collateral circulation have been of value in cases where the underlying defect appears to be in or around the spleen.

ABSENCE OF THE SPLEEN

Absence of the spleen (whether congenital or surgically induced) may be associated with increased susceptibility to fulminating infections. In the congenital form there may also be cardiac anomalies and an accessory lobe of the left lung. In the peripheral blood, Howell-Jolly bodies are seen in the red blood cells. The tendency to develop life-threatening infections is minimal in older children when the spleen is removed for trauma, idiopathic thrombocytopenic purpura, portal vein thrombosis, local tumors, or hereditary spherocytosis. The risk is significant in histiocytosis, inborn errors of metabolism, hepatitis with portal hypertension, thalassemia, and Wiskott-Aldrich syndrome. Prophylactic penicillin should be considered in all patients younger than four or five years of age who have undergone splenectomy for any reason.

LEUKEMIAS IN CHILDHOOD

Most leukemias in childhood are "acute" (97.5%). The most common types are lymphoblastic, stem cell, monocytic, and myeloblastic.

Forms with normal or reduced white blood counts ("aleukemic" or "hypoplastic") occur in 25 to 60% of patients.

Clinical Findings.
A. Symptoms and Signs: The highest incidence occurs between two and five years. Initial signs and symptoms may include anemia, fever, weakness, bleeding, and bone or joint pain or swelling. Purpura is common. Lymphadenopathy is usually less prominent than in chronic leukemias. Hepatosplenomegaly is usually present but is less marked than in chronic leukemias. C. N. S. infiltration may cause manifestations simulating meningitis and may be associated with C. S. F. pleocytosis, elevation of C. S. F. protein, and lowered C. S. F. glucose. Septicemia is common during the course of the disease.

There appears to be more than a chance association between leukemia and Down's syndrome.
B. Laboratory Findings:
  1. Blood -
     a. RBC and Hgb. - Usually low. Generally a normochromic normocytic anemia. Normoblasts occasionally.

    b. WBC - May be elevated, normal, or reduced. In some cases, large numbers of abnormal cells are seen; in others, especially with granulocytopenia, the leukocytes appear entirely normal.

    c. Platelets - Thrombocytopenia is very frequent.

2. Bone marrow - In almost all cases, 50 to 98% of nucleated cells are blast forms with marked reduction in the normal erythroid, myeloid, and platelet precursors.

3. An abnormal Ph[1]-chromosome is absent in the "juvenile" form of chronic granulocytic leukemia.

4. Serum levels of uric acid and LDH are usually elevated.

5. Cerebrospinal fluid - May show pleocytosis (consisting of blast forms), elevated protein, and decreased levels of sugar.

Treatment of Acute Leukemias.

A. Acute Lymphoblastic or Stem Cell Leukemia: Eighty-five to 95% of patients achieve complete remission following treatment with vincristine and prednisone. Therapy is continued with regular administration of 6-mercaptopurine, methotrexate, and cyclophosphamide for two to three years.

B. Central Nervous System Leukemia: Because of the significant incidence of C.N.S. leukemia (50%), patients should be treated "prophylactically" with methotrexate, 12 mg./sq. M. intrathecally weekly, with C.N.S. irradiation despite the risk of complicating encephalopathy, or both.

C. Additional Methods: Periodic elective reinduction therapy with prednisone and vincristine has been recommended. The role of host defense stimulants such as BCG or leukemic cell fractions has not been determined.

D. Relapse: If the disease recurs, another remission may be induced with methotrexate and 6-mercaptopurine or another course of vincristine and prednisone. If this is unsuccessful, L-asparaginase or adriamycin may be of value.

E. General Measures:

1. Transfusions for anemia; antibiotics to treat infections; diet and activity as tolerated.

2. Hyperuricemia due to the degradation of nucleic acid purines may occur, especially following antileukemic therapy. Allopurinol (Zyloprim®), 100 to 150 mg./sq. M. orally twice daily, is effective in reducing the hyperuricemia. Intravenous fluids, urinary alkalinization, and mannitol diuresis may also be of value.

3. Pain due to leukemic infiltration of bone may be relieved by local x-ray radiation.

Course and Prognosis.

In recent years, the survival time - particularly of acute lymphoblastic leukemia - has increased markedly, and many children are enjoying extended periods (two to four years) of disease-free life. With a combination of the presently available antimetabolites and steroids, children live from 18 to more than 36 months.

Aggressive combination chemotherapy, supportive care with blood components, and newer antibiotics have contributed to the improvement.

• • •

IMMUNOLOGIC DEFICIENCY SYNDROMES
(Antibody Deficiency Syndromes; Hypogammaglobulinemias)

Immunologic deficiency diseases are characterized by (1) increased susceptibility to bacterial, viral, fungal, and protozoal infections; (2) a generalized or selective deficiency in the serum immunoglobulins; (3) a diminished capacity (in varying degrees) to form circulating antibodies or to develop cellular immunity (delayed hypersensitivity) after an appropriate antigenic stimulus; and (4) clinical and immunologic variability. Several broad categories are definable based upon whether the defect originates with a disturbance of antibody-producing lymphoid cells ("B" cells) or with thymus-derived cells which mediate cellular immunity ("T" cells.)

Classification of Immunologic Disorders.
  A. Immunoglobulin Deficiencies:
    1. Infantile X-linked agammaglobulinemia (IgG, IgA, IgM deficiency).
    2. Selective immunoglobulin deficiency (dysgammaglobulinemia).
    3. Acquired hypogammaglobulinemia -
      a. Primary - All ages; various immunoglobulin defects; associated autoimmune disorders, sporadic and familial.
      b. Secondary - In diseases with loss of serum proteins (nephrosis, protein-losing enteropathy) or in lymphoid neoplasms.
    4. Transient hypogammaglobulinemia of infancy.
  B. Cellular Immunity Deficiency With "Normal" Immunoglobulins:
    1. Thymic dysplasia (Nezelof type).
    2. DiGeorge's syndrome (congenital absence of thymus and parathyroids; third and fourth pharyngeal pouch syndrome).
  C. Combined Immunoglobulin and Cellular Immunity Deficiencies:
    1. Congenital -
      a. Severe combined immunodeficiency.
      b. Wiskott-Aldrich syndrome (dysgammaglobulinemia and progressive cellular immunity deficiency).
    2. Acquired -
      a. Hodgkin's disease (advanced).
      b. Iatrogenic (steroid or antimetabolite therapy).

Diagnosis.
(1) Quantitative immunochemical determination of the serum levels of IgG, IgM, and IgA.
(2) Isohemagglutinin determination: These antibodies to the blood group substance belong for the most part to the IgM class. They are normally present after about one year of age in all individuals of blood groups A, B, and O. Therefore, their absence is presumptive evidence of IgM deficiency.
(3) Schick test: Normal individuals who have been adequately immunized with diphtheria toxoid should have a negative reaction on testing with Schick toxin. A positive Schick test in a well immunized individual is presumptive evidence of IgG deficiency.

(4) Absolute lymphocyte count: Normal children have 4000 to 6000 lymphocytes per cubic millimeter. Lymphocytes are reduced in cellular immunity deficiency states (especially severe combined immunodeficiency).

(5) Examination of bone marrow for plasma cells.

Confirmatory tests include: (1) Results of immunization with well characterized antigens (e. g. , diphtheria toxoid, tetanus toxoid) in terms of specific antibody produced and plasma cell development. (2) Presence of germinal center formation, plasma cells, and small lymphocytes in biopsy of regional lymph node taken one week after antigenic stimulation. (3) Reaction to candida, streptokinase-streptodornase (Varidase®), and mumps skin tests. (4) Induction of contact dermal hypersensitivity with dinitrochlorobenzene. (5) In vitro tests of lymphocyte function (PHA, antigens, allogeneic cells).

Clinical Findings.

In patients with immunoglobulin deficiency disease, recurrent pyogenic bacterial infections predominate and chronic otitis media, sinusitis, and bronchiectasis are especially common. In agammaglobulinemia, viral infections (such as measles, varicella, and mumps) are weathered without incident. In individuals with cellular immunity defects, progressive vaccinia has been a frequent complication and vaccination should be avoided. Candidal infections are not uncommon in such patients, and unusually severe infections with cytomegalovirus, herpesvirus, and pneumocystis occur as well. In the acquired forms, malignancies of the lymphoreticular system occur with increased frequency.

Treatment.

Therapy of the immunoglobulin deficiency states consists of replacement with gamma globulin (Cohn fraction II), which is chiefly IgG. Give 200 mg./Kg. (I. M. only) and then 100 mg./Kg. every three or four weeks. Preparations consisting solely of IgM and IgA are not yet available.

Because of genetically determined differences in gamma globulins from one individual to another, iso-immunization can occur as a result of giving genetically foreign gamma globulin. Since iso-immunization may have some deleterious effects, injudicious administration of gamma globulin should be avoided.

Therapy of cellular immunity deficiencies is still experimental.

18 . . .
Urogenital System

CLINICAL FINDINGS

Frequent clinical and laboratory manifestations of diseases of the urinary tract include the following: Abnormalities of urination (frequency, urgency, incontinence, dysuria, straining or dribbling, enuresis), dehydration, acidosis, edema, ascites, fever, costovertebral angle pain, lower abdominal pain, anemia, hypertension, edema, and pyuria; proteinuria,* abnormal cellular urinary elements,† fixation of the specific gravity of the urine, or inability to concentrate above 1.020.

The unspun sediment from a fresh, clean specimen of urine should be Gram stained and examined for organisms. The finding of more than one or two organisms per high dry field in the stained specimen correlates well with a positive culture. Organisms may be present even though pyuria is absent. Avoid routine catheterization, if possible. The most reliable means of collecting urine for culture is suprapubic needle aspiration of the bladder (see p. 608). Any organisms obtained by this means probably signify a urinary tract infection. Culture of a clean-voided midstream urine specimen (discarding the first few milliliters of urine) often gives helpful information, especially in males. Bacterial colony counts greater than 100,000/ml., if a pure culture of known pathogens, usually indicate infection but should be repeated in the symptomatic patient. Those between 10,000 and 100,000 are suspect and should be repeated in any patient. Those less than 10,000 are usually due to urethral contamination, and frequently indicate the need for examination of a urine specimen obtained by suprapubic aspiration.

Chemical studies may show depressed creatinine clearance, elevated B.U.N., altered serum proteins, lowered calcium and elevated phosphorus levels, and evidence of chronic acidosis or anemia.

Vague signs and symptoms such as the following should always arouse suspicion of disease of the urinary tract: failure of adequate gain in weight and height, unexplained fever, abdominal pain; a mass in the region of the bladder, ureter, or kidney; convulsions, rickets after infancy, and any change in urinary habits.

In newborn infants, congenital absence of the abdominal muscu-

---

*Surveys have shown that approximately 5% of children will exhibit proteinuria but only 20% of those with proteinuria will exhibit it on retesting. There is a greater prevalence of proteinuria between 10 and 16 years than at other ages.

†Hematuria occurring after any type of trauma requires a careful examination of the urinary tract. I.V. urograms are abnormal in one-third of such patients.

lature, single umbilical artery, abdominal masses, unexplained
dehydration, acidosis, anemia, abnormalities of the spinal cord
and lower extremities, myelodysplasia, sacral agenesis, chromosomal disorders, imperforate anus, aniridia, hemihypertrophy,
cystic disease of the liver, hepatic fibrosis, congenital ascites,
positive family history of renal disease, oligohydramnios, bilateral
pulmonary hyperplasia, or abnormalities of the ears or external
genitalia are often associated with abnormalities of the urogenital
tract and other anomalies.

SPECIAL DIAGNOSTIC STUDIES

Obstruction may occur at any level of the urinary tract. Symptoms may be absent even if infection exists. The symptoms of
obstruction are seldom diagnostic of the site of obstruction; special
tests may be necessary for diagnosis.

Voiding cystourethrogram and cinefluoroscopy may give information about vesicoureteral reflux, bladder outlet function, and the
presence of residual urine.

Intravenous urography to visualize the kidneys and upper urinary tracts may also give an estimate of renal function. *

Cystoscopic inspection will demonstrate trabeculation, diverticula, and the integrity and location of the ureteral orifices. At
this time, retrograde visualization of the upper tract may be carried out to permit examination of the upper urinary tract and give
information regarding sites of obstruction and the state of the renal
pelves and calyces.

Observe the size, regularity of flow, and force of urinary
stream.

Renal arteriography is required to visualize tumors, blood
vessels, etc., and to disclose the presence of kidneys which may
not be visualized by other radiographic technics. Radioisotope
renal scans may be of value.

NONOBSTRUCTIVE CONGENITAL MALFORMATIONS

CYSTIC KIDNEYS

Classification.
  A. Polycystic Kidneys (Infantile Type; Often Autosomal Recessive):
     The renal tissue is filled with multiple small cysts. The kid-
     neys are generally very enlarged. Polycystic disease is often
     present in the liver, pancreas, or lungs.
  B. Polycystic Kidneys (Adult Type; Often Autosomal Dominant):
     Numerous cysts involve all portions of both kidneys and, occa-
     sionally, other organs.

---

*Better x-ray films may be obtained through the gas-distended
stomach that will result after the ingestion of 150 to 240 ml. (5 to
8 oz.) of a carbonated drink.

C. Multicystic Kidneys: Multicystic disease usually affects only
one kidney, which is moderately enlarged with large cysts;
the renal parenchyma is hypoplastic or absent. The calyces
and pelvis are malformed, hypoplastic, or absent and the
ureter is atretic. The other kidney is often dysplastic.
D. Other Varieties of Cystic Kidneys: These include medullary
cystic disease (juvenile nephronophthisis), medullary sponge
kidney, dysplastic kidney, solitary renal cyst, and hamartoma-
tous cystic or multilocular kidney.

Clinical Findings.
A. Symptoms and Signs: In addition to enlargement of the kidney,
cystic diseases may be manifested by evidences of increasing
renal insufficiency such as hypertension, anemia, explained
dehydration, azotemia, tubular dysfunctions, and rickets; acid-
base imbalance; and disturbances of growth in long-standing
cases.
B. Laboratory Findings: Hematuria, fixation of the specific gravity of the urine, elevated B. U. N., acidosis, hypocalcemia,
hyperphosphatemia, and osteodystrophy. Occasionally, recurrent bacteriuria and proteinuria are seen.
C. Urograms show marked enlargement of the kidneys and deformity of the calyces and pelves to varying degrees (sometimes
resembling "spider pelvis") due to pressure of the cysts.
Excretion of dye is usually delayed.

Treatment.
Treatment is supportive and palliative. Combat renal acidosis
and insufficiency. Administer vitamin D, prevent infection, regulate diet, and treat hypertension. Transplantation may produce
improvement without recurrence.

Prognosis.
Infants with polycystic kidneys of the infantile type often die
within the first few days of life. With other forms, there is occasionally variable decrease in renal function which may not become
evident for several years.

EXSTROPHY OF THE BLADDER

In exstrophy of the bladder a split in the anterior walls of the
abdomen and bladder permits a direct passage of urine to the outside. There is usually an associated separation of the pubic rami,
as well as epispadias, undescended testes, inguinal hernia, and,
occasionally, defects of the bowel. The exposed bladder mucosa
and trigone form parts of the external abdominal wall.
Constant dribbling of urine excoriates the skin. Ulceration of
the bladder mucosa may occur. Children walk with a waddling and
unstable gait.
Renal function and I. V. urograms are generally normal for a
few years (three to ten), after which hydronephrosis and pyelonephritis usually occur. The disease may be compatible with a
normal life span in some patients.
The results of plastic reconstruction are generally poor.

PATENT URACHUS

Patent urachus is due to persistence of the embryonic connection of the bladder with the umbilicus. The connection normally is obliterated by the time of delivery. The urachus may be open at either end; may be closed at both ends with a cyst between (most common type); or may be open throughout its course, permitting urine to dribble from the umbilicus. Treatment is by surgical correction, preceded by antibacterial therapy if infection is present.

OBSTRUCTIVE CONGENITAL MALFORMATIONS

URINARY TRACT OBSTRUCTION

Uncorrected lower urinary tract obstruction is often accompanied by bilateral hydronephrosis with infection, azotemia, or both. In males, it may be produced by urethral "valves" or other urethral constriction. Neuromuscular bladder dysfunction produces similar end results.

The bladder dilates, hypertrophies, becomes trabeculated, and may develop diverticula. Residual urine is present. The ureters may dilate and become elongated and tortuous. The pelvis of the kidney enlarges; kidney tissue is eventually destroyed as a result of obstruction, infection, or both, until only a thin shell of cortex remains.

Abnormalities of urination include difficulty in starting the stream, dribbling, straining during urination (bowel movement may occur each time urine is passed), weak or thin stream, or abrupt cessation during urination. Dilatation of the bladder, ureter, or kidney may be variable and may be palpable. Infection is frequent and may be persistent or intermittent, acute or chronic. Pyelonephritis is the usual result, but chronic pyelonephritis may be completely silent and asymptomatic.

Treatment is usually both medical and surgical (see below). Renal insufficiency or hypertension may be the outcome in progressive and untreated cases. High surgical drainage is usually beneficial in spite of considerably lowered renal function. Marked improvement often results, and life may be prolonged for many years, allowing nearly normal growth and development until such time as renal transplantation becomes necessary.

UPPER URINARY TRACT OBSTRUCTIONS

Most cases are produced by obstruction of the ureter as it passes through the bladder wall or joins the pelvis of the kidney, duplication of the ureter to one kidney (with ectopia of the ureteral orifice), stricture or diverticulosis of the ureter, pressure of an aberrant blood vessel, or calculi.

ACQUIRED ABNORMALITIES OF THE
URINARY TRACT

URINARY TRACT INFECTION

Acute urinary tract infection may be limited to the lower urinary tract, but persistent or recurrent cases often progress to involve the renal pelvis and parenchyma, producing pyelonephritis. Urinary tract infections are most common between two months and two years of age and are much more frequent in girls than in boys.

Infection may be caused by a variety of organisms. Escherichia coli is the most common. Infection usually enters the kidneys through the ureters. Congenital abnormalities associated with obstruction are important predisposing factors. Meatal stenosis or distal urethral obstruction, as diagnosed by currently available technics, does not appear to be a factor of importance in most cases.

Urethral catheterization is a significant predisposing factor.

In children, reinfection with a different organism usually implies cystitis; relapse due to the same organism is more commonly due to pyelonephritis.

The value of treating asymptomatic bacteriuria found on random examination in children who do not have disease is proved.

Clinical Findings.

Urinary tract infections may occur in combination with other infections.

A. Symptoms: Symptoms may be absent, particularly in the chronic form of the disease. Onset may be gradual or abrupt. Fever may be as high as 104.5° F. (40.3° C.), accompanied by chills.

Urinary frequency, urgency, incontinence, dysuria, prostration, anorexia, and pallor may occur. Vomiting may be projectile. There may be irritability and sometimes convulsions. Any of the findings listed on p. 328 may be present. Asymptomatic bacteriuria occurs in 1% of school girls; early identification may be an important measure in preventing serious renal damage. Allergy may be a factor in recurrent genitourinary infections.

B. Signs: Signs include dull or sharp pain and tenderness in the kidney area or abdomen. Hypertension and evidence of chronic renal failure may be present in long-standing and severe cases. Jaundice may occur, particularly in early infancy.

C. Laboratory Findings: Pyuria is characteristic, but it may be absent in the majority of patients during some phase of the disease. Slight or moderate hematuria occasionally occurs. There may be slight proteinuria. Pathogenic organisms and casts of all types may be present in the urine, but the urine may be normal for long periods of time. Anemia is found in cases of long-standing infection. Leukocytosis is usually in the range of 15,000 to 35,000/cu. mm. The urinary glucose concentration is below 2 mg./ml. after incubation for eight hours in patients with significant bacteriuria. Renal biopsy is of no value.

D. Urologic Studies As Indicated:
   1. I. V. urograms and voiding cystourethrograms are indicated after the first urinary tract infection regardless of sex.
   2. Cystoscopy is indicated if pyelocaliectasis or reflux is found.

Treatment.
   A. Specific Measures: Eradicate infection with appropriate chemotherapeutic or antibiotic therapy (see Chapter 6). A prolonged course of urinary tract antisepsis (two to six months or longer) may be indicated, especially for repeated infections. Repeat urinalysis and culture 48 hours after starting treatment and at intervals of one or two months for at least a year.
   B. General Measures: Force fluids during the acute stage. If possible, have the patient shower instead of bathing. Discontinue ''bubble baths.'' Avoid constipation.
   C. Surgery: There is no clear evidence that routine surgical correction - either by bladder neck revision, dilation, urethrotomy, or meatotomy - alters the course of recurrent urinary tract infections to any significant degree, but repair of clearly obstructive lesions is probably indicated.
   D. After control of the infection, a prophylactic regimen using nitrofurantoin, sulfisoxazole, or methenamine mandelate may be of value depending on the organism; if methenamine is used, the urine should be kept acid. Nalidixic acid may be an effective substitute for methenamine. Frequent urine cultures are indicated.

   In most cases it is not sufficient to institute treatment only for clinical exacerbations since subclinical infection may persist and be associated with progressive severe renal damage.

   Reinfection in children without obstructive malformation is not uncommon and is usually due to a different organism. Recurrences with the same organism are most likely to occur when there is an underlying urologic abnormality and pyelonephritis exists. Children should be checked periodically for at least five years.

VULVOVAGINITIS

Vulvovaginitis may occur at any age. It is most commonly non-specific (75%) and is sometimes related to improper hygiene, local irritation, infections, or relative estrogen lack in prepubertal girls. Vulvovaginitis may also be an early sign of diabetes mellitus. Specific vulvovaginitis may be due to bacteria (e. g., gonococci), fungi (candida), viruses (herpes simplex, etc.), trichomonads, pinworms, allergy, or foreign body.

Clinical Findings.
   A. Symptoms and Signs: Often there are no symptoms, but the child may have any of the findings listed on p. 328. The child may be irritable and have pruritus and local irritation. The vaginal discharge may be white and mucoid, cottage cheese-like, yellow, yellow-green, purulent, thin, or thick. A blood-tinged discharge suggests a foreign body.

   In the pubescent female, a benign cottage cheese-like discharge confined to the vulva may be present. Vaginal washings show abundant desquamated, cornified epithelial cells.

B. Laboratory Findings: Bacterial, fungal, vaginal cytologic, viral, and special studies as indicated (see p. 329). Nonspecific vulvovaginitis causes contaminated urine cultures if urine is collected by the "clean catch" method.

Treatment.

Nonspecific vulvovaginitis should be treated by correcting local hygiene and treating infection elsewhere, if present. Treat locally with estrogen cream, lactic acid solution, 1 tsp. to 1 pint of water, or nitrofurazone (Furacin®) urethral inserts placed in the vagina, one daily for ten to 14 days. Antibiotics may be necessary for secondary infection.

Specific vulvovaginitis should be treated with specific therapy.

ACUTE GLOMERULONEPHRITIS*
(Acute Nephritis, Acute Hemorrhagic Nephritis)

Acute glomerulonephritis appears to be due to an immunologic reaction with a specific bacterium, most frequently a beta-hemolytic streptococcus. The disorder is sometimes found in other members of the family. As a rule, the acute symptoms of the primary infection have cleared when the nephritis appears.

The disease may occur in epidemic form following infection of the throat or skin with a type-specific streptococcus (especially types 12, 4, 25, and 49), and under such circumstances the majority of cases have abnormalities of the urine but no clinical manifestations. Acute glomerulonephritis is rare in children under three years of age.

Nephritis may also be associated with syphilis, toxins (lead, trimethadione, mercury, hydrocarbons), amyloid disease, renal vein thrombosis, anaphylactoid purpura, lupus erythematosus, various virus infections, dysproteinemias, and malignancies. Recurrent gross hematuria over periods of several years may be part of a syndrome associated with minimal physical and laboratory findings. In these cases, the episodes are frequently preceded by upper respiratory tract infections not related to group A streptococcal infections. Buerger's disease (IgG-IgA), nephropathy with focal segmental nephritis, and a benign course may occur.

Clinical Findings.

A. Uncomplicated Acute Poststreptococcal Nephritis: The intensity of the disease varies, but most patients are not markedly ill. Hematuria is generally the first symptom. There may be oliguria, slight to moderate edema (rapid weight gain may be the only indication of developing edema), hypertension, slight cardiac enlargement in first two weeks, slight headache and malaise, gastrointestinal disturbances, and fever of variable degree.

B. Acute Nephritis With Hypertensive Encephalopathy: In addition to the signs and symptoms of uncomplicated cases, there may also be restlessness, stupor, convulsions, vomiting, and

---

*Adapted from Rubin and Rapoport.

visual disturbances. Headache may be severe. Hypertensive encephalopathy may be the presenting or only clinical finding of acute nephritis. Seizures appear to be related to the rate of rise of the blood pressure.

C. Acute Nephritis With Cardiac Involvement: This form of the disease is characterized by cardiac enlargement and gallop rhythm, Ecg. changes, or attacks of pulmonary edema, peripheral edema, increasing venous pressure, hypervolemia, and cardiac enlargement. Cardiac failure can be a cause of death in acute nephritis and is usually due to persistent hypertension.

D. Acute Nephritis With Uremia: There may be no specific signs or symptoms, or there may be evidences of acidosis and decreased renal function (drowsiness, coma, stupor, muscular twitchings, and convulsions) as well as respiratory and gastrointestinal disturbances.

E. Laboratory Findings:

1. Urine - Output is decreased. Microscopic or gross hematuria is present but may be very slight during the initial phase of the disease. When hematuria is present the urine is usually brown or smoky in appearance. Specific gravity is high, although fixed specific gravity (around 1.010 to 1.012) may occur temporarily early in the disease. Moderate proteinuria is present, and there are moderate numbers of white cells and hyaline, granular, and cellular casts. Red cell casts establish the renal origin of the hematuria.

2. Blood - B.U.N. is usually increased; sedimentation rate is elevated; serum albumin is often slightly depressed; acidosis occurs in some patients; serum complement (beta$_{C'3}$ globulin) is usually decreased.

   Antistreptolysin levels are usually elevated within one or two weeks of onset. Serum ASO levels will not rise if the preceding streptococcal disease involved only the skin or if eradication of streptococci was accomplished by early treatment with antibiotics. Antistreptococcal DNase, antihyaluronidase nicotine deaminase, and antistreptococcal M-protein may be elevated in some patients in whom ASO titers are normal. The streptozyme test and evaluation of the streptococcal DNase B test are useful screening tests.

3. Renal function tests are normal in 50% of patients.

Treatment.

There is no specific therapy which influences healing of the glomerular lesions.

A. General Measures: The patient should be at bed rest until hypertension is well controlled. Give a regular diet for the age as tolerated, with sodium restriction if the patient is hypertensive. In the uncomplicated form, fluids may be taken as desired. Penicillin may be given during the acute phase of the disease. Any coexisting infection should be eradicated with appropriate antibiotic or chemotherapeutic agents (see Chapter 6).

B. Correct Hypertension: Mild hypertension may be corrected by limiting fluid and sodium intake and maintaining sedation. Moderate or severe hypertension may require reserpine and hydralazine (Apresoline®), both given I.M. as often as every six hours until the blood pressure has been controlled. In refractory cases, the addition of a ganglionic blocking agent in combination with reserpine and hydralazine may be necessary.

Treatment of Complications.
   A. Hypertensive Encephalopathy: Correct hypertension and give oxygen.
   B. Cardiac Failure: Correct hypertension and give oxygen, morphine, and digitalis. Venesection may be of value if pulmonary edema is present. Restrict sodium intake.
   C. Acute Oliguria: Correct hypertension and treat anuria. Severe oliguria should be treated in the same way as acute renal failure. Avoid administration of sodium. Maintain adequate nutrition. During the acute phase and with elevated B. U. N., protein catabolism should be reduced to a minimum to reduce the rate of accumulation of toxic end products. Give a high-calorie diet rich in carbohydrate and fat and low in protein and potassium. Transfusion should be avoided unless anemia is profound. Administer appropriate antibiotics to prevent and treat infections.

Course and Prognosis.
   Symptoms and physical signs of the disease disappear in two or three weeks. Blood chemistry returns to normal during the second week. Microscopic hematuria and traces of protein in the urine may persist for months or even years. The Addis count remains abnormal for four months or more. The sedimentation rate is elevated for about three months. The glomerular filtration rate and the level of cryoglobulins may assist in assessing progression.
   It has been commonly believed that approximately 95% of patients recover completely; 2% die during the acute phase of the disease; and 2% go on to have chronic nephritis. Recent evidence, however, suggests a higher incidence of chronicity appearing after many years.

CHRONIC GLOMERULONEPHRITIS
(Chronic Nephritis)

Chronic glomerulonephritis is a clinical diagnosis based on the finding of persistent hematuria and proteinuria. It may have no known predisposing cause or may follow an attack of acute nephritis. In some cases, exacerbations are preceded by acute upper respiratory infections with hemolytic streptococci.
   An inherited (dominant) familial progressive form of nephritis, often associated with nerve deafness and sometimes with ocular lesions, may occur; involvement is commonly severe in males and mild in females.

Clinical Findings.
   A. Symptoms: There are often no symptoms until renal failure develops. Symptoms then include weakness and easy fatigability, vomiting, headache and restlessness, muscular cramps and twitchings, drowsiness, and coma and convulsions in the terminal phases.

B. Signs: Edema of variable degree may occur. Other signs are
hypertension, renal insufficiency, retinal abnormalities
(hemorrhages, exudates, and arteriolosclerosis), poor growth
and nutrition, and anemia.

C. Laboratory Findings:
1. Urine - Hematuria and proteinuria of variable degrees.
Casts of various types; broad casts ("renal failure casts")
in late stages. Fixed specific gravity, 1.008 to 1.012.
2. Blood - After onset of renal failure, B.U.N. and other
nitrogenous substances are elevated; serum phosphorus is
elevated and serum calcium and magnesium are decreased;
serum sodium and chloride may be decreased late; serum
potassium may be elevated terminally. Resistant anemia is
present.
3. Renal function tests, especially the creatinine clearance,
show progressive renal impairment.

Treatment.

No treatment is known for the basic disease process, although,
occasionally, a favorable response has been associated with therapy
with azathioprine, cyclophosphamide, adrenocortical steroids, and/
or anticoagulants. Efforts should be directed toward the alleviation
of symptoms and the correction of chemical imbalance or the etiologic agent or mechanism when known.

Permit activity as tolerated. Provide a normal diet for age,
although restriction of proteins may be of some value. Treatment
for progressive renal failure should include correction of fluid and
electrolyte imbalance and oliguria and control of hypertension with
methyldopa or hydralazine and propranolol. Antihypertensive
agents that lower cardiac output (such as guanethidine) should be
avoided.

Aluminum hydroxide, calcium lactate, and vitamin D are valuable as means of reducing the phosphate absorption and increasing
calcium absorption from the intestinal tract. Chronic dialysis
(both peritoneal and extracorporeal) and homotransplantation may
offer effective methods of prolonging life.

Course and Prognosis.

In spite of markedly reduced renal function, the patient may
appear to do quite well until puberty, when the growth spurt and
other physiologic changes may impose a final burden upon the kidneys sufficient to cause death. Progression may be interrupted for
indefinite periods of clinical well-being. A nephrotic stage is not
infrequent during the course of the disease; minimal lesion nephrosis may have to be differentiated by renal biopsy.

NEPHROSIS
(Nephrotic Syndrome, Lipoid or
Childhood Nephrosis)

The nephrotic syndrome consists of generalized edema, marked
proteinuria, hypercholesterolemia, and hypoproteinemia. It occurs
chiefly in children between 18 months and five years of age. The
course is usually insidious, with a tendency to remissions and ex-

acerbations, but in most instances nephrosis appears as the first manifestation of renal disease in an apparently healthy child.

The cause of nephrosis is obscure. Renal biopsy usually reveals no significant glomerular abnormalities. Electron microscopy reveals fusion of the foot processes of the epithelial cells, but basement membrane thickness is normal. Immunofluorescent studies are negative.

Nephrotic syndrome may complicate many glomerulonephritides. The presence of significant hypertension, azotemia (especially hypercreatinemia), hematuria, or hypocomplementemia suggests a more serious and inflammatory glomerular lesion. The syndrome may also occur in association with amyloidosis, systemic lupus erythematosus, syphilis, renal vein thrombosis, trimethadione and other types of drug toxicity, bee stings, and poison oak dermatitis. Rarely, severe, sometimes familial forms develop in early infancy which are often refractory to treatment and invariably fatal, although maintenance of nutrition, control of infection, and transplantation have been reported to be of value.

Nephrotic syndrome may be manifest with focal sclerosis, resistance to therapy, renal failure, and recurrent nephrotic syndrome following transplantation.

Clinical Findings.

A. Symptoms: Anorexia, with diminished food intake and malnutrition; gastrointestinal disturbances, severe infections, and irritability and depression.

B. Signs: Insidious onset of edema is usually the first sign. Edema, usually periorbital in the morning, is sometimes accompanied by ascites; it eventually becomes very marked and may persist for weeks or months. Oliguria is present during periods of edema. Retinopathy and persistent hypertension are usually not present.

C. Laboratory Findings:

1. Urine - Marked selective proteinuria and many casts (granular, hyaline, fatty, hyaline containing doubly refractile bodies, and Maltese crosses [using polaroid filters]). Hematuria is absent or transient. When hematuria is present the urine is usually red with a yellow supernatant, and 70 to 90% of red cells are well preserved.

2. Renal function tests - Glomerular filtration rate is typically normal or elevated in minimal lesion nephrosis but may be depressed if severe glomerulodestructive disease exists.

3. Blood - Total serum protein reduced, serum albumin reduced, total serum globulin normal or increased (albumin-globulin ratio reversed), with increase in $alpha_2$ and beta fractions and IgE and reduction in gamma fraction; amino acid level low. Anemia absent or slight. Sedimentation rate markedly accelerated. Lipids (cholesterol, etc.) and lipoproteins increased. Serum calcium may be depressed, due chiefly to a deficit in the nondiffusible fraction bound to protein. Serum sodium, carbon dioxide, and pH may be normal or reduced. B.U.N. is usually normal. Urinary sodium is typically low due to secondary hyperaldosteronism.

Treatment.

There is no known specific therapy. These children should be permitted to lead as normal lives as possible, with activity as tolerated and an adequate diet with liberal protein intake as tolerated. Infections must be treated vigorously as they occur.

Management of edema: Sodium restriction helps limit edema formation, but no method is consistently successful in reducing edema. No salt should be added to the diet unless it is required to maintain the child's appetite. Mercurial diuretics should be avoided. Furosemide, especially with slowly administered sodium-poor albumin, may give striking (though transient) benefit; however, hypochloremia and alkalosis may result.

Thoracentesis is occasionally required for life-threatening respiratory distress. Abdominal paracentesis should be avoided except to ease respiratory difficulty. Diuresis produced with albumin and furosemide is generally safer.

Corticotropin, the adrenocortical steroids (see Chapter 22), spironolactone, and the thiazides are of value in precipitating diuresis. They should be continued for six months, although occasionally a single intensive course of corticosteroid therapy may be adequate for many children. Prednisone appears to be a satisfactory steroid. Following an initial period of daily therapy which is continued for three or four days beyond diuresis, give the total 48-hour dose once every two days for six months; then taper rapidly to physiologic levels and gradually to zero.

If relapses occur after adequate courses of therapy or if the patient becomes steroid-resistant or steroid-dependent, perform a biopsy to establish the diagnosis of minimal lesion nephrosis and to rule out glomerulonephritis. Then give chlorambucil or cyclophosphamide and administer prednisone daily through the period of diuresis and then every other day. No salt should be added to the diet until diuresis ensues. (Caution: Toxicity of cyclophosphamide includes impaired fertility, hair loss, and leukopenia.)

In some children, corticosteroid administration may produce a significant increase in proteinuria independent of a change in the status of the disease.

Course and Prognosis.

About two-thirds of patients tend to have more than one episode of edema interspersed with normal periods which may persist for months or years. Evidence of progressive renal failure may develop in children who appeared to have a pure lipoid nephrosis at onset. Proteinuria may be used as an index of improvement.

There is increased susceptibility to infections, especially pneumococcal infections, with a predisposition to peritonitis. Skin infections, often erysipeloid in nature, may occur. Attempts at femoral puncture in edematous patients may be followed by arterial thrombosis, especially in those receiving adrenocortical steroids.

Recovery can occur even though the condition has recurred for many years. Relapses may occur months or even years after control of the disease. Recovery is most likely in those patients in whom renal biopsy revealed only minimal pathologic changes.

ACUTE RENAL FAILURE
(Oliguria, Acute Tubular Necrosis)

Oliguria may be due to any of several causes, including poisonings, transfusion reactions, burns, crush injuries, glomerulonephritis, severe dehydration, and drugs (sulfonamides, ampicillin,
bismuth, carbon tetrachloride). Many cases are due to unknown
causes. Spontaneous recovery can occur after more than four
weeks of oliguria or even anuria. A diuretic phase commonly follows an initial oliguric phase. In general, the treatment of persistent marked oliguria or anuria is as follows:

Treatment (After Chasis and Other Sources).

A. Specific Measures: (Do not delay.) Treat the underlying disease if possible. Rule out total obstructive uropathy as a
   cause. Insert an indwelling bladder catheter. Reverse the
   mechanism responsible for anuria by giving blood and plasma
   transfusions for extensive thermal burns, blood loss, or
   trauma and to alleviate any prerenal components; alkalinizing
   the urine in cases of transfusion reaction; and catheterizing
   the ureters in cases of sulfonamide toxicity to determine
   whether crystals may be obstructing the ureters.

   If oliguria is not alleviated, prepare for central venous
   pressure readings and install an indwelling catheter in the
   urinary bladder. Use of mannitol, 0.5 to 1 Gm./Kg. of 25%
   solution (maximum: 25 Gm.) over 30 minutes, and furosemide,
   1 to 2 mg./Kg. I.V. initially, and then 1 mg./Kg. every four
   hours (**caution**), has been recommended until diuresis is induced. In two hours, repeat the furosemide. If improvement
   does not occur, begin a regimen which includes total restriction
   of potassium, administration of adequate calories and sodium
   polystyrene sulfonate (Kayexalate®), repeated nasogastric
   aspiration, and administration of sodium bicarbonate. Avoid
   overhydration with hypotonic solutions. Maintain electrolyte
   balance. Monitor Ecg.

B. General Measures: Control of the fluid and electrolyte balance
   and caloric intake is the most promising means of therapy (see
   Table 18-1).

   1. Administer just enough water (by mouth, vein, or intestinal
      tube) to balance sensible and insensible water losses minus
      water of oxidation plus replacement of nasogastric losses if
      present. Excessive administration of water is injurious.
         The daily water requirement of the anuric child will vary
      with the numerous factors that affect water balance (e.g.,
      activity, sweating, body temperature, metabolic rate,
      vomiting, diarrhea, and the environmental temperature
      and humidity). (See Table 18-1.)

   2. **Note:** Weigh daily so that a gain in weight indicative of ex-
      cessive fluid administration will be detected. Small amounts
      of weight should be lost each day.

   3. Determine plasma concentrations of sodium, chloride,
      bicarbonate, potassium, B.U.N., and serum and urine
      osmolality at frequent intervals. Exchange transfusion,
      peritoneal or intestinal lavage, or dialysis with the artifi-
      cial kidney may be of value (1) if hyperkalemia is intract-

TABLE 18-1. Approximate daily water and glucose
requirements in anuria at various ages (Pratt).

Age (Yrs.)	Glucose	Water
< 1	10 Gm./Kg.	30 ml./Kg.
1-2	90 Gm.	325 ml.
2-4	110 Gm.	375 ml.
4-8	140 Gm.	475 ml.
8-12	150 Gm.	525 ml.
Adult	200 Gm.	700 ml.

able and severe enough to produce changes in the Ecg. (or
is greater than 8 mEq./L.); (2) if uremia with restlessness,
lethargy, or coma is present in spite of the use of glucose,
insulin, potassium exchange resins, and intravenous calcium; or (3) if significant bleeding due to some anti-clotting
factor occurs.
4. Other measures - (1) Cation resins for hyperkalemia, (2)
calcium gluconate for hypocalcemia, (3) aluminum hydroxide
gel to prevent phosphate absorption, (4) packed red blood
cells for anemia, and (5) hydralazine plus propranolol or
reserpine for hypertension.

ORTHOSTATIC PROTEINURIA
(Lordotic Albuminuria, Postural Proteinuria)

In this condition protein appears intermittently in the urine
when the child is in the erect position; proteinuria is decreased in
the reclining position but may still be greater than in normal children. In an occasional child, the proteinuria is more marked in the
recumbent position; in others, it is not affected by changes in position. It may occur with apparently normal kidneys but is usually
not present in the morning, and it may be present in certain stages
(particularly early) of acute and chronic glomerulonephritis.

To obtain a specimen of urine for testing, have the patient void
one to two hours after assuming the recumbent position. Discard
this urine. Then collect a timed urine specimen before the patient
gets out of bed and assumes the erect position. The test should be
repeated on several occasions. Protein excretion should be less
than 0.03 mg./minute.

Note: Orthostatic proteinuria may be an early sign of progressive or healing nephritis.

RENAL TUBULAR DEFECTS

Hereditary diseases may occur with disturbances of one or a
combination of several renal functions (renal glycosuria, cystinuria,
renal tubular acidosis, diabetes insipidus, hyperphosphaturia, or
vitamin D-resistant rickets), possibly as the result of an absence

or deficiency of an essential enzyme system in the renal tubules
and perhaps elsewhere.

DE TONI-FANCONI-DEBRE SYNDROME

This disorder is characterized by vitamin D-resistant hypophosphatemic rickets, hyperchloremia, acidosis with alkaline
urine, renal glycosuria, hyperaminoaciduria, organic aciduria, and
cystinosis. The renal abnormality consists of deficient proximal
tubular reabsorption of phosphorus, amino acids, and glucose along
with a deficiency in the tubular mechanism for reabsorbing base
without acid.

Therapy, which is often ineffective, is with large doses of
vitamin D and sufficient sodium bicarbonate to correct the acid-base
disturbance.

CONGENITAL HYPERCHLOREMIC RENAL ACIDOSIS
(Renal Tubular Acidosis; Lightwood's Syndrome)

Congenital hyperchloremic renal acidosis may occur in several
diseases (chronic renal diseases, hereditary fructose intolerance,
hypergammaglobulinemic states, etc.) with a renal tubular defect in
conserving fixed base. There is failure to thrive, muscular hypotonia, anorexia, vomiting, and constipation starting in early infancy. There may also be polyuria and polydipsia. An alkaline
urine is excreted despite a metabolic acidosis. In one form of the
disease late findings include nephrocalcinosis, renal stones, osteoporosis, osteomalacia, and rickets.

Treatment is with alkali solutions (such as 10% sodium citrate
with 6% citric acid).

In Lightwood's syndrome, complete recovery may occur.

HEMOLYTIC-UREMIC SYNDROME
(Syndrome of Nephropathy, Hemolytic Anemia,
and Thrombocytopenic Purpura): See Chapter 17.

19 . . .
Eye

Examination of the eye, including visualization of the retina, is an integral part of the complete physical examination. Rapid dilation of the pupil to facilitate ophthalmoscopic examination can be accomplished by instilling two drops of 10% phenylephrine (Neo-Synephrine®) or a short-acting cycloplegic such as 1% cyclopentolate (Cyclogyl®). One percent tropicamide (Mydriacil®) is faster-acting but weaker. It is very effective for rapid dilation in older children and those with light complexions. In heavily pigmented individuals, instillation of 1% cyclopentolate (Cyclogyl®) or 5% homatropine may be needed in addition to 10% phenylephrine. (In newborns, 2.5% phenylephrine should be used instead of the 10% solution.) While poor vision is an occasional cause of failure to do well in school, parents and school nurses frequently blame impaired eyesight when other conditions are responsible. In such cases the physician, utilizing a test chart, must demonstrate the normality of eyesight to the satisfaction of the parents. In infancy it may be necessary to perform the examination under sedation or generalized anesthesia, especially if a neoplasm is suspected.

DISORDERS OF THE EYELIDS

EPICANTHUS

Epicanthus is a congenital malformation characterized by a concave bilateral lidfold at the inner angle of the lids. It is normal in the Mongolian race, is found in children with Down's syndrome, and may be observed also in otherwise normal Caucasian children, usually as a family trait.

If epicanthus is marked, it may give the appearance of a convergent squint, since the pupil is closer to the lidfold at the inner angle than at the outer angle. No therapy is indicated.

STY
(External Hordeolum)

A sty is a purulent infection of a sebaceous gland in the lid, usually caused by Staphylococcus aureus. There is localized edema, swelling, redness near the lid edge, and pain, with the point of maximum tenderness over the affected gland.

Treatment.
A. Local Measures:
    1. Hot moist compresses constitute the most effective treatment.

2. Topical antibiotics may prevent complicating conjunctivitis, hasten resolution, and prevent recurrences and involvement of other glands. Use sulfacetamide sodium (10% ointment) or an antibiotic ophthalmic ointment.
3. Never squeeze the sty.
B. Systemic antibiotics in severe cases, especially if there is a surrounding cellulitis.

Prognosis.
The acute inflammation usually resolves in four to ten days, but recurrences are frequent. Continued therapy at night with an antibiotic ointment may prevent recurrence.

INTERNAL HORDEOLUM

Internal hordeolum is an infection of a meibomian gland or duct caused by a pyogenic organism, usually Staphylococcus aureus. There is pain, tenderness, redness, and swelling on the inner side of the eyelid. There may be marked edema of the skin of the entire lid.
Internal hordeolum is an acute form of chalazion (see below).

Treatment.
A. Local Measures:
1. Warm moist compresses.
2. Local antibiotic therapy with bacitracin, neomycin, polymyxin, or sodium sulfacetamide ophthalmic ointment.
B. Surgery: Make an incision at right angle to the lid margin and drain from conjunctival side when well localized. Avoid the lid margin. If incision is necessary, it should not be done during the acute phase.
C. Occasional cases require systemic antibiotics.

Course and Prognosis.
Cure usually follows spontaneous evacuation of pus or incision and drainage.

CHALAZION

Chalazion is a relatively painless mass which may result from obstruction, retention, and chronic granulomatous inflammation of one of the meibomian glands in the upper or lower lid.
The irregularity of the lid may be cosmetically disturbing. A slight feeling of irritation of the eye may also be present.

Treatment.
A. Local Measures: When the area is chronically infected or the condition is recurrent, antibacterial ointments may be used.
B. Surgical Measures: Open the chalazion by conjunctival incision and curettage under local anesthesia.
C. Complete excision for biopsy is suggested in recurrent or unusual cases.

Prognosis.

Prognosis for eradication is good with incision and curettage or excision. Without such definitive treatment, recurrent infection and irritation are to be expected. In the absence of repeated infections, chalazion is a cosmetic problem which in itself may make surgery desirable. A large chalazion can produce astigmatism through pressure on the globe.

BLEPHARITIS
(Granulated Lids)

Chronic inflammation of the lid margins is caused by infection with pyogenic bacteria (usually Staphylococcus aureus). Pityrosporum ovale is associated with the seborrheic type of blepharitis in adolescent children. Seborrheic dermatitis and dandruff are often associated. Refractive errors may aggravate this condition, probably due to rubbing the eyes.

Blepharitis is characterized by chronic purulent discharge with matting of the eyelashes, chronic reddening and thickening of the lid margins, and frequent rubbing and irritation of the eye. Fine scales may be seen along the base of the eyelashes, and ulceration and bleeding occur at the base of the lash in severe cases.

Treatment.
A. Local Measures: Depending on the etiologic agent, local antibiotic or chemotherapeutic medication is indicated, together with warm water soaks of lid margins. The lid margins should be cleansed with cotton applicator moistened with a weak baby shampoo.
B. Treat dandruff and seborrheic dermatitis.
C. Examine and treat siblings and parents.
D. Refractive errors should be corrected.

Prognosis.

There is a marked tendency to chronicity. Treatment usually controls the condition, but complete cures are difficult to obtain. Spontaneous cures are common in staphylococcal infections. Permanent loss of the eyelashes may result from severe cases.

PTOSIS
(Drooping of the Upper Eyelids)

Ptosis is characterized by drooping lids and backward tilting of the head in an attempt to see below the upper lids. It is due to paresis or paralysis of the levator muscle of the upper lid, which is supplied by a branch of the oculomotor nerve. There may be associated weakness of the superior rectus muscle.

Practical Point: When ptosis is acquired, myasthenia gravis should be suspected and ruled out by specific tests.

Ptosis may be congenital (sometimes accompanied by a marked epicanthus) or acquired. It is generally bilateral but frequently asymmetrical. Acquired ptosis is seen less often in children than in adults and suggests neurologic disease. Slight ptosis results from interruption of cervical sympathetics (Horner's syndrome).

Treatment.
 A. Moderate or Severe: To prevent visual loss, early plastic
    surgery is indicated when ptosis interferes with vision.
 B. Milder Forms: No surgical treatment is required except for
    cosmetic reasons.

Prognosis.
 Prognosis is excellent for surgical cure whether levator paralysis is partial or complete.

TICS OF THE EYELIDS
(Blepharospasm)

 Frequent blinking may be due to refractive errors, chronic
blepharitis, or conjunctivitis, but it usually suggests emotional
tension. Correction of physical cause may lead to rapid improvement. Blepharospasm due to tension states may disappear spontaneously or with psychotherapy or tranquilizers. The parents
should be reassured of the good prognosis and urged to adopt a
more permissive attitude. Not infrequently, however, this symptom gives way to other signs of tension state in the post-adolescent
period.

. . .

OBSTRUCTION OF THE LACRIMAL APPARATUS
(Dacryostenosis)

 This is one of the most common congenital abnormalities of the
eye. It may also be acquired. Trauma concomitant to silver nitrate or penicillin instillation, as well as chronic conjunctivitis,
may predispose to the development of this disorder.
 Tearing and conjunctivitis may be noted. Mucopurulent discharge is often present or may be expressed from the lacrimal sac.
The condition may be unilateral or bilateral.

Treatment and Prognosis.
 A. Local Measures: Gentle massage of the lacrimal sac by a
    pumping action with a small finger in the lacrimal fossa. If
    infection is present, local chemotherapy with sodium sulfaceta-
    mide ophthalmic drops is advised. Correction occurs in 95%
    spontaneously or following massage.
 B. Surgical Measures: Probing is easily and safely performed
    after six to nine months of age. It is seldom performed earlier
    because the condition usually resolves spontaneously. Probing
    is successful in nearly 100% of cases; if it fails, however,
    dacryocystorhinostomy may be indicated.

CONJUNCTIVITIS OF THE NEWBORN
(Ophthalmia Neonatorum)

Classification.
 There are three main causes of conjunctivitis in the newborn:

A. Silver Nitrate: By far the most common cause. Onset is in the first two days of life, usually the first.

B. Gonococcal or Staphylococcal: The onset is at any time after birth, usually between the second and fifth days.

C. Inclusion Blennorrhea: Begins between third and fourteenth days.

Clinical Findings.

A. Signs:

1. Silver nitrate conjunctivitis - A mucopurulent discharge which may become secondarily infected and purulent.

2. Gonococcal or staphylococcal conjunctivitis - Frankly purulent and very profuse.

3. Inclusion blennorrhea - Discharge is moderately profuse. Characteristically, the conjuctiva in the lower fornix is hypertrophied.

B. Laboratory Findings:

1. Silver nitrate conjunctivitis - Smears of pus reveal cellular debris but few, if any, bacteria. Bacteriologic cultures are negative early in the course.

2. Bacterial conjunctivitis - Gram-stained smears of discharge will reveal gram-negative intracellular diplococci (gonococci) or gram-positive cocci in clusters (staphylococci). Blood agar plate cultures in duplicate are indicated, one plate being placed under low oxygen tension for incubation. This will favor the growth of gonococci.

3. Inclusion blennorrhea - The demonstration of inclusion bodies by smear of conjunctival scrapings, and a monocytic cell response, make the diagnosis. Giemsa's stain or hematoxylin-eosin stains are required.

Treatment.

Silver nitrate conjunctivitis responds well to saline irrigation and is usually self-limited. Bacterial conjunctivitis requires prompt therapy with chemotherapeutic agents such as sodium sulfacetamide, bacitracin, or tetracycline ointment four times daily for four to six days. Topical and systemic chemotherapy is advisable in gonococcal conjunctivitis. Inclusion blennorrhea should be treated with sodium sulfacetamide (10%) drops or ointment or tetracycline (1%) ointment or solution instilled every two to four hours. Cure results in two to four days.

Prophylaxis.

A. Replacement of silver nitrate with an antibiotic ophthalmic ointment has been advocated to prevent silver nitrate conjunctivitis.

B. Prepartum therapy of gonorrhea-infected mothers may prevent gonococcal conjunctivitis, but instillation of silver nitrate or an antibiotic affords an additional safeguard.

C. Inclusion blennorrhea originates from an asymptomatic subclinical infection of the mother's cervix with the specific chlamydial organism. No prophylaxis is known.

Prognosis.

The prognosis with treatment is generally very good, and cure should result within two to four days. If bacterial conjunctivitis is untreated, permanent scarring of the cornea and partial or complete loss of vision may result, depending on the severity and duration of the untreated condition.

CONJUNCTIVITIS

Conjunctivitis is most often caused by local bacterial, viral, or fungal infections (secondary to other mycotic infections), or systemic diseases.

A. Bacterial: Staphylococcus aureus, pneumococcus, beta-hemolytic streptococcus, Morax-Axenfeld diplococcus, and Koch-Weeks bacillus are the agents usually responsible for "pink-eye." Inclusion blennorrhea and trachoma are due to chlamydial infection.

B. Viral: Viruses of epidemic keratoconjunctivitis (adenovirus type 8), pharyngeal conjunctival fever (adenovirus type 3), herpes simplex.

C. Fungal:
1. Leptothrix - This is the most common cause of oculoglandular conjunctivitis (syndrome of Parinaud).
2. Streptothrix infection of canaliculi is a most important cause of unilateral canaliculitis and conjunctivitis.

D. Allergy, e.g., vernal conjunctivitis; may also be due to bacterial allergy to tuberculoprotein, giving rise to the characteristic phlyctenular keratoconjunctivitis. In the continental U.S.A., many patients with phlyctenular disease do not have hypersensitivity to tuberculoprotein but are probably sensitive to other bacterial or fungal proteins.

E. Systemic diseases, e.g., vitamin A deficiency (xerophthalmia), measles, erythema multiforme (Stevens-Johnson disease).

Clinical Findings.

A. Symptoms and Signs: Photophobia, itching, and burning; feeling of roughness underneath the lids; congestion of the conjunctivas; mucoid or mucopurulent discharge (in bacterial forms); watery discharge or none (in viral and allergic forms); small subconjunctival hemorrhages; edema of the lids, preauricular adenopathy.

B. Laboratory Findings:
1. Bacterial - Demonstration by stained smear and culture of bacterial pathogens; many polymorphonuclear leukocytes. Demonstration of inclusion bodies in conjunctival scrapings (in trachoma and inclusion blennorrhea only).
2. Viral - Cell response is predominantly lymphocytic and mononuclear. Antibody rise to adenovirus or isolation of viral agent.
3. Fungal - Stained smears of conjunctival scrapings reveal causative organisms.
4. Allergy - Eosinophils in scrapings from conjunctivas.
5. Systemic diseases - Diagnosis of the primary disease.

Treatment.

A. Specific Measures:
1. Bacterial - Local instillation of ophthalmic bacitracin, neomycin, or sulfacetamide. For trachoma and inclusion con-

junctivitis apply broad-spectrum antibiotic ointments locally four times daily.

2. Fungal - Amphotericin B drops, 2.5-5 mg./ml.; or nystatin solution, 100,000 units/Gm. Streptothrix responds to penicillin or tetracycline, but concretions in canaliculi or tear sac must be mechanically removed.

3. Allergy - Instillation of 1:4000 epinephrine hydrochloride and the systemic use of antihistaminic drugs. Topical hydrocortisone, 0.5 to 1.5% (or equivalent) every two hours, is also effective. Observe closely for complications.

4. Systemic disease - The therapy or recovery from systemic disease usually results in improvement of the eye lesion.

B. General Measures: Cool compresses (not ice), eye irrigations, and dark glasses in older children. Never use eye patches.

Prognosis.

The prognosis in all types is generally excellent if proper treatment is instituted. In the untreated case, corneal scarring and diminution or loss of vision in the affected eye may occur.

REFRACTIVE ERRORS

MYOPIA (Nearsightedness)

In myopia the focus of distant objects lies anterior to the retina, resulting in poor vision for distant objects. The focus of near objects lies closer to the retina (i.e., near-sighted). Myopia is often hereditary and is frequently associated with prematurity.

Myopia should be suspected when the condition exists in either parent. It usually results from excessive length of the eyeball, but may be caused by increased refractive power in cornea or lens, e.g., keratoconus. It tends to increase gradually during the growing period.

Clinical Findings.

A. Poor vision for distant objects, squinting, difficulty in reading blackboard at school.

B. At three years of age, fundus examination should be done with a cycloplegic.

C. Holding reading matter close up is not necessarily a sign of myopia, since children have much greater powers of accommodation than adults.

D. The refractive error in either myopia or hyperopia may be estimated using the direct ophthalmoscope. A cycloplegic is necessary in children. If the examiner is emmetropic or wearing his correction, the subject's approximate refractive error can be read in diopters as the most plus (black numbers) in the ophthalmoscope with which retinal detail can be seen clearly. (With less plus, the examiner will accommodate to maintain a clear view.) This technic of examination has definite limitations and should not be relied on completely for the diagnosis of refractive errors.

Treatment and Prognosis.

Except for mild cases, proper lenses for full correction of the refractive error should be worn at all times. In general it is the parents' distaste for eyeglasses rather than the child's lack of co-operation which interferes with early treatment. Children as young as two years usually can wear eyeglasses comfortably.

HYPEROPIA (Farsightedness)

An emmetrope has perfect vision for distance without focusing (accommodating). The hyperope also usually has perfect distant vision but has to accommodate to see clearly. Hyperopia usually results from shortness of the eyeball, but may be caused by reduced refractive power of cornea or lens. Some degree of hyperopia is normal before puberty. The condition is largely familial and should be suspected if either of the parents suffers from it.

The condition may be asymptomatic. Headache and eyestrain may be present in older children during close work. Internal strabismus (esotropia) is often related to moderate or high hyperopia.

For diagnosis with the direct ophthalmoscope, see D, above.

Treatment and Prognosis.

Only in marked degrees of hyperopia or in strabismus is optical correction required, since some improvement can be expected when the child reaches puberty.

ASTIGMATISM

Astigmatism is characterized by a difference in refractive power of one meridian of the cornea as compared with the meridian at right angles to it. The difference between the two is the degree of astigmatism, and the meridian in which a corrective cylinder is placed is the axis of the astigmatism. Optically, this causes the horizontal component to be out of focus with the vertical component (or vice versa, depending upon the meridian of astigmatism).

Astigmatism is largely familial and is usually caused by developmental variations in the curvature of the cornea. A minority of cases are lenticular rather than corneal in origin.

Clinical Findings.

Astigmatism is usually seen in children who also have either myopia or hyperopia. Common findings are headache, fatigue, eye pain, reading difficulties, and a tendency to frown.

Treatment and Prognosis.

Eyeglasses or contact lenses may be required, at least for reading and for watching television or movies. The degree of far-sightedness or nearsightedness determines whether eyeglasses must be worn constantly. No spontaneous improvement may be expected. A contact lens will correct corneal but not lenticular types of astigmatism.

CONTACT LENSES

Contact lenses can be fitted satisfactorily on any patient who is sufficiently motivated to undergo the discomforts of adaptation, but the child should be old enough to remove and insert the lenses himself. Contact lenses may be valuable in infants who have undergone unilateral cataract surgery provided understanding, cooperative parents learn technics of contact lens care. Since corneal damage may result from improper fitting or handling, contact lenses should be prescribed and fitted only by persons qualified to give critical follow-up care and to treat injury or infection early.

The newly developed soft contact lenses may be used for therapeutic purposes - protection of cornea, bandaging of corneal injury, and treatment of corneal edema. Some patients who cannot wear the conventional lenses may tolerate the soft lenses.

STRABISMUS (SQUINT)

Strabismus is characterized by ocular deviations or the failure of the two eyes to maintain parallelism. Squint before the age of six months may be spurious. Deviations after six months are true strabismus, often requiring treatment.

Because the two eyes fail to maintain parallelism, the image of the deviating eye is suppressed, with consequent progressive diminution of vision on that side leading to loss of sight (amblyopia), which may be permanent if not recognized and treated.

Etiology.
The exact cause cannot be determined in most cases. Cases of congenital or hereditary strabismus outnumber the acquired forms.
  A. Paralytic strabismus is due to congenital or acquired anomaly of a particular extraocular muscle or paresis of its nerve supply.
  B. Concomitant (Nonparalytic) Strabismus:
    1. Accommodative (due to hyperopia) - Onset at two to four years of age.
    2. Congenital (muscular, innervational) - Onset at or near birth.
    3. Anisometropia (marked difference in refractive error of the two eyes).
    4. Visual - (1) Poor vision in one eye from developmental anomaly or malignant tumor of the retina. (2) Opacities of the media, interfering with fixation and fusion.

Clinical Findings.
  A. Symptoms: Eso deviations are most common in children; older children and adults tend to develop exo deviations. Vision may be decreased on the affected side. With alternating squint good vision is maintained in both eyes. Personality disorders may occur and may be reflected in social maladjustment and poor school work.
  B. Signs: Deviation of the eye may be in any direction and may be intermittent or constant, alternating or monocular. If strabismus is paralytic and the lesion neurologic in nature, the angle

of deviation varies with the direction of the gaze, increasing in the direction of action of the paretic muscle. If concomitant, it remains unaffected by the direction of the gaze.

Treatment.

Diagnosis of the usual congenital types should be possible by six months of age, and early therapy should be instituted. Many cases become apparent with increasing near use of eyes, i.e., in school years (accommodative type). Ocular disease must be ruled out by ophthalmoscopic examination.

A. General Measures:
  1. A patch over the unaffected eye to force the child to use the deviated eye and prevent amblyopia. This patch must be kept on all day and should cover the entire eye. The use of a patch for many months may be required. Patching is generally of little value after the age of 8 years.
  2. Correction by glasses at 12 to 20 months of age is imperative where marked refractive errors are found.
  3. Exercises - Orthoptic exercises have been recommended in an attempt to avoid surgery, but children under five to seven years of age are rarely able to cooperate satisfactorily. Injudicious use of orthoptics often merely postpones definitive therapy unnecessarily.
  4. If nonoperative procedures result in improvement, surgery may be postponed.

B. Surgery: Indicated when vision is equal in both eyes and the deviation cannot be corrected by glasses, or for cosmetic reasons when vision cannot be equalized. Surgery may be done as early as one year of age. Early correction is desirable if there is a good potential for fusion. Cosmetic surgery is usually done closer to the school years.

Prognosis.

Good results are usually obtained in strabismus associated with refractive errors. Good cosmetic results usually follow surgical treatment. Binocularity depends upon sensory mechanisms, which are usually abnormal in congenital and small angle strabismus and are therefore associated with a less favorable prognosis.

MISCELLANEOUS EYE DISORDERS

INFLAMMATION OF THE CORNEA
(Keratitis)

The healthy cornea possesses no blood vessels and is clear. Any blood vessels or opacities seen in it are pathologic.

Etiology.
A. Vitamin A deficiency, occurring in malnourished children, in allergic children on restricted diets, and in children with biliary tract anomalies which interfere with absorption of vitamin A. (See also Chapter 4.)

B. **Bacterial Ulcers:** Usually follow trauma by a foreign body or injuries infected by bacteria, including pneumococcus, hemolytic streptococcus, Friedländer's bacillus, Pseudomonas aeruginosa, or Moraxella lacunata. These ulcers lead to hypopyon (pus in anterior chamber), great corneal destruction, and loss of eye if not treated intensively. Gonococcal conjunctivitis also frequently leads to corneal ulceration, hypopyon, and ultimately perforation.

C. **Phlyctenular keratitis** may be due to an allergic reaction to tuberculoprotein but also may result from sensitivity to other proteins (bacterial or fungal). Tuberculosis can also cause a deep form of keratitis.

D. **Interstitial keratitis** is associated with congenital or acquired syphilis (90%), or may follow infectious diseases such as herpes zoster, mumps, or tuberculosis.

E. **Mycotic ulcers** are usually associated with a penetration of the cover with vegetable material, e.g., a stick.

F. **Viral keratitis** (herpes simplex, vaccinia).

Clinical Findings.

A. **Symptoms and Signs:** Inflammation of the cornea, regardless of etiology, is usually characterized by pain, photophobia, tearing, and blurred vision. Defects in the epithelium stain with fluorescein. This green stain can be seen with an ordinary flashlight but is fluorescent with a cobalt-blue filter or with a Wood's lamp. Iritis is usually associated and would be suggested by the presence of a ciliary flush (limbal injection), and aqueous flare and cells (usually seen only with a slit lamp).

1. **Xerophthalmia** is characterized by a cornea which has lost luster and appears cloudy and dry (xerosis). Typically, there is little vascular reaction. Epithelial defects and secondary infection occur. As the condition progresses, these dry areas become progressively whiter (Bitot's spots) and usually are seen at the limbus on the temporal side of the cornea. The end stage is keratomalacia and obscured vision. Bitot's spots are grayish-white, foamy lesions, usually on the temporal conjunctiva adjacent to the limbus. They are associated with poor nutritional states but are not always accompanied by hypovitaminosis A.

2. **Pneumococcal serpiginous ulcers** - In the early stages there is a gray area of infiltration of the cornea associated with a dilatation of the circumcorneal blood vessels, producing the characteristic ciliary flush. There is more pain than is expected from such a small lesion, and the corneal epithelium is markedly hazy.

    The area enlarges and spreads very rapidly (creeping ulcer); a level of pus often appears in the anterior chamber (hypopyon).

3. **Phlyctenular keratitis** - The limbus is usually first affected, with the appearance of a small, vascularized, elevated nodule. Gray infiltrates with secondary vascularization may occur in the superficial layers of the corneal stroma and may progress to shallow ulcers. The ulcer extends toward the center of the cornea and results in extensive scar formation. Photophobia is most marked in phlyctenulosis.

4. Interstitial keratitis - Marked, insidious, early congestion
is present with coincident iridocyclitis and clouding of the
iris. The cornea may become so cloudy that the iris cannot
be seen. Photophobia may be severe. Deep stromal vessels
are present.

5. Viral keratitis - The dendrite is suggestive of herpes simplex, which may also present as stippling or as a geographic
corneal ulcer. Corneal hypesthesia is usually present.

B. Laboratory Findings:

1. Bacteriologic cultures of serpiginous ulcers reveal the presence of pathogenic bacteria. Direct scrapings for Gram
staining often can give more prompt specific diagnosis.

2. Serologic tests for syphilis and tuberculin testing with very
dilute (1:100,000 or greater) tuberculin material should be
done in suspected cases.

3. Vitamin A levels and tolerance tests are abnormal in vitamin A deficiency.

Complications.

Corneal involvement may give rise to an iritis and a clouding
of the central area which may lead to blindness. Purulent endoph-
thalmitis may lead to loss of the eye.

Treatment.

A. Specific Measures:

1. Xerophthalmia - Vitamin A therapy is specific. Parenteral
therapy may be required in some cases.

2. Bacterial ulcers - Early specific local and systemic antibiotic therapy is imperative and must be based on findings
obtained from scrapings and cultures from the ulcer itself.

a. Neomycin-polymyxin-bacitracin ophthalmic ointment
(Neosporin®) or gentamicin solution (2 to 10 mg./ml.)
may be used pending bacterial diagnosis. These drugs
are effective against pseudomonas ulcers and will also
combat common cocci or rods.

b. The pupil should be dilated with 1% cyclopentolate or 5%
homatropine.

c. The cortisones have been used locally in combination with
antibiotic therapy. Results remain controversial, and
caution is advised unless the organism is identified and
known to be sensitive to an antibiotic. Corticosteroids
are detrimental in some of the viral infections, especially herpes simplex.

3. Phlyctenular keratitis - Topical corticosteroids result in
dramatic improvement (one drop every two hours).
Note: Children with this condition may be hypersensitive
to tuberculin, and skin testing should be done with the greatest of caution at dilutions of 1:100,000 or greater.

4. Interstitial keratitis - Specific therapy of syphilis and tuberculosis may improve the eye lesion. Topical cortisone
probably minimizes scarring. Local use of cycloplegics is
imperative.

5. Mycotic ulcers - Topical amphotericin B, 2.5 to 5 mg./ml.

6. Herpes simplex and vaccinia - Topical use of 0.1% idoxuridine (Dendrid®, Herplex®, Stoxil®), one drop each hour dur-

ing the day and every two hours at night for 4 to 7 days. Idoxuridine ointment, 0.5%, instilled five times a day, may be equally effective. The cortisones should never be used in viral types of keratitis. They may enhance invasiveness of virus and have in many cases caused spontaneous perforation of the cornea in herpetic keratitis.

B. General Measures:
  1. Sedation and analgesia are most important in symptomatic care. Topical anesthetics are **contraindicated** as they impair corneal healing.
  2. Atropine (one drop of 1% solution instilled three to four times a day) should always be used in these conditions.
  3. Hot compresses applied for 15 minutes three or four times a day may decrease pain.
  4. Dark glasses will decrease photophobia.
  5. The routine systemic use of broad-spectrum antibiotics should be discouraged. Specific bacteriologic diagnosis should guide therapy when possible.

Course and Prognosis.
  A. Xerophthalmia: Even when marked clouding of the cornea has interfered with vision, complete regression frequently will occur after adequate vitamin A therapy.
  B. Serpiginous Ulcers: With early specific antibiotic therapy, prognosis is good. Prognosis is guarded in pseudomonas, gonococcal, and hemolytic streptococcus ulcers.
  C. Phlyctenular Keratitis. Recurrences are frequent and in many cases are of unknown etiology. The ultimate prognosis depends on the frequency and severity of these recurrences. Prognosis for vision is much better now that attacks can be controlled with the cortisones.
  D. Interstitial Keratitis: Corneal scars may interfere with vision. In many of these, however, eventual visual acuity is excellent. Corneal transplants may be of value in selected cases.
  E. Viral Keratitis: Complaints of photophobia and pain usually persist for a long time, frequently for several months, until healing has occurred. The ulcers never perforate spontaneously, but may give rise to considerable scarring. (Perforation has occurred when cortisone has been used topically.)

ORBITAL AND PERIORBITAL CELLULITIS

Cellulitis is often secondary to sinusitis and may also occur as a complication of trauma and septicemia. The most common organisms are streptococci, staphylococci, and Haemophilus influenzae.

Periorbital cellulitis is characterized by erythema and swelling of the eyelids. The conjunctiva and orbital tissues are not involved. Preauricular lymphadenopathy may be present.

Orbital cellulitis is marked by erythema and swelling of the eyelids, conjunctival chemosis, proptosis, limitation of ocular movements, fever, and leukocytosis. In cases of H. influenzae infection, the skin of the eyelids has a distinct magenta discoloration.

Complications include meningitis and cavernous sinus thrombosis.

Treatment consists of hot packs and specific systemic anti-biotic drugs. Drainage of loculated abscesses is occasionally necessary.

CATARACT

Cataract is an opacity of the lens or of its capsule which may be present at birth or may develop in childhood. Cataracts are often bilateral and symmetrical.

Clinical Findings.
A. Symptoms:
1. Diminution of visual acuity.
2. There is no pain if the cataract is uncomplicated by other diseases of the eye.
B. Signs:
1. The lens nucleus and cortex both may be opaque. If no clear lens remains it is termed "mature."
2. Strabismus may be the first indication of cataract.
3. Nystagmus (searching or pendular type) develops if visual acuity is impaired to 20/100 or worse.
4. Ophthalmoscopic examination - On dilating the pupil, the opaque areas are seen to be white by direct light (leukocoria). The red reflex of the retina is not seen if the cataract is dense.

Etiology.
A. Congenital Cataract:
1. Maternal rubella occurring during the first or early in the second trimester may result in congenital cataracts.
2. It is probable that other viral and systemic diseases may result in congenital cataracts. These causes, however, are less well explored.
B. Cataracts of Childhood:
1. Traumatic cataract - This results from penetrating wounds or other trauma to the eyeball. The cataract may develop in a short time and progress rapidly; it frequently is followed by secondary glaucoma.
2. Metabolic diseases - Diabetes, hypoparathyroidism, galactosemia, Down's syndrome, and Lowe's syndrome.
3. Poisoning - Chiefly from ingestion or inhalation of naphthalene or diphenyl.
4. As a complication of other diseases of the eye, including retinitis pigmentosa, glaucoma, uveitis, iridocyclitis, and in a late stage of retrolental fibroplasia.
5. As a complication of long-term administration of systemic corticosteroids in high doses.

Treatment.
A. General Measures: In the unusual case of dense central cataract, it is worthwhile to try to improve vision with phenylephrine (Neo-Synephrine®), 10% solution, 2 drops in the involved eye during the day. If this is successful, surgery may be postponed; the prognosis is better if surgery can be deferred until the child is over six years of age.

B. Surgical Measures: In those cases which cannot be managed temporarily with mydriatic eyedrops, surgical removal should be done early.

Prognosis.

The extent of the cataract and the presence or absence of complicating ocular disease will determine whether or not useful vision can be expected. If nystagmus has developed, vision will rarely be better than 20/200, even after successful surgery.

GLAUCOMA

Glaucoma is increased intraocular pressure involving one or both eyes, giving rise to optic nerve damage and visual field loss. Infantile congenital glaucoma (in children under 3 years) is an autosomal recessive trait and is caused by injury or disease of the eye. Most cases of congenital glaucoma are sporadic (some show a hereditary pattern).

Clinical Findings.
A. Symptoms: Photophobia is often the earliest symptom. The eyes may water. Persistent pain may be present, but more often there is none. Vision gradually deteriorates.
B. Signs: The eye may enlarge, and the corneal diameter may increase. Corneal edema may be present. The pupil is often dilated, and the sclera may be thin and bluish. The eyeball is large and firm to pressure. The difference between the normal and the affected eye in unilateral glaucoma is marked.

Treatment.
A. General Measures: Pilocarpine will control intraocular pressure in some cases of juvenile glaucoma but has no effect on congenital glaucoma. Attempts to relieve pain with analgesic drugs are usually unsuccessful. Acetazolamide (Diamox®) orally may be of value.
B. Surgical Measures: Surgery generally is required to relieve intraocular pressure. In congenital glaucoma, goniotomy or trabeculotomy may improve the function of the filtration angle. Enucleation is indicated if the eye continues to be painful and if vision has been lost.

Course and Prognosis.
Generally, glaucoma is slowly progressive. Without treatment, blindness usually occurs eventually, although impairment of vision may progress gradually over a period of many months.
With surgical treatment, vision frequently is saved.
Prognosis is always guarded.

RETROLENTAL FIBROPLASIA

This is a disease of the retina which occurs almost exclusively in premature infants of low birth weight (under 1500 Gm.) and of gestational age of six to seven months. It is invariably bilateral (may be unequally so) and leads, in its severe form, to wildly disorganized retinal overgrowth and permanent blindness. Until recently it was the most common cause of blindness in children in the U.S.A. The incidence of this disease has declined with the awareness by physicians of the toxic effects of oxygen on the retina.

High oxygen tension in the blood stream is the main precipitating factor. The disease is quite rare when supplemental oxygen therapy is not used and is uncommon when concentrations in incubators are kept below 40%. If oxygen therapy is necessary, the concentration in the incubator should be controlled by direct measurement with an oximeter rather than by monitoring the rate of flow from the tank; this has recently assumed considerable medicolegal importance. Monitoring of arterial O_2 or pCO_2 is the best method of determining oxygen tension in the blood stream.

UVEITIS

Inflammation of the uveal tissues (iris, ciliary body, and choroid) may be granulomatous or nongranulomatous. Uveitis may be due to specific infection with bacteria, viruses, fungi, or parasites; or a nonspecific inflammatory reaction may occur, probably as a hypersensitivity or autoimmune process.

Anterior involvement (iridocyclitis) is characterized by inflamed eye, photophobia, blurred vision, ciliary injection, pupillary constriction, inflammatory cells in the anterior chamber, and keratic precipitates on the back of the cornea; posterior involvement (choroiditis) by blurred vision and vitreous floaters. The vitreous is hazy on ophthalmoscopic examination. Acute choroidal lesions appear as white indistinct masses; old lesions are seen as pigmented, disorganized scar tissue of the choroid and retina.

Complications consist of glaucoma, cataracts, and retinal detachment. Optic neuritis may be associated.

Nonspecific anterior uveitis should be treated with topical administration of 1% atropine twice a day and topical corticosteroids (2.5% hydrocortisone or equivalent) 4 to 8 times a day. Posterior involvement requires systemic corticosteroids and salicylates. Treat associated disease (syphilis, tuberculosis, polyarthritis, toxoplasmosis, focal infections, etc.) specifically.

OPTIC NEURITIS

Two types of optic neuritis are seen in childhood: (1) papillitis (anterior involvement with papilledema) and (2) retrobulbar neuritis (disks appear normal). Most cases follow viral infections or represent localized encephalomyelitis. Optic neuritis may also be due to drug toxicity or associated with neurologic disease.

The symptoms consist of loss of visual acuity, field defects (central scotomas), and, occasionally, pain on movement of the eye. Papilledema is present in the anterior form only.

Treatment is nonspecific. Systemic corticosteroids are of questionable value. Possible drug causes should be eliminated. The prognosis is good.

20 . . .
Bones & Joints

INFECTIONS OF THE BONES AND JOINTS

OSTEOMYELITIS

Osteomyelitis is an inflammatory process which may involve all parts of a bone, although the initial focus is usually in the metaphysis of a bone. It is usually caused by staphylococci, although streptococci, salmonellae, and other organisms may be the causative agents. Infection generally occurs via hematogenous spread but may be due to local extension from an infected focus. A history of trauma, usually mild, is common in the hematogenous type.

Considerable areas of cortex may undergo necrosis and produce sequestra which cannot be readily absorbed and which usually must be removed surgically if not extruded. During repair, new bone is laid down beneath the elevated periosteum and tends to form an encasement (involucrum) of the necrotic area. Complete healing takes place only when all dead bone has been destroyed, discharged, or excised. A joint is not invaded unless the metaphysis lies within the confines of the capsule.

Clinical Findings.
A. Symptoms and Signs: Local inflammatory signs may be absent early. Later, there usually is localized erythema, warmth, tenderness, and swelling; fever, elevated pulse; severe, constant, throbbing pain over the end of the shaft; and limitation of joint motion.
B. Laboratory Findings: Leukocytosis may be marked. Blood cultures are generally positive early in the course. Smear of aspirated pus shows cocci or rods. Cultures (aerobic and anaerobic) of aspirated pus are positive and useful for sensitivity tests.
C. X-ray Findings: Spotty rarefaction followed shortly by periosteal new bone formation (generally absent for the first ten to 14 days of the disease; range three to 14). A considerable portion of bone is usually involved. The bone is demineralized.

Treatment.
A. Specific Measures: Aspiration of pus (using aseptic technic) provides material for smear and culture and in many cases makes possible immediate bacteriologic diagnosis. Give penicillin or other appropriate bactericidal drug intravenously in very large doses for three weeks, then orally for three months. A dropping sedimentation rate is a useful guide to the efficacy of treatment.

B. General Measures: Immobilization in a loose-fitting plaster cast may be helpful.
C. Surgical Measures: Surgical aspiration is of diagnostic value; more extensive surgical intervention is limited to cases which show progressive early localized skin changes, to those with rapidly progressive and uncontrolled bone destruction, to those which fail to show clinical response to drug therapy in 48 hours, and to cases in which the sequestra that may form do not show evidence of resorption.

PYOGENIC ARTHRITIS

Pyogenic arthritis is an infection of one or more joints by hematogenous spread (most common) or by direct extension of pathogenic bacteria. The most common organisms are Staphylococcus aureus, gonococci, meningococci, pneumococci, and Haemophilus influenzae.

Initially, there is an effusion which rapidly becomes purulent. Destruction of cartilage occurs at areas of joint contact. Bone is not affected in the early stages, but the femoral and humeral heads, if involved, may undergo necrosis and subsequent fragmentation, and pathologic dislocation. Epiphyses whose synchondroses are located within the joint capsule are particularly apt to be involved by infection and necrosis.

During the chronic phase of the disease and the phase of repair there is an organization of the exudate present in the joint, and granulation tissue appears and becomes fibrous. This may bind the joint surfaces together with a fibrous ankylosis. When motion is present, the synovial fluid tends to regenerate, but limitation of motion and associated pain generally remain as a result of the production of residual strong intrasynovial adhesions.

Clinical Findings.
A. Symptoms and Signs:
1. Slow or rapid onset of severe systemic findings (fever, malaise, vomiting).
2. Pain may be severe; motion is limited and the joint is splinted by muscular spasm. In infants this may produce a pseudoparalysis.
3. Effusion occurs but may not be palpable at first. The overlying tissues become swollen, tender, and warm.
4. Contractures and muscular atrophy may result.
B. X-ray Findings:
1. Distention of the joint capsule is the first change.
2. Subsequent course produces narrowing of the cartilage space, erosion of the subchondral bone, irregularity and fuzziness of the bone surfaces, bone destruction, and diffuse osteoporosis.

Treatment.
A. Specific Measures:
1. Prompt aspiration for diagnosis.
2. Surgical drainage is almost always indicated when pus can be aspirated from the joint.
3. Appropriate parenteral antibiotic therapy in large doses.

B. General Measures:
1. Immobilization and traction during acute phase.
2. Physical therapy when the infectious process has subsided.

SKELETAL DISORDERS

INFANTILE CORTICAL HYPEROSTOSIS
(Caffey-Smyth-Roske Syndrome)

An infantile and sometimes familial, usually benign disease of unknown etiology, starting before the sixth month of life, which produces irritability, fever, and non-suppurating, tender, painful, hard swellings. Swellings may involve almost any bone of the body, but they are seen most frequently in the mandible (100%), clavicle (50%), ulna, humerus, and ribs. The disease is limited to the shaft, does not involve the subcutaneous tissues or joints, and persists for weeks or months. Pallor, pseudoparalysis, and pleurisy may occur. Anemia, leukocytosis, increased sedimentation rate, and elevated alkaline phosphatase are usually present. Cortical hyperostosis is demonstrable by x-ray and may be evident prenatally. Cortisone is effective and should be used, especially in severe cases. The prognosis is generally good; the disease terminates without deformity. Death may occur without treatment.

Periosteal new bone may develop in one third of normal infants after the first month of life. The cause is not known.

HYPERVITAMINOSIS A

This disease is caused by excessive ingestion of vitamin A (100,000 I.U. or more daily) for prolonged periods of time and is manifested by irritability, anorexia, firm, painful, subcutaneous masses in the skull and extremities, fissuring of the lips, dry skin which is often pruritic, alopecia, jaundice, hepatomegaly, and increased C.S.F. pressure. There is cortical thickening of bone similar to that seen in infantile cortical hyperostosis (see above), but children with hypervitaminosis A are generally older and the mandible is not involved. The blood vitamin A level is very high. Fever is absent.

The only therapy necessary is discontinuation of excessive doses of vitamin A. Clinical improvement begins within a few days, but a return of the bones to normal may not occur for several months.

CONGENITAL DYSPLASIA OF THE HIP JOINT
(Congenital Dislocation of the Hip)

An abnormality of the hip, often hereditary and occurring more commonly in females. The acetabulum is shallow, the ossification center for the femoral head, which normally appears at three to five months, is delayed in its appearance, and the joint capsule is stretched. The head of the femur becomes dislocated upward and backward and comes to lie on the dorsal aspect of the ilium, where constant pressure may result in the formation of a false acetabulum.

All newborn infants should be routinely tested for instability of the hip (Ortolani's sign - a snapping of the hips as the head passes over the posterior acetabular rim).

Clinical Findings.
A. Symptoms and Signs:
1. Prior to dislocation - There may be abnormal muscular splinting of the affected hip, with diminished spontaneous movement, partial flexion of the thigh, inability to abduct the hip normally, and asymmetry of the gluteal and thigh folds. However, the normal newborn infant may also have asymmetry of skin folds (40%), unilateral extra skin fold (20%), increased acetabular angle, unequal ability to abduct legs (4%), apparent shortness of one leg (3%), and inability to abduct a full 90°. In some cases patients who develop subluxation have no abnormal signs initially.
2. Following dislocation - All of the above findings are present, plus the following: more marked asymmetry of gluteal, inguinal, and knee folds; external rotation of the leg or increased anteversion of the femoral neck, shortening of the affected leg, telescoping of the involved extremity, a clicking sound on forced abduction, a bulge of the femoral head, a positive Trendelenburg sign, and delay in learning to walk. With bilateral dislocations, lordosis and waddling gait may be marked.
B. X-ray Findings:
1. Deformity of the normally symmetrical obturator-costo-femoral curve on the deformed side.
2. Delayed appearance of the femoral epiphysial center, which is often hypoplastic.
3. Absence of the upper lip of the acetabulum, shallow acetabulum, and increase of the angle formed by the acetabular shelf with the horizontal plane.
4. Displacement of the femur, when it occurs, is upward and backward.

Treatment.
Closed reduction and maintenance of the affected hip in the position of maximum stability. In older children, open reduction may be necessary.

Maintenance of correction in position of abduction, extension, and internal rotation may be preferable to the "frog-leg" position. Open reduction is indicated if closed reduction is unsatisfactory.

COXA VARA

A disorder in which the long axis of the femoral neck is depressed to a horizontal position, allowing the greater trochanter to approach the ilium. It may be congenital, or may result from epiphysial separation, fractures, osteochondrosis, chondrodysplasia, or hypothyroidism. Debilitating disease, rickets, and obesity may be contributing factors. The congenital form is due to maldevelopment of the femoral neck and to disordered enchondral ossification of that region and is accompanied by a disordered epiphysial growth with premature fusion.

Symptoms include shortening of the leg, pain (often referred to the knee on the affected side), limp, muscle spasm, limited abduction and internal rotation of the hip, and upward tilting of the pelvis on the affected side with shortening of the leg.

Treatment.

Remove the underlying condition, if possible. Orthopedic correction may be necessary.

SLIPPED FEMORAL EPIPHYSIS

A nontraumatic separation of the femoral head, more common in males and in thin and tall or overweight children. It occurs at adolescence and may present with sudden posteromedial displacement of the epiphyses following minor trauma or a slowly progressive displacement with pain, loss of internal rotation, limp, and shortening of the leg. It may be bilateral. X-ray reveals thickening and irregularity of the epiphysial plate (early) followed by posteromedial displacement of the head of the femur.

Treatment and Prognosis.

Internal fixation of epiphysis in situ for early slip. For complete separation, closed reduction and pin fixation should be attempted, but osteotomy of the proximal femur after closure of the epiphysis may be necessary.

Cases with slight slipping have a favorable prognosis when treated early. Late cases with severe displacement often have permanent disability regardless of the form of therapy.

TRANSIENT SYNOVITIS OF THE HIP

This is the commonest cause of painful hip in children in the U.S. It is a self-limiting disease of unknown etiology lasting days (usually) to weeks which affects children between the ages of three and ten years (boys more than girls). The disease is characterized by a sudden onset of unilateral mild or severe pain in the hip, thigh, or knee, especially with movement or weight bearing. There is tenderness over the hip joint anteriorly, occasionally palpable swelling, and limp. The hip is usually held in flexion, abduction, and internal rotation. Motion is usually limited. Fever is variable and often absent. X-rays are usually normal but may show capsular swelling. Treatment is symptomatic. Traction may be necessary in severe cases. In some patients, Legg-Perthes disease has developed several months after convalescence.

COMBINED DEFECTS

Acrocephalosyndactyly.

Acrocephaly (tower skull) combined with fused or webbed fingers or toes.

TABLE 20-1. Congenital and idiopathic disorders of bone.

DISEASE	FAMILY HISTORY	CLINICAL MANIFESTATIONS	X-RAY	TREATMENT AND PROGNOSIS
Osteogenesis imperfecta (fragilitas osseum, osteopsathyrosis); congenital and tarda types	Familial in congenital type. Absent in tarda type.	Increased bone fragility and fractures. Normal healing. Blue sclerae. Flaccidity of ligaments and muscles. Deafness (due to otosclerosis and labyrinthine changes). Elevated levels of pyrophosphate.	Bones slender with thin cortices, bulbous ends, areas of demineralization. Multiple fractures and healed fractures. Exuberant callus formation.	Magnesium oxide may be of value. May die at any age or improve at puberty.
Osteopetrosis (osteitis condensans generalisata, marble bone disease, Albers Schönberg disease)	Familial and hereditary.	Bony deformities due to pathologic fractures. Myelophthisic anemia. Splenomegaly. Visual and auditory manifestations. Square head. Facial paralysis sometimes. Pigeon breast. Dwarfing. May appear at any age.	Bones show increased density, transverse bands in shaft, clubbing of ends, vertical striations (long bones). Thickening about cranial foramina. May have heterotopic calcification of soft tissues.	No treatment. Prognosis fair.
CHONDRODYSTROPHIES				
Achondroplasia (classical chondrodystrophy)	Often present.	Short arms and legs. Upper arm and thigh proportionately shorter than forearm and leg. Bowing of extremities. Waddling gait. Limitation of motion sometimes. Relaxation of ligaments sometimes. Short, stubby fingers of almost equal length. Prominent forehead. May have moderate hydrocephaly. Depressed bridge of nose. Lumbar lordosis. Mentality and sexual function normal.	Tubular bones are short and thick. Epiphysial plates generally irregular. Ends of bone are thick, broad, knoblike, and cupped. Epiphysial centers may be delayed and small in early childhood. Skull dysplasia and shortening; premature fusion of tribasilar bone. Calvarium enlarged. Fibula relatively long compared to tibia.	No treatment. Prognosis good. Deformities do not increase after puberty.
Osteochondrodystrophy (Morquio's disease)	Often present.	Appears after one year. Normal intelligence. Spine shows shortening, kyphosis, scoliosis. Moderate shortening of extremities. Sternum protrudes. Abdomen prominent. Hepatosplenomegaly, minimal involvement of skull. Waddling gait due to genu valgum and flexion and limitation of motion of hip joint.	Similar to those of achondroplasia. Wedged, flattened vertebral bodies. Abnormality of metacarpals. Irregularity of epiphyses. Lower extremities tend to be involved more than upper.	No treatment. Prognosis fair.
Gargoylism (dysostosis multiplex, Hurler's syndrome, lipochondrodystrophy)	Often present.	Mental retardation. Coarse, grotesque facies, flat nose, thickened lips, corneal opacities, big tongue, deafness, orange peel-like skin. Hepatosplenomegaly. Kyphosis. Limited extension at joints. Hirsutism. Short neck.	Elongated sella turcica, shortened vertebral bodies with concave anterior and superior surfaces; thickening of tubular bones and metacarpals with tapering of ends. Arms more involved than legs.	No treatment. Prognosis poor. The value of adrenocortical steroids remains to be determined.

Disease		Clinical features	Radiographic findings	Treatment and prognosis
		broad "claw-like" hands, slow growth. Reilly cells in blood and inflammatory sites. Increased urinary chondroitin sulfate B and heparatin sulfate.*	May show other changes of chondrodystrophy.	
Chondroectodermal dysplasia (Ellis-van Creveld syndrome)		Ectodermal dysplasia. Congenital heart disease. Polydactyly and frequently syndactyly. Teeth poorly formed. Some or all of teeth may be absent. Mental retardation.	May show changes of chondrodystrophy. Shortening and bowing of tibiae and fibulae. Hypoplastic, eccentric proximal tibial epiphyses. Fusion of carpal bones.	No treatment. Prognosis depends on type of heart disease.
Hereditary multiple exostoses (dyschondroplasia, diaphysial aclasis, osteochondroma)	Present.	Slow-growing masses, usually near joints or in spine. Generally asymptomatic but may cause pain, interference with joint function, or pressure disturbance. Deformity and shortening of long bones may occur.	Bilaterally symmetrical osteocartilaginous masses at metaphysial ends of long bones assume bizarre shapes; may be long and tapering, resembling spurs. Osteochondromosis may develop from exostoses.	Usually no treatment. Excision when symptomatic. Prognosis good. Lesion may undergo malignant degeneration.
Multiple enchondromas (Ollier's disease)	Absent.	May have hemiatrophy. May have pathologic fractures and resultant deformities. Large lesions have tendency to recur.	Islands of cartilage lie in the metaphysial ends of the shaft along the long axis of the bone. End of bone thickened. Lesions are asymmetrical and multiple and usually limited to one extremity or one side of the body.	No treatment may be needed. Prognosis good for non-growing tumors. Remove growing tumors (may be malignant).
Polyostotic fibrous dysplasia (osteitis fibrosa disseminata, McCune-Bruch-Albright syndrome)	Absent.	Large brown areas of pigmentation ("café au-lait" spots), predominantly unilateral. More common in males. Advanced bone age and short stature. Local pain or tenderness may occur. Precocious puberty in females.	Fibrous replacement of bone (predominantly unilateral). Thinning and expansion of cortex associated with multiple radiolucent areas having sclerotic margins. Base of skull may be dense.	No treatment. Prognosis good.
Osteochondrosis deformans tibiae (Blount's disease)	Absent.	Extreme bowing of the legs. Waddling gait or limp.	Proximal tibia and/or distal metaphysis of femur shows faulty growth, delayed ossification, enlarged medial condyle, and a beak-like extension of metaphysis posteriorly and caudally.	Orthopedic correction if necessary. Prognosis good.
Osteochondritis dissecans	Absent.	Boys. Late adolescence. Pain, synovial effusion, atrophy of muscles. Joint may lock or "give way."	Synovial effusion. Fragment of bone in joint. Usually involves knee.	Immobilization. May heal spontaneously. Remove bone fragments.

*May be due to a deficiency of hexosaminidase (β-galactosaminidase) activity with accumulation of mono- and distalogangliosides and glycolipids in tissues.

TABLE 20-2. Osteochondritis deformans.

A disease of unknown etiology causing aseptic necrosis of the epiphyses as a result of impairment or obliteration of the blood supply to the affected bone.

SITE	SYMPTOMS AND SIGNS	X-RAY FINDINGS	TREATMENT AND PROGNOSIS
Head of the femur (Legg-Perthes disease)	Tenderness in hip and pain in hip and/or knee. Limp. Age: 3-10 years.	Flattened, fragmented femoral head with widening of neck and increase in the joint space.	Ambulation without weight bearing; shoe lift, crutches. Usually lasts 2 to 5 years. Surgery occasionally indicated. Better prognosis with early onset.
Tibial tubercle (Osgood-Schlatter disease)	Pain, swelling, tenderness; weak knee extension, sl. limp. Freq. bilateral. Boys > girls.	Fragmentation and enlargement of tibial tubercle. Swelling of infrapatellar ligament.	Treatment symptomatic. Immobilization in severe cases. Prognosis good.
Tarsal navicular (Köhler's disease)	Pain in foot, limp. May have local swelling, redness, and heat.	Irregularity and flattening or fragmentation. Delayed maturation of ossification center.	Conservative with rest and support p.r.n. Complete healing in 5 to 8 years.
Lunate (Kienböck's disease)	Pain and/or weakness in wrist; later, limitation of motion. Age: 4-10 years.	Cysts of semilunar early. Later, irregularity, fragmentation, and increased density.	Immobilization. May require fusion of wrist. Healing in 1 to 3 years. Symptoms may persist.
Secondary epiphyses of vertebral body (Scheuermann's disease)	Usually asymptomatic. Dorsal kyphosis. May have hamstring "tightness."	Wedge-like deformity of vertebral bodies. Irregularity of superior and inferior bodies.	Prognosis good. May have residual deformity. Exercise. Brace, if severe.
Primary epiphyses of vertebral body (Calvé's disease, vertebra plana)	Usually asymptomatic. May have weakness of back. May be due to eosinophilic granuloma of vertebral body.	Destruction or collapse of vertebra with "wafer-like" appearance.	Immobilization. May need no treatment. Prognosis excellent.
Head of second metatarsal (Freiberg's infraction)	Pain and tenderness.	Increased density. Fragmentation.	Rest. Shoe support. Prognosis excellent. May produce stiff, painful metatarsophalangeal joint.
Os calcis (Sever's disease)	Heel pain and tenderness. Limp.	Fragmentation or flattening. Increased density.	Rest. Prognosis good.

Marfan's Syndrome.

This is an autosomal dominant disease due to a defect in the metabolism of acid mucopolysaccharides. Abnormal length of fingers, toes, and extremities (arachnodactyly), sometimes associated with hypermobility of the joints, subluxation of the lens, other abnormalities of the eyes (cataract, coloboma, enlarged cornea, strabismus, nystagmus), high palate, defects of the spine and chest (pigeon-breast), and congenital heart disease (particularly weakness of the media of the aorta). Serum mucoproteins may be decreased and urinary excretion of hydroxyproline increased. There may be an altered ratio of chondroitin sulfate to keratosulfate in costal cartilage.

Some of the findings of Marfan's syndrome may occur in patients with homocystinuria.

Cleidocranial Dysostosis.

Absence of part or all of the clavicle, often associated with delay of ossification of the skull. The facial bones may be underdeveloped, the sinuses absent, the palate highly arched, dentition defective, the skull enlarged (especially in the parietal and frontal regions), and other bones defective.

Craniofacial Dysostosis (Crouzon's Disease).

Acrocephaly (tower skull), hypoplastic maxilla, beaked nose, protrusion of the lower lip, exophthalmos, external strabismus, and hypertelorism. May be familial.

Klippel-Feil Syndrome.

Fusion of some or all of the cervical vertebrae or of multiple hemivertebrae into one osseous mass. The neck is short and limited in motion, and the hairline is low. Other defects, including scoliosis, cervical rib, spina bifida, torticollis, webbed neck, and congenital high position of the scapula, may be present also.

Mandibulofacial Dysostosis (Treacher-Collins Disease; Franceschetti's Syndrome).

Hypoplasia of the facial bones (especially the malar bones and mandible), anti-mongoloid slant to eyes, coloboma of the eyelids, malformation of the external ear, deafness, hypoplasia of mandibular and malar bones, groove extending from the mouth to the ear, hair growing down over the cheeks, abnormal hearing, and other anomalies (defects of palate, lip, heart, etc.). Hereditary.

Laurence-Moon-Biedl Syndrome.

Retinitis pigmentosa, polydactyly, obesity, hypogenitalism, and mental retardation. May be incomplete or associated with other abnormalities.

Pterygium Colli (Congenital Webbed Neck).

Formation of a thick fold of loose skin on the lateral aspect of the neck. It may occur alone or may be associated with **gonadal dysgenesis** (Bonnevie-Ullrich-Turner syndrome), with congenital lymphedema of hands and feet, shortness of stature, cubitus valgus, shield chest, cardiac anomalies, sexual infantilism, deep-set nails (particularly on the feet), numerous moles on the skin, telangiectasia of the bowel, short tubular bones of hands and feet, elevated excretion of urinary gonadotropins, and an XO configuration of chromosomes and negative chromatin pattern in the majority of apparent females. Estrogen therapy is indicated in puberty. (See Appendix.)

Absence of the Radii.
    May occur with congenital amegakaryocytic thrombocytopenia and leukemoid peripheral blood.

Pierre Robin Syndrome.
    Micrognathia and partial cleft palate. Tongue may fall back and cause respiratory distress. May have congenital glaucoma and retinal detachment.

Marchisani Syndrome.
    Brachydactyly, shortness of stature, stocky chest, thick spherical lens, and retardation in carpal ossification.

MISCELLANEOUS DEFECTS*

ARTHROGRYPOSIS MULTIPLEX CONGENITA
(Amyoplasia Congenita)

A congenital incomplete fibrous ankylosis (usually symmetrical) of many or all of the joints (except those of the spine and jaw). There may be contractures either in flexion or extension. The joints appear enlarged and cylindrical. The periarticular tissues show contractures and fail to develop normally, and the skin appears thickened. There may be numerous other congenital anomalies. The condition is probably due to abnormal development of muscle.

SPRENGEL'S DEFORMITY

A congenital condition in which one or both scapulae are elevated and small. The child cannot raise his arms completely on the affected side, and there may be torticollis. There is asymmetry of the shoulders.

OTHER DEFECTS

Brachydactyly (abnormal shortness), clinodactyly (deviation of the distal phalanx, usually of the fifth digit), syndactyly (webbing), and other abnormalities may involve the fingers and toes.

---

*Craniosynostosis is discussed in Chapter 21.

COMMON FOOT PROBLEMS

When a child begins to stand and walk there is a natural tendency for the long arches to seem flattened, the feet to become mildly pronated, the legs and feet to turn outward, and the knees to show a slight valgus deformity. As the child grows and muscle power develops, the feet usually lose this pronation, long arches become more evident, and the legs become straight.

FLAT FOOT
(Weak Foot, Flexible Foot, Strained Foot, Static Foot)

Flat foot occurs in most normal infants but clears spontaneously in the majority by the time walking is well established; it is characterized by a relaxed longitudinal arch which the child is unable to elevate. Flat foot in an older child may be one manifestation of a generalized state of muscular and ligamentous weakness, or it may be an inherited abnormality.

Treatment.
For persistent or severe cases, a corrective shoe will help maintain the position of the foot during growth. The shoe should be sturdy, with a longitudinal arch support and a Thomas heel with a small (3/16 to 1/4 inch) medial wedge.

TALIPES CALCANEOVALGUS

Talipes calcaneovalgus is a disorder in which there is excessive dorsal flexion at the ankle and eversion of the foot. It is often present at birth but corrects itself spontaneously in the majority of cases.

Treatment and Prognosis.
Treatment consists of passive exercise or casting prior to the age of walking. In older children, scaphoid pads and 1/8 inch or 3/16 inch inner heel and inner sole wedges are used.

CAVUS FOOT

This disorder may be due to heredity, poliomyelitis, short shoes, congenital syphilis, or neurologic conditions affecting the posterior and lateral columns of the spinal cord. It is manifested by an excessively high longitudinal arch and overactive long toe extensor tendons, which produce hyperextension at the metatarsophalangeal joint and flexion at the interphalangeal joints.

Early (conservative) treatment consists of metatarsal pads and bars and stretching exercises. Surgical transplantation of the long toe extensor tendons, together with arthrodesis, if indicated, need not be undertaken until later.

HAMMER TOE

This is a flexion deformity, usually congenital, of either or both interphalangeal joints of any toe. It is generally asymptomatic and requires no treatment except for cosmetic reasons or if a callus forms.

METATARSUS VARUS (Pigeon Toe)

This common disorder of infants is characterized by adduction of the forefoot on the rear foot.

Treatment.
  A. Postural Type: This type of deformity is flexible.
     1. If discovered early (before walking begins), treatment consists of mild overcorrection by passive manipulation or reverse last shoes.
     2. If not discovered until later, some cases require treatment as for the structural type.
  B. Structural Type: In the structural type of metatarsus varus the deformity is fixed and cannot be corrected by passive manipulation. Treatment consists of wedging with plaster casts so that the forefoot is forced into a position of overcorrection and held there for six weeks. If this treatment fails or the older child has been untreated, surgery may be indicated.

Prognosis.
  The prognosis for the postural type is excellent; for the structural type, the prognosis is good if treatment is started early.

TALIPES EQUINOVARUS (Clubfoot)

A congenital fixed deformity in which the inner border of the forefoot is turned up, the anterior half of the foot is adducted, the calcaneal tendon is shortened and the heel drawn up, and the foot is held in inversion and plantar flexion. Clubfoot may be associated with spina bifida with paralytic changes in the lower extremities.

Treatment and Prognosis.
  Treatment should be started at birth and consists of wedged plaster casts (early) and surgery as indicated (later) for residual deformity.
  Prognosis for cure is guarded.

● ● ●

SHOES

Shoes are not necessary for children with normal feet until walking is well established. Any covering for an infant's foot should be soft enough to allow the maximum in foot freedom for muscle development. The main purpose of shoes is protection.

An Oxford type, rubber-soled cloth shoe or sandal may offer an adequate covering for the normal foot.

THE BATTERED CHILD SYNDROME

The battered child syndrome occurs in young children who have received severe physical abuse and is a frequent cause of permanent injury or death. The findings are quite variable, and the syndrome should be considered in any case of possible trauma or child neglect (fracture of any bone, subdural hematoma, multiple soft tissue injuries, poor skin hygiene or malnutrition) or where there is a marked discrepancy between the clinical findings and the history. If evidence of injury is present but a history of injury is not available, or if a child dies suddenly and the cause cannot be determined, roentgenograms of the entire skeleton should be examined for characteristic multiple bony lesions in various stages of healing, cortical thickening, subperiosteal ossification, epiphysial displacements, and avulsion of parts of the provisional zone of calcification.

Parental psychiatric factors are probably of prime importance in the pathogenesis of this disorder, but parents who physically abuse their children do not necessarily have psychopathic personalities or come from lower socio-economic groups (although most published reports have involved patients in these categories). In most cases some defect in character structure is probably present; the parents may be repeating the type of child care practiced on them in their childhood.

Physicians may have great reluctance in believing that the parents were guilty of abuse and in initiating a criminal investigation. However, the physician's responsibility to the child requires a full evaluation of the problem and a reasonable guarantee that repetition will not occur.

21...
Neuromuscular Disorders

DEVELOPMENTAL DISORDERS OF
THE NERVOUS SYSTEM

Although the etiology of most developmental diseases is at
present not known, a variety of toxic mechanisms affecting the
mother during pregnancy (e.g., overexposure to x-ray radiation in
the pelvic area, uterine anoxia, infection with rubella virus or
Toxoplasma organisms) may be associated with abnormal C.N.S.
development in the fetus. Genetic factors play an important role
in some entities.

HYDROCEPHALUS

Hydrocephalus is usually due to obstruction of the circulation of
the C.S.F. anywhere along its course, due to defective development
of the ventricular foramina, neoplasm, infection, hemorrhage, or
unknown cause.

Clinical Findings.
- A. Symptoms and Signs: There may be a history of C.N.S. infection, bacterial or viral. The head may appear normal at birth,
but within two or three months an abnormal rate of enlargement
may be noted (see chart on inside front cover). Fontanelles
and sutures may be palpably widened. In congenital aqueductal
atresia (Arnold-Chiari syndrome), the infant may show macro-
cephaly at birth. Lethargy, irritability, vomiting, and disturbances of vital signs are late signs.
- B. X-ray Findings: Plain film of skull may show, in addition to
widening of fontanelles and sutures, cranial abnormalities or
intracranial calcification of toxoplasmosis or cytomegalic inclusion disease.
- C. Special Examinations:
  1. Subdural taps to rule out subdural hematoma. Transillumination may demonstrate the hematoma.
  2. Pneumoencephalography may indicate not only the extent of
the brain damage but also the location and cause of the
block.
  3. Echoencephalography, which may show ventricular dilatation, may be most useful in diagnosis and management.

Treatment.
Several operative procedures have been devised to decrease the
production of C.S.F. or to establish artificial channels for reducing
the pressure in the ventricles.

Isosorbide dinitrate, 2 mg. four times per day, may slow head enlargement.

Prognosis.

The prognosis is guarded. Spontaneous arrest may occur. Surgery at present offers the child a slightly better chance. Correction, either spontaneous or surgical, will not restore damaged and destroyed brain tissue; subsequent mental retardation of varying degree is the rule. Visual defects, cerebellar ataxia, spastic diplegia, and inappropriate behavior may become apparent in later development.

MYELODYSPLASIA
(Spina Bifida)

Myelodysplasia is a malformation of development resulting in varying degrees of failure of alar plate closure: vertebral, neural, meningeal, or cutaneous. They occur most frequently in the lumbosacral region of the spine.

Myelodysplasias are the most common developmental defects of the C. N. S., occurring about once in 1000 births.

Classification.
  A. Spina Bifida Occulta (most common type): No externally visible sac. Defective vertebrae with usually no damage to spinal cord.
  B. Meningocele: Sac composed only of meninges, with cord and nerve roots not grossly apparent. Microscopic examination reveals cord and root structures.
  C. Meningomyelocele: A soft, round, cyst-like mass the wall of which contains neural tissue of the usually imperfectly developed and damaged cord.
  D. Encephalocele: Defect at any point of the skull which may be associated with a meningocele or encephalomeningocele or have no protrusion of the C. N. S. The most common sites are at the midline in the occipital and parietal areas, but the frontal bone, orbit, or nose may be involved.
  E. Diastematomyelia: Projection of bony, cartilaginous, or fibrous septum from posterior surface of vertebral body and segmental division of cord and meninges.
  F. Dermal or pilonidal sinuses anywhere along the cerebrospinal axis should be investigated by x-ray to rule out a communication with the subarachnoid space.

Clinical Findings.
  A. Spina Bifida Occulta: Most cases are asymptomatic. There may be a lack of or gradual loss of sphincter control, becoming apparent with attempts at toilet training. Weakness or paralysis of lower extremities may be present or may gradually become apparent. X-ray studies establish the diagnosis by comparison with normal roentgen findings for age group.
  B. Meningocele: No evidence of motor weakness or sphincter disturbance. Lesion transilluminates easily. Electromyography may demonstrate subclinical asymmetric muscle denervation.

C. Meningomyelocele: Transilluminates less easily than meningocele. There may be flaccid paralysis, absent sensation, and
deformities of the legs. In cervical lesion there may be spasticity and hyperactive reflexes in lower extremities.

D. Encephalocele: Symptoms depend on location of lesion and
extent of involvement of nervous tissue.

E. Diastematomyelia: Symptoms depend on location and extent of
malformation, but usually involve lower extremities. Localized
hypertrichosis, dermal sinus, and defects of skin frequently
occur. There may be a progressive weakness and sensory
loss in the legs.

Treatment.

A. Surgical Measures: The correction of myelomeningoceles
probably should be done as quickly as possible after delivery.
Hydrocephalus or extensive paralysis contraindicates surgery.
Spina bifida occulta is usually not treated unless neurologic
abnormalities show progression. Head size should be charted
daily and x-ray studies undertaken if the circumference increases.

B. General Measures: The infant should be kept on his abdomen
and the sac covered with sterile dressings. Fluid intake should
not exceed minimum daily requirements.

Prognosis.

The prognosis is guarded at best and depends principally upon
the extent of spinal cord involvement. If there is associated hydrocephalus, the prognosis is poor. Spina bifida occulta without other
symptoms may be associated with loss of sphincter control later in
childhood.

CRANIOSYNOSTOSIS

Craniosynostosis is a developmental disorder of the skull bones
that results in closure of one or more cranial sutures in utero.
Diagnosis is based on distortion of the normal skull shape: elongation, narrowing, or broadening and shortening. X-rays confirm the
diagnosis and define the sutures involved.

Treatment is by means of surgical incision of sutures during
the first three weeks of life. In about 15% of cases, intervention
may have to be repeated because increased cranial pressure recurs.

Prognosis is usually good, but mental retardation may be apparent in 5% of children despite surgical intervention.

DEGENERATIVE DISORDERS OF
THE NERVOUS SYSTEM

The degenerative disorders primarily affecting the nervous
system have a variable but insidious onset in a child considered
normal at birth; once apparent, symptoms progress steadily. A
family history of similar disease is frequently obtained.

DEMYELINATING ENCEPHALOPATHY
(Schilder's Disease)

Schilder's disease is a massive demyelinating involvement of the cerebral hemispheres. Onset is at any time during childhood. Cortical type of blindness may be an early symptom. Gradual motor paralysis involves first the extremities and then the trunk. Headache, vomiting, and papilledema suggesting increased intracranial pressure may be observed. Central deafness occurs, and, with progression, convulsions, mental deterioration, and dementia.

No treatment is available. Death supervenes within a few years of onset. The course may be rapid, with death in months.

THE LIPIDOSES

Any one of the many types of abnormal lipid metabolism may seriously affect the C.N.S. A brief description of some of the more well-established entities follows:

Cerebromacular Degenerations.

These disorders are characterized by widespread deposits of the lipid ganglioside throughout the C.N.S. and are associated with a deficiency of hexoseaminidase A. Several sub-types occur, depending upon the age at onset of symptoms. The infantile form (Tay-Sachs disease) is apparent between the third and sixth months in an infant who was normal at birth. The onset is with apathy, lethargy, and eventually motor weakness. A cherry-red spot appears on the retina at the macula. A decerebrate state results, with death before four years of age.

If the onset occurs later in childhood or in adulthood, the course is slower (Spielmeyer-Vogt disease, Bielschowsky's disease, Kufs' disease).

Cerebromacular degenerations occur in familial distribution, primarily in individuals of Jewish ancestry, probably as an autosomal recessive trait.

Histiocytosis X (Hand-Schüller-Christian Disease): See p. 455.

Gaucher's Disease.

Gaucher's disease is a rare familial disorder which is considered to result from a deficiency of beta-galactosidase in brain and other organs, giving rise to a blocked degradation of gangliosides and accumulation of glucocerebrosides. It is more common among Jews, appears at any age, and is characterized by splenomegaly, wedge-shaped pingueculae (light yellowish-brown discolorations of the conjunctiva on either side of the cornea), pigmentation of the skin; hemorrhages, especially from the nose and mouth; pain in the extremities; and bone lesions (including thinning of the cortex and widening of the bone). Neurologic symptoms are similar to those of cerebromacular degeneration. Mental retardation is prominent when the disease starts in early childhood. Anemia, leukopenia, and thrombocytopenia may occur. Levels of total fats, cholesterol, and lecithin of the blood are usually normal. Typical Gaucher cells containing abnormal amounts of kerasin can often be demonstrated by splenic or bone marrow puncture or biopsy.

Treatment is symptomatic. Removal of the spleen is indicated only because of its excessive size. Patients may live many years, but progressive neurologic involvement leading to death is the rule in the infantile form.

Niemann-Pick Disease.

Niemann-Pick disease occurs mainly in Jewish infants. It is due to a sphingomyelinase deficiency, with accumulation of sphingomyelin in the brain and other organs and is characterized by hepatosplenomegaly, lymphadenopathy, abdominal distention, weight loss, and mental retardation. Infants appear normal at birth and for the first few weeks or months of life. A cherry-red spot is sometimes found in the region of the macula. The symptoms of C. N. S. involvement are similar to those of cerebromacular degeneration. There is moderate anemia and leukopenia or leukocytosis. Foamy Niemann-Pick cells may be found in the bone marrow or spleen and occasionally in the blood. X-rays of the lungs may reveal disseminated nodules which resemble miliary tubercles.

No treatment is effective, and death usually occurs in 2 years although chronic forms of the disease have been reported.

Metachromatic Leukodystrophy.

This is a sulfatide lipidosis due to lack of aryl sulfatase. The accumulated material is found in the white matter of the brain, peripheral nerves, and renal epithelium. Onset is in late infancy, with development of ataxia, spasticity, mental deterioration, and peripheral neuropathy. Diagnosis based on decreased enzyme levels in urine and on nerve biopsy. No treatment is known. Death occurs within two or three years of onset.

HEPATOLENTICULAR DEGENERATION
(Wilson's Disease)

Wilson's disease is a recessively inherited disorder which results from a defect in copper-containing enzymes in the respiratory chain, resulting in an abnormal accumulation of copper within the body.

Onset is in late childhood, with symptoms of cirrhosis of the liver, including hepatomegaly and jaundice. Neurologic signs, including dysarthria, tremors, emotional lability, and eventually extensive muscular rigidity, may be intermittent in early stages and then persist. Pericorneal pigmentation with a narrow, gray-green zone overlying the outer margin of the iris (Kayser-Fleischer ring) is a diagnostic finding.

Treatment is with penicillamine (Cuprimine®) given orally until urinary copper levels reach normal.

The prognosis is poor, with death usually occurring in three to five years.

SPINOCEREBELLAR DEGENERATIVE DISEASE
(Hereditary Ataxias)

This is a group of related diseases characterized by degeneration of various parts of the C. N. S., including the ascending and descending tracts of the spinal cord, the cerebellum, and the optic nerves. Several clinical entities are recognized.

Friedreich's Ataxia.

This is the most common type. Friedreich's ataxia is a familial hereditary disease with onset in childhood between five and 15 years of age. Early symptoms affect the lower limbs, with ataxic gait. Nystagmus is usually present. Speech is jerky, explosive, and indistinct. The disease progresses to the upper limbs and spinal muscles, and death occurs in ten to 15 years.

Hereditary Spastic Paraplegia.

This disorder often affects several siblings. It is characterized by weak spastic lower extremities and a stiff gait. Contracture eventually confines the patient to bed. Death occurs after many years.

CEREBRAL PALSY

Cerebral palsy is a term applied to the neuromotor components resulting from various types of brain damage and is characterized by paralysis, weakness, incoordination, or ataxia. Convulsions, mental retardation, visual defects, hearing defects, and emotional disturbances may also be present. Cerebral palsy is the largest cause of crippling disease in children in the U. S. A. Of those affected, about one-third are mentally retarded, one-third are capable of considerable improvement, and one-sixth are so mildly affected that treatment is not necessary. One-sixth are so severely affected as to be bedridden.

Etiology.
A. Prenatal Factors: These include radiation to the mother, intrauterine hypoxia or bleeding, Rh or ABO incompatibility, maternal rubella infection, toxoplasmosis, or cytomegalic inclusion disease.
B. Natal Factors: Hypoxia due to anesthetic or to analgesic drugs, cerebral trauma during delivery, or hyperbilirubinemia due to blood incompatibility.
C. Postnatal Factors: Brain contusion or hemorrhage, infection, and poisoning.

Clinical Symptoms.
The symptoms are related to the area of the brain affected.
A. Spastic Type With Pyramidal Tract Involvement: Hyperactive stretch reflex.
B. Extrapyramidal Involvement and Basal Ganglia: Involuntary, incoordinated, and uncoordinated movement of muscle groups.
C. Dystonias: Rigid postural attitude, with resistance to passive motion.
D. Ataxias: Involvement of cerebellum and loss of balance.
E. Dystonia Musculorum Deformans: This genetic disease is transmitted as a dominant trait with a very slow course or as an autosomal recessive trait in Jewish children with a very rapid course after onset in childhood. The disease begins in the form of hypertonia of leg muscles and spreads progres-

sively to the trunk, the back, and, eventually, the arms.
Spasticity and involuntary movement are accentuated by emotional and physical activity. Characteristically, spasticity and
involuntary movement disappears in sleep; if relaxation is
maintained, strength, coordination, and reflexes are normal.

Topographical classification of cerebral palsy includes mono-
plegia, paraplegia, hemiplegia, triplegia, quadriplegia, and diplegia.

Treatment.
Treatment in all types of cerebral palsy is difficult and must be
planned individually over a period of years. Physical therapy to
establish automatic motion and eliminate unwanted motions is most
important. Speech training requires much time and the use of
special skills on the part of the trainer. Diazepam (Valium®), two
to four times a day, may reduce uncontrollable motions.
Orthopedic surgery offers much improvement and the hope of a
more normal life in many cases. Bracing, splinting, and recon-
structive procedures (e. g. , muscle and tendon transfers, joint
arthrodesis, and denervations) are all potentially applicable.

TRAUMATIC DISORDERS OF
THE NERVOUS SYSTEM*

SUBARACHNOID HEMORRHAGE

Bleeding into the spinal fluid of the subarachnoid space from
blood vessels on the surface of the brain may be the result of
trauma or may be due to spontaneous rupture of an aneurysm or
arteriovenous malformation. Bleeding can also occur with blood
dyscrasias, leukemia, or hypertension.

Clinical Findings.
A. Symptoms and Signs: Onset may be sudden or gradual up to 48
   hours after trauma. Headache and nausea and vomiting appear
   first, followed by increasing lethargy or periods of delirium
   and finally coma. Signs of meningeal irritation (see p. 505)
   are present; fever up to 101° F. (38.3°C.) may be present.
   Onset sudden with rupture of congenital aneurysm or with
   hypertensive hemorrhage.
      There may be no symptoms in cases where bleeding is
   slight and occurs for only a short period of time.
B. Laboratory Findings: Spinal fluid shows blood which does not
   diminish in concentration with continued flow of fluid. Samples
   of C. S. F. taken at five-minute intervals will show no change in
   the red cell count or in the gross color. Xanthochromia will
   be noted on centrifugation. Microscopic examination early
   shows crenated red cells and few white cells.

---

*Battered child syndrome is discussed in Chapter 20.

Treatment.

The underlying hemorrhagic disease should be treated if present. Measures to combat cerebral edema are most important: restrict fluids, elevate the head, and give corticosteroids, Urevert®, or mannitol. Further lumbar puncture is contraindicated unless infection or renewed bleeding is suspected.

Surgical correction of blood vessel abnormalities may be possible following demonstration by angiography.

Prognosis.

If hemorrhage is not massive and is self-limited, prognosis is excellent. With massive hemorrhage, large areas of the brain may be permanently damaged, with resultant sequelae such as cerebral palsy or convulsive disorders.

SUBDURAL HEMATOMA

Unilateral or bilateral collection of blood between the dura and the piarachnoid, resulting from physical trauma at any age, including the newborn period (birth trauma). In infancy, especially if the history is inconsistent, consider the battered child syndrome (see Chapter 20).

Clinical Findings.

Subdural hematoma is suggested by abnormal enlargement of the head in association with any of the symptoms listed below.

In older children, a history of trauma to the head may be elicited, preceding onset of symptoms by two to four weeks.

A. Symptoms and Signs: Insidious onset of signs and symptoms apparently unrelated to the C.N.S. makes the diagnosis difficult.

1. In infancy, early symptoms may be regarded as a "feeding problem," with irritability, anorexia, vomiting, and failure to gain weight. Head size increases, and the anterior fontanel may bulge and pulsate. Retarded motor development, retinal hemorrhages, and hyperactive reflexes are also found.

2. In older children, symptoms of increasing intracranial pressure such as lethargy, anorexia, headache, and vomiting slowly become apparent.

3. Convulsions and coma may occur early in infants but later in older children.

B. Special Diagnostic Procedures: Diagnosis is established by bilateral subdural tap. In infants this procedure may be done in the treatment room, with surgical precautions. In older children, it is necessary to make burr holes through the skull before a needle is introduced. The electroencephalogram is frequently abnormal. Carotid angiography shows a filling defect.

Treatment.

Treatment usually consists of subdural taps, with removal of 10 to 20 ml. of fluid daily until the quantity and the protein content of the withdrawn fluid remain constant over a period of three or four days. With bilateral hematomas, tap one side every other day. Remnants of the clot and the surrounding membrane often require surgical removal. Hemoglobin and total protein should be determined frequently.

If the quantity of fluid obtainable decreases steadily, surgical removal may not be necessary.

Prognosis.

Generally excellent with the above treatment, although mental retardation, convulsions, ocular abnormalities, or paralysis may become apparent, depending upon the damage to the underlying brain suffered with the initial insult.

EXTRADURAL HEMATOMA

Bleeding from dural or emissary veins or from middle meningeal vessels, usually a complication of a closed head injury.

Clinical Findings.
A. Symptoms and Signs: There may be local evidence of head trauma and a history of momentary unconsciousness, followed by a lucid interval of 30 minutes to several hours, and then increasing drowsiness. Hemiparesis, unequal pupils, hyperactive deep tendon reflexes, and positive Babinski signs may be found. Weak, rapid pulse, low blood pressure, and respiratory irregularity are ominous signs. Drowsiness may rapidly progress to stupor, coma, and convulsions.
B. Laboratory Findings: Lumbar puncture is not necessary since the findings will not change the management of the case. Cerebral angiography will establish the diagnosis.

Treatment.
Surgical intervention may be an emergency procedure but should not be done until I.V. infusion has been started and blood for transfusion is available.

TOXIC DISORDERS OF
THE NERVOUS SYSTEM

LEAD POISONING
(Lead Encephalopathy)

Lead poisoning in children - especially those under five years of age - produces an encephalopathy. The onset is insidious. Early manifestations include weakness, irritability, loss of weight, and vomiting, which may eventually become projectile. Personality changes and developmental regression with generalized convulsions and coma are late signs of increased intracranial pressure.

Symptoms may be precipitated by infection or acidosis. A history of pica involving flaking paint in older homes, lead toys, yellow and orange crayons, artists' paints, leaded gasoline, or fruit tree sprays can often be obtained.

Blood and urine tests show increased lead concentration.

C. S. F. indicates an elevated white blood cell count, usually < 100 cells/cu. mm. Lumbar puncture should be performed with extreme caution because of the increased pressure.

X-ray may demonstrate increased density in the metaphyses of the long bones, and lead may be seen in the gastrointestinal tract.

Treatment.

A. Specific Measures:

1. Combined therapy with calcium disodium edetate (EDTA, Calcium Disodium Versenate®) plus dimercaprol (BAL) is effective. First inject BAL, 4 mg./Kg. I. M. (available as BAL in oil for I. M. use only); beginning 4 hours later and every 4 hours thereafter for five to seven days, inject same dose of BAL plus EDTA, 12.5 mg./Kg. I. M. (with a final concentration of procaine of 0.5%) at separate sites. Start chelation therapy after urine flow is initiated.

   If blood lead concentration exceeds 100 μg./100 ml. whole blood on the 14th or 25th day, give a second five-day course of BAL-EDTA.

   Do not administer medicinal iron while BAL is being given.

2. For initial control of seizures, diazepam (Valium®) in frequent doses is preferred whenever there is significant increase in muscle tone or muscle twitching. Phenobarbital or diphenylhydantoin sodium may be necessary.

3. Avoid overhydration during therapy. Renal toxicity due to edathamil treatment is indicated by increasing hematuria and proteinuria. Daily urinalyses should be performed and the dosage of edetate reduced if signs of toxicity appear.

4. Surgical decompression, hypothermia, urea, or mannitol (see p. 385) may be necessary in severe cases with markedly increased intracranial pressure.

5. Oral penicillamine may be of value in asymptomatic children with chronic lead poisoning.

B. General Measures: **Prevent reexposure to lead** and give anticonvulsants (see Table 21-4). High-calcium, high-phosphorus diet (milk) and large doses of vitamin D assist in removing lead from the blood by depositing it in the bones.

Prognosis.

The prognosis is poor in the child under two years of age; the mortality rate in this age group is 25%. In the older child - and in cases of peripheral neuritis without encephalopathy - the prognosis for recovery is excellent.

BENIGN INTRACRANIAL HYPERTENSION
(Pseudotumor Cerebri, Otitic Hydrocephalus)

Benign intracranial hypertension is a clinical syndrome of elevated intracranial pressure, otherwise normal C. S. F. findings, and a midline ventricular system of normal or small size. Clinical findings include sudden onset of headache, vomiting, papilledema, and sixth nerve paresis, together with ataxia, drowsiness, or stupor. Convulsions and focal neurologic abnormalities are uncommon. The EEG may be abnormal. Treatment with serial spinal punctures, corticosteroids, fluid restriction, hypertonic solutions, and the administration of diuretics have all been used. Surgical decompression may occasionally be necessary. An increased incidence in obese prepubertal females has been described. The prognosis is excellent, although long-standing emotional disturbances may develop.

The condition may occur one to two weeks after various infections, particularly of the middle ear; withdrawal of corticosteroid therapy; or trauma to the jugular vein. In some cases, no apparent cause can be discovered.

Similar clinical findings may occur with hypoparathyroidism, Addison's disease, vitamin A overdosage, and the administration of tetracycline.

ACRODYNIA
(Pink Disease)

Acrodynia (rare in the U.S.A.) is a disease of early childhood characterized by marked irritability, restlessness, or apathy; symmetric swelling and marked erythema of the hands, feet, and the tip of the nose; pain and desquamation of the hands and feet which may go on to loss of nails and portions of the digits; photophobia, inflammation in the mouth, excessive perspiration, hypertension, and profuse salivation. The child has marked hypotonia, often assumes a "penknife" position, and squirms constantly in an attempt to allay the intensive itching. Chronic mercurial poisoning is the cause of many if not all cases, and treatment with dimercaprol (BAL) is indicated. Liver, dried yeast, and ultraviolet irradiation have also been recommended.

CHOREA
(Sydenham's Chorea, St. Vitus' Dance)

Chorea is an encephalopathy characterized by quick, twitching, involuntary, incoordinate movements of the face, trunk, and extremities. More common in girls than boys, and in the age group from six to ten years. Often associated with rheumatic fever. Tests for precise muscle control, such as finger-to-nose or buttoning clothes, will demonstrate involuntary actions in mild cases. Gait and speech may be markedly impaired. Muscle strength is diminished. Emotional instability, confusion, irritability, and insomnia are common.

Treatment includes bed rest, sedation with chlorpromazine or phenobarbital, and penicillin prophylaxis as for rheumatic fever.

The prognosis is good for eventual recovery. Recurrent episodes are not uncommon. Associated rheumatic fever or rheumatic heart disease may complicate the situation.

ENCEPHALITIS IN CHILDREN

Infectious encephalitis results from direct invasion of brain tissue by an infectious agent (see Table 21-1). Evidence of a chronic viral encephalitis has been demonstrated in Western equine

TABLE 21-1. Infectious encephalitis in the U. S. A.	TABLE 21-2. Para-infectious encephalitis.
Arthropod-borne	Antigen-antibody type
Western equine encephalitis	Accompanying or following:
St. Louis encephalitis	Rubeola
Eastern equine encephalitis	Varicella
Enterovirus	Rubella
Echovirus	Infectious mononucleosis
Coxsackievirus	Herpes zoster (?)
Poliovirus	Roseola infantum (?)
Myxovirus	Following:
Mumps	Vaccinia inoculation
Miscellaneous viruses	Pertussis vaccine
Herpes simplex	Rabies vaccine
Lymphocytic choriomeningitis	Yellow fever vaccine
Rabies	Toxic type
Other agents	Influenza
Torulosis (cryptococcosis)	Shigellosis
Toxoplasmosis	Salmonellosis
Mycoplasma pneumoniae (?)	Scarlet fever
(Eaton agent, primary atypical pneumonia)	

encephalitis and in Japanese B encephalitis. Chronic, continuing viral activity might be extremely important in explaining some of the serious and slowly developing sequelae of infectious encephalitis in children.

Para-infectious encephalitis, as the name implies, is associated with an infection but is not due to direct invasion of the nervous system by the infecting agent. These cases are of two basic types: (1) those probably due to an antigen-antibody reaction associated with a systemic infection, and (2) those due to the direct effect of a toxin which is the by-product of bacterial or viral proliferation in a systemic infection (see Table 21-2). Postvaccinal encephalitis is included in this category because it is clearly related to an infectious agent and because the pathologic process is similar to encephalopathy that follows or accompanies an acute infection such as rubeola or varicella. The encephalopathy that follows inoculation of killed pertussis vaccine is unique in that the pathologic process is entirely similar to that associated with a systemic infection.

Clinical Findings.
A. Symptoms and Signs: The essential clinical feature of encephalitis is impairment of brain function, affecting the state of consciousness and the activity of the cerebral cortex. Hence the symptoms are usually those of lethargy, coma, and convulsions. The earliest signs are headache, nausea, and vomiting, and are related to the cerebral edema accompanying the inflammatory process. In very early childhood, headache may be manifested by irritability. Anorexia, nausea, and vomiting may be the first symptoms noted by the mother. An inflammatory reaction of the meninges produces the classic stiffness of neck and back together with varying degrees of impairment of straight leg raising. Severe encephalitis can produce a confusing array of neurologic phenomena. Cerebral edema alters

TABLE 21-3. Laboratory and clinical clues
to causes of encephalitis.

	CSF		Routine Clinical or Laboratory Findings Suggest Cause
	Usual WBC per ml.	Glucose	
Infectious			
Arthropod-borne*			
Western equine St. Louis Eastern equine	<200	Normal	No
Enteroviruses			
Coxsackievirus	<400		Yes (pleurodynia and herpangina syndromes)
		Normal	
Echovirus†	200-1000		Yes (morbilliform rash)
Poliovirus	<200		Yes (asymmetric, flaccid paralysis)
Mumps*	200-3000	Normal	Yes (CSF)
Lymphocytic choriomeningitis*	200-3000	Normal	Yes (CSF)
Herpes simplex*	<200	Normal	Yes (eruption)
Rabies*	<100	Normal	
Other agents:			
Toxoplasmosis*	50-200	Normal	Yes (?)
Cat-scratch disease	100-200	Normal	Yes (lymphadenopathy)
Torulosis*	10-150	Decr.	Yes (CSF)
Para-infectious			
Antigen-antibody†			
Rubeola, rubella, varicella, infectious mononucleosis, herpes zoster, roseola infantum, vaccinia, pertussis vaccine, rabies vaccine, yellow fever vaccine	<150	Normal	Yes (primary disease symptoms, history, and routine blood count)
Toxic*			
Shigellosis, salmonellosis, scarlet fever	<50	Normal	Yes (clinical and culture)

*Serologic tests and culture technics often available.
†Serologic tests and culture technics available only under special conditions.

brain function in various areas at random. A wide variety of signs may be elicited such as the Babinski, loss of deep tendon reflexes, tremors of the extremities, and even sensory changes. Findings may vary from hour to hour as small changes occur in the degree of cerebral edema.

B. Laboratory Findings: See Table 21-3.

Treatment.
A. Specific Measures: None known.
B. General Measures:
   1. Give initial treatment as for bacterial meningitis of unknown type, until viral etiology is clear (see p. 506).
   2. Increased intracranial pressure may be relieved as a temporary measure for periods up to four hours by hypertonic intravenous infusions of urea or mannitol. Give 0.5 to 1.5 Gm. urea/Kg. in a 30% solution in water by intravenous drip over 20 to 25 minutes. Mannitol, which may have a more prolonged effect, is given in a dosage of 1.5 to 2 Gm./Kg. as a 20% solution in water intravenously over 10 to 15 minutes. Use these agents cautiously in case of impaired urinary flow due to marked dehydration or electrolyte imbalance.
   3. Convulsions should be controlled with phenobarbital (see Table 21-4) or diphenylhydantoin, 10 mg./Kg. body weight I.V. at a rate not to exceed 50 mg./minute. The maintenance dose of diphenylhydantoin is 7-8 mg./Kg./day.
   4. Maintenance of airway is the most important consideration and may require tracheostomy if the usual technics are not effective.
   5. General hygiene includes care to avoid bedsores and to keep the skin well cleansed. The patient should be isolated to prevent other infections.

Prognosis.
The prognosis following encephalitis should always be guarded. The severity of the damage apparent in convalescents is not a guide to long-term prognosis. Subtle impairment of C. N. S. function can become increasingly apparent with increasing age. In contrast, children with apparently serious damage have occasionally shown remarkable improvement with the passage of time.

REYE'S SYNDROME

This is a rare fulminant encephalopathy of unknown cause which may be associated with influenza or varicella viruses. The onset is abrupt, with rapidly deepening coma. The C. S. F. may occasionally show a pleocytosis of less than 30 white cells. Hepatic involvement is characteristic, with elevated serum transaminase and fatty degeneration of the liver demonstrable on biopsy or autopsy. Cerebral edema is severe. Hypoglycemia occurs.

Treat as for other types of encephalitis (see above) and for hepatic failure. Peritoneal dialysis and exchange transfusion have been recommended, but their value is not proved. Hypoglycemia should be corrected.

The prognosis is poor. Mortality rates in reported series are over 75%.

CONVULSIVE DISORDERS
(See also Fig 30-2.)

Convulsive seizures are relatively common in children. They may be of unknown cause, genetic, or related to the following: (1) C.N.S. and other infections (meningitis, encephalitis, brain abscess, tetanus), (2) fever, (3) trauma to and vascular accidents in the brain, (4) tumors of the C.N.S., (5) disturbances in physiology of the brain (hypoxia, hypoglycemia, water intoxication, changes in CO_2 tension, hypocalcemia), (6) drugs and poisonings (Metrazol®, lead, strychnine), (7) defective development and vascular anomalies of the brain, (8) hypertensive encephalopathy, (9) progressive degenerative diseases (Tay-Sachs disease, Niemann-Pick disease, Gaucher's disease, tuberous sclerosis, Schilder's disease, and others), and (10) pyridoxine deficiency and dependency.

EPILEPSY
(Idiopathic Convulsive State)
(Paroxysmal Cerebral Dysrhythmia)

Epilepsy refers to recurrent or paroxysmal seizures of cerebral origin which usually involve involuntary movements of muscles and impairment of consciousness, memory, or vegetative function, either singly or in various combinations.

Clinical Findings. (See also Fig 30-2.)
A family history can often be elicited. Attack may be precipitated by overhydration, vasomotor reactions, illness, fatigue, emotional tension, hyperventilation, or autonomic disturbances.
A. Types of Seizures and Manifestations:
1. Generalized convulsion (grand mal) (most common) - Generalized tonic-clonic convulsions are frequently preceded by a motor or sensory aura, staring or deviation of the eyes, loss of consciousness, and a short tonic convulsion. The child may salivate, bite the tongue, and have urinary or fecal incontinence. Seizure is followed by headache, confusion, or deep sleep.
2. Typical petit mal seizure - Staring and loss of consciousness for a few seconds. There may be slight rhythmic motor disturbances (head nodding, eye blinking). Child may be unaware of the attacks, and there is no aura or drowsiness.
3. Akinetic seizures - Sudden, brief loss of consciousness and muscle tone. There are no tonic or clonic movements. Post-convulsion somnolence may occur.
4. Myoclonic seizures - Brief involuntary contractions of limbs or groups of muscles, sometimes localized to one side of the body. These may result in falling or injury, but there may or may not be loss of consciousness.
5. Psychomotor seizures ("epileptic equivalent," "psychic variant") - Brief period of increased muscular tonicity preceded by an aura and visceral symptoms (nausea, vomiting, epigastric sensation) and followed by movements of the mouth and integrated but confused, semi-purposeful move-

ments during a period of impaired awareness or amnesia.
A history of birth trauma and C.N.S. infection is frequently
present. Seizures may be predominantly subjective or may
progress to a generalized convulsion. Personality disturbances, especially an overactive, aggressive type, may be
present between seizures.

6. Jacksonian seizures (focal seizures) - Motor or sensory
disturbance which begins locally in one part of the body and
spreads or extends according to a fixed pattern. This may
eventually involve the entire body and be indistinguishable
from a grand mal seizure.

B. Electroencephalogram: Although abnormal patterns may be
found in apparently normal individuals, and although individuals with idiopathic convulsive state may have a normal
pattern, there is usually a characteristically abnormal tracing.
With the exception of petit mal, there are no specific abnormalities characteristic of a specific clinical syndrome. Hyperventilation tends to bring out and accentuate the abnormality.

C. Other Studies: Spinal tap should be done after the first seizure
or in the presence of fever to rule out infection. A subdural
tap should be done if there is a history of trauma and evidence
of increased intracranial pressure. The pattern of seizures
may indicate a relationship to hypoglycemia (fasting blood
glucose is low). Pneumoencephalography and arteriography
are indicated if persistent localizing signs are found on neurologic examination. Radioisotope brain scan may be of value.

Treatment.

The goal of treatment is the prevention of seizures; if seizures
can be prevented for a long enough time, they may not recur. Prolonged use of sedative drugs does not cause mental retardation.

A. Management of Individual Seizures: Except in status epilepticus,
give no treatment except to protect the patient from injury.

B. Drugs: (See Table 21-4.) The type of convulsion determines
to some extent the drug used, but the response of the patient is
the most important criterion.

C. Management of Status Epilepticus:
1. Diazepam (Valium®), 0.2 mg./Kg. I.V. and repeated in 10 to
20 minutes as necessary, is the treatment of choice.
2. Paraldehyde, 4% I.V., may be of value.
3. After emergency is controlled, start diphenylhydantoin
(Dilantin®) I.M. every three hours or phenobarbital I.M.
every six to eight hours.

D. General Measures: The family and the child must be impressed
with the necessity for faithful adherence to the treatment regimen. The patient should avoid excessive fatigue and keep in
optimum physical condition. Acetazolamide (Diamox®) may be
useful in addition to other anticonvulsant drugs, especially in
petit mal. The suggested daily dose is 8 to 30 mg./Kg. orally
in divided doses to a maximum of 1 Gm./day.

Prognosis.

Although death may occur during status epilepticus or as a
result of accidents, the outlook for life is generally good. The
majority of patients can be controlled with drug therapy. Frequent

TABLE 21-4. Anticonvulsant drugs for children.*

Drug	Age (yrs.)	Starting Dose†	Maximum Dose (t.i.d.)	Indications and Precautions	Toxic Reactions
Phenobarbital	< 3 3-6 > 6	15 mg. 30 mg. b.i.d. 30 mg.	30 mg. 65 mg. 0.1 Gm.	One of the safest drugs for all epilepsies, especially as adjunct. Drug of choice for initial trial.	Toxic reactions are rare. Drowsiness, increased excitability, dermatitis may occur.
Mephobarbital (Mebaral®)	< 3 3-6 > 6	30 mg. 65 mg. 65 mg.	65 mg. 0.12 Gm. 0.2 Gm.	Phenobarbital derivative. No advantage over phenobarbital.	As phenobarbital.
Diphenyl-hydantoin sodium (Dilantin®)	< 6 6-12 > 12	30 mg. 0.1 Gm. b.i.d. 0.1 Gm.	0.1 Gm. 0.2 Gm. 0.4 Gm.	Good drug for management of grand mal and many cases of psychomotor epilepsy. May accentuate petit mal. Often used with phenobarbital.	Few reactions: Gum hypertrophy, nervousness, ataxia, rash, nystagmus, nausea and vomiting.
Primidone (Mysoline®)	< 6 > 6	125 mg. b.i.d. 250 mg.	125 mg.	Second choice for grand mal and complicated major seizures. Useful in psychomotor seizures.	Urticaria, diarrhea, nausea and vomiting.
Ethosuximide (Zarontin®)	< 6 > 6	250 mg. once a day 250 mg. once a day	250 mg. 500 mg.	First choice for true petit mal. Dosage must be individualized by working up until seizures are controlled.	Leukopenia, nausea, vomiting, headache, drowsiness, liver dysfunction.

*Modified from Livingston and other sources.
†t.i.d., except as noted.

major seizures may result in eventual mental deterioration, but with control, in spite of long-continued drug administration, the mental status remains unchanged. Therapy may need to be continued for several years until long-continued freedom from attacks and eventual disappearance of the abnormal EEG pattern suggest that drugs may be gradually discontinued.

BREATH-HOLDING SPELLS
(Infantile Syncope)

Breath-holding spells may occur in some children when they are frightened, hurt, or angered; they cry vigorously for a short time and then "hold their breath." After a few seconds they may become slightly cyanotic or pallid, lose consciousness, and become limp. This may be followed by a few jerks of the limbs, a short period of increased tonus, or even opisthotonos. Micturition occasionally occurs. There is no postictal confusion. The spells occur most commonly between the ages of six months and two years and usually stop by the age of five years. In contrast to an epileptic seizure, cyanosis precedes the seizure rather than follows it. The EEG is normal.

Treatment with drugs is not indicated.

• • •

MENTAL RETARDATION

Etiology. (See Table 21-5.)
  A. Natal:
    1. Maternal infections - Maternal infections affecting the fetus or newborn include acute bacterial infections, tuberculosis, specific viral infections (rubella, influenza, poliomyelitis, herpes simplex, chickenpox, mumps, measles, vaccinia, cytomegalic inclusion virus), nonspecific viral infections, as well as those due to spirochetes and protozoa (e.g., toxoplasmosis).
    2. Iso-immunization (Rh, ABO).
    3. Down's syndrome (mongolism).
    4. Hypoxia - Maternal, placental, or due to respiratory obstruction.
    5. Breech delivery with delay in delivery of the head.
    6. Cerebral hemorrhage - Traumatic (obstetric), cephalopelvic disproportion, precipitate delivery, prematurity.
  B. Postnatal:
    1. C.N.S. infection.
    2. Brain trauma.
    3. Cerebral degenerative disease (Tay-Sachs).
    4. Hypoxia - Recurrent convulsions or hypoglycemia.
    5. Toxic encephalopathy - Lead poisoning.
  C. Unknown Etiology: Cretinism, primary amentia.

Classification.
  The classical terms moron (I.Q. 51-75), imbecile (I.Q. 21-50), and idiot (I.Q. 0-20) have been abandoned in favor of a less pejorative terminology. A child with an I.Q. of 70-85 is now classified

TABLE 21-5. Biochemical disorders often associated with C.N.S. symptoms and mental retardation (MR).*

Syndrome	Amino Acids Increased in Plasma	Amino Acids or Organic Acids Incr. in Urine	Biochemistry	Clinical Features and Treatment
Sulfur-Containing Amino Acids				
Cystathioninuria		Cystathionine	Cystathionine cleavage enzyme deficiency	Congenital malformation, talipes, deafness, abnormal ears and sensation. One case with high phenylalanine, one with thrombocytopenia and renal calculi. Treat with large doses of pyridoxine.
Homocystinuria	Methionine	Homocystine	Cystathionine synthetase deficiency	MR, spastic paraplegia, occasional convulsions, cataracts, lenticular dislocation, friable hair, malar flush, thromboembolic disease, bone changes. Treat with low-methionine, cystine-supplemented diet or with large doses of pyridoxine.
Methionine malabsorption syndrome		α-Hydroxybutyric acid in excess in urine and feces	Methionine, leucine, isoleucine, and valine are rejected by bowel wall.	Convulsions, episodic diarrhea, hyperventilation, MR, and odor as in oasthouse syndrome.
Urea Synthesis Cycle				
Argininosuccinic-aciduria		Argininosuccinic acid, citrulline	Argininosuccinate lyase deficiency	MR, ataxia, convulsions, friable hair, rough skin, coma due to ammonia intoxication. Treat with low-protein diet.
Ornithine transcarbamoylase deficiency		Generalized aminoaciduria	Ornithine carbamoyltransferase deficiency	Episodes of vomiting, restlessness, ataxia, and coma in early life from ammonia intoxication. Treat with low-protein diet.
Congenital lysine intolerance	Lysine	Lysine, ornithine, arginine, cystine, GABA, ethanolamine	Not known exactly, but excess lysine inhibits arginase.	Vomiting, convulsions, MR. Responds to low-protein intake.
Citrullinuria	Citrulline, methionine	Citrulline, alanine, aspartic acid, glycine, glutamic acid, histidine	Argininosuccinate synthetase deficiency	MR, episodes of severe vomiting and coma due to ammonia intoxication. Treat with low-protein diet.

				Possible deficiency	Clinical features
Tryptophan Metabolism					
Congenital tryptophanuria	Tryptophan after oral load		Tryptophan	Possible tryptophan oxygenase deficiency	MR, photosensitivity, rough hyperpigmented skin, telangiectasia of conjunctivas. Treat with nicotinic acid.
Hartnup disease			All neutral amino acids	Tryptophan rejection by bowel and renal tubular epithelium	MR in some, pellagra-like skin rash, ataxia, and other cerebellar signs. Treat with nicotinic acid and low-protein diet.
Proline Metabolism					
Hyperprolinemia Type A	Proline		Proline, hydroxyproline, glycine	Proline oxidase deficiency	Familial nephritis, deafness, renal hypoplasia, epilepsy, abnormal EEG.
Type B	Proline		Proline, hydroxyproline, glycine	Δ^1-Pyrroline-5-carboxylic acid dehydrogenase	Convulsions, coma, MR.
Hydroxyprolinemia	Hydroxyproline		Hydroxyproline, 1-methylhistidine	Hydroxyproline oxidase deficiency	MR, moderate hematuria and pyuria.
Histidine Metabolism					
Histidinemia	Histidine		Histidine, alanine, and threonine	Histidase deficiency	Slurred, inarticulate speech, variable incidence of MR.
Formiminoglutamic-aciduria Type A	Normal		FIGLU after histidine load	Formiminotransferase deficiency	Somatic and intellectual retardation, round face, obesity, hypersegmentation of PMN's.
Type B	Normal		FIGLU before and after histidine load	Folic acid transport defect (?)	Ataxia, megaloblastic anemia, MR, convulsions.
Phenylalanine Metabolism					
Phenylketonuria		Phenylalanine	Phenylalanine	Phenylalanine hydroxylase deficiency	Usually severe MR, convulsions, eczema, fair hair and complexion. Urine smells musty. Treat with low-phenylalanine diet.
Tyrosinosis (several clinical types)	Tyrosine, methionine		Normal for age	Transient p-hydroxyphenylpyruvic acid oxidase deficiency	General failure to thrive, convulsions. Temporarily respond to low-phenylalanine diet.

*Modified from D. O'Brien: Rare Inborn Errors of Metabolism in Children with Mental Retardation. U.S. Dept. of Health, Education, and Welfare, Children's Bureau, 2nd ed., 1968.

TABLE 21-5 (cont'd.). Biochemical disorders often associated with C.N.S. symptoms and mental retardation (MR).

Syndrome	Amino Acids Increased in Plasma	Amino Acids Increased in Urine	Biochemistry	Clinical Features and Treatment
Oasthouse syndrome	Not reported	Phenylalanine, methionine, tyrosine*	Not known	Infantile spasms with interim flaccidity and unresponsiveness, sparse hair, MR, general unawareness.
Miscellaneous Hyperglycinemia 1. Ketotic		Glycine	Methylmalonyl-Co A isomerase or propionyl-Co A carboxylase deficiency	Vomiting, acidosis, ketosis, infections, somatic and MR.
2. Nonketotic		Glycine	Defect in conversion of glycine to serine	Seizures, MR.
Hypervalinemia	Valine		Not known	Failure to thrive, hypotonia, unresponsiveness, nystagmus, loss of vision, MR.
Glutamicacidemia	Glutamic acid	Slight generalized increase in total amino nitrogen	Not known	Sparse, coarse, unpigmented hair, MR, failure to thrive, other congenital malformations.
Elevated C.S.F. glutamic acid	Proline, perhaps glutamine, leucine	Slight generalized increase in total amino nitrogen	Not known	Hypertonia, hyperreflexia, failure to thrive, MR.
Sarcosinemia	Sarcosine (methylglycine)		Sarcosine oxidase deficiency	Hypotonia, mental and physical retardation.
Maple syrup urine disease	Leucine, isoleucine, valine, and their keto acids		Defective onward metabolism of branched chain keto acids	Hypoglycemia, acidosis, convulsions; if untreated, death usually occurs in the newborn period. Urine smells like maple syrup. Dietary treatment.
β-Alaninemia	β-Alanine	β-Alanine, BAIB, taurine, GABA	Possible β-alanine-α-ketoglutarate transaminase deficiency	Lethargy, somnolence, hypotonia, hyporeflexia, grand mal seizures.
Isovalericacidemia	Isovaleric acid after protein-rich meal	Isovaleric acid much increased	Isovaleric acid dehydrogenase deficiency	Intellectual and motor retardation. Odor of "sweaty feet" on breath and skin. Leucine load precipitates coma. Dietary treatment.

*Perhaps also leucine, isoleucine, α-hydroxybutyric acid.

as dull normal; one with an I.Q. of 50-69 is considered borderline defective; and one with an I.Q. of below 35 is considered severely mentally defective.

Clinical Findings.

Familiarity with the potential causes of mental retardation should enable the physician to recognize mental deficiency at an early age and to plan with the family for future care and therapy.

In the absence of clinical evidence of disease associated with mental deficiency, mental retardation usually becomes apparent to family and physician in a slow and insidious manner.

A. Developmental: Neuromuscular coordination does not develop consistently at a normal rate (see Figure 3-2).
B. Educational: Failure to profit from experience and instruction.
C. Social: Failure to achieve social standards of maturation at successive age levels. Best noted by comparison with children of similar age and manifested by lack of reliance, unacceptable conduct, and inability to "get along with others."
D. Psychometric and audiologic testing is necessary to clearly establish the diagnosis and avoid tragic misdiagnosis.

Treatment and Prognosis. (See also p. 166.)

Except for severely retarded children (I.Q. below 35), most of the mentally retarded can be taught to take a place in society. Care within the family requires emotional adjustment. Institutional care is indicated when the child has a serious behavior or personality disorder or when there are no community facilities to aid the family in management and education.

Many communities have established special parent groups and special classes for the mentally retarded. Treatment is possible in many types of chemical disorders (see Table 21-5).

DOWN'S SYNDROME
(Mongolism)

Down's syndrome occurs in about one of every 600 live births in all races. It is associated with trisomy of chromosome 21, and is most common among first-born infants of older women. There is mental retardation and a characteristic facies with slanted palpebral fissures, prominent epicanthic folds, and a small brachycephalic head. The hands are broad, with a short, incurved fifth finger and a rudimentary second phalanx. There is a wide space between the first and second toes and increased mobility of the joints. Other findings present in most patients with Down's syndrome include small or absent ear lobes, constantly open mouth, red cheeks, irregular alignment of teeth, high-arched palate, raucous voice, Brushfield spots (circle of silver-gray spots near the periphery of the iris) in young infants, flat nipples, delayed development of frontal sinuses, hypoplasia of the base of the skull, and reduced acetabular angles of the hip joint. Leukemia occurs more frequently in these patients than in the general population. Interatrial septal defect of the primum type is common.

Down's syndrome must be differentiated from congenital cretinism, which it resembles in some ways.

The child with Down's syndrome may be quite adaptable to living at home and can be trained to socially acceptable behavior in the family and community. The average maximum mental age attained is about eight years, and at any chronologic age beyond this point the patient should be treated as an eight-year-old child.

MINIMAL BRAIN DYSFUNCTION

This condition does not produce gross motor or sensory deficits or generalized impairment of intellect. There are, however, demonstrable limited alterations of behavior or intellectual functioning. These alterations may be combinations of impaired perception, conceptualization, language, memory, impulse, or motor function.

Diagnostic Evaluation. *

Diagnostic evaluation should include the following:

A. Medical Evaluation:
  1. Histories -
      a. Medical - Include pre-, peri-, and postnatal information. Details of all childhood illnesses should be obtained, including age of child at time of illness, symptoms, severity, course, and care (such as physician in attendance, hospitalization).
      b. Developmental - Include details of motor, language, adaptive, and personal-social development.
      c. Family and social - This should include information regarding acculturation factors, interpersonal family dynamics, and interpersonal family stresses.
  2. Physical examination -
      a. General - Special attention should be given to possible systemic disease.
      b. Neurologic - Special attention should be given to possible specific disorders of the nervous system and to evaluation of integrated motor acts as opposed to simple reflexes.
  3. Special examinations -
      a. Ophthalmologic - Include visual acuity, fields, and fundus examination.
      b. Otologic - Include audiometric and otoscopic examinations.
  4. Routine laboratory tests -
      a. Serologic.
      b. Urinalysis.
      c. Hematologic.
  5. Special laboratory tests (only when specifically indicated) -
      a. Electroencephalographic - Include wake, sleep, and serial tracings.
      b. Radiologic.
      c. Pneumoencephalographic (rarely indicated).
      d. Angiographic (rarely indicated).
      e. Biochemical - Urine and serum amino acids.
      f. Genetic assessment (chromosome analysis).
B. Behavioral Assessment:
  1. Academic history - Involves child's teachers and principal,

---

*Report of National Institute of Neurological Diseases and Blindness, U.S. Dept. of Health, Education, and Welfare.

with their observations regarding school behavior as well
as academic progress and achievement. The child's school
records, including samples of schoolwork and test results,
should be available to the diagnostic team.

2. Psychologic evaluation - The following items represent the
   core of the psychologic evaluation:
   a. Individual comprehensive assessment of intellectual
      functioning.
   b. Measures of complex visual-motor-perceptual functioning.
   c. Behavioral observations in a variety of settings.
   d. Additional indices of learning and behavior as indicated.
3. Language evaluation - Detailed assessment of speech and
   language behavior. Includes audiometric screening; assessment of articulation, voice quality, and rate; and the ex-
   pressive and receptive aspects of language.
4. Educational evaluation - An educational diagnostician should
   conduct detailed analyses of academic abilities, including
   achievement assessment for details of levels and methods
   of skill acquisition, e.g., reading, number concepts,
   spelling, and writing.

Treatment.
Treatment involves special educational technics and programs.
The following references are useful:
> Cruickshank, W. M., & others: A Teaching Method for Brain
> Injured and Hyperactive Children. Syracuse Univ. Press,
> 1961.

TABLE 21-6. Evaluation of weakness by anatomic area.*

Corticospinal pathways
Hyperactive stretch reflexes. Increased resistance to passive
motion. Abnormal reflexes. Weakness usually greater than
atrophy.

Lower motor neuron
Anterior horn cell
Fasciculation. Hypoactive or absent reflexes. Usually distal
or generalized distribution. Atrophy usually in proportion to
weakness.
Peripheral nerve
Above plus sensory changes.

Myoneural junction (myasthenia gravis)
Extraocular musculature usually involved. Fatigue easily fol-
lowing contraction. Strength increases following rest.
Variable and fluctuating course.

Muscle fiber
Hypoactive or absent reflexes. Atrophy usually in proportion
to weakness. Usually proximal distribution.

Functional
Cogwheel response. Inconsistencies. Hoover sign. Bizarre
gait. Slowness of motion. Overflow of activity.

*Reproduced, with permission, from W. M. Fowler, Jr.: Muscle
weakness and atrophy: Clinical and laboratory evaluation. California
Med. **108**:25-31, 1968.

Birch, H. G. (editor): Brain Damage in Children. Williams & Wilkins, 1964.

Strauss, A., & Lehtinen, L.: Psychopathology and Education of the Brain Injured Child. Grune & Stratton, 1962.

DISEASES OF THE MUSCLES

Disorders of muscle are universally characterized by weakness. This symptom is also characteristic of a number of disorders of the nervous system such as spinal cord disease, motor neuron dysfunction, and peripheral nerve damage. In approaching a possible muscular disease, the neuroanatomic site of dysfunction must be determined first. Table 21-6 outlines this approach.

PROGRESSIVE MUSCULAR DYSTROPHY

Progressive muscular dystrophy is the most common of the X-linked recessive disorders. The onset is between three and six years. The first symptoms are usually in the lower extremities, with difficulty in walking. Trunk muscle weakness produces the classical "Gowers' sign," with the child "climbing up" his lower extremities with his hands. The muscles of the hands and feet are usually not affected, even in advanced cases. There is no sensory disturbance or loss of sphincter control.

The juvenile form has an onset in late childhood in which the proximal muscles of the shoulders and legs are affected first. It may be pseudohypertrophic early and then atrophic.

The facioscapulohumeral type (autosomal dominant) has an onset between seven and 20 years of age. It is first manifested in the facial muscles, producing a flat and mask-like appearance. The muscles of the shoulder girdle are next affected, and the spinal muscles last.

Serum enzymes (SGOT, creatine phosphokinase, lactate dehydrogenase) may be elevated, especially in the progressive type of disease.

Treatment is most unsatisfactory. A high-protein diet with supplementary vitamins should be given. Physical therapy may strengthen and improve the function of unaffected muscles. Death usually occurs within five to ten years.

WERDNIG-HOFFMANN DISEASE
(Infantile Progressive Spinal Muscular Atrophy)

This is a disease of the lower motor neurons with resultant effects upon muscle tissue development. Hypotonicity is usually apparent at birth or in early infancy. The muscles of the lower extremities are affected first and most severely. Deep reflexes are absent, and there is no response to faradic or galvanic stimulation of the affected muscles.

Serum enzymes are normal. Electromyography will show lower motor neuron damage. Biopsy is necessary for diagnosis.

There is no specific treatment, and the disease is usually fatal. In mild forms, braces for the back and neck may be of some help.

MYOTONIA CONGENITA
(Thomsen's Disease)

This is a hereditary disease characterized by an inability to relax the muscles following a forceful contraction.

Clinical Findings.
Onset between three and six years of age may be insidious in mild forms. The disease may progress until puberty and then show variation in severity throughout life.

Sustained contractions may last up to 30 seconds, followed by relaxation. Movements become more normal with repetition. The muscles of the lower extremities are most frequently involved, but any of the voluntary muscles may be affected. The child starts walking first hesitantly and then with a more normal gait. Symptoms are aggravated by cold and emotional stress. Tendon reflexes are normal. There is no atrophy (sometimes hypertrophy).

There is no specific treatment. Physical therapy and muscle training may occasionally be of some help.

Mild cases may be quite compatible with a normal life, but in severe cases the child is bedridden.

MYASTHENIA GRAVIS

Myasthenia gravis is an uncommon disease in childhood which involves striated muscles; there is weakness and rapid fatigue but no atrophy. Transient myasthenia gravis (for about six weeks) often occurs in infants born to women with myasthenia gravis.

Clinical Findings.
Onset may be at any age, but usually not until after puberty. Muscles supplied by the cranial nerves are usually first and most severely affected, with ptosis of eyelids, diplopia, and dysphagia.

A therapeutic test with neostigmine (Prostigmin®), 0.5 to 1 mg. subcut., with atropine sulfate, will cause temporary disappearance of symptoms and signs within minutes.

Treatment.
A. Specific Measures:
1. Neostigmine bromide, 5 to 15 mg. orally in two to four doses daily. Regulate according to response.
2. Neostigmine methylsulfate, 0.5 to 1.5 mg. subcut. two to four times per day if tablets are ineffective.
3. Ephedrine sulfate, given simultaneously with neostigmine preparations, may enhance the effect of the latter.
B. General Measures: Surgical removal or irradiation of the thymus has been reported to produce improvement.

Prognosis.
With treatment, usually good. Despite treatment, death may occur from respiratory failure in progressive disease.

FAMILIAL PERIODIC PARALYSIS

This is a rare autosomal dominant disease which usually appears first in adolescence. It is characterized by recurrent attacks of flaccid paralysis with normal musculature and no apparent weakness between attacks, and is most commonly due to an intermittent increase in the secretion of aldosterone, with retention of sodium and lowering of serum potassium. Tumors of the adrenal glands may be present.

Treatment.
Treatment of acute attack consists of potassium chloride, 5 Gm. by mouth, or 50 ml. of a 2% solution **very slowly** I. V. **This is a dangerous procedure.**

Prophylaxis.
Potassium chloride, 2 to 4 Gm. per day by mouth with meals. Adrenal tumors must be removed.

Prognosis.
Excellent with treatment. Death due to cardiac or respiratory failure may occur during an attack. Paralytic episodes may become less frequent and less severe in adult life.

FAMILIAL DYSAUTONOMIA
(Riley-Day Syndrome)

Familial autonomic dysfunction is a recessive disease of unknown etiology occurring chiefly in Jewish children and characterized in almost all cases by defective lacrimation, skin blotching, excessive perspiration, drooling, emotional instability, motor incoordination, hyporeflexia, and relative indifference to pain. Most children also exhibit hypertension, urinary frequency, breath-holding spells in infancy, frequent pulmonary infections, frequent unexplained fever, cyclic vomiting, mental retardation, short stature, and convulsions. Treatment is symptomatic. Psychotherapy for the patient and his family may be very important. Chlorpromazine may control cyclic vomiting.

TORTICOLLIS
(Wryneck)

Torticollis is malposition of the head due to spasm or shortening of the cervical or sternocleidomastoid muscles. A congenital type noted in the neonatal period may be associated with a bony abnormality of the neck but is usually due to a hematoma in the sternocleidomastoid muscle, especially following a breech delivery.

Acquired torticollis may develop at any age and is secondary to atrophy of the cervical or sternocleidomastoid muscles following nerve injury or poliomyelitis. Stretching of the affected muscle by the mother four to six times daily for several months may be successful. If not, surgery after the age of one year is usually necessary.

22...
Endocrine
& Metabolic Disorders

DISTURBANCES OF GROWTH
AND DEVELOPMENT

Disturbances of growth and development are the most common presenting complaints in the pediatric endocrine clinic. It is estimated that over one million children in the U. S. A. have abnormally short stature and that there are at least ten million children whose growth is potentially abnormal.

Failure to thrive is a term usually reserved for infants who fail to gain weight and is most often due to undernutrition (see p. 402).

Tall stature is a much less frequent presenting complaint than short stature and is usually a matter of concern only to adolescent girls. The recent trend toward acceptance of tall stature in women has decreased the number of young people evaluated and treated for this condition.

SHORT STATURE

Abnormally short stature in relation to age is a common finding in childhood. In most instances it is due to a normal variation from the usual pattern of growth. The possible roles of such factors as sex, race, size of parents and other family members, nutrition, pubertal maturation, and emotional status must all be evaluated in the total assessment of the child.

The causes of unusually short stature are given in Table 22-1. In most instances, the causes can be differentiated on the basis of significant findings in the history and physical examination and by observation of skeletal maturation (bone age).

1. CONSTITUTIONAL SHORT STATURE

Many children have a constitutional delay in growth and skeletal maturation. Puberty is delayed. In all other respects, they appear entirely normal. There is often a history of a similar pattern of growth in one of the parents or other members of the family. Normal puberty eventually occurs, and these children usually reach normal adult height although at a later than average age.

TABLE 22-1. Causes of short stature.

Familial, racial, or genetic

Constitutional with delayed adolescence

Endocrine disturbances
Hypopituitarism
Hyposomatotropinism - isolated or
with other pituitary deficiencies
Hypothyroidism
Adrenal insufficiency
Cushing's disease and syndrome (in-
cluding iatrogenic causes)
Sexual precocity
Diabetes mellitus (poorly controlled)
Diabetes insipidus
Hyperaldosteronism

Primordial short stature
Intrauterine growth retardation
Primordial dwarfism with pre-
mature aging
Progeria (Hutchinson-Gilford
syndrome)
Progeroid syndrome
Werner's syndrome
Cockayne's syndrome
Without associated anomalies
With associated anomalies (e.g.,
Seckel's bird-headed dwarfism, lep-
rechaunism, Silver's syndrome,
Bloom's syndrome, Cornelia
de Lange syndrome, Hallerman-
Streiff syndrome)

Inborn errors of metabolism
Altered metabolism of calcium or
phosphorus (e.g., hypophosphatemic
rickets, hypophosphatasia, infantile
hypercalcemia, pseudohypoparathyroidism)
Storage diseases
Mucopolysaccharidoses (e.g., Hurler's syndrome, Hunter's
syndrome)
Mucolipidoses (e.g., generalized
gangliosidosis, fucosidosis,
mannosidosis)
Sphingolipidoses (e.g., Tay-Sachs
disease, Niemann-Pick disease,
Gaucher's disease)
Miscellaneous (e.g., cystinosis)
Aminoacidemias and aminoacidurias
Epithelial transport disorders (e.g.,
renal tubular acidosis, cystic
fibrosis, Bartter's syndrome, vasopressin resistant diabetes insipidus, pseudohypoparathyroidism)
Organic acidemias and acidurias (e.g.,
methylmalonic aciduria, orotic
aciduria, maple syrup urine disease, isovaleric acidemia)

Metabolic anemias (e.g., sickle
cell disease, thalassemia,
pyruvate kinase deficiency)
Disorders of mineral metabolism
(e.g., Wilson's disease, magnesium malabsorption syn-
drome)
Body defense disorders (e.g.,
Bruton's agammaglobulinemia,
thymic aplasia, chronic granulomatous disease)

**Constitutional (intrinsic) diseases
of bone**
Defects of growth of tubular bones
or spine (e.g., achondroplasia,
metatropic dwarfism, diastro-
phic dwarfism, metaphyseal
chondrodysplasia)
Disorganized development of
cartilage and fibrous components of the skeleton (e.g.,
multiple cartilaginous exostoses, fibrous dysplasia with
skin pigmentation, precocious
puberty of McCune-Albright)
Abnormalities of density of cortical diaphyseal structure or
metaphyseal modeling (e.g.,
osteogenesis imperfecta congenita, osteopetrosis, tubular
stenosis)

**Associated with chromosomal de-
fects**
Autosomal (e.g., Down's syndrome, cri du chat syndrome,
trisomy 18)
Sex chromosomal (e.g., Turner's
syndrome-XO, penta X, XXXY)

**Chronic systemic diseases, congen-
ital defects, and malignancies**
(e.g., chronic infection and infestation, inflammatory bowel
disease, hepatic disease, cardiovascular disease, hematologic disease, C.N.S. disease,
pulmonary disease, renal disease, malnutrition, malignancies, collagen vascular disease)

**Psychosocial dwarfism (maternal
deprivation)**

Miscellaneous syndromes (e.g.,
arthrogryposis multiplex congenita, cerebrohepatorenal syndrome, Noonan's syndrome,
Prader-Willi syndrome, Riley-
Day syndrome)

2. PITUITARY DWARFISM
(Growth Hormone Deficiency)

Growth hormone (GH) deficiency is an uncommon cause of short stature; approximately half of cases are idiopathic (rarely familial); the remainder are secondary to pituitary or hypothalamic disease (craniopharyngioma, infections, tuberculosis, sarcoidosis, toxoplasmosis, syphilis, trauma, reticuloendotheliosis, vascular anomalies, and other tumors such as gliomas). GH deficiency may be an isolated defect or may occur in combination with other pituitary hormone deficiencies. Idiopathic growth hormone deficiency affects both sexes equally. The idiopathic form associated with multiple hormone deficiencies is more common in males.

At birth, affected subjects are of normal weight but length may be reduced. Growth retardation is evident during infancy, and there may be infantile fat distribution, youthful facial features, small hands and feet, and delayed sexual maturation. Excessive wrinkling of the skin is present in older individuals. Dental development and epiphyseal maturation ("bone age") are delayed to a greater degree than height age (median age for patient's height). In cases resulting from C. N. S. disease, headaches, visual field defects, abnormal skull x-rays, and symptoms of posterior pituitary insufficiency (polyuria and polydipsia) may precede or accompany the growth hormone deficiency.

Growth hormone deficiency is associated with low levels of GH in the serum and a failure of GH rise in response to arginine. Low levels occur also in insulin-induced hypoglycemia and during normal psysiologic sleep.

Treatment is with human pituitary growth hormone. Protein anabolic agents (testosterone, fluoxymesterone, oxandrolone, etc.) may be effective in promoting linear growth, but these drugs may cause acceleration of epiphyseal closure with limitation of growth potential and short stature in adult life.

3. HYPOTHYROIDISM
(See also p. 411.)

Hypothyroidism in childhood is invariably associated with poor growth, and osseous maturation is more delayed than height age. In occasional cases, short stature may be the principal finding.

4. PRIMORDIAL SHORT STATURE

Primordial short stature may occur in a number of disorders, including craniofacial disproportion (e. g. , Seckel's bird-headed dwarfism), Silver's syndrome, some cases of progeric and cachectic dwarfism (e. g. , Hutchinson-Gilford dwarfism), or may occur in individuals with no accompanying significant physical abnormalities. Children with these conditions are small at birth; both birth weight and length are below normal for gestational age. They grow parallel to but below the third percentile. Plasma growth hormone levels are usually normal but may be elevated. There is an increased incidence of ketotic hypoglycemia. In most instances, skeletal maturation ("bone age") corresponds to chronologic age or is only mildly retarded, in contrast to the striking delay often present in children with GH and thyroid deficiency.

There is no satisfactory treatment for primordial short stature.

5. SHORT STATURE DUE TO EMOTIONAL FACTORS
(Psychosocial Short Stature; Deprivation Dwarfism)

Psychologic deprivation with disturbances in motor and personality development may be associated with short stature. Growth retardation in some of these subjects is the result of undernutrition; in others, undernutrition does not seem to be a factor. In some instances, in addition to being small, the child may have increased (often voracious) appetite and a marked delay in skeletal maturation. These children are of normal size at birth and grow normally for a variable period of time before growth stops. A history of feeding problems in early infancy is common. Emotional disturbances in the family are the rule. Polydipsia and polyuria are sometimes present.

Placement in a foster home or a significant change in the psychologic and emotional environment at home usually results in significantly improved growth, a decrease of appetite and dietary intake to more normal levels, and personality improvement.

LABORATORY STUDIES IN DIAGNOSIS OF SHORT STATURE

When the cause is not apparent from the history and physical examination, the following laboratory studies, in addition to bone age, are useful in detecting or categorizing the common causes of short stature: (1) Complete blood count; (2) erythrocyte sedimentation rate; (3) urinalysis; (4) stool examination for occult blood, parasites, and parasite ova; (5) serum electrolytes; (6) blood urea nitrogen; (7) buccal smear and karyotyping - these should be performed in all short girls with delayed sexual maturation with or without clinical features of Turner's syndrome; (8) thyroid function tests (PBI and T_4); and (9) growth hormone evaluation.

FAILURE TO THRIVE (FTT)

There are many reasons for failure to thrive, although a specific cause often cannot be established.

Classification and Etiologic Diagnosis.

The diagnosis of failure to thrive is usually apparent on the basis of the history and physical examination. When it is not, it is helpful to compare the patient's chronologic age with the height age (median age for the patient's height), weight age, and head circumference. On the basis of these measurements, three principal patterns can be defined which provide a starting point in the diagnostic approach.

Group 1. (Most common type.) Normal head circumference; weight reduced out of proportion to height: In the majority of cases of failure to thrive, malnutrition is present as a result of either deficient caloric intake or malabsorption.

Group 2. Normal or enlarged head circumference for age; weight only moderately reduced, usually in proportion to height: Structural dystrophies, constitutional dwarfism, endocrinopathies.

Group 3. Subnormal head circumference; weight reduced in proportion to height: Primary C. N. S. deficit; intrauterine growth retardation.

An initial period of observed nutritional rehabilitation, usually in a hospital setting, is often helpful in the diagnosis. The child should be placed on a regular diet for age and his intake and weight carefully plotted for one to two weeks. During this period, the presence of lactose intolerance is determined by checking pH and the presence of reducing substances in the stools. If stools are abnormal, the child should be further observed on a lactose-free diet. Caloric intake should be increased if weight gain does not occur but intake is well tolerated. The following three patterns are often noted during the rehabilitation period. Pattern 1 is by far the most common.

Pattern 1. (Most common type.) Intake adequate; weight gain satisfactory: Feeding technic at fault. Disturbed infant mother relationship leading to decreased caloric intake.

Pattern 2. Intake adequate; no weight gain: If weight gain is unsatisfactory after increasing the calories to an adequate level (based on the infant's ideal weight for his height), malabsorption is a likely diagnosis.

  If malabsorption is present, it is usually necessary to differentiate pancreatic exocrine insufficiency (cystic fibrosis) from abnormalities of intestinal mucosa (celiac disease). In cystic fibrosis, growth velocity commonly declines from the time of birth and appetite usually is voracious. In celiac disease, growth velocity is usually not reduced until six to 12 months of age and inadequate caloric intake may be a prominent feature.

Pattern 3. Intake inadequate: (1) Sucking or swallowing difficulties: C. N. S. or neuromuscular disease; esophageal or oropharyngeal malformations. (2) Inability to eat large amounts is common in patients with cardiopulmonary disease or in anorexic children suffering from chronic infections, inflammatory bowel disease, and endocrine problems (e. g., hypothyroidism). Patients with celiac disease often have inadequate caloric intake in addition to malabsorption. (3) Vomiting, spitting up, or rumination: Upper intestinal obstruction (e. g., pyloric stenosis, hiatus hernia, chalasia), chronic metabolic aberrations and acidosis (e. g., renal insufficiency, diabetes mellitus and insipidus, methylmalonic acidemia), adrenogenital syndrome, increased intracranial pressure, psychosocial abnormalities.

TALL STATURE

Tall stature is usually of concern only to adolescent and pre-adolescent girls. The upper limit of acceptable height of both sexes appears to be increasing, but there are occasions when the patient and her parents desire to influence the pattern of growth. Although there are several conditions (Table 22-2) which may produce tall stature, by far the most common cause is a constitutional variation from normal.

On the basis of family history, previous pattern of growth, stage of physiologic development, assessment of epiphyseal development ("bone age"), and standard growth data, the physician should make a tentative estimate of the patient's eventual height. If the predicted height appears to be excessive, hormonal therapy with conjugated estrogenic substances (e.g., Premarin®), 1.25 to 5 mg. daily orally (continuously or cyclically), may be tried if the physiologic age - as determined by stage of sexual maturity and epiphyseal development - has not reached the 12-year-old level.

TABLE 22-2. Causes of tall stature.

Constitutional (familial, genetic)	Genetic causes
	Klinefelter's syndrome
Endocrine causes	Syndromes of XYY, XXYY
Somatotropin excess (pituitary gigantism)	(tall as adults)
Androgen excess (tall as children, short as adults)	**Miscellaneous syndromes and entities**
True sexual precocity	Marfan's syndrome
Pseudosexual precocity	Cerebral gigantism (Soto's syndrome)
Androgen deficiency (normal height as children, tall as adults)	Total lipodystrophy
Klinefelter's syndrome	Diencephalic syndrome
Anorchidism (infection, trauma, idiopathic)	Homocystinuria
Hyperthyroidism	

DIABETES INSIPIDUS

Diabetes insipidus may result from deficient secretion of vasopressin (ADH), lack of response of the kidney to ADH, or failure of osmoreceptors to respond to elevations of osmolality. Hypofunction of the posterior lobe of the pituitary with deficiency of vasopressin may be idiopathic or may be associated with lesions of the posterior pituitary or hypothalamus (trauma, infections, suprasellar cysts, tumors, xanthomatosis, or some developmental abnormality). Congenital ADH deficiency may be transmitted as an autosomal dominant trait. In nephrogenic diabetes insipidus, a hereditary (dominant) disease affecting both sexes but more severe in males, the renal tubules fail to respond to vasopressin and no lesion of the pituitary or hypothalamus can be demonstrated.

Onset is often sudden with polyuria, intense thirst, constipation, and evidences of dehydration. High fever, circulatory collapse, and secondary brain damage may occur in young infants on an ordinary feeding regimen. Serum osmolality may be elevated (above 305 mOsm./L.), but urine osmolality remains below 280 mOsm./L. (specific gravity approximately 1.010 even after a seven-hour test period of thirsting. Rate of growth, sexual maturation, and general body metabolism may be impaired, and hydroureter and bladder distention may develop.

Diabetes insipidus may be differentiated from psychogenic polydipsia and polyuria by permitting the usual intake of fluid and then withholding water for seven hours or until weight loss (3% or more) demonstrates adequate dehydration. With neurogenic or nephrogenic diabetes insipidus the urine osmolality does not increase above 300 mOsm./L. even after the period of dehydration. Normal children and those with psychogenic polydipsia will respond to the dehydration with a urinary osmolality above 450 mOsm./L. Patients with longstanding psychogenic polydipsia may be unable to concentrate urine initially, and the test may have to be repeated on several successive days. Eventually, dehydration will increase urine osmolality well above plasma osmolality. The vasopressin and hypertonic saline tests may be employed to distinguish between the various forms of diabetes insipidus. The administration of carbamazepine (Tegretol®), clofibrate (Atromid-S®), or nicotine, which are direct stimuli for vasopressin release, or chlorpropamide, which augments the action of ADH, may be of value in picking up cases due to primary osmoreceptor failure.

Replacement therapy with lysine-8 vasopressin nasal spray (lypressin, Diapid®) or Linguets® (preferable), vasopressin tannate (Pitressin Tannate®), or posterior pituitary is of value for cases with a deficiency of vasopressin. Chlorpropamide, 150 to 400 mg./day orally before breakfast, may be effective in controlling symptoms in mild cases; watch for hypoglycemia and treat by reducing dose. The cautious use of the chlorothiazides and ethacrynic acid may be of value in nephrogenic diabetes insipidus. (Check serum electrolytes, uric acid, and blood glucose periodically.) For nephrogenic diabetes insipidus, also administer abundant quantities of water at short intervals and feedings containing limited electrolytes and minimum (but nutritionally adequate) amounts of protein. X-ray and drug therapy is used for some cases of tumor (e.g., reticuloendotheliosis). When no specific cause can be found, the search for an underlying lesion should be continued for many years.

. . .

SEXUAL PRECOCITY

Sexual precocity is either gonadotropin-mediated (i.e., hypothalamopituitary, hepatoma, etc.) and classified as true sexual precocity, or it is nongonadotropin-mediated (e.g., gonadal or adrenal tumor) and classified as pseudosexual precocity. Of the gonadotropin-mediated types, there are three subtypes, the most common occurring without definable cause and termed idiopathic or constitutional. Constitutional precocious puberty is nine times more common in girls than boys, but a positive family history is more common in the latter. The remainder of cases with true sexual precocity are due to C.N.S. lesions, extra-C.N.S. tumors, or drug administration.

A variety of C.N.S. lesions and anomalies may result in sexual precocity, and, unlike the situation in the female, when sexual precocity occurs in a male a C.N.S. lesion is not uncommon. For this reason, extensive evaluation of the C. N. S. is indicated for males presenting with sexual precocity.

Sexual precocity may occur at any age. Breast development is usually the first sign in females, but the pattern of development is variable, and, because of the variable pattern of progression, sexual precocity may be confused with premature thelarche or adren-- arche (see below). Height may be normal initially, but it is often increased; osseous maturation may be even more advanced. Psychologic development tends to correspond to chronologic age. Ovarian luteal cysts of the ovaries may be present; their role in the production of the precocity is not clear. When sensitive assays are employed, urinary and serum gonadotropins are elevated for age and 17-ketosteroids may be elevated to the pubertal range. The EEG is frequently abnormal, particularly in males.

Of the "pseudo" types of sexual precocity, adrenal lesions are etiologically the most common (see pp. 421-430). Gonadal tumors are uncommon causes, and the granulosa cell and theca lutein cell tumors of the ovary are perhaps the most common. These tumors are generally unilateral, of low malignancy, and produce excessive amounts of estrogen. In almost all instances, the tumor can be palpated transabdominally or rectally, but it is advisable to examine the girl in the well-sedated or anesthetized state. Treatment is directed at the underlying cause, and in the idiopathic variety is often unnecessary although the administration of medroxyprogesterone acetate (Depo-Provera®), 100 to 150 mg. every ten days, may arrest and reverse the precocious sexual development. (Caution: May cause hypertension and not alter the increased acceleration of bone age.) Psychologic management of the patient and family is important. Children who initially have no definable causative lesion should be examined (abdominal examination, skull x-ray, eye examination, visual fields, EEG) at periodic intervals for evidence of previously occult abdominal mass or C. N. S. lesion.

Precocious Development of the Breast (Premature Thelarche).

Precocious development of one or both breasts may occur at any age; in most cases the onset is in the first two years of life, and in two-thirds breast development is obvious in the first year. The condition is not associated with other evidence of sexual maturation. It may represent unusual sensitivity of the breasts to normal amounts of circulating estrogen or a temporarily increased secretion of estrogen. Both breasts are usually involved, and enlargement may persist for months or years; the nipples generally do not enlarge. In contrast with sexual precocity, rapid growth, advanced skeletal maturation, and menstruation do not occur. Diagnostic tests are seldom warranted; no treatment is necessary. Puberty occurs at the normal time.

Premature Adrenarche (Premature Pubarche).

Premature development of sexual hair may occur at any age and in both sexes (in females more often than males). About a third of cases occur in organically brain-damaged children. It may result from a premature slight increase in production of adrenal androgens or increased sensitivity of sexual hair follicles to normal levels of androgens. Pubic hair usually develops first, but axillary hair is present in about half of cases when they are first seen. True virilization does not develop; children are of normal stature, and osseous development is not advanced. 17-Ketosteroid and testosterone excretion is normal. Premature adrenarche requires no treatment.

Menstruation.

The age at menarche ranges from nine to 16 years, and menarche is considered delayed if it has not occurred by age 17 years. Primary amenorrhea is the result of gonadal lesions (i.e., gonadal dysgenesis) in approximately 60% of subjects, and in such cases serum and urine gonadotropin levels are elevated. In the remaining 40% of cases of primary amenorrhea, extragonadal abnormalities are present (e.g., pituitary-hypothalamic hypogonadotropinism, congenital anomalies of the tubes, uterus, or vagina, androgen excess, or other endocrine imbalance and chronic systemic disease or pelvic inflammatory disease).

Once regular periods are established, amenorrhea (i.e., secondary amenorrhea; see Table 22-3) during adolescence is often the result of either pregnancy or significant organic or psychiatric disease. Secondary amenorrhea should therefore be viewed as a symptom requiring prompt evaluation and, when possible, treatment.

TABLE 22-3. Secondary amenorrhea.

I. Decreased ovarian function.
  A. Gonadotropins Elevated (primary ovarian insufficiency).
    1. Ovarian agenesis and dysgenesis* (e.g., Turner's syndrome).
    2. Acquired diseases (radiation castration, surgical removal of ovaries, destruction of ovaries by infection or tumor, "premature menopause").
  B. Decreased Gonadotropins (secondary ovarian insufficiency).
    1. Organic and idiopathic hypothalamic and/or pituitary disease.*
    2. "Functional abnormalities of hypothalamic-pituitary axis" ("psychogenic").
    3. Hypothalamic-pituitary disease secondary to chronic systemic illness.
      a. Nutritional (e.g., anorexia nervosa).
      b. Chronic infection or systemic disease (e.g., collagen vascular disease, malignancy, inflammatory bowel disease).
    4. Secondary to endogenous hormones (e.g., androgen excess, feminizing or masculinizing ovarian tumor).
    5. Secondary to exogenous drugs (e.g., long-term contraceptive drugs, estrogens, androgens, tranquilizers).

II. Congenital and acquired lesions of the fallopian tubes and uterus, including cases of chromosomal intersex (e.g., testicular feminization syndrome, cryptomenorrhea, hysterectomy, congenital absence of the uterus, adhesions, or synechia of the uterus).

*Usually or often associated with primary amenorrhea.

Menstruation is likely to occur when girls reach a mean weight of about 47 Kg.

THE GONAD

Deficiency of gonadal tissue or function may result from a genetic or embryologic defect; from hormone excess affecting the fetus in utero; from inflammation and destruction following infection (mumps, syphilis, tuberculosis); from trauma, irradiation, trauma, or tumor; or as a consequence of surgical castration. Secondary hypogonadism may result from pituitary insufficiency (destructive lesions in or about the anterior pituitary, irradiation of the pituitary, or starvation), diabetes mellitus, androgen excess (e.g., adrenogenital syndrome), or insufficiency of either the thyroid or adrenals.

CRYPTORCHISM

Most cases of cryptorchism (undescended testes) are not due to an endocrine disturbance. When cryptorchism persists into adult life, there will be a failure in spermatogenesis even though testicular androgen production may remain normal. The undescended testis is frequently abnormal at any age.

Cryptorchism may be caused by delayed descent, prevention of normal descent by some mechanical lesion such as adhesions, short spermatic cord, or fibrous bands; or by endocrine disorders causing hypogonadism (uncommon). Pseudo-cryptorchism is withdrawal of the testes from the scrotum by the cremasteric muscles.

Clinical Findings.

In palpating the scrotum for the testes, the cremasteric reflex may be elicited, with a resultant ascent of the testes into the abdomen (pseudo-cryptorchism). To prevent this, the fingers first should be placed across the upper portion of the inguinal canal to prevent ascent. Examination in a hot bath is also helpful.

With unilateral cryptorchism, the scrotum on that side is frequently smaller.

Treatment.

The best age for medical or surgical treatment has not been determined. Although there is a difference of opinion about whether lack of descent until puberty will cause damage to the testes, delaying treatment for five to ten years (or even longer) probably involves no greater risk of sterility than early surgical correction, with the hazard of surgical injury to the testis. Surgical repair may be indicated for persistent cryptorchism (beyond puberty) since the incidence of malignancy is greater in those glands which remain in the abdomen. The presence of an associated local abnormality (e.g., hernia, ectopic position) is an indication for surgical correction of the cryptorchism.

A. Unilateral: Most cases are due to local mechanical lesions.

1. Apply heat (hot water bottle to perineum or hot sitz bath) for a few minutes before reexamining patient.
2. Surgical repair may be indicated in the second decade if descent does not occur after application of heat.
3. Surgery may be preceded by administration of gonadotropins (see below).

B. Bilateral: Most cases will descend spontaneously by puberty, and so conservative therapy generally will be successful.
1. Examine after application of heat.
2. Chorionic gonadotropins, 500 units two or three times per week I. M. for five to eight weeks. When descent is produced by gonadotropin therapy, it indicates that the testes would have descended spontaneously in a similar manner.
3. The value of surgical repair has not been proved.
4. Testosterone is indicated only after puberty as androgen replacement therapy in hypogonadism.

C. Pseudo-cryptorchism: No treatment is necessary.

Prognosis.

Following surgery, the prognosis must be guarded in respect to spermatogenesis in the involved testis.

KLINEFELTER'S SYNDROME

A syndrome (occasionally familial) appearing during puberty and characterized by atrophic sclerosis of the seminiferous tubules with normal Leydig cells and normal masculinization; it is accompanied by bilateral gynecomastia (50 to 67%) and abnormally small testes, and is associated with high anterior pituitary follicle-stimulating hormone, normal or somewhat diminished 17-ketosteroid excretion, and aspermatogenesis. Many patients are mentally retarded. They have an extra X (female) chromosome (most commonly an XXY chromosome pattern) and a positive nuclear chromatin pattern. There is no satisfactory treatment, but methyltestosterone, 20 to 40 mg./day orally for several months, may produce positive physical and behavioral changes and reduce gynecomastia. If it does not, surgical mastectomy for cosmetic purposes is indicated.

Klinefelter's syndrome must be differentiated from the physiologic gynecomastia which occurs in some boys at puberty as well as from feminizing tumors of the adrenal or testes.

Typical histopathologic changes may occur in adults whose only complaint is sterility.

DISEASES OF THE THYROID

GOITER

Goiter is not uncommon in children and adolescents and is most commonly due to chronic lymphocytic thyroiditis. It may also result from acute inflammation, infiltrative processes, neoplasms,

or an inborn error in thyroid metabolism (familial goiter). With
the exception of hyperthyroidism, thyroid enlargement results from
the stimulation of excess thyroid stimulating hormone (TSH). Regardless of the cause, patients may be clinically and biochemically
euthyroid, hypothyroid, or hyperthyroid.

Familial goiter results from enzymatic defects in hormonogen-
esis, e.g., (1) iodide trapping, (2) iodide organification, (3) coupling, (4) deiodination, and (5) production of thyroglobulin and serum
carrier protein. Patients with any of these defects display an
autosomal recessive mode of inheritance; the organification defect
may be associated with severe congenital deafness (Pendred's syndrome). The age of presentation of hypothyroidism is variable.

Goiter may also result from the ingestion of excessive amounts
of goitrogenic substances, such as cabbage, soybeans, PAS, resorcinol, phenylbutazone, and iodides (particularly in individuals
who have also received adrenocortical steroids), or drugs that
interfere with iodide trapping (e.g., thiocyanates).

Clinical Findings.

The thyroid, especially in children with goiters who exhibit
normal thyroid function, is usually large and soft; bruits and thrills
may be present, and occasionally a nodule may be palpable. Pressure symptoms due to goiter are relatively uncommon in childhood.
Serum protein-bound iodine and radioiodine (^{131}I) uptakes are usually normal but may be elevated or reduced.

Nodular goiter may occur in childhood. The likelihood that a
nodule is malignant increases when the nodule is single, hard,
associated with paratracheal lymph node enlargement, or does not
concentrate radioactive iodide.

Treatment of Goiter.

A. Remove or avoid precipitating factors if possible.
B. Desiccated thyroid, 60 to 180 mg. daily, is of value when treatment is necessary.
C. Iodine therapy alone is usually not effective.
D. Surgery is occasionally necessary if significant pressure symptoms persist or for possible malignancy if a nodular lesion fails
   to regress despite therapy with a large dose of thyroid hormones for a period of one to four months.

Prophylaxis.

Prophylaxis in endemic areas consists of the use of bread containing iodides or iodized salt containing 1 mg. of iodine per 100
Gm. of salt, or the administration of 1-2 drops of Lugol's solution
or saturated solution of potassium iodide per week. Iodinization of
the water supply is also a satisfactory preventive measure.

Course and Prognosis.

The simple adolescent goiter usually subsides without treatment, but therapy will hasten shrinking. Iodine is specific for
goiters due to iodine deficiency.

NEONATAL GOITER

Neonatal goiter may result from the transplacental passage, from mother to infant, of iodides, goitrogens, antithyroid drugs, or long-acting thyroid stimulator (LATS). Transplacental passage of LATS occurs in pregnancies in which the mother has or previously had Graves' disease. The offspring may temporarily be hyperthyroid with exophthalmos. The goiter is usually diffuse and relatively soft but may be large and firm enough to compress the trachea, esophagus, and adjacent blood vessels. Treatment with iodides or antithyroid drugs (or both) for a few weeks may be indicated. In all other instances, the infant is euthyroid or hypothyroid, and regression usually occurs in a few weeks. It may be hastened by the administration of small doses of thyroid. Occasionally, surgical division of the thyroid isthmus may be necessary.

HYPOTHYROIDISM

Hypothyroidism may be either congenital or acquired. Congenital hypothyroidism may be due to aplasia, hypoplasia, or maldescent of the thyroid resulting from an embryonic defect of development; the administration of radioiodine to the mother; or, possibly, an autoimmune disease; or it may be caused by defective synthesis of thyroid hormone (familial goiter) (see p. 410).

Other cases of congenital hypothyroidism may result from the maternal ingestion of medications (goitrogens, propylthiouracil, methimazole, iodides), iodide deficiency (endemic cretinism), or thyroid hormone unresponsiveness. Thyroid tissue in an aberrant location is present in most patients with sporadic "athyrotic" cretinism.

Acquired (juvenile) hypothyroidism is most commonly the result of chronic lymphocytic thyroiditis (see p. 416) but may be the result of surgical removal, thyrotropin deficiency (usually associated with other pituitary tropic hormone deficiencies), the ingestion of medications (e. g., iodides, cobalt), or a deficiency of iodides.

Clinical Findings.
The severity of the findings depends on age at onset.
A. Symptoms and Signs:
  1. Functional changes - Findings include physical and mental sluggishness; pale, gray, cool skin; decreased intestinal activity (constipation), large tongue, poor muscle tone (protuberant abdomen, umbilical hernia, lumbar lordosis), hypothermia, bradycardia, diminished sweating (variable), carotenemia, decreased pulse pressure, hoarse voice or cry, slow relaxation on eliciting tendon reflexes (normal: 180 to 360 msec. for children as measured by photomotogram; reflex time shorter in boys and in younger children); and transient deafness. Nasal obstruction and discharge, large fontanels, and persistent jaundice may be present in the neonatal period.
    Even with congenital absence of the thyroid gland, the first finding may not appear for several days or weeks.

2. Retardation of growth and development - Findings include shortness of stature, infantile skeletal proportions with relatively short extremities, infantile naso-orbital configuration (bridge of nose flat, broad, and undeveloped; eyes seem to be widely spaced), retarded "bone age," epiphysial dysgenesis, especially of hip (centers of ossification may show multiple small centers or a single stippled, porous, or fragmented center), retarded dental development, and large fontanels in the neonate. Slowing of mental responsiveness and retardation of development of the brain may occur.

3. Sexual retardation (rarely, precocity). Menometrorrhagia in older girls.

4. Other changes - Myxedema of tissues; skin may be dry, thick, scaly, and coarse, with a yellowish tinge from excessive deposition of carotene; hair is dry, coarse, brittle (variable), and may be excessive. The axillary and supraclavicular pads may be prominent. Muscular hypertrophy (Debré-Sémélaigne syndrome) occasionally is present. Pseudoanorexia nervosa and psychosis secondary to myxedema have been described.

B. X-ray Findings: Epiphysial development ("bone age") is delayed; the cardiac shadow increased; epiphysial dysgenesis; coxa vara and coxa plana may occur. The pituitary fossa may be enlarged.

C. Laboratory Findings: T_4, PBI, and RAI uptake reduced. (PBI and RAI uptake may be normal or elevated in goitrous cretinism and in some cases of thyroiditis.) Serum cholesterol elevated (but often low or normal in infants and sometimes in older children); rise above original (untreated) levels occurs six to eight weeks after cessation of therapy. B.M.R. low (unreliable in children). TSH levels may be elevated. Urinary creatine excretion is decreased, creatinine increased. Serum alkaline phosphatase reduced. Erythrocyte glucose-6-phosphate dehydrogenase activity decreased. Sweat electrolytes are often increased. Circulating autoantibodies to thyroid constituents present in about 50% of patients. Urinary hydroxyproline reduced. Plasma growth hormone levels and growth hormone response to insulin-induced hypoglycemia and arginine stimulation may be normal.

Treatment.

A. Levothyroxine Sodium (Synthroid® Sodium): Levothyroxine is a reliable synthetic agent for thyroid replacement therapy. Older children, adolescents, and adults require 0.15 to 0.25 mg. daily in one dose; infants require 0.05 to 0.1 mg. daily. In hypothyroid subjects, particularly myxedematous infants, low doses (0.025 to 0.05 mg.) should be used initially and increased weekly in small increments. Therapeutic range is evaluated by clinical response (appearance, growth, development), sleeping pulses, and thyroid function tests. (T_4 levels, when a euthyroid state has been reached, are 25% higher than accepted "normal" levels in untreated individuals.) Improvement usually occurs in one to three weeks. If a patient can tolerate appreciably more than the above doses, the diagnosis of hypothyroidism should be questioned, since hypothyroid individuals show signs of toxicity on larger doses while those who are normal can take comparatively large doses of thyroid without evidence of overage.

B. Other Thyroid Drugs: Desiccated thyroid, triiodothyronine (Cytomel®), and combinations of synthetic thyroxine and triiodothyronine (e.g., Proloid® and Euthroid®) may also be used. The doses of the synthetic combinations are the same as those given for levothyroxine; 65 mg. of desiccated thyroid is approximately equal to 0.1 mg. of levothyroxine. Triiodothyronine is four times as potent and the normal T_4 range will be proportionately lower when triiodothyronine is used. (Triiodothyronine is probably contraindicated in infants.)

Course and Prognosis.

A. Congenital: With adequate replacement therapy, growth and motor development can be returned to normal; the prognosis for mental development is guarded. Early therapy gives a greater chance for intellectual advancement.

B. Acquired: Restoration of physical and mental function to the pre-disease level is to be expected following replacement therapy.

HYPERTHYROIDISM

The etiology of hyperthyroidism has not been determined, but psychic trauma, psychologic maladjustments, immunologic alterations, disturbances in pituitary function, infectious disease, heredity, and imbalance of the endocrine system all have been incriminated. Transient congenital hyperthyroidism with or without exophthalmos may occur in infants of thyrotoxic mothers.

Hyperthyroidism (with normal T_4 levels) may result from isolated hypersecretion of T_3 (T_3 toxicosis).

Clinical Findings.

A. Symptoms and Signs: The disease is much more common in females and between the ages of 12 and 14 years. It is most often rapid in development. Findings include "nervousness" (inability to sit still, marked variability of mood, and tremor), warm and moist skin and flushed face, exophthalmos, palpitation, tachycardia (even during sleep), and systolic hypertension with increased pulse pressure; weakness, goiter (diffuse, usually firm; bruit and thrill may be present), accelerated growth and development (variable), loss of weight in spite of polyphagia, and poor school performance. Amenorrhea is common in adolescent girls.

B. Laboratory Findings: T_4 above 6.4 µg./100 ml.; PBI above 8 µg./100 ml.*; T_3 resin test elevated; RAI uptake above 35%†

---

*Certain organic iodine compounds (Teridax® [iophenoxic acid], etc.) may cause prolonged elevation of the PBI. If administered to the mother, they may cross the placenta in significant amounts to affect the infant's PBI for many months.

†In many parts of the U.S.A., the upper limit of normal of RAI uptake of normal individuals is significantly lower than it was a few years ago.

and suppressed less than 40% after administration of triiodothyronine, 25 μg. three or four times daily for seven days.
Free thyroxine levels elevated. B. M. R. is elevated, serum
cholesterol low, urinary creatine excretion elevated. Glycosuria may occur. Agglutinating antibodies found in most patients. Enlargement of the pituitary fossa on skull x-rays in
some cases with pituitary disease. Increased activity of erythrocyte glucose-6-phosphate dehydrogenase. Circulating LATS
(long-acting thyroid stimulator) usually elevated. Serum TSH
levels are low. Urinary hydroxyproline increased. Norepinephrine excretion not increased. Moderate leukopenia.
Serum tyrosine elevated.

Treatment.

Antithyroid drugs, radioactive iodine, and surgical methods are
equally capable of eliminating the manifestations of hyperthyroidism
and yield approximately equal numbers of "cured" patients.

A. General Measures:
  1. Restricted physical activity - Especially in severe cases,
     in preparation for surgery, or at the beginning of a medical
     regimen.
  2. Diet - High in calories, proteins, and vitamins.
  3. Sedation - Large doses of barbiturates or tranquilizers may
     be necessary to control nervousness.
  4. Sympatholytic drugs (e. g. , propranolol, reserpine, guan-
     ethidine) may diminish symptoms without altering thyroid
     function.

B. Medical Management:
  1. Propylthiouracil - This drug may be used in the initial
     treatment of the patient with hyperthyroidism, but if the PBI
     fails to return to a normal range, or if PBI rises rapidly
     with reduction in drug dosage after 36 to 48 months of ther-
     apy, surgery may be necessary. Relapses occur in 10 to
     30%, and severe cases may not respond. Therapy should be
     continued for at least two to three years with the minimum
     drug dosage that will produce a euthyroid state.
     a. Initial dosage - 75 to 300 mg. a day in three or four
        divided doses six or eight hours apart until tests of thy-
        roid function are normal and all signs and symptoms
        have subsided. Larger doses may be necessary.
     b. Maintenance - 50 to 100 mg. a day in two or three divided
        doses. The drug may be continued at higher levels until
        hypothyroidism has resulted and then a supplement of
        oral thyroid added. Thyroid hormone should also be
        given if the gland remains large after one to two months
        of propylthiouracil therapy.
  2. Methimazole (Tapazole®) may be used in $1/15$ to $1/10$ the
     dosage of propylthiouracil. However, toxic reactions may
     be more common with this drug than with the thiouracils.
  3. Iodine is generally not recommended.
  4. With medical treatment, clinical response may be noted in
     about two to three weeks, and adequate control may be
     achieved in one to three months. The thyroid gland fre-
     quently increases in size after initiation of treatment, but
     it usually decreases in size eventually.

C. Surgery: Subtotal thyroidectomy is considered by some to be the treatment of choice for children, especially if close follow-up is difficult or impossible. The patient should be prepared first with bed rest, diet, and sedation (as above) and with pro-pylthiouracil (for two to four weeks) and iodide (2 to 10 drops daily of strong iodine [Lugol's] solution or saturated solution of potassium iodide for 10 to 21 days). Continue for one week after surgery.

D. Radiation Therapy: Radioactive iodine (^{131}I or ^{125}I) is currently recommended by many as initial treatment if medical therapy fails. Regardless of the dose or type of RAI employed, hypo-thyroidism generally can be anticipated at variable periods after treatment.

E. Antithyroid drugs, antibiotics, sedation, propranolol, reser-pine, and guanethidine may be of value for the treatment of thyroid storm.

Course and Prognosis.

It has been claimed that approximately one-third of adults will respond without specific therapy; the results of similar management in children are not available. Without treatment there will be par-tial remissions and exacerbations for several years. With medical treatment alone, prolonged remissions may be expected in about half of cases. The actual increased risk of developing leukemia or carcinoma of the thyroid after treatment with radioactive iodine has not been determined.

CARCINOMA OF THE THYROID
(See also p. 455.)

Carcinoma of the thyroid is uncommon. It is most likely to occur following irradiation of the neck and chest. Findings include goiter, neck discomfort, dysphagia, and voice changes. Surgical extirpation of the entire gland and removal of all involved nodes is the treatment of choice. A radical neck dissection is seldom neces-sary. Postoperatively the patient may be allowed to become hypo-thyroid, and a diagnostic scan with radioactive iodine may be car-ried out; metastases, if present, can be treated with ^{131}I or re-moved surgically, if feasible. Subsequent thyroid replacement therapy should be maintained. Papillary carcinoma has a good prognosis for prolonged ($>$ 10 years) survival.

Medullary carcinoma may be familial and associated with Marfan-like body habitus, nodularities (mucosal neuromas), of the tongue and mucous membranes and a pheochromocytoma or visceral ganglioneuromas.

GOITROUS CRETINISM:
See Familial Goiter, p. 410.

THYROIDITIS

Acute thyroiditis produces an acute inflammatory goiter and may be due to almost any pathogenic organism (viral or bacterial) or may be nonspecific or idiopathic. It is usually unassociated with any endocrine disturbance. Specific antibiotic therapy and adreno-cortical steroids may be of value.

Subacute thyroiditis (pseudotuberculous, De Quervain's giant cell thyroiditis) is characterized by mild and transient manifesta-tions of hypermetabolism and an enlarged, very tender, firm thy-roid gland. PBI is elevated and ^{131}I uptake is markedly reduced. Aspirin (mild cases) and adrenocortical steroids and thyroid hor-mone (severe disease) may be of value.

Chronic thyroiditis (lymphomatous or Hashimoto's struma, autoimmune thyroiditis) is being seen with increasing frequency, particularly during puberty ("adolescent goiter"). It is character-ized by firm, nontender, diffuse or nodular, "pebbly" enlargement of the thyroid with variable activity. There may be symptoms of mild tracheal compression. PBI is variable; the difference between PBI and T_4 or BEI levels is often increased, and ^{131}I uptake may be elevated. Circulating antibodies against one or more thyroid com-ponents (particularly immunofluorescent) often develop. A needle biopsy is of questionable diagnostic value.

Treatment is with desiccated thyroid; rarely, adrenocortical steroids are necessary.

Hypothyroidism is often an end result and treatment may need to be lifelong.

DISEASES OF THE PARATHYROIDS

HYPOPARATHYROIDISM

Hypoparathyroidism may be idiopathic, may result from para-thyroidectomy, or may be one feature of a general autoimmune dis-order associated with candidiasis, Addison's disease, pernicious anemia, diabetes mellitus, thyroiditis, and alopecia. Transient hypoparathyroidism may occur in the neonate, particularly in the offspring of diabetic mothers as a result of parathyroid gland immaturity.

Clinical Findings.
  A. Of Tetany: Numbness, cramps and twitchings of extremities, carpopedal spasm, laryngospasm, positive Chvostek's sign (tapping of the face in front of the ear produces spasm of the facial muscles), positive peroneal sign (tapping the fibular side of the leg over the peroneal nerve produces abduction and dorsi-flexion of the foot), positive Trousseau's sign (prolonged com-pression of the upper arm produces carpal spasm), positive Erb's sign (use of a galvanic current to determine hyperexcita-bility), unexplained bizarre behavior, diarrhea, photophobia, irritability, loss of consciousness, and convulsions.
  B. Of Prolonged Hypocalcemia: Tetany (see above and Chapter 9); photophobia, blepharospasm, diarrhea, and chronic conjuncti-vitis; cataracts, numbness of the extremities, poor dentition, skin rashes, ectodermal dysplasias, fungus infections (can-dida), "idiopathic" epilepsy, symmetric punctate calcifications

of basal ganglia, adrenal insufficiency, steatorrhea, or a pernicious anemia-like picture.

C. Laboratory Findings: (See Table 22-4.) Confirmatory tests:

1. Ellsworth-Howard test - Markedly increased excretion of urinary phosphorus following the injection of parathyroid extract, 2 ml. (200 units) I.V. False-negative results are common.

2. Parathyroid extract test - Rise in serum calcium, fall in serum phosphorus, and increase in urine phosphate following the injection of parathyroid extract, 5 to 10 ml. (100 units/ml.) in divided doses I.M. daily for three to four days.

3. Urinary cyclic AMP normally rises five- to 50-fold following the administration of parathyroid hormone. Failure to rise indicates severe renal disease or end organ unresponsiveness to the hormone.

Treatment.

The objective of treatment is to maintain the serum calcium at a low normal level. A simple, practical method of regulating therapy is with the Sulkowitch urine test, but it may not always accurately reflect hypercalciuria, particularly in infants.

A. Acute or Severe Tetany: Immediate correction of hypocalcemia. Give calcium I.V. and orally.

B. Maintenance of Hypoparathyroid and Chronic Hypocalcemia:

1. Calciferol (most valuable) or dihydrotachysterol (see Drug Dosages in Appendix).

2. Diet -
   a. High-calcium, with added calcium lactate or gluconate.
   b. Low-phosphorus - Omit milk, cheese, and egg yolk.

3. Aluminum hydroxide gel, 2 to 8 ml. ($1/2$ to 2 tsp.) with each meal, removes phosphorus from the gastrointestinal tract, enhancing calcium absorption.

PSEUDOHYPOPARATHYROIDISM
(Seabright Bantam Syndrome)

This is a familial X-linked dominant syndrome in which there is no lack of parathyroid hormone but a failure of response of adenyl cyclase in the end organs (e.g., the renal tubule). The symptoms, physical findings, and chemical findings are the same as in idiopathic hypoparathyroidism. These patients have round, full faces, stubby fingers (shortening of the first, fourth, and fifth metacarpals), shortness of stature, delayed and defective dentition, and early closure of the epiphyses. X-rays may show dyschondroplastic changes in the bones of the hands, demineralization of the bones, thickening of the cortices, exostoses, and ectopic calcification of the basal ganglia and subcutaneous tissues. Corneal and lenticular opacities may be present.

Treatment is with vitamin D (1α, $25[OH]_2 D_3$), calciferol, and supplementary oral calcium lactate.

Pseudohypoparathyroidism type II, resulting from an intracellular defect in the response to cyclic AMP with failure of parathyroid hormone administration to produce a phosphaturic effect but with a urinary rise in cyclic AMP, has been described.

418 Endocrine & Metabolic Disorders

TABLE 22-4. Laboratory findings in hypocalcemia.*

Condition	Serum Concentration			Urinary Excretion		Bone Pathology
	Ca^{++}	P	P-ase	Ca^{++}	P	
Hypoparathyroidism	dec.	inc.	N	dec.	dec.	Possible inc. density.
Pseudohypoparathyroidism (Types I and II)	dec.	inc.	N	dec.	dec.	Tendency to congenital malformations.
Renal insufficiency (glomerular)	N or dec.	inc.	N or inc.	dec.	dec.	Possible osteitis fibrosa.
Renal insufficiency (tubular)	dec.	dec.	inc.	inc.	inc.	Rickets, osteomalacia.
Infantile rickets	N or dec.	dec.	inc.	dec.	dec.	Rickets.
Tetany of newborn	dec.	inc.	N	N or dec.	N or dec.	
Steatorrhea	dec.	N or dec.	inc.	dec.	dec.	Rickets, osteomalacia.
Postacidotic hypocalcemia	dec.	dec.	N	dec. (?)	dec. (?)	
Hypoproteinemia	Total, dec. Ionized, N	N	N	N	N	
Familial vitamin D resistant rickets	dec.	dec.	N	N	inc. or N	Rickets.
Hereditary vitamin D dependent rickets	dec.	dec.	inc.	inc. or N	inc. or N	Rickets.

*Tubular reabsorption of phosphate (TRP) normally is 83 to 98%; the lower values are associated with higher serum levels of phosphorus. In hypoparathyroidism, TRP varies from 40 to 70%. Low values for TRP are also found in some forms of inherited renal tubular disease.

HYPERPARATHYROIDISM

Hyperparathyroidism may be primary (occasionally familial) or secondary. Primary hyperparathyroidism may be due to adenoma or diffuse parathyroid hyperplasia. The most common causes of the secondary form are chronic renal disease (glomerulonephritis, pyelonephritis), congenital anomalies of the genitourinary tract, pseudohypoparathyroidism, and vitamin D dependent rickets. Rarely, it may be found in osteogenesis imperfecta, malignancies with bony metastases, and rickets.

Clinical Findings.
  A. Symptoms and Signs:
    1. Due to hypercalcemia* - Hypotonicity and weakness of

*Hypercalcemia may also be secondary to immobilization, excess intake of vitamin D, sarcoidosis, milk-alkali syndrome, extensive fat necrosis of the newborn, or certain malignancies, or it may occur as a familial disease.

TABLE 22-5. Laboratory findings in hypercalcemia.

Condition	Serum Concentration			Urinary Excretion		Bone Pathology
	Ca^{++}	P	P-ase	Ca^{++}	P	
Hyperparathyroidism	inc.	dec.	N or inc.	inc.	inc.	Generalized osteitis fibrosa
Hyperparathyroidism with impaired renal function	inc.	N or inc.	inc.	inc.	inc.	Generalized osteitis fibrosa
Excessive vitamin D	inc.	inc.	N	inc.	N or inc.	
Excessive A.T.10	inc.	dec.		inc.	inc.	
Neoplasms of bone	N or inc.	N	N or inc.	inc.	N or inc.	Bone destruction
Hyperproteinemia	Total, inc. Ionized, N	N	N	N	N	
Idiopathic hypercalcemia	inc.	N	N	inc.	N	See below.

muscles; nausea, vomiting, and poor tone of gastrointestinal tract, with constipation; loss of weight, hyperextensibility of joints, bradycardia, and shortening of Q-T interval.

2. Due to increased calcium and phosphorus excretion - Polyuria, polydipsia, and precipitation of calcium phosphate in renal parenchyma or as urinary calculi (i.e., sand or gravel).

3. Related to changes in the skeleton - Osteitis fibrosa, absence of lamina dura around the teeth, spontaneous fractures, and "moth-eaten" appearance of skull. If patient drinks adequate quantities of milk, renal stones will occur but bone disease will not.

B. Laboratory Findings: Urinary phosphorus, cyclic AMP, and hydroxyproline excretion are increased. (See also Table 22-5.)

C. X-ray Findings: Bone changes usually do not occur in children with an adequate calcium intake. When bone changes occur, one finds a generalized demineralization with a predilection for the subperiosteal cortical bone. The distal clavicle is usually first affected.

Nephrocalcinosis is the most important x-ray finding.

Treatment.

Complete removal of tumor or subtotal removal of hyperplastic parathyroid glands. Preoperatively, fluids should be forced and the intake of calcium restricted. Postoperatively, the diet should be high in calcium, phosphorus, and vitamin D.

Treatment of secondary hyperparathyroidism is directed at the underlying disease. Diminish the intake of phosphate with aluminum hydroxide orally and by reduction of milk consumption.

Course and Prognosis.

Although the condition may recur, the prognosis following sub-total parathyroidectomy or removal of an adenoma is usually quite good. The prognosis in the secondary forms depends on correcting the underlying defect. Renal function may remain abnormal.

.   .   .

IDIOPATHIC HYPERCALCEMIA

Idiopathic hypercalcemia is an uncommon disorder probably related to either excessive intake or increased sensitivity to vitamin D. The disease is characterized in its severe form by peculiar facies (receding mandible, depressed bridge of nose, relatively large mouth, prominent lips, hanging jowls, large low-set ears, "elfin" appearance), failure to thrive, mental and motor retardation, irritability, purposeless movements, constipation, hypotonia, polyuria, polydipsia, hypertension, and heart disease (especially supravalvular aortic stenosis). Generalized osteosclerosis is common, and there may be premature craniosynostosis and nephrocalcinosis with evidence of urinary tract disease. Hypercholesterolemia, azotemia, and elevation of serum vitamin A may be present. Familial benign hypercalcemia has been reported.

Clinical manifestations may not appear for several months. Severe disease may end in death. Mild disease may occur without the typical facies and other findings and has a good prognosis.

Treatment is by rigid restriction of dietary calcium and vitamin D and, in severely involved children, the administration of corticosteroids in high doses. Other methods of treatment that have also been reported to be of value include addition of sodium sulfate to the diet, administration of thyroxine, and the use of furosemide (especially for its acute effect).

HYPOPHOSPHATASIA

Hypophosphatasia is an uncommon heritable condition characterized by rickets and a specific deficiency of alkaline phosphatase. The earlier the age at onset, the more severe the condition. Failure to thrive, premature loss of teeth, widening of the sutures, bulging fontanels, convulsions, bony deformities, dwarfing, and renal lesions have been reported. Premature closure of cranial sutures may occur. Late features include osteoporosis, pseudofractures, and rachitic deformities. Signs and symptoms may be similar to those of idiopathic hypercalcemia. Serum calcium is frequently elevated. Urinary hydroxyproline is low in infancy. The plasma and urine contain phosphoethanolamine in excessive amounts. No specific treatment is available; adrenocorticosteroids may be of value.

.   .   .

THE ADRENALS

ADRENOCORTICAL STEROIDS AND
CORTICOTROPIN (ACTH)

Controls to Minimize Dangers in Use of Corticosteroids.
A. Determine the following at periodic intervals: Blood pressure, weight, height, red cell count and sedimentation rate, urinary glucose, serum potassium and CO_2 content (if prolonged therapy with large doses is necessary), stool for occult blood.
B. Other Recommendations:
  1. If adrenocortical steroids have been administered for more than one week, terminate gradually. Abrupt withdrawal may cause a severe ''rebound'' of the disease or produce symptoms of adrenal insufficiency.
  2. When treating less severe disorders, give steroids during the daytime only since this causes less suppression of endogenous ACTH. Withdraw the evening dose first. Whenever possible, give entire 48-hour dose as a single dose every other morning. (See Dosage, below.)
  3. Give adrenocortical steroids to any child undergoing surgery, severe infection, or other significant stress who has received prolonged therapy with adrenocortical steroids during the past six months to two years.
  4. If edema develops, place the patient on a low-sodium diet or administer mercurial diuretics or chlorothiazide.
  5. Give potassium in divided doses if prolonged therapy or high dosage is employed.
  6. If a child receiving steroids develops chickenpox, the dosage of the steroid should not be reduced but increased (unless it is already at a high level). Steroid withdrawal in these circumstances may have a fatal outcome. Gamma globulin should also be administered.
  7. When prolonged therapy with adrenocortical steroids is necessary, the administration of short-acting drugs may be advantageous.
  8. Sodium fluoride has been reported to stimulate calcium retention in some patients with corticosteroid-induced osteoporosis.
  9. Liberal intake of protein may decrease the risk of developing osteoporosis.

Dosage.
  The exact dosage of these drugs in various diseases has not been determined. The following data may be used as a guide for the therapy of most diseases. (See specific diseases for additional recommendations.) Maintenance dosage should be altered depending upon the clinical response and the effect desired; if possible, it should be no higher than the minimum dosage required for adequate control of the disease (as shown by symptoms, signs, and laboratory evidence of activity). The total two-day dose of corticosteroid for long-term maintenance therapy may be administered as a single dose once every 48 hours without diminishing the thera-

TABLE 22-6. Adrenocorticosteroids.

Generic and Chemical Names	Trade Names	Potency/mg. Compared to Hydrocortisone*	
		Gluco-corticoid Effect	Mineralo-corticoid Effect
Glucocorticoids			
Hydrocortisone (cortisol, compound F)	Cortef®, Cortril®, Hydro-cortone®, Solu-Cortef®	1	1
Cortisone (compound E)	Cortogen®, Cortone®	4/5	1
Prednisone	Deltasone®, Deltra®, Meticorten®, Paracort®	4-5	2/5
Prednisolone	Delta-Cortef®, Hydeltra®, Meticortelone®, Para-cortol®, Prednis®, Sterane®, Sterolone®	4-5	2/5
Methylprednisolone†	Medrol®	5-6	Minimal effect
Triamcinolone†	Aristocort®, Kenacort®, Kenalog®	5-6	Minimal effect
Paramethasone	Haldrone®	10-12	
Fluprednisolone	Alphadrol®	13	
Fludrocortisone	Alflorone®, F-Cortef®, Florinef®	15-20	100-200
Dexamethasone	Decadron®, Deronil®, Dexameth®, Gamma-corten®, Hexadrol®	25-30	Minimal effect
Betamethasone†	Celestone®	33	
Mineralocorticoids			
Desoxycorticosterone	Percorten®	---	15
Desoxycorticosterone pivalate (trimethyl-acetate)			
Desoxycorticosterone acetate	Doca®	--- ---	15 15
Aldosterone	Electrocortin®	30	500

*To convert hydrocortisone dosage (see below) to equivalent dosage in any of the other preparations listed in this table, divide by the potency factors shown.
†There is no indication that these preparations offer any advantage over prednisone and prednisolone.

peutic efficiency, but with diminished side-effects (including normal growth and decreased tendency to cushingoid appearance).

A great many topical corticosteroids are available in various strengths for the treatment of inflammatory skin conditions. A significantly large amount of corticosteroid may be absorbed through both normal and inflamed skin.

See above for conversion of other adrenocortical steroids to hydrocortisone equivalents.

A. Corticotropin (ACTH) Gel: 0.5 units/Kg. or 15 to 20 units/sq. M. intramuscularly daily in two equal doses 12 hours apart, or synthetic corticotropin (Cortrosyn®, Synacthen®), 250 μg./sq. M./dose I.M. or I.V.

B. Hydrocortisone:

1. Physiologic replacement -

a. I.M. - 0.44 mg./Kg. or 13 mg./sq. M. once daily.
b. Orally* - 0.66 mg./Kg. or 20 mg./sq. M./day.
2. Therapeutic -
a. I.M. - 4.4 mg./Kg. or 130 mg./sq. M. once daily.
b. Orally* - 6.6 mg./Kg. or 200 mg./sq. M./day.
3. Therapeutic maintenance -
a. I. M. - 1.3-2.2 mg./Kg. or 40-65 mg./sq. M. once daily.
b. Orally* - 2-3.3 mg./Kg. or 60-100 mg./sq. M./day.
4. Development of infection while on a large dose of steroid -
Give about $1\frac{1}{2}$ to 2 times the physiologic maintenance
dose for three or four days and then resume larger dose.

C. Corticosteroids in Patients With Adrenocortical Insufficiency
Who Undergo Surgery:
1. Preoperatively - Give cortisone acetate I. M. as follows
(single dose):
a. Twenty-four hours before surgery, 100% of maintenance.
b. Twelve hours before surgery, 100% of maintenance.
c. One hour before surgery, 200% of maintenance.
2. During operation - Give hydrocortisone sodium succinate
(Solu-Cortef®), 1 to 2 mg./Kg. by I. V. infusion over a six-
to 12-hour period.
3. Postoperatively - Give cortisone acetate I. M., 100 to 200%
of maintenance daily, for one to two days. Begin oral preparation as soon as possible and give full maintenance doses
daily. If the maintenance dose is unknown, give 1.25 mg./
Kg. I.M. as follows: 100% of total at 8:00 A.M.; 50% of
dose at 2:00 P.M. and at 10:00 P.M. If significant stress
occurs postoperatively, give three to five times the maintenance dose.

DISEASES OF THE ADRENAL CORTEX

ADRENOCORTICAL INSUFFICIENCY
(Adrenal Crisis, Addison's Disease)

Adrenocortical hypofunction may be due to atrophy (toxic); destruction of the gland by a tumor, hemorrhage (Waterhouse-
Friderichsen syndrome), or an infection (e. g. , tuberculosis); congenital absence of the adrenal cortex (see p. 428); congenital hyperplasia of the cortex associated with androgen excess. It may occur
with some tumors as a consequence of inadequate secretion of
corticotropin (ACTH) due to anterior pituitary or hypothalamic disease. Any acute illness, surgery, trauma, or exposure to excessive heat may precipitate an adrenal crisis. A temporary salt-
losing disorder (possibly due to hypoaldosteronism) with normal excretion of adrenal steroids may occur during infancy.

Clinical Findings.
A. Acute Form (Adrenal Crisis): Signs and symptoms include

---

*In four equal doses six hours apart (preferred) or three equal doses
every eight hours.

nausea and vomiting, diarrhea, dehydration; fever, which may be followed by hypothermia; circulatory collapse, and confusion or coma.

B. Chronic Form (Addison's Disease): Adrenogenital syndrome with associated adrenal insufficiency, congenital adrenocortical insufficiency, and neoplasms are the most common causes. Addison's disease may be associated with hypoparathyroidism, lymphocytic thyroiditis, candidiasis, pernicious anemia, and diabetes mellitus. Anti-adrenal antibodies and antiparathyroid antibodies may be present.

Signs and symptoms include vomiting, which becomes force-ful and sometimes projectile; diarrhea, weakness, fatigue, failure to gain or loss of weight, increased appetite for salt, dehydration, rarely opisthotonos, increased pigmentation (both generalized and over pressure points and on mucous mem-branes), hypotension, and small heart size.

C. Laboratory Findings:
  1. Suggestive of adrenal insufficiency -
     a. Decreased serum sodium, chloride, carbon dioxide.
     b. Increased serum potassium* and N. P. N.
     c. Urinary sodium elevated despite low serum sodium.
     d. Eosinophilia and moderate neutropenia. †
     e. Fasting blood glucose generally normal; may be low in crisis.
  2. Confirmatory tests (measurement of the functional capacity of the adrenal cortex) -
     a. Urinary 17-hydroxycorticosteroid and ketogenic steroid excretion is decreased.
     b. 17-Ketosteroid output - Decreased (see p. 646) except in cases due to congenital hyperplasia or tumor of the cortex; of no value in younger children, who may nor-mally excrete less than 1 mg./day.
     c. Circulating eosinophils elevated - If there are fewer than 50 eosinophils/cu. mm. of blood, the diagnosis of pri-mary adrenocortical insufficiency is doubtful.
     d. Corticotropin and metyrapone tests - See pp. 659 and 660.
     e. Prolonged corticotropin (ACTH) test - 17-Hydroxycorti-coids or ketogenic steroids on the day before and on the day of ACTH infusion are compared. A rise of 150% or more in 17-hydroxycorticoids excludes primary adrenal insufficiency. Acute allergy will not affect this test.

Treatment.
A. Acute Form (Adrenal Crisis):
  1. Treat infections with large doses of the appropriate anti-biotics or chemotherapeutic agents.
  2. Waterhouse-Friderichsen syndrome with fulminant infec-tions - Adrenal steroids and isoproterenol (Isuprel®) should be used in the presence of adrenal insufficiency, but not for

---

*Hyperkalemia may persist for two or three months in infants with the adrenogenital syndrome despite treatment with cortisone, DCA, and supplemental salt.

†A normal number of eosinophils the first day after operation or in the presence of a severe infection is also suggestive of insufficiency.

fulminant infections alone.
3. Replacement therapy -
   a. Hydrocortisone hemisuccinate (Solu-Cortef®), 25 to 50 mg. diluted in 2 to 10 ml. water I. V. or I. M. over two to five minutes. Follow with hydrocortisone free alcohol (Infusion Concentrate Hydrocortone®, Cortef® sterile solution) or Solu-Cortef®, 25 to 50 mg. in 5% glucose in physiologic saline solution by I. V. infusion over a period of two to eight hours. Hydrocortisone or cortisone acetate, 1 mg./Kg. I. M., may also be given at the onset of treatment for more prolonged and persistent action.
   b. Repeat I. M. medication (see p. 422 for dosage) every 24 hours until control is achieved and then reduce gradually.
   c. On the second to fourth day of treatment, give desoxycorticosterone acetate, 1 to 2 mg. I. M. per day, and regulate dose depending on hydration, weight, heart size, and serum and urinary electrolytes.
4. Combat hypotension with phenylephrine (see p. 628) or isoproterenol (Isuprel®), 1 mg. in 500 ml. of 5% dextrose (final concentration, 1:500,000). **Caution.**
5. Plasma or blood transfusion, 5 to 22 ml./Kg.
6. Fluids and electrolytes - See Chapter 5. **Caution:** Avoid overtreatment. Total parenteral fluid should not exceed the fluid requirement of the normal child.
7. Fruit juices, ginger ale, milk, and soft foods should be started as soon as possible.
B. Chronic Form (Addison's Disease): Maintenance therapy: Following initial stabilization, the most effective substitution therapy generally requires the use of an adrenocortical steroid together with a high sodium chloride intake or supplementary DCA or a fluorinated steroid.
   1. Cortisone acetate (aqueous suspension), 15 mg./sq.M. (2.5 to 10 mg. I.M. once or twice daily), or cortisone acetate, 20 mg./sq.M. (1 to 5 mg. orally four times daily). Increase to two to four times regular dosage during periods of intercurrent illness or other periods of stress.
   2. Desoxycorticosterone (DCA) -
      a. DCA in oil, 0.5 to 3 mg. I. M. per day and increase or decrease gradually to the amount needed to maintain hydration, normal blood pressure, heart size, and weight. DCA also comes in propylene glycol for sublingual administration and as Linguets® or Buccalets®.
      b. Desoxycorticosterone trimethylacetate or pivalate may be given following prolonged regulation. (25 mg./ml. of this long-acting macrocrystalline suspension I. M. every three to four weeks corresponds to about 1 mg. DCA in oil I. M. daily.) Hypertension (without hypernatremia) may occur following the administration of mineralocorticoids to patients with congenital adrenal hyperplasia and may persist for months following their discontinuation.
      c. Pellets of DCA may be implanted.
      d. Fludrocortisone, 0.05 to 0.2 mg. daily, may be used with glucocorticoids in place of DCA.
   3. Sodium chloride (as enteric-coated salt pills if they can be taken), 1 to 3 Gm./day. Reduce dose if edema appears.

4. Additional DCA, sodium chloride, or cortisone may be necessary with acute illness, surgery, trauma, exposure to sudden change in temperature, or other stress reactions.

ADRENOCORTICAL HYPERFUNCTION

CUSHING'S SYNDROME

The principal findings in Cushing's syndrome in children result from excessive secretion of the carbohydrate-regulating (glucocorticoid) and androgenic (mineralocorticoid) hormones, leading to depletion of body protein stores and abnormal carbohydrate and fat metabolism. There may also be lesser degrees of overproduction of the salt- and water-controlling fraction and of androgens.

Cushing's syndrome is more common in females; in children under 12, it is usually due to adrenal tumor or to an ectopic ACTH-producing tumor. Hemihypertrophy may be present. It may be secondary to therapy with corticotropin (ACTH) or one of the cortisones. Rarely, it may be associated with an apparently primary adrenocortical hyperplasia or hyperplasia secondary to a basophilic adenoma of the pituitary gland. Spontaneous remission has been described.

Clinical Findings.
A. Symptoms and Signs:
   1. Due to excessive secretion of the carbohydrate-regulating hormones: "buffalo type" adiposity, most marked on the face, neck, and trunk (a fat pad in the interscapular area is characteristic); easy fatigability and weakness, striae, plethoric facies, easy bruisability, osteoporosis, hypertension, growth failure, diabetes (usually latent), and pain in back.
   2. Due to excessive secretion of androgens (mild): hirsutism, acne, varying degrees of clitoral or penile enlargement and deepening of the voice. Menstrual irregularities occur in older girls.
   3. Due to excessive production of salt- and water-controlling fractions: sodium retention with hypertension (rarely edema).
B. Laboratory Findings:
   1. Serum chloride and potassium may be lowered.
   2. Serum sodium, pH, and carbon dioxide content may be elevated.
   3. Plasma cortisol is increased and plasma and urinary diurnal variation may not occur.
   4. Excretion of urinary 11-oxysteroids and 17-hydroxycorticosteroids or hydrocortisone-like substances is increased. Urinary 17-ketosteroids may be normal, elevated, or low. Increased secretion of corticotropin (ACTH) occurs in patients in the later stages of adrenal hyperplasia and with ACTH-secreting nonendocrine tumors but not with other adrenal tumors. Suppression of 17-hydroxycorticosteroids

by high doses of dexamethasone occurs with adrenal hyperplasia but not with adrenal tumors.

5. Polymorphonuclear leukocytosis with lymphopenia.
6. Eosinophil count below 50/cu. mm.
7. RBC may be elevated.
8. Glycosuria alone or with carbohydrate intolerance and hyperglycemia may be present ("diabetic" type of glucose tolerance curve).
9. Urograms may be abnormal.

Treatment.

Since almost all cases of primary hyperfunction in childhood are due to tumor, surgical removal, if possible, is indicated. Corticotropin (ACTH) has been recommended for pre- and postoperative use to stimulate the nontumorous adrenal cortex, which is generally atrophied. Adrenocortical steroids should be administered for one or two days before surgery and continued during and after operation. Supplemental potassium, saline, and DCA may be necessary.

Pituitary irradiation may be of value to control Cushing's disease resulting from adrenal hyperplasia. If ineffective, bilateral adrenalectomy and hypophysectomy have been recommended. The use of o, p′-DDD (dichlorodiphenyldichloroethane) for the treatment of adrenal hyperplasia and tumors has been suggested.

Prognosis.

If the tumor is malignant, the prognosis is poor; if benign, cure should result following proper preparation and surgery.

ADRENOGENITAL SYNDROME

The congenital form of the adrenogenital syndrome is an autosomal recessive disease due to an inborn error of metabolism with a deficiency of an adrenocortical enzyme. Various types are recognized, including the following:

(1) Deficiency of 21-hydroxylase (approximately 80% of cases), resulting in inability to convert 17-hydroxyprogesterone into compound S (11-desoxycortisol). Mild forms result in androgenic changes (virilization) alone, but severe cases are associated with salt loss and electrolyte imbalance.

(2) Deficiency in 11β-hydroxylation and a failure to convert compound S to compound F (cortisol). Associated with virilization and usually with hypertension but no disturbance of electrolytes. Desoxycorticosterone and its metabolites are present.

(3) A defect in 17-hydroxylase, with the enzyme deficiency in both the adrenals and the gonads. Hypertension, virilization, and eunuchoidism may be present. Serum aldosterone levels may be low.

(4) A defect in 3β-hydroxysteroid dehydrogenase activity and a failure to convert Δ5-pregnenolone to progesterone. Associated with incomplete masculinization, with hypospadias and cryptorchidism, in the male. Some degree of masculinization may occur in the female. Severe sodium loss occurs, and the infant mortality rate is high.

(5) Cholesterol desmolase deficiency with congenital lipoid adrenal hyperplasia. Clinical features are similar to those of 3β-hydroxysteroid dehydrogenase deficiency (above). Urinary corticosteroid excretion does not occur.

Adrenogenital Syndrome in Females.

A. Congenital Bilateral Hyperplasia of the Adrenal Cortex (Pseudo-hermaphroditism): Abnormalities of the external genitalia include an enlarged clitoris with partial to complete labial fusion and a common urogenital sinus. Growth in height is excessive, bone age advanced, and patients become muscular and well developed. Pubic hair appears early, acne may be excessive, and the voice may be deep.

Pseudohermaphroditism in the female may also be produced as a result of the administration of androgens, progestins, stilbestrol, and related hormones to the mother during the first trimester of pregnancy or as a result of virilizing maternal tumors. In these cases, the condition regresses after birth.

B. Postnatal Adrenogenital Syndrome (Virilism): May be due to adrenal hyperplasia or tumor, or arrhenoblastoma (extremely rare). Enlargement of the clitoris occurs, but other changes of the genitalia are not found. The family history is negative. If a tumor is present, it may be palpably enlarged. Other findings are similar to those of pseudohermaphroditism.

Adrenogenital Syndrome in Males (Macrogenitosomia Praecox).

In males, precocious sexual development is along isosexual lines. With congenital bilateral hyperplasia of the adrenal cortex, the infant may appear normal at birth, but during the first few months of life the penis enlarges, the scrotum darkens, and the rugae become more prominent. Spermatogenesis does not occur. Other symptoms and signs are similar to those of the congenital form in females. If an adrenal or testicular tumor is the cause, the tumor may be palpable and masculinization may occur at a later age. Rarely, an adrenal tumor in either sex produces feminization, with gynecomastia resulting in males.

Laboratory Findings.
A. Urine:
1. 21-Hydroxylase deficiency - 17-Ketosteroids, pregnanetriol, and testosterone levels are elevated. (Note: During the first three weeks of life, normal infants may excrete up to 2.5 mg./day. Urinary pregnanetriol levels are sometimes normal in the neonatal period.) Aldosterone may be reduced, and excessive sodium loss occurs in salt-losing forms.
2. 11β-Hydroxylase deficiency - 11-Desoxycortisol (compound S), tetrahydro-compound S, desoxycorticosterone, and 17-ketosteroids and testosterone levels elevated.
3. 17-Hydroxylase deficiency - 17-Ketosteroid and aldosterone levels decreased; corticosterone and desoxycorticosterone levels increased.
4. 3β-Hydroxysteroid dehydrogenase deficiency - 17-Ketosteroid levels moderately elevated.
5. Cholesterol desmolase deficiency - All steroid excretion is markedly decreased.

6. Tumor - Excretion of dehydroepiandrosterone may be greatly elevated.
7. Urinary excretion of gonadotropins may be elevated.
B. Blood: Plasma renin activity may be elevated with 21-hydroxylase defect and decreased in the hypertensive form of the disease.
C. Dexamethasone Suppression Test: If the administration of dexamethasone, 2 to 4 mg./day in four doses for seven days, reduces 17-ketosteroids to normal, hyperplasia rather than adenoma is the probable diagnosis.
D. Buccal Smear: In female pseudohermaphrodites, the nuclear chromatin pattern is positive.
E. Nuclear Chromatin Pattern: Positive in female pseudohermaphroditism.

X-Ray Findings.

Genitograms using contrast media may indicate the presence of a urogenital sinus. Defects in the urogram, displacement of the kidney, and calcification in the area of the adrenal may be seen on x-rays of patients with tumors. Bone age is advanced with 21- and 11β-hydroxylase defects but may not be evident in the first year. Extraperitoneal pneumography may demonstrate adrenal pathology.

Treatment.

A. Congenital Hyperplasia of the Cortex:
1. Give cortisone acetate. Approximately 30 to 40 mg./sq.M./day will produce adrenal suppression and normal linear growth. Dosages of 10 to 25 mg./day to infants and 25 to 100 mg. daily to older children initially are usually necessary. The drug may be given orally in divided doses several times a day or I.M. (aqueous suspension) every three or five days.
2. Mineralocorticoids In salt-losing forms, desoxycorticosterone or fludrocortisone and sodium chloride therapy may be necessary (see p. 425).
3. Partial clitoridectomy is occasionally indicated in a girl with an abnormally large or sensitive clitoris but may be delayed for one or two years until the effect of therapy is determined. Surgical correction of the labial fusion and urogenital sinus may require several operations.
4. Other aspects of treatment are as for Addison's disease.
B. Tumor: Because the malignant lesions cannot be distinguished clinically from the benign ones, surgical removal is indicated whenever a tumor has been diagnosed. Preoperative and postoperative treatment are as for Cushing's syndrome due to a tumor (see p. 426).

Course and Prognosis.

Untreated cases of congenital hyperplasia will show precocious virilization throughout childhood, and these individuals will be tall as children but short as adults. Adequate adrenocorticosteroid treatment permits normal growth and sexual maturation.

Female pseudohermaphrodites mistakenly raised as males for more than three years may have serious psychologic disturbances if their sex is changed after that time.

When the adrenogenital syndrome is caused by a tumor, progression of signs and symptoms will cease after surgical removal; evidences of excessive masculinization may persist, however.

PRIMARY ALDOSTERONISM

Primary aldosteronism may be caused by an adrenal tumor or by adrenal hyperplasia. It is characterized by paresthesias, tetany, weakness, periodic "paralysis" with low serum potassium, hypertension, and hyposthenuria with alkaline urine and proteinuria, metabolic alkalosis, suppressed plasma renin activity, and low specific gravity which does not respond to vasopressin. Urinary aldosterone is elevated, but other steroid levels are variable. Treatment of tumor is surgical removal. With hyperplasia, subtotal or total adrenalectomy is recommended if glucocorticoid therapy is ineffective after two months.

A form of secondary hyperaldosteronism occurs in which both renin and aldosterone levels are elevated in the absence of hypertension (Bartter's syndrome). There is associated renovascular disease and hyperplasia of the juxtaglomerular apparatus and renal electrolyte wasting.

DISEASES OF THE ADRENAL MEDULLA

PHEOCHROMOCYTOMA
(Chromaffinoma)

Pheochromocytoma is an uncommon tumor which may be located wherever there is any chromaffin tissue (e.g., adrenal medulla, sympathetic ganglia, carotid body). The condition may be familial, and in children the tumors are often multiple and bilateral.

Clinical manifestations of pheochromocytoma are due to excessive secretion of epinephrine or norepinephrine. Attacks of anxiety and headaches should arouse suspicion. Other findings are palpitation, dizziness, weakness, nausea, vomiting, diarrhea, dilated pupils with blurring of vision, abdominal and precordial pain, rapid pulse, hypertension (usually persistent), and discomfort from heat. The symptoms may be sustained, producing all of the above findings plus papilledema, retinopathy, and cardiac enlargement.

Urine and serum catecholamines are elevated. The 24-hour urine collection shows increased urinary excretion of metanephrines and vanillylmandelic acid. Attacks may be provoked by mechanical stimulation of the tumor or by histamine or tyramine (**caution**). The phentolamine (Regitine®) test is abnormal, but it may be positive in other hypertensive states and not be necessary for diagnosis (**caution**). Displacement of the kidney may be shown by routine x-ray or after presacral insufflation of air.

Surgical removal of the tumor is the treatment of choice but is a dangerous procedure, and may produce a sudden paroxysm and death. The oral administration of phentolamine (Regitine®) preoperatively has been recommended to prevent the extreme fluctuations of blood pressure which sometimes occur during surgery.

Medical treatment includes phenoxybenzamine (Dibenzyline®) to reduce hypertension, and propranolol (Inderal®) to lessen tachycardia and ventricular arrhythmias.

Complete relief of symptoms except those due to long-standing vascular or renal changes is the rule after recovery. If untreated, severe cardiac, renal, and cerebral damage may result.

• • •

DIABETES MELLITUS

Diabetes mellitus is a generalized hereditary metabolic disorder which leads to derangement of carbohydrate, protein, and fat metabolism, followed by glycosuria, dehydration, ketoacidosis, coma, and eventually death. The administration of insulin corrects these deficiencies but is not curative.

Diabetes in the newborn may be transient; may not require insulin; and may disappear after weeks or months. In some cases diabetes has resulted from ingestion of inappropriately diluted powdered formula. Transient hyperglycemia, acetonuria, and glycosuria (in the absence of diabetic symptoms) have been noted in young children who have received phenylephrine or asparaginase.

Heredity is an important predisposing factor in the onset of diabetes, but the precise mode of inheritance has not been determined.

Clinical Findings.
A. Early Manifestations in Chemical and Overt Disease (one to two months or less): Thirst and polydipsia, polyuria and nocturia or enuresis, loss of weight or failure to gain, increase in appetite (less common than in adults; anorexia is often noted), lassitude and easy fatigability, cramping pains in the limbs or abdomen, dizziness, confusion, hyperventilation, and sudden coma or stupor (due to diabetic acidosis).

   Spontaneous hypoglycemia may occur as an early manifestation of diabetes in childhood.
B. Chronic Complications: Stunting of growth and poor development are found in patients with uncontrolled diabetes of long standing. Serious psychologic difficulties are not infrequent. Characteristic "small vessel" changes occur. Diabetic retinopathy usually develops in the majority of juvenile diabetics after ten years of known disease. There may also develop intercapillary glomerulosclerosis (Kimmelstiel-Wilson changes), with hypertension, edema, proteinuria, and atherosclerosis, although the latter is not as frequent as in adults.
C. Laboratory Findings: Glycosuria, fasting hyperglycemia (a fasting blood glucose level > 120 mg./100 ml. in the absence of obesity or drug is generally indicative of diabetes mellitus), and hyperglycemia two hours after a meal. (A normal fasting blood glucose level does not rule out diabetes.) Other findings include abnormal glucose tolerance tests, ketonuria, hyperlipidemia, hemoconcentration, and lactic acidemia.

   Both low and high plasma insulin concentrations have been reported depending on the stage of the disease.

TABLE 22-7. Action of insulin after subcutaneous injection.*

Official or Generic Name	Synonym or Trade Name	Activity (Hours)		
		Onset	Maximal	Duration
Insulin injection	Insulin Insulin hydrochloride Regular or unmodified insulin	1/2-1	2-4	5-8
Insulin zinc suspension, prompt	Semi-lente insulin	1/2-3/4	4-8	12-18
Globin zinc insulin	Globin insulin	1-2	6-10	10-20
Isophane insulin suspension	Isophane insulin NPH insulin	1/2-2	8-12	16-24
Insulin zinc suspension	Lente insulin	1-2	12-18	20-24
Protamine zinc insulin suspension	Protamine zinc insulin	4-8	14-24	24-36+
Insulin zinc suspension, extended	Ultra-lente insulin	5-8	14-20	34-36+

*Modified from various sources.

Treatment.
A. Insulin: Insulin therapy is necessary in almost all cases of childhood diabetes. Initially (seven to 14 days), the insulin requirements may be high, followed by a period of considerably lower needs, but requirements will soon rise again after that. The initial dose of insulin may be determined primarily by trial and error in relation to urine glucose and occasional blood glucose determinations; in many cases it will be approximately 1 unit daily for every 30 Calories of food taken. The juvenile diabetic should usually be started at once on long-acting preparations, preferably equal proportions of semi-lente and ultra-lente or regular and NPH insulin one-half hour before breakfast. Crystalline insulin is generally reserved for emergency situations and as a supplemental dose with injections for other critical changes. In patients who require more than 60 units of insulin daily, pork insulin may be more effective than beef insulin.

The average juvenile diabetic who has had the disease for several years must use between 40 and 80 units of insulin daily.
B. Oral Hypoglycemic Agents: These drugs play a minimal role in the management of juvenile diabetes, although they are occasionally employed in the adolescent.
C. Diet: The diet should be well balanced, allowing approximately 1000 Calories plus an additional 100 Calories/year of age. Give 45 to 55% as carbohydrate, 35 to 45% as fat, and 15 to 20% as protein. Many believe that the patient may be allowed freedom to eat according to appetite but within sensible limits. Intermittent mild glycosuria (without ketosis) is permitted. The patient should know about the American Diabetes Association

exchange diet, which uses household measurements rather than weights. With the use of long-acting or intermediate insulin, one must give a bedtime feeding to prevent hypoglycemia during the night. A small feeding in the afternoon or before exercise may also be indicated.

In general, diabetic patients should be kept at normal or slightly subnormal weight levels. An attempt should be made to maintain normal serum lipoprotein and cholesterol levels.

D. Other Factors Influencing the Regulation of Diabetes:

1. Activity - Strenuous exercise tends to lower the insulin requirement; a sedentary existence may increase the requirement. Exercise in moderation (and without significant day-to-day variations) is beneficial. However, patients should be cautioned against strenuous exercise unless they take extra carbohydrate beforehand.

2. Infection - Any infection is serious in a diabetic patient; it completely upsets the equilibrium established by therapy, always increasing the need for insulin, and is one of the most common precipitating causes of ketosis and acidosis. During severe infections it is often necessary to add small doses of supplemental crystalline insulin before two of the major meals in order to overcome the insulin resistance that goes with severe infections. Enough crystalline insulin should be given to compensate for most of the postprandial glycosuria.

3. Surgery of the diabetic patient - Prior to elective surgery the patient should be given half the usual dose of long-acting insulin in the morning; following this, 5 or 10% dextrose in water should be administered slowly I.V. prior to, during, and after surgery to cover the insulin. If the patient is unable to return to oral food intake promptly, I.V. glucose and electrolytes are continued and glycosuria is controlled by small amounts of crystalline insulin given on the basis of spot tests for glucose every four hours, as follows: 4+, give 0.3 units/Kg. of crystalline insulin; 3+, give 0.2 units/Kg.; 2+, give 0.1 units/Kg.; 1+, give no insulin. On the day after surgery, the usual amount of long-acting insulin should be administered. It may have to be supplemented by crystalline insulin if the urine shows more than 2+ glucose in the majority of tests. As soon as possible, feedings by mouth should be reinstituted and an early return to the exclusive use of long-acting insulin anticipated.

4. Suspect occult hypoglycemia, posthypoglycemic hyperglycemia ("Somogyi effect"), and overdosage with insulin in diabetic children with conspicuous fluctuations in glycosuria.

DIABETIC ACIDOSIS
(Diabetic Coma)

Clinical Findings.

A. Symptoms and Signs: Diabetic acidosis is characterized by marked thirst and polyuria followed by nausea and vomiting, abdominal pain, and general malaise. Dehydration and acidosis develop rapidly. Respirations then become long, deep and labored; headache, irritability, drowsiness, stupor, and finally coma may develop. On physical examination the patient is irritable, drowsy, or unconscious, and there is marked dehydration. The skin and mucous membranes are usually dry, lips cherry red, eyeballs soft, blood pressure low, pulse usually rapid and thready, hyperventilation present, temperature low, and a sweetish ("fruity") acetone breath may be detected. The abdomen may show diffuse spasm and tenderness suggestive of an acute abdominal disorder. The signs and symptoms of the precipitating cause (infection, trauma, etc.) will also be found.

A syndrome of hyperosmolar nonketotic diabetic coma in children has been described. It is characterized by the presence of hyperglycemia, severe dehydration, and metabolic acidosis. The duration of illness is short. There is little or no polydipsia and polyuria, and these children are frequently insulin-resistant. In treatment, sufficient insulin (and isotonic parenteral fluid initially) should be used to normalize glucose metabolism.

B. Laboratory Studies: Glycosuria, ketonemia, ketonuria, hyperglycemia. Serum sodium, chloride, and plasma carbon dioxide content low. Serum potassium and inorganic phosphorus may be elevated initially, but there is a major total body depletion of these elements. Total protein, hemoglobin, and B.U.N. may be elevated. Leukocytosis and increased hematocrit are often present.

Treatment.

A. Objectives: Restoration of circulation, correction of fluid and electrolyte deficit, reestablishment of normal carbohydrate metabolism, and eradication of the cause of acidosis and the hyperosmolar state.

B. Emergency Measures:

1. Hospitalize patient - Keep warm, but avoid excessive warmth. Do not give narcotics or barbiturates.

2. Treat shock, if present, with plasma and other anti-shock measures (see Chapter 2).

3. Evaluate the degree of dehydration and shock by physical examination, weight of child, and hematocrit.

4. Obtain urine for estimation of glucose, ketones, acetone, and diacetic acid, specific gravity, and evidence of infection or acute tubular necrosis.

5. Take blood for determination of pH, carbon dioxide content, sodium, chloride, potassium, blood glucose, serum inorganic phosphorus, B.U.N., and ketone bodies. Measurement of blood lactic acid level may also be of value, especially in the acidotic nonketotic patient.

6. Insulin -
   a. Immediate - Regular insulin, 0.75 to 1 unit/Kg. ideal body weight; give half subcut. and half I.V. in the first parenteral solution. In a new diabetic patient, first try a small dose (0.1 to 0.2 unit/Kg. I.V.) and observe the effect before giving larger amount. Relatively larger doses of insulin (1.25 units/Kg.) may be necessary later in infants. Intramuscular insulin in a dose of 0.05 to 0.2 units/Kg./hour may be administered effectively under

close observation.

b. Follow-up in severe states - In severely acidotic patients it may be necessary to give insulin, 0.5 to 1 unit/Kg., every two to four hours. Regulation in these patients should be based on the degree of ketosis and on repeated blood glucose levels (not urine glucose levels unless no parenteral carbohydrate has been given).

7. Gastric lavage is advisable early to relieve distention of the stomach and to reduce vomiting.

8. Fluids and electrolytes -

a. From balance studies the deficits of fluid and electrolyte resulting from severe diabetic acidosis would appear to be about as follows:*

Water deficit of 100 to 125 ml./Kg. ideal body weight.
Sodium deficit of 6 to 12 mEq./Kg.
Chloride deficit of 4 to 9 mEq./Kg.
Potassium deficit of 2 to 7 mEq./Kg.
Bicarbonate deficit = 24 (normal level of bicarbonate minus patient's bicarbonate) × 0.6 ("bicarbonate space") × weight in Kg.

However, only 80% of the deficit of water, sodium, and chloride, and 50% of the deficit of potassium, should be replaced in the first 24 hours; 30% may be given during the first two to four hours. On the first day, the patient should also receive maintenance and concurrent loss replacement (see Chapter 5).

b. First correct extracellular dehydration, shock, anoxia, and impaired renal function with:

(1) Normal sodium chloride solution or solution containing 150 mEq./L sodium, 100 mEq./L. chloride, and 50 mEq./L. bicarbonate. Give 20 to 30 ml./Kg. over the first one or two hours of therapy.

(2) Then give the same solution at a rate calculated to restore deficits (see above) and supply maintenance amounts and replace intercurrent losses.

c. When urine flow and circulatory efficiency are satisfactory and signs of hyperpnea have begun to subside (generally in two to four hours), replace intracellular electrolytes (potassium and phosphorus). Although serum potassium and phosphorus† are usually normal or high early in acidosis, they may drop to low levels. Give potassium phosphate solution with glucose, 40 ml./Kg., subcut., during the second to seventh hours of therapy.‡ Potassium must not be given until shock has been overcome.

d. Replace the remainder of the water deficit and, if the glucose level is falling toward normal, administer 5% glucose during the second to seventh hours.

---

*The larger amounts are indicated for the infant; the smaller amounts for the older child.
†Phosphorus: Serum phosphorus tends to parallel potassium; therefore, potassium phosphate is the choice for the replacement of both ions.
‡The solution is made by adding 20 ml. of potassium phosphate solution (Abbott) to 1000 ml. of 5% glucose in water.

C. General Measures:
1. Ascertain the precipitating cause of the acidosis and initiate appropriate treatment.
2. Glucose - Although the patient with acidosis may have a high blood glucose level, the total carbohydrate stores are depleted. When the blood glucose has begun to fall (200 to 600 mg./100 ml.), glucose or invert sugar should be given. If the blood glucose is above 600 mg./100 ml., parenteral glucose should not be given. In the presence of hypoglycemia, give 1 to 2 ml./Kg. of 50% glucose diluted half-and-half with water or 0.5 N saline.
3. Indwelling catheter if spontaneous voidings are not possible.
4. Whole blood transfusion or plasma, 10 to 20 ml./Kg., may be indicated after initial hydration is well under way. In the presence of shock, transfusions should be given at once. Fresh blood is preferable since stored bank blood contains a higher level of potassium in the plasma.
5. Determine urinary glucose and acetone, blood glucose and carbon dioxide, and serum electrolytes at frequent intervals.
6. Continuous or intermittent Ecg. monitoring is helpful to follow the effect of potassium therapy.
7. Fluids and electrolytes - After the first seven hours of therapy, continue giving parenteral fluids slowly until the remainder of the calculated first day's total deficit, ongoing losses, and maintenance fluids and electrolytes have been given.
8. Oral fluids - After 12 to 18 hours, if there is no vomiting, the remainder of the day's fluid and electrolyte requirements may be given orally in a suitable vehicle (orange juice, ginger ale, or milk). Vomiting generally subsides after ketosis has been corrected.
9. Further fluid therapy - Continued fluid and electrolyte therapy (see Chapter 5).

Prognosis.

With prompt and adequate therapy, the prognosis is good. The largest number of serious side-effects and sequelae result from delayed or inadequate correction of fluid and electrolyte losses and overzealous correction of the hyperglycemia and ketoacidosis. Recurrent episodes of acidosis are due to failure to take the proper insulin or diet or to chronic or repeated infections.

HYPOGLYCEMIA AND HYPERINSULINISM
(See also Neonatal Hypoglycemia, p. 155.)

Hypoglycemia may be induced by overdosage with insulin in the treatment of diabetes mellitus or when the diabetic fails to eat or exercises too strenuously; by hyperplasia of the pancreatic islands; by benign or malignant tumors of the pancreatic islands (uncommon in childhood, malignant tumors very rare), in certain patients after the administration of leucine alone or in a mixed protein, occasionally in salicylism or alcohol intoxication or after the administration of other drugs, in association with ketosis, or in patients with a deficiency in glucagon or epinephrine production. It may also be caused by instability of the carbohydrate metabolism of the body (idiopathic), diseases of the liver which interfere with the storage or utilization of glycogen (including glycogen storage disease, fructose intolerance, and galactosemia), diseases of the adrenal cortex or of the anterior pituitary which interfere with normal gluconeogenesis, diseases of the gastrointestinal tract with abnormalities of absorption, diseases with defective tubular reabsorption, with certain nonpancreatic tumors, as an idiopathic form in infancy (often familial), in infants with cretinism, with C. N. S. disease, and by inanition. Functional hypoglycemia (without symptoms or signs) is common in the newborn period and may appear transiently after feedings in older children. There is an increased incidence of hypoglycemia in low birth weight infants and in the smaller of twins.

Ketotic hypoglycemia may occur as a familial condition and is more common in low birth weight (SGA) infants. The onset is usually in infancy, and the incidence is higher in low birth weight infants. It is characterized by early morning seizures, ketosis, and hypoglycemia occurring spontaneously or within 24 hours after institution of a ketogenic diet.

Clinical Findings.

A. Signs and Symptoms: Weakness, hunger, irritability, faintness, sweating, changes in mood, epigastric pain, vomiting, nervousness, hypothermia, unsteadiness of gait, semiconsciousness, tremors, and convulsions. All of these are relieved by the administration of glucose. If left untreated, hypoglycemia may lead to extensive C. N. S. damage. Symptomatic hypoglycemia is more commonly associated with mental deterioration, disintegration of the personality, and death, but some infants may have prolonged and severe hypoglycemia and subsequently develop normally. Brain damage appears to result more frequently from second or subsequent episodes of hypoglycemia than from the first. It has been suggested that in some cases the C. N. S. dysfunction is primary and may play an etiologic role in the production of the hypoglycemia.

B. Laboratory Findings. (See Table 22-8.)

1. Blood glucose is low during an attack. There is no sharp dividing line below which a blood glucose level can be regarded as abnormal, but consistent or repeated levels below 50 mg./100 ml., except in the neonatal period, generally are considered to be significantly lowered.

2. Serum insulin levels may be inappropriately elevated in hyperinsulinemic states when compared with the simultaneous glucose level.

3. No single test of blood glucose regulation reliably confirms the diagnosis of hypoglycemia, and no combination of tests reliably establishes the mechanism of hypoglycemia.

Treatment.

Caution: Do not attempt to feed an unconscious patient.

Long-term treatment for the specific type is outlined in Table 22-8. Acute treatment is usually necessary prior to definitive diagnosis and includes:

A. Glucose:

1. Infuse 10 to 20% dextrose via peripheral vein, at a constant

TABLE 22-8. Hypoglycemia.

Classification	Clinical and Laboratory Features	Treatment
I. Antenatal period Fetal malnutrition (placental insufficiency) Sepsis Offspring diabetic mothers Erythroblastosis fetalis Neonatal cold injury Hypoglycemia, cardiomegaly and pulmonary edema	Offspring of diabetic mothers and infants with erythroblastosis fetalis may have hyperinsulinemia with rebound hypoglycemia to insulinogenic stimuli; blood insulin:glucose ratios are elevated. The other conditions listed have in common depleted fat hepatic glycogen stores and fasting hypoglycemia.	(1) 10 to 20% glucose infusion by peripheral vein; frequent oral feedings. (2) Avoidance or cautious administration of insulinogenic agents (e.g., arginine, 50% dextrose) in hyperinsulinism states.
II. Primary neurologic disorders ("central")	Hypoglycemia is frequently observed in children with neurologic disorders of various types. No definite pattern or consistent metabolic abnormality has been demonstrated, although hyperinsulinemia has not been a feature.	(1) Frequent feedings. (2) Anticonvulsants when indicated.
III. Idiopathic spontaneous hypoglycemia	(1) Fasting hypoglycemia occurring with the first two years in 90% of cases. (2) No determinable cause.	(1) Frequent high carbohydrate feedings.
IV. Metabolic disorders (1) Liver glycogen storage disease (2) Liver glycogen synthetase deficiency (3) Fructose intolerance (4) Maple syrup urine disease (5) Deficiency of liver 1,-6-diphosphatase activity	Definitive diagnosis is dependent on enzyme determination. Blunted hyperglycemia response to glucagon is found in 1, 2, and 5. History of hypoglycemia after fructose ingestion in No. 3 and a characteristic odor in No. 4 are helpful.	(1 & 2) Frequent feedings high in carbohydrates, hyperalimentation, portacaval diversion in severe type I may be indicated. (3 & 4) Rigid avoidance of offending substrate.

V. Endocrine insufficiency syndromes (1) Hypopituitarism (2) Hypopituitarism and hyper-insulinemia (3) Adrenocortical insufficiency (4) Adrenomedullary insuffi-ciency (Broberger-Zetterström) (5) Congenital hypothyroidism (6) Glucagon deficiency	Definitive diagnosis is dependent on biochemical establishment of hormone deficiency. History of failure to thrive, growth retardation, and features of hypopituitarism (1 & 2), excessive tanning (3), and abnormal weight for gestational age (4) are helpful clinical features.	Replacement of deficient hormone or hormones.
VI. Ketotic hypoglycemias	History of low birthweight for gestational age; onset between ages 2 and 6 years. Triad of hypoglycemia, ketosis, and blunted glycemic response to glucagon. May have abnormalities in gluconeogenesis with abnormalities in hepatic handling of alanine during a fast.	Frequent feeding with diet high in carbohydrate and protein.
VII. Severe malnutrition states (1) Chronic diarrhea (2) Liver disease	Characterized by fasting hypoglycemia and depleted glycogen and fat stores.	(1) Nutritional rehabilitation.
VIII. Hyperinsulin states (1) Islet cell hyperplasia (2) Islet cell adenoma or adeno-carcinoma (3) Islet cell nesidioblastosis (4) Leucine sensitivity (5) Beckwith-Weidemann-Coombs syndrome	As a whole, this group is prone to fasting hypo-glycemia and rebound hypoglycemia to insulino-genic stimuli. Diagnosis dependent on finding of abnormally elevated insulin or proinsulin levels during fasting state or following insulin provocation with glucose, amino acids (i.e., leucine, arginine), glucagon, or tolbutamide. Clinically, No. 5 is characterized by the EMG triad of exomphalos, macroglossia, and gigantism with abdominal organomegaly.	(1) Avoidance of insulinogenic stimuli. (2) Catecholamines and diazoxide. (3) Pancreatectomy.

rate, maintaining a blood sugar level that controls C. N. S. symptoms (e. g. , newborn 30 mg./100 ml. , children 40 to 50 mg./100 ml.). If hyperinsulinemia is suspected or is a possibility, avoid bolus (''push'') infusions of concentrated dextrose solutions. (Fifty percent dextrose solutions are seldom necessary during infancy and childhood.)

2. Rectal feeding - If the patient is unconscious and a physician is not available, glucose by rectum may be life-saving. Add 1 oz. (2 tbsp.) of syrup, honey, or sugar to a pint of warm water and give slowly, using a rectal tube.

3. If a diagnosis of hypoglycemia not due to hyperinsulinism has been established, carbohydrates can be safely administered via any route without risk of hypoglycemic rebound.

4. If a diabetic patient is seen unconscious, and if a diagnosis of coma or insulin reaction is impossible or in doubt, give 50% glucose I. V. This will definitely overcome the insulin reaction and will not harm the patient in diabetic acidosis.

B. Drugs:

1. In general, drug therapy should be employed only after a definite diagnosis (Table 22-8) is established.

2. If the cardiorespiratory status permits, catecholamines (oral ephedrine sulfate; subcutaneous epinephrine in oil [Sus-Phrine®]) may be useful and have the unique advantage in the undiagnosed case of avoiding insulin stimulation.

3. Adrenocorticosteroids, ACTH, and glucagon may be helpful in controlling hypoglycemia, but they may stimulate insulin, and the action of glucagon in the neonate is unpredictable (see pp. 421-423 and p. 621 for dosage).

4. In severe chronic hyperinsulin states, diazoxide (Hyperstat®) is useful. Diazoxide, a nondiuretic benzothiadiazine, may be of value in controlling chronic idiopathic hypoglycemia and certain cases of hyperinsulinism, including leucine-sensitive hypoglycemia. The dosage has varied from 5 to 20 mg./Kg./day. Side-effects include hypertrichosis, advancement of epiphyseal maturation, hyperuricemia, fluid retention, neutropenia, and depression of immunoglobulin G. Failure of adequate response to therapy with diazoxide should prompt consideration of subtotal pancreatectomy.

5. Sedatives and anticonvulsant therapy may be helpful to reduce convulsions and neuromuscular irritability. (Diphenylhydantoin has the added effect of reducing insulin stimulation.)

C. Diet: High-protein, high-caloric, high-fat. In leucine-sensitive patients, however, a low-leucine diet is indicated. In ketotic hypoglycemia, use a liberal carbohydrate diet and place a moderate restriction on ketogenic foods.

1. Give no concentrated forms of carbohydrate in order to avoid stimulation of the pancreas to elaborate insulin. Rapidly utilized carbohydrates are replaced by slow-acting ones.

2. Give small frequent feedings (six or more meals a day). It may be necessary to feed the patient at regular intervals throughout the 24 hours and to give small carbohydrate feedings 30 to 45 minutes after regular meals.

D. Surgical removal of a portion of the pancreas (or of a tumor if present) should be undertaken for any individual who cannot be controlled by the above measures.

Prognosis.

Excellent results have been reported in some treated cases of the idiopathic form of the disease and following removal of a tumor. Otherwise the results depend on the underlying condition.

• • •

GALACTOSEMIA
(Galactose Diabetes)

Galactosemia is a hereditary (recessive) disease due to congenital absence of the activity of the enzyme galactose-1-phosphate uridyl-transferase, which is necessary to convert galactose-1-phosphate to glucose-1-phosphate. In certain types, enzyme activity may be decreased in red cells but not in the tissues. There is decreased activity of the enzyme in the heterozygous individual. It is characterized by feeding difficulties, hepatomegaly with or without splenomegaly, cataracts, mental retardation (not universal), and jaundice in the neonatal period. Pseudotumor cerebri may occur. There is galactosemia and hypoglycemia (**total** reducing substance in blood may be normal or even elevated), galactosuria, aminoaciduria, albuminuria, and increased levels of galactose-1-phosphate in erythrocytes.

Treatment consists of excluding galactose (especially milk and its derivatives) from the diet. This prevents the development of the signs and symptoms of the disease or may result in improvement after they have developed. A more normal diet may be tolerated later in childhood. Administration of progesterone may minimize progression of cataract formation and mental deficiency.

The mother of a known galactosemic child should be on a restricted galactose diet during subsequent pregnancies.

GLYCOGEN STORAGE DISEASE

Types of Glycogen Storage Diseases. (Adapted from O'Brien and Ibbott.)

Type I. Von Gierke's disease. Most common. Involves liver and kidneys. Deficiency in glucose-6-phosphatase. Epinephrine and glucagon tolerance curves are flat. Elevated blood lactic and pyruvic acid levels. Abnormal glycogen deposition in liver. May be associated with debranching enzyme deficiency. Doll face, stunted growth, normal development. May be improved with a portacaval shunt.

Type II. Pompe's disease. Generalized glycogenosis. Muscle weakness; cardiomegaly; macroglossia; hepatomegaly; normal mental development. Deficiency of the lysosomal enzyme alpha-1,4-glucosidase.

Type III. Cori's disease. Involves liver, striated muscle, and red blood cells. Clinical features similar to type I but less severe. Defect in debranching enzymes (amylo-

1, 6-glucosidase or oligo-1, 4-glucantransferase).
Hepatomegaly.

Type IV. Amylopectinosis. Andersen's disease. Abnormal glycogen in liver and reticuloendothelial system. Diminished response to glucagon and epinephrine. Defect of
branching enzyme (amylo-1, 4 → 1, 6-transglucosi-
dase?). Hepatosplenomegaly; cirrhosis, ascites.
Normal mental development.

Type V. McArdle's syndrome. Involves skeletal muscle. Defect in muscle phosphorylase.

Type VI. Hers' disease. Clinically similar to type I but less
severe. Deficiency in liver phosphorylase.

Type VII. Other types involving reduced activity of phosphoglu-
comutase, phosphofructokinase, or phosphohexoiso-
merase may have weak muscles, partial defect of
other glycolytic enzymes, and elevated SGOT, serum
aldolase, and phosphocreatine kinase.

Type I glycogen storage disease is an autosomal recessive disease. It starts at birth or in early infancy and is characterized by
anorexia, weight loss, vomiting, convulsions, and coma. There is
organomegaly (liver and kidneys), retardation of growth, obesity
with a "doll-like" appearance, and bleeding tendencies. Laboratory
findings may include acetonuria, hypoglycemia, hyperlipemia, inadequate response to epinephrine and glucagon, and impaired glucose tolerance with insulinopenia. Cardiac failure, intermittent
cyanosis, muscular weakness, neurologic abnormalities, hepatic
cirrhosis, and marked enlargement of the tongue may occur in
some types. Treatment includes frequent feedings, and sodium
bicarbonate to combat acidosis. The prognosis in type I is generally
poor, although there is a tendency to improve at puberty and some
patients live for many years.

PHENYLKETONURIA
(Phenylpyruvic Oligophrenia)

Phenylketonuria is a hereditary (recessive) familial disease
caused by a deficiency of phenylalanine hydroxylase. Affected
children (most often blond and blue-eyed) appear normal at birth
but soon develop vomiting, irritability, a peculiar odor, patchy
eczematous lesions of the skin, convulsions, a schizoid-like personality, and EEG abnormalities. Mentality is retarded. (An
occasional patient may have normal intelligence without treatment.)
The children are hyperactive, with unpredictable, erratic behavior.
Perspiration is excessive. Serum and urinary phenylalanine levels
are markedly high as determined by ferric chloride test, Pheni-
stix® paper strip, or Guthrie bacterial inhibition assay test (of particular value in young infants). Some normal infants, particularly
those with physiologic jaundice of the newborn, may have transiently
elevated (> 6 mg./100 ml.) blood levels of phenylalanine. Ortho-
hydroxyphenylacetic acid is usually present in the urine.

A diet low in phenylalanine (approximately 70 to 90 mg. of
phenylalanine/Kg.) should keep plasma phenylalanine levels around
8 mg./100 ml. , and, when started in the first weeks of life, pre-

vents severe retardation. The diet should be titrated against the nutritional status of the child and the serum phenylalanine levels to ensure that the diet is restricted enough to prevent manifestations of the disease but liberal enough to prevent hypophenylalaninemia with resultant malnutrition and cerebral damage. In established cases such a diet may arrest the condition and produce improvement in personality and in symptoms other than the mental deficiency. It may be discontinued after several years.

The blood phenylalanine levels of phenylketonuric females should be maintained in the normal range during the childbearing years to decrease the risk of abnormalities (e. g. , growth and mental retardation, microcephaly) in their offspring who may be non-phenylketonuric.

Hyperphenylalaninemia may be a transient phenomenon in some newborns who have normal urinary metabolites and do not require treatment.

23 ...

Neoplastic Diseases &
Reticuloendothelioses*

Cancer in children differs biologically from cancer in adults.
(See Fig 23-1.) Neoplastic disease is the second leading cause of
death in the pediatric age group in the U.S.A. Solid tumors represent 60% of cases and acute leukemia the remaining 40%.

NEUROFIBROMATOSIS
(Von Recklinghausen's Disease)

Neurofibromatosis is a hereditary autosomal dominant disorder
characterized by the gradual development of numerous pedunculated
soft tissue tumors. It is frequently associated with small areas of
skin pigmentation (café au lait spots) and sometimes with mental

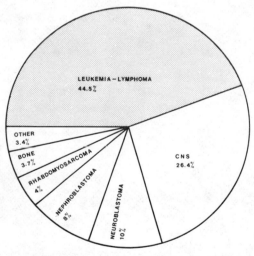

FIG 23-1. **Relative frequencies of malignancies in childhood.** (Tumor experience at Children's Hospital, Denver, from 1931 to
October 1, 1972. Total cases: 867. Courtesy of B. Favara, M.D.)

---

*With the assistance of Charlene P. Holton, MD, Assistant Clinical
Professor of Pediatrics, University of Colorado Medical Center,
and Director of Clinical Oncology, Children's Hospital, Denver.

deficiency. Lesions are found in the skin and subcutaneous tissues (mollusca fibrosa), bones, peripheral nerves (neurofibromas), and the spinal canal. Neurofibromas are formed in the sheaths of the peripheral nerves and may rarely undergo malignant degeneration to form sarcomas. Glioma of the C.N.S. is frequently associated with neurofibromatosis.

Clinical Findings.

Skin lesions are of two types: (1) areas of smooth-bordered brown discoloration (café au lait spots) and (2) multiple fibromas. Many findings are caused by pressure on adjacent structures. Their location and size determine the severity of symptoms. There may be loss of function of the area supplied by a nerve that is compressed, or sensory and motor changes due to compression on spinal cord roots. Eighth nerve involvement is common.

Treatment.

Localized lesions may be excised to relieve pressure. Recurrences are frequent.

Course and Prognosis.

The prognosis for life varies depending on the presence or absence of malignant degeneration and pressure symptoms. Peripheral neurofibromas are generally devoid of serious complications and have a good prognosis. However, in the presence of associated intraspinal or intracranial tumors, the prognosis is poor.

BRAIN TUMORS
(See Table 23-1.)

Over 75% of brain tumors of childhood are gliomas. Almost all of these are characteristically found in the posterior fossa. The most prominent general symptom of C.N.S. tumor of childhood is headache. The two most prominent physical findings are enlargement of the head and papilledema.

In the newborn, the various forms of hydrocephalus are the most common cause of abnormal enlargement, but tumors may cause enlargement. If abnormal skull enlargement occurs between two months and one year of age, subdural hematoma is more likely responsible. The most common cause of abnormal increase in the size of the head after one year of age is tumor.

Diagnostic Points.
A. An elevated white blood cell count and a rapid sedimentation rate, even in the absence of fever, suggest a diagnosis of pyogenic brain abscess rather than neoplasm.
B. Papilledema occurs in internal hydrocephalus due to brain tumor but not in idiopathic internal hydrocephalus.
C. The "cracked pot" percussion note elicited in internal hydrocephalus (Macewen's sign) has previously been considered diagnostic of this condition, but it is also present in subdural hematoma and in some normal children with open sutures.

TABLE 23-1. Brain tumors.

Part Affected	Symptoms and Signs	Radiologic Findings	Tumor Type and Characteristics	Treatment and Prognosis
Cerebellum and fourth ventricle	Evidence of increased intracranial pressure.* Cerebellar signs.† Signs due to pressure on adjacent structures in posterior fossa.‡ Personality and behavioral changes. Occasionally emaciation.	Skull films: signs of increased intracranial pressure.§ Brain scan of posterior fossa may be helpful. Ventriculography or positive pressure encephalography may show tumor and hydrocephalus. Brachial angiography often useful in demonstrating hydrocephalus, abnormal vascular patterns, and herniation.	Astrocytoma: slow growth, frequently cystic. Medulloblastoma: rapid growth; primarily 2-6 years; about 75% in boys; seeds along C.S.F. pathways. Less common: ependymoma, hemangioblastoma, choroid plexus papilloma.	Surgical removal. Follow by intensive x-ray therapy if removal incomplete. Prognosis good if removal complete. Surgical decompression of posterior fossa and x-ray therapy to site, cerebrum, and spinal canal. Chemotherapy. Shunt (ventriculopleural, etc.) to relieve C.S.F. obstruction. Prognosis grave: rare 5-year survivors. Surgical cure possible with hemangioblastomas and choroid plexus papilloma.
Brain stem	Cranial nerve palsies (IX-X, VII, VI, V; primarily sensory root), pyramidal tract signs (hemiparesis), and cerebellar ataxia. Signs of increased intracranial pressure (rarely).*	Pneumoencephalographic demonstration of posterior fossa and displacement of cerebral aqueduct (aqueduct of Sylvius) and fourth ventricle.	Astrocytoma (varying grades; polar spongioblastoma): usually rapid growth and recurrence.	X-ray therapy to site results in remission for short periods. Prognosis grave: average survival 1 year, particularly when medulla is involved.
Midbrain and third ventricle	Personality and behavioral changes (often early). Evidence of increased intracranial pressure.* Pyramidal tract signs and cerebellar signs.† Inability to rotate eyes upward. Sudden loss of consciousness. Seizures rare.	Skull films: signs of increased intracranial pressure.§ Brain scan and echoencephalography are helpful. Air and contrast ventriculography in third ventricle masses. Pineal gland rarely calcified in childhood.	Astrocytomas, teratomas, including pinealoma (macrogenitosomia praecox in boys), ependymoma. Choroid plexus papilloma and colloid cyst.	Shunt procedure (ventriculocisternal, etc.) for relief of C.S.F. obstruction and intensive x-ray therapy. Prognosis poor. Prognosis good with total surgical removal.

Region	Clinical Features	Diagnostic Procedures	Tumor Types	Treatment/Prognosis
Diencephalon	Emaciated; good intake; often very active, euphoric. Few neurologic findings. Pale, without anemia. Frequently: eosinophilia, low PBI and pulmonary reserve.	Pneumoencephalography shows defect in floor of third ventricle and other midline findings. Echoencephalography may be useful. Brain scan, EEG, and angiography usually not diagnostic.	Usually astrocytomas; less common: oligodendroglioma, glioma, ependymoma, glioblastoma.	X-ray treatment. C.S.F. shunt for block. Prognosis variable; generally poor.
Suprasellar region	Visual disorders (visual field defects, optic atrophy). Hypothalamic disorders (including diabetes insipidus, adiposity). Pituitary disorders (growth arrest, hypothyroidism, delayed sexual maturation). Evidence of increased intracranial pressure.*	Skull films: suprasellar calcification in about 90%. Deformity of sella turcica frequent. Enlarged optic foramens in optic gliomas. Pneumoencephalography in absence of increased intracranial pressure; otherwise, ventriculography.	Optic glioma: high incidence of café au lait spots. Craniopharyngioma: often dormant for years.	X-ray if optic chiasm involved. Surgical removal if only one optic nerve is involved. Prognosis fair to good. Conservative approach advised. Complete excision with hormone replacement now often feasible; or drainage of cyst and irradiation. Prognosis good with complete removal.
Cerebral hemispheres and lateral ventricles	Evidence of increased intracranial pressure.* Seizures (generalized, psychomotor, focal) in about 40%. Neurologic deficits include hemiparesis (40%), visual field defects, ataxia, and personality changes.	Signs of increased intracranial pressure.§ Occasionally calcifications. Angiography preferred where lateralizing signs are present. Brain scan may be helpful, as may echoencephalogram and EEG. Ventriculography, especially for lesions in ventricles. Pneumoencephalography in absence of increased pressure.	Gliomas; primary astrocytomas; glioblastomas in 10%; meningiomas rare. Leptomeningeal sarcoma. Ependymoma and choroid plexus papilloma.	Surgical biopsy or excision where possible. X-ray treatment. Chemotherapy: BCNU, 150 mg./sq.M. I.V., and CCNU, 120 mg. orally every 4-6 weeks. Prognosis varies with tumor type. Surgical excision of choroid plexus papilloma; occasionally, hydrocephalus persists and requires shunt procedure.

*Headache, vomiting (often without nausea and before breakfast), blurred vision, and papilledema and personality changes, including irritability, apathy, and frequent disturbances in sleep and eating patterns. If head circumferences have been plotted, sudden head enlargement may be noted when sutures are still open or after they have split. Other signs are alterations of consciousness and stiff neck with tonsillar herniation.

†i.e., ataxia and nystagmus. Truncal ataxia in the absence of lateralizing signs is most common in vermis tumors.

‡May include head tilting, cranial nerve signs, pyramidal tract signs, and suboccipital tenderness.

§Splitting of sutures, erosion of the posterior clinoids, and thinning of the sphenoid wings. Increased digital markings are an unreliable sign.

Differential Diagnosis of Intracranial Lesions.

The entire symptom complex of an intracranial space-consuming lesion, including vomiting, increase in intracranial pressure, and papilledema, can be caused by lesions which are not neoplastic. The principal ones are granulomatous abscess (including tuberculoma), pyogenic abscess, hemorrhage (subdural hematoma), C.N.S. infections, and venous sinus thrombosis.

TUMORS OF THE SOFT TISSUE

The most common malignant soft tissue tumor seen in children is rhabdomyosarcoma. The child usually presents with a firm mass on an extremity, in the head and neck region, or in the pelvic area. Patients should be evaluated with skeletal survey, intravenous urograms, chest x-ray with oblique views, bone marrow aspiration, and liver function tests, including creatine phosphokinase (CPK), LDH, BUN, and uric acid. Treatment consists of en bloc surgical resection when possible, followed by high-energy radiation therapy of 4000 to 6000 rads over a period of five to eight weeks. Chemotherapy with vincristine, dactinomycin, and cyclophosphamide is used for one or two years.

Fibrosarcomas and liposarcomas are rare lesions and should be surgically excised when possible. Electron beam therapy (4000 to 6000 rads) has also been used.

Benign tumors are slow-growing and nontender. Most commonly seen are the fibromas and lipomas. These may be excised if they are symptomatic.

TUMORS OF BONE

The most frequent age group seen with a malignant bone tumor is the preadolescent, adolescent, and the young adult group. Osteosarcoma, Ewing's sarcoma, chondrosarcoma, fibrosarcoma, and synovial sarcoma may all present with a painful mass, limitation of motion, and x-ray changes in the bones involved. Metastatic disease contraindicates radical surgery and should be ruled out. Survival rates with surgery alone have been poor: 5 to 15% five-year survivals are reported. These tumors tend to spread to lungs, soft tissues, and other bones. Ewing's tumor has had an increase in survival rate in recent years with radiation therapy, 5000 rads to the entire bone involved concurrently with vincristine and cyclophosphamide chemotherapy; amputation is not done.

Osteosarcoma survival rates have not changed with surgical amputation. Therefore, some centers are using electron beam radiation therapy with the betatron, followed by delayed amputation in four to six months if no metastatic disease is apparent. Adjunctive chemotherapy is being explored with adriamycin. Immunotherapy with tumor vaccines and BCG is also under investigation.

Many fibrous, cartilaginous, and osseous benign tumors are seen. Some have classical x-ray findings; others should be excised to rule out the possibility of a malignant tumor.

OTHER TUMORS

WILMS'S TUMOR
(Nephroblastoma)

The most common abdominal masses encountered in early childhood are hydronephrosis, neuroblastoma, and Wilms's tumor.
Wilms's tumor is believed to be embryonal in origin, develops within
parenchyma, and enlarges with distortion and invasion of adjacent
renal tissue. This tumor may be associated with congenital anomalies such as hemihypertrophy, aniridia, ambiguous genitalia, hypospadias, undescended testes, duplications of ureters or kidneys,
horseshoe kidney, and Beckwith's syndrome.

Clinical Findings.
  A. Symptoms: Abdominal mass, malaise, flank pain, fever, and
     pallor.
  B. Signs: A solid or (rarely) cystic, nontender, firm mass is
     present in the flank. It rarely crosses the midline, but may
     be bilateral in 2% of patients. Hematuria is rare as compared
     to renal tumors in the adult. Hypertension is unusual.
  C. Laboratory Findings: Urinalysis is usually normal, but hema-
     turia or pyuria may be found if trauma or infection has oc-
     curred within the tumor mass. BUN is usually normal; uric
     acid and erythropoietin levels may be increased.
  D. X-ray Findings: A soft tissue mass may be seen on a plain
     film of the abdomen, and calcification may occur in a marginal
     concentric fashion. Hepatomegaly may be present if the liver
     has extensive metastases. Intravenous urography may show
     distortion and displacement of the renal pelvis and calyces in
     any direction; hydronephrosis may also be present. Chest
     x-ray may reveal metastases; oblique views are often helpful.

Treatment.
     Surgical excision of the mass after clinical staging is the treat-
ment of choice. A transabdominal approach is essential to allow
early ligation of the renal vessels, prevent excess manipulation of
the tumor, and allow examination of abdominal viscera, nodes, and
the opposite kidney.
     Radiation therapy to the tumor bed should be given postopera-
tively with megavoltage equipment in dosages of 2000 to 3500 rads
depending upon the age of the patient and the stage of the tumor.
If the tumor is ruptured, the entire abdomen should be treated with
proper shielding to the remaining kidney.
     Adjunctive chemotherapy with dactinomycin and vincristine in
courses of six to 12 weeks for one to two years has increased survival rates.

Prognosis.
     The two-year survival rate is better in children under two
years of age with localized disease. Survival rates are improving
where radiation therapy and chemotherapy are used concurrently.

NEUROBLASTOMA

Neuroblastoma is a tumor arising from cells in the sympathetic ganglia and adrenal medulla. It is the third most frequent pediatric neoplasm. The tumors may spontaneously regress in 5 to 10% of cases. The prognosis is much better in a child under two years of age. This tumor may be seen in the newborn or young child.

Clinical Findings.
A. Symptoms and Signs: General symptoms include failure to thrive, anorexia, black eyes, fever of unknown origin, diarrhea, hypertension, pallor, irritability, and masses.
   1. Cervical tumors commonly present with a mass in the neck and may be associated with Horner's syndrome.
   2. Thoracic tumors may present with respiratory symptoms: cough, croup, dysphagia, and fatigue.
   3. Abdominal tumors may cause abdominal swelling from adrenal or paraspinal tumor. They may be very large and cross the midline or may be deep and difficult to palpate. Other findings include abdominal pain, change in bowel habits, delay in walking, paraplegia, or shock if a large tumor is ruptured.
B. Laboratory Findings: Anemia or pancytopenia may represent a myelophthisic picture because of marrow involvement with tumor or may be on a dietary basis. Bone marrow may reveal classical rosettes or sheets of anaplastic neuroblasts. The patient should be placed on a restricted catecholamine diet and a 24-hour urine collected for catecholamine levels. A vanillylmandelic acid test is a helpful screening test. Urinary cystathionine should also be measured. BUN and uric acid as well as liver function should be evaluated as baseline studies.
C. X-ray Findings: Multiple destructive lesions of bone with a moth-eaten appearance may be seen in all bones. Pathologic fracture may also occur.
   1. Thoracic tumors - Chest x-ray shows soft tissue areas with clear borders and scattered calcifications close to the spine and in the upper chest. There may be erosion and separation of posterior ribs.
   2. Abdominal tumor - Abdominal x-ray reveals a soft tissue mass in the region of the adrenal gland or along the spine. Many tumors show calcification. Intravenous urograms reveal downward and lateral displacement of the kidney.

Treatment.
Total surgical removal followed by megavoltage radiation to the tumor bed or area of regional spread followed by vincristine and cyclophosphamide therapy is advocated in all stages. In cases with marrow involvement, the primary should be treated with radiation prior to surgical intervention. Palliative x-ray therapy to painful bone lesions or proptotic eye lesions, along with prednisone (40 mg./sq.M. orally daily), may make a terminal child more comfortable.

Course and Prognosis.
The major problem in control of this potentially curable disease is the fact that 75% of patients presenting with symptoms related to

metastasis are over two years of age. Until physicians treating
children become more aware of the cancer problem in children,
the progress that has been made in treatment cannot be utilized
to its fullest extent.

ADRENOCORTICAL TUMORS

Tumors of the adrenal cortex are characterized by the excessive production of hormones which, in turn, cause marked physiologic and anatomic changes. Metastases may be local or pulmonary,
and usually occur relatively early in the disease.

GANGLIONEUROMA

This functional neurogenic tumor may cause chronic severe
diarrhea due to increase in circulating norepinephrine and epinephrine. Renal acidosis and the celiac syndrome may also occur.
Urinary vanillylmandelic acid and vanilphenylethylamine are elevated.

PHEOCHROMOCYTOMA (Chromaffinoma)
(See Chapter 33.)

HODGKIN'S DISEASE

This disease occurs twice as frequently in men as in women,
with its peak incidence in the third decade. It has been reported
in children as young as three years of age. The cause is not
known. The clinical staging and histologic classification have
recently been revised (see Tables 23-2 and 23-3).

Clinical Findings.
   A. Symptoms and Signs: Variable degrees of anorexia, weight
      loss, fatigue, weakness, fever, malaise, pruritus, night
      sweats, and pain on ingestion of alcohol are noted. The most
      common site of nodal involvement is the cervical region. In-
      volved nodes are usually firm and nontender and may produce
      pressure symptoms depending upon their location, which may
      be anywhere. Hepatosplenomegaly and extranodal disease in
      any organ may be present.
   B. Laboratory Findings: Hematologic findings may be normal or
      may show anemia, leukocytosis, leukopenia, thrombocytosis,
      thrombocytopenia, eosinophilia, or elevated sedimentation
      rate. Kidney and liver function tests or scans may reflect
      abnormalities if involved with disease.
      Immunologic defects as a reflection of abnormalities of the
      cell-mediated immune responses may be seen in abnormal
      delayed hypersensitivity to PPD, candidal extract, and strep-
      tokinase-streptodornase skin test antigens. Hemolytic anemia
      and abnormal levels of immunoglobulins may also occur.
      The diagnosis is confirmed by biopsy of the involved node
      followed by bone marrow biopsy, clinical staging, and laparot-

TABLE 23-2. Histologic classification of Hodgkin's disease.

Jackson and Parker	Rye, 1965	Distinctive Features and Relative Frequency	
Paragran-uloma	Lymphocyte predomi-nance	Abundant stroma of mature lympho-cytes, histiocytes, or both; no ne-crosis; Reed-Sternberg cells may be sparse.	10 to 15%
	Nodular sclerosis	Nodules of lymphoid tissue, par-tially or completely separated by bands of doubly refractile collagen of variable width; atypical Reed-Sternberg cells in clear spaces ("lacunae") in the lymphoid nodules.	20 to 50%
Granuloma	Mixed cellu-larity	Usually numerous Reed-Sternberg and atypical mononuclear cells with a pleomorphic admixture of plasma cells, eosinophils, lymphocytes, and fibroblasts; foci of necrosis commonly seen.	20 to 40%
Sarcoma	Lymphocyte depletion	Reed-Sternberg and malignant mono-nuclear cells usually, though not always, numerous; marked paucity of lymphocytes; diffuse fibrosis and necrosis may be present.	5 to 15%

*Reproduced, with permission, from Kempe, C., Silver, H.K., & D. O'Brien: Current Pediatric Diagnosis & Treatment, 3rd ed. Lange, 1974.

TABLE 23-3. Clinical staging of Hodgkin's disease.*†

Stage I	Involvement of a single lymph node region (I) or of a single extralymphatic organ or site (I-E).
Stage II	Involvement of 2 or more lymph node regions on the same side of the diaphragm (II), or solitary involve-ment of an extralymphatic organ or site and of one or more lymph node regions on the same side of the dia-phragm (II-E).
Stage III	Involvement of lymph node regions on both sides of the diaphragm (III), which may also be accompanied by in-volvement of the spleen (III-S) or by solitary involve-ment of an extralymphatic organ or site (III-E), or both (III-SE).
Stage IV	Multiple or disseminated foci of involvement of one or more extralymphatic organs or tissues, with or with-out associated lymph node involvement.

*Reproduced, with permission, from Kempe, C., Silver, H.K., & D. O'Brien: Current Pediatric Diagnosis & Treatment, 3rd ed. Lange, 1974.
†Stages are subclassified as A (absence) or B (presence) of sys-temic symptoms (fever, night sweats, 10% or greater weight loss).

omy with multiple abdominal node biopsies, liver biopsy, and splenectomy.
C. X-ray Findings: Chest x-ray may show parenchymal or mediastinal nodal disease. Skeletal survey may show bone involvement. The intravenous urogram may show diversion of the ureter or bladder; a lateral view is often helpful to show anterior displacement. Lymphangiography may reveal a "foamy" enlarged node which implies tumor filling the node.

Treatment.

After the patient is properly staged, he should receive the optimum benefits of megavoltage extended field radiation by a therapist skilled in the treatment of the growing child to minimize side-effects.

Combination chemotherapy is superior to single agent drug therapy. Agents commonly used are vincristine, cyclophosphamide, procarbazine, and prednisone. The use of combination chemotherapy concurrent with or following radiation therapy is being explored.

Prognosis.

In adequately treated patients, five-year survival rates have improved greatly. In stages I and II, rates range from 85 to 90%; in stage II-A, the average survival rate is 70%; and in stage III-B, the survival rate is 40 to 50%. The duration of symptom-free life is also being lengthened by combination chemotherapy in stage IV disease.

NON-HODGKIN'S LYMPHOMA

A new classification of this diverse group of lymphomas proposed by Gall and Rapport is based on the architecture of the node, whether the disease is nodular or diffuse, and the cytologic differentiation of lymphocytes and histiocytes. This group includes the former "lymphosarcomas"—reticulum cell sarcomas or tumors with giant follicular cell patterns.

Burkitt's tumor (African lymphoma) is a special type of childhood lymphoma found principally in Africa. A few cases have been reported in the U.S.A. This tumor is responsible for half of all cancer deaths in children in Uganda and Central Africa. A viral etiology has been assumed, and Epstein-Barr virus is under scrutiny. The tumor is characterized by (1) primary involvement of abdominal nodes and viscera, (2) predilection for the facial bones and mandible, and (3) massive proliferation of primitive lymphoreticular cells and phagocytosis on histologic examination.

Clinical Findings.
A. Symptoms and Signs: The primary site of involvement differs from that of Hodgkin's disease in its mode of presentation. The gastrointestinal tract in the region of the terminal ileum, cecum, appendix, ascending colon, and mesenteric nodes is the most common site. Boys outnumber girls 9:1. Acute abdominal pain, intussusception, gastrointestinal tract perforation, and hemorrhage may occur. Involvement of the tonsillar region, cervical nodes, and nasopharynx may be diagnosed by the pres-

ence of a mass or compression symptoms. The mediastinum and retroperitoneal nodes may be involved as well as any superficial nodal chain. The incidence of marrow involvement with a leukemia-like picture is 20 to 50% of cases; this is most frequently seen when the mediastinum is involved. The C.N.S. may also be involved; lumbar puncture or brain scan may be helpful in confirming this diagnosis.

B. Laboratory Findings: These patients should be studied as Hodgkin's patients with the exception of routine exploratory laparotomy and splenectomy. Laboratory findings depend on organ, nodal, or marrow involvement.

Treatment.

Surgical resection of extranodal disease, when possible, is advocated, followed by megavoltage radiation therapy to the tumor bed or regional nodes. Combination chemotherapy should be started as soon as possible and continued for two to three years. The drugs most commonly used are vincristine, 1.5 mg./sq.M. I.V. weekly for six weeks and then every two weeks; prednisone, 40 mg./sq.M. orally daily in three divided doses; cyclophosphamide, 300 mg./ sq.M. I.V. weekly for six weeks and then every two weeks; and procarbazine, 100 mg./sq.M. I.V. weekly for six weeks and then every two weeks. Mercaptopurine, methotrexate, cytarabine, CCNU, adriamycin, and bleomycin are used for resistant disease or in maintenance combinations.

Prognosis.

The prognosis in non-Hodgkin's lymphoma is not as good as in Hodgkin's disease, and many children die with a conversion to a leukemic phase.

TUMORS OF THE OVARY

Tumors of the ovary constitute only 1% of all childhood tumors. The three main types are benign teratoma (dermoid), cysts, and malignant tumors. Granulosa cell tumors may be malignant or benign.

Tumors of the ovary are characterized by an enlarging palpable mass in the lower abdomen or pelvis. Severe abdominal pain may occur due to a twisted pedicle. Sexual precocity, uterine bleeding, and advanced bone age as a result of excessive estrogen production occur only in granulosa cell tumors (which are almost always large enough to palpate).

Treatment is by surgical removal of the tumor. If the tumor is malignant and inoperable, postoperative irradiation may be used. Combination chemotherapy with vincristine, cyclophosphamide, dactinomycin, thiotepa, and fluorouracil has been helpful in some patients. Intercavitary chemotherapy is no longer advocated.

TUMORS OF THE TESTICLE

Testicular tumors vary from highly malignant (adenocarcinoma, seminoma, or malignant teratoma) to relatively benign (Leydig cell

tumor or benign teratoma). Paratesticular rhabdomyosarcoma
may also present as a scrotal mass in the male child. Tumors
are characterized by painless, solid swelling of the testicle which
does not transilluminate and appears to have a purplish discoloration. Although evidence of endocrine activity usually is absent,
pseudoprecocious puberty occasionally occurs. Pregnancy tests
are positive in embryonal carcinoma and choriocarcinoma.

Orchiectomy with high ligation of the cord is indicated in all
testicular tumors. Retroperitoneal node dissection is indicated
for staging and adequate resection. Radiation therapy to involved
nodes and chemotherapy with vincristine, dactinomycin, cyclophosphamide, and bleomycin are also useful.

Alpha-fetoprotein may be elevated in embryonal carcinomas
and some teratomas and may be followed for activity of disease.

The prognosis is good in seminomas but poor in other forms
of malignant testicular tumors. Metastases may occur to the lungs,
mediastinum, and regional and abdominal lymph nodes.

CARCINOMA OF THE THYROID

Carcinoma of the thyroid may occur spontaneously or following
irradiation of the neck or upper chest. Any thyroid nodule should
be suspected of being a tumor. If it occurs in an adolescent with
goiter, therapy with thyroid preparations is indicated. If the nodule
does not respond to therapy, surgical removal is indicated. Thyroid
carcinoma occurring at other ages or in adolescents without an
accompanying goiter nodule should be treated by subtotal thyroidectomy. Lesions found in the cervical lymph nodes should be treated
by radical radiation therapy. Palliative treatment with radioiodine
is indicated for distant metastases which take up radioiodine or can
be induced to do so by thyroidectomy plus the use of TSH or one of
the thiourea derivatives. However, only about 10% of metastatic
cancers of the thyroid will take up radioiodine in quantities sufficient to warrant treatment with this agent.

The prognosis for patients with completely removed thyroid
tumors is excellent. The prognosis for patients in whom metastases have occurred is questionable. The prognosis for patients
with widespread tumor, regardless of method of treatment, is poor.

RETICULOENDOTHELIOSES
(Histiocytosis X)

The diseases to be discussed under this heading comprise a
heterogeneous group of proliferative disorders of the reticuloendothelial system of unknown cause. Eosinophilic granuloma of bone,
Hand-Schüller-Christian disease, and Letterer-Siwe disease constitute a complex of diseases of unknown cause, of histiocytic proliferation, and of unpredictable prognosis. Lichtenstein has grouped
them under the term histiocytosis X. Although foam cells containing cholesterol are found in these disorders, it is currently believed
that the storage cells are not the result of a primary disturbance
of lipid etabolism but are secondary to increased intracellular
cholesterol synthesis or to inhibition of cholesterol from necrotic
tissue.

TABLE 23-4. Antineoplastic agents.*

Agent	Dosage and Route	Spectra	Toxicity
BCNU (carmustine, bischloroethyl-nitrosourea)	150-300 mg./sq. M. I.V. every 6 weeks.	Malignant gliomas, medullo-blastoma, advanced Hodgkin's disease and other sarcomas, neuroblastoma, malignant melanoma.	Nausea and vomiting in the first 24 hours after administration. Delayed marrow suppression with a peak at 3-4 weeks. Hepatotoxicity. Chemical dermatitis.
CCNU (lomustine, chloroethyl-cyclohexyl-nitrosourea)	130 mg./sq. M. orally every 6 weeks.	Same as above.	Nausea and vomiting 24-48 hours after administration. Delayed marrow toxicity with a peak at 3-4 weeks. Hepatotoxicity.
Cyclophospha-mide (Cytoxan®)	75-100 mg./sq. M./day orally or 300 mg./sq. M./week I.V.	Leukemia, Hodgkin's lymphoma, neuroblastoma, sarcomas, retinoblastoma, hepatoma, rhabdomyosarcoma, Ewing's sarcoma.	Nausea, vomiting, anorexia, alopecia, bone marrow depression, hemorrhagic cystitis.
Cytarabine (Cytosar®)	100-150 mg./sq. M./week I.V. or I.M.; 5-50 mg./sq. M. once or twice weekly intra-thecally for C.N.S. leukemia until C.S.F. clears.	Acute myeloblastic and acute lymphocytic leukemia.	Nausea, vomiting, anorexia, bone marrow depression, hepatotoxicity.
Dactinomycin (Cosmegen®)	0.4 mg./sq. M./week I.V. in 6 doses in phases with varying rest periods.	Wilms's tumor, sarcomas, rhabdomyosarcoma.	Nausea, vomiting, anorexia, bone marrow depression, alopecia, chemical dermatitis if leakage at intravenous site, tanning of skin if used with radiation therapy.
Fluorouracil (Efudex®)	300-360 mg./sq. M. I.V. Dosage should be scheduled based upon the specific disease stage. Maximum dose: 800 mg./day.	Hepatoma, gastrointestinal carcinoma.	Nausea, vomiting, oral ulceration, bone marrow depression, gastroenteritis, alopecia, anorexia.

Mercaptopurine (Purinethol®)	50-100 mg./sq. M./day orally.	Acute myeloblastic and acute lymphocytic leukemias.	Nausea, vomiting, rare oral ulcerations, bone marrow depression.
Methotrexate	15-20 mg./sq.M. orally or I.V. twice a week until relapse. Give 12 mg./sq.M./week intrathecally for C.N.S. leukemia until C.S.F. clears.	Acute lymphocytic leukemia, C.N.S. leukemia, lymphomas, choriocarcinoma, brain tumors, Hodgkin's disease.	Oral ulcers, gastrointestinal irritation, bone marrow depression, hepatotoxicity. Do not use in presence of impaired renal function.
Prednisone	40 mg./sq.M./day orally in 3 divided doses for 4-6 weeks.	Acute myeloblastic and lymphocytic leukemia, lymphoma, Hodgkin's disease, bone pain from metastatic disease, C.N.S. tumors.	Increased appetite, sodium retention, hypertension, provocation of latent diabetes or tuberculosis, osteoporosis.
Procarbazine (Matulane®)	100-125 mg./sq.M./day orally for 4-6 weeks depending on schedule.	Hodgkin's disease, lymphomas.	Nausea, vomiting, anorexia, bone marrow depression (3-week delay). Do not give with narcotics or sedatives; has "Antabuse® effect." Monitor liver and renal function.
Vincristine (Oncovin®)	1.5 mg./sq.M./week I.V. for 4-6 weeks, then every 2 weeks. Maximum dose: 2 mg.	Acute lymphocytic and myeloblastic leukemia, lymphoma (Hodgkin's), rhabdomyosarcoma, Wilms's tumor, neuroblastoma, Ewing's sarcoma, retinoblastoma, hepatoma, sarcomas.	Alopecia, constipation, abdominal cramps, jaw pain, paresthesia, myalgia and muscle weakness, neurotoxicity, decrease in deep tendon reflexes, chemical dermatitis. Do not use in presence of severe liver impairment.

*Modified and reproduced, with permission, from Kempe, C., Silver, H.K., & D. O'Brien: Current Pediatric Diagnosis & Treatment, 3rd ed. Lange, 1974.

Certain patients present primarily with signs and symptoms of lytic lesions limited to the bones - especially the skull, ribs, clavicles, and vertebrae. These lesions are well demarcated and occasionally painful. Biopsy reveals eosinophilic granuloma, which may be the only lesions the patient will develop, although further bone and even visceral lesions may occur.

Another group of patients often present with otitis media, seborrheic skin rash, and evidence of bone lesions, usually in the mastoid or skull area. They frequently also have visceral involvement, which may be indicated by lymphadenopathy and hepatosplenomegaly. This chronic disseminated form is usually known as Hand-Schüller-Christian disease and is associated with "foamy histiocytes" on biopsy. The classical triad of Hand-Schüller-Christian disease (bony involvement, exophthalmos, and diabetes insipidus) is rarely seen; however, diabetes insipidus is a common complication.

A third group of patients present early in life primarily with visceral involvement. They often have a petechial or macular skin rash, generalized lymphadenopathy, enlarged liver and spleen, pulmonary involvement, and hematologic abnormalities such as anemia and thrombocytopenia. Bone lesions can occur. This acute visceral form, Letterer-Siwe disease, is often fatal.

In all three groups, the tissue abnormality is proliferation of histiocytes; aggregations of eosinophils, lymphocytes, and plasma cells; and collection of foam cells.

The principal diseases to be differentiated from histiocytosis X are bone tumors (primary or metastatic), lymphomas or leukemias, granulomatous infections, and storage diseases. The diagnosis is established by biopsy of bone marrow, lymph node, liver, or mastoid or other bone.

Almost any system or area can become involved during the course of the disease. Rarely, these will include the heart (subendocardial infiltrates), bowel, eyes, mucous membranes such as the vagina or vulva, and dura mater.

Isolated bony lesions are best treated by curettage and local radiotherapy. Multiple bony involvement and visceral involvement often respond well to prednisone, vinblastine, cyclophosphamide, and methotrexate. The current treatment of choice at the authors' institution is prednisone and vinblastine, given in repeated courses or continuously until healing of lesions occurs.

If diabetes insipidus occurs, treatment with vasopressin gives good control.

In idiopathic histiocytosis, the prognosis is often unpredictable. Many patients with considerable bony and visceral involvement have shown apparent complete recovery. In general, however, the younger the patient and the more extensive the visceral involvement, the worse the prognosis.

24 ...
Infectious Diseases:
Viral & Rickettsial

VIRAL DISEASES

ROSEOLA INFANTUM (Exanthem Subitum)

An acute febrile disease of infants and young children which is characterized by a high sustained or spiking fever of one to five days' duration followed by a faint rash. The incubation period is estimated to be seven to 17 days.

Clinical Findings.
   A. Symptoms and Signs:
   1. Onset sudden, with fever as high as 106° F. (41.1° C.). Fever persists for one to five days (average: 3 days), falls by crisis, and then is usually subnormal for a few hours just before the rash appears.
   2. Rash appears when temperature returns to normal. It is faintly erythematous, macular, and diffusely disseminated, starting on and principally confined to the trunk. Individual macules resemble those of rubella.
   3. Physical findings may be entirely normal except for the rash, although many children have mild pharyngitis, enlargement of the postoccipital nodes, and irritability.
   B. Laboratory Findings: Progressive leukopenia to 3000 to 5000 white cells, with a relative lymphocytosis as high as 90%.

Complications.
   Convulsions are the principal complication (may be first sign of illness) and are related to the rapidly rising temperature. A para-infectious type of encephalopathy has been reported (see Chapter 21).

Treatment.
   A. Specific Measures: None.
   B. General Measures:
   1. Restricted activity until rash appears.
   2. Aspirin for temperature of over 103° F. (39.4° C.).
   3. Tepid water sponge bath or alcohol rub for high fever uncontrolled by aspirin.
   C. Treatment of Complications: Barbiturate sedatives may prevent convulsions resulting from hyperpyrexia, especially in children with convulsive tendencies (see Table 21-4).

Prognosis.
   The prognosis is excellent.

MEASLES (Rubeola)

A highly communicable disease with highest incidence between the ages of two and 14 years. It is easily spread from person to person by droplets and by contact with articles freshly soiled by nose and throat secretions of an infected individual during a prodromal period of three to five days. The incubation period is eight to 14 days, with a majority of cases occurring ten days after exposure.

Clinical Findings.
A. Symptoms and Signs:
    1. Prodrome (three to five days) -
        a. Fever is usually the first sign and persists throughout the prodrome. It ranges from 101 to 104° F. (38.3 to 40° C.), tending to be higher just before the appearance of the skin rash, and may be lower after eruption of the rash.
        b. Sore throat, nasal discharge, and dry, "barking" cough are common during the prodrome.
        c. Nonpurulent conjunctivitis appears toward the end of the prodrome and is accompanied by photophobia.
        d. Lymphadenopathy of posterior cervical lymph nodes.
    2. Koplik's spots, fine white spots on a faint erythematous base, appear first on buccal mucosa opposite molar teeth and later may spread over entire inside of mouth by about the third or fourth day of the prodrome. They usually disappear as the exanthem becomes well established.
    3. Rash appears on about the fifth day of disease: a pink, blotchy, irregular, macular erythema which rapidly darkens and characteristically coalesces into larger red patches of varying size and shape. The eruption fades on pressure.
        a. First appears on the face and behind the ears; spreads to chest and abdomen, and finally to the extremities.
        b. Lasts from four to seven days and may be accompanied by mild itching.
        c. A fine branny desquamation, especially of face and trunk, may follow, lasting two or three days; light-brown pigmentation may then appear.
B. Laboratory Findings: Leukopenia is present during the prodrome and early stages of the rash. There is usually a sharp rise in the white count with the onset of any bacterial complication. In the absence of complication, the white cell count slowly rises to normal as the rash fades.

Complications.
A. Bacterial (commonest in the respiratory tract): Manifested by recurrence of fever and leukocytosis.
    1. Otitis media - Appears toward end of prodrome or during the course of the rash; may be due to a variety of organisms.
    2. Tracheobronchitis - Besides the specific inflammation due to rubeola, there may be secondary bacterial involvement. This is usually accompanied by more productive cough.
    3. Bronchopneumonia - While rubeola virus itself often causes a specific pneumonitis, involvement of the lower bronchial tree by secondary bacterial invasion with resultant bronchopneumonia is a relatively common complication.

B. Encephalitis: (See Chapter 21.) Occurs in about one out of 3,000 cases (no relation to severity of measles). The first sign may be increasing lethargy or convulsions. Lumbar puncture shows 0 to 200 cells, mostly lymphocytes.

C. "Hemorrhagic Measles": A rare form with a high mortality rate characterized by generalized bleeding and purpura.

D. Aggravation of active pulmonary tuberculosis.

Treatment.

A. Specific Measures: None available.

B. General Measures:
1. Isolation for one week from onset of rash.
2. Rest until afebrile.
3. Aspirin for discomfort or for temperature over 103°F. (39.4°C.).
4. Saline sponges for the eyes. Darkness is not necessary but may make the child more comfortable.
5. Saline irrigations for soreness of the mouth and throat.
6. Vasoconstrictor nose drops.
7. Warm, moist air (steam) for cough. Sedative cough mixture may be of some help.

C. Treatment of Complications:
1. Bacterial complications are usually due to group A streptococcus. Prophylaxis of bacterial infection may be instituted in children with pre-existing pulmonary conditions or other debilitating diseases.
2. Encephalitis - See Chapter 21.

Prophylaxis.

Measles vaccine should be given routinely as outlined in Chapter 7. Passive immunization with immune serum globulin (human gamma globulin; see p. 108) may prevent the disease or result in a mild, modified rubeola syndrome with reduced incidence of bacterial complications.

Prognosis.

In uncomplicated cases or those with bacterial complications, excellent. In encephalitis the prognosis is guarded, with incidence of permanent sequelae high.

RUBELLA (German Measles)

A mild febrile virus infection which frequently occurs in epidemics but is not as contagious as rubeola or chickenpox. Transmission is probably by droplet route. The incubation period is from 12 to 21 days (average: 16).

Clinical Findings.

A. Symptoms and Signs: Prodrome (slight malaise, occasional tender postero-occipital lymph nodes, no catarrhal symptoms), if present, lasts only a few days. In younger children the prodrome may not be noted by parents. Rash may be the first sign of disease and consists of faint, fine, discrete, erythematous macules appearing first on the face and spreading rapidly over the trunk and extremities. Macules are only slightly raised; eventually they blend. The rash may suggest measles on the first day and scarlet fever on the second. It generally disappears by the third day. Temperature rarely exceeds 101° F. (38.3° C.) and usually lasts less than two days.

Rubella without rash (rubella sine eruptione) occurs as a febrile lymphadenopathy which may persist for a week or more. During epidemics, this syndrome may represent over 40% of cases with infection.

Congenital rubella is a syndrome involving an infant born to mothers affected with rubella in the first trimester of pregnancy. The majority of infants show growth retardation, hepatosplenomegaly, and purpura, in addition to congenital defects of the heart, eye, and ear. Marked thrombocytopenia is a common finding. X-ray of the long bones shows an irregularity in trabecular pattern, with longitudinal areas of radiolucency in the metaphysis. Rubella virus is easily isolated from such patients and they must be considered to have a highly contagious disease which can spread to other patients and to personnel.

B. Laboratory Findings: Transient leukopenia is generally noted.

Complications.

A. During Pregnancy: If rubella occurs during the first month of pregnancy, there is a 50% chance of fetal abnormality (cataracts, congenital heart disease, deafness, mental deficiency, microcephaly). By the third month of pregnancy the risk of abnormalities decreases to less than 10%.

B. Encephalitis and thrombocytopenic purpura are rare. Polyarthritis occurs in 25% of cases in persons over 16 years of age.

Treatment.

A. Specific Measures: None.

B. General Measures:

1. Isolation is usually not necessary, but susceptible women must not be exposed in the first trimester of pregnancy.

2. Symptomatic measures are rarely necessary.

C. Treatment of Complications:

1. Bacterial - As for those associated with rubeola.

2. Encephalitis (see Chapter 21) and purpura (see Chapter 17).

Prophylaxis.

A live attenuated rubella virus vaccine is recommended for use in children between the ages of one year and puberty. A history of "German measles" should not be considered a contraindication to the use of this preparation.

Gamma globulin, 20 ml. I. M. given shortly after exposure, has been claimed to prevent the disease in pregnant women. Since the globulin does not prevent viremia, little benefit to the fetus can be expected; this measure, therefore, is not recommended. Determination of rubella antibody in the serum of exposed women may establish a state of immunity; in the absence of such antibody, therapeutic abortion should be considered. Pregnant women should avoid exposure to clinical rubella regardless of their presumed immunity.

Prognosis.

The prognosis is excellent.

ERYTHEMA INFECTIOSUM
(Fifth Disease)

A mild, afebrile contagious disease of viral etiology, usually occurring in family or institutional epidemics. The incubation period is estimated to be from seven to 14 days.

Clinical Findings.
A. Symptoms and Signs: There is usually no prodrome. The first symptom is the rash, which has a characteristic appearance and course:
1. Rash -
a. Appears first on the cheeks as very red coalescent macules which are warm and slightly raised. Circumoral pallor is marked. This eruption fades within four days.
b. Following the eruption on the face by one day, a maculo-papular erythematous rash appears on the extensor surfaces of the extremities, spreading, over two to three days, to the flexor surfaces and trunk. Macules develop a pale central area. Palms and soles are rarely involved. Rash lasts three to seven days and may recur after seven to ten days, with irritation of the skin.
2. The patient is almost invariably otherwise asymptomatic and without fever.
B. Laboratory Findings: WBC is normal.

Treatment and Prognosis.
No treatment is indicated. There are no complications, and the prognosis is excellent.

VARICELLA (Chickenpox)

An acute, extremely communicable disease caused by the varicella-zoster virus. It is spread from person to person by droplets from a respiratory source or by direct contact with freshly contaminated articles. Varicella is communicable from 24 hours before until six days after appearance of the rash. The incubation period is 14 to 21 days (average: 15).

With rare exceptions, immunity to varicella after attack is probably lifelong, although the individual with a history of varicella may later develop herpes zoster.

Clinical Findings.
A. Symptoms and Signs:
1. Prodrome is usually not apparent; there may be slight malaise and fever for 24 hours.
2. Rash - Usually the first sign. Lesions tend to appear in crops (two to four crops in two to six days), and all stages and sizes may be present at the same time and in the same vicinity. They occur first on the scalp and mucous surfaces, then on the body. They are numerous over the chest, back, and shoulders; less numerous on the extremities; and are

seldom seen on the palms and soles. Successive stages
(usually over a period of one to four days) are as follows:
  a. Macular (small red blotches).
  b. Papular (raised skin eruption).
  c. Vesicular - Lesions are very fragile, generally not um-
     bilicated, appearing as a drop of water on a slightly red
     base; the top may be readily scratched off.
  d. Pustular, with crust formation - This stage may be
     reached within a few hours after the appearance of the
     macule. Scabs fall away by the ninth to thirteenth days.
  3. Pruritus is minimal at first but may become severe in the
     pustular stage.
  4. Fever may occur when most vesicles reach the pustular
     stage, but constitutional reactions are usually minimal; the
     rash is often noted by chance.
B. Laboratory Findings: Leukopenia early. White blood count
   may rise with extensive secondary infection of vesicles.

Complications.

Secondary infection of vesicles. Encephalitis is rare. Severe
disease with high mortality has been associated with the use of medications which alter the immune mechanism (steroid and antime-
tabolite therapy).

Treatment.
A. Specific Measures: None available at present.
B. General Measures:
  1. Pruritus may be relieved by local application of calamine
     lotion, mild local anesthetic ointments, or systemic anti-
     histamines.
  2. Cut nails short, and have patient wear gloves if necessary
     to prevent excoriation.
  3. Mouth and perineal lesions may be treated by rinses, gar-
     gles, and saline soaks.
  4. Sponge baths with antiseptic detergent such as pHisoHex®
     relieve itching and reduce the incidence of secondary bacte-
     rial infection.
C. Treatment of Complications:
  1. Secondary infection of skin - Local broad-spectrum antibi-
     otics; if secondary infection is suspected, give systemically
     (penicillin for group A streptococcus) (see Chapter 6).
  2. Encephalitis - For general measures, see Chapter 21.

Prophylaxis.

Prophylaxis with immune globulin has been reported to modify
or prevent the disease. The dosage is 0.5 ml./lb. given within six
days of exposure.

Prognosis.

In uncomplicated disease, excellent. Scarring from secondary
infection of eruption is not uncommon. In encephalitis, prognosis
is poor with high incidence of sequelae in surviving patients. Death
has been reported in cases of varicella occurring in children receiving long-term therapy with cortisone.

VARIOLA (Smallpox)

Variola major is an acute disease with a febrile prodrome of sudden onset. It varies from a mild disease to a most severe one and lasts three to six weeks. The virus of variola is related to a number of agents producing similar disease in animals (i.e., vaccinia or cowpox). In addition to the typical variety, there are severe cases in which the lesions become confluent or hemorrhagic. The mild form in an unvaccinated person is called variola minor (alastrim); mild, modified smallpox in a previously vaccinated person is known as varioloid. The incubation period is usually 12 days (range: seven to 18).

The disease is spread easily from person to person, probably by droplet, but virus is also present in skin and in dried scabs, in urine and feces, and in the bodies of fatal cases. It may also be spread by direct contact with freshly contaminated articles, and is communicable from first symptoms to disappearance of all scabs.

Clinical Findings.

Recent successful vaccination **usually** excludes diagnosis.

A. Symptoms and Signs:
1. Prodrome is febrile, lasting up to five days, with severe constitutional symptoms. Onset is sudden, with fever and severe chills in adults and convulsions in children. Backache, nausea and vomiting, and severe prostration occur. After three to four days, symptoms diminish and temperature tends to return to normal.
2. Rash - Appears first on the head or around the wrists as a red papule which persists for one to four days. Distribution is centrifugal, and density is greatest on extremities and face. On any given area all lesions tend to appear at the same time and are at the same stage. Stages are as follows:
   a. Papular stage - Four to 24 hours.
   b. Vesicular stage - One crop, lasting one or two days. Vesicles are symmetrical, hard to rupture, umbilicated, and extend into the underlying skin.
   c. Pustular stage - Three to five days, with scab formation. Scabs persist as long as 40 days. After they fall away, there may be pitting and permanent scarring.

B. Laboratory Findings: Leukopenia early, but leukocytosis is common in the pustular stage. Mononuclear cells predominate.

Complications.

A. Secondary bacterial infection of skin.
B. Septicemia.
C. Albuminuria.
D. C.N.S. complications are uncommon.
E. Hemorrhagic form of disease early in course, with purpuric rash and high mortality.

Treatment.

A. Specific Measures: None available at present.
B. General Measures: Strict isolation must be enforced. Energetic fluid and electrolyte therapy is essential so that a good urinary output may be maintained (see Chapter 5). An indwelling plastic gastric tube will facilitate hydration in the dysphagic ill child.

C. Treatment of Complications: Secondary bacterial infections are
treated with appropriate antibiotics. Eczema vaccinatum, generalized vaccinia, and vaccinia necrosum should be treated
with vaccinia immune gamma globulin (human).

Prophylaxis.
Vaccination is discussed in Chapter 7. Treatment of exposed
individuals with methisazone (Marboran®) is reported to be a highly
effective prophylactic measure.

Prognosis.
The mortality rate is high in severe disease in unvaccinated
children and in the hemorrhagic form (40 to 70%). In mild disease,
the prognosis is good.

EPIDEMIC PAROTITIS (Mumps)

Mumps is an acute virus disease which may involve many organ
systems but which commonly affects the salivary glands, chiefly
the parotid (about 60%), and frequently the C.N.S. It is uncommon
before three and after 40 years of age. It is probably not as contagious as measles and chickenpox. It is spread directly from person
to person and by direct contact with contaminated articles. It is
communicable from two days before the appearance of symptoms to
the disappearance of salivary gland swelling. Disease without salivary gland involvement is also communicable. The incubation
period is usually 12 to 24 days (average: 16 to 18).

Clinical Findings.
A. Symptoms and Signs:
  1. Parotid - (Submaxillary and sublingual glands may be in-
     volved also or in the absence of parotid involvement.)
     a. Prodrome of one or two days may precede the swelling
        and is characterized by fever, malaise, and pain in or
        behind the ear on chewing or swallowing.
     b. Involvement of salivary glands with tender swelling and
        brawny edema which contrasts with the more sharply
        defined enlargement of a lymph node. Pain is referred
        to the ear and is aggravated by chewing, swallowing, or
        opening the mouth. Aggravation by sour substances (e. g.,
        lemon) is not a reliable symptom. Tenderness persists
        for one to three days, and swelling is present for seven
        to ten days. Skin over the gland is normal.
     c. Openings of ducts of involved gland and especially the
        papilla of Stensen's duct (opposite upper second molar)
        may be puffy and red.
     d. Fever may be absent or as high as 104° F. (40° C.).
     e. Malaise, anorexia, and headache may be present.
  2. "Inapparent" mumps infection has a short course, with
     fever lasting one to five days.
  3. Mumps encephalitis may precede, accompany, or follow in-
     flammation of the salivary glands but may occur without
     such involvement. Asymptomatic C.N.S. inflammation with
     pleocytosis may be found in over half of cases of mumps.

a. The onset of meningeal irritation is usually sudden. Headache, vomiting, stiff neck and back, and lethargy are characteristic. Fever recurs or increases, up to 106° F. (41.1° C.). Symptoms seldom last more than five days.

b. C.N.S. involvement by mumps virus must be suspected in every case of nonbacterial "meningitis." Transient paresis may suggest poliomyelitis.

4. Other organs which may be involved include -

a. Testicles and ovaries - Usually during or after adolescence, but orchitis can occur in childhood. This may occur in absence of distinctive salivary gland involvement.

b. Pancreas - Sudden onset of mid- or upper abdominal pain, with vomiting, prostration, and usually fever.

c. Kidney - Nephritis is rare and mild, with complete recovery in most cases.

d. Ear - Deafness occasionally occurs and may be permanent.

B. Laboratory Findings:

1. WBC - Usually leukopenia and relative lymphocytosis.

2. Serologic tests to confirm diagnosis.

3. Skin testing is unreliable as an indication of immunity in exposed persons (see p. 113).

4. C.S.F. findings (see Appendix, Table 5).

Complications.

A. With C.N.S. involvement paresis of the facial nerve has been reported.

B. A fatal outcome with C.N.S. involvement is extremely rare.

C. Testicular involvement, usually unilateral, may produce atrophy but sterility is rare.

Treatment.

A. Specific Measures: None available.

B. General Measures:

1. Isolate patient until salivary swelling is gone.

2. Bed rest during febrile period.

3. Aspirin or codeine analgesics when pain is severe.

4. Local warm or cold applications.

5. Saline mouth wash.

C. Treatment of Complications:

1. C.N.S. involvement - Symptomatic for mild encephalitis. Lumbar puncture may be useful in reducing headache.

2. Orchitis -

a. Cortisone is dramatic in some cases (see Table 22-6).

b. Suspension of scrotum in a sling or suspensory.

c. Codeine or morphine analgesia.

d. Infiltration around spermatic cord at external inguinal ring with 10 to 20 ml. of 1% procaine solution may produce dramatic relief.

3. Pancreatitis and oophoritis - Symptomatic only.

Prophylaxis.

A. A live attenuated mumps virus vaccine is highly effective. It is especially recommended for children approaching adolescence who have no history of mumps.

B. Mumps hyperimmune globulin has been suggested to reduce incidence in exposed susceptibles, but results are most unpredictable.

Prognosis.
Excellent even with extensive organ system involvement. Very rare sterility in post-adolescent male following orchitis.

COXSACKIEVIRUS INFECTION

Coxsackieviruses have been shown to be the cause of several general types of clinical disease (see below), usually occurring in epidemic form during the summer months. There are many immunologic types grouped into group A and group B.

The pathogenesis of coxsackievirus infections in man is not clearly understood, but the virus is believed to be transmitted in a manner similar to that of poliomyelitis virus. It may be found in the stool up to six weeks after the onset of symptoms.

Clinical Findings.
A. Herpangina (Caused by Group A Viruses): Onset of fever (up to 104° F. [40° C.]) is abrupt and lasts one to four days. Older children may complain of moderately severe sore throat. There may be vomiting and abdominal pain. The pharynx shows characteristic hyperemia of the anterior pillars of the fauces with discrete vesicular eruptions. The gingival or buccal mucous membranes are not involved, as they are in herpes simplex infection.
B. Hand-Foot-Mouth Syndrome: Papulovesicular eruption in those areas (group A).
C. "Summer Grippe": An acute, brief febrile illness lasting one to four days without other signs or symptoms. This may represent the commonest form of infection with these viruses. Diagnosis depends upon knowledge of a community or family epidemic with more characteristic syndromes present in other individuals.
D. Pleurodynia (Epidemic Myalgia, Bornholm Disease): Pleurodynia is more common in older children and adults. Onset is abrupt, with fever, dyspnea, and often headache. Acute pain occurs most commonly around the lower ribs and is intensified by respiratory movement. The thoracic type may simulate pneumonia or pleuritis. Abdominal pain occurs in about 50% of cases and may simulate appendicitis, cholecystitis, or hepatitis. After fever subsides, pain may recur up to two weeks after onset. Pleurodynia may be accompanied by central nervous system symptoms (see below).
E. Aseptic Meningitis: Onset is usually abrupt, with fever, headache, nausea, and vomiting. Abdominal or chest pain may be early symptoms. Stiffness of the neck or back may follow after 24 hours. Spinal fluid may show increase in cells, usually monocytes, but rarely exceeding 100 per ml. Aseptic meningitis must be differentiated from poliomyelitis and bacterial meningitis. Asymmetric flaccid paralysis has been reported in rare cases.
F. Myocarditis and/or Pericarditis (see Chapter 13) Caused by A or B Viruses: Except in the neonatal period, the prognosis is generally good although sudden death has been reported.
G. Generalized Infection in Newborn With Myocarditis, Encephalitis, Hepatitis, and Pneumonia: Reported as epidemic in newborn nurseries. The mortality rate is high.

Treatment.
  A. Specific Measures: None available.
  B. General Measures: Bed rest during the febrile period and
     aspirin or codeine analgesics when pain is severe. Warm
     applications to back and chest may bring relief.

Prophylaxis.
     Since little is known about how these viruses are spread, little
can be done to prevent infection. Good hygiene (rest and nutrition)
and avoidance of crowds during epidemic seasons are advisable.

Prognosis.
     Prognosis is excellent. The disease is usually self-limited,
and recovery is complete. In small infants, myocarditis due to
these viruses often has a fatal termination. Transient paresis has
been reported.

ECHOVIRUS INFECTIONS

     Many types of echoviruses have been found on tissue culture
of human stools. Several types have clearly been shown to cause
human disease of different clinical categories. Transmission from
human to human is probably by the enteric-oral route. Like poliomyelitis virus and coxsackievirus epidemics, infections are most
common during the summer months.

Clinical Findings.
  A. Aseptic Meningitis Syndrome: Usually is due to echovirus type
     6 but is common with type 4 and has been rarely found with
     type 9 and type 16. Onset is sudden, with fever to 103° F.
     (39.4° C.), vomiting, headache, and stiff neck. There may
     be a morbilliform rash resembling that of rubella and lasting
     from one to six days. The rash is found mostly on face and
     trunk. All symptoms usually subside within one week.
       Paralytic disease - consisting of paresis in the extremities -
     has been described involving types 2, 4, 6, 9, and 16. The
     weakness is usually temporary and does not persist beyond
     one month in most cases.
  B. Exanthematous Disease: Echovirus type 9 or 16 (Boston ex-
     anthem) has been found to be the cause of a febrile disease
     characterized by sudden onset of fever to 103° F. (39.4° C.),
     sore throat, and nausea. A discrete macular, morbilliform
     rash soon appears, with distribution mostly over the face and
     trunk. This rash lasts from one to ten days. The disease may
     be differentiated from rubeola by absence of catarrhal respir-
     atory symptoms and Koplik's spots, and from rubella by per-
     sistence beyond the third day.
  C. Diarrheal Disease of Infants: Type 18 echovirus has been
     associated with epidemic diarrheal disease in infants under one
     year of age. There is a sudden onset of diarrhea unaccompan-
     ied by fever. Stools show no pus and rarely blood.
  D. Echovirus types 8 and 20 have been shown to cause outbreaks of
     acute upper respiratory disease.

TABLE 24-1. Enteroviral exanthems and enanthems.*

Exanthem	
Rubelliform	Coxsackieviruses A and B
	All echovirus types
Vesicular	Coxsackieviruses A4, 5, 9, 16; B1, 4
Petechial	Coxsackieviruses A9, B3
	Echoviruses 4, 9, 11
Urticarial	Coxsackieviruses A9, 16; B5
	Echovirus 11
Enanthem	
Herpangina	Coxsackieviruses A2, 4, 5, 6, 8, 10; B4
	Echovirus 17
Nodular pharyngitis	Coxsackievirus 10
Stomatitis	Coxsackieviruses A3, 5

*After Horstman.

Treatment.

No specific measures are available. General measures include bed rest during the febrile period and, in the case of the diarrheal disease, infants' dietary measures as for other enteric infections (see Chapter 16).

Prognosis.

Prognosis is excellent. Asymmetric paresis with complete recovery has been reported but is rare.

VIRAL HEPATITIS

An acute contagious disease often occurring in epidemics and characterized by liver involvement and jaundice. It is caused by a virus.

Two "phases" of the virus are recognized: "short incubation" infectious hepatitis (IH), transmitted principally by the oral route; and "long incubation" serum hepatitis (SH), transmitted principally by the parenteral route following transfusion with blood or blood products other than globulin. (See Table 24-2.) An antigenic entity called Australia (Au) antigen is found in serum hepatitis.

Clinical Findings.
A. Symptoms and Signs: Fever, malaise, chills, anorexia, vomiting, and headache. Upper abdominal pain and hepatomegaly are common. Jaundice appears in two to five days when fever is subsiding and may last several weeks. Infection without jaundice is probably most common in childhood and may be detectable only by laboratory tests of liver function. Fulminant infection, with rapid onset of liver involvement, acute yellow atrophy, and death, is rare.
B. Laboratory Findings:
   1. Sedimentation rate increased.
   2. Liver function studies show evidence of hepatocellular disease. The sulfobromophthalein test is the first to become abnormal and the last to become normal (see Appendix).

TABLE 24-2. **Differentiation of infectious hepatitis (IH)
and homologous serum hepatitis (SH).**

	Infectious Hepatitis	Serum Hepatitis
Incubation period	30 to 40 days Average: 32	40 to 110 days Average: 65
Usual portal of entry	Oral: from GI tract (parenteral also possible)	Parenteral: by injection or transfusion (oral also possible)
Contagion	High	None, except by injection. Parenteral drug abuse is common source.
Age incidence	Below 30 years	Any age
Virus demonstrable	In stool	In blood
Type of onset	More abrupt: malaise, anorexia, nausea, fever	Insidious: recurrent anorexia, low fever, arthralgia, and urticarial rash
Transaminase levels	Elevated less than 3 weeks	Elevated for 1 to 6 months
Prophylaxis with gamma globulin	Effective	Ineffective
Resistance to infection after previous infection with IH virus	Present	Absent
Resistance to infection after previous infection with SH virus	Absent	Present

3. Occasional false-positive Wassermann or Kahn test.
4. Transaminase (SGOT) level is increased early, usually to above 200 units.

Complications.

A. Hemorrhagic Manifestations: Due to low prothrombin level.
B. Acute Hepatic Failure and Acute Yellow Atrophy: This condition is often fatal and has widespread hemorrhagic manifestations.

Treatment.

A. Specific Measures: None available.
B. General Measures:
1. Reduce physical activity and stress bed rest in children with moderate to severe symptoms. In these children, sedatives may be necessary. Give phenobarbital but avoid sedatives and hypnotics which are detoxified by the liver (e.g., pentobarbital). In children without moderate to severe symptoms, physical activity as tolerated will probably not interfere with a smooth convalescence.
2. Balanced and palatable diet with adequate protein-sparing carbohydrate. If patient is unable to retain oral feedings -
a. Give 5% glucose and 5% protein hydrolysate solutions by intravenous infusion.

   b. Tube feeding - Protein hydrolysate and skimmed milk
      mixture by plastic nasogastric tube.
3. When patient is able to take food by mouth, give restricted
   oral feedings. Finally, give a full diet high in carbohydrates
   and proteins.
4. Supplementary vitamins, particularly B complex.
5. In severely ill patients with anorexia, nausea, and vomiting,
   give corticosteroids for five days, and then rapidly reduce
   the dosage.
C. Treatment of Complications:
   1. Hemorrhagic manifestations -
      a. Transfusion of fresh whole blood (see p. 17).
      b. If possible, increase donor prothrombin level by admin-
         istration of vitamin K to donor prior to drawing blood.
      c. Irradiated plasma has limited value and should not be
         used in view of danger of superimposed serum hepatitis.
   2. Acute hepatic failure and possible acute yellow atrophy -
      Although the prognosis is extremely poor, liver function can
      improve and recovery can take place in some cases. Pro-
      tein intake should be sharply restricted. Protein breakdown
      by bacteria in the bowel should be inhibited by enema as well
      as by administration of neomycin. Corticosteroids should
      be administered in full dosage. Intravenous glucose should
      be stressed. Exchange transfusions may be most useful.

Prophylaxis.

   Passive immunization of exposed susceptibles (who have no
history of the disease) with immune serum globulin. Results are
not always predictable. Give 0.01 ml./Kg. body wt. (I.M.) and repeat at four-week intervals if exposure continues.

Prognosis.

   Viral hepatitis is usually a self-limited disease. In the absence
of acute hepatic failure, the prognosis is good. Chronic progressive or recurrent liver disease may be associated with these viral
agents, especially when Australia antigen is present.

HERPES SIMPLEX INFECTION

   An acute and sometimes chronic disease caused by a dermo-
tropic and neurotropic virus. Transmission is probably by direct
contact with skin or mouth lesions.

Clinical Findings.
A. Symptoms and Signs: There may be a history of exposure to
   young children with stomatitis or to an older child or adult
   with "fever sores."
   1. Primary infection - The primary infection may manifest
      itself as gingivostomatitis, vulvovaginitis, keratoconjuncti-
      vitis, meningoencephalitis, rhinitis, dactylitis, eczema
      herpeticum (Kaposi's varicelliform eruption), or as a severe
      generalized disease of the newborn. Herpes is the most
      common cause of severe gingivostomatitis in children under
      five years of age. The onset is insidious, with fever of 100

to 104° F. (37.8 to 40° C.), malaise, and sore throat. The gums are quite red and swollen and bleed easily. Multiple small vesicles develop on the palate, tongue, and gums, and rupture to become small white ulcers. The breath is fetid. Ingestion of food is very painful. Fever usually subsides in one week, but mouth lesions may persist as long as two weeks.

2. Recurrent infection (herpes febrilis, "cold sores," "fever sores") - Local lesions are mild and constitutional symptoms are absent.

   a. Recurrent papulovesicular eruption at mucocutaneous junction is most common and is related to various host factors (e.g., fever due to other infection, pneumococcal infection, menses, sunburn, emotional stress).

   b. Recurrent ulcer on mucous membrane of the mouth ("canker sore").

   c. Recurrent eruption of the skin on almost any area of the body and consistently at the same site.

   d. Differentiate from herpangina (coxsackievirus) by presence of gingivitis in herpes simplex infection.

3. Generalized herpetic infection in the newborn, often associated with herpes vaginitis in the mother, is usually a fatal disease characterized by encephalopathy, chorioretinitis, papulovesicular rash, pneumonia, and stomatitis. Virus can be demonstrated throughout the entire body.

4. Herpes simplex virus may account for almost 10% of cases of viral encephalitis in the United States. Symptoms and signs are not distinctive. For treatment, see Chapter 21. Diagnosis may be established by laboratory tests (Table 21-3).

B. Laboratory Findings:

1. Routine laboratory procedures contribute little; there may occasionally be leukopenia at onset.

2. Virus studies involve inoculation of material from skin lesions on the rabbit cornea or the demonstration of antibodies. They are not generally available.

Treatment.

A. Specific Measures:

1. For localized skin or mucous membrane infection, photodynamic inactivation with 0.1% proflavine or neutral red has been widely used and may be effective although there is serious question of the possibility of premalignant change as a result of this method of treatment. The technic is to unroof the lesions, apply the dye, and then expose the lesion to light from a 15 watt fluorescent bulb for about 15 minutes. The procedure is done twice, either morning and afternoon or on successive days.

2. Idoxuridine in aqueous solution may be used as a wet dressing over the skin eruption and ruptured vesicles. This treatment has been suggested to shorten the course of the disease. In newborn infants, treatment of herpesvirus generalized infection with idoxuridine has been reported successful.

B. General Measures:

1. Stomatitis, primary - Mouth hygiene by saline rinse and cleansing with Zephiran® Chloride, 1:1000, after eating; analgesics (aspirin), and sedation (barbiturates).

2. Herpes febrilis ("fever sore") or other local eruptions -
   a. Compound tincture of benzoin locally.
   b. Secondary bacterial infection - Broad-spectrum anti-
      biotics systemically (see Chapter 6).
   c. Saline compresses if larger areas are involved.
3. Herpetic conjunctivitis - Use of corticosteroid preparations
   should be strictly avoided.

Prophylaxis.
   Widespread distribution of virus in humans and ignorance of
methods of spread make prophylaxis almost impossible. Avoid
contact with open skin lesions or abrasions.

Prognosis.
   In usual case, excellent. In severe generalized eruption,
prognosis depends upon control of secondary bacterial infection.
In C.N.S. involvement and in systemic disease in newborn, prognosis is very poor.

CAT SCRATCH FEVER
(Benign Lymphoreticulosis)

   Cat scratch fever is an acute illness characterized by low-
grade fever, malaise, an erythematous papular or pustular cutaneous lesion at the site of contact, and regional adenopathy occurring
about two to four weeks later. Viral etiology has long been assumed,
but the agent may be a member of the psittacosis–LGV group. The
lymph nodes are usually not painful, but they may become warm,
fixed to surrounding tissue, and suppurative; this enlargement may
persist for one week to several months. A history of cat scratch,
cat bite, or contact with healthy cats a few days before onset is
characteristic.

   Heat-inactivated purulent material from enlarged and fluctuant
lymph nodes has served as a skin test antigen under research conditions and produces a tuberculin-like reaction in convalescent
cases. No specific therapy is known. Surgical removal or needle
evacuation of the affected node will usually be followed by marked
improvement.

   An encephalopathy associated with cat scratch fever has been
reported and a conjunctivitis associated with inoculation on the face
has also been described.

   Complete recovery usually occurs within a few months.

DENGUE

   An acute febrile disease with sudden onset, short duration, and
excellent prognosis, occurring potentially wherever the vectors and
infected individuals exist (mostly in the tropics and subtropics).
Dengue is characterized by the triad of morbilliform rash, bradycardia, and leukopenia. Transmission of the virus is through the
bite of a mosquito, and prophylaxis consists of mosquito control.

Clinical Findings.
   A. Symptoms and Signs: Incubation period is five to nine days

after the bite of the mosquito. Onset is very sudden, with rise in temperature to 102 to 105° F. (38.9 to 40.6° C.), severe headache, and joint pains. Initial rash is an irregular blotchy congestion on the face. On the third or fourth day, the temperature falls to normal, with profuse diaphoresis. After one to three days, fever recurs, accompanied by a faint morbilliform rash which spreads from hands and feet to the trunk, and by a definite bradycardia (around 50 per minute). This stage lasts four to six days. Convalescence is marked by depression and anorexia.

B. Laboratory Findings: Leukopenia by the second day of fever.

Treatment.

Control temperatures above 103° F. (39.4° C.) to prevent possible convulsions due to hyperpyrexia. Increase fluid intake to allow for deficiency caused by profuse diaphoresis.

YELLOW FEVER

An acute febrile disease which is of varying severity but usually causes hepatic necrosis and renal damage. It is endemic in Brazil, Colombia, Venezuela, and parts of Africa. The virus is transmitted through the bite of the Aedes aegypti mosquito. Blood of an infected individual is infectious from two days prior to fever until four days after onset. The mosquito may transmit the disease ten to 20 days after biting an infected person. The incubation period is from three to six days after the mosquito bite.

Clinical Findings.

A. Symptoms and Signs: There is a short prodrome with mild malaise, followed by a rise in temperature, headache, and joint pains. The temperature rises to about 104° F. (40° C.) by the second day and persists for about four days. Pulse rate falls as temperature rises.

The second phase follows after one to three days, with increasing fever at onset and jaundice by the fifth day of disease. Nausea and vomiting are prominent. Icterus is not intense. Bleeding tendency may be prominent, with gastrointestinal hemorrhage. Hypoglycemia is common at this stage.

The disease ends by crisis in the second week. In mild cases with only slight fever and headache, clinical diagnosis is almost impossible.

B. Laboratory Findings: Initial polymorphonuclear leukocytosis followed in six days by leukopenia; urinary casts and increasing albuminuria; and hypoglycemia.

Complications.

A. Hemorrhage, usually from gastrointestinal tract, may be extensive and fatal.

B. Severe renal damage with anuria.

Treatment.

A. Specific Measures: None available.

B. General Measures:

1. Ample fluid intake, with stress on glucose to combat hypo-

glycemia. Parenteral route should be used without hesitation.
2. Strict bed rest.
C. Treatment of Complications: Transfusion to compensate for gastrointestinal bleeding (see p. 17).

Prophylaxis.
A. Control the insect vector.
B. Control individuals entering from endemic areas.
C. Active immunization (see p. 104).

Prognosis.
Guarded until seven days after onset, when severity of liver involvement will be apparent. Hemorrhagic tendency at this stage may be cause of death. Clinical improvement after ten days is an excellent sign. One attack produces lifelong immunity.

INFECTIOUS MONONUCLEOSIS

This is an infectious but not very contagious disease or syndrome with several possible causes. Toxoplasma gondii and cytomegalovirus are known to cause this syndrome in young adults and children. The Epstein-Barr virus (EBV) of the Burkitt lymphoma syndrome of West Africa has been demonstrated to be the cause of mononucleosis with a positive heterophil antibody test. It may occur at any age up to 30 years but is rare in infancy. The usual case is characterized by a gradual onset of fever to $102°$ F. $(38.9° C.)$, malaise, sore throat, and enlarged lymph nodes and spleen. Many cases have clinical liver involvement with hepatomegaly and jaundice. A morbilliform, scarlatiniform, or petechial rash may appear.

The most reliable criterion of diagnosis is the appearance on a stained blood smear of large, immature, vacuolated lymphocytes. Leukocytosis with predominant lymphocytosis is usually present. A rising titer in serum of heterophil agglutinin usually appears by the second week. Titers of 1:112 are significant and 1:160 diagnostic, but 20 to 40% of cases never show appreciable rises. Horse serum injection will stimulate a similar antibody which can be differentiated by absorption tests. A simple slide agglutination test is available which demonstrates the same antibody and can be used for diagnostic screening purposes.

No specific treatment measures are available. In severe cases, give methylprednisolone (Medrol®), 1 mg./Kg. Stat. and the same dosage daily for five days. Bed rest should be continued until the patient has been afebrile for four days. Hepatitis is benign and requires no special treatment even when laboratory abnormalities persist. Severe pharyngitis may be complicated by group A streptococcus infection, which should be treated with penicillin (see Chapter 6). In severe streptococcal pharyngitis, methylprednisolone, 0.25 mg./Kg./day in four divided doses for five days, will produce rapid subsidence of symptoms and fever.

The disease usually runs its course in two to four weeks but may be prolonged over several months. Recurrences are rare. Prognosis is excellent in most cases.

CYTOMEGALOVIRUS DISEASE

Cytomegalovirus disease, once thought to be a rare type of congenital infection which was usually fatal, is now recognized as the cause of several types of disease of which the congenital variety is perhaps the least common.

Cytomegalovirus is isolated easily from the urine of the acutely ill patient as well as the body tissues. The virus can also be isolated from the urine for many months after the acute illness or after birth in the case of the congenital disease. Characteristic large inclusion bodies are present in the epithelial cells found in the urinary sediment.

Clinical Findings.
A. Congenital Disease: Rapid onset of jaundice shortly after birth with hepatosplenomegaly, purpura, hematuria, and signs of encephalitis. Laboratory findings include thrombocytopenia, erythroblastosis, bilirubinemia, and marked lymphocytosis. Downey type abnormal lymphocytes are present in large numbers. Sequelae include intracranial calcifications, microcephalus, mental retardation, convulsive states, and optic atrophy. The prognosis is poor.
B. Acute Acquired Cytomegalovirus Disease: This resembles the syndrome of infectious mononucleosis (see above). There is a sudden onset of fever, malaise, joint pains, and myalgia. Pharyngitis is minimal, and respiratory symptoms are absent. Lymphadenopathy is generalized. The liver shows enlargement and often slight tenderness. Laboratory findings include the hematologic picture of mononucleosis as well as bilirubinemia. Heterophil antibody does not appear.

Treatment.
No specific treatment measures are available. General measures should include analgesic and antipyretic procedures and control of convulsions (see Table 21-4). Corticosteroids have been reported to produce amelioration of symptoms and are especially indicated in the congenital disease where the prognosis is so poor.

INFLUENZA

An acute systemic virus disease which usually occurs in epidemics and is caused by a distinct class of viruses divided into three groups and many subtypes. The clinical disease is characteristic, and in epidemics the symptoms are quite consistent.

Clinical Findings.
Onset is abrupt, with sudden fever to 103-104°F. (39.4-40°C.), extreme malaise, myalgia, headache, and a dry, nonproductive cough. Small infants may exhibit only fever, cough, and marked irritability. Physical findings are minimal and usually include only a red pharynx. In small children the neck and back may appear to be stiff (myalgia).

Complications.
Primary complications due specifically to the influenza virus are rare but may include an extensive hemorrhagic type of pneumonia

with rapid downhill course, myocarditis, and toxic encephalopathy. Secondary complications due to bacterial agents include bronchial pneumonia and otitis media. The bacterial agent most often responsible is Staphylococcus aureus. Bacterial complications should be considered if temperature remains elevated longer than four days and if the WBC is greater than 12,000/cu.mm.

Treatment.

No specific measures are available. General measures include analgesic and antipyretic measures, use of mist and steam, as in croup (see p. 254); and bed rest for at least one week. For bacterial complications, treat as for specific agent. If bacteriologic laboratory diagnosis is not available, treat with penicillin and chloramphenicol (see Chapter 6 for dosage). In the rare event of encephalopathy, treat as for toxic encephalopathy. Amantadine hydrochloride (Symmetrel®) has been reported to show promising results. It is given in the same dosage used for prophylaxis (see below).

Prophylaxis.

Influenza vaccine has been demonstrated to have varying efficacy in the past, but improved technics offer continuing promise for more reliable active immunization in the future. It is recommended for any child with chronic respiratory or cardiovascular disease.

Amantadine hydrochloride (Symmetrel®) has been shown to prevent infection with influenza Type A_2 when given after exposure, especially in previously immunized individuals. It appears to exert its effect by preventing penetration of the virus into the host cell. For children under 9 years of age, give 2 to 4 mg./lb. body weight/day in 2 or 3 equal doses. For children 12 years of age and over, give 100 mg. twice a day. Continue this drug for at least 10 days following a known exposure. It can be used for a maximum of 30 days in a persistent epidemic with recurrent exposure.

ACUTE INFECTIOUS LYMPHOCYTOSIS

A rare benign disease, probably of viral origin, with symptoms lasting one to three days and a distinct lymphocytosis lasting from three to seven weeks. Few symptoms are found, but the onset may be marked by fever and irritability. Abdominal pain or symptoms of upper respiratory tract infection may also occur. The condition must be differentiated from lymphatic leukemia and mononucleosis. The white blood count is diagnostic, with totals to 40,000 per cu. mm. and occasionally to over 100,000 per cu. mm., predominantly adult lymphocytes. Lymph node or splenic enlargement is absent. Heterophil agglutination test is negative. The prognosis is excellent; long-term follow-up shows no evidence of leukemia or other blood disease.

COLORADO TICK FEVER

An acute viral disease, relatively common in the western U.S.A., which is transmitted by a wood tick. It is characterized by a sudden onset of fever lasting two to three days, followed by an afebrile period (24 to 48 hours) and then a second febrile period of two or three days. Rarely, C.N.S. involvement or maculopapular rash may be present. Leukopenia is invariably present.

There is no treatment. The prognosis is excellent.

VIRAL INFECTIONS
OF THE CENTRAL NERVOUS SYSTEM*

POLIOMYELITIS

An acute viral infection of the spinal cord and brain stem which in its severe form leads to neuron destruction and irreversible muscular paralysis and, in 10% of the paralytic forms, to death.

Clinical Findings.

Poliomyelitis is more common between May and October in the northern hemisphere. Investigation may uncover a history of community or family exposure. There is no other common cause for asymmetrical, scattered flaccid paralysis accompanied by signs of meningeal irritation and fever.

A. Nonparalytic Poliomyelitis: Believed by many to be the most common form of the disease. There is no clinical or laboratory evidence of invasion of the C.N.S. Diagnosis can rarely be established except by inference in epidemics.

B. Paralytic Poliomyelitis (Spinal Type):
   1. Symptoms and signs -
      a. Paralysis may occur without obvious antecedent illness, especially in infants. It usually begins and progresses during the febrile stage of the illness.
      b. Tremor upon sustained effort may be first clue to diagnosis and may be present before weakness occurs.
      c. Muscle tightness and pain on stretching may cause malfunction and stimulate paralysis.
   2. Laboratory findings - C.S.F. findings (see Appendix). Cell count may be normal in 10 to 15% of cases.

C. Bulbar Polioencephalitis: Paralytic poliomyelitis which includes involvement of the cranial nerves and brain stem. Significant lower spinal involvement may be absent. Any cranial nerve may be affected, but swallowing difficulties predominate. This form of poliomyelitis is more likely to occur in the patient who has had his tonsils removed. Polioencephalitis is the term applied when there is impairment of cerebral function. It follows a fulminant course.

Respiratory Difficulty in Poliomyelitis.

May occur with the following:

A. Paralysis of Intercostal Muscles: Manifested by anxiety, in-

---

*See also coxsackievirus infection (p. 468) and echovirus infection (p. 469).

creased respiratory rate, and reluctance to vocalize. Upper
arm and shoulder muscles are often involved. Diagnosis is
made by observation in oblique light with examiner splinting
the abdomen to exaggerate chest motion. Determination of
vital capacity and tidal volume and their relationship to the normal for age and size of patient is very important. Normal
standards for tidal volume should be increased 5% for each degree of fever. More indirect clues include frequent inspiration
in normal conversation and the inability of the older child to
count to 40 after one inspiration.
  B. Paralyses of the Diaphragm: Are easily overlooked and usually
     associated with intercostal paralysis. Fluoroscopic examina-
     tion may be necessary to demonstrate this.
  C. Damage to Medullary Respiratory Center:
     1. Severe form - Irregular, shallow, spasmodic breathing.
     2. Mild form - Affecting sensitivity of center to low carbon
        dioxide tension. Patient "forgets" to breathe.
  D. Obstruction of pharynx or trachea due to aspiration of saliva
     secondary to pharyngeal and/or palatal paralysis may simulate
     any of the above conditions.

Treatment.
  A. Specific Measures: None are known.
  B. General Measures: Many cases of poliomyelitis can be cared
     for in the home. The need for isolation in special hospitals is
     questionable, since the virus is universally distributed in epi-
     demic conditions. Special facilities and trained professional
     personnel are required for the severely involved patient.
     1. Bed rest - May limit paralytic involvement. Observe care-
        fully for further paralysis during first week of disease.
     2. Heat - May relax extremely tender and tight muscles so that
        physiotherapy may be undertaken.
        a. Hot packs (Sister Kenny treatment) - Wool cloths cut in
           appropriate size and shape are heated in boiling water,
           wrung "dry" in a wringer or spinner, and applied quickly
           to areas of muscle tightness and tenderness. The cloths
           should be hot enough to be mildly painful but not hot enough
           to cause burns, usually 110 to 140° F. (43.3-60° C.).
           They are then covered with oiled or rubberized material,
           and the patient wrapped in blankets. Applications should
           be made as often as adequacy of nursing personnel per-
           mits; fever is not a contraindication.
        b. Hot tub (mild ambulatory cases) - Water at 105 to 110° F.
           (40.6 to 43.3° C.) relieves hamstring, calf, or back pain.
        c. Dry heat (also mild cases) - Heat lamp or electric
           heating pad. Do not use heating pad with hot wet packs.
     3. Physiotherapy - Most important single factor in "cure."
        Passive motion is begun during acute stage to point of pain
        only. All extremities must be exercised to prevent joint
        immobilization. Active motion is begun when pain subsides.
        Uncoordinated or unnatural function must be avoided as long
        as possible. Postpone resistance type exercises until all
        tightness has subsided.

4. Orthopedic measures - Immobilization is very important in some cases. Patients with back symptoms need a bed-board. Foot or leg involvement requires foot-board if patient is old enough to cooperate. If not, a splint may be needed. Braces and surgery are indicated only after orthopedic consultation and preferably not until physiotherapy has been attempted.

C. Treatment of Respiratory Difficulties:

1. Intercostal or diaphragm paralysis - Artificial respiration before cyanosis appears.

   a. Tank type - Experienced personnel needed.
      (1) Rate, 16 to 18 per minute.
      (2) 10 to 15 cm. negative pressure for children.
      (3) 2 cm. positive pressure. Increase to 8 cm. with shock.
      (4) Removal of patient from tank depends upon degree of impairment and recovery rate. If vital capacity is below 10% of normal, removal will require many months. Above 10% of normal, progressive removal may be started with return of temperature to normal. Length of time out is determined by signs of fatigue, increased pulse rate, anxiety, and cyanosis.

   b. Chest respirator (cuirass) - About 60% as efficient as tank. It is useful in rehabilitation and simplifies the problem of nursing care.

   c. Rocking bed - May be used alone or in conjunction with tank or chest respirator in rehabilitation.

2. Severe respiratory center involvement - If intercostal muscles are not paralyzed, results with tank respirator are very poor due to incoordinate muscle action.

   a. Electrophrenic stimulation is very useful.

   b. Chondodendron tomentosum extract, purified (Intocostrin®), 1 U./Kg. as necessary to eliminate incoordinate intercostal action, may be useful.

3. Tracheostomy - Paralysis of muscles of swallowing and need for tank respirator usually requires tracheostomy for efficient removal of aspirated material. In bulbar cases, observe for respiratory difficulty; tracheostomy is best done before putting patient in tank. In younger children and infants for whom inability to swallow will mean more chance of massive aspiration, tracheostomy may be done without the customary indication of need for artificial respiration.

Prophylaxis.

Protection from paralytic consequences of infection with poliomyelitis virus is possible.

A. Vaccine (see Chapter 7).

B. Previous infection with any one of the three known strains of poliomyelitis virus appears to afford protection against paralysis upon subsequent exposure to the same strain or strains.

C. Good hygiene (rest and nutrition) and avoidance of crowds during epidemic seasons.

Prognosis.

Prognosis as to paralysis is guarded until pain subsides. In the bulbar form, prognosis is good if complications are overcome.

Polioencephalitis usually has a poor prognosis for survival. If the respiratory center is severely involved, prognosis is very poor.

VIRAL ENCEPHALITIDES

The most important types are those carried by an insect vector, usually a mosquito. The arthropod-borne encephalitides include a large number of diseases caused by antigenically distinct viruses: Western equine encephalomyelitis virus, Eastern equine encephalitis virus, St. Louis encephalitis virus, Australian X disease virus, Venezuelan virus, Japanese B encephalitis virus, and West Nile fever virus. Encephalitis in children is discussed in Chapter 21.

LYMPHOCYTIC CHORIOMENINGITIS

An acute viral infection involving principally the meninges. It is transmitted by direct contact with house mice in certain geographic areas; it occurs rarely west of the Mississippi.

The clinical picture is dominated by signs of meningeal irritation. Malaise and fever are usually not great. Encephalitic symptoms are rare. The course is short and benign.

C.S.F. (see Appendix) shows high cell count, predominantly lymphocytes, as in mumps meningoencephalitis.

Differentiation from mumps is made on serologic and epidemiologic grounds.

No specific treatment is available. Prognosis is excellent.

RABIES

An acute viral disease of the C.N.S. occurring in dogs and a variety of wild animals. It is usually transmitted to man by a bite from the diseased animal, which in most cases dies within ten days. Human rabies infections could be essentially eliminated by compulsory vaccination of dogs.

For C.S.F. findings in rabies, see Appendix, Table 5.

Clinical Course in Humans.
The incubation period of rabies is four to eight weeks.
A. Prodrome: Numbness, tingling, irritability, salivation, and perspiration.
B. Excitation Phase: Apprehension, stiff neck, twitchings and convulsions, spasm of muscles of deglutition, and fever to 105° F. (40.6° C.).
C. Terminal Phase: Within five days of onset, coma and death in virtually all symptomatic cases.

Prophylaxis. (Vaccine, see p. 101. Hyperimmune serum, see p. 109.)
Early and adequate local treatment of the wound, local epidemiologic factors, veterinary consultation, adequate field investigation, and the facts and circumstances associated with the bite may modify the physician's judgment with regard to the systemic treatment indicated in individual cases. The following is intended only as a guide.

A. Local Treatment of the Wound: If the animal is not overtly rabid and has been impounded, cleanse the wound carefully with bland soap and water and irrigate copiously with saline solution. Debride devitalized tissues. Give tetanus prophylaxis (see p. 110). If the animal is known to be rabid, or if the attack was unprovoked and the animal has been killed or has escaped, cauterize the wound with fuming nitric acid, irrigate copiously with saline, and cleanse with soap and water.

B. Antirabies Immunization:*
   1. No lesion (indirect contact; licks of unabraded skin) - No treatment even if animal is overtly rabid.
   2. Licks of abraded skin, scratches, mucosa - No treatment if animal remains healthy. Start vaccine at first sign of rabies in animal.
   3. Bites **other than** multiple bites or face, head, or neck bites -
      a. Start vaccine at first sign of rabies in animal.
      b. Stop treatment on fifth day after exposure if the animal at first showed signs suggestive of rabies but is normal after five days.
      c. Start vaccine immediately if the animal is overtly rabid or if he has escaped, was killed, or cannot be identified.
   4. Multiple bites or face, head, or neck bites -
      a. Start serum immediately. Give no vaccine as long as the animal remains normal.
      b. Start vaccine at first sign of rabies in animal.
      c. Stop vaccine if animal is normal on fifth day after exposure.
      d. Give serum immediately, followed by vaccine, if the animal is rabid, escaped, killed, or unknown; or for bites by a wild animal (especially a skunk or bat).

RICKETTSIAL DISEASES

The rickettsiae are very small intracellular organisms which otain irregularly gram-negative They are divided immunologically into distinct groups and sub-groups. While most groups stimulate the production in humans of agglutinins against strains of Proteus vulgaris, the determination of complement-fixing antibodies is a more accurate and acceptable serologic testing method.

EPIDEMIC TYPHUS

An acute febrile disease characterized by a generalized rash and caused by Rickettsia prowazeki, which is transmitted in louse feces from person to person by inoculation through abraded skin. The incubation period is five to 15 days.

---

*Modified from recommendations of the California State Department of Public Health, May, 1960. Physicians in rabies-enzootic areas are advised to consult WHO Technical Report Series No. 121, 1957, prepared by the Expert Committee on Rabies of the World Health Organization.

Clinical Findings.

A. Symptoms and Signs (usually mild in children): Onset is sudden, with nausea, vomiting, headache, nosebleeds, and cough. Fever rises in severe cases to 103 to 104° F. (39.4 to 40° C.) by the second day and lasts in untreated cases for about 14 days. Rash appears on the fourth to sixth days, first on the trunk near the axillae and spreading to the extremities. The lesion appears first as a pale macule which blanches easily and then becomes darker red or hemorrhagic. It lasts about seven days, fading slowly and leaving a brown spot.

B. Laboratory Findings:

1. WBC usually reduced in first week.
2. Agglutinins against Proteus OX-19 rise during second week.
3. Complement fixation titer rises by the end of the first week.

Complications.

A. Cardiac damage, appearing in the second week in more severe cases, with dyspnea and Ecg. changes.

B. Bronchopneumonia, which results from secondary bacterial infection.

C. Renal insufficiency, developing in the second and third weeks of disease, is the most common terminal event and is accompanied by increasingly deep coma.

Treatment.

A. Specific Measures: Tetracycline drugs.

B. General Measures: Bed rest for ten days. Otherwise, symptomatic and supportive.

C. Treatment of Complications:

1. Cardiac involvement - Unless failure is apparent, digitalis is not indicated. Bed rest should be maintained until Ecg. changes are no longer noted.
2. Bronchopneumonia - Appropriate antibiotics should be given.

Prophylaxis.

Typhus vaccine is very effective; booster doses should be given every six months in endemic areas. Delouse susceptibles and clothing with DDT powder in endemic areas.

Prognosis.

Excellent in cases developing in vaccinated individuals and in unvaccinated children who are treated early in the disease. In cases with renal failure, prognosis is poor.

ENDEMIC TYPHUS

An acute febrile disease clinically indistinguishable from mild epidemic typhus and caused by Rickettsia mooseri. Transmission is through the bite of the rat flea.

Clinically the disease is a mild one with no complications and excellent prognosis. Treatment is the same as for epidemic typhus. Vaccines are not available; prophylaxis consists of rat control.

ROCKY MOUNTAIN SPOTTED FEVER
(Kenya Typhus, South African Tick Fever, Tobia Fever, Pinta Fever, Sao Paulo Typhus)

An acute febrile disease caused by Rickettsia rickettsii. Transmission is through a tick bite. In eastern U.S.A., the dog tick, Dermacentor variabilis, is the most common vector; in western U.S.A., the wood tick, Dermacentor andersoni.

Clinical Findings.
A. Symptoms and Signs: Incubation period is three to 14 days (average: 7 days). Onset is sudden with febrile course, as in typhus, and lasting, in untreated cases, for three to seven weeks. In children, Rocky Mountain spotted fever is more severe than typhus. The rash appears on the third or fourth day, first on the extremities and spreading to trunk. The lesion is a small, bright-red macule which becomes hemorrhagic or even necrotic. Tick or evidence of bite is present.
B. Laboratory Findings:
  1. WBC - 12,000 to 14,000.
  2. Rising complement fixation titer by second week.
  3. Appearance of agglutinins against Proteus OX-2, OX-19, and OX-K in second week.

Complications.
In severe cases, a shock-like state from markedly disturbed fluid and electrolyte balance.

Treatment.
A. Specific Measures: Tetracyclines.
B. General Measures: Symptomatic care.
C. Treatment of Complications: In severe cases with shock and dehydration, liberal but careful use of parenteral fluid therapy, including plasma, is extremely important (see Chapter 2).

Prophylaxis.
Vaccine (see p. 101) is very effective in children. In tick-infested areas, the body should be examined frequently for ticks.

Prognosis.
Excellent with early therapy. In severe cases, the outcome will depend upon the success of fluid and electrolyte therapy, in addition to the specific antibiotic in use.

Q FEVER

An acute febrile disease caused by Coxiella burnetii. Animal reservoirs such as sheep, goats, and cattle excrete large numbers of organisms in feces which are then dust-borne to humans. Infected cattle excrete organisms in milk, which carries the infection to humans if not pasteurized.

Clinical Findings.
A. Symptoms and Signs:
  1. Mild cases - Most cases of Q fever resemble mild attacks

of influenza. There may be fever for two to six days with slight respiratory symptoms.
2. Severe cases - The onset is sudden, with high fever, characteristically spiking to 103 to 104° F. (39.4 to 40° C.), and chills. Fever lasts, in children, three to seven days. A faint, generalized, morbilliform rash appears rarely. Clinical or x-ray evidence of pneumonitis may be present.
B. Laboratory Findings:
1. WBC is usually within normal range.
2. Complement fixation titer rises during second week.

Treatment.
Give tetracyclines (see Chapter 6) and symptomatic care.

Prophylaxis.
Vaccine (see p. 101), dust control measures, detection of animal vector sources, and pasteurization of milk.

Prognosis.
Excellent with specific antibiotic therapy. Severe cases are very rare in children.

RICKETTSIALPOX

An acute febrile disease caused by Rickettsia akari and characterized by a red papule at the site of an infected mite's bite which slowly changes to a black eschar and an accompanying vesicular rash resembling that of varicella. Transmission is through the bite of the rodent mite (Allodermanyssus sanguineus) from a mouse reservoir. This disease has been detected only in the New York City area up to the present time. Prophylaxis consists of control of rodent reservoirs. Prognosis is excellent.

Clinical Findings.
A. Symptoms and Signs: Incubation period is ten to 14 days. On the seventh to ninth days a large, rapidly ulcerating papule appears at the location of the bite, with concomitant enlargement of regional lymph nodes. Febrile onset is sudden, with fever to 103 to 104° F. (39.4 to 40° C.) which is maximal every evening and which lasts seven to ten days in untreated cases. Malaise and generalized aching are severe. Photophobia may occur. Rash appears on the third to fourth days, first papular and then papulovesicular. The lesion resembles that of varicella except that crusts are black.
B. Laboratory Findings: WBC is usually low; complement fixation titer rises during second week.

Treatment.
A. Specific Measures: Tetracycline drugs.
B. General Measures: Symptomatic care.

25...
Infectious Diseases: Bacterial & Spirochetal

BACTERIAL DISEASES

STREPTOCOCCAL DISEASES
(Streptococcosis)

A variety of disease states directly or indirectly ascribed to streptococci are very important in the pediatric age groups. These are spread from person to person by droplets but may occasionally be transmitted by contact with soiled articles.

Etiology.

Streptococci are gram-positive and characteristically appear in chains. They may be classified as follows:

A. Hemolytic strains causing "beta" hemolysis on blood agar plates are divided into groups A, B, C, D, E, F, G, H, K, L, M, and N. Group A most commonly occurs in older children, while group B may cause severe disease in the newborn.

B. Hemolytic strains causing "green" hemolysis and known as viridans streptococci. These are divided into nine strains including the common Str. viridans, Str. SBE, and Str. MG.

C. Non-hemolytic strains, principally found in the intestinal tract and including Streptococcus D (may be hemolytic; see above), which is sometimes pathogenic in humans.

Clinical Findings.

A. Symptoms and Signs: Streptococci produce a variety of clinical conditions. The primary disease usually involves the upper respiratory tract. Certain clinical entities show a definite prediliction for specific age groups.

1. Early childhood type - Insidious onset with mild constitutional symptoms, mucopurulent nasal discharge, and many suppurative complications (otitis media, lymphadenitis). Exudative tonsillitis is uncommon, sore throat apparently absent. Rheumatic fever, nephritis, and scarlet fever rarely occur in association with this form of the disease.

2. Middle childhood type -
   a. Onset is usually sudden, with temperature over 102°F. (39°C.). Throat is moderately sore and beefy red, with edema of anterior pillars and palatal petechiae. Exudative tonsillitis, with a white-yellow membrane, is relatively frequent.
   b. Anterior cervical lymph nodes usually large and tender.
   c. Suppurative and nonsuppurative complications (rheumatic fever, nephritis) occur in 10 to 30% of untreated cases.

       d. Vomiting is frequently present.

       e. **Scarlet fever** consists of streptococcal pharyngitis plus a rash due to susceptibility to erythrogenic toxin and not to the presence of any particular strain of streptococcus.

          (1) The rash appears 12 to 48 hours after the onset of fever in the areas of warmth and pressure, spreads rapidly to involve the entire body below the chin line, and reaches its maximum in one or two days. It is characterized by a diffuse erythema of the skin with prominence of the bases of the hair follicles. It fades on pressure and does not involve the circumoral region. Transverse lines which do not fade on pressure are found at the elbow (Pastia's sign). The exanthem usually is followed by desquamation beginning in the second week; peeling of the finger tips has greatest diagnostic significance.

          (2) The tongue may be coated but then desquamates and becomes beefy red.

   3. Adult type - Usually occurs after age ten but may occur in much younger children who have had repeated streptococcal infections. The course is similar to the pharyngitis described above; exudative tonsillitis is common. Complications are usually non-suppurative, e.g., rheumatic fever and nephritis. Scarlet fever is uncommon.

B. Laboratory Findings:

   1. White blood count - Usually elevated (12,000 to 15,000) with uncomplicated upper respiratory tract infection; may go to 20,000 or higher with suppurative complications.

   2. Titer of antibodies - Antistreptolysin titer will rise above 150 Todd Units in the course of a streptococcal infection of any sort. If the titer later drops, the test may be used as a measure of recent uncomplicated streptococcal infection.

   3. Culture of the throat - Positive for streptococcus. The more predominant this organism is in the populations of organisms in the culture, the more likely that streptococcus is playing an etiologic role.

Complications.

    A wide variety of clinical conditions may result from the presence of streptococci in the upper respiratory tract of the patient or from contact with the carrier. There is no relationship to age.

A. Pyoderma:

   1. Impetigo.

   2. Secondary infection of eczema - Multiple papulovesicular lesions resembling Kaposi's varicelliform eruption.

   3. Furuncles and cellulitis - These appear less commonly than with staphylococcal infections.

B. Otitis Media: Commonly caused by streptococci as complication of upper respiratory tract infection.

C. Adenitis (usually cervical): Streptococci are the most common cause of this condition in childhood.

D. Septicemia: Especially in the debilitated or the very young.

E. "Metastatic foci," such as meningitis, pyogenic arthritis, and osteomyelitis.

F. Vaginitis.

Sequelae.

Rheumatic fever and nephritis are believed to be sensitivity states resulting from exposure to streptococci.

Treatment.

A. Specific Measures:

1. Penicillin is the drug of choice. In order to decrease the incidence of sequelae the drug should be given for seven to ten days even though clinical manifestations of the disease have disappeared before that time. In usual infections, procaine penicillin is adequate. In severe infections a high blood level of penicillin can be obtained by administration of procaine penicillin G twice daily or penicillin G in more frequent dosage I. M. (see Chapter 6). Oral penicillin preparations may sometimes be used in superficial, minor throat infections, especially when preceded by an initial dose of procaine penicillin G by injection. Benzathine penicillin G (Bicillin®, Permapen®) may be adequate for maintenance therapy following one or more initial doses of procaine penicillin G by injection.

2. In cases of penicillin sensitivity, give erythromycin orally or cephalothin (Keflin®) parenterally.

B. General Measures: Symptomatic only.

C. Treatment of Complications: Treat as for specific infection. Cervical adenitis will require higher blood levels and a longer course of treatment than simple throat infection. Incision and drainage of local foci are rarely necessary when adequate dosage of penicillin has been used. Organisms may persist in the throat culture of ten percent of adequately treated cases.

D. Treatment of Carrier of Streptococci: There is no unanimity of opinion regarding the therapy of the carrier state. Some recommend full therapeutic doses of penicillin for adequate therapy; others feel that the strain of organisms carried does not produce clinical disease and may increase immunity to future infection.

Prophylaxis.

No immunizing agent against the hemolytic streptococcus is at present available. In certain cases, antibiotic prophylaxis may be indicated (e. g. , rheumatic fever; see Chapter 29). The complications and sequelae of streptococcal disease are less likely to occur if the patient is treated promptly and adequately with antibiotics.

Prognosis.

A. Early Childhood and Adult Types: Excellent with penicillin.

B. Middle Childhood Type: Uncomplicated cases subside in four to five days with or without specific treatment.

PNEUMOCOCCAL DISEASES

Like the streptococcus, the pneumococcus produces a number of clinical entities, principally diseases of the respiratory tract. It does not cause diseases of the skin, however.

Pneumococci are gram-positive, encapsulated organisms occurring in pairs. They are divided into more than 75 types on the basis of specific capsular polysaccharides. The higher types are more commonly pathogenic in children, the lower types in adults.

The disease is spread from person to person by droplets. When active disease is present the carrier rate is usually high.

Clinical Findings.
A. Symptoms and Signs:
1. Upper respiratory tract infection - Sudden onset, with fever of 102 to 104° F. (39 to 40°C.) malaise, and obvious signs of upper respiratory tract infection such as rhinitis, usually with a profuse mucoid discharge and pharyngitis.
2. Pneumonia.
   a. Usually peribronchial in the child under the age of six.
   b. Typical lobar pneumonia occurs more commonly in older children.
3. Meningitis, usually secondary to infection in the respiratory tract.
4. Bacteremia with fever and with no obvious localized site of infection.
5. Peritonitis, especially in cases of chronic glomerulonephritis and nephrosis.
6. Vaginitis in pre-adolescent girls.
B. Laboratory Findings: Leukocytosis, with polymorphonuclear neutrophils predominating.

Complications.
A. Otitis media and mastoiditis secondary to upper respiratory tract infection.
B. Sinusitis secondary to upper respiratory tract infection.
C. Empyema following pneumonia.

Treatment.
A. Specific Measures: Penicillin is the drug of choice; it is given as in streptococcal infections.
B. General Measures: Symptomatic.
C. Treatment of Complications: Treat as for specific infection.

Prophylaxis.
There is probably no indication for active immunization in childhood, although type-specific carbohydrate substances have been used in the aged.

STAPHYLOCOCCAL DISEASES

These organisms characteristically produce a localized type of infection, but like other gram-positive cocci are capable of producing a wide variety of clinical disorders. Staphylococcal septicemia with multiple metastatic abscesses may also occur.

The staphylococci are gram-positive organisms which are divided into several types. Coagulase-positive Staph. aureus is the most common pathogen.

Staphylococci are common in the environment and are normally found in the throat and on the skin.

Clinical Findings.

A. Symptoms and Signs:

1. Pyoderma (most common type of infection) -
   a. Furuncle, folliculitis, or carbuncle.
   b. Impetigo, especially in the neonatal period (see Chapter 12).
2. Osteomyelitis as a result of blood streat spread from local inoculation.
3. Food poisoning - The organism produces an exotoxin known as "enterotoxin," which is probably the most common cause of "food poisoning." The usual source is creamed foods or custards. Vomiting, prostration, and diarrhea usually appear within four hours of ingestion of the contaminated food and rarely last more than six hours. Antibiotics are not necessary.
4. Pneumonia, usually peribronchial. (Commonest type of pneumonia during early infancy.)
5. Septicemia with focal abscesses; often a terminal event in the debilitated.
6. Enterocolitis in small infant; often the result of modification of intestinal flora by broad-spectrum antibiotics.

B. Laboratory Findings:

1. Leukocytosis in systemic infections.
2. Smear of pus from local infection shows organism.

Treatment.

A. Specific Measures: In recent years many strains have become resistant to the usual blood levels of penicillin. The use of two or more antibiotics is better than a single drug, as it will delay development of resistant strains. Local skin infections should not be treated with antibiotics.

1. Organisms assumed or known not to be penicillinase producers - Give penicillin G, phenethicillin, or ampicillin. Use the parenteral route for at least five days in osteomyelitis, pneumonia, meningitis, peritonitis, and empyema.
2. Organisms assumed or known to be penicillinase producers (penicillin resistant) - Give cloxacillin or oxacillin orally or, in severe infections, methicillin parenterally.
3. Enterocolitis - Neomycin orally.
4. Combined medical and surgical treatment (thoracotomy) is usually necessary for staphylococcal pneumonia.

B. General Measures:

1. In any local infection, heat, especially moist heat, will hasten localization and prevent systemic spread.
2. Food poisoning - Treat symptomatically (see Table 16-2).

Prophylaxis.

For prophylaxis of recurrent furunculosis, see Chapter 12. Prevent food poisoning by adequate refrigeration and sanitation.

Prognosis.

In usual local infection with adequate local treatment, excellent. Septicemia has become a serious disease with poor prognosis due to development of antibiotic-resistant strains of the organism. In staphylococcal food poisoning, prognosis is also excellent.

PERTUSSIS
(Whooping Cough)

Bordetella pertussis is a gram-negative bacillus. Transmission is by droplets during the catarrhal and paroxysmal stages of whooping cough. Pertussis is communicable from one week before to three weeks after onset of paroxysms. The incubation period is seven to ten days. A pertussis-like syndrome may be caused by Bordetella parapertussis, Haemophilus hemolyticus, or several respiratory viruses.

Clinical Findings.
A. Symptoms and Signs:
1. Insidious onset of symptoms of a mild catarrhal upper respiratory tract infection with rhinitis, sneezing, lacrimation, slight fever, and irritating cough.
2. Within two weeks the cough becomes paroxysmal, with repeated series of many coughs during one expiration followed by a sudden deep inspiration with characteristic crowing sound or "whoop."
3. Eating often precipitates paroxysms, which may also cause vomiting. Tenacious mucus may be coughed and vomited up.
4. Paroxysmal stage lasts from two to six weeks, but a habit pattern of coughing may continue for many weeks.
B. Laboratory Findings:
1. Very high WBC with predominant lymphocytosis.
2. Positive nasopharyngeal culture on Bordet-Gengou medium. Cultures are best obtained by nasopharyngeal swab and are generally positive during the catarrhal stage and the first week or two of the paroxysmal stage. The fluorescent antibody test may give a rapid diagnosis.
3. Sedimentation rate may be low.

Complications.
A. Pneumonia accounts for 90% of the deaths due to pertussis.
B. Atelectasis, emphysema, and bronchiectasis are other pulmonary complications.
C. Convulsions, which are probably due to cerebral anoxia during paroxysms. Permanent brain damage may occur.
D. Hemorrhage, usually into the conjunctivae or from the nose during paroxysms.

Treatment.
A. Specific Measures:
1. Tetracycline drugs or erythromycin may be given to young children or those with severe infections, but the value of such therapy has not been determined.
2. Pertussis immune gamma globulin may be given, but there is no clear evidence that it is of value.
B. General Measures:
1. Because of anoxic periods during paroxysms, infants under 18 months require constant attendance and sometimes such measures as insertion of airway, artificial respiration, and suction of oropharynx.
2. In severely ill children and all infants under the age of 18 months, use an oxygen tent with high humidity.

3. Parenteral fluids - Severe paroxysms may prevent adequate oral intake of fluids and necessitate parenteral therapy.
4. Sedatives - Phenobarbital for younger children and early in the disease, and codeine for older children in the latter phases of the illness, are often of value.
5. An abdominal binder may help to shorten paroxysms.
6. General hygienic measures are of importance because of the extended course of the disease.
7. Feedings - Frequent small feedings are less likely to cause vomiting than the usual three-meals-a-day schedule. Thick feedings are often retained better than more fluid ones.
8. Refeeding - If vomiting occurs during or immediately after a feeding, the child should be refed. Paroxysms are less likely to occur at this time.

C. Treatment of Complications:
1. Treat pulmonary complications with broad-spectrum antibiotics (see Chapter 6).
2. The liberal use of oxygen in severe cases will reduce the severity of cerebral anoxia and hence the incidence of convulsions and brain damage.
3. If convulsions occur despite the use of oxygen, give parenteral sodium phenobarbital (see Table 5-9).

Prophylaxis.

A. Active immunization in early infancy (see Table 7-1).
B. In exposed susceptibles under five years of age, give pertussis immune globulin, 2.5 ml. I.M., and five-day course of tetracyclines or erythromycin.
C. In exposed immunized children, give a booster injection of pertussis vaccine.

Prognosis.

Untreated severe disease in infants under one year of age has a very poor prognosis. Adequate treatment in this age group gives a good prognosis. Over one year of age, prognosis in uncomplicated case is good.

EXOTOXIC DISEASES
(DIPHTHERIA, TETANUS, GAS GANGRENE)

In this group of diseases, the dominant pathologic process is due to a product of bacterial metabolism (exotoxin) rather than the actual invasion of the host by the organism. The successful treatment of these diseases depends primarily upon neutralization of the effects of such toxins rather than the elimination of the organisms.

DIPHTHERIA

An acute febrile infection, usually of the throat, which is most common in the winter months in temperate zones. Infants born of immune mothers are relatively immune for about six months. With active immunization in early childhood, the disease is becoming more common in adolescence and in adults.

Diphtheria is caused by a gram-positive, pleomorphic rod, Corynebacterium diphtheriae, which shows barred forms on staining with methylene blue. It grows best on Löffler's medium. The organism produces a powerful necrotizing toxin which, unless it is neutralized by circulating antitoxin, is fixed on tissues. The disease is transmitted by droplets from the respiratory tract of a carrier or patient. The organism resists drying; contaminated articles may therefore serve as transmitting agents. The incubation period is one to seven days (average: 3 days).

Clinical Findings.

A. Symptoms and Signs:
  1. Pharyngeal -
    a. Mild sore throat.
    b. Moderate fever to 101 to 102° F. (38.5 to 39° C.).
    c. Rapid pulse and severe prostration.
    d. Exudate - A membrane forms in the throat and spreads from the tonsils to the anterior pillars and uvula. It is typically dirty gray or gray-green when fully developed but may be white early in the course. The edges of the membrane are slightly elevated, and bleeding results if it is scraped off. (This procedure is contraindicated, as it will hasten absorption of toxin.)
  2. Nasal (potent source of infection to others) -
    a. Serosanguinous nasal discharge that excoriates the upper lip.
    b. Membrane visible on turbinates.
    c. Constitutional manifestations are slight.
  3. Laryngeal (most serious) -
    a. Hoarseness or aphonia, croupy cough.
    b. Fever up to 103 to 104° F. (39.5 to 40° C.) and marked prostration.
    c. Cyanosis, difficulty in breathing, and eventually respiratory obstruction.
    d. Brawny edema of neck.
    e. Membrane may be visible in pharynx.
  4. Cutaneous, vaginal, or wound - Ulcerative lesions with membrane formation; lesions are persistent and often anesthetic.
B. Laboratory Findings:
  1. WBC is normal or there may be a slight leukocytosis.
  2. Smear of exudate stained with methylene blue shows rods with midpolar bars.
  3. Culture on Löffler's medium positive.

Complications.

A. Myocarditis: A direct result of the effect of the toxin. Clinical diagnosis is discussed in Chapter 13. Ecg. shows T-wave changes and partial or complete A-V block.
B. Neuritis: Usually a late development. Both sensory and motor paralysis develop rapidly once neuritis becomes apparent. Complete recovery is possible eventually.
  1. Pharyngeal and palatal muscles - Earliest to become involved; manifested by nasal voice, dysphagia, and nasal regurgitation of fluids.
  2. Extrinsic eye muscles - Diplopia and strabismus.

3. Skeletal muscles (legs and arms) - May end in quadriplegia.
C. Bronchopneumonia.
D. Albuminuria: Usually clears as fever returns to normal, but nephritis may occur.

Treatment.

A. Specific Measures (All Types):
1. Antitoxin in sufficient dosage must be given promptly. The longer the time between onset of disease and administration of antitoxin, the higher the mortality. Give antitoxin if disease is considered possible from clinical manifestations; do not wait for reports of cultures. Dose: 10,000 to 100,000 units for any age, depending on site, severity, and duration of the disease. Always test for horse serum sensitivity before administration (see p. 105). It may be given I.M., but the I.V. route is used in laryngeal diphtheria, in extensive nasopharyngeal involvement, when there is extensive cervical adenitis, when hemorrhage is present, and in all patients treated after the third day of illness.
2. Erythromycin (best) or procaine penicillin G should be used in treatment and to shorten the carrier state. The administration of these antibiotics before culture is taken may prevent diagnosis of diphtheria by inhibiting growth of the organisms.
3. Diphtheria may not confer immunity. Therefore, if Schick test (see p. 114) is positive, given toxoid inoculations in convalescence (see p. 99).

B. General Measures:
1. Give fluids parenterally if not taken by mouth.
2. Strict bed rest for at least four weeks followed by a gradual return to normal activity. During this period the child should be fed, bathed, and handled with utmost caution. Voluntary activity should be cut down to an absolute minimum.
3. Examine frequently for appearance of possible complications.
4. Special measures for laryngeal form -
   a. Avoidance of sedation.
   b. Aspiration of larynx as necessary.
   c. Tracheostomy for respiratory obstruction.
   d. Atmosphere with high humidity.
   e. Expectorant drugs.

C. Treatment of Complications:
1. Myocarditis - Give oxygen by tent, and glucose, 10%, 200 to 500 ml. I.V. daily. Avoid digitalis. Fluid balance should be maintained by parenteral administration.
2. Neuritis - Dysphagia may necessitate indwelling polyethylene nasogastric tube. Intercostal paralysis may necessitate the use of a mechanical respirator (see p. 481).
3. Cutaneous and wound diphtheria requires the use of antitoxin as for pharyngeal infection.

Prophylaxis.

A. Active immunization in early childhood (see Table 7-1).
B. Discovery and treatment of carriers.

Prognosis.

Always guarded, varying with day of disease on which antitoxin treatment is given. After six days without treatment, mortality is almost 50%. Myocarditis within first ten days is an ominous sign.

TETANUS

An acute disease characterized by painful muscular contractions. All ages are susceptible, including the newborn.

Clostridium tetani is an anaerobic, spore-forming, gram-positive organism which produces a very powerful neurotoxin.

Bacilli and spores are widely distributed in soil and dust and are present in the feces of animals and humans. Inoculation of a wound with dirt or dust is most likely to occur with puncture wounds. In many cases the original wound may have been very minor or overlooked entirely. In the newborn, transmission may occur by contamination of the umbilical cord, which, as it becomes necrotic, permits growth of the organism.

Clinical Findings.
A. Symptoms and Signs: The incubation period varies from five days to five weeks, depending upon the size of the inoculum and the rapidity of its growth. The onset may be with spasm and cramp-like pain in the muscles of the back and abdomen or about the site of inoculation, together with restlessness, irritability, difficulty in swallowing, and sometimes convulsions. A gradual increase in muscular tension occurs in the following 48 hours, with stiff neck, positive Kernig's sign, tightness of masseters, anxious expression of the face, and stiffness of arms and legs. Facial expression is modified by inability to open mouth (trismus). Swallowing is difficult. Recurrent tetanic spasms occur which last five to ten seconds and are characterized by agonizing pain, stiffening of body, retraction of the head and opisthotonus, clenching of the jaws, and clenching of the hands. Fever is usually low grade but may rarely be as high as 104°F. (40°C.). Auditory or tactile stimuli may initiate convulsions.
B. Laboratory Findings:
   1. WBC - 8000 to 12,000.
   2. C. S. F. - Slight increase in pressure; normal cell count.
   3. Anaerobic culture of excised necrotic tissue may yield organism.

Treatment.
A. Specific Measures:
   1. Antitoxin - See also Chapter 7. Human antitoxin is preferred at doses of 5000 to 10,000 units I.M. Precautions should be taken against serum reactions before injecting horse antitoxin. Use bovine antiserum if horse serum sensitivity is apparent and human antitoxin is not available.
   2. Surgical exploration of the wound, with excision of necrotic tissue and cleaning and drainage, is indicated after sufficient relaxation has taken place. There is no conclusive evidence that local therapy with antitoxin is indicated.
   3. Intramuscular penicillin or tetracyclines for at least seven days.

B. General Measures:
1. Keep patient in quiet, dark room. Minimize handling.
2. Sedation - Barbiturates in large doses may control severe spasms or convulsions, but may inhibit respiration and should be discontinued if the respiratory rate decreases. Meprobamate parenterally has been reported to markedly reduce the incidence of spasms. The dosage is 50-100 mg. every three hours up to five years of age; 200-300 mg. every three hours for ages five to 12 years; and 400 mg. every three hours for over 12 years of age.
3. Gentle aspiration of secretions in nasopharynx as required.
4. Oxygen should be available.
5. I. V. fluids as required.
6. Tracheostomy may be a life-saving measure for removal of secretions in the tracheobronchial tree, prolonged spasm of respiratory muscles, laryngeal obstruction, or coma.

Prophylaxis.
A. Active immunization (see Table 7-1) and an occasional recall injection will prevent tetanus in children and adults.
B. Antitoxin should be administered to all persons with compound fractures, deep, penetrating, or lacerated wounds, or wounds containing much devitalized tissue unless the child has previously been actively immunized. Repeated doses may be necessary if the site of possible infection cannot be adequately debrided. Active immunization should also be started.

Prognosis.
Mortality rate among children is about 35%, with death due to pulmonary infection.

GAS GANGRENE

Gas gangrene is caused by infection with any of the anaerobic clostridia, which produce powerful necrotizing toxins. It is characterized by a sudden onset of fever to 104°F. (40°C.), tachycardia, and toxemia developing after a contaminated wound (usually deep puncture wounds). The wound is tender, painful, and swollen, with a watery or purulent discharge, and has a musty, sickeningly sweet odor. Gas bubbles are palpable (crepitus). Gas gangrene is less common in children than in adults.

Treatment consists of thorough debridement of all potentially infected wounds and the administration of polyvalent gas gangrene antitoxin if infection with gas gangrene bacilli is suspected. If gas gangrene develops, surgical intervention is required, with multiple incisions to aerate the infected part; antibiotic therapy with penicillin G, 300,000 units/Kg./day in eight doses given every three hours, together with sulfonamide mixtures in full doses; and therapeutic doses of polyvalent gas gangrene antitoxin. Hyperbaric oxygen therapy has been reported to be successful in medical centers equipped to administer it. Unless specific measures are started early, the prognosis is poor.

• • •

SALMONELLOSIS

This term designates the group of disease states caused by organisms of the genus Salmonella, gram-negative bacilli.

Salmonellosis is spread from the feces of the sick person or fecal carrier to the mouths of other individuals. Epidemics have been traced to contaminated water, ice, milk, and various improperly prepared foods. Flies frequently carry the organism.

Etiology.

The salmonellae are divided into groups, replacing the old terminology in which only two types, Paratyphoid A and Paratyphoid B, were described.

A. Group A: S. paratyphi A; infrequent.
B. Group B:
   1. S. schottmülleri (Paratyphoid B); infrequent.
   2. S. typhimurium; common.
C. Group C: A large number of sporadically encountered species.
D. Group D: S. typhi, the cause of typhoid fever.
E. Other groups are only rarely encountered in human disease.

Clinical Findings.

A. Symptoms and Signs: Salmonella infections are of four types:
   1. Enteric fevers (e.g., typhoid fever) - After an incubation period of eight to 16 days, fever appears to 104° F. (40° C.) accompanied by anorexia, vomiting, abdominal distention, and extreme malaise. In many cases these are the only symptoms; however, after about five days a rash may appear, usually on the abdomen and consisting of red macules which blanch easily ("rose spots"). At this point the patient is usually very sick, sometimes with coma or convulsions. Physical findings include splenomegaly and a relative bradycardia. Diarrhea is rarely prominent, but may develop in the third week of the untreated case.
   2. Septicemia (particularly common in children) - Sudden onset, often with convulsions and spiking fever to 103-105° F. (39.5-40.5° C.). May accompany localized infectious processes (see below).
   3. Acute gastroenteritis and enterocolitis - Probably the most common form of salmonellosis and probably much more common than statistical records indicate. After an incubation period of one to three days there is a sudden onset of vomiting, diarrhea, and fever to 104° F. (40° C.). Abdominal cramps and prostration are common. Stools usually contain pus and blood (see Table 16-2).
   4. Localized salmonella infections - Salmonellae may cause localized infections in practically any part of the body. These include osteomyelitis, meningitis, pyelitis, appendicitis, peritonitis, bronchitis, and pneumonia. Children with sickle cell anemia are particularly susceptible to salmonella osteomyelitis.
B. Laboratory Findings:
   1. Enteric fever (typhoid) - Leukopenia at onset; positive blood, stool, urine, or bone marrow cultures. Serologic test for antibodies (Widal test) is best done with "H" and "O" antigens. Classic Widal test includes both antigens and

does not differentiate antibodies from active immunization ("H"). A single specimen any time during illness with titer above 1:100 against "O" antigen is indicative of acute enteric fever.
2. Septicemia - Positive blood culture during febrile phase.
3. Gastroenteritis - Moderate leukocytosis, w.b.c.'s in rectal smear. Culture of stools often positive. Multiple negative cultures do not rule out this etiology.
4. Localized infections - Leukocytosis. Culture of involved area positive. Serologic test positive.

Complications.
A. Of Typhoid Fever: In third week, hemorrhage or perforation of the intestines (rare in childhood).
B. Of Septicemia: Localized infectious process such as meningitis, osteomyelitis, pleural infection, abscess in any organ.
C. Of Gastroenteritis: Dehydration and acidosis as in any severe diarrhea.

Treatment.
A. Specific Measures:
   1. For enteric fever, septicemia, and meningitis, chloramphenicol (Chloromycetin®) should be given in usual doses until temperature has been normal for at least three days and for a maximum of ten days.
   2. Gastroenteritis - Dietary therapy is the most important factor. Chloramphenicol (Chloromycetin®) or ampicillin may be used. Prolonged carrier state is often found despite antibiotic therapy.
B. General Measures: Control fever and treat shock as necessary (see Chapter 2). Strict isolation of patients and careful disposal of excreta will protect other patients.

Prophylaxis.
Discovery and supervision of cases and carriers and sanitary disposal of their excreta. Protection and purification of food and water supplies. Supervision of food-handlers.
Active immunization is discussed on p. 104.

Prognosis.
In enteric fever, prognosis is usually good with antibiotics.
In septicemia, prognosis is guarded; local salmonella infections are particularly difficult to treat.
In gastroenteritis, prognosis is usually good with adequate measures to control diarrhea. Carrier state is common in young children and should be determined by repeated stool cultures. Treatment of carrier is most unsuccessful and not necessary. Family hygiene in such cases should be reviewed and improved by instruction.

SHIGELLOSIS
(Bacillary Dysentery)

Bacillary dysentery is spread from human feces of the sick person or fecal carrier to the mouths of other individuals. Epidemics have been traced to contaminated water, ice, milk, and various foods. Flies frequently carry the organisms.

The dysentery bacilli are divided into four pathogenic groups: Shigella dysenteriae (Shiga's bacillus), S. paradysenteriae (the various types of Flexner's bacillus and Boyd types), S. ambigua (Schmitz's bacillus), and S. sonnei (Sonne-Duval bacillus). The incubation period is one to six days (usually less than four).

Clinical Findings.
A. Symptoms and Signs:
   1. In severe and fulminant cases, the onset is sudden, with prostration, fever to 103° F. (39.5° C.), vomiting; profuse bloody diarrhea, colic, and tenesmus. The patient may be in shock very early in the course of the illness. Meningismus, deep drowsiness, coma or convulsions may occur. Generalized abdominal tenderness is usually present and, at times, rigidity.
   2. Mild form of the disease may show only slight fever and a mild, watery diarrhea.
B. Laboratory Findings:
   1. Pus and blood in smear of stool.
   2. Leukocytosis (10,000 to 16,000) and polymorphonuclear increase in the majority of patients.
   3. Cultures of the stool are usually positive; several cultures should be obtained in suspected cases before antibiotic is administered.

Complications.
A. A chronic, recurrent form of shigellosis may occur.
B. Localization of the disease in a joint, eye, respiratory tract, C.N.S., or urinary tract occurs but is not common.

Treatment.
A. Specific Measures: (See Chapter 6.)
   1. Ampicillin.
   2. Alternative drugs include sulfonamides, tetracycline, and chloramphenicol.
B. General Measures: In fulminant cases, treat shock (see Chapter 2). Control the diarrhea with dietary measures (see Chapter 16). Treat dehydration early and vigorously (see Chapter 5).

Prophylaxis.
Control of cases and carriers is most important. No active immunizing agent is in use as yet.

Prognosis.
When treatment is begun early in the disease, the prognosis is good. In infancy and old age, the mortality rate is highest if therapy is delayed. Relapse or reinfection occurs in 10% of cases.

GONORRHEA

Neisseria gonorrhoeae is a gram-negative, coffee bean-shaped diplococcus usually found both intracellularly and extracellularly in purulent exudate. The infection may be acquired during delivery by direct contact with infected material in the vagina; in childhood by contact with infected vaginal or urethral discharge or from infected bedpans and toilet seats.

Clinical Findings.

A. Symptoms and Signs: There are two principal forms of gonococcal infection in infancy, childhood, and adolescence:
1. Gonococcal conjunctivitis of the newborn.
2. In males, urethritis with purulent discharge.
3. Gonorrheal vulvovaginitis - While the vaginal mucosa in adults is resistant to infection with the gonococcus, both the vagina and the vulva are readily infected before puberty (most commonly from birth to five years). The infection is spread by contact with contaminated articles or infected children or adults and is manifested by itching and burning of the vulva and vagina. The mucous membranes of the vulva and vagina are red and edematous, and there is a profuse, yellow, purulent discharge. Must be differentiated from the more common nonspecific vulvovaginitis due to improper hygiene.
4. In postpubertal girls, infection is usually inapparent or may cause pelvic abscess in more rare instances.

B. Laboratory Findings:
1. Smear of purulent exudate may show intracellular organisms.
2. Cultures on Thayer-Martin medium should be carried out on any suspected case.

Complications.

A. Of Conjunctivitis: Corneal ulceration and opacity.
B. Of Vaginitis: Spread to regional organs or (through blood stream) to joints.
C. Septicemia: Septicemia with purulent arthritis and distinctive skin lesions can occur. The skin lesions have an erythematous base with central hemorrhage which later becomes necrotic and vesicular. Arthritis involves ankles, knees, and wrists and is migratory. Tenosynovitis is also common.

Treatment.

A. Conjunctivitis, Vaginitis, and Urethritis:
1. Procaine penicillin, 1.2 million units in a single dose at several intramuscular sites if necessary. Give probenecid, 25 mg./Kg., 1 hour before penicillin.
2. If there is sensitivity to penicillin compounds, give tetracycline for four days.

B. Arthritis and Sepsis:
1. Penicillin G I.V. for five days.
2. As an alternative, give tetracycline for ten days.
3. Arthritis may persist or recur. Intra-articular injection of penicillin G may be useful; repeat three times every two days.

Prophylaxis.

A. Conjunctivitis: See Chapter 19.
B. Vaginitis: Examination of contacts, to prevent recurrence or infection of other children, and of mother prior to delivery.

Prognosis.

Excellent with penicillin treatment. Untreated conjunctivitis may result in corneal scarring.

TULAREMIA

The causative agent is Francisella tularensis, a gram-negative rod. The infection is transmitted through direct contact with the blood of an infected rabbit, ground squirrel, or other small animal; through bites of infected insects, such as flies and ticks; or through ingestion of improperly cooked rabbit meat (usually wild rabbit). The incubation period is one to seven days (average: 3 days).

Clinical Findings.

A. Symptoms and Signs: Onset is sudden, with fever to 104 to 105° F. (40 t0 40.5° C.), vomiting, chills in older children, and convulsions in the rarely infected infant. Cutaneous eruptions of various types occur in about 10% of children. The clinical picture depends upon portal of entry:

1. Ulceroglandular type - Lesion on extremity where the bacteria enter the skin; it is at first papular but rapidly breaks down and becomes a punched-out ulcer, and is accompanied by enlargement and tenderness of regional lymph nodes and sometimes by nodules along the course of the lymphatics. Without therapy, suppuration of the lymph nodes frequently occurs. In some cases there is lymphadenopathy, but no primary lesion can be detected.

2. Pharyngotonsillar type - Ulceration and formation of a membrane on pharynx and tonsils, accompanied by enlargement of cervical lymph nodes.

3. Oculoglandular type (acquired when material is rubbed into the eye) - Acute conjunctivitis with edema; photophobia; itching and pain in the eye and swelling of the upper lid, which may show scattered small yellow nodules; enlargement of lymph glands of neck, axilla, and scalp.

4. Cryptogenic type - Point of entry of the organisms cannot be recognized, and the symptoms are entirely systemic.

B. Laboratory Findings:

1. WBC may be normal or there may be a slight leukocytosis.

2. Positive agglutination test with rising titer, beginning around seven days from onset. The test may give cross reaction with brucellosis.

Treatment.

A. Specific Measures: Streptomycin, 60 mg./Kg. body wt./day I. M., produces rapid effect; it should be continued for at least seven days. Tetracyclines are usually administered concurrently (see p. 94), especially in seriously ill patients.

B. General Measures: Symptomatic and supportive.

Prophylaxis.

A. Proper handling and cooking of wild rabbits.

B. Extreme care in handling laboratory material from case.

C. Avoid early surgical incision of suppurating lesions.

Prognosis.

With streptomycin treatment, excellent. Without treatment the fever may last one month and glandular enlargement four months.

PLAGUE

Plague is a disease primarily of rats and other small rodents. It is transmitted to man by a variety of fleas. The organism is present in ground squirrels and other rodents in the U.S.A. The pneumonic form of the disease may be transmitted from person to person by the inhalation of infected droplets.

The causative agent is Pasteurella (Yersinia) pestis, a gram-negative, bipolar-staining, pleomorphic bacillus.

Clinical Findings.
A. Symptoms and Signs: Incubation period is two to ten days. There are three clinical syndromes of the disease:
   1. Bubonic plague - Sudden onset with chills, fever to 104°F. (40°C.), vomiting, and lethargy; and tender, firm enlargement of inguinal, axillary, and cervical lymph nodes (buboes) by third day. Meningismus, convulsions, and delirium may occur.
   2. Pneumonic plague - As above, but with absence of bubo and onset of cough on first day. Blood-tinged, mucoid, or thin, bright-red sputum may be brought up. Clinical signs of pneumonia may be absent at first.
   3. Fulminant (septicemia) - Onset as above but with overwhelming blood stream invasion before enlargement of nodes or pneumonia.
B. Laboratory Findings:
   1. Leukocytosis early to as high as 50,000, mostly P.M.N.'s.
   2. Positive blood culture early.
   3. Organisms on smear of lymph node contents, sputum, and sometimes from C.S.F.

Treatment.
A. Specific Measures:
   1. Combined streptomycin, 50 mg./Kg. body weight/day in four I.M. doses, and tetracyclines in full doses; give parenterally if necessary.
   2. Tetracyclines alone are the therapy of second choice.
B. General Measures: Symptomatic treatment, with strict isolation of pneumonic case and disinfection of all discharges.

Prophylaxis.
Control of rats and fleas, active immunization (see p. 100), and re-immunization every six months in endemic areas. Upon recovery from plague, the patient will be immune to further attacks.

Prognosis.
If treatment can be started early enough in the disease, prognosis is excellent. Delay in treatment may result in death from fulminant form of disease. Without treatment, prognosis is poor.

CHOLERA

The causative agent is Vibrio cholerae (V. comma), a gram-negative, curved organism with a terminal flagellum which is actively motile in suspension. Transmission, as in other enteric infections, is by contaminated food or water.

Clinical Findings.
A. Symptoms and Signs: During the incubation stage (one to three days), a mild diarrhea may be present. During the diarrheal stage, there is severe cramping and profuse diarrhea, the stools becoming almost clear fluid and albuminous ("rice water"). Vomiting is severe. In the collapse stage, diarrhea ceases and shock appears within two to 12 hours after onset of diarrhea. During the recovery stage the stools become more normal during the course of a week.
B. Laboratory Findings: There is little change in blood picture, and the stools show no pus cells.

Treatment.
Emergency intravenous therapy with massive infusions of physiologic saline solution is the single most important consideration. Saline must be given via cut-down and allowed to run as rapidly as possible (ten to 20 times the usual speed), and may need to be repeated. Potassium and bicarbonate supplements may be necessary. If tolerated, oral tetracycline given for five days may hasten recovery.

Prophylaxis.
Active immunization, boiling all water and potentially contaminated foods, and screening in endemic areas.

Prognosis:
In untreated case, mortality is 25 to 50%. With early and adequate treatment, the prognosis is good.

BRUCELLOSIS
(Undulant Fever, Malta Fever)

Brucellosis is caused by one of the three strains of gram-negative brucella organisms (Brucella abortus, B. melitensis, and B. suis). Although these varieties are most commonly found in cattle, goats, and hogs, respectively, they have also been isolated in other species of animals. The incubation period is five to 20 days.
Transmission is by direct contact with diseased animals, their tissues, or unpasteurized milk from diseased cows and goats.

Clinical Findings.
A. Symptoms and Signs: In the acute disease the onset is gradual and insidious, with fever and loss of weight. Fever at first may be low-grade and present in the evening only, but in the course of days or weeks it may reach 104° F. (40° C.) and present a wave-like character over a period of two to four days. The chronic disease is manifested by low-grade fever, sweats, malaise, arthralgia, depression, splenomegaly, and leukopenia.
B. Laboratory Findings: Agglutination and complement fixation tests are of value; skin tests are of limited value (see p. 111). Serologic tests may give cross reaction with tularemia. Blood cultures should be repeated at least three times.

Treatment.
A. Specific Measures: Combined therapy with streptomycin and a tetracycline drug is the treatment of choice. Continue treatment for two to three weeks. For dosages see Chapter 6.
B. General Measures: Bed rest during acute stage, and high vitamin intake.

Prophylaxis.
Pasteurization of milk and milk products.

Prognosis.
In acute form prognosis is good with adequate treatment. Response of chronic form to treatment may be poor, although the disease is not fatal.

BACTERIAL INFECTIONS
OF THE CENTRAL NERVOUS SYSTEM

GENERAL CONSIDERATIONS IN MENINGITIS

The most important step in diagnosis of infection of the central nervous system is to suspect that it may be present.

Symptoms and Signs of Meningitis.
A. "Meningeal" Signs: Stiffness of neck (inability to touch chin to chest), stiffness of back (inability to sit up normally), positive Kernig's sign (inability to extend knee when leg is flexed anteriorly at the hip), and positive Brudzinski's sign (when the head is bent forward, flexure movements of the lower extremity are produced).
B. Increased Intracranial Pressure: Bulging fontanelles in small infant, irritability, headache (may be intermittent), projectile vomiting (or vomiting may be absent), diplopia, "choking" of the optic disks, "cracked pot" percussion note over skull (sometimes in normal children also), slowing of pulse, and irregular respirations.
C. Change in Sensorium: From mild lethargy to coma.
D. Convulsions: Usually generalized. More common in infancy.
E. Fever: Onset of high or low-grade fever may be sudden or insidious, or there may be a marked change in pattern during a minor illness.
F. Shock: May appear in the course of many types of infection of the central nervous system.
G. In infancy, a high-pitched cry, irritability, poor feeding, or vomiting may be the only signs. Fever may be absent or low-grade.

Examination of Cerebrospinal Fluid. (See Appendix.)
When infection of the C.N.S. is suspected, lumbar puncture and examination of the C.S.F. must be performed to establish the diagnosis. The gross appearance, Pandy test for globulin, cell count, and microscopic examination of a concentrated sediment for

bacteria may all be performed immediately after this procedure. Fluorescent antibody technics, if available, may reveal the specific cause. The determination of glucose content should be done **at once;** the degree of depression of the glucose level will determine the urgency of treatment. A poor prognosis is related to the degree of depression also.

C.S.F. and Blood Culture.

C.S.F. must be cultured both aerobically and anaerobically. The organism causing the C.N.S. infection may grow in a blood culture and not in cultures of the C.S.F.

Complications of Meningitis.

C.N.S. infection may produce hydrocephalus, especially in infants (uncommon since advent of specific therapy; see p. 372); subdural accumulation of fluid, especially in a patient under two years of age (see p. 379); deafness (see p. 232), paralysis of various muscles, mental retardation (see p. 389), focal epilepsy (see p. 387), and psychologic residua. Persistent fever may be due to brain abscess, lateral sinus thrombosis, mastoiditis, drug reaction, or continued sepsis.

General Plan of Treatment.

A. Emergency Measures: **Treat shock.** (See Chapter 2.) (For treatment of possible endotoxic shock, see p. 507.) Avoid overhydration.

B. Infection With Known Organism: Treat according to regimen given under specific disease (see below).

C. Suspected Infection With Undetermined Organism: **Obtain diagnostic material first.** Urgency in starting treatment depends upon presumed duration of disease; presence and depth of coma; age of the patient, with infancy an indication for urgency; and the degree of depression of the C.S.F. glucose.

 1. For infants under six months, give ampicillin I.V. and kanamycin.

 2. For children over six months of age, give ampicillin I.V.

 3. If tuberculosis is a strong possibility, treat accordingly.

D. Increased intracranial pressure may produce death before antimicrobial treatment takes effect. Treat as for encephalitis.

MENINGOCOCCAL MENINGITIS

Clinical Findings.

A. Symptoms and Signs: Any of the findings described above may be present. Most cases have a sudden onset, high temperature, and petechial or purpuric rash. Herpes labialis is commonly associated. Meningococcemia with petechiae and morbilliform rash without C.N.S. involvement may occur.

B. Laboratory Findings: C.S.F. abnormalities are usually characteristic of acute purulent bacterial meningitis (see Appendix, Table 5). Organisms usually can be seen in smear of C.S.F. and may be demonstrated within polymorphonuclear leukocytes in blood smears obtained by puncturing the center of petechiae. Leukocytosis is present. Blood cultures are usually positive.

Complications.

Any of the complications listed above may develop. In addition, arthritis, conjunctivitis, and toxic myocarditis may be present. Diffuse thromboembolic lesions with disseminated intravascular clotting may involve many organs. The course may be fulminant, with Waterhouse-Friderichsen syndrome, in which case the blood stream may be so infected with organisms that they can be seen in a blood smear. Hemorrhagic phenomena are a prominent feature of this form of the disease, with rapidly spreading purpura and hemorrhage into body cavities and organs. Hemorrhage of the adrenal glands creates a shock-like state. The chronic, recurrent form is uncommon.

Treatment.

A. Specific Measures:
   1. Penicillin G in maximum parenteral dosage (see Chapter 6).
   2. Sulfadiazine should be given in addition to penicillin. Give by a parenteral route if possible. (See p. 93 for dosage.) It is apparent that infection with the organism and resultant carrier state is not the most important factor in the production of disease. Eradication of the carrier state cannot be considered an easily attainable preventive measure to eliminate cases of disease.
   3. If penicillin allergy is present, give chloramphenicol.
   4. Continue antimicrobial therapy for ten days.
B. General Measures: Symptomatic therapy as indicated.
C. Treatment of Complications:
   1. Arthritis - Paracentesis for relief of pain.
   2. Conjunctivitis - See Chapter 19.
   3. Toxic myocarditis - None available.
   4. Endotoxic shock may occur with any gram-negative organism, including meningococci. The clinical picture is that of shock plus hemorrhagic phenomena, including purpura and hemorrhagic pneumonia. Disseminated intravascular clotting also takes place. Treatment is as follows:
      a. Treat for primary shock (see p. 16). Use dextran-70 as a plasma expander because this substance will inhibit platelet aggregation and adherence to injured surfaces.
      b. Give hydrocortisone in doses of 30 to 50 mg./Kg. I.V. repeated every 30 minutes until clinical improvement occurs or for 12 hours.
      c. Heparin sodium given I.V. in repeated dosage of 100 units/Kg. every 4 hours. Increase in platelet count will indicate success of this agent; dosage should be reduced or discontinued depending on repeated counts.
      d. Vasodilators such as isoproterenol or phenoxybenzamine have been recommended.

Prophylaxis.

For close contacts in the family and exposed attendants, sulfadiazine, 0.5 Gm. twice daily for two days, may be given if the infecting strain is determined to be sensitive to sulfonamides. For strains resistant to sulfonamides, give rifampin (Rimactane®, Rifadin®). Give single daily doses as follows: adults, 600 mg.; children, 10 to 20 mg./Kg., not to exceed 600 mg.

Prognosis.

Except for fulminating type, prognosis is good. The prognosis in endotoxic shock is poor but improves markedly if the patient can survive the first 24 hours.

PNEUMOCOCCAL, STREPTOCOCCAL, AND STAPHYLOCOCCAL MENINGITIS

Clinical Findings.

Clinical findings are similar in all three types. Differential diagnosis is made on the basis of laboratory examination.

A. Symptoms and Signs: A history of upper respiratory tract infection, sinusitis, pneumonia, otitis, or other infection, or of skull fracture or meningocele may be obtained. Any of the findings described on p. 505 may be found. Onset is less acute than with meningococcal meningitis. Petechial rash is rare.

B. Laboratory Findings: C.S.F. abnormalities are characteristic of acute purulent bacterial meningitis (see Appendix, Table 5). Smear usually shows large numbers of gram-positive cocci in pairs (pneumococci), chains (streptococci), or clumps (staphylococci).

Complications.

Any of those listed on p. 505 may develop, particularly if therapy is inadequate or started late. Infection of the middle ear and sinusitis (see Chapter 14) are especially common. There may also be localization in the pleural, pericardial, or peritoneal cavities, or arthritis.

Treatment.

A. Specific Measures:
   1. Penicillin G in large dosage. Give 300,000 units/Kg./day in eight divided doses I.V. for ten days or until cerebrospinal fluid sugar level is normal.
   2. Occasional use of intrathecal dose of penicillin at onset in young children or small infants. For dosage, see p. 88.
   3. In staphylococcal infection with resistant strain, use methicillin, oxacillin, or nafcillin.

B. General Measures: Symptomatic therapy, as indicated.

C. Treatment of Complications: Large doses of drugs and in some instances surgical drainage of abscess or empyema. In pneumococcal or streptococcal meningitis, mastoidectomy should be considered even in the absence of localizing signs.

Prognosis.

With early, adequate therapy complete recovery occurs. Otherwise, prognosis for life or residua depends on severity and duration.

HAEMOPHILUS INFLUENZAE MENINGITIS

Clinical Findings.

A. Symptoms and Signs: Usually occurs in children under two years of age (almost unknown over ten years). Onset may be insidious or quite abrupt following an upper respiratory infection (usually mild). Coma occurs within a few hours. Any of the findings listed on p. 505 may be present. Young infants may have persistent unexplained fever, irritability, difficulties with feeding, or a high-pitched cry and no clear evidence of meningitis.

B. Laboratory Findings: Nose and throat cultures are usually positive. Smear of spun sediment from cerebrospinal fluid usually shows gram-negative, pleomorphic, encapsulated coccobacilli in pairs or chains. Quellung reaction with specific antiserum. Blood culture is frequently positive. Severity of infection may be determined by glucose test (see p. 505) on spinal fluid; the lower the C.S.F. glucose, the more severe the infection.

Complications.

Subdural effusion, a collection of fluid (often sterile) in the subdural space, may occur especially if initial therapy has been delayed or inadequate. Symptoms include recurrence of fever, vomiting, lethargy, or enlargement of the head in infants. In younger children with open fontanelles, a subdural tap (see Chapter 32) will establish the diagnosis. In older children, bur holes are required. Recent reports suggest that post-meningitis effusions are more likely to occur when large amounts of C.S.F. (> 5 ml.) are removed at the time of the "diagnostic" spinal puncture.

Any of the complications listed on p. 506 may develop.

Treatment.

A. Specific Measures:
1. Ampicillin - For dosages, see Chapter 6.
2. Alternative method - Streptomycin and sulfonamides given simultaneously for five days and followed by chloramphenicol for an additional ten to 14 days. Chloramphenicol may be given in addition to streptomycin and sulfonamides during the first five days and continued when these latter drugs are stopped. (For dosages, see Chapter 6.)
B. Local Measures: Otitis media may require myringotomy.
C. General Measures: Symptomatic therapy as indicated.
D. Treatment of Complications: Subdural empyema is treated by repeated aspiration. In some cases a membrane forms which may have to be removed, as in subdural hematoma (q.v.).

Prognosis.

Usually favorable with early and adequate therapy.

MENINGITIS DUE TO GRAM-NEGATIVE BACTERIA

Meningitis may also be caused by Escherichia coli, Pseudomonas aeruginosa, Enterobacter aerogenes, and Proteus morgani. Any of the findings listed on p. 505 may be present. A history of local infection (infected navel, diaper area pyoderma), meningomyelocele (in infants), or urinary tract infection (in older children) can be obtained. Laboratory confirmation is very important. Smear of C.S.F. shows numerous gram-negative rods. Growth on culture is usually rapid. Sensitivity to various antibiotics should be determined. Treatment depends largely on the results of antibiotic sensitivity tests and clinical experience with these agents (see Chapter 6). Intrathecal administration of antibiotic may be necessary.

The prognosis depends upon the type and severity of infection. For endotoxic shock, see p. 507.

MENINGITIS DUE TO KLEBSIELLA PNEUMONIAE
(Friedländer's bacillus)

Clinically indistinguishable from meningitis due to gram-negative organisms (see above). Only bacteriologic studies can identify the organism and determine the treatment.

Treatment with sodium cephalothin (Keflin®) is the method of choice. Sulfonamides and streptomycin are also effective (see Chapter 6 for dosage).

MENINGITIS DUE TO LISTERIA MONOCYTOGENES

Listeria monocytogenes produces a clinical picture resembling those of the other purulent meningitides (see p. 505). Only bacteriologic studies can identify the organism, which is gram-positive, rod-shaped, and non-spore-forming. The organism may be misinterpreted as a "diphtheroid" and concluded to be a contaminant.

Penicillin in large doses in combination with erythromycin is the treatment of choice. Tetracyclines are also effective. (See Chapter 6.)

TUBERCULOUS MENINGITIS

Clinical Findings.
  A. Symptoms and Signs: A history of exposure to an adult case of pulmonary tuberculosis is common. Any of the findings listed on p. 505 may be present. Onset is often gradual, with irritability, change in personality, and drowsiness. Symptoms referable to the central nervous system may be minimal or may suggest encephalitis. As the disease advances, the irritative symptoms subside, and stupor becomes more pronounced. Positive tuberculin skin test in a child under ten years with C.N.S. disease is very suggestive of tuberculous meningitis (see p. 115). An associated tuberculous pneumonitis is usually present. Marked dermatographia (tache cérébrale) is common.
  B. Laboratory Findings: Lumbar puncture should be performed in any child with known tuberculosis who shows change in temperature pattern or any C.N.S. symptoms. An occasional tubercle bacillus may be found in the pellicle or web of C.S.F. which forms on standing (see Appendix, Table 5). Culture or guinea pig inoculation of spinal fluid is positive.

Treatment.
  A. Specific Measures: (Combined therapy.)
    1. Isoniazid (INH), 8 mg./Kg. for one day and then 20 mg./Kg./day for one year.
    2. Ethambutol (Myambutol®), 15 mg./Kg./day in two doses for one year. Check vision monthly.

3. Streptomycin sulfate, 200 mg./Kg./week I.M. in daily doses for eight weeks.
4. Dexamethasone (Decadron®) - Give in doses of 2 to 5 mg. I.V. depending on age and weight repeated at four-hour intervals for 14 days.
5. When treatment has been delayed or in severely ill patients, more intensive therapy may be necessary. Among the recommended methods are: intrathecal streptomycin, 2 mg./Kg./day; intrathecal isoniazid, 20 to 40 mg./day; fibrinolytic enzymes (streptokinase or streptodornase); ventricular drainage for relief of intracranial pressure, and intrathecal tuberculin (PPD). The exact value of these procedures has not been determined.

B. General Measures: Maintenance of nutrition is important because of protracted course. Gavage feedings may be necessary. Blood transfusion and electrolyte management are indicated. Give pyridoxine, 10 to 25 mg./day, and thiamine hydrochloride, 10 mg./day. Occupational and play therapy is indicated according to the physical and psychologic tolerance of the patient.

Prognosis.

Without treatment, mortality is 100%. With early, adequate treatment, recovery is to be expected. Long-term follow-up is necessary to determine recurrences, treat as the initial disease.

BRAIN ABSCESS

Brain abscess is usually caused by one of the common pyogenic bacteria: streptococci, pneumococci, staphylococci, or Esch. coli. The source of infection is usually a septic focus elsewhere in the body (e.g., otitis media, pneumonia, osteomyelitis, SBE, or furuncles). Organisms may enter following skull fracture through the sinuses or middle ear.

Clinical Findings.

A. Symptoms and Signs: May be few and diagnosis difficult. Onset is gradual, with fever, vomiting, lethargy, and coma. Increased intracranial pressure is usually present, manifested by bulging fontanelles (infants) or papilledema (older children). Neurologic signs relating to special areas of the brain may be present, and a focal type of convulsion may occur (see p. 386). A history of infection elsewhere in the body should be sought.
B. Laboratory Findings: Leukocytosis and C.S.F. changes (see Appendix, Table 5).
C. X-ray Findings: Cranial sutures may be widened. Brain scan and arteriography may give specific diagnosis and location.

Treatment.

A. Specific Measures: If the organism is known, treat with specific antibiotic of choice (see Chapter 6). If not known, treat with large doses of penicillin, as for streptococcal meningitis (see p. 508), until specific etiologic diagnosis can be made. Surgical drainage will usually be necessary.
B. General Measures: Anticonvulsants (see Table 21-4).

Prognosis.

When the organism is known and is susceptible to antibiotics and treatment is early, the prognosis is good. Otherwise, prognosis is at best guarded. Extensive brain damage may occur, with resultant mental retardation.

SPIROCHETAL DISEASES

SYPHILIS

Childhood infection with Treponema pallidum may be either congenital or, rarely, acquired.

A. Congenital: Transmitted by direct inoculation into the blood through the placenta during the latter half of pregnancy. If the infection of the mother is recent, the infant is almost always affected. The longer the intervals between infection of the mother and the birth of the child, the greater the likelihood that the infant will be free of the disease.

B. Acquired: Introduced through an abrasion or laceration by contact with infected nipples, through kissing, or by sexual contact.

Clinical Findings.

A. Symptoms and Signs: Childhood syphilis may be considered in two forms: early and late. Specific signs and symptoms may be mistaken for a variety of other conditions. As a rule, several are present in combination and suggest the diagnosis.

1. Early congenital syphilis - Signs appear before the sixth week. The more severe the infection, the earlier the onset.

   a. Rhinitis or "snuffles," a profuse, persistent, mucopurulent nasal discharge, is usually the first symptom. The discharge may be blood-tinged.

   b. Skin rash, following onset of rhinitis and appearing as maculopapular or morbilliform eruption, heaviest over the back, buttocks, and backs of thighs. Bullous lesions on hands and feet are suggestive.

   c. Bleeding ulcerations and fissures of mucous membranes of mouth and anus and contiguous areas.

   d. Anemia; erythroblasts may be present in large numbers.

   e. Osteochondritis and/or periostitis, with pseudoparalysis, pathologic fractures, and a characteristic x-ray appearance of increased density, widening of the epiphysial line, and scattered areas of decreased density.

   f. Hepatomegaly and splenomegaly; jaundice may be prominent.

   g. Chorioretinitis with eventual optic atrophy.

2. Late congenital syphilis - Symptoms do not usually occur until after the third month.

   a. Maldevelopment of bones of nose (saddle nose) and of legs (saber shins).

   b. Neurosyphilis with clinical evidence of meningitis, paresis, or tabes, or with a slowly developing hydrocephalus.

   c. Teeth - Decidious teeth are normal. Permanent dentition may show "Hutchinson's teeth," in which upper central incisors have characteristic V-shaped notch in a peg-shaped tooth. The first permanent molars may have multiple cusps ("mulberry molar").

    d. Rhagades, or scars around mouth and nose.

    e. Interstitial keratitis, usually between six and 12 years of age; early conjunctivitis which gradually infiltrates deeply into the cornea, producing opacity.

  3. Acquired syphilis - Symptoms are similar to and as variable as those in the adult.

B. Laboratory Findings:

  1. Serologic tests - A routine Wassermann test on cord blood obtained at birth will detect passively acquired antibodies from treated or untreated syphilis in the mother as well as actively acquired antibodies from the infection in the infant. If the mother has been adequately treated during pregnancy and the infant shows no evidence of disease, repeated serologic testing should be performed and treatment delayed for two to three months. By that time passively acquired antibodies will have been lost, and a positive reaction indicates active disease. Quantitative tests demonstrate a declining titer of passively acquired antibodies.

  2. Scrapings from mucous lesions and nasal discharge may show Treponema pallidum.

C. X-ray Findings: These are typical. All of the long bones may be affected. Changes are apparent early in the disease. Epiphysial line shows increased density, with decreased density proximal to it. In severe cases, destructive lesions occur near the ends of long bones. Periostitis appears as a widening of the shaft of the long bones, with eventual calcification and distortion of the normal curvature.

Treatment.

A. Specific Measures:

  1. Penicillin - Give procaine penicillin G, 600,000 units per day for eight days in early cases, or aqueous penicillin G, 50,000 units I.M. every three hours for eight days.

  2. In presence of sensitivity to penicillin, give tetracyclines for 14 days.

B. Treatment of Neurosyphilis: Continue with penicillin for 14 days.

C. Follow-up Treatment: Serologic tests at intervals of three months for at least one year and evaluation and treatment of maternal disease.

Prophylaxis.

Case-finding in adults, especially early in pregnancy so that treatment may be completed before delivery. The chances of preventing the disease in the newborn are excellent even if treatment is not given until the seventh or eighth month of pregnancy.

Prognosis.

Rapid treatment of early congenital syphilis in infancy will usually result in a cure and normal growth and development.

The prognosis for late congenital syphilis in childhood is good for cure of the spirochetal infection, but pathologic changes in bones, nervous system, and eyes will remain throughout life.

SPIROCHETAL MENINGITIS
(Leptospirosis: Lept. canicola, Lept. icterohaemorrhagiae, Lept. grippotyphosa, and Lept. mitis)

This disease is now recognized to be more common than was formerly believed to be the case. It is transmitted by ingestion of water or food contaminated with the urine of dogs, usually male, seriously ill, with polyuria; or of rats. All degrees of severity may occur. Any of the findings listed on p. 505 may be present, as well as jaundice, albuminuria, oliguria, and episcleral injection ("conjunctivitis").

Lept. canicola appears to be the cause of an appreciable number of cases of meningitis, and should particularly be considered in so-called "benign aseptic meningitis."

Leptospira may be found in the blood by dark-field examination of fresh specimens or in thick, dry, stained films early in the disease. They may also be isolated by animal inoculation.

Antibodies may appear any time after the first week of infection, reach a peak in several weeks, and then fall slowly.

The exact value of the various antibiotics used in treatment has not been determined, but tetracyclines or penicillin in large doses have been reported to be effective when given early (see Chapter 6).

SPIROCHETAL JAUNDICE
(Weil's Disease)

An acute febrile disease usually caused by Leptospira icterohaemorrhagiae of rats. Transmission is through ingestion of food or water contaminated with the urine of infected rats. Ingestion may occur while bathing. Rat bites are also a source. Infectious jaundice may also be caused by L. canicola, probably as a result of ingestion of food or water contaminated with dog urine.

The incubation period is six to 12 days. Onset is sudden, with fever to 103 to 105° F. (39.5 to 40.5° C.). Jaundice appears in at least 50% of cases by the fifth day, sometimes with hemorrhagic tendency. Rash, sometimes morbilliform, appears in the first seven days. Meningeal involvement produces signs of meningitis (see p. 505). The WBC may rise to 50,000, with occasional immature forms. C.S.F. may show 100 to 200 cells, mostly lymphocytes. Leptospirae in the blood may be seen on a smear with Wright's stain in the first four days, and in the urine from the tenth to twentieth days. Direct inoculation of animals and serologic methods are available for final diagnosis.

Renal involvement, with marked reduction in urinary output or even anuria, may occur after the third day. This grave prognostic sign is accompanied by a 50% mortality rate.

Treatment is with penicillin in the usual doses for seven days. As alternative therapy, give tetracycline.

With early treatment, the prognosis is good. Recurrences should be re-treated for the seven-day course.

RELAPSING FEVER

Relapsing fever is endemic in many parts of the world. The causative organism is Borrelia recurrentis and the reservoir is rodents or other human beings sick with the disease. Transmission to humans occurs by mites or ticks and occasionally by contact with the blood of infected rodents.

After an incubation period of two to fourteen days, the onset of disease is abrupt, with fever, chills, tachycardia, nausea, vomiting, arthralgia, and cough. A morbilliform rash appears usually within the first two days and maximally over the trunk and extremities. Petechiae may also occur. Without treatment, the fever falls by crisis in three to ten days. Relapse then characteristically occurs at intervals of one to two weeks and may involve as many as ten such episodes in the absence of treatment.

Diagnosis depends upon the clinical course and the observation of spirochetes in the peripheral blood by dark-field examination or the usual Wright's stain.

Treatment with penicillin, tetracyclines, or chloramphenicol is successful.

Prognosis is good except in debilitated states.

26...
Infectious Diseases:
Protozoal & Metazoal

PROTOZOAL DISEASES

MALARIA

An acute or chronic febrile disease caused by one of four types of plasmodia: Plasmodium vivax, P. malariae, P. falciparum, and P. ovale. Transmission occurs through the bite of the female Anopheles mosquito, in which the sexual cycle of the parasite occurs. The asexual cycle occurs in man.

Clinical Findings.

In children malaria does not always present the classical clinical picture seen in adults.

A. Symptoms and Signs: Sudden onset of paroxysms of fever to 103 to 105° F. (39.5 to 40.5° C.) accompanied by convulsions in the very young. Chill is sometimes present, lasts at least two to four hours, and is followed by sweating. In young children, paroxysms may be continuous or very irregularly recurrent. In older children, recurrence of paroxysms varies with type of infection: P. vivax, P. falciparum, and P. ovale, 48 hours; and P. malariae, 72 hours. Diarrhea and vomiting are frequent, and splenomegaly is usually present.

B. Laboratory Findings:
1. Rapid onset of anemia and increased serum bilirubin.
2. Thin and thick blood smears and bone marrow smears show parasites.

Complications.

''Blackwater fever'' is rare in childhood. It is usually associated with P. falciparum infection and is characterized by hemoglobinuria and a shock-like state.

Treatment.

A. Specific Measures:
1. Chloroquine diphosphate (Aralen®), given once daily orally for four days, is the drug of choice for P. vivax and P. falciparum infections, which it completely eradicates. Toxic symptoms include nausea, vomiting, and diarrhea. Dosage:
   a. Give 10 mg./Kg. as initial dose, followed by 5 mg./Kg. once daily for three days.
   b. If oral therapy is not possible, give chloroquine hydrochloride, 2 mg./Kg. I. M. or I. V. Stat. and the same dosage once each day.

2. In chloroquine-resistant falciparum infection, fever persists over 48 hours. Change treatment to quinine.
   a. Quinine sulfate, 0.6 Gm. t. i. d. orally for five to seven days.
   b. Quinine dihydrochloride, 0.5 Gm. I.V. diluted in 100 ml. (3 oz.) or more of physiologic saline. Give slowly. Use only for patients unable to take oral medication. Follow with oral medication. A **very dangerous drug.**
3. Primaquine diphosphate - A drug used in combination with chloroquine in P. vivax infections only. It is reported to eradicate the infection and prevent relapses.
   a. Dosage - Give orally once daily for 14 days.
      (1) Up to 15 lb. - 2 mg.
      (2) 15 to 40 lb. - 4 mg.
      (3) 40 to 80 lb. - 6 mg.
      (4) 80 to 120 lb. - 10 mg.
      (5) Over 120 lb. - 20 mg.
   b. Toxicity - Primaquine is a toxic drug and must be used with careful laboratory follow-up.
      (1) Never use in Negroes.
      (2) If anemia, leukopenia, or methemoglobinemia appear, discontinue drug immediately.
      (3) Never use with quinacrine hydrochloride or within five days of quinacrine therapy.
B. General Measures:
   1. Fluid therapy is most important. Urge oral intake and, if not satisfactory, give parenteral fluids.
   2. Control high fever.
   3. Treat anemia with iron.

Prophylaxis.

A. Control of mosquito vectors
B. Suppressive Therapy: Most of the drugs used to treat the disease may be used prophylactically in endemic areas.
   1. Chloroquine - Doses as above, at weekly intervals.
   2. Quinine - 0.3 to 0.6 Gm. daily.
   3. Amodiaquin - 0.6 Gm. every two weeks (one dose).
   4. Quinacrine and pyrimethamine, although not recommended for the acute attack, may be used for prophylaxis.
      a. Quinacrine hydrochloride (Atabrine®) - Give orally once daily with meals. Begin treatment two weeks before entering endemic area.
         (1) One to five years - 0.07 Gm.
         (2) Five to ten years - 0.15 Gm.
         (3) Over ten years - 0.3 Gm.
      b. Pyrimethamine (Daraprim®) - For children, give 12.5 mg. weekly (may be dissolved in syrup).
C. Chloroquine diphosphate, 10 mg./Kg. body wt., is indicated before giving a transfusion of whole blood in endemic areas or from a donor recently arrived from an endemic area.

Prognosis.

In majority of cases, excellent with proper therapy. In small infants and in the presence of malnutrition or chronic debilitating disease, the prognosis is more guarded.

AMEBIASIS

An acute and chronic enteric infection with Entamoeba histolytica. Transmission from an infected case or a carrier is through the cysts, which are excreted in feces. The cyst may survive as long as one month in water. The disease is acquired by oral route through contamination of food or drinking water.

Clinical Findings.
A. Symptoms and Signs:
    1. Acute amebic dysentery is characterized by a sudden onset of diarrhea which is not usually explosive or accompanied by tenesmus and which lasts about one week. Frequency of stool varies with age of child, being higher in infants and occurring only two or three times daily in older children. This diarrheal phase is followed by an asymptomatic phase and, usually, a recurrence. Fever is usually not significant. Hepatomegaly may be present.
    2. Atypical amebiasis is common in children, with mild recurrent diarrhea, irritability, anorexia, and slight abdominal pain (most often RUQ).
B. Laboratory Findings: Stool examination in acute stage may show trophozoites. Cysts are excreted in cycles, and repeated stool examinations may be necessary. Biopsy of rectal mucosa sometimes provides a definitive diagnosis.

Complications.
Amebic abscess is rare in early childhood but should always be considered. Early symptoms include relief of hunger by extremely small amounts of food, and hiccupping as a result of diaphragmatic irritation. Liver scanning with radioisotopes is the most useful diagnostic approach.

Treatment.
A. Specific Measures: Drugs available for treatment are not consistent in results, and careful follow-up of cases, with examination of stools for cysts two to four weeks after cessation of therapy, is required. Diarrhea may not cease until several days after trophozoites have disappeared from the stool.

    Combined treatment with one of the tetracyclines (or other broad-spectrum antibiotics) and chloroquine is the most commonly used regimen. There are, however, wide variations in recommendations, and a variety of other drugs are reported to be effective.
    1. Metronidazole (Flagyl®) is very effective and has few side-effects. The dosage is 10 to 15 mg./Kg./day given in three doses for five to ten days, usually following a course of chloroquine.
    2. Tetracycline given three times daily for ten days.
    3. Chloroquine phosphate (Aralen®) given for ten days.
        a. Up to five years - See dosages below; give correspondingly smaller dosage.
        b. Five to ten years - Give half the adult dosage.
        c. Over ten years (adult dosage) - 1 Gm. followed by 0.5 Gm. after six to eight hours and then 0.5 Gm. on the next two days (2.5 Gm. in three days).

4. Emetine hydrochloride is of value (with chloroquine) in acute dysentery. Like chloroquine, it has less effect on the intestinal phase and should therefore be used with tetracycline as above.

    a. The patient should be in hospital during administration of emetine. Pulse and blood pressure should be followed carefully. Upon increase in pulse rate or fall in blood pressure, discontinue the drug. An Ecg. should be taken at start of therapy and after four days of treatment. Changes in QRS complex, ST segment, and conduction time are indications for cessation of treatment.

    b. Give 1 mg./Kg. body wt. once daily (not to exceed 0.06 Gm. per day) subcut. or I. M.

5. Carbarsone given orally in capsule form in two doses per day for ten days. The dose per day is 0.06 Gm./20 lb. body wt.

B. General Measures:

    1. Dietary measures for diarrhea as in Chapter 16.

    2. Precautions as to disposal of stools and care of diapers.

C. Treatment of Complications: Amebic hepatitis should be treated with erythromycin or chloroquine. Regulate diet as for other types of acute hepatitis.

Prognosis and Prophylaxis.

The prognosis is excellent with adequate treatment and follow-up. Proper disposal of excreta and precautions in regard to drinking water are preventive measures.

TOXOPLASMOSIS

A variety of clinical entities are caused by infection with the protozoon Toxoplasma gondii, which is widespread in animals and birds. Human adults are relatively resistant to infection, but it is more common in children and occurs also as a congenital infection of the fetus.

Clinical Findings.

A. Symptoms and Signs:

    1. Congenital disease (acquired through infection in mother) -

        a. C. N. S. disease - A variety of syndromes from fatal encephalitis to meningeal symptoms only may occur. Symptoms in the neonatal period may include jaundice, hepatosplenomegaly, chorioretinitis, and convulsions. Microcephaly or porencephaly may result from asymptomatic acute infection in the mother.

        b. Chorioretinitis - Found in all cases of C. N. S. disease but sometimes occurs as the sole manifestation. The vitreous is cloudy and the retina eventually shows large defects and scars.

    2. Acquired disease -

        a. Febrile lymphadenopathy resembling infectious mononucleosis but with a more prolonged course, sometimes two to six months and with intermittent exacerbations.

        b. Febrile disease without symptoms or signs of specific organ system involvement. Transient morbilliform rash may appear. A prolonged and recurrent course is not uncommon.

c. Chorioretinitis with acute onset in children or young adults; may be recurrent and prolonged (almost pathognomonic of toxoplasmosis).

B. Laboratory Findings:

1. WBC and differential may resemble infectious mononucleosis (see Chapter 24) or be entirely normal.
2. Heterophil antibody titer rarely elevated.
3. Sabin-Feldman dye test becomes positive after initial infection and is positive in mother with congenital infection.
4. Liver function tests may be abnormal (see Appendix).
5. In C.N.S. disease, C.S.F. shows up to 500 WBC.
6. Complement fixation antibodies may also be demonstrated.
7. X-ray of skull shows intracranial calcifications in recovered congenital infection.

Treatment.

Chemotherapy has not proved effective. Pyrimethamine (Daraprim®) has shown promise in animals. Sulfonamides have been suggested. In chorioretinitis, give prednisone, 1 mg./Kg. for ten days, then reduce dosage to stop the drug in five more days.

Prognosis.

In congenital disease, sequelae are common in survivors. Mental retardation, blindness, and convulsive states have all been ascribed to this disease.

In acquired disease the prognosis is guarded for sequelae but good for survival. Systemic disease without specific organ involvement has a good prognosis.

METAZOAL DISEASES

I. NEMATODES

OXYURIASIS (Pinworms)

Asymptomatic infestation with Enterobius (Oxyuris) vermicularis is a common disease. Symptoms occasionally do occur and may require treatment.

The fertile eggs, laid outside the anus, are distributed from person to person by dust, the anus-to-mouth route from contaminated articles, and by direct contact with infected individuals. About 20% of children in the U.S.A. harbor the worm.

Clinical Findings.

A. Symptoms and Signs: Several members of the family are usually infected. Pruritus ani is the most common symptom and is usually most intense at night, when the worms are laying their eggs. There may be involvement of the vagina, with itching and discharge, or dysuria. Massive infestation may cause abdomi-

nal pain or even appendicitis, as well as variable, vague nervous symptoms.
B. Laboratory Findings:
1. Demonstration of eggs should be attempted. The customary technic is to press a small piece of pressure-sensitive cellulose tape (Scotch® tape) around the anus in the early a.m., preferably before bowel movement, and to examine the tape under the microscope on a glass slide. Eggs appear as elongated ovals with the embryonic worm inside.
2. Eosinophilia may be present.

Treatment.
A. Specific Measures: Use one of the following methods:
1. Piperazine citrate or phosphate (Syrup of Antepar®) (100 mg./ml.) - Give daily for seven days, withdraw for seven days, and then give again for seven days.
   a. One to five years - 2.5 ml. three times daily.
   b. Five to ten years - 5 ml. three times daily.
   c. Ten years and over - 7.5 ml. three times daily.
2. Pyrvinium pamoate (Povan®), 5 mg./Kg. body weight orally (maximum dose, 250 mg.); repeat in two weeks. Nausea, vomiting, and cramping may occur.
3. Gentian violet - 0.01 Gm./day/year of age. Enteric-coated tablets, which must be swallowed intact, are given in divided doses two or three times per day with meals: give daily for eight days, discontinue for eight days, and then give a second course for eight days. Side-effects include nausea, vomiting, and abdominal pain; if these occur, the drug should be stopped for a period of five days and then resumed.
B. General Measures:
1. Wash hands carefully before each meal and after bowel movement.
2. Keep fingernails short and well scrubbed.
3. Launder and boil all bed linen twice weekly; avoid shaking bed linen when removing it from bed.
4. Avoid scratching involved area and putting hands in mouth and nose.
5. Scrub toilet seats daily.

Prognosis and Prophylaxis.
The prognosis is excellent, and complications are extremely rare. Most infestations are not recognized or treated. A high carrier rate makes control measures difficult.

ASCARIASIS (Roundworms)

Infestation with Ascaris lumbricoides, a large roundworm, which may produce no symptoms. The eggs are excreted in feces, and the highly infective larvae are developed in the soil. Human-to-human transmission occurs in childhood by ingestion of larvae from soil-contaminated fingers, toys, etc.

Clinical Findings.
A. Symptoms and Signs: Passage of adult worm is usually the only sign of infestation. Colicky, recurrent abdominal pain due to

adult worms in intestine, or respiratory symptoms due to passage of larval stage through the lungs in the course of the normal life cycle may occur. Bile duct obstruction with the adult worm may occur.

B. Laboratory Findings: Eggs found in feces are round and have a prominent outer membrane with a wave-like contour.

Treatment.
  A. Specific Measures:
    1. Piperazine syrup (citrate or phosphate) (Antepar®) - Give once daily for three days in same dosage as for oxyuriasis (see p. 520).
    2. Hexylresorcinol - Alternate method. Supplied as enteric-coated crystoids. Give saline purge (15 to 30 Gm. sodium sulfate in water) on the night before therapy. Crystoids (0.2 Gm.) must be swallowed intact. Dose is given once. Withhold all food until four hours after treatment is given. Examine feces two weeks after therapy to be sure that treatment has been successful. Dosage:
      a. One to five years - 0.2 to 0.4 Gm.
      b. Six to ten years - 0.6 to 0.8 Gm.
      c. Over ten years - 1 Gm.
    3. Thiabendazole (Mintezol®) - Alternate method. Give 25 mg./Kg. orally twice daily for two days.
  B. General Measures: Intestinal decompression with a Levin tube may be helpful in cases of massive infestation with partial intestinal obstruction and during the first 24 hours of drug therapy.

Prognosis.
  The prognosis is excellent for eradication by the first course of drug therapy.

ANCYLOSTOMIASIS (Hookworms)

Infestation with Ancylostoma duodenale (Europe) or Necator americanus (America). Eggs are passed in feces and develop in soil to form larvae. Larvae pass through the intact skin of the bare feet in contact with contaminated soil. Coexisting deficiency diseases and malnutrition may contribute to some of the symptoms.

Clinical Findings.
  A. Symptoms and Signs: Passage of larvae through the skin of the feet may produce itching and papular eruption. An early sign is soft and sometimes tarry feces (melena). Apathy, pallor, anorexia, and failure to grow are noted, and the abdomen may be protuberant.
  B. Laboratory Findings: Examination of stool reveals eggs in great quantity. They are oval and thin-walled, with cells or embryos inside. Early, leukocytosis with eosinophilia is present. Later, hypochromic microcytic anemia appears.

Treatment.
  A. Specific Measures: Treatment should be undertaken only after general supportive measures have been carried out.

1. Bephenium hydroxynaphthoate (Alcopara®) is highly effective against Ancylostoma, and it may be used with tetrachloroethylene in Necator infection. Give a 5 Gm. dose twice in a single day. For children weighing less than 50 lb., give a 2.5 Gm. dose twice. The drug is best given mixed with some flavored liquid, fruit juice, or milk.
2. Hexylresorcinol, as for ascariasis, is only slightly less successful than above.
3. Tetrachloroethylene - (Do not give in presence of Ascaris; in mixed infections, treat ascariasis first.) Saline purge of 15 to 30 Gm. sodium sulfate on the night before therapy. Withhold all food. Give 0.2 ml. per year of age as a single dose, in capsule form or as liquid with syrup, followed by bed rest for 24 hours. Two hours after therapy, repeat saline purge.

B. General Measures: Iron for hypochromic anemia, with transfusions if degree of anemia is severe; and good diet with supplementary vitamins.

Prognosis and Prophylaxis.

Prognosis is excellent for cure and anemia responds to therapy with eradication of disease. Shoes should be worn in endemic areas, and re-infection can occur.

TRICHINOSIS

A very common infestation, most often unrecognized, with Trichinella spiralis acquired through ingestion of inadequately cooked infested hog meat. Larvae migrate from bowel to blood stream to muscle, where they encyst to form a fibrotic nodule.

Clinical Findings.
A. Symptoms and Signs:
1. Acute manifestations - May be quite mild or may be fatal. Gastrointestinal symptoms appear early, followed in a few days by nausea, vomiting, cramps, diarrhea, and flatulence; chills and fever, weakness, rash; edema, especially of the face and about the eyes; conjunctivitis and photophobia, splinter hemorrhages, pain and tenderness in the muscles, and central or peripheral nerve involvement with severe headache.
2. Chronic manifestations - Most cases have no symptoms. Weakness may be present, as well as other symptoms referable to multiple organ involvement.
B. Laboratory Findings: Eosinophilia is present in both forms.
1. Acute form - Trichinella skin test gives a delayed reaction (12 to 24 hours) early in the disease (third to seventh days).
2. Chronic form - Trichinella skin test gives an immediate reaction (five minutes) late in the disease (seventeenth day on). Muscle biopsy may demonstrate organisms. Complement fixation and precipitin tests are of value after the fourth week of infection.

Treatment.
- A. Specific Measures: None available.
- B. General Measures: Hospitalization and optimum nursing care for severe acute cases.
- C. Corticotropin (ACTH) and one of the cortisones (cortisone, hydrocortisone, prednisone) provide effective relief for the acute symptoms of trichinosis (see Chapter 22). A reduction of the eosinophil count, disappearance of fever and splinter hemorrhages, if present, and a general improvement in the clinical state of the patient are guides which should be employed to determine the efficacy of treatment.
  1. Acute form - Treat with relatively large doses of either drug for first 24 to 48 hours.
  2. Subacute form - Therapy may have to be continued for several days or weeks on a reduced dosage to prevent recurrence of symptoms.

Prognosis and Prophylaxis.
The prognosis is excellent for subsidence of symptoms. All pork should be thoroughly cooked and stored at sub-freezing temperatures to kill the larvae.

II. CESTODES

TAENIASIS (Tapeworms)

Infestation with Taenia saginata (beef) and T. solium (pork), the tapeworms. Transmission is by ingestion of larvae in inadequately cooked beef or pork. Larvae develop into adults in about three months.

Clinical Findings.
- A. Symptoms and Signs: History of consumption of raw or incompletely cooked beef or pork.
  1. Acute manifestations - Diarrhea, fever.
  2. Chronic manifestations - Vague gastrointestinal and C.N.S. symptoms.
- B. Laboratory Findings:
  1. Acute phase - Leukocytosis and eosinophilia.
  2. Chronic phase - Mild to severe anemia and gravid proglottids in feces or on underclothing.

Treatment.
- A. Niclosamide (Yomesan®): The drug of choice for all tapeworms. Give orally in a dosage of 1 Gm. for children two to eight years of age; 1.5 Gm. for children over eight; and 2 Gm. for older children and for adults. The drug is given on an empty stomach on the morning following a light nonresidue supper. Post-treatment purgation is required only in the case of T. solium infection. The toxicity of niclosamide is slight in therapeutic doses.
- B. Quinacrine: If niclosamide is not available, give quinacrine (Atabrine®), 10 to 15 mg./Kg. orally up to a maximum of 800

mg., either as a single dose or two divided doses one hour apart on an empty stomach in the morning. A saline cathartic is recommended for both T. solium and T. saginata infections.

Prognosis.

Excellent, with successful eradication of all worms, although sometimes several courses of treatment may be necessary.

DIPHYLLOBOTHRIASIS
(Fish Tapeworm Disease)

Infestation with Diphyllobothrium latum, the fish tapeworm, the larvae of which exist in muscles of fish. Inadequate cooking allows transmission to man.

Few symptoms are apparent in children. Anemia may produce secondary symptoms of anorexia and lethargy. Stool examination shows characteristic oval eggs, with many cells visible inside. Leukopenia with eosinophilia is present.

Treatment is with niclosamide (or quinacrine), administered as for taeniasis (see above).

VISCERAL LARVA MIGRANS
(Toxocara, Larval Granulomatosis) (See also p. 250.)

Visceral larva migrans may produce an illness in young children which is characterized in most cases by a benign course with hepatomegaly; chronic, persistent leukocytosis; eosinophilia, hyperglobulinemia, and eosinophilic granulomatous lesions of the liver. The disease is self-limited. Severe cases may be treated with thiabendazole (Mintezol®), 25 mg./Kg. orally twice daily for five to seven days.

Infection results from the ingestion of embryonated toxocara eggs present in soil contaminated with the excrement of infected cats and dogs. The prognosis is good.

PNEUMOCYSTIS PNEUMONIA

This is an interstitial pneumonitis occurring in infants or children with low resistance syndromes such as when receiving corticosteroids, prolonged antibiotic therapy, or cytotoxic drugs for neoplasms. It is caused by the protozoon Pneumocystis carinii. Multiple cases in newborn nurseries have been reported.

X-rays show an interstitial pneumonitis, but physical signs are rare. The diagnosis may be established by lung puncture biopsy or open lung biopsy.

Treatment with pentamidine isethionate (Lomidine®) has been reported to be successful. Give 4 mg./Kg. I.M. daily for 14 days. The cause of the lowered resistance should be eliminated if known. Transfusions are sometimes necessary.

27 . . .

Infectious Diseases: Mycotic

COCCIDIOIDOMYCOSIS (Valley Fever)

An acute or chronic illness caused by Coccidioides immitis, the spores of which are highly infectious in the saprophytic phase and are spread in the dust of the arid areas in Southwestern U.S.A. Inhalation of the dust is the means of infection. Only about 30% of infected persons show symptoms.

Clinical Findings.
A. Symptoms and Signs:
1. Primary form - Incubation period is one to four weeks. In about two-thirds of infected persons there are no clinical manifestations. In others there may be sudden onset with fever, chills, and prostration. Cough is common, usually of the nonproductive, "barking" type. Physical examination usually is non-contributory. In the presence of cough fine rales or scattered areas of dulness may be found on examination of the chest. Morbilliform or scarlatiniform rash may appear in the first three days of disease. Erythema nodosum and/or erythema multiforme occur in some patients two weeks after onset of symptoms and after the febrile phase has subsided.
2. Chronic or granulomatous form - 0.2% of primary cases progress to the granulomatous stage. Lungs, chest wall, and other structures are involved. Organisms are present in the infected tissues or in the discharge from the lesions.
B. Laboratory Findings:
1. Sedimentation rate is elevated during acute phase of infection.
2. X-ray findings in primary form of the disease include enlarged hilar nodes and soft parenchymal densities simulating, primary tuberculosis. Cavities are characteristically thin-walled.
3. Coccidioidin skin test is positive in primary and chronic disease. In meningitis and other forms of disseminated disease, this test is characteristically negative.
4. Precipitin test is positive early (one to two weeks) and complement-fixation test is positive late (six to 14 weeks).

Complications.
A. Pleural effusion is usually asymptomatic but may cause some embarrassment of respiration.
B. Disseminated coccidioidomycosis is a rare and very serious complication, occurring usually within six months of the primary infection.

1. Coccidioidin skin test is usually negative. Serologic tests are positive.
2. Skin lesions appear as multiple nodules which rapidly break down into chronic, draining "cold" abscesses; they are accompanied by fever to 102° F. (39° C.) and prostration.
3. Meningitis or lesions of bones may be the only manifestation of dissemination.

Treatment.
A. Specific Measures: Amphotericin B (Fungizone®) in severe or disseminated cases. For reasons of toxicity it should not be used in mild forms. The daily dosage is 1 mg./Kg. I.V. in a solution of 5% glucose over a six-hour period. Give one-fourth of the calculated daily dosage for five days before the full dosage is given. Continue treatment for three to six months. For small children, an indwelling polyethylene catheter has proved to be of value. For meningitis the drug must be given intrathecally, 10 to 20 mg. daily for three months.
B. General Measures: Symptomatic care. Bed rest during symptomatic phase of primary infection for at least two weeks or until temperature has been within normal range for five days.
C. Treatment of Complications: Supportive and symptomatic.

Prophylaxis.
None available.

Prognosis.
Primary coccidioidomycosis without dissemination, excellent. In disseminated coccidioidomycosis with skin lesions only, fair; with meningitis, guarded.

ACTINOMYCOSIS

A focal purulent infection caused by Actinomyces bovis, which is universally distributed in the soil and is commonly found in the mouths of humans without evidence of disease. It is thought to result from contamination of a wound on the skin or in the mouth.

Clinical Findings.
A. Symptoms and Signs:
1. Cervicofacial type (about 50% of all cases) - Gradual onset of hard swelling of the jaw and neck, which becomes red and only slightly tender. Eventual development of fluctuant areas, with breakdown and draining of sinuses.
2. Abdominal type (about 30%) - Often follows an appendectomy. Gradual development of a non-tender mass, usually in the right lower quadrant. Involvement and enlargement of liver and spleen. Chronic draining sinuses may develop.
3. Thoracic type (about 20%) - Resembles pulmonary tuberculosis at onset. Involvement of pleura, with breakdown through the chest wall and chronic draining sinuses, eventually occurs.
B. Laboratory Findings: Examination of unstained discharge shows mycelial filaments and "sulfur granules."

Treatment.
A. Specific Measures: Penicillin and sulfadiazine is the treatment
regimen of choice.
1. Penicillin, two to 20 million units I.V. daily, depending on
age, for ten to 15 days. Procaine penicillin, 600,000 units
daily for 30 days, followed by phenoxymethyl penicillin, 250
mg. orally three times a day for one year.
2. Give sulfadiazine three times a day for 30 days.
B. General Measures: Symptomatic; irradiation in well-localized
type of disease.

Prognosis.
In sharply localized lesion, where surgical removal may be
used in conjunction with antibiotic therapy, prognosis is excellent.
In the cervicofacial form, with long-term follow-up and retreatment of possible recurrence, prognosis is fair. In thoracic
and abdominal types and the rare case with involvement of meninges, prognosis is very poor with available methods of treatment.

NOCARDIOSIS

Nocardiosis is a chronic disease, rare in childhood, usually
manifest as pulmonary or brain abscesses. It is caused by No-
cardia asteroides, which is a gram-positive, acid-fast, branching
form of actinomycete. The treatment of choice is with sulfonamides. Prognosis is grave.

HISTOPLASMOSIS

Infection with Histoplasma capsulatum is usually asymptomatic
but occasionally disseminates and produces a generalized, severe
disease. The mode of transmission is not clear at present. The
organism is present in many animals, including dogs, and has been
found in the soil. It may be dust-borne. Cases are found in all
parts of the U.S.A., especially in Midwestern and Southern areas.

Clinical Findings.
A. Symptoms and Signs:
1. The benign form of the disease may be the most common,
with unrecognized or minimal symptoms and with resultant
skin sensitivity to histoplasmin (see p. 113). It may be
responsible for calcified lesions in the chest, including
those resembling miliary tuberculosis.
2. The severe form of the disease has a gradual onset, with
malaise, weight loss, mild diarrhea, and enlargement of
the abdomen. Irregular fever rises to 101 to 103°F. (38.5
to 39.5°C.). Physical examination shows hepatosplenomegaly and lymphadenopathy.
B. Laboratory Findings:
1. Leukopenia and relative lymphocytosis. Mononuclear and
polymorphonuclear cells may show phagocytized yeast-like
cells in the cytoplasm.
2. Hypochromic anemia.

3. Yeast phase of fungus may be found on bone marrow aspiration (see Chapter 32) or in biopsy of lymph node.

Treatment.

In disseminated cases, give amphotericin B (Fungizone®) as for coccidioidomycosis. In mild cases treatment is given for two to three weeks. In severe or prolonged cases treatment is continued for 16 weeks.

Prognosis.

In the benign form the prognosis is excellent; in the severe form death usually occurs within six months.

CRYPTOCOCCOSIS
(Torulosis)

Infection with Cryptococcus neoformans almost always involves the C. N. S. in the form of a chronic meningitis with intermittent exacerbations and remissions, sometimes for several years. Spinal fluid examination shows high protein and low glucose levels and the organism, which is round or ovoid and is enclosed in a thick capsule.

A granuloma of the skin may be an early sign of infection or may accompany C. N. S. disease.

Treatment with amphotericin B as for coccidioidal meningitis has given most promising results. Flucytosine is useful as an alternative treatment. The prognosis is guarded at best. All untreated patients will eventually succumb.

CANDIDIASIS

Candidiasis, which is caused by Candida (Monilia) albicans, commonly causes stomatitis, vulvovaginitis, onychomycosis, and paronychia. Intertriginous skin eruption and "diaper rash" are also common. Less common systemic involvement includes pneumonia, meningitis, endocarditis, and gastroenteritis, often associated with immunosuppressive therapy.

For treatment of skin and mucous membrane involvement, see p. 196. Systemic manifestations are treated with amphotericin B or with flucytosine.

The prognosis for skin and mucous membrane involvement is excellent. For systemic disease, the prognosis is grave, even with treatment.

28 . . .
Allergic Diseases

GENERAL CONSIDERATIONS

Predisposing Factors.

The development of allergic symptoms depends upon inheritance and on the nature of the allergen, the degree, duration, and nature of exposure, and a number of poorly understood nonhereditary factors. All persons are potentially allergic, but the susceptibility to certain types of allergic disorders (e.g., hay fever and asthma - "atopic" disorders) varies widely, depending largely upon constitutional factors. Inherited predisposition is not itself sufficient to produce hypersensitivity; adequate contact with allergenic agents is necessary.

A. Pathogenesis: Active sensitization can be brought about by inhalation, ingestion, absorption through mucous membranes, or parenteral injections of foreign substances. Characteristically, some time is required between the initial contact with an allergen and the establishment of a sensitized state.

B. Passive Sensitization: Transient hypersensitivity may be acquired through blood transfusions.

C. Increased permeability of the intestinal wall after severe gastrointestinal disturbances may permit the ready entrance of unchanged protein into the blood stream and so facilitate the development of sensitivity.

D. Psychologic factors may aggravate allergic conditions and should be carefully evaluated in the general work-up of the patient.

Prophylaxis.

Allergy is rarely "cured" but may be kept under control so as not to produce symptoms. Some very sensitive persons may be forced to avoid allergens completely, but most allergic patients can tolerate slight or moderate contact with their allergens. Therefore, partial removal of an allergen is better than none.

A. Early Prophylaxis: If members of the family are known to be allergic, breast feeding is especially advisable in offspring. The infant should not be given cow's milk in the period before breast feeding is established, since sensitization to cow's milk may occur at this time. In potentially allergic children, the avoidance in early infancy of milk and milk products, chicken, cow products, and wheat-containing foods appears to result in a lower incidence of asthma and allergic rhinitis. Avoid the early introduction (before six to nine months) of other foods known to be of high allergic potential such as fish, chocolate, nuts, and eggs. New foods should be added to the diet singly and not in mixtures.

530

B. Dietary Care*: In infancy and early childhood, single additions to the diet every four to seven days should be in the form of simple foods rather than combinations of foods such as mixed vegetables or cereals. If possible, avoid common allergens such as wheat, chocolate, oranges, eggs, fish, and nuts.

Skin Testing.
A. Reactivity: In general, positive allergy skin tests with inhalants are more meaningful clinically than positive tests to foods.
B. Interpretation: Reactions must be interpreted in the light of clinical findings. As a general rule, large reactions, especially on "scratch" testing, are more likely to reflect clinical sensitivity than minimal reactions. However, the intensity of a given reaction is not an indicator of the severity of symptoms elicited by the allergen. A positive reaction to a particular antigen does not necessarily indicate a clinical problem.

Characteristics of an Atopic Individual.
These patients should receive routine childhood immunizations. Smallpox vaccination is contraindicated in the presence of eczema.
A. Family History: Most allergic children have a positive family history. However, the child's allergens need not be the same as those of other allergic members of the family, nor are the allergic manifestations always the same.
   There is a high incidence (10 to 35%) of a positive family history among "nonallergic" individuals.
B. Clinical Findings:
   1. Some stereotyped clinical manifestation.
   2. Different allergic symptoms and signs may appear at different ages. For example, a patient may have eczema as a baby, hay fever as a child, and asthma as an adult. Conversely, new sensitivities may appear, while previous sensitivities may remain or may be lost.
   3. Nonallergic factors (irritants, infections, psychologic conditions) characteristically play significant roles in worsening symptoms.
C. Diagnostic Tests: Allergic patients usually react positively to skin and mucous membrane tests with appropriate allergens. Provocative tests (nasal, conjunctival, or bronchial challenge; feeding of possible food allergens) are helpful but may be dangerous; they should only be performed under close supervision.
D. Laboratory Findings: Eosinophilia of peripheral blood is common in atopic reactions. Eosinophilia of nasal mucous membrane is an especially important finding in patients with allergic rhinitis. Eosinophilia of bronchial mucus is present in children with asthma. Serum IgE concentrations may be elevated.

General Treatment of Allergic State.
A. Removal of the Offending Allergens: This is potentially the most effective method of managing all allergic syndromes.

---

*It has been suggested that sensitivity to certain foods, especially milk and chocolate, may cause a "tension-fatigue" syndrome with chronic fatigue, leg aches and pains, recurrent headache, abdominal discomfort, and, occasionally, low-grade fever.

Relief of symptoms can be expected to be proportionate to the extent of allergen removal and depends on the sensitivity to the allergen. When dietary manipulation is deemed necessary, care must be taken to ensure that the diet is nutritionally adequate.

B. Altering the Response Toward the Offending Allergen: (Effective in some cases.)
1. Disturbed emotional patterns should be improved.
2. Certain drugs, including antihistamines, methylxanthines, sympathomimetic amines, and the corticosteroids, may be beneficial.
3. Treat bacterial infection if present.

C. Decreasing Sensitization to Specific Known Antigens That Cannot Be Avoided: Immunotherapy ("hyposensitization") aimed at reducing the allergic child's sensitivity to offending allergens is frequently of value. Initial dose (give subcutaneously) equals the smallest amount which will produce a positive intradermal test. Increase each subsequent dose by 50% (assuming that it did not produce a severe reaction) up to a maintenance dose (highest tolerated dose). The interval between doses is three to seven days while dosage is being increased and three to six weeks when maintenance amounts are being given. In pollen sensitivities, treatment may be given preseasonally or perennially (preferred), but the maximum dose should be reached just before the start of the pollen season.

Preparation of Dust-Free Room.

The preparation and maintenance of a dust-free room is usually of benefit to the allergic child. The house-dust mite is a major allergen in house dust. The patient must not sleep in any bed that is not prepared like his own.

A. The Room: Remove all rugs (especially if underlying pads contain horse or cattle hair), fabric floor, wall, or window coverings, cleaning equipment, and unnecessary furniture and clothes (especially furs) from the room and closet. Only the patient's clothes in daily use should be left in the room. Clean the room completely, including ceiling and walls. Dust the room daily, using an oiled or damp cloth, and clean it thoroughly once a week in the patient's absence.

B. Bed and Bedding: The bed should be of wood or metal without cloth or fabric covering. Clean mattress and box springs and enclose each with dustproof, nonporous encasing. Blankets and pillows should be made of synthetic fibers (e.g., Dacron®) or cotton. Blankets, bedspreads, and sheets must be washed often. Do not use comforters or mattress pads.

C. Furniture and Other Articles: Use wood or metal chairs without fabric covers, and dust frequently. Overstuffed furniture should be removed. Plain light curtains of nonallergenic washable material may be used.

D. Pets and Toys: Do not allow pets with wool, hair, or feathers in a room or house, even if child shows no evidence of existing sensitivity. Allow only washable toys (not fuzzy or stuffed) or those stuffed with synthetic material.

E. Miscellaneous: Keep doors closed to prevent excessive passage of dust into room. The patient must always sleep in his own "dust-free" bedroom. Close off forced-air furnace inlets or

cover with several thicknesses of cheesecloth. Sleep with
windows shut during the pollen season if pollen-sensitive.
Electrostatic precipitators may be particularly helpful at this
time.

ECZEMA
(Atopic Dermatitis)

Atopic dermatitis most commonly appears during the second
or third month of life; most cases begin to clear spontaneously by
the third year.

The incidence of eczema may be somewhat more common in
infants completely artificially fed with cow's milk than in breast-
fed infants. Eczema may be easily confused with seborrheic dermatitis in infancy.

See also General Considerations, p. 530.

Etiology. *†
- A. The etiology of most cases of infantile eczema is obscure.
  Foods, inhalants, contact with various irritants, trauma, and
  infection of the skin all may play a role.
- B. In the older child, environmental allergens (inhalants, various
  irritants, trauma, etc.) appear to be more important than
  foods.

Clinical Findings.
- A. Skin Lesions: In many cases initial lesions are on cheeks,
  forehead, and scalp. Flexor surfaces of arms and legs are
  frequently involved; later, the entire skin surface, with the
  exception of the palms and soles, may be covered. The lesions
  are very pruritic, and the child may be very uncomfortable. In
  older children lesions may be limited to flexor surfaces.
  1. Early - An erythematous, papular, and subsequently exuda-
     tive eruption of the skin which becomes crusted. Secondary
     infection may occur.
  2. Later - Skin becomes dry, thickened, and scaly.
- B. Adenopathy may be marked in the area draining the infected
  lesion.

Treatment.
- A. General Measures:
  1. Attention and affection - These children should be handled,
     fondled, and played with liberally.
  2. Prevent scratching - On occasion, restraint may be neces-
     sary both day and night. If so, the following measures may
     be helpful:

---

*Wiskott-Aldrich syndrome: A familial, X-linked recessive disease
with an eczematoid rash, thrombocytopenia, bloody diarrhea, re-
current infections (especially of ears), leukopenia with decreased
lymphocytes, decreased IgM level, and deficient cellular maturity.
Most patients succumb to overwhelming infection at an early age.
Those who survive through infancy are apt to develop malignancies.
† Typical eczematoid lesions may occur in phenylketonuria and
X-linked agammaglobulinemia.

      a. Cut fingernails short.
      b. Use elbow splints to prevent scratching.
      c. Antipruritic drugs and sedation at bedtime (with diphen-
         hydramine, promethazine, trimeprazine, cyproheptadine,
         or hydroxyzine hydrochloride) may be necessary. Chloral
         hydrate may be of value.
  3. Cover as much of skin as possible (including part of face)
     with nonallergenic lightweight cloth.
  4. Avoid soap. Use soap substitutes (Lowila Cake®, Neutra-
     gena®, Cetaphil®) or mineral oil baths to cleanse and lubri-
     cate the skin. Even these may irritate. Avoid excessive
     bathing. Daily bathing, followed by application of a thin layer
     of bland cream, may help to hydrate the skin in dry climates.
  5. Avoid exposure to skin irritants (including inhalants such as
     house dust, feathers, wool, epidermals, flannel, and silk).
  6. Avoid overdressing and overheating.
  7. Diet - Carefully scrutinize the dietary history for possible
     offending allergens. Although foods can seldom be impli-
     cated as the cause of infantile eczema, a trial of removal of
     milk, eggs, and wheat may be of value. Be certain that the
     diet is nutritionally adequate during such trials.
  8. Drugs -
      a. Antibiotics for secondary infection (see Chapter 6).
      b. Systemic corticosteroids should be avoided except for
         cases with extensive involvement resistant to other
         forms of therapy.
  9. Avoid smallpox vaccination in the child, family members,
     or other close contacts and protect child from herpes sim-
     plex infection.
B. Local Therapy: Local therapy is the mainstay of the treatment
  of eczema.
  1. Acute inflamed, moist lesions, particularly with severe itch-
     ing - Aluminum acetate (Burow's) solution soaks, applied for
     20 minutes as often as every two hours in severe cases, may
     be helpful.
  2. Topical corticosteroids are extremely effective in treating
     subacute and chronic stages of the disease.
  3. Chronic, dry, thickened, localized areas - Crude coal tar,
     1 to 5% in a hydrophilic ointment, may be useful for lichen-
     ified lesions.
  4. Iodochlorhydroxyquin cream for local infection.

Prognosis.
    There is a tendency for the condition to clear spontaneously
toward the end of the third year of life, with lesions subsequently
being limited to the flexor surfaces of the elbows and knees. Infants
with eczema frequently go on to develop asthma or allergic rhinitis.

URTICARIA (Hives)

    Urticaria may result from a variety of allergic and non-allergic
causes. In those cases where the cause can be identified, it is most
commonly caused by food (especially shellfish, nuts, berries,

chocolate, eggs, and milk) or drug (most commonly, penicillin) allergy. Insect stings, plants, infections, injected foreign serums, vaccines, physical agents, and ill-defined psychogenic factors may be responsible. Hereditary angioneurotic edema is due to deficiency of an inhibitor of C_1 esterase of the complement system.

Urticaria is usually transitory but may recur over many weeks and months.

Clinical Findings.
A. Urticaria: Lesions may be macular and erythematous, with little edema, or the wheal reaction may be the predominant feature. Wheals are usually multiple, but may coalesce to involve large areas of the body. Pruritus usually is marked and may begin prior to the appearance of the skin lesion.
B. Angioneurotic edema is a giant hive which occurs most commonly on the tongue or larynx or over some part of the face. The lesion is tense and pale and does not itch. In extreme cases, laryngeal edema may cause respiratory obstruction and death.

Treatment.
A. See Prophylaxis (p. 530) and General Treatment of Allergic State (p. 531).
B. Epinephrine gives most rapid relief. If necessary, it may be repeated every 20 minutes for 3 or 4 doses.
C. Antihistamines by mouth or injection if needed.
D. Ephedrine sulfate orally.
E. Hydroxyzine may be of value in chronic urticaria.
F. Cyproheptadine, in particular, is frequently beneficial in cold urticaria.
G. The corticosteroids may be of value in severe reactions.
H. Saline cathartic and enema may be of value if an ingestant is responsible.

ALLERGIC RHINITIS

Allergic rhinitis may occur in the first year of life but more commonly appears after one or two years. It may be seasonal (hay fever), due to pollens, or perennial, due to other inhalant allergens such as house dust. (See also General Considerations, p. 530.)

Clinical Findings.
A. Symptoms:
1. Cardinal symptoms are itchiness of eyes, nose, palate, or pharynx, nasal congestion, rhinorrhea, and paroxysms of sneezing (especially in the early morning hours). Symptoms may be mistaken for "frequent colds."
2. Attacks are recurrent and may be seasonal, perennial, or occur at a certain time of day.
3. There may be a history of recurrent epistaxis or recurrent otitis media. Frequent headaches and lethargy may be reported.

B. Signs:
  1. Nasal mucous membranes may show only slight hyperemia in mild cases but are often pale, boggy, and swollen.
  2. Nasal discharge is typically clear and watery, but may become purulent if secondarily infected.
  3. Erythema of the conjunctivas may occur.
  4. Polyps occasionally are found in older children, particularly with infection of the paranasal sinuses or aspirin sensitivity.
  5. Tonsils may be enlarged but not inflamed.
  6. Sinus x-rays may show mucosal thickening and even fluid levels without overt symptoms of sinus disease.

Treatment.
  A. Specific and General Measures:
    1. See Prophylaxis, General Treatment of Allergic State, and Preparation of Dust-Free Room elsewhere in this chapter.
    2. Electrostatic precipitators may be of value.
    3. "Hyposensitization" should be considered when symptoms are severe and when elimination is not feasible.
  B. Drugs:
    1. Antihistamines with or without decongestants as symptoms warrant.
    2. Constricting agents to nasal mucous membranes on a short-term basis only.
    3. Topical corticosteroid therapy for severe allergic rhinitis unresponsive to other measures; short-term oral therapy only for refractory cases.

ASTHMA

Asthma is a diffuse obstructive disease of the airway characterized by a high degree of reversibility. The obstruction results from edema of the mucous membranes of the airway, increased secretion of mucus, and smooth muscle spasm. The obstruction in asthma is more prominent on expiration - hence the typical expiratory wheeze and prolonged expiratory phase. Inspiratory wheezing is frequently also present. (Overt wheezing does not necessarily occur.) The obstructive process leads to hyperinflation of the lungs. The "barrel chest" deformity in children that is a result of chronic hyperinflation may be mistakenly diagnosed as emphysema, a condition which is rarely seen in children with asthma. Allergic asthma can frequently be shown to be due in part to inhalant sensitivity to pollens, epidermals (cat, dog, feathers), molds, or household inhalants (house dust). The importance of foods as a causative factor in asthma is highly controversial; most experts do not consider them to be a major causative factor. Frequently - especially in small children - no definite etiologic agent can be determined. Characteristically, the airway of children with asthma is hyperreactive to a variety of stimuli, both allergic and nonallergic (e.g., smoke, air pollutants, cold air, emotions). In older children, aspirin may provoke asthma.

Etiology.
Asthma may be evoked by inhalants, infection, ingestants (particularly egg, wheat, and milk), or physical or intrinsic factors.

The most common causes of asthma in children are pollens and the household inhalant group of substances, chiefly house dust, feathers, and animal danders. These are derived mainly from mattresses, box springs, pillows, upholstered furniture, fuzzy and stuffed toys, rugs and rug pads, cats and dogs, and birds.

Although many positive skin tests to foods are obtained, a high percentage of these are entirely without etiologic significance.

Emotional factors and exercise may be important in precipitating or aggravating asthma. Inhaled irritants (e.g., smoke) are also important. The role of infection remains to be clarified.

Clinical Findings.

A. Symptoms:
1. Insidious onset - Slight cough, sneezing, nasal congestion.
2. Acute onset - Dyspnea, cough; noisy, wheezing respirations.
3. Severe attack - Patient is anxious, sits up to improve aeration, perspires, and may be markedly cyanotic.

B. Signs:
1. Chest is distended and hyperinflated.
2. Cough may be prominent.
3. Costal retractions may be noted.
4. Percussion note is hyperresonant.
5. On auscultation, there is wheezing with prolonged, sibilant, musical rales; these may not be evident in the infant with profound obstruction or in the older child with very severe disease in whom air exchange may be so reduced as to diminish the intensity of wheezing.
6. Atelectasis may result from plugging of a bronchus with thick, tenacious mucus.

C. Pulmonary Function Studies: During acute attack, vital capacity, FEV_1, and peak flows are decreased and residual volume and functional residual capacity are increased.

Treatment.

A. For general treatment of the allergic state, see p. 531. The patient with a chronic problem should be educated to live with it in the best possible way.

B. Initial Treatment of the Acute Attack:
1. Epinephrine, 0.1 to 0.2 ml of a 1:1000 solution subcut. every 20 minutes as required for three or four doses, will give the most effective relief and should be tried first. It may be effective after an initial refractory period.
2. Epinephrine, 1:200, 0.05 to 0.2 ml. (maximum) or 0.004 ml./Kg., may be used when an effect that is both immediate and prolonged is desired.
3. Aerosolized adrenergic agents (e.g., isoproterenol, isoetharine) by hand or pressurized nebulizer is effective in relieving acute symptoms.
   Caution: The patient must be warned against excessive use of aerosolized catecholamines, since this can increase bronchial obstruction and has been implicated in some asthmatic deaths.
4. Aminophylline (theophylline) rectally (fluid form only, **not** suppositories) in patients resistant to epinephrine or for sustained relief in those who responded well. Discontinue drug if vomiting occurs. Avoid overdosage.

5. Ephedrine sulfate, 8 to 25 mg., is useful for mild attacks of asthma and for the relief of cough in conjunction with amino-phylline.

6. Expectorants are important in subacute and chronic cases because they help liquefy the sticky bronchial secretions and for their expectorant effect. Saturated aqueous solution of potassium iodide, 5 to 15 drops three times daily in fruit juice, may be of value. (Solution contains 1 gr./drop.) A liberal fluid intake is important.

C. Treatment of Hospitalized Patient: If the response to the above measures is inadequate, the patient should be hospitalized.

1. If possible, place patient in an allergen-free room with high humidity. Avoid cold foods and drinks.

2. Humidified oxygen (40%) is indicated for hypoxemia (always present when there is respiratory distress).

3. **Adequate hydration is of utmost importance** (parenterally, if necessary) to compensate for decreased intake, the increased work of breathing, and greatly increased insensible water loss through the lungs. Use sodium bicarbonate therapy for correction of acidosis.

4. Aminophylline, 4 mg./Kg. I.V. over a 10- to 15-minute period. Should be repeated every four to six hours.

5. Isoproterenol in physiologic saline by intermittent positive pressure breathing is useful if the patient is so obstructed as to prevent adequate inspiratory effort using a hand nebulizer. **Caution:** Avoid overdosage.

6. Corticosteroids should be used I.V. in high doses (e.g., hydrocortisone sodium succinate, 4 mg./Kg. every 4 hours) in patients already receiving corticosteroids or those who have been on chronic corticosteroid therapy within four to six months, and also in life-threatening asthma. Use for as short a time as possible.

7. In general, sedation should not be used unless facilities for monitoring blood gases and pH are available. If a sedative is required, chloral hydrate appears to be the safest drug. The best sedative for the anxious asthmatic patient is the relief of airway obstruction.

8. Obtain a chest x-ray to rule out complications (e.g., atelectasis, pneumothorax, or mediastinal emphysema).

    Bronchoscopy, constant intravenous isoproterenol drip, or nasotracheal intubation (rarely) and mechanical ventilation may be necessary. These procedures are hazardous and should be performed with extreme caution. Postural drainage may be effective in relieving obstruction due to inspissated mucus.

9. Monitoring of arterial paO_2, $paCO_2$, and pH are mandatory in severe asthma since clinical judgment of the severity of the illness is frequently misleading.

10. Treatment in an intensive care unit with an anesthesiologist in attendance makes a favorable outcome more likely.

D. Interim Measures:

1. Antihistaminic drugs may help to prevent attacks but should be avoided during an attack, when they may serve to further dry and thicken already viscid secretions.

2. Control of any infections present is very important.
3. Children with chronic or recurrent asthma should be instructed in breathing exercises to ensure maximal ventilation.
4. Children with severe asthma may require continuous bronchodilator therapy with theophylline, alone or in combination with ephedrine or cromolyn sodium (or both) by inhalation.
5. Corticosteroid therapy may be necessary in refractory cases. Giving the total 48-hour dose once every two days in the early morning may be effective for steroid-dependent asthmatics and produce less adrenal suppression than the same dosage in multiple divided doses.

Steroids should be used with great caution in both acute and chronic cases; their long-term use may be associated with an increased incidence of status asthmaticus. Corticosteroids are effective when administered as aerosols, but this route may also be associated with significant adrenal suppression.

Course and Prognosis.

The long-term prognosis for childhood asthma is good. The disease lessens in severity in the majority of patients. In some it appears to disappear entirely. Because of difficulty in predicting which childhood asthmatic will improve spontaneously, all children with asthma should have the benefit of an allergy investigation designed to determine the cause of the illness. Asthma uncomplicated by infection rarely leads to irreversible destructive lung disease (emphysema). Children whose asthma is intractable frequently benefit from study and treatment at a residential care center.

Hyposensitization therapy may be of value for children with seasonal and perennial bronchial asthma.

INSECT STING ALLERGY

Insect sting allergy may include urticaria, generalized pruritus, laryngeal edema, dysphagia, wheezing, tightness in the chest, dyspnea, nasal congestion, sneezing, abdominal cramps, nausea and vomiting, incontinence, circulatory collapse, and death or a delayed serum sickness-type reaction. Hymenoptera (bees, wasps, hornets, yellow jackets, and fire ants) is the order most likely to cause serious reactions. The sting of a single insect may sensitize an individual to the entire Hymenoptera group. Skin testing is of limited value, since individuals may have positive reactions to skin test extracts without any clinical sensitivity. Insects should be avoided; susceptible individuals should keep as much skin covered as possible, wear white clothes with a hard finish, should not use scented drug items, should stay away from flowers, flowering trees, and shrubs, and should avoid walking barefoot in grass. Hyposensitization therapy is indicated for all who have suffered a systemic reaction and should be continued indefinitely. Emergency treatment includes epinephrine, an antihistamine by injection, and the use of a tourniquet when the sting is on an extremity. The highly sensitive individual should have these in a kit which he carries. Steroids may be of value.

SERUM SICKNESS

Serum sickness is a symptom complex originally described following the therapeutic use of horse serum antitoxins. The term is now used to describe a similar clinical picture that may occur following administration of drugs such as penicillin and certain foreign proteins. Serum sickness does not appear to be more common in atopic than in nonatopic individuals, and virtually 100% of the population can develop serum sickness if a sufficient antigenic dose is given repeatedly over a period of time. The symptoms have been shown to be due to biologically active "toxic" antigen-antibody complexes in the circulation. These complexes, acting in conjunction with complement components and polymorphonuclear leukocytes, are responsible for the pathologic lesions.

Clinical Findings.

The incubation period is six to ten days after injection of the offending agent (e.g., horse serum), but the onset of symptoms may be earlier if the patient is already sensitized. The offending agent frequently produces wheal and flare reactivity on skin testing.

A. Urticarial skin eruption is the most common symptom. Other types of eruptions (erythematous, morbilliform, or scarlatiniform) may occur but are less common.

B. Angioneurotic edema, itching, generalized lymphadenopathy, splenomegaly, fever, and malaise as well as pain, swelling, and redness of joints are not infrequent.

C. Neurologic complications (especially peripheral neuritis) and glomerulonephritis may be present in severe cases.

D. Fatal reactions to foreign serum usually occur only in atopic individuals already sensitive to serum or dander from that particular animal species.

Treatment.

Give epinephrine for acute symptoms and ephedrine and anti-histamines for milder cases or to control symptoms. Corticosteroids are indicated for severe cases. Cold compresses (5% sodium bicarbonate) give symptomatic relief.

Course and Prognosis.

Serum sickness is self-limited, usually lasting one to seven days. Evidences of damage to the C.N.S. may persist for months.

29 . . .

Collagen Diseases

Since the "collagen diseases" are not limited pathologically to alterations of collagen but also involve changes in the connective tissue (i. e., in the fibrillar and cellular elements as well as the interstitial ground substance), they are often called connective tissue diseases. However, although many diseases involve the connective tissue, six disorders with similar characteristics can accurately be called collagen diseases: rheumatic fever, rheumatoid arthritis, polyarteritis (periarteritis) nodosa, disseminated lupus erythematosus, scleroderma, and dermatomyositis. The similarities can be summarized as follows:

    (1) Frequently overlapping clinical features.

    (2) Chronicity with relapses.

    (3) Changes in immunologic state.

    (4) Common pathologic features (fibrinoid degeneration, granulomatous reaction with fibrosis, vasculitis with proliferation of plasma cells).

    (5) Improvement with steroids (often only symptomatic).

RHEUMATIC FEVER

Rheumatic fever is the most common cause of symptomatic acquired heart disease in childhood. Even though its incidence has been decreasing, it is still responsible for a significant percentage of cardiac fatalities in the pediatric age group. It is clear that group A beta-hemolytic Streptococcus is implicated in the etiology of rheumatic fever, but the mechanism by which it initiates rheumatic fever remains obscure. There is evidence that the cell wall proteins of the group A beta-hemolytic streptococci contain antigens that cross-react with the membranes of cardiac muscle cells and with the muscle layers of small arteries. Gamma globulins from rheumatic fever patients and antibodies to these cell wall proteins have been shown to bind to these same myocardial and arterial components. This relation to a specific bacterial component sets rheumatic fever apart from the other collagen diseases.

A beta-hemolytic streptococcal infection invariably precedes by one to three weeks the initial attack and subsequent relapses of rheumatic fever, although not all of these infections are clinically manifest. Since rheumatic fever disease represents a hypersensitivity reaction, it is reasonable to assume that several infections with group A beta-hemolytic streptococci are necessary to trigger the first episode of rheumatic fever.

Predisposing Factors.

    A. Family History: Familial predisposition and heredity play important roles in susceptibility to the disease.

B. Age: Rheumatic fever is most common between the ages of four and 15 years but may occur, usually in a much milder form, in adulthood. The median age of onset has apparently decreased over the past decade; initial diagnoses under three years of age are no longer rare.
C. Race: All racial groups are susceptible.
D. Economic Status: The disease occurs most commonly among children living in crowded areas (probably by increasing the number of intimate exposures to the beta-hemolytic Streptococcus), especially among economic groups with poor diets.
E. Climate and Geographic Incidence: Rheumatic fever has an eclectic distribution in terms of geography and climate; it is found in abundance in temperate, subtropical, and tropical zones.
F. Season: Peak incidence in the temperate zones is during the winter months.
G. Previous Attacks: Rheumatic recurrences following reinfection with a beta-hemolytic Streptococcus are frequent (30 to 60%) in children who have had a previous acute episode of rheumatic fever, as compared with the relatively small number of cases (0.5-3%) of rheumatic fever occurring as a complication of all cases of streptococcal pharyngitis.

Clinical Findings.
The diagnosis is usually certain if the child has either (a) two major or (b) one major and two minor of the following (modified after Jones):
A. Major Manifestations:
1. Signs of active carditis.
2. Polyarthritis - Inflammation of the large joints (ankles, knees, hips, wrists, elbows, and shoulders), usually in a migratory fashion involving one or two joints at a time. Occasionally involvement is monarticular.
3. Subcutaneous nodules.
4. Erythema marginatum.
5. Chorea (see p. 382).
B. Minor Manifestations:
1. Fever.
2. Arthralgia.
3. Ecg. changes, particularly prolonged P-R interval (see p. 212). Ecg. examination should be done early in the course of the disease; serial studies may reveal useful information regarding progress. S-T or T wave changes are noted if pericarditis is present. Arrhythmias are usually minor, but occasionally second or third degree heart block occurs.
4. Abnormal blood tests - The sedimentation rate is greatly accelerated. The white blood cell count is raised, showing a variable polymorphonuclear leukocytosis. C-reactive protein and gamma globulin are elevated. Antistreptococcal antibodies are elevated. (Antistreptolysin O titer is usually 250 Todd units or higher.) A mild or moderate degree of anemia (normochromic or normocytic) is found.
5. Beta-hemolytic streptococci are often present and can be isolated from the upper respiratory tract of the child or his family contacts.

Associated manifestations include erythema multiforme, abdominal, back, or pericordial pain, dyspnea on exertion, nontraumatic epistaxis, purpura, pneumonitis, with or without acute pleural effusion, and a family history of rheumatic fever.

There is no specific laboratory test for rheumatic fever. Combined use of clinical and laboratory findings may aid in diagnosis and subsequent evaluation of the degree of rheumatic activity. Echocardiography has recently added a new dimension in that the posterior mitral valve leaflet thickens and separates from the anterior leaflet.

Treatment.

A. Specific Measures:

1. Steroids - Steroids should be administered for management of acute-onset congestive heart failure associated with carditis. They are useful in controlling the exudative phase of acute severe myocarditis in critically ill patients. However, long-term controlled studies show no benefit from steroid therapy in preventing chronic rheumatic heart disease.

    Thus, in patients with carditis who are not in congestive heart failure, steroids are not recommended since ultimately they do not modify the incidence or severity of residual cardiac damage.

    Once initiated, steroid therapy should be continued for about six weeks (although some recommend a much shorter course); thereafter it should be reduced rapidly. To prevent the typical "rebound phenomenon" accompanying weaning, salicylates should be given in full dosage during the last two weeks of steroid therapy.

    Since retention of fluid during steroid therapy may aggravate cardiac failure, restriction of dietary salt is recommended. Excessive potassium losses should be replaced if necessary.

2. Salicylates - The salicylates markedly reduce fever, alleviate joint pain, and reduce joint swelling. The rapid response of rheumatic fever to salicylates is usually quite dramatic and is a useful diagnostic test in differentiation from rheumatoid arthritis, which responds much more slowly. They should be continued as long as necessary for the relief of symptoms. If withdrawal of salicylates results in a recurrence, they should immediately be reinstituted.

    a. The average dose of aspirin is 90-120 mg./Kg./day every four to six hours. The highest dosage is recommended for the first 48 hours. Symptomatic improvement, blood levels, and signs of toxicity are useful criteria for modifying dosage.

    b. Early symptoms of toxicity include tinnitus, nausea, vomiting, and hyperpnea. Since gastrointestinal hemorrhages are frequently seen in chronic salicylate therapy and can be massive, stools should be periodically examined for blood using the guaiac test.

3. Penicillin in full dosage should be used in all cases for ten days followed by daily prophylaxis to prevent recurrences (see below). Serious and inapparent infections may occur during steroid therapy, but are uncommon in rheumatic fever treated as described.

B. General Measures:

1. Rest - Resumption of full activity should be gradual and related to the severity of the attack, particularly if a significant degree of carditis is present. Currently, most children with mild to moderate carditis are fully ambulatory six weeks after treatment has started. The child's tolerance for exercise will dictate the speed with which activities should be resumed. Strict, prolonged bed rest until biological signs of rheumatic activity have disappeared is unwarranted.

2. Diet - Maintain good nutrition, with particular emphasis on adequate intakes of vitamin C and protein. Overfeeding a child on reduced activity frequently leads to obesity and the development of undesirable behavior problems.

3. Emotional factors - Careful planning of a home program will help to prevent behavior disorders during the long therapy period and is particularly important in patients with chorea. Home teachers, play therapy, and occupational therapy are all of importance in the total care of children with rheumatic fever. Parents and siblings should maintain a cheerful attitude; quiet recreation (e. g., radio, phonograph, or television) should be provided; and too much attention must not be paid to the heart.

Prophylaxis.

The main principle of prophylaxis is the prevention of infection with beta-hemolytic streptococci.

A. General Prophylaxis:

1. Avoid persons who have upper respiratory tract infections.
2. If possible, live in a warm climate and under relatively uncrowded conditions.

B. Prevention of Beta-streptococcal Infections:

1. The unequivocal treatment of choice is benzathine penicillin G (Bicillin®), I. M. every 28 days; 1,200,000 units are sufficient for school-age children. Oral penicillin G, 200,000 units twice daily, is considerably less effective and is a poor second choice.
2. Erythromycin, 125 to 250 mg. orally per day, is of value in children who cannot tolerate penicillin.
3. Sulfonamides may be used as more economical prophylactic agents.

Course and Prognosis.

The course varies markedly from patient to patient. It may be fulminating, leading to death early in the course of the acute rheumatic episode, or entirely asymptomatic, the diagnosis being made in retrospect on the basis of pathologic findings. Most attacks last two to three months.

With adequate penicillin prophylaxis, recurrences are virtually eliminated. Therapeutic doses of penicillin are recommended before tooth extraction or other surgery if valvular involvement is present.

The prognosis for life largely depends on the intensity of the initial cardiac insult and the prevention of repeated rheumatic recurrences. In general, the incidence of cardiac damage is in inverse proportion to the age at onset of the first episode. An actual overall reduction in the incidence of rheumatic fever in the population has recently been observed, presumably because of the early use of antibiotic therapy in children with beta-streptococcal infections and because of the gradual improvement in the social and economic conditions in many parts of the country.

RHEUMATOID ARTHRITIS

Rheumatoid arthritis in childhood is a slowly progressive generalized collagen disease of unknown etiology. It is likely to be related to a normal response of antibody-forming cells to modified self antigens. Rheumatoid factor is an antibody directed against gamma globulins altered by as yet unknown mechanisms. Classical rheumatoid factor is an IgM immunoglobulin, but antibodies with similar specificities have been found in all three major immunoglobulin classes.

Rheumatoid arthritis commonly has its onset between two and five years in both sexes and around adolescence in girls. There is the strong suggestion of a hereditary factor, with a definite family history of arthritis and related diseases in many cases. Other predisposing or triggering factors are not usually found.

Rheumatoid arthritis may be related to ankylosing spondylitis in some as yet unexplained manner. Ankylosing spondylitis is more common in males. It is sometimes familial and affects the spine (particularly the sacroiliac joints). Transient and nondeforming peripheral arthritis usually confined to a few large joints occurs in about one-half of patients; it may occur before back complaints appear. Iritis and aortitis are characteristic extra-articular manifestations, but psoriasis, inflammatory bowel disease (e.g., ulcerative colitis, regional enteritis), and Reiter's syndrome may be associated conditions in older individuals. Rheumatoid nodules and a positive rheumatoid factor are rare. Treatment with phenylbutazone (Butazolidin®) and indomethacin (Indocin®) may be of value.

Clinical Findings.

A. Symptoms: Onset may be acute or insidious, and symptoms vary markedly in severity.
1. Fever, frequently spiking and accompanied by chills, may precede all other findings by weeks or months.
2. Shifting joint pains, especially of hands and feet, but single joint involvement also occurs.
3. Weight loss.
4. Clamminess of skin.
5. Muscle aches and tremors.
6. Patients frequently exhibit marked passivity and depression with underlying anxiety or great lability.
B. Signs: Joint involvement usually consists of symmetrical involvement of various joints, including fingers and toes, knees, ankles, wrists, hip, and mandibular joint; in the very young patient, involvement is often monarticular (usually the knee) or asymmetrical. Cervical spondylitis may be present. Joints are slightly swollen and tender and motion limited; increased warmth is often present. Within one to three months after on-

set of involvement of the fingers, the joints become character-istically spindle-shaped with shiny smooth skin over them.

Subcutaneous nodules are present, especially along the ulna, the spine, or occasionally the occiput. A recurrent, fleeting, salmon-pink, discrete maculopapular, nonurticarial rash is frequently present over the extremities, trunk, and face and may precede other signs. Iridocyclitis (particularly in patients with monarticular or pauciarticular disease), band keratopathy, and pericarditis are relatively common, serious manifestations and may precede joint involvement. Amyloidosis may develop in chronic cases.

Other signs include tachycardia, lymphadenopathy, pneu-monitis, splenomegaly, and hepatomegaly (occasionally).

C. Laboratory Findings: Ecg. is usually normal unless cardiac involvement is present. Echocardiography often shows peri-carditis, and mitral valve prolapse has recently been demon-strated. In addition, there is polymorphonuclear leukocytosis, the sedimentation rate is accelerated, and gamma globulin and alpha$_2$ globulin are increased (in 25% of cases). Moderate anemia is present. Hemolytic anemia with jaundice is occa-sionally present. Antistreptolysin levels are low (under 120 Todd units) except in the presence of incidental streptococcal disease. The Rose sensitized sheep erythrocyte agglutination test and the latex fixation test for "rheumatoid factor" are seldom positive ($<$ 15% of the time) in children. Synovial fluid may show either an inflammatory or a noninflammatory re-action; synovial biopsy is often not diagnostic.

D. X-ray Examination:
   1. Early phase usually shows swelling of periarticular soft structures, synovitis, and slight widening of the joint spaces. Accelerated epiphysial maturation, increase in size of ossi-fication centers, and disproportionate longitudinal bone growth may occur.
   2. Later, obliteration of the joint space and ground-glass ap-pearance of trabeculated ends of the bones. Generalized osteoporosis of all bones of the involved area.

Treatment.
A. Drug Therapy:
   1. Salicylates - Aspirin is the most satisfactory suppressive agent. It should be given in the same dosage as recomended for rheumatic fever (see p. 543). The response of rheuma-toid arthritis to salicylates occurs within three to four days and is usually not as dramatic as in rheumatic fever.
   2. Gold salts and antimalarials are being used with increasing frequency in patients who do not respond to salicylate treat-ment. Phenylbutazone and indomethacin do not have a place in the treatment of this disease. Cyclophosphamide (Cytox-an®) is being used successfully in adult rheumatoid arthritis but has no established role in the treatment of juvenile rheu-matoid arthritis. The gonadal toxicity of the latter must be borne in mind at all times.
   3. Steroids - Since steroids do not alter the natural remission rate, the length of the illness, or the ultimate prognosis, they are seldom indicated. However, there is a place for

them (e.g., prednisone, 2 to 3 mg./Kg./day) in cases of myocarditis, in iritis, and in any case where the disease appears to be life-threatening. Steroids do not appear to enhance the incidence of amyloidosis; however, if long-term administration is accompanied by numerous undesirable side-effects, a therapeutic trial in which steroids are given every other day is warranted after the life-endangering manifestations have abated. Intra-articular steroids have a place in the management of juvenile rheumatoid arthritis when there is a monarticular involvement or when one or two joints appear to retard rehabilitation.

B. General Measures:
1. Physical therapy - The patient should exercise even if fever is present. A hospital program for physiotherapy is insufficient; exercise at home daily or twice daily is mandatory. Assisted exercise with no weight bearing on the joints of the lower extremities should be followed by active exercise and then resisted exercise. Heat and hydrotherapy should be useful adjuvants to a well-planned exercise program.
2. Orthopedic care - The wearing of splints during the night will ensure proper alignment of joints. Traction and cylindrical casts may be necessary.
3. Ophthalmic care - Periodic slit lamp examination is the only means for early diagnosis of iridocyclitis, which may otherwise continue undiagnosed until vision fails.
4. Rest - Since there is evidence that exertion may bring about flare-ups, rest should be stressed. However, bed rest should be discouraged because it can lead to osteoporosis, renal calculi, muscle atrophy, or joint deformities.
5. Psychologic care - In view of the long duration of this disease, the family should understand the necessity of fulfilling the patient's social, educational, and psychologic needs.
6. Diet - There is no special diet. Ferous sulfate should be given if hypochromic anemia is present.
7. Infections - It has been stated that reactivation of the disease is occasionally associated with group A beta-hemolytic streptococcal infection. Prophylactic therapy with penicillin may be indicated.

Course and Prognosis.

The average duration of an attack of rheumatoid arthritis varies from months to years. Once it has passed, the chances of having a second episode are slightly less than 50%.

With good medical management, one can expect that more than 70% of patients will have complete functional recovery and less than 10% will be severely disabled. Deaths are reported in the pediatric age group, but they are rare.

POLYARTERITIS NODOSA

Polyarteritis (periarteritis) nodosa is a rare systemic disease characterized by inflammatory damage to blood vessels, with resulting injury to involved organs. Pathologically, there is segmental inflammation of small and medium sized arteries with fibrinoid changes and, more rarely, necrosis in the vessel wall.

Clinical Findings.

Clinical manifestations vary, depending on the location of the involved arterioles.

A. Symptoms: Generally those of a rapidly progressive, wasting disease: fever, lassitude, weight loss, and generalized pains in extremities and/or abdomen.

B. Signs: Skin eruptions of the urticarial or macular type occur. Subcutaneous nodules are frequently present along the course of the blood vessels. Additionally, there are moderate hypertension, convulsions and occasionally hemiplegia, muscular weakness or paralysis as a result of polyneuritis, rhinitis and conjunctivitis, pericarditis and congestive heart failure, ischemic gangrene of an extremity, and asthma or pneumonia.

C. Laboratory Findings: These include anemia with moderate leukocytosis and eosinophilia; accelerated sedimentation rate; albuminuria; intermittent microscopic hematuria and showers of casts; elevated nonprotein nitrogen; sterile blood cultures; cardiomegaly on x-ray. Muscle biopsy is sometimes helpful.

Treatment.

One of the cortisones (cortisone or prednisone) usually produces symptomatic improvement and may prolong life. The response to steroids is unpredictable and quite variable. (For dosages and precautions, see Chapter 22.)

Prognosis.

Prognosis is poor, although spontaneous and steroid-induced remissions are seen.

DISSEMINATED LUPUS ERYTHEMATOSUS
(Systemic Lupus Erythematosus)

A multisystem progressive disease whose protean symptomatology and relentless course is a diagnostic and therapeutic challenge. The disease often coincides with rheumatoid arthritis or polyarteritis nodosa. Pathologically, fibrinoid degeneration and necrosis are found extensively. S. L. E. is nine times more common in females than in males. A lupus erythematosus-like syndrome (including positive lupus preparations and antinuclear antibodies) may occur during procainamide hydrochloride therapy.

Clinical Findings.

A. Symptoms:
1. Prolonged, irregular fever with remissions of variable duration.
2. Recurrent joint pains.
3. Edema may be found in the presence of renal insufficiency.
4. Weakness, fatigue, and weight loss frequently occur.

B. Signs:
1. The signs are protean and may be related to any system.
2. Erythematous rash on the face, characteristically over the bridge of the nose and cheeks (butterfly distribution) and especially on areas exposed to sun. Lesions may also be seen on fingers and palms but may be absent in as many as half of patients. Oral lesions are common.

3. Renal involvement in three-fourths of cases or more.
4. Central nervous system signs in one-third of patients. This disease is probably the second most common cause of chorea in children.
5. Recurrent appearance of polyarthritis, varieties of carditis, pleural effusion, and pulmonary infiltration.
6. Although generalized lymphadenopathy is relatively rare, hepatosplenomegaly occurs in one-third to one-half of patients, with derangement of hematopoiesis in many.

C. Laboratory Findings:
1. Antinuclear antibodies present in most cases.
2. Demonstration of the lupus erythematosus (L. E.) cell containing a metachromatic cytoplasmic inclusion body which displaces the nucleus of the cell. The L. E. cell is considered diagnostic of disseminated lupus erythematosus, but it is sometimes present in patients with rheumatoid disease.
3. Anemia (autoimmune hemolytic), leukopenia, and thrombocytopenia; positive Coombs test.
4. Microscopic hematuria, cylindruria, and albuminuria.
5. Sedimentation rate is markedly accelerated in the presence of a relatively low C-reactive protein response.
6. Blood urea level and serum globulin elevated.
7. A false-positive Wassermann reaction (but not T. P. I.).

Treatment.

This disease is now diagnosed more on the basis of a few sensitive, relatively specific laboratory tests than on the severity of the symptomatology, and a wider spectrum of severity is found.

No treatment should be given to asymptomatic patients. Aspirin should be given to the rare patient with only mild joint pain. Prednisone in doses of at least 60 mg./sq. M./day not only suppresses the acute inflammatory manifestations but in many cases also modifies or halts progressive glomerular involvement. Antibiotics should be used at the first sign of an infection. Chloroquine may be of value.

The idea that lupus is the classical autoimmune disorder has led to trials with immunosuppressive agents. Both azathioprine (Imuran®) and cyclophosphamide (Cytoxan®) are effective in controlling renal and systemic manifestation of the disease in some children who are resistant to steroids alone.

It is now known that certain drugs (anticonvulsants, hydralazine, methyldopa, and certain long-acting sulfonamides) can produce a lupus-like picture. Patients should not be given these drugs, and, because of their well-known photosensitivity, they should stay away from the sun.

Course and Prognosis.

Death is usually due to a combination of cardiac and renal failure. The disease is particularly fulminating in adolescent girls. With good medical management, the average survival time is over five years and can be as long as 15 years.

SCLERODERMA

A collagen disease chiefly involving the skin and characterized by minimal systemic symptoms. Interstitial and perivascular fibrosis may occur in the viscera. In local benign scleroderma (morphea) there is a linear distribution of lesions which first show erythema and edema and subsequent scarring and shrinking. In the progressive generalized form (sclerodactylia) there is more extensive thickening and induration of the skin followed by contractures.

Trophic ulcers, calcific deposits, and Raynaud's phenomenon are common. Skin involvement is usually greatest, but any organ may be involved. Disturbances in esophageal motility lead to dysphagia, and small bowel involvement leads to malabsorption. Arthralgia and hoarseness are common manifestations.

There is no specific therapy. Physiotherapy given early may minimize contractures. Steroids are of little value. Phenoxybenzamine (Dibenzyline®) has been used to relieve peripheral vasospasm. Bethanechol (Urecholine®) has been used for dysphagia.

The prognosis is excellent for local scleroderma but only fair for the severe generalized form, in which death may occur within a year. Some deformity may occur with the former and is the rule with the latter.

DERMATOMYOSITIS

Dermatomyositis is a chronic inflammatory disease of unknown etiology involving primarily the muscles, skin, and subcutaneous tissues. The pathological process can and sometimes does involve the gastrointestinal tract and the central nervous system. Theoretically, since dermatomyositis appears to be a vascular process leading to arteritis and phlebitis, any organ could be involved. Muscles show segmental or focal necrosis, inflammation, fibrinoid changes in their capillaries, and finally denervation atrophy,

Clinical Findings.

The diagnosis is suggested by the presence of muscle tenderness and induration accompanied by dermatitis, but a biopsy of the area most intensely involved may be required to establish the diagnosis conclusively.

A. Symptoms: Fever; muscle tenderness and pain; malaise and weight loss; weakness or pseudoparalysis, sometimes involving muscles of respiration and deglutition; Raynaud's phenomenon; arthralgia.

B. Signs:

1. Dermatitis and erythema, frequently around the eyes (violaceous hue of upper lids) and over the bridge of the nose, accompanied by edema. Skin lesions eventually occur elsewhere as well and include urticaria. Erythematous nodules - areas of dark pigmentation and telangiectasia - are frequently seen over the extensor surfaces of the joints.

2. Loss of reflexes.

3. Calcinosis eventually occurs along tendons or ligaments and near the joints.

4. Firm and atrophic muscles, with contractures.

C. Laboratory Findings: Anemia, eosinophilia, increased sedimentation rate, increased serum globulin. Muscle biopsy confirms diagnosis; muscle enzymes are not always elevated.

Treatment.

Corticosteroid therapy is indicated in all patients with acute or active disease. The nonspecific suppressive effect of corticosteroids on systemic and local inflammatory phenomena is best achieved early in the course of the disease. Azathioprine (Imuran®) has been used with some success, but it is still too early to recommend it as replacement for conventional therapy.

Physiotherapy is a very important part of the treatment; the principles outlined in the section on rheumatoid arthritis should be followed.

Course and Prognosis.

The natural course of the disease is not predictable. Twenty-five to thirty per cent of patients with severe disease die within one or two years. It appears that those most severely affected either die or eventually develop calcinosis and are therefore more severely incapacitated. Affected children seldom escape some degree of crippling.

30 ...
Pediatric Emergencies

Most pediatric medical emergencies other than poisonings are associated with coma, convulsions, or dyspnea. Other pediatric medical emergencies include disorders due to heat or cold, those resulting from electric shock, and drowning.

Adequate professional help must be promptly mobilized to manage the emergency efficiently. Usually three individuals can best perform the many diagnostic and therapeutic steps required.

Emergency Management.
A. Maintain Adequate Aeration:
1. Free airway - Tidal volume should be 10-15 ml./Kg./minute.
2. Oxygen - The routine use of oxygen in high concentration immediately upon admission is of value while history is being obtained and physical examination is being done. This is also a valuable supportive measure should there be an unavoidable delay before specific diagnosis can be made.
B. Treat shock when present (see Chapter 2).

Diagnostic Measures.
A. History: An essential case history must be obtained before rational treatment is possible. Among other items, the history should include the following:
1. Time and nature of onset.
2. Previous occurrence and method of treatment, if any.
3. History of recent illness.
4. History of drug therapy, including insulin, penicillin, etc.
5. If poisoning is suspected (see p. 570), obtain details of exposure; if possible, obtain container with list of contents and manufacturer's name and address.
6. History of pica.
B. Physical Examination: A rapid but careful physical examination is essential. If possible, examination should include -
1. General evaluation of state of consciousness and shock, hydration, etc.
2. Ophthalmoscopic examination.
3. Estimation of cardiorespiratory function including blood pressure determination.
4. Examination of chest for retraction, dullness, and rales.
5. Examination of the abdomen for size of liver, masses, bladder enlargement, and areas of tenderness.
C. Laboratory:
1. Determination of the hematocrit. A complete blood count is often of value. A sample of blood for typing and cross-matching should be obtained on admission in anticipation of possible future transfusions.

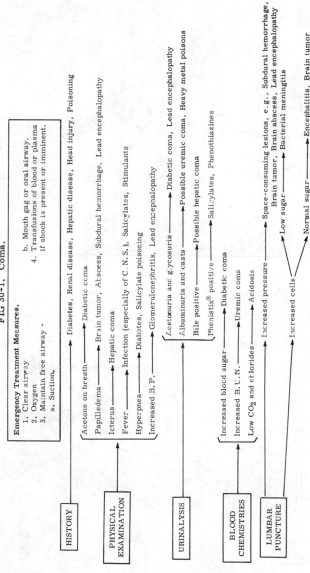

FIG 30-1. Coma.

Emergency Treatment Measures.
1. Clear airway
2. Oxygen
3. Maintain free airway –
   a. Suction.
   b. Mouth gag or oral airway.
4. Transfusions of blood or plasma if shock is present or imminent.

HISTORY → Diabetes, Renal disease, Hepatic disease, Head injury, Poisoning

Acetone on breath → Diabetic coma

PHYSICAL EXAMINATION →
Papilledema → Brain tumor, Abscess, Subdural hemorrhage, Lead encephalopathy
Icterus → Hepatic coma
Fever → Infection (especially of C.N.S.), Salicylates, Stimulants
Hyperpnea → Diabetes, Salicylate poisoning
Increased B.P. → Glomerulonephritis, Lead encephalopathy

URINALYSIS →
Acetonuria and glycosuria → Diabetic coma, Lead encephalopathy
Albuminuria and casts → Possible uremic coma, Heavy metal poisons
Bile positive → Possible hepatic coma
Phenistix® positive → Salicylates, Phenothiazines

BLOOD CHEMISTRIES →
Increased blood sugar → Diabetic coma
Increased B.U.N. → Uremic coma
Low CO_2 and chlorides → Acidosis

LUMBAR PUNCTURE →
Increased pressure → Space-consuming lesions, e.g., Subdural hemorrhage, Brain tumor, Brain abscess, Lead encephalopathy
Low sugar → Bacterial meningitis
Increased cells ⟨ Normal sugar → Encephalitis, Brain tumor

FIG 30-2. Management of convulsions.

Emergency Treatment. (Do complete neurological examination. Take B.P.)

1. Free airway.
   a. Suction.
   b. Mouth gag or oral airway.
   c. Padded tongue blade or gag to prevent injury.
2. Oxygen.
3. Restraints or padding to prevent injury.
4. Diazepam (Valium®), 0.1-0.2 mg./Kg. I.M. or I.V., has largely replaced amobarbital in the treatment of status epilepticus.
5. Barbiturates –
   a. Subcut. or I.M. – Pentobarbital sodium, amobarbital sodium, or phenobarbital sodium, 5-7 mg./Kg. May repeat half this amount every 20-30 minutes (not exceeding 15 mg./Kg.).
   b. Rectally – Sodium pentobarbital, secobarbital (Seconal®), etc., 13 mg./Kg. Make sure feces are cleared out of rectum first.
6. Antipyretic measures if indicated.

AFEBRILE CONVULSIONS

LUMBAR PUNCTURE*

NORMAL FINDINGS ⟶ BLOOD CHEMISTRIES (B.U.N., calcium, sugar)

NORMAL: Consider poisonings, tetanus, alkalosis, allergy, breathholding, asphyxia, brain injury, degenerative C.N.S. disease, epilepsy.

ABNORMAL:
B.U.N. high: Uremia.
Calcium low: Tetany.
Sugar low: Insulin reaction, pancreatic adenoma, leucine sensitivity, tumors, hypoglycemia.

INCREASED PRESSURE, NORMAL OR INCREASED PROTEIN: (Look for evidence of pineal shift, calcification, fracture, or increased pressure on skull x-ray.) Subdural hematoma, brain tumor, brain abscess, lead encephalopathy.

BLOODY SPINAL FLUID (all 3 tubes): Cerebrovascular accident (e.g., subarachnoid hemorrhage; fluid may not be bloody in infants), traumatic puncture.

*Caution: See bottom of p. 555.

FEBRILE CONVULSIONS

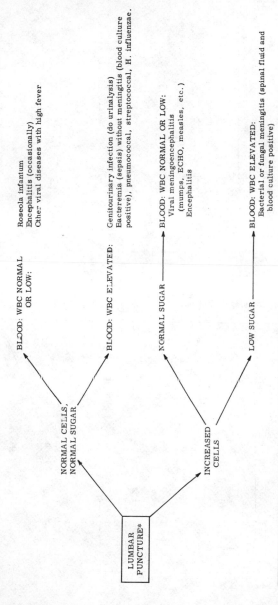

LUMBAR PUNCTURE*

NORMAL CELLS, NORMAL SUGAR

BLOOD: WBC NORMAL OR LOW:
- Roseola infantum
- Encephalitis (occasionally)
- Other viral diseases with high fever

BLOOD: WBC ELEVATED:
- Genitourinary infection (do urinalysis)
- Bacteremia (sepsis) without meningitis (blood culture positive), pneumococcal, streptococcal, H. influenzae.

INCREASED CELLS

NORMAL SUGAR

BLOOD: WBC NORMAL OR LOW:
- Viral meningoencephalitis (mumps, ECHO, measles, etc.)
- Encephalitis

LOW SUGAR

BLOOD: WBC ELEVATED:
- Bacterial or fungal meningitis (spinal fluid and blood culture positive)

*Caution: Withdraw fluid very slowly or not at all if ophthalmoscopic examination or skull x-ray shows evidence of increased pressure.

556

FIG 30-3. Dyspnea.

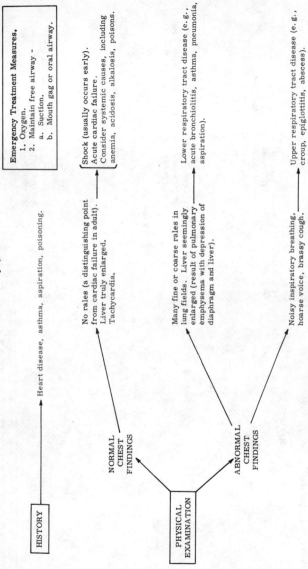

HISTORY → Heart disease, asthma, aspiration, poisoning.

PHYSICAL EXAMINATION

NORMAL CHEST FINDINGS

No rales (a distinguishing point from cardiac failure in adult).
Liver truly enlarged.
Tachycardia.

→ Shock (usually occurs early).
Acute cardiac failure.
Consider systemic causes, including anemia, acidosis, alkalosis, poisons.

Emergency Treatment Measures.
1. Oxygen.
2. Maintain free airway -
   a. Suction.
   b. Mouth gag or oral airway.

ABNORMAL CHEST FINDINGS

Many fine or coarse rales in lung fields. Liver seemingly enlarged (result of pulmonary emphysema with depression of diaphragm and liver).

→ Lower respiratory tract disease (e.g., acute bronchiolitis, asthma, pneumonia, aspiration).

Noisy inspiratory breathing, hoarse voice, brassy cough.

→ Upper respiratory tract disease (e.g., croup, epiglottitis, abscess).

2. Urinalysis (for sugar, acetone, microscopic examination).
An indwelling catheter may be needed to obtain specimens
promptly.
3. Blood chemistries, as indicated in Figs. 30-1, 30-2, and
30-3.

DISORDERS DUE TO HEAT

BURNS

Burns are tissue injuries due to heat and may be graded as
follows:
A. Classification by Depth:
1. First degree - Erythema without blistering.
2. Second degree - Erythema with blistering.
3. Third degree - Destruction of deeper tissues.
B. Classification by Extent:
1. Minor burns involve less than 15% of body surface and are
first degree.
2. Extensive burns involve over 15% of body surface and are
second and third degree.

MINOR (FIRST DEGREE) BURNS

Local application of ice for 30 to 60 minutes markedly decreases
the development of the burn and produces relief of pain. Blebs
should be protected or, if open, treated under sterile conditions
since the fluid is an excellent culture medium.

EXTENSIVE (SECOND AND THIRD DEGREE) BURNS*

When tissues are burned, plasma is lost into the burned area
and from the surface of the burn. This leads to hypoproteinemia,
which remains as long as a granulating surface is present. In turn
the granulating surface heals poorly as long as there is hypoproteinemia. The loss of plasma results in a reduced blood volume,
hemoconcentration, low cardiac output, decreased blood flow, oliguria, elevated N.P.N., and leukocytosis. Although anemia due to
hemolysis may occur in the first two to four days, it more commonly becomes apparent about the fifth day. Immobilization may
produce hypercalcemia with resultant hypertension. Secondary
infection frequently occurs and must be treated promptly. Death
may result in an adult when 30% or more of the body surface is
involved. In an infant, 10% burns may be associated with very
severe effects.
The course of a severe burn may be divided as follows:
1. Neurogenic shock (immediate).
2. Burn shock (first 48 hours).

---

*Modified from A.W. Farmer, Management of Burns in Children.
Pediatrics **25**:886, 1960.

3. Toxemia (occurring about the third day).
4. Sepsis (about the third day).
5. Healing and restoration of function.

Treatment.
A. Emergency Measures:
1. Prompt hospitalization is indicated. Child should be wrapped in a large clean sheet for transportation.
2. Give meperidine (Demerol®) I.M. if analgesia is indicated. Morphine is contraindicated since it stimulates antidiuretic hormone and favors fluid retention.
3. Oxygen by mask, cafheter, or tent.
4. Begin treatment for shock immediately by giving plasma and electrolytes. If patient fails to respond to these measures, hydrocortisone and levarterenol bitartrate (Levophed®, norepinephrine), I.V., may produce striking improvement (see Chapter 2).
5. Prompt cooling of the affected part (e.g., by immersion in cool water or application of ice or cool compresses) appears to be beneficial.
B. General Measures:
1. Determine hemoglobin and hematocrit, utilizing venous blood.
2. Determine specific gravity of urine if specimen can be obtained.
3. Determine the surface area involved by the table in Fig 30-4.
4. Dressings - It is the present practice to employ open treatment of burns and to allow air drying but to do so with strict sterile precautions. This is a departure from the use of pressure dressings, the use of fats and oils, or tannic acid, all of which have been shown not to decrease the loss of electrolytes and proteins from the burned areas.
5. Topical application of silver nitrate, 0.5%, to second and third degree burns is useful. Severity of secondary infections is reduced. Wet dressings are applied promptly except in infants, in whom a two- or three-day delay for electrolyte therapy is desirable. (**Caution:** Electrolyte imbalance as a result of this therapy may be severe; constant monitoring is required.)
Mafenide acetate (Sulfamylon® cream) may be used as an alternative to silver nitrate. It has considerable antibacterial activity and the advantages of being nonstaining and readily washed off with water. Mafenide acetate is less likely to cause hyperchloremic acidosis than was the first marketed preparation, mafenide hydrochloride. Skin sensitivity can occur. Mafenide acetate should be applied by hand with a sterile glove once or twice daily to a thickness of one-sixteenth of an inch. The burned area should be continuously covered. Treatment is continued until healing is progressing well or until the burn site is ready for grafting. Silver sulfadiazine (Silvadene®) may be used in a similar manner.
6. Replacement fluid therapy -
a. Route - Electrolyte solutions should be given rapidly I.V. (via I.V. catheter for young children). Gravity drip may

be too slow, in which case a syringe may be used to accelerate the injection.

b. Solutions and dosage -
   (1) Lactated Ringer's injection (see Table 5-9 for composition) - Twenty-four hour requirement: 4 ml./10 lb. body wt./% surface area burned.
   (2) Colloid (whole blood, plasma, albumin, dextran, or mixtures thereof) - Twenty-four hour requirement: 4 ml./10 lb. body wt./% surface area burned.

FIG 30-4. Lund and Browder modification of Berkow's scale for estimating extent of burns.

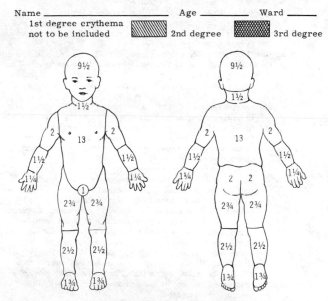

Name _____ Age _____ Ward _____

1st degree crythema not to be included [///] 2nd degree [###] 3rd degree

Infant Less Than One Year of Age

AREA*	Age in Years					
	0	1	5	10	15	Adult
Head area	19%	17%	13%	11%	9%	7%
Trunk area	26%	26%	26%	26%	26%	26%
Arm area	7%	7%	7%	7%	7%	7%
Thigh area	$5\frac{1}{2}$%	$6\frac{1}{2}$%	$8\frac{1}{2}$%	$8\frac{1}{2}$%	$9\frac{1}{2}$%	$9\frac{1}{2}$%
Leg area	5%	5%	5%	6%	6%	7%

Total 3rd degree burns _____ %
Total 2nd degree burns _____ %   TOTAL BURNS _____ %

*The neck, hands, buttocks, genitalia, and feet are not included in this chart.

(3) Water - Give 5% glucose in water I. V., supplemented
by oral sips, to a total minimum twenty-four hour
requirement of 110-130 ml./Kg. (for small children)
or 75-90 ml./Kg. (for children over ten years of age).
In hot weather or in patients who are febrile or whose
renal output is reduced (see below), these amounts
must be increased. The rate of replacement of water
is as follows:
   (a) One-half in the first eight hours after the burn.
   (b) One-half in the next 16 hours.
   (c) In the second 24 hours, give one-half the calculated
       total of the first 24 hours.

7. Fluid should also be given by mouth, if possible. The criteria for fluid needs are as follows -
   a. Increase in hematocrit - If the packed cell volume re-
      mains over 55, plasma therapy has been inadequate and
      shock and oliguria may result unless prompt additional
      intravenous therapy is given.
   b. Renal output - This is the most sensitive index and should
      be followed at hourly intervals by checking the volume and
      specific gravity of urine. Specimens **must be** collected
      from an indwelling catheter. Three possibilities may
      occur:
      (1) Adequate fluids - Output exceeding 2 to 3 ml./Kg./hour
          indicates adequacy of therapy.
      (2) Inadequate fluids (or lower nephron nephrosis) -
          Falling or decreased hourly output calls for increase
          in therapy even though the packed cell volume may not
          appear to have changed.
              A lowered output continuing for many hours in the
          face of continuing therapy suggests either inadequate
          therapy or developing acute renal failure. These may
          be differentiated by administering 25 ml./Kg. of 5%
          glucose in water in approximately one hour. If there
          is a rise in hourly urine volume within the next few
          hours, the maintenance therapy is inadequate and
          should be increased. If no other response occurs,
          acute renal failure has developed (see p. 340).
      (3) Overhydration - Hourly urine outputs of over 3 to 6
          ml./Kg./hour for more than six hours signify over-
          treatment, in which case prompt decrease in fluid
          therapy is indicated.

8. Maintenance fluids - Best given in the form of 5% glucose in
   0.45% saline. Oral fluids ad lib. are preferable in lesser
   burns.

9. Blood therapy - Hemolytic anemia occurs during the first
   two to four days after the burn, while hypoplastic anemia
   usually occurs in the later phase. The blood deficit in the
   initial period is approximately 5% of the total red blood cell
   mass for each 25% of surface area burned. The total red
   blood cell mass needed may be calculated by assuming that
   it equals 3% of body weight, as follows -

Body wt. (in Kg.) × 3% of burned area × 1000 =
ml. of red cell mass needed.

Example: (3 years old, 14 Kg., 40% burned)
14 × 0.03 × 0.40 × 1000 = 168 ml.

If the red cells are replaced as part of a transfusion (200 ml. red cell mass for each 500 ml. transfusion), the plasma (300 ml. of each 500 ml. of blood) is considered as replacing part of the early fluid deficit.

10. Antibiotics are indicated only if infection is present. Choice depends on frequent bacterial cultures of blood and burned area.
11. Gamma globulin in large doses (1 ml./Kg.) may be helpful and should be repeated in three to five days.
12. Tetanus toxoid booster or, in the unimmunized, tetanus hyperimmune human globulin (Hyper-Tet®):
    a. Under 5 years, 75 units.
    b. 5-10 years, 125 units.
    c. Over 10 years, 250 units.
    d. After severe exposure or delayed therapy, 500-1000 units.
13. Feedings - A calorie intake chart is kept on all patients with severe burns. Efforts should be made to maintain at least normal intake of calories and protein.

HEAT EXHAUSTION

Heat exhaustion is caused by sustained exposure to heat and is characterized by collapse of peripheral circulation and secondary salt depletion and dehydration.

Clinical Findings.
A. Symptoms and Signs:
1. Weakness, dizziness, and stupor.
2. Headache.
3. No muscle cramps.
4. Profuse perspiration.
5. Cool, pale skin.
6. Oliguria.
7. Tachycardia.
B. Laboratory Findings: Hemoconcentration, salt depletion. In some instances, serum sodium levels are not strikingly low.

Treatment.
A. Specific Measures:
1. Treat shock when present.
2. Give sodium chloride solution, 0.3%, by mouth (approximately ½ tsp. table salt/qt. of water), or physiologic saline, 200 to 1000 ml. I.V. Hypertonic saline may be indicated in those instances where there has been a large salt loss with water replacement.
3. Sodium deficit may be calculated as follows: 140 − Patient's sodium × 0.6 × Wt. in Kg. = Sodium deficit.
B. General Measures:
1. Place the child at rest in a cool, shady place.
2. Elevate feet and massage legs.

HEAT STROKE
(Sunstroke)

Heat stroke is caused by prolonged exposure to high temperatures and is characterized by failure of the heat-regulating mechanism.

Clinical Findings.
  A. Symptoms and Signs: Sudden loss of consciousness, hyperpyrexia; hot, flushed, and dry skin; rapid, irregular, and weak pulse; and cessation of sweating (an index of the failure of the heat-regulating mechanism). There may be premonitory headache, dizziness, nausea, and visual disturbances. Rectal temperatures may be as high as 108 to 110°F. (42.2 to 43.3°C.).
  B. Laboratory Findings: Hydration and salt content of the body are normal.

Treatment.
  Treatment is aimed at reducing high temperature.
  A. Specific Measures: None.
  B. General Measures:
    1. Place child in cool, shady place and remove all clothing. Cool the child by fanning after sprinkling with water. Immerse in tepid water or sponge thoroughly to reduce body temperature. **Caution:** Discontinue all antipyretic measures when 102°F. (39°C.) is reached.
    2. Avoid sedation (unless the child is having convulsions, at which time diazepam may be used), since this further disturbs the heat-regulating mechanism.
    3. Maintenance intravenous fluids should be provided with careful electrolyte monitoring.
    4. Avoid immediate re-exposure to heat. Inability to tolerate high temperatures may remain for a long time.

DISORDERS DUE TO COLD

Keeping the child warm and dry will prevent most disorders due to cold. In cold climates the child should be taught to exercise the extremities (including fingers and toes) to maintain circulation and warmth.

FROSTBITE

Frostbite is injury of the superficial tissues caused by freezing. There are three grades of severity:
    1. First degree - Freezing without blistering or peeling.
    2. Second degree - Freezing with blistering or peeling.
    3. Third degree - Freezing with necrosis of skin and/or deeper tissues.
Mild cases of frostbite are characterized by numbness, prickling, and itching. More severe degrees of frostbite may produce

paresthesia and stiffness. As the member thaws, tenderness and burning pain become severe. The skin is white or yellow, and the involved joints are stiff. Hyperemia, edema, blisters, and necrosis may appear. Localized frostbite may prove difficult to diagnose. The most common areas are on the face under hat straps and buckles.

Treatment.
Treatment is best instituted during the stage of reactive hyperemia, as thawing begins.
A. Local Measures:
1. **Do not** rub or massage parts or apply ice, snow, or heat.
2. Protect injured part from trauma and secondary infection and loosen all constricting garments.
3. Return to warm environment.
   a. In mild cases, warm the exposed part with natural body heat (e.g., place the patient's hands in his axillas, next to his abdomen, or in his groin).
   b. In severe cases, keep affected parts uncovered at room temperature (74 to 80° F.). Fairly rapid thawing at temperatures slightly above that of body heat may lessen extent of necrosis.
4. Elevate affected part.
5. Warm drinks, including hot toddy (whisky or rum and tea or warm milk).
6. Sedation.
B. General Measures: Heparin sodium may prevent secondary thrombosis in surrounding areas but has no effect on frostbitten areas or on gangrene. The initial dose is 0.5 mg./Kg. I.V. every one to three hours, keeping the clotting time between 20 and 35 minutes. Depoheparin may have a very erratic effect on children and is not advised.
C. Surgical Measures:
1. Amputation should not be rushed. Necrosis and gangrene may be very superficial, and the tissue may heal well.
2. Sympathetic and paravertebral block are contraindicated.

DROWNING AND ELECTRIC SHOCK

DROWNING

Treatment.
A. Emergency Measures: Prompt institution of artificial respiration (resuscitation) should immediately follow the clearing of the upper respiratory tract and the pulling forward of the tongue. Resuscitation replaces spontaneous respiration and supplies needed oxygen to the tissues until the paralyzed respiratory center can again resume its normal function. Artificial respiration must be carried on for many hours, even in the absence of any sign of life. Only absolute signs (i.e., rigor mortis and persistent hypothermia) justify discontinuing efforts.
Various technics of artificial respiration have found favor.

Mouth-to-mouth insufflation is one of the most efficient methods. It is superior to the prone pressure method, the rocking method, and the arm-lift-back-pressure method.

Manual artificial respiration, as outlined above, should never be postponed in waiting for the arrival of a mechanical resuscitator.

B. General Measures:

1. Oxygen - Administration of oxygen during manual artificial respiration is of great value. It is necessary only to maintain a free flow of oxygen close to the mouth and nose. Administration of CO_2 is contraindicated.

2. External cardiac massage may be helpful. Massaging the legs toward the heart may stimulate circulation.

3. Stomach contents should be emptied to minimize aspiration.

4. Both metabolic and respiratory acidosis may develop. Blood gas determinations should be closely monitored. Metabolic and respiratory acidosis should be treated aggressively.

5. Plasma or whole blood may be needed to treat shock associated with the onset of pulmonary edema. (Mannitol, low molecular weight dextran, and diuretics are not indicated.)

6. Morphine may be used as necessary to control agitation, but only if ventilation is being controlled.

7. Antibiotics are indicated when signs of infection appear. Direct culturing is recommended if near drowning occurs in contaminated water.

8. Pulmonary edema is treated with positive pressure (CPAP or volume respiration) and diuretics.

9. Stimulants and corticosteroids are not useful.

C. Fresh Water Drowning vs. Salt Water Drowning: Contrary to some published reports, there is no essential difference between near drowning in salt water or fresh water, and the treatment is the same for both. Differences may arise in the amounts of fresh or sea water absorbed from the stomach. The basic problems are hypoxemia, acidemia, and severe laryngospasm associated with retrograde pulmonary edema.

ELECTRIC SHOCK AND ELECTRIC BURNS

Direct current is much less dangerous than alternating current. Alternating current of high frequency or high voltage is less dangerous than alternating current of low frequency or low voltage. With alternating currents of 25 to 300 cycles, low voltages tend to produce ventricular fibrillation; high voltages (over 1000), respiratory failure; intermediate voltages (220 to 1000), both.

Clinical Findings.

A. Symptoms: Electric burns are usually small, round or oval, sharply demarcated, painless gray areas without associated inflammatory reaction. Little happens to them for several weeks; sloughing then occurs slowly and in a fairly wide area.

Electric shock may produce loss of consciousness, which may be momentary or prolonged. With recovery there may be muscular pain, fatigue, headache, and nervous irritability, the so-called postshock psychosis.

B. Signs: The physical signs vary.
   1. Ventricular fibrillation - No heart sounds or pulse can be found, and the patient is unconscious; the respirations continue for a few minutes, becoming exaggerated as asphyxia occurs and then ceasing as death intervenes.
   2. Respiratory failure - Respirations are absent and the patient is unconscious; the pulse can be felt, but there is a marked fall in blood pressure; the skin is cold and cyanotic.

Treatment.
A. Emergency Measures:
   1. Interrupt current.
   2. Give artificial respiration (mouth-to-mouth) and administer oxygen if available.
   3. Treat shock promptly.
   4. External cardiac massage (see inside back cover).
B. Local Measures:
   1. Simple burn - The affected area of skin and mucous membrane should be treated if necessary.
   2. Severe burn - Treat conservatively. Infection is usually not present early. Granulation tissue should be well established before surgery is attempted. Hemorrhage may occur late and may be severe. Debridement may be necessary and should be left to the surgeon.

SURGICAL EMERGENCIES

DOG BITE

Perhaps the greatest service the physician can render to the patient who has been bitten by a dog is to have the dog impounded by the local health department so that it may be observed for the development of clinical signs of rabies. The dog must **never** be destroyed, except in self defense or to prevent its escape. The examination of the dog's brain at the proper time by the state department of health or a university medical center may allow a histological or immunological diagnosis of rabies to be made.

Treatment.
A. Specific Measures:
   1. Hyperimmune serum (see p. 109).
   2. Antirabies vaccine (see p. 101).
B. Local Measures:
   1. Clean the wound thoroughly with soap and water, **using a syringe to force water into the wound.**
   2. Debride the wound to remove dead tissue and dirt.
   3. A tetanus toxoid booster should be administered if the patient has been immunized previously. Tetanus immune globulin (human) is required if tetanus immunization has not taken place.
   4. The use of gas gangrene antitoxin may be indicated if the wound is extensive.
   5. In the case of extensive wounds it may be necessary to give oral antibiotics such as ampicillin.

HUMAN BITE

Minimal abrasions of the skin resulting from bites among children require only local care and generally heal promptly. However, penetrating bites cause some of the most severe of all infections because of the wide variety of pathogenic organisms in the human mouth. Prompt and vigorous treatment is necessary to prevent prolonged infections.

Treatment.
  A. Specific Measures: Give broad-spectrum antibiotics in full
    doses (see Chapter 6).
  B. Local Measures:
    1. Cleanse wound thoroughly with soap and water, **using a
      syringe to wash water forcibly into wound.**
    2. Surgical debridement as indicated.

ACUTE HEAD INJURIES

Head injuries may be classified as open or closed. Both types are often seen in the same patient and may require consideration jointly. Attention should always be given to the possibility of injury elsewhere, particularly to the cervical spine.

OPEN WOUNDS OF THE HEAD

Treatment of Extensive Wounds.
  A. First Aid: Apply a compression bandage to control bleeding.
  B. Local Measures: The measure here described represents
    definitive treatment and may lead directly to a neurosurgical
    procedure. When the child's general condition permits, treat-
    ment should be undertaken as follows:
    1. Shave scalp widely about the wound.
    2. Cleanse wound with soap and water and irrigate thoroughly.
    3. Infiltrate margins of wound with procaine or lidocaine.
    4. Debride thoroughly.
    5. Gently explore the outer table of the skull for fracture.
    6. If no fracture is found, close wound snugly in one or two
      layers with interrupted sutures of non-absorbable material.
  C. General Measures:
    1. Tetanus - Give tetanus toxoid booster (to children previously
      immunized) or 500 units of tetanus hyperimmune human
      globulin (Hyper-Tet®).
    2. Broad-spectrum antibiotics in massive doses (see Chapter
      6) only if wound is dirty.
  D. Surgical treatment of associated extensive brain injury requires
    prompt neurosurgical consultation as well as special equipment.
    Leakage of cerebrospinal fluid from the nose or ears poses a
    special problem of incipient bacterial meningitis. Prompt use
    of massive antibiotic prophylaxis is justified to prevent this
    serious complication. The child should be kept in a sitting
    position. Leakage usually improves spontaneously within ten
    days. Neurosurgical consultation should be sought.

CLOSED WOUNDS OF THE HEAD

The chief dangers of closed head injuries are from immediate destruction of brain tissue (contusion, laceration) and progressive secondary damage due either to anoxia or to cerebral compression (from intracranial hemorrhage or edema).

Anoxia is one of the most frequent causes of death from head injuries. It is induced by (1) obstruction of the respiratory tract and/or respiratory center involvement, leading to reduction of the oxygen concentration of the blood; or (2) decrease in the capacity of the contused brain to utilize oxygen.

Diagnosis of Progressive Intracranial Bleeding.

The single best indication of progressive intracranial bleeding is a change in the level of consciousness. The appearance of focal signs such as seizures or weakness is also important.

Treatment.

A. Emergency Measures:

1. Maintain an adequate airway to minimize hypoxia due to mechanical respiratory obstruction. Tidal volume = 10 to 15 ml./Kg./minute.

   a. Position in bed - If possible, elevate the child's head. This will allow better venous return from the head, but it may make drainage of respiratory secretions difficult and obstruct the airway. The latter consideration is of overriding importance.

   b. Early tracheostomy allows adequate tracheal suction, administration of oxygen through a free airway, and elevation of the head to reduce intracranial pressure. The use of an endotracheal tube is limited to 3 to 5 days, at the end of which time the comatose child will require tracheostomy. Constant nursing attention with a suction apparatus for the removal of mucus is required.

2. Oxygen - Hypoxia of the brain may exist in the absence of noticeable peripheral cyanosis. The most satisfactory route for oxygen administration is by nasal catheter, but this may be difficult in a small child.

3. Shock - Surgical shock (peripheral vascular collapse) is rare in head injuries per se and usually indicates associated traumatic injuries demanding primary consideration. When present, it must be promptly and vigorously treated.

4. Hyperthermia - This indicates a disturbed temperature-regulating mechanism. It increases the metabolic and oxygen requirements of tissues which already suffer from oxygen lack and may result in peripheral vascular collapse and further increase brain hypoxia. Treatment must be prompt and energetic. Remove blankets and sponge the child with tepid water or use a cooling blanket. If hyperthermia persists, controlled hypothermia should be employed. Aspirin rectally in doses of 65 mg./year of age may be of some value, with careful monitoring of salicylate level to keep it below 25 mg./100 ml. If hydration and urine output are not normal, chronic salicylism is a danger. Chlorpromazine may be a useful adjunct.

B. General Measures: X-rays of the skull are indicated only after an airway is established and the immediate threats to life controlled. X-rays are especially useful when progressive bleeding is suspected which might have been produced by possible rupture of the middle meningeal artery. In such a case, identification of a fracture line may be of localizing diagnostic significance.

1. Fluid balance - Should be maintained by parenteral administration of fluids designed to provide maintenance sodium requirements and to replace losses via lungs, kidneys, or skin, and through vomiting - without, however, flooding the patient with excessive amounts. Maintenance fluids should be two-thirds to three-fourths of normal maintenance to assist in decreasing cerebral edema.

2. Feeding - Gastric feeding of a high-protein diet by nasal catheter is indicated in prolonged coma. Tracheostomized patients can more readily be maintained in this fashion because the danger of aspiration of vomitus is decreased. Small gastric tubes are less likely to contribute to the formation of tracheo-esophageal fistula in the presence of a tracheostomy. Intravenous hyperalimentation may also be utilized.

3. Spinal puncture - Considerable controversy prevails concerning the indications for and the merits or disadvantages of spinal fluid puncture in the diagnosis or treatment of head injuries in children, and neurosurgical consultation should be sought.

Spinal puncture is indicated if infection is suspected following basal skull fracture.

Technic is described on p. 602. Stop just before entry into the subarachnoid space, remove the stilet, and attach a manometer. Enter the space slowly and allow the fluid to rise in the manometer. One or 2 ml. are sufficient for a cell count. Withdraw the needle with the manometer in place. One should note color of fluid, initial pressure, final pressure, and amount withdrawn. Jugular compression tests should not be carried out unless one suspects injury to the spinal column. The sudden rise in spinal fluid pressure which follows jugular compression may be harmful after head injury, and these tests give no information of value with reference to the brain. Spinal puncture should not be attempted if resistance to the procedure is expected, because of the undesirable rise of spinal fluid pressure which may result from straining.

4. Sedation - Restless children may constitute a difficult nursing problem. Sedation should be avoided if possible. Restlessness may, however, be a symptom of anoxia; it may also accompany urine retention. (Consider catheterization or suprapubic aspiration.)

   a. Paraldehyde (rectally) or barbiturates (I.M. or I.V.) are satisfactory. Barbiturates or I.V. Dilantin® are particularly indicated for the control of convulsions. (See Appendix for dosages.) Diazepam (Valium®), in a dose of 0.05 to 0.2 mg./Kg. I.V. to a maximum of 10 mg./dose, is quite useful in controlling severe seizures.

     b. Avoid morphine and codeine; they may depress respiration, may cause edema of the larynx, and the attendant alteration of pupil size is undesirable for diagnostic reasons.

C. Follow-up Measures: Clinical response in the first few hours will generally indicate whether urgent surgical intervention is necessary. Medical and nursing care should include the following:

1. Take pulse and respiration every 15 minutes; temperature every 30 minutes; blood pressure every hour.

2. Test level of consciousness by ability to rouse.

3. An indwelling urinary catheter is usually necessary.

4. Oxygen inhalation should be continued. A free airway should be maintained and the patient suctioned when necessary.

5. Restraints are not usually indicated.

6. Worsening of the child's condition, with progressive stupor, convulsions, focal paralysis, and disturbance of vital signs (such as alterations of pulse, respiration, and blood pressure) require neurosurgical intervention as a lifesaving measure.

7. Hypothermia is contraindicated since the oxygen requirements at 93°F. (34°C.) are much greater than at the isothermic temperature of 98.6°F. (37°C.). True hypothermia of 82 to 84°F. (28 to 30°C.) is of questionable value in this situation.

31 . . .

Poisons & Toxins*

Poisons of all types are the third most common cause of accidental deaths in the home; 350 to 500 children die each year from poisoning. Nonfatal poisonings are 100 to 200 times as frequent as fatal poisonings. Medicines account for about 50% of all cases of poisoning (aspirin, 20%); cleaning and polishing products, 17%; pesticides, 10%; and petroleum products, 10%.

Accidents involving household poisons, especially in children under five years of age, are attributable to three main factors: (1) Improper storage, (2) poor lighting, and (3) human factors, including failure to return a poison to its proper place, failure to read the label properly, and failure to recognize the substance as poisonous.

Even the child who survives an episode of poisoning may be left with a permanent disability, e.g., stricture of the esophagus following lye ingestion, permanent liver and kidney damage caused by poisons such as chlorinated hydrocarbons, and bone marrow depression after benzene poisoning.

Prevention.

Instructions in poison prevention and poison-proofing of homes should be given prior to or at the six-month check-up. As a child grows developmentally, further areas of discussion should be raised with the parents, e.g., when the child begins climbing, the danger of medicine cabinet storage should be discussed; after walking, storage in other areas of the house should be discussed. Parents should be asked about the poison-proof status of each of the following areas: under the sink storage of drain cleaners, etc.; kitchen pantries and cleaning supplies; bathroom cabinets containing medicines, antiseptics, etc.; basements and utility rooms containing paints, thinners, etc.; garages containing antifreeze and other automotive supplies; storage sheds containing garden sprays, etc.

Following the discussion of these areas, general concepts should be discussed, such as provision of locked storage; safe disposal of old medicines and products; labelling of containers, especially when not in original container; impropriety of tasting or eating things without parental consent; and how and when to use syrup of epicac - always following a call to the doctor or poison control center. The physician should give the parent (or prescribe) a 1 oz. bottle of syrup of ipecac.

The peak age of accidental poisoning is 2 years of age. If a child ingests a poison, there is a 25% chance of a repeat poisoning in one year. If adequate prevention has been discussed, child battering or neglect should be considered with a second ingestion.

---

*With the assistance of Barry H. Rumack, M.D., Assistant Professor of Pediatrics, University of Colorado Medical Center.

GENERAL MANAGEMENT OF POISONINGS

The child is frequently found near the source of the poison shortly after having eaten it. Containers suspected of containing the poisonous substance should be brought to the hospital or office with the patient, since poisonous ingredients are almost always listed on the labels and specific antidotes are frequently given.

If the ingredients are not listed on the label or have been obliterated, call the nearest Poison Control Center or call the manufacturer or the local representative collect. The initial history correlates with the actual agent ingested less than half of the time. It is best to compare the clinical condition of the patient with a suspected ingestant and determine if they correspond. An experienced person at the Poison Control Center may provide the best up-to-date data.

Diagnosis.

In the absence of a definite history of ingestion or of contact with the poison, the differential diagnosis presents many difficulties. Most symptoms of poisoning are not diagnostic and may occur also in a number of diseases of childhood. Frequent clues to the presence of an unsuspected poisoning are as follows:

A. Gastrointestinal disturbances, including anorexia, abdominal pain, nausea, vomiting, and diarrhea.

B. Circulatory or respiratory symptoms, including cyanosis, shock, collapse, sudden loss of consciousness, or convulsions.

C. Evidence may be obtained from the appearance, smell, or analysis of vomitus, gastric washings obtained by lavage, or urine. Characteristic odors of some poisons may be detected on the patient's breath. Ingestion of corrosives is suggested by blood in gastric washings and stools.

D. Chemical Analyses: Analysis of blood, urine, gastric washings, or fat obtained at biopsy may be useful in establishing a diagnosis.

E. Clinical Laboratory Tests: Tests for urinary porphyrins (lead), red cell stippling (lead), cholinesterase levels (organo-phosphates), and salicylate levels are available in the general laboratory.

F. In cases of chronic lead and bismuth poisoning, x-ray examinations of the bones may be of great help.

G. Alopecia is present in cases of chronic thallium, arsenic, and selenium poisoning.

H. The use of ferric chloride (Phenistix®) may be helpful in urine testing for salicylates and phenothiazines.

Induced vomiting is much more effective than lavage with a small bore nasogastric tube. However, a large bore orogastric tube is more effective for emesis.

The immediate management of acute poisoning in children should include the following:

Emergency Treatment.

Specific types of poisoning are discussed on the following pages. Emergency care should be supervised by a physician (not delegated to office personnel, e.g., those taking emergency telephone calls). This is best done in a hospital, where complete facilities and antidotes are available.

Table 31-1. Symptoms and signs of acute poisoning
by various substances.*

Symptoms and Signs	Substance or Other Cause
Albuminuria	Arsenic, mercury, phosphorus
Alopecia	Thallium, arsenic, selenium, radiation sickness
Blood changes	
Anemia	Lead, naphthalene, chlorates, favism, solanine and other plant poisons, snake venom
Cherry-red blood	Cyanide. (The lips in carbon monoxide poisoning are usually dusky and not cherry-red.)
Hematuria or hemo-globinuria	Heavy metals, naphthalene, nitrates, chlorates, favism, solanine and other plant poisons
Hemorrhage	Warfarin, thallium
Methemoglobinemia	Nitrates, nitrites, aniline dyes, methylene blue, chlorates
Breath	
Bitter almonds odor	Cyanide
Garlicky odor	Arsenic, phosphorus
Burns of skin and mucous membranes	Lye, hypochlorite, other corrosive agents
Cardiovascular collapse	Arsenic, boric acid, iron, phosphorus, food poisoning, nitrates
Cyanosis	Barbiturates, opiates, nitrites, aniline dyes, chlorates
Eyes	
Lacrimation	Organic phosphates, nicotine, mushroom poisoning
Ptosis	Botulism, thallium
Pupillary constriction	Opiates, parathion and other organic phosphates, mushrooms and some other plant poisons
Pupillary dilation	Atropine, nicotine, antihistamines, phenylephrine (Neo-Synephrine®), mushrooms, thallium, oleander
Strabismus	Botulism, thallium
Visual disturbances	Atropine, parathion and other organic phosphate insecticides, botulism
Fever	Atropine, salicylates, food poisoning, antihistamines, tranquilizers, camphor
Flushing	Atropine, antihistamines, tranquilizers
Gastrointestinal tract	
Abdominal cramps	Corrosive substances, food poisoning, lead, arsenic, black widow spider bite, boric acid, carbon tetrachloride, organic phosphates, phosphorus, nicotine, castor beans, fluorides, thallium

*Arena, JM., The clinical diagnosis of poisoning. P. Clin. North
America 17:477-494, 1970.

TABLE 31-1 (cont'd.). Symptoms and signs of acute
poisoning by various substances.

Symptoms and Signs	Substance or Other Cause
Gastrointestinal tract (cont'd.)	
Diarrhea	Food poisoning, iron, organic phosphates, arsenic, naphthalene, castor beans, mercury, boric acid, thallium, nicotine, nitrates, solanine and other plant poisons, mushrooms
Dry mouth	Atropine, antihistamines, ephedrine
Hematemesis	Corrosive substances, warfarin, aminophylline, fluorides
Stomatitis	Corrosive substances, thallium
Vomiting	Aminophylline, food poisoning, organic phosphates, nicotine, digitalis, arsenic, boric acid, lead, mercury, iron, phosphorus, thallium, DDT, dieldrin, nitrates, castor beans, mushrooms, oleander, naphthalene
Headache	Carbon monoxide, organic phosphates, atropine, lead, dieldrin, carbon tetrachloride
Heart	
Bradycardia	Digitalis, mushrooms
Tachycardia	Atropine
Other irregularities of rhythm	Nitrates, oleander
Jaundice	Phosphorus, chlordane, favism, mushrooms
Muscles	
Cramps	Lead, black widow spider bite
Spasm, dystonia	Phenothiazines
Nervous system	
Ataxia	Lead, organic phosphates, antihistamines, thallium
Coma	Barbiturates, carbon monoxide, cyanide, opiates, ethyl alcohol, salicylates, hydrocarbons, parathion and other organic phosphate insecticides, lead, mercury, boric acid, antihistamines, digitalis, mushrooms
Convulsions	Aminophylline, amphetamine and other stimulants, atropine, camphor, boric acid, lead, mercury, parathion and other organic phosphate insecticides, nicotine, phenothiazines, antihistamines, arsenic, DDT, dieldrin, kerosene, fluorides, nitrates, barbiturates, digitalis, salicylates, solanine and other plant poisons, thallium

TABLE 31-1 (cont'd.). Symptoms and signs of acute
poisoning by various substances.

Symptoms and Signs	Substance or Other Cause
Nervous system (cont'd.) Delirium	Aminophylline, antihistamines, atropine, salicylates, lead, barbiturates, boric acid
Depression	Barbiturates, kerosene, tranquilizers, arsenic, lead, boric acid, DDT, naphthalene
Mental confusion	Alcohol, barbiturates, atropine, nicotine, antihistamines, carbon tetrachloride, mercury, digitalis, mushrooms
Paresthesias	Lead, thallium, DDT
Weakness	Organic phosphates, arsenic, lead, nicotine, thallium, nitrates, fluorides, botulism
Pallor	Lead, naphthalene, chlorates, favism, solanine and other plant poisons, fluorides
Proteinuria	Arsenic, mercury, phosphorus
Salivation and sweating	Parathion and other organic phosphate insecticides, muscarine and other mushroom poisoning, nicotine
Respiratory tract Aspiration pneumonia	Kerosene
Cough	Hydrocarbons, mercury vapor
Respiratory difficulty	Barbiturates, opiates, salicylates, ethyl alcohol, organic phosphates, dieldrin
Respiratory failure	Cyanide, carbon monoxide, antihistamines, thallium, fluorides
Respiratory stimulation	Salicylates, amphetamine and other stimulants, atropine, mushrooms
Shock	Food poisoning, iron, arsenic, fluorides
Skin erythema	Boric acid

A. Ingested Poisons: Speed is essential for effective therapy.
   1. Emesis (in the home) - **Contraindications** to emesis include
      absent gag reflex, coma, convulsions, and ingestion of strong
      acids or strong bases. Telephone instructions must be given
      when the poisoning is first reported. **Caution: Do not** administer more than 30 ml. of syrup of ipecac. If the child does
      not vomit, then see the patient. **Do not use** mustard water,
      salt water, etc. These "emetics" may be dangerous. **Do
      give:** 15 ml. syrup of ipecac **orally** followed by **oral fluids,**
      10 to 15 ml./Kg. Keep the child walking; do not put to bed.
      Repeat in 20 minutes if emesis does not occur. Instruct
      the mother to recover the regurgitated vomitus in a pan for

later analysis and bring the child to the hospital along with the vomitus and the container with the remainder of the uningested material.

2. Emesis (in the hospital) - Give syrup of ipecac and follow the same procedure outlined in ¶ 1. This produces an average recovery of 30% of an ingested agent.

3. Lavage - This should be performed in a left-sided, head-down position with a large bore orogastric tube. Lavage with a 16 to 18 F nasogastric tube is worthless except for liquids and dispersed powders and solutions; 28 to 36 F orogastric tubes should be employed with a minimum of 5 to 10 L. of warm saline. One hundred ml. should be instilled and withdrawn with each exchange. In the position described, no residue should be left in the stomach. **Endotracheal intubation** should precede lavage if the patient is comatose or convulsive or has lost the gag reflex.

4. Catharsis - Sodium sulfate or magnesium sulfate should be administered orally at 250 mg./Kg.

5. Activated charcoal (**not** universal antidote, which is contraindicated) should be given or instilled at five to ten times the estimated weight of the ingested material or a minimum of 10 to 15 Gm. in a water slurry. Cherry syrup may be added just before it is given and will not interfere with adsorptive ability.

B. Surface Poisons: Remove by washing in large amounts of water or with soap and water. Alcohol is used on water insoluble substances such as phenol after initial copious washing has mechanically removed some of it. **Caution:** Do not use chemical antidotes; the heat liberated by the reaction may increase the extent of injury.

C. Inhaled Poisons: Remove the patient from exposure, remove constricting clothing, and give artificial respiration (see p. 563) or utilize an Ambu® bag or other positive pressure device if necessary.

References Useful in Clinical Poisonings.

Arena, J.M.: Poisoning: Toxicology—Symptoms—Treatments. (Thomas, 1970.)

Dreisbach, R.H.: Handbook of Poisoning: Diagnosis & Treatment, 8th ed. (Lange, 1974.)

Gleason, M.N., Gosselin, R.E., and Hodge, H.C.: Clinical Toxicology of Commercial Products (with Supplements), 4th ed. (Williams and Wilkins, 1975.)

Goodman, L., and Gilman, A.: The Pharmacological Basis of Therapeutics, 4th ed. (Macmillan, 1971.)

The Merck Index of Chemicals and Drugs, 8th ed. (Merck & Co., 1968.) [Very useful for identification and antidotes.]

The Merck Manual, 11th ed. (Merck Sharp & Dohme Research Laboratories, 1966.)

Rumack, B.H., editor: Poisindex: A Computer-Generated Microfiche Poison Information Source. (Micromedex, Inc., 1975.)

SPECIFIC EMERGENCY MEASURES

Ingestion.
1. Syrup of ipecac in all cases except corrosives, coma, or seizures.
2. Lavage only if semiconscious or in coma, after endotracheal tube is inserted.
3. "Activated" charcoal.

Inhaled Irritants.
1. Oxygen therapy.
2. Mouth-to-mouth resuscitation.
3. Humidity.
4. Observe for pneumonitis and pulmonary edema.

Local Irritants.
1. Copious water irrigation.
2. Careful eye examination.
3. No chemical "antidotes."

Available Consultants.
1. Poison control centers.
2. State health departments.
3. Medical center consultants.
4. Pharmaceutical houses.
5. U. S. agricultural office.
6. Medical examiner (coroner's office, toxicologist).
7. See references in text.

Specific "Antidote" Treatment Available.
1. Carbon monoxide (see oxygen, p. 581).
2. Phenothiazines (see diphenhydramine, p. 591).
3. Amphetamines (see chlorpromazine, p. 577).
4. Cyanide (see amyl nitrite, sodium nitrite, sodium thiosulfate, p. 581).
5. Narcotics (see nalorphine, p. 586). **Note:** Naloxone (Narcan®), 5 μg./Kg., is a new effective narcotic antagonist which does not cause respiratory depression.
6. Nitrites (see methylene blue, p. 587).
7. Spider and snake bites (see antivenins, pp. 590 and 591).
8. Heavy metals (for arsenic, see dimercaprol, p. 578; iron, see deferoxamine, p. 582; lead, see edetate, p. 380; mercury, see dimercaprol, p. 578).
9. Phosphate esters (see atropine, pralidoxime, p. 589).
10. Belladonna alkaloids (see physostigmine, p. 580).
11. Tricyclic antidepressants (Tofranil®, Elavil®, etc.) (See physostigmine, p. 592).

MANAGEMENT OF SPECIFIC COMMON TYPES OF POISONING IN CHILDREN

ACIDS, CORROSIVE

The strong mineral acids exert primarily a local corrosive effect on the skin and mucous membranes. Classically, acids cause oral and esophageal burns, the majority of which resolve; however, pyloric constriction with obstruction and vomiting regularly occurs at three weeks. This is due to pylorospasm occurring immediately after ingestion which "hangs" the acid in this area and produces the burn.

Symptoms include severe pain in the throat and upper gastrointestinal tract, marked thirst, bloody vomitus; difficulty in swallowing, breathing, and speaking; discoloration and destruction of skin and mucous membranes in and around the mouth; collapse, and shock. Milder burns may result in fewer symptoms but serious sequelae.

Treatment.

Do not give emetics or lavage. Dilute acid immediately with copious amounts of water or milk. Avoid carbonates or bicarbonates internally since these form gas and cause distention of a perhaps weakened stomach wall. Diagnostic esophagoscopy may be performed as indicated within the first 12 to 24 hours. Prednisone (2 mg./Kg./day for 21 days) is indicated if the esophagus has been burned or if esophagoscopy is not performed.

ALCOHOL, ETHYL

Incoordination, slow reaction time, blurred vision, staggering gait, slurred speech, hypoglycemia, convulsions, and coma are the common results of overdosage. The diagnosis of alcoholic intoxication is commonly overlooked in children.

Treatment.

Supportive treatment and aggressive management of any degree of hypoglycemia are usually the only treatment required. Forced diuresis increases the clearance rate for alcohol. Peritoneal dialysis or hemodialysis is very useful in severe ingestions.

AMPHETAMINES

Central nervous system stimulation is the most significant result of overdosage. There may be extreme, unmanageable hyperactivity and anxiety as well as flushing, arrhythmias, cardiac pain, hyperpyrexia, hypertension, and eventual circulatory collapse. Abdominal cramps, nausea, and vomiting are frequent.

Treatment.

Small amounts (1 mg./Kg. subcutaneously) of chlorpromazine (Thorazine®) may dramatically quiet the patient. Acid-forced diuresis increases amphetamine excretion in the urine. If amphetamine has been ingested in a preparation also containing a barbiturate, the dose of chlorpromazine should be 0.5 mg./Kg. Do not give intravenously. If there is a question about what has been ingested, do **not** give chlorpromazine, as synergistic hypotension occurs in the presence of congeners such as MDA, STP, and DMT. Hyperpyrexia must not be treated with salicylates.

ANOVULATORY PREPARATIONS

The only toxic effects noted are nausea, vomiting, and, in females, vaginal bleeding.

ANTIHISTAMINES

The effects of poisoning with these agents are variable, but all will show anticholinergic or sympathomimetic effects. Atropine-like toxic effects such as dry mouth, fever, and dilated pupils may predominate. Signs of C.N.S. toxicity include ataxia, hallucinations, and convulsions followed by coma and respiratory depression. Especially in older children, depression comparable to that seen with poisoning due to tranquilizers may be prominent.

Prolonged toxic manifestations may be caused by sustained-action tablets.

Treatment.

Treatment consists of emesis or lavage, charcoal, and catharsis; the latter are important when prolonged-action tablets have been ingested. Convulsions should be controlled with diazepam (Valium®). Stimulants are contraindicated. Avoid salicylates; decrease fever with fluids and sponge baths. Physostigmine, 0.5 to 2 mg. I.V. **slowly**, will reverse coma, hallucinations, arrhythmias, convulsions, and hypertension. Repeat doses should be given to reverse these toxic manifestations only.

ARSENIC

Acute arsenic intoxication is characterized by severe gastrointestinal symptoms and may be accompanied by a metallic taste, hoarseness, dysphagia, renal damage, shock, and fever. Increased capillary permeability, dehydration, protein depletion, garlic odor of breath, and hypotension may be noted. Chronic toxicity is characterized by peripheral neuritis, weight loss, and sometimes involvement of the skin, kidneys, and gastrointestinal tract.

Laboratory determination of arsenic levels in vomitus, urine, and tissues is confirmatory.

Arsine gas causes massive hemolysis and must be treated rapidly with exchange transfusion once serum hemoglobin rises or hemolysis is documented.

Treatment.

Treatment consists of anti-shock therapy and specific therapy with dimercaprol (BAL), 2.5 mg./Kg. I.M. Stat. and then 2 mg./Kg. I.M. every four hours. After four to eight injections, give twice daily for five to ten days or until recovery. Penicillamine (Cuprimine®), 100 mg./Kg./day orally on an empty stomach to a maximum of 1 Gm./day for five days, is an effective chelating agent when oral medication can be given.

BARBITURATE POISONING

Treatment of barbiturate intoxication must be divided into two groups: (1) short-acting drugs, detoxified in the liver, e.g., pentobarbital, secobarbital; and (2) long-acting drugs, cleared via the kidneys, e.g., phenobarbital. The general symptoms are similar in both types and consist of drowsiness, ataxia, difficulty in thinking clearly, depression of spinal reflexes, respiratory depression, hypotension, and coma, which should be classified by the Reed Classification (Table 31-2).

Since histories are usually unreliable, treatment decisions based on estimated amount ingested may be risky. Any amount in excess of 10 to 15 mg./Kg. may produce more than therapeutic depression. Following suspected ingestion, close observation should be continued for four to six hours.

A. Short-Acting Drugs:
   1. Emesis, lavage, charcoal, and cathartics should be administered as under emergency treatment (see p. 571).
   2. Analeptic agents such as doxapram, nikethamide, caffeine, etc., are contraindicated in all cases.
   3. Respiratory assistance should be provided by respirator if necessary. Tidal volume of less than 10 to 15 ml./Kg. is inadequate.
   4. Hypotension is common and should be treated with fluids, plasma, etc. Vasopressors may be utilized if fluids are inadequate.
   5. Shock lung with pulmonary edema may occur and may require positive end-expiratory pressure.
   6. Forced diuresis is ineffective since less than 3% is excreted via this route. Fluids should be held to three-fourths of maintenance since cerebral edema may be a complication, especially following anoxia.
   7. Continuous monitoring of vital signs should be maintained until 24 hours of symptom-free time have elapsed and charcoal stools have been passed.

TABLE 31-2. Clinical classification of coma.
(After Reed.)

Symptoms	Class
Asleep, but can be aroused and can answer questions.	0
Comatose, does not withdraw from painful stimuli, reflexes intact.	1
Comatose, does not withdraw from painful stimuli, no respiratory or circulatory depression, most reflexes intact.	2
Comatose, most or all reflexes absent but without depression of respiration or circulation.	3
Comatose, reflexes absent, respiratory depression with cyanosis, and circulatory failure or shock (or both).	4

8. Coma lasts approximately 10 hours for each milligram above the therapeutic level of 0.5 to 2 mg./100 ml.

B. Long-Acting Drugs:

1-5. As above.

6. Forced alkaline diuresis improves clearance by three times. Urine output should be 3 to 6 ml./Kg./hour, preferably 6 ml./ Kg./hour. Alkalinization may be performed with sodium bicarbonate to a urine pH greater than 7.5.

7. Hemodialysis may be useful if the patient is not responsive to the above procedures. It is rarely needed and should not be based on blood levels but rather on deteriorating clinical condition.

8. Therapeutic levels are 2 to 4 mg./100 ml., but patients with tolerance may have considerably higher levels without toxicity. Correlate levels with clinical status before utilizing them to classify severity of toxicity.

BELLADONNA DERIVATIVES
(Atropine and Scopolamine)

The belladonna alkaloids are parasympathetic depressants with variable C.N.S. effects. The patient complains of dryness of mouth, thirst, difficulty in swallowing, and blurring of vision. The physical signs include dilated pupils, flushed skin, tachycardia, fever, delirium, delusions, weakness, and stupor. Symptoms are rapid in onset but may last for long periods because they delay gastric emptying.

Treatment.
Provide emergency emesis as outlined on p. 574. Physostigmine, 0.5 to 2 mg. I.V., dramatically reverses the central and peripheral effects of belladonna alkaloids. Forced diuresis is ineffective with the synthetic alkaloids.

BORIC ACID

Toxicity can result from ingestion or absorption through inflamed skin. Manifestations include severe gastroenteritis, C.N.S. irritation, and fiery red rash (toxic epidermal necrolysis). Shock, convulsions, coma, and death may follow.
Note: There is no justification for keeping boric acid solution or powder where infants and children can be accidentally exposed to it. This drug has no medical value.

Treatment.
Gastric lavage or induced emesis (or both) is the immediate therapy. Supportive therapy (for ingestion or absorption) includes maintenance of fluid and electrolyte balance and circulation.
Excretion of ingested or absorbed boric acid can be facilitated with exchange transfusion, hemodialysis, or peritoneal dialysis.

CARBON MONOXIDE

This gas combines with hemoglobin to form carboxyhemoglobin, which fails to carry oxygen and results in tissue anoxia. Levels of carboxyhemoglobin can be easily measured, and they correlate well with degree of toxicity. The patient is asymptomatic with levels of 10 to 20%; 20 to 30% indicates mild symptoms, 30 to 40% moderate, and 40 to 50% severe symptoms. Symptoms are more severe if the patient has exercised or taken alcohol or resides at high altitudes. Symptoms consist of headache, lethargy, depressed sensorium, nausea, vomiting, and occasionally seizures. After prolonged exposure, psychotic behavior may be noted. A bright cherry-red color is typical of blood with high levels of carboxyhemoglobin. Although said to be characteristic of carbon monoxide poisoning, cherry-red lips are rarely seen in living patients. The lips are usually dusky.

Treatment.

Therapy consists of exposure to air and administration of oxygen. The half-life of carboxyhemoglobin is 40 minutes in 100% oxygen and 180 minutes in air. Delayed effects are not uncommon and are reflective of anoxia. SGOT, CPK, etc. will be elevated, and variable C.N.S. effects will be seen, with residual effects depending upon the degree of anoxia.

CYANIDE

Cyanide specifically inhibits the cytochrome oxidase system, causing cellular anoxia. The onset of symptoms after ingestion or inhalation is rapid. Symptoms include giddiness, hyperpnea, headache, palpitation, and unconsciousness. The breath may smell of bitter almonds. Poisoning may be caused in children by the ingestion of relatively few (five to ten) bitter almonds. Death usually occurs in 15 minutes unless treatment is immediate.

Treatment.

Initially, inhalation of one ampule of amyl nitrite for 30 seconds of every minute produces 5% methemoglobinemia, which binds cyanide better than hemoglobin. Cyanide kits (Lilly) contain material and directions for therapy; dosage given is for adults, and children should receive proportionately less. Intravenous sodium nitrite is given first, followed by sodium thiosulfate. The pediatric dose is 10 mg./Kg. (0.33 ml./Kg.) of 3% sodium nitrite I.V. (2 to 5 ml./minute, which produces approximately 30% methemoglobinemia), followed by 50 ml. of 25% sodium thiosulfate I.V., which then produces a harmless thiocyanate. Oxygen should be administered.

DETERGENTS

Fatalities due to poisoning with anionic and nonionic detergents have not been reported. However, the detergents used in the household may contain alkalies. Cationic detergents are common antiseptics (Diaparene®, Zephiran®, etc.), and acute poisoning can cause gastroenteritis, convulsions, burns, and strictures.

Treatment.

Dilution with water or, preferably, milk is the primary treatment of cationic (quaternary ammonium) detergents followed by esophagoscopy and definitive care if burns are detected.

Anionic and nonionic detergents generally cause emesis but have no toxicity other than gastroenteritis.

FERROUS SULFATE

Accidental ferrous sulfate poisoning may be toxic in amounts as low as 60 mg./Kg. of elemental iron. Five phases of intoxication are described: (1) Hemorrhagic gastroenteritis shortly after ingestion (30 to 120 minutes). Shock due to blood loss may be present. (2) Recovery phase lasting from two to 12 hours after ingestion. (3) Delayed shock may occur 12 to 24 hours after ingestion and may be due to a vasodepressant action of ferritin or unbound ionic iron. (4) Liver damage with onset at three to five days. (5) Delayed gastric obstruction, usually at three weeks after ingestion.

The history is the most important diagnostic clue. X-ray of the abdomen may show the radiopaque tablets in the gastrointestinal tract. Laboratory determination of serum iron and total iron binding capacity allows calculation of free iron, an excess of which is diagnostic.

Treatment.

Remove by induced vomiting and lavage with a large bore tube and saline cathartic. Sodium bicarbonate left in the stomach may decrease absorption. Supportive measures (blood, plasma, saline, and vasopressors as indicated) are imperative. Exchange transfusion may be useful if the patient does not respond to standard measures. Deferoxamine (Desferal®) is useful in severe intoxications. The dose is 15 mg./Kg./hour as a drip - not a push - during the first 12 to 24 hours. As long as chelation occurs, the urine shows a reddish "vin rose" color.

FLEA BITES, FLY BITES; YELLOW JACKET, WASP, BEE, AND HORNET STINGS

These insects produce a small wheal with a small red dot in the center and cause only itching in most older children and adults. However, in young children and in some hypersensitive children there may be an allergic response of two types: (1) Local, with intense swelling and itching and a large wheal; or (2) systemic, in which miliaria-like or papular urticaria may appear over other areas of skin (small, hard, blanched or pink papules resembling a vesicle but not easily ruptured). A generalized reaction may occur, with fever and intense swelling at the site of the bite, as well as anaphylactic shock with respiratory and circulatory compromise.

Prevention.

Flea or bee antigens may be of value when given to children who are bitten frequently and develop severe reactions. Patients with known severe reactions should carry a kit containing epinephrine on an outing.

Treatment.

Treatment is seldom indicated. An excessive local reaction may be treated with anesthetic ointment. For systemic reactions, antihistamines should be given orally or, if necessary, parenterally. Epinephrine, 0.05 to 0.5 ml. subcut., or hydrocortisone I.V. may be lifesaving for anaphylactic reaction to bee sting.

FLUORIDES

Fluorides are found in agricultural poisons and insect powders. Clinical features include nausea, vomiting, colicky abdominal pain, diarrhea, cyanosis, excitement, and convulsions. A variable rash may be present, and fever may be significant.

Treatment.

Give calcium chloride, calcium gluconate, or milk in large quantities, 10 to 15 ml./Kg. orally. Induced vomiting or gastric lavage with a large bore tube should be employed. Calcium gluconate, 10%, should be injected slowly I.V. as necessary, and repeated if tetany occurs. Support respiration and treat shock. Give sodium sulfate, 15 to 30 Gm. in 100 to 200 ml of water, as cathartic orally.

GLUE SNIFFING

Toluene was the most common organic solvent used in "glue sniffing," but it has largely been replaced by nontoxic substances. Most frequently, it causes blurred vision, lack of coordination, hallucinations, and renal tubular acidosis.

Treatment.

Eliminate exposure to the solvent. Conservative management is indicated. Epinephrine should not be used, since it may have an adverse effect on a sensitized myocardium.

HALLUCINOGENS*

Marihuana has stimulant, depressant, and hallucinogenic properties, but usually the depressant properties predominate. Euphoria, mood swings, and distortion of time and space commonly occur. Performance skills may be affected. Panic states or psychotic reactions are uncommon.

LSD (lysergic acid diethylamide) causes euphoria, mood swings, loss of inhibitions, and depersonalization. Flashbacks (recurrence of initial effects), panic states, and hallucinations occur in some individuals.

---

*Amphetamines, barbiturates, belladonna derivatives, glue sniffing, narcotics, tranquilizers, and tricyclic antidepressants are discussed under individual headings.

DMT (dimethyltryptamine) is a short-acting drug which primarily produces excitation and exhilaration.

STP (2, 5-dimethoxy-4-methylamphetamine) is a long-acting hallucinogen which causes euphoria, confusion, and hallucinations.

Mescaline typically produces nausea, vomiting, exhilaration, anxiety, and hallucinations. Mescaline ingestion can sometimes mimic appendicitis.

PCP (phencyclidine) is a veterinary anesthetic which causes a marked paranoid state, hallucinations, and sometimes self-destructive behavior.

Psilocybin causes nausea, vomiting, headaches, and hallucinations.

Many samples of street drugs supposedly containing one of these agents may contain another.

Treatment.

Patients ingesting hallucinogens must often be treated without identification of the specific drug used. Histories are often unreliable. Although most of the commonly abused drugs cannot be readily identified in biological fluids by standard laboratories, the following can be identified in urine: mescaline, amphetamine, belladonna alkaloids, and tricyclic antidepressants. Others may be identified by laboratories dealing with forensic cases. Patients ingesting any of these drugs can have hallucinations.

Most patients ingesting hallucinogens are brought to the emergency room because of panic states or uncontrollable hyperactivity. In many cases, the only treatment required is reassurance ("talking the patient down") and placement in a neutral environmental setting. Physical restraints usually do more harm than good. Sometimes diazepam (Valium®) is helpful in controlling hyperactivity. Chlorpromazine may cause marked hypotension if STP, MDA, or DMT has been ingested and should not be used unless hard evidence exists that these have **not** been ingested. In planning long-term management of drug abusers, it should be remembered that drug abuse is a symptom, not a disease. Although serious questions have been raised, there is no conclusive evidence that LSD or other hallucinogens cause permanent chromosomal damage or birth defects in humans.

LEAD: See p. 380.

LYE AND BLEACHES

Ingestion of lye and bleaches may result in ulceration and perforation of the gastrointestinal tract and in long-term complications of stricture of the esophagus. Burns in the mouth indicate an absolute need for esophagoscopy, but many patients have been reported who have not sustained oral burns but have developed esophageal burns.

Treatment.

Avoid emetics. Dilute with water or, preferably, milk. Then order nothing by mouth and obtain assistance with esophagoscopy in the first 24 hours. Corticosteroids may be helpful and, if used, should be given early and continued for three weeks. Antibiotics are **not** indicated unless an infection is demonstrated. Give supportive therapy with sedation and analgesia as necessary. Intravenous nutrition and fluids may be necessary in early stages. Early tracheostomy may be indicated in cases of severe ingestion. See recommendations for Corrosive Acids.

MEPROBAMATE
(Miltown®, Equanil®)

Respiratory depression, coma, cardiac arrhythmia and, occasionally, convulsions associated with hyperexcitability occur. Death results from cardiac or respiratory failure. Severe metabolic acidosis with very rapid onset may occur.

Treatment.
Gastric lavage with a large bore tube should be performed. Recovering patients may relapse and die from delayed absorption of the drug; thus, charcoal and cathartics must be administered (see pp. 571 and 574). Although supportive treatment may be sufficient in mild intoxications, hemodialysis or peritoneal dialysis and forced diuresis are indicated in severe cases, especially when they are unresponsive to standard therapy.

MERCURY

Acute symptoms of mercury poisoning include metallic taste, severe gastrointestinal irritation, and shock. Severe acidosis and leukocytosis occur. Delayed symptoms (after 12 hours) include a mercury gum line, lower nephron nephrosis, ulcerative colitis, hepatic damage, and shock. Chronic symptoms are those of gastrointestinal irritability, a blue-black gum line, salivation, stomatitis, nephrosis, and irritability. Acrodynia occurs in children following chronic exposure to small amounts of mercury, including topically applied medication.

Treatment.
Treat acute poisoning with dimercaprol (BAL) and penicillamine (Cuprimine®) as for arsenic poisoning.

MUSHROOMS

Mushrooms are responsible for rare deaths and somewhat more common nonfatal poisonings. However, a history of mushroom ingestion always arouses concern, which is intensified because some toxins present in mushrooms may not show their effects until many hours after ingestion and because it is often not known exactly what kind of fungus was ingested.

The most common intoxicating American species are delineated. Almost 90% of childhood accidental ingestions are nontoxic puffballs or nontoxic "little brown mushrooms." The services of a mycologist through a botanical garden must be obtained to determine exact identification.

Clinical Findings According to Type.

A. Bulb Agarics (Amanita verna [U.S.] or A. phalloides [U.S. and Europe]): Toxins are cyclopeptides. Vomiting and severe diarrhea occur after a latent period of six to 20 hours, followed by liver and kidney damage.

B. Fly Agarics (A. muscaria or A. pantherina): These fungi are variably toxic and may contain muscarine, in which case they will cause parasympathomimetic manifestations. At least as commonly, they contain an atropine isomer, in which case they cause the anticholinergic syndrome (see p. 580). Hallucinations may occur with either.

C. False Morels: These are variably toxic, causing hemolysis and gastrointestinal irritation. The toxin can sometimes be removed by cooking or drying.

D. Hallucinogens: Psilocybin, a serotonin congener, is the active principle of the ritual mushroom found in Mexico and has also been implicated in poisoning in a West Coast incident.

Treatment.

A. Induce emesis or lavage with a large bore orogastric tube. Save stomach contents for spore analysis.

B. Atropine sulfate, 50 μg./Kg. subcut. Stat. and then as required, should be used only if muscarinic signs appear. Discontinue if signs of atropine poisoning appear.

C. Specific therapy for other major groups is in a state of flux, and consultation should be obtained. Generally, supportive care may be instituted, but specific procedures are becoming available for the cyclopeptide group.

NARCOTICS

Intoxication with narcotics (e.g., morphine, codeine, and diphenoxylate [in Lomotil®]) produces respiratory depression, hypotension, pinpoint pupils, skeletal muscle relaxation, decreased urinary output, and occasionally shock. Additionally, propoxyphene (Darvon®) is associated with convulsions in 40 to 60% of cases of overdosage.

Treatment.

Acute overdosage is treated similarly to barbiturate intoxication. Respiratory assistance and maintenance of adequate blood pressure are mandatory. Naloxone (Narcan®), 5 μg./Kg., is an effective narcotic antagonist that does not cause respiratory depression and has no known toxicity even in overdosage. Nalorphine should no longer be used because it causes synergistic depression with barbiturates and may cause depression itself if used too frequently. Diazepam (Valium®) may be of value to reduce withdrawal symptoms in heroin abusers.

NITRITES AND NITRATES

Methemoglobin is produced by the administration of a nitrite compound or a nitrate which is converted to a nitrite in the large bowel. Sodium nitrite, food preservatives, phenacetin, home remedies such as spirits of nitre, and high concentrations of nitrite in water have been reported to cause production of methemoglobin. The onset may be gradual and symptoms may be deceiving. The color of the child gradually changes to an ashen gray. There are no specific clinical findings other than a weak, lethargic child with some respiratory and cardiac difficulty. Symptoms depend on the amount of available normal hemoglobin to carry oxygen but generally do not occur until approximately 30% of the hemoglobin has been converted to methemoglobin. A drop of patient's blood will appear brown compared to a drop of physician's blood dried on a filter paper at levels of 15% or greater.

Treatment.

Intravenous methylene blue allows electron transfer to reverse methemoglobinemia. A 1% solution is administered in the amount of 0.1 ml./Kg. and may be repeated 30 minutes later to reverse symptoms. Persistence of methemoglobinemia at high levels in a symptomatic patient is an indication for exchange transfusion. Laboratory determinations for methemoglobin are available. This is the only known condition in which a colorless solution (spirits of nitre) produces a gray baby with brown blood and a blue medication turns the child pink. The results of treatment are dramatic.

PETROLEUM DISTILLATE POISONING
(Including Kerosene, Paint Thinner, Charcoal Starter, Turpentine, and Related Products)

The petroleum distillates are mixtures of saturated and unsaturated hydrocarbons of the aliphatic and aromatic series. The following products are common causes of poisoning: Kerosene, light oils, turpentine and other pine products, gasoline, lighter fluid, insecticides with petroleum distillate bases, benzine, naphtha, and mineral spirits.

It is essential to remember that just a few drops aspirated into the pulmonary tree can cause a severe and fatal pneumonia, a complication to which infants and children are particularly prone. In fatal poisonings, death usually occurs in two to 24 hours. Studies in experimental animals suggest that significant pulmonary complications do not occur secondary to gastrointestinal absorption of kerosene.

Kerosene and other products are more likely to cause spontaneous emesis in about 90% of patients in one hour.

Pulmonary complications are reported with greater frequency among children who ingest kerosene or mineral seal oil than in those who ingest other petroleum distillate products with higher viscosity.

In general, ingestion of more than 1 oz. (30 ml.) of a petroleum distillate is associated with a higher incidence of C.N.S. complications. C.N.S. involvement is reported most frequently among patients who ingest light oils and kerosene. Lethargy is found in over 90% of patients with C.N.S. involvement; semicoma in 5%; coma in 3%; and convulsions in 1%.

Clinical Findings.

Ingestion of petroleum distillates causes local irritation with a burning sensation in the mouth, esophagus, and stomach; vomiting; and occasionally diarrhea with blood-tinged stools. With C.N.S. involvement there is lethargy, confusion, disorientation, semi-coma, coma, and death (usually due to respiratory arrest). Pulmonary involvement is usually indicated by cyanosis, rapid breathing, tachycardia, and fever. Basilar rales may rapidly progress to massive pulmonary edema or pneumonic hemorrhage, infiltration, and secondary infection. In severe poisoning there may be cardiac dilatation, hepatosplenomegaly, proteinuria, formed elements in the urine, and cardiac arrhythmias associated with congestive heart failure.

Treatment.

Although controversial, induced emesis is more effective in life-threatening ingestions and is less dangerous than gastric lavage. Gastric lavage should be performed only if a cuffed endotracheal tube is inserted because there is no such thing as a "careful gastric lavage" in children. If the amount ingested is small - a difficult thing to estimate in children - a saline cathartic is all that is necessary (see p. 568).

At the conclusion of the lavage, give a saline cathartic (e.g., sodium sulfate) in water.

For C.N.S. depression, supportive care is indicated. Do not give epinephrine as a stimulant because it may have adverse effects on the sensitized myocardium.

"Prophylactic" antibiotic therapy is of questionable value and does not speed resolution when pneumonitis exists. Oxygen and mist are helpful. Corticosteroids are probably useless and may be harmful. Hospitalization is only indicated if the child has taken a large amount or is symptomatic. Fever, etc. may continue for as long as ten days without infection, and pneumatoceles may develop three to five weeks after pneumonitis.

Withhold digestible fats, oils, and alcohol, which may promote absorption from the bowel or cause aspiration pneumonitis on their own.

The rapidity of recovery depends upon the degree of pulmonary involvement. Resolution may take as long as four weeks.

PHOSPHATES, ORGANIC
(Parathion, Malathion, TEPP, HEPT, etc.)

Many insecticides contain organic phosphates; parathion is one of the most toxic examples. All inhibit cholinesterase, resulting in parasympathetic and C.N.S. stimulation. Symptoms include headache, dizziness, blurred vision, diarrhea, abdominal pain, dyspnea, chest pain, bronchial constriction, pulmonary edema, respiratory failure, convulsions, cyanosis, coma, loss of reflexes and sphincter control, sweating, salivation, miosis, tearing, muscle fasciculations, and even generalized collapse.

Lowered red cell cholinesterase activity confirms the diagnosis.

Treatment.

The patient **must** be decontaminated with soapy water or tincture of green soap as soon as possible to prevent further absorption.

Complete atropinization is mandatory. Begin with 50 μg./Kg. I.V. in a small child and 1 to 2 mg. I.V. in an older child. Repeat every 15 to 30 minutes until dry mouth, mydriasis, and tachycardia appear. In addition, pralidoxime (2-PAM), 500 mg. I.V. injected slowly (over a five-minute period), should be given if symptoms are severe but may be delayed until confirmation of red cell cholinesterase depression has been confirmed. Repeated administration of atropine may be necessary for three to four days following the onset of illness. 2-PAM should be continued in accordance with instructions.

Supportive measures include oxygen, artificial respiration, postural drainage of secretions, and measures to combat shock.

RAUWOLFIA DERIVATIVES

Rauwolfia derivatives produce parasympathetic effects: nasal congestion, salivation, sweating, bradycardia, abdominal cramps, and diarrhea. Parkinsonian symptoms occasionally develop. Give supportive treatment and remove the poison by emesis and lavage.

RIOT CONTROL DRUGS

Several riot control drugs are now available. In general they consist of a chemical in a hydrocarbon solvent, such as kerosene, and in some cases a propellant, such as Freon® gas. The chemical agent typically causes lacrimation, photophobia, and, in some instances, nausea and vomiting. Skin sensitization and corneal scarring can occur, particularly when the chemical is released close to the victim's face or skin.

Treatment.

The most effective treatment is prompt removal from the sprayed area and careful decontamination of the patient. After removing all clothes, the patient should shower carefully, using copious amounts of soap and water. An ophthalmologist should examine the eyes for possible corneal damage. Medical personnel involved in decontamination should wear surgical scrub suits and should also shower with copious amounts of soap and water when the decontamination is completed.

SALICYLATES: See p. 67.

SCORPION STINGS

The toxin of the less venomous species of scorpions causes only local pain, redness, and swelling; that of the more venomous species causes generalized muscular pains, convulsions, nausea, vomiting, variable C.N.S. involvement, and collapse.

Treatment.

Keep the patient recumbent and quiet. Treatment of the wound is as for snake bite. If absorption has occurred, give a slow I. V. infusion. Hot baths and 20 ml. of 10% magnesium sulfate may be given I. V. for relief of pain. Provide adequate sedation and institute supportive measures. Hot compresses of sodium bicarbonate solution will relieve local pain if there is no systemic involvement. Corticotropin (ACTH) or the corticosteroids may be of value in severe cases.

SNAKE BITE

Snake venom may be neurotoxic or hemotoxic. Neurotoxin (cobra, coral snake) causes respiratory paralysis; hemotoxin (rattlesnake, copperhead, moccasin, pit viper) causes hemolysis, tissue destruction, and damage to the endothelial lining of the blood vessels. Manifestations consist of local pain, thirst, and nausea and vomiting, profuse perspiration, local swelling and redness, abdominal cramps, urticaria, dilated pupils, stimulation followed by depression, extravasation of blood, respiratory difficulty, muscle weakness, hemorrhage, and circulatory collapse.

Note: Seventy percent of snake bites do not result in envenomation. Crotalid bites can be expected to show local hemorrhage if envenomation occurred.

Treatment.

Keep the patient recumbent and quiet. Treat shock or respiratory failure with all available means. A tourniquet that occludes venous and lymphatic return should be applied, although its value is questionable. (If envenomation of the arterial tree is suspected or if prolonged delay in definitive treatment is unavoidable, the tourniquet should completely occlude arterial supply.) The tourniquet should be left on until antivenin is given. Release of the tourniquet prior to administration of the antivenin can cause shock and death. It is better to lose a limb than a life.

Immobilize the bitten part in a dependent position if possible. The value of ice packs is very dubious and, if prolonged, may cause frostbite. Incision for suction is probably useless. With compromise of circulation due to swelling of a limb, a joint-to-joint splitting fasciotomy may be used.

Administer polyvalent horse serum antivenin (Wyeth Laboratories) or coral snake antivenin (available from Charity Hospital, New Orleans) as indicated. A skin test should be performed first. The first dose should be large; the smaller the victim, the larger the dose. Three to five vials (10 ml. each) may be required in a 20 to 40 lb. child. Seven to ten have been given as the first dose. Inject the dose I. M. If the patient is seen late, antivenin may be given I.V. diluted in 5% dextrose in water. An additional vial of antivenin should be given every one to two hours if swelling or pain continues to progress. Concurrent administration of corticosteroids may lessen the risks associated with administration of the antivenin. A dosage of 1 Gm. of hydrocortisone sodium succinate (Solu-Cortef®) initially is suggested. Cortisone, 50 to 100 mg. every six to eight hours, is helpful.

Give supportive measures (fluids, sedatives) and tetanus and gas gangrene prophylaxis as indicated. Transfusions may be necessary to counteract hemotoxic venom.

SPIDER BITES

Black Widow Spider.

The bite of a female black widow spider (Latrodectus mactans) causes pain at the site of injection. Clinical manifestations include generalized muscular pains with severe abdominal cramps, irritability, nausea and vomiting, variable C. N. S. symptoms, profuse perspiration, labored breathing, and collapse. Convulsions may occur, especially in children.

Examination reveals a small papule at the area of the bite, board-like rigidity of the abdomen, restlessness, and hyperactive deep reflexes.

Keep the patient recumbent and quiet. Antivenin (Latrodectus mactans), 2.5 ml. I. M., repeated in one hour if symptoms have not markedly improved, although traditional, may not be of value and should be reserved for seriously symptomatic patients. Morphine or codeine may help control pain. Keep the child recumbent and quiet with adequate sedation. A tetanus toxoid booster should be given to the previously immunized child if a booster has not been given in four years, and antitoxin to the nonimmunized. Corticosteroids may relieve symptoms. Ten percent calcium gluconate I. V. may reduce muscle irritability and may be repeated as needed. Diazepam, 0.1 mg./Kg./dose, may decrease muscle spasm.

Brown Spider.

The North American brown recluse spider (violin spider, Loxosceles reclusus) is most commonly seen in the central and midwestern areas of the U. S. A. Its bite characteristically produces a localized reaction with progressively more severe pain within eight hours. The initial bleb on an erythematous ischemic base is replaced by a black eschar within a week. Systemic signs include cyanosis, a morbilliform rash, fever, chills, malaise, weakness, nausea and vomiting, joint pains, hemolytic reactions with hemoglobinuria, jaundice, and delirium.

There is no specific antivenin. Hydrocortisone, 1 Gm./24 hours I.V., is indicated for systemic complications. Hydroxyzine (Vistaril®), 1 mg./Kg./day orally, is reported to be useful for its muscle relaxant, antihistaminic, and tranquilizing effects. The advisability of total excision of the lesion at the fascial level to minimize necrosis is debatable but should not be delayed if circulatory compromise occurs as a result of swelling.

TRANQUILIZERS
(Phenothiazine Compounds)

Phenothiazine compounds produce extrapyramidal motor symptoms (opisthotonos, oculogyric crisis, torticollis, trismus, rigidity) and convulsions. Diphenhydramine (Benadryl®), 10 to 25 mg. I.V. or orally, or other antiparkinsonism drugs may dramatically reverse the extrapyramidal symptoms.

This therapy is **not** helpful in cases where overdosage of phenothiazine produces C.N.S. and respiratory depression. Only supportive measures are indicated in these situations and emergency treatment (p. 571) should be followed.

TRICYCLIC ANTIDEPRESSANTS
(Imipramine [Tofranil®], Amitriptyline [Elavil®], Nortriptyline [Aventyl®], Doxepin [Sinequan®], etc.)

This group of drugs characteristically causes cardiac arrhythmias, central nervous system abnormalities (agitation, hallucinations, seizures, and coma), and other signs of atropinism such as dilated pupils, malar flushing, dry mouth, hyperpyrexia, and urinary retention.

Treatment.

Give 0.5 mg. of physostigmine salicylate intravenously over two minutes. This dose may be repeated every five minutes until a total dose of 2 mg. has been given. Repeated doses at 20- to 30-minute intervals may be necessary because the drug is rapidly metabolized. The lowest effective dose should be given, and the drug should only be used to control convulsions, severe coma, hallucinations, and arrhythmias. Physostigmine may be repeated as indicated. Sodium bicarbonate administration is also helpful in correcting and preventing recurrence of cardiac arrhythmias.

32...
Pediatric Procedures*

INTRAVENOUS THERAPY†

Gravity Method.

For most infants and children a gravity apparatus or special equipment (Vacoset® to deliver fluids slowly and Pedatrol® which permits controlled administration of fluid) is best for giving large amounts of fluid slowly over a long period. Fluids are best administered through a No. 21 or 23 gauge needle.

A. Site: For small infants, a scalp vein or one on the wrist, hand, foot, or arm will usually be most convenient (see Fig 32-1). Any accessible vein may be used in an older child. If vein can not be entered, blood may be given intraperitoneally in an emergency.

B. Equipment: A gravity apparatus is used with a closed drip bulb in the tubing not far below the container, so it will hang perpendicularly. The bulb should be one-fourth to one-third full and the tubing below it free of air. Flow is regulated by a screw clamp on the tubing or the clamp which comes with special I.V. tubing.

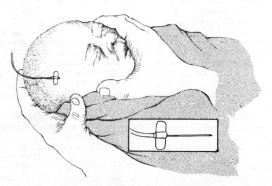

FIG 32-1. Intravenous fluids into scalp vein.

---

*Revised by Ronald W. Gotlin, MD.
†Note: Catheterization of vessels is associated with an increased risk of thrombosis of large vessels. Infusion via large vessel catheters should not be used as a substitute for infusion into peripheral veins for fluid therapy.

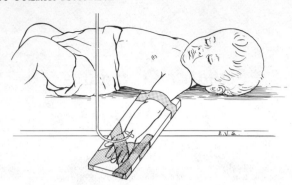

FIG 32-2. Intravenous fluids into wrist vein.

C. Technic: Use a Pediatric Scalp Vein Infusion Set (Cutter) with
a 21 gauge needle and rubber finger grip connected to plastic
tubing or a short No. 21 to 24 gauge needle. Tape the needle
firmly in place. Sandbags will be useful in holding the head and
sandbags or a padded board for the extremities.

D. Rate: A rate of 15 drops per minute from an ordinary I. V.
setup with a No. 21 needle will deliver about 60 ml./hour and
1440 ml. in 24 hours. The Vacoset® can be regulated to deliver 1 drop per minute (1 ml./hour). Microdrop bulbs which
deliver 60 drops/ml. (number of drops administered/minute =
ml./hour) are of value when small volumes are being given.

E. Precaution: The rate of flow should be checked frequently. An
accurate record must be kept of the amount of fluid added. For
small infants (particularly if premature), never have more
than one-third of daily fluid requirements in container at any
one time. Phlebitis usually develops after a few days. It is
best to remove the needle and change location each 48 to 72
hours. If possible, avoid hypertonic solutions.

For greater comfort for the patient receiving fluids in an
extremity, use foam rubber to maintain the limb in a position
of comfort. Inspect the limb at regular intervals for evidence
of undue pressure and circulatory embarrassment.

Pump Method.

In small infants, veins may be too small for the administration
of fluids by the gravity method despite maximum elevation of reserve bottle; in these cases the solution can be pumped in slowly by
syringe. In the neonate, a precision-controlled infusion pump
(Howard) is helpful.

A. Equipment: Most convenient for this purpose is a setup with a
pediatric scalp vein needle and catheter connected to a three-
way stopcock.

B. Technic: One operator enters the vein and holds or tapes the
scalp vein needle in place. A second person pumps the solution in by a syringe on the stopcock inserted farther up the

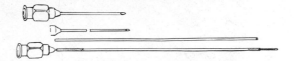

FIG 32-3. Intravenous needle and flexible polyethylene tubing.

tubing. If only one person is available, he can pump from the
stopcock after taping the scalp vein needle in place and restraining the limb.
C. Amount: 20-30 ml./Kg. body wt. (except blood and plasma;
see p. 18) **slowly** over the course of several minutes.

Cut-Down Intravenous.

For small infants or if fluids are urgently needed by a seriously ill older child and difficulty is encountered in entering a vein,
expose a vein surgically and tie in a piece of polyethylene tubing, or
enter the vein subcutaneously with a plastic catheter equipped with
an inner needle stylet.
A. Site: The internal saphenous vein running anterior to the medial
   malleolus of the tibia to a groove between the upper medial end
   of the tibia and the calf muscle will be found the most satisfactory. It can be entered at any point along its course. Hence, by
   starting at the ankle, the same vein can be used two or three
   times if necessary.
B. Equipment:
   1. Sterile solution, container, tubing, drip bulb, and clamp
      are prepared as for continuous venoclysis (see p. 593).
   2. Thin polyethylene tubing with the end cut on the slant is
      easiest to use and least irritating. A No. 19 gauge tubing
      is preferred, but tubing as small as No. 22 may be used.
C. Technic:
   1. Preparation - Apply tourniquet, sterilize the skin and drape
      the leg as for a surgical procedure, using sterile precau-
      tions. The foot can be securely taped to a sandbag or board

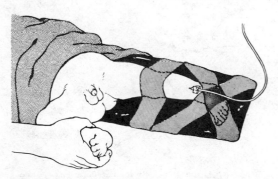

FIG 32-4. Intravenous fluids into ankle vein.

FIG 32-5. Position and taping of leg for cut-down incision.

splint (see Fig 32-5). Make a large wheal with 1 or 2% procaine solution in the skin over the vein.

2. Incision - With a scalpel, make an incision about 1 cm. long
   just through the skin. The incision should be at a right angle
   to the direction of the vein. Using a small, curved, sharp-
   pointed scissors or fine forceps, spread the incision widely.
3. Identifying the vein - Usually the vein is seen lying on the
   fascia. Some dissection of subcutaneous fat may be necessary. Insert curved clamp to periosteum and bring vein to
   the surface. Be certain it is a vein, not a nerve or tendon,
   by noting the flow of blood. Using a small hook or hemostat
   (e.g., strabismus hook), dissect the vein free for a length of
   1.5 to 2.5 cm. In small infants the vein is small and fragile,
   and great care must be taken in handling it (see Fig 32-6).
4. Placing ties - Using No. 00 black silk, tie the vein off at
   the extreme distal (lower) end of the exposed portion. Leave
   the ends of the suture long so that they may be used later for
   traction. At the proximal end of the vein, loop a piece of

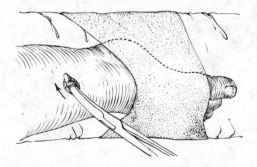

FIG 32-6. Isolation of vein for cut-down intravenous.

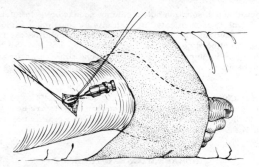

FIG 32-7. Cut-down intravenous with ligatures tied.

suture loosely around the vein (see Fig 32-7).
5. Nicking the vein - Using a fine-pointed scissors, sterile razor blade, or sharp-pointed scalpel blade, make a small incision through the wall of the vein a few mm. above the lower ligature. Make certain that the lumen has been entered by lifting the vein on the handle of the hook or other instrument used so as to flatten it and draw it taut. Release tourniquet after tubing is in the vein.
6. Fixing the cannula - Insert the polyethylene tubing for a distance of 2 cm. Blood will usually drip from it; if not, note whether a small amount of the solution can be injected easily with a syringe and rubber adapter without producing a wheal. Tie the upper proximal suture firmly around the vein and tubing to hold it in place. Connect the tubing from the reservoir of fluid to the polyethylene tubing in the vein with care to avoid pulling and tearing the vein.
7. Closing the wound - Close the wound with fine silk sutures which are removed in three to four days. The tubing must be firmly strapped in place. When using a needle or cannula, a pad of gauze under the hilt will keep it in alignment with the vein. Cover the wound with gauze and roller bandage. Do not restrain foot so as to interfere with adequate circulation or to cause pressure sores.

HYPODERMOCLYSIS

For Small Infants.
A. Site: For small infants, hypodermoclysis may be given by syringe, using the subcutaneous tissues of the axillas, upper back, thighs, or lower abdomen. In most instances the intravenous route is preferred, since hypodermoclysis may cause a marked shift in body fluids.
B. Equipment: A 20 or 50 ml. syringe and a No. 20 gauge needle.
C. Technic: **Caution:** Use only isotonic solutions. Inject slowly; if the center of the injected area becomes pale, change the position of the needlepoint. Gentle massage will help to diffuse the fluid into the tissues. (Hyaluronidase may be used to facilitate

spread and absorption but is seldom necessary.) In infants, up
to 50 ml. can be injected in each site at one time. Rigid aseptic precautions are necessary. The infant must be restrained
to prevent bending or breaking the needle.

D. Dose: 30 to 40 ml./Kg. body wt. at one time. Larger amounts
can be given over a longer period by a gravity apparatus with
a Y-tube and two needles.

For Older Children.

For older children, fluids by hypodermoclysis are best given
slowly in the outer aspect of the mid-thigh by a gravity apparatus,
using a Y-tube and two needles.

INTRAPERITONEAL THERAPY

Isotonic fluids and blood may be administered by the intraperitoneal route, but the intravenous route is generally preferred.

VENIPUNCTURE

The antecubital, femoral, and external or internal jugular veins
are used most frequently for venipuncture and withdrawal of blood.
In some instances, blood may be withdrawn from other veins in the
extremities.

Large, accessible veins are best for purposes of injection and
for the withdrawal of considerable quantities of blood. **Caution:** Do
not inject materials into internal jugular, sagittal sinus, or other
deep veins.

The skin should be cleansed thoroughly with soap and water and
a disinfectant (e.g., an iodinated organic compound or isopropyl
alcohol). In an uncooperative patient, the use of a catheter between
the needle and the syringe will facilitate entry into the vein.

Antecubital Vein Puncture.

If available, this is the best vein for the purpose of venipuncture
in larger infants and children and is often easily entered even in the
neonate.

Femoral Vein Puncture.

Caution: This is a hazardous procedure, particularly in the
neonate, and should be employed only in emergencies.

Place the child on a flat, firm table. Abduct the leg so as to
expose the inguinal region. Use strict sterile precautions.

Locate the femoral artery by its pulsation. The vein lies immediately medial to it. Be certain of the position of the femoral
pulse at the time of puncture. Insert a short-beveled needle into
the vein (perpendicularly to the skin) about 3 cm. below the inguinal
ligament; use the artery as a guide (see Fig 32-8). If blood does
not enter the syringe immediately, withdraw the needle slowly,
drawing gently on the barrel of the syringe; the needle sometimes
passes through both walls of the vein, and blood is obtained only
when the needle is being withdrawn. Use a 10 to 20 ml. syringe to
produce adequate suction to withdraw blood.

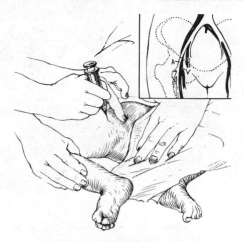

FIG 32-8. Femoral vein puncture.

After removing the needle, exert firm, steady pressure over the vein for three to five minutes. If the artery has been entered, check the limb periodically even longer. If blanching of the extremity occurs, the application of heat may be of value.

Great care should be exercised in cleansing the skin prior to the venipuncture so as to decrease the risk of osteomyelitis and arthritis of adjacent structures.

External Jugular Vein Puncture.

Wrap the child firmly so that arms and legs are adequately restrained. The wraps should not extend higher than the shoulder girdle. Place the child on a flat, firm table so that both shoulders

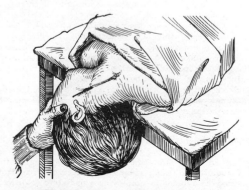

FIG 32-9. External jugular puncture.

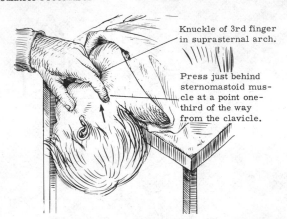

Knuckle of 3rd finger in suprasternal arch.

Press just behind sternomastoid muscle at a point one-third of the way from the clavicle.

FIG 32-10. Direction of needle for internal jugular puncture.

are touching the table; the head is rotated fully to one side and extended partly over the end of the table so as to stretch the vein (see Fig 32-9). Adequate immobilization is essential.

Use a very sharp No. 21 or 23 gauge needle for withdrawing blood. The child should be crying and the vein distended when entered. First thrust the needle just under the skin; then enter the vein. Pull constantly on the barrel of the syringe and be certain that air is not drawn into the vein during aspiration.

After removing the needle, exert firm pressure over the vein for three to five minutes while the child is in a sitting position.

Internal Jugular Vein Puncture. (See Fig 32-10.)
Prepare the child as for an external jugular vein puncture (see Fig 32-9). Insert needle beneath the sternocleidomastoid muscle at a point marking the junction of its lower and middle thirds. Aim at the suprasternal notch and advance the needle until the vein is entered. Avoid the trachea and the upper pleural space. Do not use this method in the presence of a hemorrhagic diathesis.

If no blood is obtained on inserting the needle, withdraw slowly and continue to pull on the barrel of the syringe. Not infrequently the needle passes through both walls of the vein and blood is obtained only when the needle is being withdrawn.

After completing the procedure, remove the needle and exert firm pressure over the area for three to five minutes with the child in a sitting position so as to reduce pressure in the vein.

COLLECTION OF MULTIPLE SPECIMENS OF BLOOD

When a number of simultaneous samples must be obtained over a short period of time (e.g., glucose tolerance test), multiple venipunctures may be avoided by employing a pediatric scalp vein infusion needle. The needle is inserted in an arm or hand vein in the usual manner (see p. 593) and a two- or three-way stopcock is inserted into the catheter end. A syringe is used to fill the system with normal saline or heparinized saline (10 units per ml.) and the stopcock is closed. Blood may be withdrawn at intervals by applying a tourniquet, opening the stopcock, and drawing off and discarding the saline solution. A syringe is then used to obtain the desired quantity of blood. The line is subsequently cleaned with saline and the stopcock is closed until the next specimen is needed.

EXCHANGE TRANSFUSION FOR ERYTHROBLASTOSIS FETALIS

After adequate preparation of the infant (respirations and temperature stabilized and maintained, gastric contents removed, proper restraint, humidified oxygen being administered), drape the umbilical area. Cut off the cord about one-half inch or less from the skin. Control any bleeding. Identify vein (the two arteries are white and cordlike; the single vein is larger and thin-walled). If the vein cannot be visualized in the cord stump, make a small transverse incision above the umbilicus. Cannulate vein gently (usually to a distance of 6 to 8 cm.) with polyethylene tubing. Determine venous pressure and maintain below 10 cm. with the child at rest.

Employing sterile packaged equipment specifically prepared for this procedure, remove 10 to 20 ml. of blood at a time (save for laboratory studies) and replace with an equivalent amount of fresh heparinized blood or blood preserved with anticoagulant acid-citrate-dextrose (ACD) less than five days old. Use type-specific or Group O Rh-negative blood to which A and B soluble substances may be added. Give twice the blood volume (blood volume = approximately 85 to 100 ml./Kg.) for a "complete" exchange. When the infant is severely affected, a full exchange should not be attempted immediately after birth. Instead, small doses of sedimented erythrocytes should be given, alternating with slow withdrawal of the infant's blood until the venous pressure is less than 10 cm. water. Determine pulse rate every 20 ml. and venous pressure every 100 ml. exchanged; if venous pressure is elevated or if hemorrhagic manifestations or respiratory distress develop, gradually establish a deficit (10 to 100 ml.). If the infant becomes irritable, administer calcium gluconate, 1 to 2 ml. of 10% solution, slowly through the polyethylene tubing (rinsing tubing with saline solution before and after the drug is introduced). Do not give any further calcium if there is slowing of the pulse. Stop exchange if irritability, changes in respiration, yawning, pallor, or cyanosis develop. If signs of distress do not disappear, discontinue the exchange. Cardiac arrest occasionally occurs and should be treated with tracheal intubation and the administration of oxygen by artificial ventilation; closed chest massage; intravenous or intracardiac sodium bicarbonate to correct acidosis; and supportive measures as indicated. If ACD blood is used, buffering it with 10 ml. of 1 to 1.2 M. tromethamine immediately prior to transfusion may be of value to prevent severe acidosis. If heparinized blood is used, give protamine sulfate, 0.5 to 1 mg. I.M., at the termination of the exchange transfusion. Prophylactic postexchange antibiotics are recommended by some.

OBTAINING SPINAL FLUID

When making a puncture for spinal fluid, the lumbar area should be used whenever possible.

Lumbar Puncture in Children and Older Infants.

Restrain the patient in the lateral recumbent position on a firm, flat table (see Fig 32-11). Draw an imaginary line between the two iliac crests and use the intervertebral space immediately above or below this line. Prepare the skin surrounding this area as for a surgical procedure with iodine and alcohol or other suitable antiseptic.

Scrub and wear sterile gloves. Drape area with sterile towels. Infiltrate the skin and subcutaneous tissues with 1% procaine (not necessary in infants and young children).

Insert lumbar puncture needle with stilet in place (see Fig 32-12) just below the vertebral spine in the midline (use short No. 21 to 23 gauge needle for infants; long No. 21 for older children). Keep the needle perpendicular to both planes of the back, or pointing a little towards the head. A distinct "give" is usually felt when the dura is pierced; if in doubt remove the stylet to watch for fluid.

Cardiorespiratory function should be monitored throughout the procedure.

Lumbar Puncture in Small Infants.

For small infants lumbar puncture may be performed at the level of the superior iliac crests with the patient in a sitting position and leaning forward. C.S.F. may flow very slowly, and the "give" may not be felt in small infants. Gentle aspiration with a small syringe may be necessary.

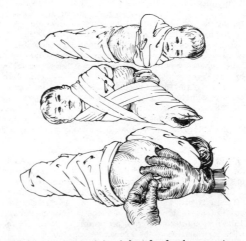

FIG 32-11. Restraining infant for lumbar puncture.

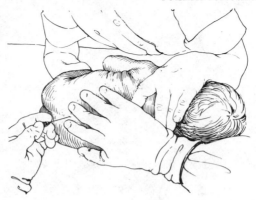

FIG 32-12. Lumbar puncture with assistance of nurse.

Cisternal Puncture.

Although lumbar puncture is generally preferable, cisternal puncture may be used to advantage for drainage and treatment when there is a block below this level. Cisternal puncture is easier than lumbar puncture in the patient with marked opisthotonos, and there is less danger of medullary impaction when the intracranial pressure is high. However, the needle may pierce and damage vital centers in the medulla, and arterial damage with hemorrhage into the cistern or fourth ventricle may be fatal. Whenever possible, use the lumbar route instead.

Hold the patient in the lateral recumbent position on a firm, flat table. Place a folded sheet or small firm pillow under his head to bring the cervical spine in line with the thoracic, with the whole spine horizontal. Use sterile precautions. Hold the patient very firmly if not fully cooperative, with the neck strongly flexed.

Insert a long No. 21 gauge lumbar puncture needle immediately below the suboccipital notch and stay in the sagittal plane, i. e., parallel to the table surface, aiming toward a line drawn between the two external auditory meatuses. The forward progress of the needle must be under complete control by having one fingertip of the carrying hand resting firmly against the patient's neck or head. A distinct "give" will usually be felt and perhaps heard when the needle pierces the dura. Do not go any farther. If in doubt at any stage, withdraw the stylet to see if any fluid appears. If none appears, withdraw the needle and make a fresh start.

Subdural Puncture.

Shave the anterior two-thirds of the scalp. Use sterile precautions as for any surgical procedures. Restrain the child in the position shown in Fig 32-13.

Insert a short No. 19 or 21 gauge lumbar puncture needle with a very short bevel for a distance of 0.2 to 0.5 cm. at the extreme lateral corner of the fontanel or farther out through the suture line, depending on the size of the fontanel. Piercing the tough dura is

FIG 32-13. Subdural puncture.

easily recognized. Normally not more than a few drops (up to 1 ml.)
of clear fluid are obtained. If a subdural hematoma is present, the
fluid will be grossly xanthochromic or bloody and more abundant.
For children over two in whom the fontanel has closed, a trephine
opening usually is necessary.

Repeat the procedure on the other side. Do not remove more
than 10 to 15 ml. of fluid at any one time.

Remove the needle, exert firm pressure for a few minutes,
and apply a sterile collodion dressing.

BODY CAVITY PUNCTURES

Thoracentesis.

Used for removing pleural fluid for diagnosis or treatment, to
inject antibiotics in cases of empyema, or to induce pneumothorax.

A. Site: Locate the fluid by physical examination and by x-ray if
necessary. If entering at the base, locate the bottom of the
opposite uninvolved lung as a guide so the puncture will not be
below the pleural cavity.

B. Dangers: Introduction of a new infection, pneumothorax and/or
hemothorax from tearing of the lung, hemoptysis, syncope
(pleuropulmonary reflex or air embolus), and pulmonary
edema (from too rapid removal of large amounts of fluid).
None of these are common if reasonable care is taken. If the
patient starts to cough, the needle should be removed.

C. Equipment: Use a No. 18 to 19 gauge needle with a very short
bevel and a sharp point. The needle and a 10 or 20 ml. syringe
are attached to a three-way stopcock (10 ml. syringe is easier).
If much fluid is to be removed, it can be pumped through a

rubber tube attached to the side arm of the stopcock, thereby avoiding leakage of air into the pleural space.

D. Procedure: The patient should sit up, if possible, with a bed-stand or chairback to lean against. If too ill to sit up, he can lie on his uninvolved side on a firm flat surface with a small pillow under his chest to widen the upper interspaces.

Use strict sterile precautions; scrub and wear sterile gloves. Prepare the skin surgically and use suitable drapes, preferably a large drape with a hole in the center. Infiltrate with 1% procaine, into the skin and down to the pleura.

Insert the needle in an interspace, passing just above the edge of the rib. The intercostal vessels lie immediately below each rib. Usually it is not difficult to know when the pleura is pierced, but suction on the needle at any stage will show whether or not fluid has been reached. In cases of long-standing infection, the pleura may be thick and the fluid may be loculated, necessitating more than one puncture site. To prevent accidental penetration of the lung after the needle is in place, put a clamp on the needle adjacent to the skin. Pleural fluid is apt to coagulate unless it is frankly purulent, and an anticoagulant should be added after removal to facilitate examination. If a large amount of fluid is present, it should be removed slowly at intervals, 100 to 500 ml. each time, depending on the size of the patient.

Pericardial Puncture.

For diagnosis and treatment of purulent pericarditis, or to relieve cardiac embarrassment due to collection of large amounts of blood or other fluid.

A. Site: The common site of aspiration is the fifth left interspace 1 to 2 cm. inside of the left outer border of percussion dullness or x-ray shadow. Other sites of entrance are just outside the apex beat; from below, in the chondroxiphoid angle; and occasionally from the back if a very large collection has collapsed the lung against the posterior chest wall.

B. Procedure: The patient sits at a 60° angle supported by bed or pillows. Using sterile technic, infiltrate the skin and subcutaneous tissue with 1% procaine. Connect a 50 ml. syringe, three-way stopcock, and a No. 18 gauge needle. Insert the needle slowly at the lower border of the interspace just above the edge of the rib, directing the needle posteriorly and toward the spine. Aspirate, and then turn the stopcock to discharge fluid via the rubber tubing. When fluid is being aspirated with ease, attach a surgical clamp to the needle next to the skin to prevent the needle from slipping farther.

Peritoneal Puncture.

This procedure can be used as a therapeutic measure to remove excessive fluid in cases of nephrotic syndrome or hepatic cirrhosis or for diagnostic evidence of blood. Infrequently it may be used as a diagnostic measure to obtain bacteriological specimens in peritonitis, but this involves the danger of puncturing the distended bowel, which is adherent to the abdominal wall. Rarely, blood, albumin, or fluids may be administered by this route.

Use rigid surgical technic. The procedure is dangerous if the intestines are distended or if the bladder is not empty. Use a No. 18 or No. 19 gauge needle with a short bevel and a sharp point. Enter at a level about half-way between the symphysis and the umbilicus in the lower quadrant or in the midline. The needle should enter obliquely to avoid leakage afterward. Ascitic fluid will flow out readily. Pus can be aspirated with a sterile syringe.

BONE MARROW PUNCTURE

Bone marrow puncture is indicated in the diagnosis of blood dyscrasias, neuroblastoma, lipidosis, reticuloendotheliosis, lupus erythematosus, and to obtain cultures. The procedure should be done with great caution when a defect of the clotting mechanism is suspected.

Sites for Punctures.
A. Iliac Crest: The method of choice for children. Restrain the child on its side with the hips slightly bent. Find the iliac crest and mark a spot about 1 to 2 cm. posterior to the mid-axillary line and approximately 1 cm. below the crest.
B. Sternal Marrow: Rarely indicated in children.
C. Tibia: Between the tibial tubercle and the medial condyle over the anteromedial aspect. Recommended by some for infants.
D. Lumbar spinous process in the midline.

Procedure.
Prepare the skin surrounding the area as for a surgical procedure. Scrub and wear sterile gloves. Infiltrate with 1% procaine solution, through the skin and tissues down to the periosteum.

Insert a needle with stylet in place perpendicular to the skin, through the skin and tissues, down to the periosteum. (Use No. 21 gauge lumbar puncture needle for infants; No. 18 or 19 gauge special marrow needle with a short bevel for older children.) Push the needle through the cortex, using a screwing motion with firm, steady, and well-controlled pressure. Generally some "give" is felt as the needle enters the marrow; the needle will then be firmly in place.

Immediately fit a dry syringe (20 to 50 ml.) onto the needle and apply strong suction for a few seconds. A small amount of marrow will come up into the syringe; this should be smeared on glass coverslips or slides for subsequent staining and counting.

Remove needle after withdrawing marrow and exert local pressure for three to five minutes or until all evidence of bleeding has ceased, and apply a dry dressing.

RESTRAINT AND POSITIONING

The optimal care of children logically includes an understanding of specific procedures often required in diagnosis and management. In most cases of failure to complete a procedure successfully, the fault lies in undue haste in preparing a struggling or crying patient. The physician should therefore acquaint himself with various methods of restraining pediatric patients. Before starting any proce-

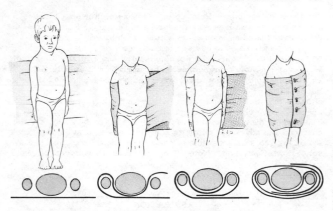

FIG 32-14. This method of body restraint can also be employed to leave an extremity available for venipuncture.

dure, all items of equipment that may be needed should be set out for immediate use as required.

The commonly employed methods of restraint and immobilization are shown in Figure 32-14. Following immobilization of an extremity, the digits should be examined for adequate circulation by noting the temperature, color, and capillary pressure in the nail bed. In using total body restraint, the physician must be certain that cardiorespiratory function is not impaired; a stethoscope may be taped to the chest for this purpose.

Whenever drugs are employed (e.g., procaine, lidocaine), a history of reactions to the drugs should be ascertained. Equipment (e.g., suction apparatus, oral airways or endotracheal intubation device, laryngoscope, tourniquet, and epinephrine, 1:1000 solution) should be readily available to manage any untoward reaction.

After the procedure has been completed, the physician should personally observe the child long enough to be certain that no untoward reaction has developed.

PROCEDURE FOR URINE COLLECTION IN INFANTS

Equipment.

Pediatric Urine Collector® (a Sterilon product), a plastic bag with a round opening surrounded by an adhesive surface to adhere to the skin, may be used. After application the diaper may be reapplied.

Urine may also be collected with a bird cup (for girls) or test tube (for boys) fitted in a specimen band.

Procedure.

Remove diaper. Fit test tube or cup into band. Place child on his back and adjust band and container. Pin band tightly around

child with safety pins. Prop up in bed in semi-Fowler position.
Restrain arms and legs with diapers if necessary. Remove restraints and band as soon as specimen is obtained.

If a specimen is to be used for culture, the genitalia should first
be cleansed thoroughly with soap and water and a mild disinfectant.
Whenever possible a mid-stream specimen should be obtained.
Catheterization is seldom necessary and should be avoided if possible.

If a metabolic bed is not available for collection of a 24-hour
specimen, the chamber of a plastic transfusion set (Baxter V-18
Vacoset® or similar apparatus) may be used. In the male, cut the
chamber and cover the rim with adhesive tape to prevent injury.
Insert the penis into the tube and tape in place. Prop up in bed in
semi-Fowler position. **Note:** This apparatus may be kept in place
for several days.

SUPRAPUBIC PERCUTANEOUS BLADDER ASPIRATION

Suprapubic percutaneous bladder aspiration is preferable to
catheterization when urine is required for culture and bacterial
count, and when possible urethral contamination is to be avoided.
The bladder must be full before the procedure is attempted. Cooperative patients should be urged to drink liberal quantities of fluid
without voiding. In infants, the bladder should be palpably enlarged
above the pubis before the attempt is made to aspirate urine. Local
anesthesia may be used but is generally not necessary. Inadvertent
perforation of a distended adjacent viscus may occur if the bladder
is not sufficiently distended.

The procedure is as follows: (1) Prepare the skin carefully as
for a spinal puncture. Remove hair if necessary. (2) The patient
should be lying supine with the lower extremities held in the frog-
leg position. (3) Firmly introduce a sterile No. 21 long (4 $\frac{1}{2}$ inch)
spinal needle with obturator in place 1 or 2 cm. above the pubis in
the midline, with the needle perpendicular to the skin. After the
skin and anterior wall have been penetrated, the tip of the needle
will be lying against the bladder. (4) With a quick, firm motion,
enter the bladder for a distance of 3 to 4 cm. (5) Remove the obturator and aspirate the urine with a sterile syringe. (6) After
urine has been obtained, withdraw the needle with a single, swift
motion.

Appendix

DRUG THERAPY

Precautions.

Older children should never be given a dose greater than the adult dose. Adult dosages are given below to show limitation of dosage in older children when calculated on a weight basis. All drugs should be used with caution in children, and dosage should be individualized. In general, the smaller the child, the greater the metabolic rate; this may increase the dose needed. Dosage may also have to be adjusted for body temperature (metabolic rate is increased about 10% for each degree centigrade); for obesity (adipose tissue is relatively inert metabolically); for edema (depending on whether the drug is distributed primarily in extracellular fluid); for the type of illness (kidney and liver disease may impair metabolism of certain substances); and for individual tolerance (idiosyncrasy). The dosage recommendations on the following pages should be regarded only as estimates; careful clinical observations and the use of pertinent laboratory aids are necessary. Established drugs should be used in preference to newer and less familiar drugs.

Drugs should be used in early infancy only for significant disorders. In both full-term and premature infants, detoxifying enzymes may be deficient or absent; renal function relatively inefficient; and the blood-brain barrier and protein binding altered. At any age, oliguria requires a reduction of dosage.

Dosages have not been determined as accurately for newborn infants as for older children.

Whenever possible, reference should also be made to the printed literature supplied by the manufacturer, particularly for drugs that are used infrequently.

Determination of Drug Dosage. *

A. Surface Area: This is probably the most accurate method of estimating the dose for a child. (See Table 1 and Figs 1 and 2.)

$$\text{Child dose} = \frac{\text{Surface area of child in sq. M.} \times \text{adult dose}}{1.75}$$

or

$$\text{Surface area in sq. M.} \times 60 = \text{Percentage of adult dose}$$

B. Dose in mg./Kg. if Adult Dose is 1 mg./Kg. (After Leach and Wood):

Age:	
Adult	1
12 years	1.25
1-7 years	1.5
2 weeks-1 year	2

---

*To convert dose in Gm./Kg. to dose in gr./lb., multiply Gm. dosage by 7.

TABLE 1. Determination of drug dosage
from surface area. *

Weight		Approx. Age	Surface Area (sq. M.)	% of Adult Dose
Kg.	lb.			
3	6.6	Newborn	0.2	12
6	13.2	3 months	0.3	18
10	22	1 year	0.45	28
20	44	5.5 years	0.8	48
30	66	9 years	1	60
40	88	12 years	1.3	78
50	110	14 years	1.5	90
65	143	Adult	1.7	102
70	154	Adult	1.76	103

*If adult dose is 1 mg./Kg., dose for three-month-
old infant would be 2 mg./Kg.

Administration of Drugs.

A. Route of Administration:
1. Oral - Tablets may be crushed between spoons and given
   with chocolate, honey, jam, or maple or corn syrups. Many
   regularly prescribed drugs are commercially available in
   special pediatric preparations. The parent should be warned
   that the attractively flavored drug must be kept out of reach
   of children in the home.
   a. Avoid administering drugs with important foods.
   b. The powdered drug should be mixed in the vehicle and
      held between two layers, not floated on the top.
   c. Attempt to administer the entire dose in one spoonful.
2. Parenteral administration of certain drugs may sometimes
   be necessary, especially in the hospital. Its use as a matter
   of convenience should be evaluated in the light of the psychic
   trauma which may result.
3. Rectal administration is often very useful, especially for
   home use. (Rectal dosages are approximately twice the
   amount given orally.) The physician must make certain,
   however, that rectal absorption is adequate before depending
   upon this route for a specific drug. Drugs may be given
   rectally in corn starch solution (not more than 60 ml.); they
   are best given through a tube, but an enema bulb may be
   used.
B. Flavoring Agents for Drugs: Drugs for children should be
   attractive in flavor. Syrups are more useful as flavoring
   agents than alcoholic elixirs, which have a burning taste.

Refusal of Medications.

The administration of a drug to a child requires tact and skill.
The parent or nurse should proceed as if she does not anticipate
protest from the child. Persuasion before it is necessary sets the
stage for struggle. The child must understand that the drug will be
given despite his protest, but great care should be exercised in a
struggling child to avoid aspiration.

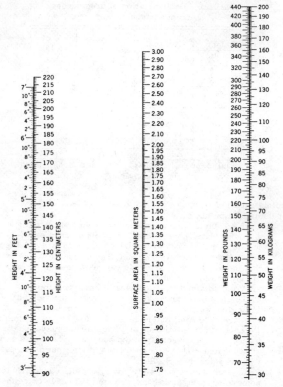

FIG 1. Nomogram for the determination of body surface area of children and adults. (Reproduced, with permission, from W. M. Boothby and R. B. Sandiford, Boston M. & S. J. 185:337, 1921.)

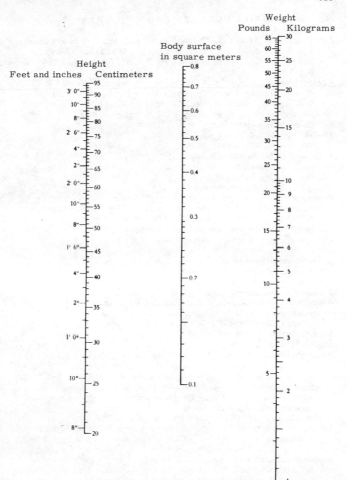

FIG 2. Nomogram for the determination of body surface area of children. (Reproduced, with permission, from E. F. Dubois, Basal Metabolism in Health and Disease. Lea & Febiger, 1936.)

DRUG DOSAGES FOR CHILDREN

Acetaminophen (Tempra®, Tylenol®): 25 mg./Kg./day in 4-6 doses. Under 1 year, 60 mg./dose; 1-3 years, 60-120 mg./dose; 3-6 years, 120 mg./dose; 6-12 years, 240 mg./dose. (Adult = 0.3-0.6 Gm. t. i. d.)

Acetazolamide (Diamox®): 5-30 mg./Kg./day orally divided in 1-4 doses. (Adult = 5 mg./Kg./day.) For hydrocephalus: 20-55 mg./Kg./day orally in 2 or 3 divided doses. In salicylate intoxication: 5 mg./Kg. every 4 hours 3 times daily I.M. after diuresis is established.

Acetylsalicylic acid: See Aspirin.

ACTH: See pp. 421-423.

Actinomycin D: See Dactinomycin.

Adanon®: See Methadone.

Adrenaline: See Epinephrine.

Adroyd®: See Oxymetholone.

Aerosporin®: See Polymyxin B.

Albumin, salt-poor: 0.5-1 Gm./Kg. of 25 Gm./100 ml. solution I.V., up to 100 ml. (Adult = 50 Gm./day I.V.)

Alcopara®: See Bephenium hydroxynaphthoate.

Aldactone®: See Spironolactone.

Aldomet®: See Methyldopa.

Aldosterone (Electrocortin®): See Table 22-6.

Alflorone®: See Fludrocortisone.

Alphadrol®: See Fluprednisolone.

Aludrine®: See Isoproterenol hydrochloride.

Aluminum hydroxide gel: 2-8 ml. orally with meals. (Adult = 4-8 ml.)

Amantadine (Symmetrel®): See p. 96.

Amethopterin: See Methotrexate.

Amidon®: See Methadone.

Aminophylline: (1) Orally, 2-5 mg./Kg./dose. (Adult = 0.25 Gm.) (2) I.V., 2-6 mg./Kg. initially (try intermediate dose); 9 mg./Kg./day in isotonic saline as maintenance. (3) I.M., 2-3.5 mg./Kg./dose. (Adult = 0.25 Gm.) (4) Rectally, 6 mg./Kg./dose. (Adult = 0.5 Gm.) Do not repeat in less than 6 hours. **Caution** in younger children.

Aminosalicylic acid (PAS): See pp. 79, 268.

Ammonium chloride: 75 mg./Kg./day orally in 4 doses. Single expectorant dose, 0.06-0.3 Gm. orally/dose. (Adult = 0.3 Gm.) As diuretic, 60-75 mg./Kg./day orally. (Adult = 4 Gm./day.)

Amobarbital sodium (Amytal®): 3-12 mg. ($1/20$-$1/5$ gr.)/Kg./dose I.V. (slowly) or I.M. (Adult = 0.125-0.5 Gm.) Use freshly prepared 10% solution and give slowly. Try smaller dose first. Orally, 6 mg./Kg./day.

Amodiaquin: See p. 517.

Amphetamine sulfate (Benzedrine®): 0.5 mg./Kg./day in 3 doses orally (not over 15 mg./day). (Adult = 5-15 mg.)

Amphotericin B (Fungizone®): 0.25 mg./Kg./day I.V. slowly. Increase to 1-1.5 mg./Kg./day diluted 1 mg. in 10 ml. (Adult = 50-100 mg. I.V. daily.) **Caution:** Toxic. (See p. 79.)

Ampicillin: See p. 89.

See Precautions, p. 610.

Amytal®: See Amobarbital sodium.

Anadrol®: See Oxymetholone.

Ancobon®: See Flucytosine.

Anhydrohydroxyprogesterone (ethisterone, Pranone®, Progesto-ral®, Lutocyclol®): 5-25 mg./day orally. (Same as adult dose.)

Ansolysen®: See Pentolinium.

Antepar®: See Piperazine.

Apomorphine: (1) Subcut., 0.06-0.1 mg./Kg./dose. (2) Orally, 3-5 mg. (Adult = 5 mg.) May cause depression or excitability and potentiate the depressant action of C.N.S. depressant drugs. Should give levallorphan tartrate after vomiting is produced. (See p. 623.)

Apresoline®: See Hydralazine.

AquaMephyton®: See Phytonadione.

Aralen®: See Chloroquine.

Aramine®: See Metaraminol bitartrate.

Arfonad®: See Trimethaphan.

Aristocort®: See Triamcinolone.

Ascorbic acid (vitamin C): See pp. 48, 51.

Asparaginase: 5000-10,000 I.U./sq. M. I.V. daily to weekly.

Aspirin: As analgesic, 65 mg. (1 gr.)/year of age/dose. (Adult = 0.3-0.65 Gm.) For rheumatic fever, 65-130 mg. (1-2 gr.)/Kg./day to maintain a blood level of 20-30 mg./100 ml. (Adult = 6-8 Gm.) As antipyretic, up to 30-65 mg./Kg./day. Try smaller dose first. Obtain blood levels for higher doses.

A.T. 10: See Dihydrotachysterol.

Atabrine®: See Quinacrine.

Atarax®: See Hydroxyzine.

Atropine sulfate: 0.005-0.02 mg./Kg./dose subcut. or orally. Maximum total dose: 0.4 mg. (Adult = 0.3-1 mg.) **Caution.**

Azathioprine (Imuran®): 3-5 mg./Kg./day orally initially.

Azulfidine®: See Salicylazosulfapyridine.

Bacitracin: See p. 79.

Bactrim®: See Trimethoprim with sulfamethoxazole.

BAL: See Dimercaprol.

Banthine®: See Methantheline.

BCNU (carmustine, bischloroethylnitrosourea): See Table 23-4.

Belladonna tincture: 0.1 ml./Kg./day orally in 3 divided doses. (Adult = 0.6 ml. t.i.d.) Do not give over 0.6 ml./dose or 3.5 ml./day.

Benadryl®: See Diphenhydramine.

Benemid®: See Probenecid.

Benodaine Hydrochloride®: See Piperoxan hydrochloride.

Bentyl®: See Dicyclomine.

Benzathine penicillin G: See p. 91.

Benzedrine®: See Amphetamine sulfate.

Bephenium hydroxynaphthoate (Alcopara®): Under 23 Kg.: 1.0-2.5 Gm./day; over 23 Kg.: 5 Gm./day.

Betamethasone (Celestone®): See Table 22-6.

Bethanechol chloride (Urecholine Chloride®): (1) Orally, 0.6 mg./Kg./day in 3 divided doses. (Adult = 10-30 mg. 3-4 times daily.) (2) Subcut., 0.15-0.2 mg./Kg./day. (Adult = 2.5-5 mg.)

Bicillin C-R®: See Benzathine penicillin G.

See Precautions, p. 610.

Bisacodyl (Dulcolax®): 0.3 mg./Kg. orally or rectally.

Bismuth glycolylarsanilate (Milibis®): Adults, 0.5 mg. t. i. d.

Bonine®: See Meclizine.

Brewer's yeast (dried yeast tablets): See pp. 50, 51.

Bromides: (1) Orally, 50-100 mg./Kg./day in 3 divided doses. (Adult = 1 Gm.) (2) Rectally, 40 mg./Kg. t. i. d. (Adult = 2 Gm.)

Brompheniramine (Dimetane®): Children under 6 years: 0.5 mg./ Kg./day. Children over 6 years: 4 mg. 3-4 times daily. (Adult = 4-8 mg. 3-4 times daily.)

Busulfan (Myleran®): 0.06 mg./Kg./day orally. (Adult = 2 mg. 1-3 times daily.)

Cafergot®: See Ergotamine-caffeine.

Calciferol (vitamin D₂): 25-200 thousand units/day.

Calcium chloride (27% calcium): Newborn, 0.3 Gm./Kg./day orally as a 2-5% solution. Infants, 1-2 Gm./day as dilute solution. Children, 2-4 Gm./day. (Adult = 2-4 Gm. t. i. d.) **Caution:** See p. 155.

Calcium EDTA (Versenate®): See p. 381.

Calcium gluconate (9% calcium): (1) Orally: Infants, 3-6 Gm./day. Children, 6-10 Gm./day in divided doses as a 5-10% solution. (Adult = 8 Gm. t. i. d.) (2) I. V.: 0.1-0.2 Gm./Kg./dose (not over 2 Gm.) as a 10% solution. Inject slowly and stop if bradycardia occurs. (Adult = 5-10 ml.) **Caution.**

Calcium lactate (13% calcium): 0.5 Gm./Kg./day in divided doses orally in dilute solution. (Adult = 4-8 Gm. t. i. d.)

Calcium mandelate: 2-8 Gm. daily orally, depending on age. (Adult = 3 Gm. q. i. d.)

Caprokol®: See Hexylresorcinol.

Carbacrylamine resins (Carbo-Resin®): Over 5 years: 0.25 Gm./ Kg./dose t. i. d. orally. (Adult = 8-16 Gm. t. i. d.)

Carbarsone: 10 mg./Kg./day in divided doses. (See p. 519.)

Carbenicillin: See p. 81.

Carbo-Resin®: See Carbacrylamine resins.

Carisoprodol (Soma®): 25 mg./Kg./day orally.

Carmustine: See BCNU.

Cascara sagrada aromatic fluidextract: Infants, 1-2 ml./dose orally. Children, 2-8 ml./dose orally. (Adult = 4-8 ml. orally.)

Castor oil: Infants, 1-5 ml./dose orally. Children, 5-15 ml./dose orally. (Adult = 15-60 ml. orally.)

CCNU (lomustine, chloroethylcyclohexylnitrosourea): See Table 23-4.

Celestone®: See Betamethasone.

Celontin®: See Methsuximide.

Cephalexin (Keflex®): See p. 82.

Cephaloridine (Loridine®): See p. 82.

Cephalothin (Keflin®): See p. 82.

Charcoal, activated: 10 Gm. mixed in water.

Chloral hydrate: Orally or rectally, 12.5-50 mg./Kg. as single hypnotic dose (not over 1 Gm.) (adult = 0.5-2 Gm.); or 4-20 mg./Kg. as single sedative dose (not over 1 Gm.) (adult = 0.25-1 Gm.). May repeat in 1 hour to obtain desired effect, then every 6-8 hours.

Chlorambucil (Leukeran®): 0.1-0.2 mg./Kg./day. (Adult = 0.2 mg./ Kg.)

See Precautions, p. 610.

Chloramphenicol (Chloromycetin®): See p. 83.
Chlordiazepoxide (Librium®): Over 6 years, 0.5 mg./Kg./day orally in 3-4 doses.
Chloroethylcyclohexylnitrosourea: See CCNU.
Chloromycetin®: See Chloramphenicol.
Chloroquine (Aralen®): 10 mg./Kg./day orally.
Chlorothiazide (Diuril®): 7-40 mg./Kg./day in 2 divided doses orally or I. V. (Adult = 0.5-1 Gm. once or twice a day.)
Chlorpheniramine (Chlor-Trimeton®, Teldrin®): Infants, 1 mg. 3-4 times daily. Children, 0.35 mg./Kg./day in 4 doses orally or subcut. (Adult = 2-4 mg. 3-4 times daily; long-acting, 8-12 mg. 2-3 times daily.)
Chlorpromazine (Thorazine®): (1) Orally, 0.5 mg./Kg. every 4-6 hours. (2) I. M., up to 5 years: 0.5 mg./Kg. every 6-8 hours p. r. n. (not over 40 mg./day). 5-12 years: not over 75 mg./day. (3) Rectally, 2 mg./Kg. (Adult = 10-50 mg.)
Chlorpropamide: Initially: 8 mg./Kg./day in 3 divided doses. Caution. (Adult = 250 mg./day.)
Chlorprophenpyridamine: See Chlorpheniramine.
Chlor-Trimeton®: See Chlorpheniramine.
Cholestyramine (Cuemid®, Questran®): Children over 6 years: 240 mg./Kg./day orally in 3 divided doses. (Adult = 4 Gm. 3-4 times daily.)
Citrovorum factor: 1-6 mg./day orally. (Adult = 3-10 mg.)
Clindamycin (Cleocin®): See p. 84.
Cleocin®: See Clindamycin.
Cloxacillin: See p. 92.
Codeine phosphate: (1) Orally, 0.8-1.5 mg./Kg. as a single sedative or analgesic dose: 3 mg./Kg./day. (Adult = 8-60 mg.) (2) Subcut., 0.8 mg./Kg. (Adult = 30 mg.) (3) For cough, 0.3 mg./Kg./dose.
Colace®: See Dioctyl sodium sulfosuccinate.
Colistimethate: See Colistin.
Colistin (Coly-Mycin®): See p. 84.
Coly-Mycin®: See Colistin.
Compazine®: See Prochlorperazine.
Compound E: See Cortisone.
Compound F: See Hydrocortisone.
Cortef®: See Hydrocortisone.
Corticosteroids: See pp. 421-423.
Corticotropin: See p. 422.
Cortisone (Compound E, Cortogen®, Cortone®): See Table 22-6.
Cortogen®: See Cortisone.
Cortone®: See Cortisone.
Cortril®: See Hydrocortisone.
Cosmegen®: See Dactinomycin.
Cotazym® (pancreatic replacement): 0.3-0.6 Gm. with each feeding. (Adult = 1-3 capsules with meals.)
Cuemid®: See Cholestyramine.
Cuprimine®: See Penicillamine.
Curare: See Tubocurarine.
Cyclizine (Marezine®): 3 mg./Kg./day in 3 divided doses orally.

Cyclophosphamide (Cytoxan®): 2-8 mg./Kg./day orally or I.V. for 7 or more days or 20-50 mg./Kg./dose once a week. (See also Table 23-4.)

Cycloserine (Seromycin®): 15-25 mg./Kg./day orally. (Adult = 250 mg. b.i.d.)

Cyproheptadine (Periactin®): 0.25 mg./Kg./day in 3 or 4 doses orally. (Adult = 12-16 mg./day.)

Cytarabine (cytosine arabinoside, Cytosar®): 2 mg./Kg./day by direct injection. 0.5-1.0 mg./Kg./day by infusion. See also Table 23-4.

Cytomel®: See Triiodothyronine.

Cytosar®: See Cytarabine.

Cytosine arabinoside: See Cytarabine.

Cytoxan®: See Cyclophosphamide.

Dactinomycin (actinomycin D; Cosmegen®): 0.015 mg./Kg./day I.V. for 5 days. (Same as adult dose.) (See also Table 23-4.)

Daraprim®: See Pyrimethamine.

Darvon®: See Propoxyphene.

DCA: See Desoxycorticosterone.

Decadron®: See Dexamethasone.

Decapryn®: See Doxylamine succinate.

Deferoxamine mesylate (Desferal®): 20 mg./Kg. I.M. (preferred) or I.V. infusion slowly as initial dose.

Delalutin®: See Progesterone-17-caproate.

Delatestryl®: See Testosterone enanthate.

Delestrogen®: See Estradiol valerate.

Delta-Cortef®: See Prednisolone.

Deltasone®: See Prednisone.

Deltra®: See Prednisone.

Demerol®: See Meperidine.

Dendrid®: See Idoxuridine.

Depo-Provera®: See Medroxyprogesterone acetate.

Deronil®: See Dexamethasone.

Desferal®: See Deferoxamine mesylate.

Deslanoside: See Table 13-4.

Desoxycorticosterone (DCA, Percorten®): See Table 22-6 and p. 425.

Desoxycorticosterone acetate (Doca®): See Table 22-6.

Dexameth®: See Dexamethasone.

Dexamethasone (Decadron®, Deronil®, Dexameth®, Gammacorten®, Hexadrol®): See Table 22-6.

Dexedrine®: See Dextroamphetamine sulfate.

Dextroamphetamine sulfate (Dexedrine®): 2-15 mg./day in 3 divided doses orally. (Adult = 5-15 mg./day.)

Dextromethorphan hydrobromide (Romilar®): 1 mg./Kg./day.

Dextropropoxyphene: See Propoxyphene.

Diamox®: See Acetazolamide.

Dianabol®: See Methandrostenolone.

Diazepam (Valium®): 0.12-0.8 mg./Kg./day orally in 4 divided doses. I.M. (deeply slowly) and I.V. (slowly), 1 mg./year of age to maximum of 10 mg. (Adult = 2-10 mg. 2-4 times daily.)

Diazoxide (Hyperstat®): 2.5-10 mg./Kg./dose I.V.

See Precautions, p. 610.

Dicloxacillin: See p. 92.

Dicodid®: See Hydrocodone bitartrate.

Dicyclomine (Bentyl®): Infants, 5 mg. as syrup 3-4 times daily. Children, 10 mg. 3-4 times daily. (Adult = 10-20 mg. 3-4 times daily.)

Diethylcarbamazine (Hetrazan®): 15 mg./Kg./day as single dose for 4 days for ascariasis. 6 mg./Kg./day in 3 divided doses for filariasis.

Diethylstilbestrol: See Stilbestrol.

Digitalis preparations: See Table 13-4.

Dihydrocodeinone bitartrate: See Hydrocodone bitartrate.

Dihydrotachysterol: 1-4 ml. (1.25 mg./ml.) orally daily initially; 0.5-1 ml. 3-5 times weekly as maintenance. (Adult = 4-10 ml. initially and then 1-2 ml.)

Diiodohydroxyquin (Diodoquin®): 40 mg./Kg./day orally in 2-3 doses. (Adult = 0.2 Gm./15 lb./day.)

Dilantin®: See Diphenylhydantoin sodium.

Dimenhydrinate (Dramamine®): 5 mg./Kg./day in 4 divided doses orally. (Adult = 50-100 mg.)

Dimercaprol (BAL): See pp. 381, 578.

Dimetane®: See Brompheniramine.

Dioctyl sodium sulfosuccinate (Colace®, Doxinate®): 3-5 mg./Kg./day in 3 divided doses orally. (Adult = 60-480 mg. daily.)

Diodoquin®: See Diiodohydroxyquin.

Diodrast®: See Iodopyracet.

Diphenhydramine (Benadryl®): 4-6 mg./Kg./day orally in 3-4 divided doses; 2 mg./Kg. I.V. over 5 minutes as an antidote for phenothiazine toxicity. (Adult = 100-200 mg./day orally.)

Diphenoxylate (in Lomotil®): Caution. Older children: 2.5 mg. 3 to 5 times daily. Decrease dose as relieved. (Adults = 5 mg. 3-4 times daily and reduce.)

Diphenylhydantoin sodium (Dilantin®): 2-8 mg./Kg./day orally in 3 divided doses. Try smaller dose first. I.M. or I.V., 1-5 mg./Kg./day. Rectally, 8-15 mg./Kg./day. (Adult = 0.3-0.5 Gm./day) (See also Table 21-4.)

Diuril®: See Chlorothiazide.

Doca®: See Desoxycorticosterone acetate.

Doxinate®: See Dioctyl sodium sulfosuccinate.

Doxylamine succinate (Decapryn®): 2 mg./Kg./day orally.

Dozar®: See Methapyrilene hydrochloride.

Dramamine®: See Dimenhydrinate.

Dulcolax®: See Bisacodyl.

Durabolin®: See Nandrolone.

Edathamil (edetate): See p. 381.

Edecrin®: See Ethacrynic acid.

Edetate: See p. 381.

Edrophonium chloride (Tensilon®): Test dose for infant: 0.2 mg./Kg. I.V. Give only one-fifth of dose slowly initially; if tolerated, give remainder. (Adult = 5-10 mg. I.V.)

EDTA (edetate): See p. 381.

Efudex®: See Fluorouracil.

Electrocortin®: See Aldosterone.

Emetine: See p. 519.

See Precautions, p. 610.

Ephedrine sulfate: Orally, 0.5-1 mg./Kg./dose. May repeat every
4-6 hours. (Adult = 25 mg.) I.M., 0.2 mg./Kg. every 6 hours.
I.V., 50 mg./1000 ml. Adjust drip rate to patient's response.

Epinephrine in oil injection, 1:500: For 1-year-old: 0.1 ml.; 2-
year-old: 0.15 ml.; 5-year-old: 0.25 ml., I.M. (Adult = 1
ml.)

Epinephrine solution, 1:1000 (aqueous): 0.01-0.025 ml./Kg. (maximum dose: 0.5 ml.) subcut. (Adult = 0.5-1 ml.)

Epinephrine solution, 1:200 (aqueous) (Sus-Phrine®): 0.05-0.1 ml.
subcut., one dose only. Use smallest effective dose.

Equanil®: See Meprobamate.

Ergotamine-caffeine (Cafergot®): Adults: 2-4 tablets containing
1 mg. ergotamine and 100 mg. caffeine per tablet, but no more
than 6 per attack.

Erythromycin (Erythrocin®, Ilosone®, Ilotycin®, Pediamycin®):
See p. 85.

Esidrix®: See Hydrochlorothiazide.

Estinyl®: See Ethinyl estradiol.

Estradiol valerate (Delestrogen®, Lastrogen®): 10 mg./month I.M.
for teen-age girl. (Adult = 10-20 mg. I.M. every 2-3 weeks.)

Ethacrynic acid (Edecrin®): Children: Initial: 25 mg. Maintenance: increase by increments of 25 mg. **Caution.** (Adults:
Initial: 50-100 mg. Maintenance: 50-200 mg. on continuous
or intermittent schedule.)

Ethambutol (Myambutol®): See p. 85.

Ethinyl estradiol (Estinyl®): 0.02-0.05 mg./dose orally 1-3 times
daily for teen-age girl. (Adult = 0.05 mg. 1-3 times daily.)

Ethionamide (Trecator®): See p. 85.

Ethosuximide (Zarontin®): Under 6 years, 250 mg./day orally as
starting dose. Over 6 years, 250 mg. b.i.d. as starting dose.

Ethotoin (Peganone®): 25-75 mg./Kg./day orally in divided doses.
(Adult = 0.5 Gm. orally 4-6 times daily.)

F-Cortef®: See Fludrocortisone.

Ferrous salts: See p. 316.

Flagyl®: See Metronidazole.

Florinef®: See Fludrocortisone.

Flucytosine (Ancobon®): See p. 86.

Fludrocortisone (Alflorone®, F-Cortef®, Florinef®): See Table 22-6.

Fluorescein: 2 ml. of 5% solution I.V. (Adult = 3-4 ml. of 20%
solution.)

Fluorouracil (Efudex®): Adults: 15 mg./Kg. daily for 4 days. Not
to exceed 1 Gm./day. If no toxicity occurs, give 7.5 mg./Kg. on
sixth, eighth, tenth, and twelfth days of treatment. Discontinue
at end of twelfth day even if no toxicity is apparent. May repeat
in 6 weeks after last injection of previous course if no toxicity
is reported. (See also Table 23-4.)

Fluoxymesterone (Halotestin®, Ultandren®): Up to 0.15 mg./Kg./
day orally in 2 divided doses in prepuberal children and up to
0.1 mg./Kg./day in puberal children. (Adult = 2-10 mg./day.)

Fluprednisolone (Alphadrol®): See Table 22-6.

Folic acid: 10-15 mg./day orally. (Adult = 10-15 mg./day.)

Fulvicin®: See Griseofulvin.

Fungicides: See pp. 192-196.

See Precautions, p. 610.

Fungizone®: See Amphotericin B.

Furadantin®: See Nitrofurantoin.

Furazolidone (Furoxone®): 5 mg./Kg./day divided in 4 doses.

Furosemide (Lasix®): Children: Contraindicated until safety is established. (Adults = Diuretic: 40-80 mg. in a.m. Hypertension: 40 mg. twice daily.)

Furoxone®: See Furazolidone.

Gammacorten®: See Dexamethasone.

Gamma globulin: See pp. 106-110, 327.

Gantanol®: See Sulfamethoxazole.

Gantrisin®: See Sulfisoxazole.

Garamycin®: See Gentamicin.

Gemonil®: See Metharbital.

Gentamicin (Garamycin®): See p. 86.

Gentian violet (methylrosaniline chloride): 2 mg./Kg./day orally in 3 divided doses. Not more than 90 mg. should be given. (Adult = 65 mg.)

Glucagon: (1) Newborn, 0.025-0.1 mg./Kg. as single dose I.V. Try smaller dose first. May repeat in 30 minutes. (2) Older child, 0.25-1 mg. subcut., I.M., or I.V. as single dose.

Glucocorticoids: See Table 22-6.

Glycerin: 1-1.5 Gm./Kg. as single oral dose.

Gold sodium thiosulfate: 1 mg./Kg. weekly.

Gonadotropin, chorionic: 500-1000 units 2-3 times/week for 5-8 weeks I.M.

Grifulvin®: See Griseofulvin.

Grisactin®: See Griseofulvin.

Griseofulvin (Fulvicin®, Grifulvin®, Grisactin®): See pp. 87, 193, 195.

Guanethidine sulfate (Ismelin®): 0.2 mg./Kg./day orally as single dose. Increase dose at weekly intervals by same amount. (Adult = 10 mg. daily.) Larger doses possible for hospitalized adults. Caution.

Haldol®: See Haloperidol.

Haldrone®: See Paramethasone.

Haloperidol (Haldol®): Children: Contraindicated in children under 12 years of age; safety is not yet established. (Adults: No more than 15 mg./day. Initial: 1-2 mg. 2 or 3 times daily. Maintenance: 1-2 mg. 3-4 times daily.)

Halotestin®: See Fluoxymesterone.

Heparin: (1) I.V., 0.5 mg./Kg./dose. This ~~me.~~ ~~repeated every~~ hour. One mg./Kg. every 4 hours clotting ~~time for 20-24~~ vascular clotting: Control ~~...~~ (2) Subcut., 4 mg./K~~...~~ hours. ~~...~~

Herplex®: Se~~...~~ ~~arbamazine.~~ ~~...methasone.~~

Hetacil~~...~~ Caprokol®): 0.1 Gm./year of age orally. Do not ~~...~~ 1 Gm. (Adult = 1 Gm.)

H~~...~~: See Methapyrilene.

~~...~~**mine:** Provocative test: 0.02 mg./sq.M. I.V. Caution: Phentolamine should be available.

HN2: See Mechlorethamine.

Hyaluronidase (Wydase®): 500 viscosity units or 150 turbidity-reducing units in 1 ml. sterile water or saline at site of fluid administration.

Hycodan®: See Dihydrocodeinone bitartrate.

Hydeltra®: See Prednisolone.

Hydralazine (Apresoline®): (1) Orally, 0.15 mg./Kg./dose q.i.d. Increase to tolerance. (2) I.M. or I.V. with reserpine: 0.1-0.2 mg./Kg. every 6-24 hours. (3) I.V. or I.M. alone: 1.5-3.5 mg./Kg./day in 4-6 divided doses. (Adults: Initial parenteral dose = 10-20 mg.; single oral dose = 100 mg.)

Hydriodic acid: 1-5 ml. of 1.4% syrup every 4 hours in fruit juice.

Hydrochlorothiazide (Esidrix®, Hydro-Diuril®): One-tenth of chlorothiazide dose. (Adult = 25-200 mg./day.)

Hydrocodone bitartrate (Dicodid®, Hycodan®): 0.6 mg./Kg./day orally. (Adult = 5-10 mg.) **Caution.**

Hydrocortisone (compound F, Cortef®, cortisol, Cortril®, Hydrocortone®, Solu-Cortef®): See p. 422 and Table 22-6.

Hydrocortone®: See Hydrocortisone.

Hydro-Diuril®: See Hydrochlorothiazide.

Hydroxyzine (Atarax®): 1-2 mg./Kg./day orally in 3 divided doses. Preoperative, 1 mg./Kg./day I.M. (Adult = 25-50 mg. t.i.d.)

Hykinone®: See Menadione sodium bisulfite.

Hyoscine: See Scopolamine.

Hyperstat®: See Diazoxide.

Idoxuridine (Dendrid®, Herplex®, Stoxil®): 50 mg./Kg./day by continuous I.V. drip over 4 days for newborn. (Adult maximum = 600 mg./Kg. total dose.) (Investigational drug.)

Ilosone®: See Erythromycin.

Ilotycin®: See Erythromycin.

Imferon®: See p. 316.

Imipramine (Tofranil®): Children: Not generally recommended for children under 6 years. Initial dose: 25 mg./day; may increase to 50 mg./day for preadolescents and 75 mg./day for adolescents. (Adult = 75 mg. initially increased up to 150 mg. daily.)

Imuran®: See Azathioprine.

Inderal®: See Propranolol.

INH: See Isoniazid.

Ins____: See p. 432.

Iodine: See p. 432.

Iodopyracin, strong (Lugol's solution): See p. 415.

aortogra____rast®): 35% for I.V. urography and retrograde with hyaluro____ 15-?% for I.V. angiocardiography. 7% in saline

I____c: Syrup: Ambulate. ~ subcut. injection. water. (lavage) If not vomited, orally. (Adult = 20-30 ml.) Give fluidextract of ipecac as e____ minutes p.r.n. Recover dose

Iron: See pp. 48, 316. ____ ml.) **Caution:** Never use

Iron-dextran complex: See p. ___6.

Ismelin®: See Guanethidine sulfate.

Isoniazid (INH, Nydrazid®): 15-20 mg./Kg./ necessary) divided into 3-4 doses. Maxim____

See also pp. 87, 268, 510.

See Precautions. p. 610.

Isoproterenol hydrochloride (Aludrine®, Isonorin®, Isuprel®, Norisodrine®, Proternol®): 2-10 mg./dose sublingually t.i.d. for older children (not oftener than every 3-4 hours). Oral inhalation, 5-15 breaths of 1:200 solution (not more than 0.5 ml.). (Adult = 15 mg. sublingually q.i.d.) Rectal, 5-15 mg. 4 times a day. Subcut., 0.1-0.5 mg.

Isoproterenol sulfate (Isonorin®, Norisodrine®): 1:200 or 1:400, 1-2 inhalations.

Kanamycin (Kantrex®): See p. 87.

Kayexalate®: See Sodium polystyrene sulfonate.

Keflex®: See Cephalexin.

Keflin®: See Cephalothin.

Kenacort®: See Triamcinolone.

Kenalog®: See Triamcinolone.

Konakion®: See Phytonadione.

Lasix®: See Furosemide.

Lastrogen®: See Estradiol valerate.

Latrodectus antivenin: See p. 591.

Leucovorin calcium: See Citrovorum factor.

Leukeran®: See Chlorambucil.

Levallorphan (Lorfan®): 0.02-0.05 mg. I.V. or I.M. for infant and repeat if necessary. (Adult = 1-2 mg.) May give levallorphan tartrate 1 minute after vomiting begins as result of administration of apomorphine for treatment of poisoning.

Levarterenol (norepinephrine, Levophed®): See p. 20.

Levophed®: See Levarterenol.

Levothyroxine sodium (Letter®, Synthroid Sodium®): 0.1 mg. = 65 mg. (1 gr.) Thyroid, U.S.P. = 25-30 µg. triiodothyronine.

Lidocaine (Xylocaine®): 1 mg./Kg. I.V. slowly for arrhythmia. Repeat as needed. (Adult = 50-100 mg. I.V. slowly.)

Lincocin®: See Lincomycin.

Lincomycin (Lincocin®): See p. 88.

Liothyronine: See Triiodothyronine.

Liquid petrolatum, liquid paraffin: See Mineral oil.

Liquiprin®: See Salicylamide.

Liver injection, crude: 2 ml./day I.M. (Adult = 2 ml./day.)

Lomotil®: See Diphenoxylate.

Lomustine: See CCNU.

Lorfan®: See Levallorphan.

Loridine®: See Cephaloridine.

Lugol's solution: See p. 415.

Lutocyclol®: See Anhydrohydroxyprogesterone.

Lypressin (lysine-8 vasopressin; Syntopressin®): 30-55 units/day as a nasal spray.

Magnesium hydroxide: See Milk of magnesia.

Magnesium sulfate: As anticonvulsant or for hypertension: 0.1-0.4 ml./Kg. of 50% solution I.M. every 4-6 hours if renal function is adequate. I.V., 10 ml. (100 mg.)/Kg. I.V. slowly as 1% solution. Caution: Check blood pressure carefully and have calcium available. As cathartic: 250 mg./Kg./dose orally.

Mandelamine®: See Methenamine mandelate.

Mannitol: Test dose for oliguria, 0.2 Gm./Kg. I.V. Edema, 1-2.5 Gm./Kg. I.V. over 2-6 hours. Cerebral edema, 1-2.5 Gm./Kg. over 1/2-6 hours.

See Precautions, p. 610.

Marboran®: See Methisazone.

Marezine®: See Cyclizine.

Matulane®: See Procarbazine.

Mebaral®: See Mephobarbital.

Mechlorethamine (nitrogen mustard, HN2, Mustargen®): Inject slowly, diluted, 0.1 mg./Kg./day for 4 days I.V. (Adult = 0.1 mg./Kg./day for 4 days.)

Mecholyl®: See Methacholine chloride.

Meclizine (Bonine®): 2 mg./Kg. every 6-12 hours orally. (Adult = 25-50 mg.)

Medrol®: See Methylprednisolone.

Medroxyprogesterone acetate (Depo-Provera®): Under 4 years, 100-150 mg. per injection every 2 weeks. Over 4 years, 150-200 mg. per injection every 2 weeks.

Mellaril®: See Thioridazine.

Menadiol sodium diphosphate (vitamin K analogue; Synkayvite®): 1 mg. I.M. Not for infants. (Adult = 3-6 mg.)

Menadione sodium bisulfite (Hykinone®): 1 mg. I.M. Not for infants. (Adult = 0.5-2 mg. I.M.)

Mepacrine: See Quinacrine.

Meperidine (Demerol®): 0.6-1.5 mg./Kg. I.M. or orally, as single analgesic dose; up to 6 mg./Kg./day. (Adult = 50-100 mg.)

Mephenesin (Tolserol®): (1) Orally, 40-130 mg./Kg./day in 3-5 doses. (2) I.V., 1-3 ml./Kg. as 2% solution slowly. (Adult = 1-3 Gm. t. i. d.)

Mephentermine sulfate (Wyamine Sulfate®): 0.4 mg./Kg. orally, I.M., or slowly I.V. as single dose. (Adult = 15-20 mg. I.M.)

Mephenytoin (Mesantoin®): 3-10 mg./Kg./day orally. Start smaller dose and gradually increase. (Adult = 0.1-0.3 Gm. t.i.d.)

Mephobarbital (Mebaral®): 2-8 mg./Kg./day orally. (Adult = 0.3-0.5 Gm./day.) (See also p. 388.)

Mephyton®: See Phytonadione.

Meprobamate (Miltown®, Equanil®): Over 3 years: 7-30 mg./Kg./day in 2-3 doses orally. (Adult = 400-800 mg. t.i.d.)

Meralluride (Mercuhydrin®): See Mercurial diuretics.

Mercaptomerin sodium: See Mercurial diuretics.

Mercaptopurine (6-M.P., Purinethol®): 2.5-4 mg./Kg./day orally in 3 divided doses. (Same as adult dose.) **Caution.** (See also Table 23-4.)

Mercuhydrin® (meralluride): See Mercurial diuretics.

Mercurial diuretics (including mercaptomerin sodium and Mercuhydrin®): Below 3 Kg., 0.125 ml.; 3-7 Kg., 0.125-0.25 ml.; 7-15 Kg., 0.25-0.5 ml.; 15-25 Kg., 0.5-0.75 ml.; 25-35 Kg., 1 ml. Give I.M. daily to once weekly. (Adult = 1-2 ml.)

Mesantoin®: See Mephenytoin.

Mestinon®: See Pyridostigmine.

Metandren®: See Methyltestosterone.

Metaraminol bitartrate (Aramine®): 0.04-0.2 mg./Kg. subcut. or I.M.; 0.3-2 mg./Kg. in 500 ml. solution is I.V. infusion. (Titrate by effect or by blood pressure readings.) (Adult = 2-10 mg. I.M., 0.5-5 mg. I.V.)

Methacholine chloride (Mecholyl®): For arrhythmia in young child, 0.1-0.4 mg./Kg. subcut. or I.M. May be increased by 25% every 30 minutes. Oral starting dose: approximately 18 times greater.

See Precautions, p. 610.

Methacycline (Rondomycin®): See p. 88.

Methadone (Adanon®, Amidon®): 0.7 mg./Kg./day orally in 4-6 doses for analgesia.

Methandrostenolone (Dianabol®): 0.04 mg./Kg./day orally. (Adult = 2.5-5 mg. daily.)

Methantheline (Banthine®): 4-8 mg./Kg./day orally or I.M. in 4 divided doses. (Adult = 50-100 mg. t.i.d.)

Methapyrilene hydrochloride (Histadyl®, Dozar®, Thenylene®): 0.2-0.3 mg./Kg./dose. Up to 5 doses/day.

Metharbital (Gemonil®): 5-12 mg./Kg./day orally in divided doses. (Adult = 1.2 Gm. 2-3 times daily orally.)

Methdilazine (Tacaryl®): 0.3 mg./Kg./day in 2 doses orally.

Methenamine mandelate (Mandelamine®): 60 mg./Kg./day orally in 4 divided doses. Maintain acid urine. (Adult = 1-1.5 Gm. q.i.d.)

Methicillin: See p. 91.

Methimazole (Tapazole®): 0.4 mg./Kg./day divided in 3 doses. Maintenance, one-half initial dose. (Adult = 15-60 mg.)

Methionine: 250 mg./Kg./day in 3-4 divided doses orally. (Adult dose to acidify urine = 12-15 Gm./day orally.)

Methisazone (Marboran®): See p. 96.

Methocarbamol (Robaxin®): 40-65 mg./Kg./day in 4-6 divided doses orally. (Adult = 1.5-2 Gm. 3-4 times daily.)

Methotrexate (amethopterin): Orally or I.M., 0.12 mg./day. (Adult = 5-10 mg./day.) (2) Intrathecally, 0.25-0.5 mg./Kg./day. (3) I.V., 3-5 mg./Kg. as single dose every other week. **Caution:** Toxic. (See also Table 23-4.)

Methoxamine hydrochloride (Vasoxyl®): 0.25 mg./Kg. I.M. as single dose. (Adult = 15 mg. I.M.)

Methsuximide (Celontin®): 20 mg./Kg./day orally in divided doses. (Adult = 300 mg. 1-3 times daily.)

Methylatropine nitrate: 1:10,000 alcoholic solution. Initial dose: 0.05 mg.; increase to 0.3 mg. p.r.n. subcut. (Adult = 1-2.5 mg. every 3-4 hours.)

Methylcellulose: See p. 278.

Methyldopa (Aldomet®): 2-4 mg./Kg. I.V. initially. Double dose in 4 hours if no effect. Dilute in 50-100 ml. fluid and infuse over 30-60 minutes. Children: 10 mg./Kg./day orally in divided doses every 6 hours, increasing at 2-day or more intervals to 65 mg./Kg./day. For crises, 20-40 mg./Kg./day in divided doses every 6 hours, continuing with oral doses when controlled. **Caution.** (Adult = 0.5-1 Gm./day initially; adjust at 2- to 7-day intervals.)

Methylene blue: 0.1-0.2 ml./Kg./dose of 1% solution I.V. (Adult = 100-150 mg.)

Methylphenidate (Ritalin®): 0.25-0.75 mg./Kg./dose orally; 0.5 mg./Kg./dose I.M. or slowly I.V. (Adult = 10 mg. t.i.d.) **Caution.**

Methylphenylethylhydantoin: See Mephenytoin.

Methylprednisolone (Medrol®): See Table 22-6.

Methyltestosterone (Metandren®, Oreton®): 0.08-0.15 mg./Kg./day sublingually. (As much as 10-20 mg./day has been used in preadolescents.) (Adult = 5-10 mg.)

See Precautions, p. 610.

Methysergide (Sansert®): Children: Dosage has not been established. (Adult = 4-8 mg./day.) Do not continue for more than 6 months; then stop for 3-4 weeks and begin again. Precede drug-free interval with dosage reduction.

Meticortelone®: See Prednisolone.

Meticorten®: See Prednisone.

Metronidazole (Flagyl®): See p. 88.

Milibis®: See Bismuth glycolylarsanilate.

Milk of magnesia: 0.5-1 ml./Kg./dose orally. (Adult = 30-60 ml.)

Milontin®: See Phensuximide.

Miltown®: See Meprobamate.

Mineralocorticoids: See Table 22-6.

Mineral oil: 0.5 ml./Kg./dose orally. (Adult = 15-30 ml.)

Mintezol®: See Thiabendazole.

Morphine sulfate: 0.12-0.2 mg./Kg. every 4 hours p.r.n. subcut. No more than 10 mg./dose. (Adult = 10-15 mg.) Infants, start with half the dose. I.V., 0.2 mg./Kg./dose. May repeat once.

Mustargen®: See Mechlorethamine.

Myambutol®: See Ethambutol.

Mycifradin®: See Neomycin.

Mycostatin®: See Nystatin.

Myleran®: See Busulfan.

Mysoline®: See Primidone.

Nafcillin: See p. 91.

Nalidixic acid (NegGram®): See p. 87.

Nalline®: See Nalorphine.

Nalorphine (Nalline®): 0.1-0.2 mg./Kg./dose I.V. or I.M. Repeat in 15 minutes if necessary. Use I.V. for shocky infant.

Naloxone (Narcan®): 0.01 mg./Kg./dose.

Nandrolone (Durabolin®): Infants, 12.5 mg. every 2-4 weeks I.M. Children, 25 mg. every 2-4 weeks I.M.

Narcan®: See Naloxone.

NegGram®: See Nalidixic acid.

Nembutal®: See Pentobarbital sodium.

Neobiotic®: See Neomycin.

Neo-cultol®: See p. 278.

Neolin®: See Penicillins.

Neomycin (Mycifradin®, Neobiotic®): See p. 88.

Neostigmine (Prostigmin®): (1) Orally, 0.25 mg./Kg./dose. (Adult = 15 mg.) (2) I.M., 0.025-0.045 mg./Kg./dose. (Adult = 0.25-1 mg.) For myasthenia test, 0.04 mg./Kg./dose I.M. **Caution:** Atropine should be available.

Neo-Synephrine®: See Phenylephrine.

Niacinamide (nicotinamide): See pp. 48, 51.

Niclosamide (Yomesan®): See p. 524.

Nicotinamide (niacinamide): See pp. 48, 51.

Nitrofurantoin (Furadantin®): See p. 88.

Nitrogen mustard: See Mechlorethamine.

Noctec®: See Chloral hydrate.

Norepinephrine (Levophed®, levarterenol): Start at 0.05 µg./Kg./minute and titrate rate by blood pressure. (See also p. 19.)

Norethandrolone (Nilevar®): 0.4-0.8 mg./Kg./day orally. (Adult = 30-50 mg. daily.)

Norisodrine®: See Isoproterenol.
Nydrazid®: See Isoniazid.
Nystatin (Mycostatin®): See p. 89.
Oleandomycin: See p. 89.
Omnipen®: See Penicillins.
Oncovin®: See Vincristine.
Opium tincture, camphorated: See Paregoric.
Oreton®: See Methyltestosterone.
Osmitrol®: See Mannitol.
Ouabain (strophanthin): 0.01 mg./Kg. I.V. Give one-half dose
   initially. Check Ecg. frequently.
Oxacillin: See p. 92.
Oxandrolone: 0.05-0.10 mg./Kg./day.
Oxymetholone (Adroyd®, Anadrol®): 0.1-0.3 mg./Kg./day orally.
   (2.5 mg. for children weighing less than 20 Kg. and 3.75 mg.
   for those over 20 Kg.)
Pancreatin (pancreatic enzymes): 0.3-0.6 Gm. with each feeding.
   Increase as necessary. (Adult = 2-5 Gm.)
Papaverine: 1-6 mg./Kg./day orally, I.V., or I.M. in 4 divided
   doses. (Adult = 0.1 Gm.)
Paracort®: See Prednisone.
Paracortol®: See Prednisolone.
Paradione®: See Paramethadione.
Paraldehyde: (1) Orally, 0.1-0.15 ml./Kg./dose. (Adult = 4-16 ml.)
   (2) Rectally, 0.3-0.6 ml./Kg./dose in 1 or 2 parts of vegetable
   oil. (Adult = 16-32 ml.) (3) I.M., 0.1 ml./Kg. as single anti-
   convulsant dose (not over 10 ml.). (Adult = 4-10 ml.) (4) I.V.,
   0.02 ml./Kg. **Very slowly.** (Adult = 1-2 ml.) **Caution:** I.V.
   administration may cause respiratory distress or pulmonary
   edema. Avoid plastic equipment.
Paramethadione (Paradione®): Same dose as Trimethadione.
Paramethasone (Haldrone®): See Table 22-6.
Parathyroid injection: 50-300 units subcut. or I.M., and then 20-
   40 units every 12 hours. (Adult = 50-100 units 3-5 times daily.)
Paregoric (opium tincture, camphorated) (0.4 mg. morphine/ml.):
   Up to 12 months, 0.06 ml./month of age. 5 years of age, 2
   ml./dose. May repeat every 3-4 hours if no drowsiness or
   respiratory depression. (Adult = 4 ml.) **Caution.**
PAS: See Aminosalicylic acid.
Pediamycin®: See Erythromycin.
Peganone®: See Ethotoin.
Penbritin®: See Penicillins.
Penicillamine (Cuprimine®): Infants over 6 months: 250 mg./day.
   Older children and adults: 1 Gm./day in 4 doses orally. In-
   crease as indicated.
Penicillin G: See p. 90.
Penicillins: See p. 89.
Pentobarbital sodium (Nembutal®): 1-1.5 mg./Kg. orally. Up to
   3-5 mg./Kg. as single sedative dose. (Adult = 100 mg.)
Pentobarbitone sodium: See Pentobarbital sodium.
Pentolinium (Ansolysen®): (1) Orally, 1 mg./Kg./day. (Adult =
   20-200 mg. t.i.d.) (2) I.M. or subcut., 0.035-0.15 mg./Kg.
   dose. (Adult = 2.5-10 mg.) Start smaller dose and increase
   gradually.

Pentothal®: See Thiopental sodium.
Pentylenetetrazol (Metrazol®, Pentrazol®): 20 mg./Kg./dose diluted I.V. slowly. **Caution.**
Percorten®: See Desoxycorticosterone.
Periactin®: See Cyproheptadine.
Permapen®: See Penicillins.
Pethidine hydrochloride: See Meperidine.
Phenacemide (Phenurone®): 20-30 mg./Kg./day orally. 5-10 years, 0.25 Gm. t.i.d. orally initially. (Adult = 0.5 Gm. 2-4 times daily.)
Phenergan®: See Promethazine.
Phenobarbital: As sedative, 0.5-2 mg./Kg. as single dose orally every 4-6 hours. Anticonvulsant: 3-5 mg./Kg./dose I.M. (I.V. only with extreme caution). Epilepsy: Starting doses: Under 3 years, 16 mg. t.i.d.; 3-6 years, 32 mg. b.i.d.; over 6 years, 32 mg. t.i.d. (Adult = 30 mg.) Hypnotic: 3-6 mg./Kg./dose orally. (Adult = 100-200 mg.) (See also Table 21-4.)
Phenobarbital sodium: (1) Subcut. or I.M., 4-10 mg./Kg. as anticonvulsant. (2) Orally, 1-5 mg./Kg. as single sedative dose. (Adult = 15-100 mg.) (3) I.M. or rectally, 1 mg./Kg. as single sedative dose. (Adult = 30 mg.) (4) Rectally, 3-5 mg./Kg. as anticonvulsant. Acts more rapidly than phenobarbital. (Adult = 0.3 Gm.)
Phenobarbitone: See Phenobarbital.
Phenoxymethyl penicillin: See p. 91.
Phensuximide (Milontin®): 20-40 mg./Kg./day orally in divided doses. (Adult = 0.5-1 Gm. 2-3 times daily.)
Phentolamine (Regitine®): (1) Test dose: 0.1 mg./Kg. I.V. **Caution.** (2) Therapeutic, 5 mg./Kg./day orally in 4 divided doses. (Adult = 5 mg. I.V.)
Phenurone®: See Phenacemide.
Phenylephrine (Neo-Synephrine®): 0.1 mg./Kg. I.M. or subcut.; 1 mg./Kg./day orally in 6 divided doses; 3-10 mg. orally for nasal vasoconstriction. (Adult = 10-25 mg.)
Phenylpropanolamine hydrochloride (Propadrine®): See p. 237.
Phytonadione (AquaMephyton®, Mephyton®, Konakion®): Prophylactic dose, 0.5-5 mg. **I.M.**; therapeutic dose, 5-10 mg. I.M., I.V., or orally.
Pilocarpine hydrochloride: 0.5, 1, and 2% as eyedrops. 0.1 mg./Kg. as single I.M. or subcut. dose.
Piperazine citrate or phosphate (Syrup of Antepar®): See pp. 521, 522.
Piperoxan hydrochloride (Benodaine Hydrochloride®): Test dose, 0.25 mg./Kg. I.V. slowly. (Same as adult.)
Pitressin® and Pitressin Tannate®: See Vasopressin injection and Vasopressin tannate.
Pituitary, posterior, powder: Small pinch (approximately 40-50 mg.) nasally q.i.d., p.r.n. (Adult = 30-60 mg. 2-3 times daily.)
Plasma: 10-15 ml./Kg. I.V.
Polycillin®: See Penicillins.
Polymyxin B (Aerosporin®): See p. 92.
Posterior pituitary: See Pituitary, posterior.
Potassium chloride: See pp. 61, 70-72, 398.

See Precautions, p. 610.

Potassium iodide (saturated solution): 0.1-0.3 ml. orally in cold
    milk or fruit juice. (Adult = 0.3 ml.)

Povan®: See Pyrvinium pamoate.

Pralidoxime (Protopam®): 25-50 mg./Kg. as 5% solution I.V.

Pranone®: See Anhydrohydroxyprogesterone.

Prednis®: See Prednisolone.

Prednisolone (Delta-Cortef®, Hydeltra®, Meticortelone®,
    Paracortol®, Prednis®, Sterane®, Sterolone®): See Table 22-6.

Prednisone (Deltasone®, Deltra®, Meticorten®, Paracort®): See
    Tables 22-6 and 23-4.

Primidone (Mysoline®): 12-24 mg./Kg./day. Under 8 years, start
    with 125 mg. b.i.d.; over age 8, 250 mg. b.i.d. Increase
    slowly p.r.n. (Adult = 250 mg. as initial dose.)

Priscoline®: See Tolazoline.

Pro-Banthine®: See Propantheline.

Probenecid (Benemid®): Initial dose, 25 mg./Kg., then 10 mg./Kg.
    every 6 hours orally. (Adult = 1-2 Gm. initially, then 0.5 Gm.
    every 6 hours.)

Procainamide (Pronestyl®): (1) Orally, 8-15 mg./Kg. every 4-6
    hours. (2) I.M., 6 mg./Kg. every 4-6 hours. (3) I.V., for
    emergency use only: 2 mg./Kg., at a rate not to exceed 0.5-1
    mg./Kg./minute. Monitor by continuous Ecg. and blood pres-
    sure recording every minute.

Procaine penicillin G: See p. 91.

Procarbazine (Matulane®): 8 mg./Kg. orally as initial dose.
    Caution. (See also Table 23-4.)

Prochlorperazine (Compazine®): 0.25-0.375 mg./Kg./day orally or
    rectally in 2-3 doses. (Adult = 25 mg. rectally b.i.d. or 5 mg.
    orally 3-4 times daily.) I.M., 0.25 mg./Kg./day. **Toxicity:**
    Parkinsonism and tetanus-like seizures. Avoid overdosage.

Progesterone: See Anhydrohydroxyprogesterone.

Progesterone-17-caproate (Delalutin®): 125 mg. I.M. for teen-age
    girl.

Progestoral®: See Anhydrohydroxyprogesterone.

Promethazine (Phenergan®): Antihistaminic, 0.5 mg./Kg. at bed-
    time orally; 0.1 mg./Kg. orally t.i.d. For nausea and vomit-
    ing, 0.25-0.5 mg./Kg. rectally or I.M. For sedation, 0.5-1
    mg./Kg. I.M.

Pronestyl®: See Procainamide.

Propadrine®: See Phenylpropanolamine hydrochloride.

Propantheline (Pro-Banthine®): 1-2 mg./Kg./day orally in 4 divided
    doses p.c. (Adult = 15-30 mg. 3-4 times daily.)

Propoxyphene (Darvon®): 3 mg./Kg./day in divided doses every
    4-6 hours orally. (Adult = 32-65 mg. 3-4 times daily.)

Propranolol (Inderal®): Adult: Arrhythmias, 10-30 mg. 3-4 times
    daily, before meals and at bedtime. Stenosis, 20-40 mg.
    3-4 times daily before meals and at bedtime. (Pediatric dosage
    has not been established; 2 mg./Kg./day has been used.)

Propylthiouracil: 6-7 mg./Kg./day in 3 divided doses at intervals
    of 8 hours. Maintenance 1/3-1/2 initial dose. See also p. 414.

Prostaphlin®: See Penicillins.

Prostigmin®: See Neostigmine.

Protamine sulfate: 2.5-5 mg./Kg., then 1-2.5 mg./Kg. I.V.
    (Adult = 50 mg. every 4-6 hours I.V.)

Proternol®: See Isoproterenol hydrochloride.
Protopam®: See Pralidoxime.
Pseudoephedrine hydrochloride (Sudafed®): 4 mg./Kg./day in 4 doses.
Purinethol®: See Mercaptopurine.
Pyribenzamine®: See Tripelennamine.
Pyridostigmine (Mestinon®): 7 mg./Kg./day in 6 doses. Increase as necessary. (Adult = 600 mg./day.)
Pyrimethamine (Daraprim®): See p. 517.
Pyronil®: See Pyrrobutamine.
Pyrrobutamine (Pyronil®): 0.6 mg./Kg./day. (Adult = 15 mg. 3-4 times daily.)
Pyrvinium pamoate (Povan®): 5 mg./Kg./day. (Adult = 5 mg./Kg.)
Questran®: See Cholestyramine.
Quinacrine (mepacrine, Atabrine®): Giardiasis, 8 mg./Kg./day for 5 days in 3 doses orally. (Maximum, 300 mg./day.) Tapeworm, 15 mg./Kg. in 2 doses orally. (Maximum, 800 mg.) See also pp. 517, 524.
Quinidine sulfate: Test dose, 2 mg./Kg. orally. If tolerated, give 3-6 mg./Kg. every 2-3 hours. (Adult = 200 mg.) Therapeutic dose, 30 mg./Kg./day divided into 4-5 doses.
Quinine sulfate: 1 year, 0.13 Gm. t.i.d. orally. 5-10 years, 0.3-0.6 Gm. t.i.d. (Adult = 0.6 Gm. t.i.d. for 5-7 days.)
Regitine®: See Phentolamine.
Reserpine (Serpasil®, etc.): (1) Orally, 0.005-0.03 mg./Kg./day in 4 doses. (2) I.M., 0.02-0.07 mg./Kg. every 12-24 hours. Initially, try smaller dose (except in life-threatening situations) and double in 4-6 hours if response is inadequate. May give with hydralazine (Apresoline®). (Adult = 0.1-0.5 mg. daily.) See also p. 335.
Resistopen®: See Penicillins.
Rifampin: See p. 92.
Ritalin®: See Methylphenidate.
Robaxin®: See Methocarbamol.
Romilar®: See Dextromethorphan.
Rondomycin®: See Methacycline.
Salamide®: See Salicylamide.
Salicylamide (Liquiprin®, Salamide®, Salrin®): 65 mg./Kg./day in divided doses or 65 mg./year/dose 3 or 4 times daily orally. (Adult = 0.3-0.6 Gm. orally 3-4 times daily.)
Salicylazosulfapyridine (Azulfidine®): 50-100 mg./Kg./day at 4- to 6-hour intervals. (Adult = 1 Gm. 4-6 times daily.)
Salrin®: See Salicylamide.
Sansert®: See Methysergide.
Scopolamine: 0.006 mg./Kg. as single dose orally or subcut.
Secobarbital sodium (Seconal®): (1) Orally, 2-6 mg./Kg. as a single sedative or light hypnotic dose. (Adult = 100 mg.) (2) Rectally, 6 mg./Kg. as a minimal hypnotic dose. (Adult = 200 mg.)
Seconal®: See Secobarbital.
Septra®: See Trimethoprim with sulfamethoxazole.
Seromycin®: See Cycloserine.
Serpasil®: See Reserpine.
Sodium bicarbonate: See p. 138.

Sodium nitrite: 10 mg./Kg. for every 12 Gm./100 ml. hemoglobin. May repeat one-half dose in 30 minutes.

Sodium phosphate: 150-200 mg./Kg./dose orally. (Adult = 4-8 Gm.)

Sodium polystyrene sulfonate (Kayexalate®): Children: 1 mEq. potassium/Gm. resin. Calculate dose on base of desired exchange. Instill rectally in 10% glucose. May be administered every 6 hours. Adult: 15 Gm. orally 1-4 times daily in small amount of water or syrup (3-4 ml./Gm. resin).

Sodium salicylate: As a single analgesic or antipyretic dose, 65 mg./year of age orally. (Adult = 0.3-0.6 Gm.) For rheumatic fever, 90-130 mg./Kg./day orally to maintain a blood level of 20-30 mg./100 ml. (Adult = 6-8 Gm.)

Sodium sulfate: 150-200 mg./Kg./dose orally. Give a 50% solution. (Adult = 8-12 Gm.)

Solu-Cortef®: See Hydrocortisone.

Soma®: See Carisoprodol.

Spectinomycin (Trobicin®): See p. 93.

Spironolactone (Aldactone®): (1) Diagnostic test, 0.5-1.5 Gm./sq.M./day in divided doses orally. (2) Edemas and ascites, 1.7-3.3 mg./Kg./day orally in divided doses. Start with smaller dose. **Caution.** (Adult - 25 mg. 3-6 times daily orally.)

Stanozolol (Winstrol®): 0.1 mg./Kg./day.

Staphcillin®: See Penicillins.

Sterane®: See Prednisolone.

Sterolone®: See Prednisolone.

Stilbestrol: 0.1-1 mg./day. (Adult = 0.5-1 mg.)

Stoxil®: See Idoxuridine.

Streptomycin sulfate: See p. 93.

Strophanthin: See Ouabain.

Sudafed®: See Pseudoephedrine hydrochloride.

Sulfadiazine: See p. 93.

Sulfamethoxazole (Gantanol®): See p. 93.

Sulfisoxazole (Gantrisin®): See p. 93.

Sulfonamides: See p. 93.

Sus-Phrine®: See Epinephrine.

Symmetrel®: See Amantadine.

Synkayvite®: See Menadiol sodium diphosphate.

Synthroid Sodium®: See Levothyroxine sodium.

Syntopressin®: See Lypressin.

Tacaryl®: See Methdilazine.

Tapazole®: See Methimazole.

Teldrin®: See Chlorpheniramine.

Tempra®: See Acetaminophen.

Tensilon®: See Edrophonium chloride.

Testosterone: (1) Testosterone enanthate (Delatestryl®): 200 mg. I.M. every 4 weeks for teen-age male. (2) Testosterone cypionate: 50-200 mg. I.M. every 2-4 weeks for teen-age male. (3) Testosterone propionate in oil: 10-50 mg. 2-6 times a week I.M. for adult or teen-age male. (4) Testosterone microcrystals in aqueous suspension: 100 mg. I.M. every 2-3 weeks. (5) Testosterone pellets: 300 mg. every 3 months.

Tetrachloroethylene: See p. 523.

Tetracyclines: See p. 94.

See Precautions. p. 610.

Tetraethylammonium chloride: Test dose, 250 mg./sq.M., I.V.
   Caution: Phentolamine should be available. (Adult = 10-15 mg./Kg. I.V. or I.M.)

Thenylene®: See Methapyrilene hydrochloride.

Theophylline: 10 mg./Kg./day orally in 2-3 divided doses.

Thiabendazole (Mintezol®): 44 mg./Kg./day (maximum, 3 Gm.) in divided doses. See also p. 525.

Thiamine hydrochloride: See pp. 48, 50.

Thiopental sodium (Pentothal®): 10-20 mg./Kg. rectally **slowly** for basal anesthesia.

Thioridazine (Mellaril®): Children 2-12 years: 0.5-3 mg./Kg./day; increase until maximum therapeutic effect is obtained. Older children: 20-40 mg./day (not for children under 2 years). (Adult = 20-200 mg./day. Psychoses: 200-800 mg./day.)

Thorazine®: See Chlorpromazine.

Thyroid: See pp. 410, 412.

L-Thyroxine sodium: See Levothyroxine sodium.

Tigan®: See Trimethobenzamide.

Tofranil®: See Imipramine.

Tolazoline (Priscoline®): Up to 5 years, 2-10 mg.; over 5 years, 5-15 mg. orally or I.M. Increase by 2-10 mg. every 4 hours p.r.n. until flush or "goose-pimples" appear. (Adult = 12.5 mg. t.i.d.)

Tolserol®: See Mephenesin.

Toluidine blue: Initial dose, 2.5-7.5 mg./Kg./day I.V. Subsequent dose, 2-5 mg./Kg./day I.V. (Adult = 6-8 mg./Kg.)

Trecator®: See Ethionamide.

Triamcinolone (Aristocort®, Kenacort®, Kenalog®): See Table 22-6.

Tribromoethanol: 65-100 mg./Kg. rectally. (Adult = 60 mg./Kg.) Not over 8 Gm. should be given.

Trichlormethiazide: 0.03-0.1 mg./Kg./day orally. (Adult = 2-8 mg. daily.)

Tridione®: See Trimethadione.

Triethylenemelamine (TEM): Initial dose, 5 mg./day orally. Subsequent dose, 1 mg./day or 0.04 mg./Kg. orally. (Adult = 5 mg., then 2.5 mg.) **Caution.**

Triiodothyronine (liothyronine, Cytomel®): 25-30 μg. are equivalent to 65 mg. thyroid, U.S.P., or 0.1 mg. levothyroxine sodium.

Trimethadione (Tridione®): 15-50 mg./Kg./day orally. Start with smaller dose and increase gradually. (Adult = 0.3-2 Gm.)

Trimethaphan (Arfonad®) camsylate: Adult = 1-15 mg./minute I.V.

Trimethobenzamide (Tigan®): 15 mg./Kg./day in divided doses. Children weighing less than 15 Kg., one-half suppository (100 mg.) t.i.d. Children over 15 Kg., 100 mg. t.i.d. orally or 100-200 mg. t.i.d. rectally.

Trimethoprim with sulfamethoxazole (Bactrim®, Septra®): See p. 93.

Tripelennamine (Pyribenzamine®): 3-5 mg./Kg./day orally in 3-6 divided doses. (Maximum, 300 mg./day.) (Adult = 50 mg. q.i.d.)

Trisulfapyrimidines: See Sulfonamides.

Tubocurarine (curare): 0.2-0.4 mg./Kg./day I.M. or subcut. **Caution.** (Adult = 6-9 mg.)

Tylenol®: See Acetaminophen.

Ultandren®: See Fluoxymesterone.

See Precautions, p. 610.

Unipen®: See Penicillins.

Urea: (1) 0.8 Gm./Kg./day in 3 divided doses orally. (Adult = 8 Gm.) (2) 0.5-1.5 Gm./Kg. I.V. over a period of 30-60 minutes. (Adult = 1-1.5 Gm./Kg.)

Urecholine Chloride®: See Bethanechol chloride.

Valium®: See Diazepam.

Vancocin®: See Vancomycin.

Vancomycin (Vancocin®): See p. 94.

Vasopressin (Pitressin®) injection: 0.125-0.5 ml. (20 units/ml.) I.M. Short duration. (Adult = 0.25-0.5 ml.)

Vasopressin (Pitressin®) tannate injection: 0.2-2 ml. (5 units/ml. in oil) every 2-4 days p.r.n., I.M. Start with smaller doses and increase. Effective 1-3 days. (Adult = 0.3-1 ml.)

Vasoxyl®: See Methoxamine hydrochloride.

Velban®: See Vinblastine.

Versenate® (edathamil): See p. 381.

Vinblastine (Velban®): 0.1-0.2 mg./Kg./week as single dose I.V. (Adult = 0.1-0.15 mg./Kg. I.V. weekly.)

Vincristine (Oncovin®): 0.05-0.15 mg./Kg./week as single dose I.V. (Same as adult.) (See also Table 23-4.)

Viokase® (pancreatic replacement): 0.3-0.6 Gm. with each feeding. (Same as adult dose.)

Vitamin A: See pp. 48, 50, 189.

Vitamin C: See Ascorbic acid.

Vitamin D: See pp. 48, 52.

Vitamin D_2: See Calciferol.

Vitamin K_1: See Phytonadione.

Winstrol®: See Stanozolol.

Wyamine®: See Mephentermine sulfate.

Wydase®: See Hyaluronidase.

Xylocaine®: See Lidocaine.

Yomesan®: See Niclosamide.

Zarontin®: See Ethosuximide.

NORMAL BLOOD CHEMISTRY VALUES*
(And Miscellaneous Other Hematologic Values)
Values vary with the procedure employed.

(S) = Determination made on sample of serum.   (P) = Plasma.
(B) = Whole blood.   (RBC) = Red blood cells.
(Hgb.) = Hemoglobin.

Acetone bodies (as acetone). (S)
1-6 mg./100 ml.

Acetylcholinesterase. (Hgb.)
(Kaplan):
0-3 days: 3.4-5.2 units/Gm.
Hgb. $\times 10^2$
3-9 weeks: 3-4 units/Gm.
Hgb. $\times 10^2$
10-17 weeks: 4.9-6.3 units/Gm.
Hgb. $\times 10^2$
Adults: 5.3-7.3 units/Gm.
Hgb. $\times 10^2$

Adenosine triphosphate. (RBC)
Premature: 5.66 μM./Gm. Hgb.
Adults: 3.86 μM./Gm. Hgb.

Albumin: See Proteins.

**Albumin binding capacity
reserve.** (S)
Cord blood: 220-328 μg. PSP
bound/ml.

ACTH: See Corticotropin, p. 636.

Aldolase. (S)
0.15-0.8 μM. fructose diphosphate
split/ml. serum/hour.

Aldolase. (P)
Newborn: 4 × adult
Children: 2 × adult
Adults: 1.8-4.9 I.U./L.

Aldolase. (P or S)
Cord blood, male: 8.8-18.2
Bruns units/ml.
Cord blood, female: 14.5-22.1
Bruns units/ml.
Birth-2 years: 18 Bruns units/ml.
2-15 years: 7-13 Bruns units/ml.
Adults: 3-8 Bruns units/ml.

Aldosterone. (P)
First year: 25-140 ng./100 ml.
Second year: 9-25 ng./100 ml.
0.03-0.08 μg./100 ml.

Amino acid nitrogen. (P)
Children: 3.4-5.4 mg./100 ml.
Adults: 4-6 mg./100 ml.

δ-Aminolevulinic acid. (S)
Children: 4-20 μg./100 ml.

δ-Aminolevulinic acid dehydrase. (P)
Children: 0.056 μg./ml. plasma
(mean)

Ammonia. (B)
Full-term: 90-150 μg./100 ml.
Children: 45-80 μg./100 ml.
Adults: 40-70 μg./100 ml.; 0.75-
1.96 μg. ammonia nitrogen/ml.

Ammonia nitrogen. (S)
0.1-0.2 mg./100 ml.

Amylase. (P)
First 3 days (S): 6-60 Somogyi
units
After 1 year: 70-200 Somogyi
units (6-33 Close-Street
units)/100 ml.
Adults: 40-140 Somogyi units/100
ml.

Androstenedione. (P) (Fraser)
Prepubertal females: 30 ± 4
mμg./100 ml.

Androsterone sulfate. (P)
3.4-16.5 μg./100 ml.

Antidiuretic hormone. (B)
1.6 ± 0.6 μg./ml. after 8 hours
of dehydration

**Antihemophilic globulin
(Factor VIII).** (P)
Children: 107 ± 25 units/100 ml.
plasma

Ascorbic acid. (S)
0.4-1.5 mg./100 ml.

Base, bicarbonate-bound. (S)
19-30 mEq./L.

Base, total fixed. (S)
Children: 143-160 mEq./L.
Adults: 145-160 mEq./L.

Bicarbonate. (P)
18-23 mM./L.

---

*Adapted from O'Brien, Ibbott, & Rodgerson and many other sources.

Bilirubin, total. (S)
Premature:
  Birth: up to 3.5 mg./100 ml.
  1st day: up to 8 mg./100 ml.
  2nd day: up to 12 mg./100 ml.
  3rd-5th days: up to 25 mg./
    100 ml.
Full-term:
  Birth: up to 3.5 mg./100 ml.
  1st day: up to 5 mg./100 ml.
  2nd day: up to 9 mg./100 ml.
  3rd-5th days: up to 13 mg./
    100 ml.
Children and adults:
  Conjugated: 0-0.3 mg./100 ml.
  Unconjugated: 0.1-0.7 mg./100
    ml.

Bleeding time.
1-3 min.

Bromide. (S)
0.7-1 μg./100 ml.

Butanol-extractable iodine (BEI).
  (S)
Premature at birth.
  After 24-34 weeks of gesta-
    tion: 2.9-4.6 μg./100 ml.
  After 35-38 weeks of gesta-
    tion. 4.2-8.0 μg./100 ml.
Full-term at birth: 7.0 ± 1.15
  μg./100 ml.
2-5 days:
  After 24-34 weeks of gesta-
    tion: 4.0-9.5 (mean, 5.8)
    μg./100 ml.
  After 35-38 weeks of gesta-
    tion: 7.0-12.0 (mean, 8.8)
    μg./100 ml.
  After full-term gestation:
    7.2-15.2 (mean, 11.5) μg./
    100 ml.
8 weeks-6 months: 4.5-8.0 μg./
  100 ml.
Children after 6 months: 4.5-7.3
  μg./100 ml.
Adults: 3.2-6.4 μg./100 ml.

Calcium. (S)
Premature:
  Birth: 4.7 ± 0.4 mEq./L.
  6-10 days: 4.1 ± 0.6 mEq./L.
  20-25 days: 4.5 ± 0.5 mEq./L.
Full-term: 3.7-6 mEq./L.
  (7.3-12 mg./100 ml.)
Infants: 5-6 mEq./L.
  (10-12 mg./100 ml.)
Older children: 4.5-5.8 mEq./L.
  (9-11.5 mg./100 ml.)

Calcium. (Cont'd.)
Adults: 4.5-5.7 mEq./L.
  (9-11.5 mg./100 ml.)

Calcium, unbound. (S)
50-58% of total calcium

Carbon dioxide content, arterial
    blood.
1.5-3.4 years: 16-21 mM./L.
Older children: 19-22 mM./L.

Carbon dioxide content, total. (P)
Premature: 12.5-25 mM./L.
  (28-56 Vol.%) (P)
Infants: 18-27 mM./L.
  (40-60 Vol.%) (P)
Older children: 21-28 mM./L.
  (47-64 Vol.%) (B)
Adults: 24-29 mM./L.
  (55-65 Vol.%) (P)

Carbon dioxide tension, arterial
    blood.
1.5-6.4 years: 34-41 mm. Hg
6.5-12 years: 35-41 mm. Hg
12.5-17 years: 38-44 mm. Hg

Carbonic anhydrase activity. (B)
First week: 1000-1800 microactivity units/ml.
Adults: 2500-3000 microactivity
  units/ml.

pCO$_2$ (sea level). (S)
Children: 40 mm. Hg

Carotene. (P)
Full-term: 70 μg./100 ml.
1-6 months: 10-300 μg./100 ml.
6-18 months: 100-670 μg./100 ml.
Older children and adults: 50-300
  μg./100 ml.

Cephalin flocculation. (S)
0-1+ units

Ceruloplasmin (copper oxidase). (P)
Male children: 28 ± 5 mg./100 ml.
Female children: 35 ± 6 mg./100 ml.

Ceruloplasmin. (P)
0.370 ± 0.06 absorbance units in
  1-cm path cells. (Absorbance
  units × 87.5 = mg. cerulo-
  plasmin/100 ml.)

Chloride, as Cl⁻. (S)
Premature: 95-110 mEq./L.
  (339-393 mg./100 ml.)
Full-term: 96-116 mEq./L.
  (343-413 mg./100 ml.)
Children: 98-105 mEq./L.
  (350-375 mg./100 ml.)
Adults: 98-108 mEq./L.
  (348-386 mg./100 ml.)

Cholesterol esters. (S)
70-78% of total cholesterol

Cholesterol, total. (P)
Full-term: 45-167 mg./100 ml.
Infants: 70-190 mg./100 ml.
Older children: 110-205 mg./
100 ml.
Adults: 150-250 mg./100 ml. (May
be higher in older individuals.)

Cholinesterase.
Children (S): > 0.8 pH unit
Adults (P): 0.5-1.3 pH units
Adults (RBC): 0.5-1.0 pH unit

Christmas factor (Factor IX). (P)
Children: 100 ± 22 units/100 ml.
plasma

Circulation time, Decholin®.
3-6 years: 8-12 seconds
6-12 years: 7.5-15 seconds
12-15 years: 10-16 seconds

Circulation time, fluorescein.
Upper limit of normal:
10 Kg.: 8 seconds
20 Kg.: 8.4 seconds
40 Kg.: 11.3 seconds

Citric acid. (S)
Full-term: 1.5-4.5 mg./100 ml.
2-16 years: 1-3.5 mg./100 ml.
Adults: 1.7-3 mg./100 ml.

Citrulline. (P)
0.3-1 mg./100 ml.

Coagulation time (test tube method).
3-9 min.

Complement. (S)
1-3.5 units

Copper. (S)
0-6 months: < 70 μg./100 ml.
6 months-5 years: 27-153 μg./100
ml.
5-17 years: 94-234 μg./100 ml.
Adult males: 70-140 μg./100 ml.
Adult females: 84-165 μg./100 ml.

Copper oxidase: See Ceruloplasmin.

Coproporphyrin, erythrocytic. (RBC)
0.5-2.0 μg./100 ml.

Corticosterone (mean). (P)
Cord blood: 5.8 μg./100 ml.
3-7 days: 13.1-14.9 μg./100 ml.
1 week to 10 years: 11.5-12.7 μg./
100 ml.
Adults: 5-18 μg./100 ml.
All ages: 10-20 μg./100 ml.
(Visser)

Corticotropin (ACTH). (P)
Children (A.M. value): 20-120
μμg./ml.
Adult: Less than 0.9 (average 0.6)
mU./100 ml.

Cortisol. (P)
Cord blood: 12.9 μg./100 ml.
3-7 days: 14 ± 0.87 μg./100 ml.
4-14 days: 5.2 ± 2.4 μg./100 ml.
(Hirose)
1 week to 10 years: 11.7 ± 1.5
μg./100 ml.
Adults: 11.7 ± 1.5 μg./100 ml.

Cortisol secretion rate.
Basal (all ages): 5-30 mg./day
(8-17.5 mg./sq.M. surface
area/day)
Maximum after corticotropin (ACTH):
125-200 mg./day

Creatine, as creatinine. (S)
Adult males: 0.17-0.5 mg./100 ml.
Adult females: 0.35-0.93 mg./100
ml.

Creatine + creatinine. (B)
5-8 mg./100 ml.

Creatine kinase. (P)
Males: 5-75 I.U./L.
Females: 6-50 I.U./L.

Creatine phosphokinase. (S)
Adults: up to 0.72 mU.

Creatinine. (P)
Children: 0.4-1.2 mg./100 ml.
Adults: 0.7-1.5 mg./100 ml.

Dehydroepiandrosterone sulfate. (P)
Girls: 4.2-27.6 μg./100 ml.

Epinephrine. (P)
Premature: 0.86 ± 1.21 μg./L.
Full-term: 0.35 ± 0.64 μg./L.
Children: < 0.1 μg./L.

17β-Estradiol. (P)
Young adult males: 0.015 ± 0.012
μg./100 ml.

Estrone. (P)
Young adult males: 0.042 ± 0.009
μg./100 ml.

Fats (lipids), total. (S)
Full-term: 170-440 mg./100 ml.
Infants: 240-800 mg./100 ml.
Older children: 490-1090 mg./100
ml.
Adults: 450-1000 mg./100 ml.

Fats, neutral. (S)
Full-term: 10-150 mg./100 ml.
Infants: 0-400 mg./100 ml.
Older children: 150-250 mg./100
ml.

Fatty acids. (P)
Children: 7.1-17.1 mEq./L.
(190-456 mg./100 ml.)
Adults: 7.3-36.9 (mean, 12.3)
mEq./L. (192-972 mg./100 ml.)

Fatty acids, "free." (P)
Newborn: 1627 ± 155 μg./ml.
Below 4 years: 180-430 μg./ml.
Older children: 230-380 μg./ml.

Fibrinogen (Factor I). (P)
Full-term: 0.26 Gm./100 ml.
Children: 0.2-0.5 Gm./100 ml.
Adults: 0.2-0.4 Gm./100 ml.

Folic acid. (S)
Adults: 5-21 mμg./ml.

**Follicle-stimulating hormone
(FSH).** (P)
Birth: Mean 32.9 ng./ml.
Boys: Mean 9.0 ng./ml.
Girls: Mean 1.5 ng./ml.
Prepuberal children: 0-20 μg./
100 ml. (Albert)
Menstruating girls, follicular
phase: 3.3 ng./ml.
Menstruating girls, luteal phase:
1.4 ng./ml.
Menstruating girls, midcycle:
8.6 ng./ml.

Galactose. (P)
< 20 mg./100 ml.

Galactose-1-phosphate. (RBC)
Newborn: 1-10 μg./ml. packed
cells
Infants: 0-2 μg./ml. packed
cells
Older children: < 1 mg./100 ml.
packed RBC lysate

Galactose-1-P-uridyl transferase.
(RBC)
1.7-9 units/Gm. Hgb.
308-475 I.U./Gm. Hgb.

Globulin: See Proteins.

Glucose (Folin-Wu). (Venous blood.)
Children and adults: 80-120 mg./
100 ml.

Glucose (true). (B or S)
Premature: 20-80 mg./100 ml.
Full-term: 30-100 mg./100 ml.
1 day: 30-65 mg./100 ml.
Children: 60-105 mg./100 ml.
Adults: 60-100 mg./100 ml.

Glucose-6-phosphate dehydrogenase.
(Hgb.) (Kaplan)
0-3 days: 9.8-14.4 units/Gm. Hgb.
3-9 weeks: 6.3-10.3 units/Gm. Hgb.
10-17 weeks: 7.8-11.6 units/Gm.
Hgb.
Children: 4.8 ± 0.5 units/Gm. Hgb.
Adults: 5.5-9.3 units/Gm. Hgb.

Glucose-6-phosphate dehydrogenase.
(RBC)
150-250 units/100 ml. packed RBC
Adults (B): 250-500 units/10^9 cells

Glutamic acid. (P)
1 day: 0.3-15 mg./100 ml.
1 month: 0.7-1.3 mg./100 ml.
Adult: 0.2-2.8 mg./100 ml.

Glutamine. (P)
1 day: 8-97 mg./100 ml.
Children: 6-12 mg./100 ml.
Adults: 6-10 mg./100 ml.

α-Glutamyl transpeptidase. (S)
0-750 μg./100 ml. (mean = 225
μg./100 ml.)

Glutathione. (B)
Adults: 24-37 mg./100 ml.

Glutathione peroxidase. (RBC)
Premature: 480 ± 107 units/100
ml. RBC
Full-term: 530 ± 163 units/100
ml. RBC
Adults: 611 ± 106 units/100 ml.
RBC

Glutathione, reduced (GSH). (RBC)
48-84 mg./100 ml. packed cells

Glutathione reductase. (RBC)
Cord blood: 24-44 units
Children: 35-81 units
Adults: 40-64 units

Glycine. (P)
1 day: 1.9-3.7 mg./100 ml.
1 month: 0.9-2.2 mg./100 ml.
Adult: 0.9-4.1 mg./100 ml.

Glycogen. (RBC)
Full-term: 48-361 μg./Gm. Hgb.
Infants: 32-134 μg./Gm. Hgb.
Older children: 22-109 μg./Gm. Hgb.
Adults: 20-105 μg./Gm. Hgb.

Growth hormone. (P)
Cord blood: 23 ± 3.5 pg./ml.
Children: 3.2 ± 3.8 pg./ml.

Haptoglobin. (S)
Adults: 40-170 mg./100 ml. as
Hgb.-binding capacity

Hemoglobin A₂.
Adults: 1.8-3.7% of total Hgb.

Hemoglobin, fetal. (Hgb.)
Newborn: 50-85% of total Hgb.
2 months: 35-50% of total Hgb.
1 year: < 15% of total Hgb.
Up to 2 years: < 5% of total Hgb.
Over 2 years: < 2% of total Hgb.

Hemoglobin, fetal. (P)
< 3 mg./100 ml.

Hexokinase. (Hgb.)
Premature: 1.85 μM./Gm. Hgb.
Children: 0.5 ± 0.07 μM./Gm. Hgb.
Adults: 0.95 μM./Gm. Hgb.

Histamine. (B)
Adults: Approx. 4-7 μg./100 ml.

α-Hydroxybutyric dehydrogenase. (S)
Adults: 140-350 units

17-Hydroxycorticosteroids. (P)
3-7 days: 4.2-6.8 μg./100 ml.
3 months to 17 years: 9-20 μg./
100 ml. between 8 A.M. and
9 A.M.
Adults: 5-25 μg./100 ml.

Immunoglobulins: See Proteins.

Insulin. (P)
First day: 7 ± 1 μU./ml.
Children: 10-19 μU./ml.

Insulin. (P)
Children: 5-40 μU./ml.

Iodine: See Butanol-extractable
iodine (BEI) and Protein-
bound iodine (PBI).

Iodine, T₄ (by column). (S)
3.2-6.4 μg./100 ml.

Iron. (S)
Full-term 190 ± 80 μg./100 ml.
3 months: 50 μg./100 ml.
Children: 50-180 μg./100 ml.;
183 ± 96 μg./100 ml. (by
atomic absorption).
Adults: 65-175 μg./100 ml.

Iron-binding capacity. (S)
Full-term: 120-250 μg./100 ml.
Children: 187-653 μg./100 ml.
Adults: 250-410 μg./100 ml.

Iron, % saturation. (S)
Older children: 13-32%
Adults: 20-55%

Isocitric dehydrogenase. (S)
Cord blood: 5.1-11.1 units
Children: 2.9-8.1 units
Adults: 2.8-7.6 units

Isoleucine. (P)
1 day: 0.4-0.7 mg./100 ml.
1 month: 0.6-1.0 mg./100 ml.
Adult: 0.5-1.3 mg./100 ml.

α-Ketoglutaric acid. (B)
8-10 mg./100 ml.

Ketones. (S)
Children: < 10 mg./100 ml.

17-Ketosteroids. (P)
Adults: 25-125 μg./100 ml.

Lactate. (S)
Children: 1.1-2.2 mEq./L.
(10-20 mg./100 ml.)
Adults: 0.44-1.8 mM./L.
(4-16 mg./100 ml.)

Lactate dehydrogenase. (S)
First week: 308-2540 I.U./L.
Thereafter, slowly falling to adult
levels by age 14.
Adult males: 98-186 I.U./L.
Adult females: 87-178 I.U./L.
(Values expressed in I.U./L. at
30°C.)

Lead.
0-50 μg./100 ml. blood; 1-3 μg./
100 ml. serum

Leucine. (P)
1 day: 0.6-1.4 mg./100 ml.
1 month: 1.2-2.0 mg./100 ml.
Adult: 1.0-2.2 mg./100 ml.

Leucine aminopeptidase. (P or S)
Newborn: $44 \pm$ I.U./L. (O'Brien)
1 month-adult: 15-50 I.U./L.
(O'Brien)
Infants: < 200 units
Adult males: 75-230 units
Adult females: 80-210 units

**Lipalbumin, as % of total lipo-
protein.** (S)
Adult males: 12-24%
Adult females: 17-30%

Lipase. (S)
Infants: 0.2-1.6 S.T. units
Children: 20-136 S.T. units (based
on 4-hour incubation). (O'Brien)
Older children: 0.3-1.6 S.T. units
Adults: < 0.5 unit

Lipids: See Fats (lipids).

Lipoprotein lipase. (P or S)
Children and adults: 0.26-0.34
mEq./ml./minute

Lipoproteins, total. (S)
Newborn: 170-440 mg./100 ml.
Infants: 240-800 mg./100 ml.
Older children: 490-1090 mg./
100 ml.
a. **Lipoproteins, alpha.** (S)
Full-term: 71-176 mg./100 ml.
Infants: 67-281 mg./100 ml.
Older children: 147-327 mg./
100 ml.
b. **Lipoproteins, beta.** (S)
Full-term: 51-176 mg./100 ml.
Infants: 122-450 mg./100 ml.
Older children: 225-541 mg./
100 ml.
As % of total:
Adult males: 36-59%
Adult females: 29-53%
c. **Lipoproteins, omega.** (S)
Full-term: 48-106 mg./100 ml.
Infants: 51-247 mg./100 ml.
Older children: 98-268 mg./
100 ml.

Long-acting thyroid stimulator (LATS).
Adults: None detectable

Luteinizing hormone. (S)
Males:
Under 9 years: 2.5-4.2 mI.U./
ml.
9-10 years: 3.5-7.0 mI.U./ml.
11-16 years: 4.0-14.0 mI.U./
ml.
Adults: 6-23 mI.U./ml.
Females:
2-9 years: 1.1-4.0 mI.U./ml.
10-12 years: 1.6-12.0 mI.U./
ml.
13-15 years: 3.0-22 mI.U./ml.
Adults: 3.0-20 mI.U./ml.

Magnesium. (S)
Infants (first week): 2.1-2.4
mg./100 ml. (Tsang)
Infants (first week): 1.4-1.7 mg./
100 ml. (Bajpal)
Children: 1.2-2.5 mEq./L.
(1.5-3.1 mg./100 ml.)

Magnesium. (Cont'd.)
Children: 1.40 ± 0.18 mEq./L.
(O'Brien)
Adults: 1.5-2.4 mEq./L.
(1.8-2.9 mg./100 ml.)

Malic dehydrogenase. (S)
Children: 52-98 units
Adults: 27-59 units

Manganese. (S)
Adults: 0.04-0.09 μg./100 ml.

β-Melanocyte-stimulating hormone.
(P)
Children (A.M. value): < 90 pg./
ml.

Methemoglobin. (B)
Premature: < 4.7 Gm./100 ml.
Full-term: 0.0-2.8 Gm./100 ml.
After neonatal period: 0.0-0.3
Gm./100 ml.
Infants and young children: 0-2.8%
of total Hgb.
Adults: < 3% of total Hgb.

Methionine. (P)
1 day: 0.2-0.6 mg./100 ml.
Adult: 0.1-0.6 mg./100 ml.

Milliosmols. (P)
270-290 mOsm./L. plasma water

Mucoprotein. (S)
Adults: 8-14 mg./100 ml. in
terms of galactose-mannose

Mucoprotein, carbohydrate. (S)
15.5-28.1 mg./100 ml.

Mucoprotein, protein. (S)
46.3-104.3 mg./100 ml.

Mucoprotein, tyrosine. (S)
2.3-4.3 mg./100 ml.

Nonprotein nitrogen. (S or P)
Full-term: 25-65 mg./100 ml.
Children: 18-35 mg./100 ml.
Adults (S): 20-35 mg./100 ml.
Adults (B): 25-50 mg./100 ml.

Norepinephrine. (P)
0.3-0.6 μg./L.

5'-Nucleotidase. (S)
Adults: Up to 1.6 units

Ornithine carbamyl transferase. (S)
Adults: < 5 nanomols

Osmolarity. (P)
270-290 mOsm./L. plasma water

Oxygen capacity. (B)
1.33 Vol. %/Gm. Hgb.
19-22 Vol. %

Oxygen content. (B)
Adults: 15-23 Vol. % (arterial);
10-18 Vol. % (venous)

Oxygen saturation. (B)
Full-term: 7-17.2 Vol. %
(33-80% saturated)
Children: 11.5-16.5 Vol. %
(60-85% saturated)

**Parathyroid hormone, radio-
immunoassayable.**
Cord blood: 15 ± 3 μl Eq./ml.
Children: 25 ± 0.7 μl Eq./ml.
Assayable levels not present
in 30% of normal children.

Partial thromboplastin time. (P)
Children: 48 ± 6 sec.

Pepsinogen. (P)
Adults: 200-425 units/ml.

pCO$_2$. (B)
40 mm. Hg (at sea level)
First 3 days: 23-52 mm. Hg

pH. (B, S, or P)
First 3 days: 7.25-7.55
Children and adults: 7.31-7.45

pH. (S from arterial blood)
1.5-3.4 years: 7.30-7.40
Older children: 7.35-7.43

Phenylalanine. (S)
Premature: 0-5 days, 1-6 mg./
100 ml.; 5-21 days, 3-27
mg./100 ml.; > 21 days, 2-7
mg./100 ml.
Newborn: < 0.35 mM./L.
(< 6 mg./100 ml.)
2-10 days: 0.06-0.3 mM./L.
(1-7 mg./100 ml.)
Children: 0.03-0.2 mM./L.
(0.7-3.5 mg./100 ml.)
Adults: < 0.24 mM./L.
(< 4 mg./100 ml.)

Phosphatase, acid. (S)
Full-term: 13.4 ± 3 I.U./L.
2-13 years: 10.8 ± 2.2 I.U./L.
Adult males: 0.5-11 I.U./L.
Adult females: 0.2-9.5 I.U./L.
Adults: 0-1.1 Shinowara units
Adults: 0-5 King-Armstrong
units.
(One I.U. = 16.7 Bessey-
Lowry units; 1 Bessey-
Lowry unit = approx.
1.8 Bodansky units.)

Phosphatase, alkaline. (S)
Premature: 33-83 I.U./L.
Full-term: 83-217 I.U./L.
Infants: 73-226 I.U./L.
Older children: 57-151 I.U./L.

Phosphatase, alkaline. (Cont'd.)
Puberty: 57-258 I.U./L.
Adults: 13-40 I.U./L. (1 I.U. =
16.7 Bessey-Lowry units)
Adults: 2-9 Shinowara units

Phosphatides.
Newborn: 75-170 mg./100 ml.
Up to 1 yr.: 100-275 mg./100 ml.
Children: 180-295 mg./100 ml.

Phosphogalactose isomerase. (S)
Adults: 1.4-2.8 μM./100 ml.

Phosphohexose isomerase. (RBC)
< 18 months: 40-110 units
> 18 months: 40-90 units
Adults: 47-79 units

Phospholipids. (P)
Newborn: 1.34 ± 0.36 μM./ml.
Infants: 122-276 mg./100 ml.
3-20 years: 2.49-4.36 μM./ml.
(O'Brien)
Adults: 145-200 mg./100 ml.

Phosphorus, inorganic. (S)
Premature: Birth, 6.8 ± 0.6
mg./100 ml.; 1-3 days,
8.1 ± 1.2 mg./100 ml.;
6-10 days, 8.9 ± 1.4 mg./
100 ml.; 20-25 days, $8 \pm$
0.7 mg./100 ml.
Full-term: 2.4-4.8 mEq./L.
(4.2-8.6 mg./100 ml.)
6-12 days: 6.9 ± 1.0 mg./100 ml.
Infants (2 weeks to 5 months)
(mean): 3.9 mEq./L.
(6.8 mg./100 ml.)
Older infants: 2.3-3.9 mEq./L.
(4-6.7 mg./100 ml.)
Children: 2-3.2 mEq./L.
(3.7-5.7 mg./100 ml.)
Adults: 1.4-2.6 mEq./L.
(2.5-4.5 mg./100 ml.)

Plasminogen. (S)
Premature cord blood: 0-9.2 units
$\times 10^{-3}$/ml.
Full-term cord blood: 2.8-10.4
units $\times 10^{-3}$/ml.
Adults: 12-24.4 units $\times 10^{-3}$/ml.

Porphyrin, total. (P)
Adults: < 7 μg./100 ml.

Potassium. (S)
Premature: 4.5-7.2 mEq./L.
(18-28 mg./100 ml.)
Full-term: 3.7-5.2 mEq./L.
(15-21 mg./100 ml.)
Children: 3.5-5.8 mEq./L.
(14-23 mg./100 ml.)
Adults: 3.5-5.5 mEq./L.
(14-21.5 mg./100 ml.)

Potassium. (RBC)
86-104 mEq./L.

Pressors. (P)
Newborn: (ng./ml.)
Umbilical artery: 1.6 ± 0.4
Umbilical vein: 1.1 ± 0.2

Proaccelerin (Factor V). (P)
Children: 94 ± 33 units/100 ml.

Progesterone. (p)
Cord: 435-2000 ng./ml.
Mean = 1130
Third day: 0-11 ng./ml.

Proline. (P)
1.4-3.3 mg./100 ml.
54.0 ± 20 μg./ml. by colorimetric assay

Proteins.
a. **Total.** (S)
Premature: 4.3-7.6 Gm./100 ml.
Full-term: 4.6-7.4 Gm./100 ml.
Infants: 4.8-7.7 Gm./100 ml.
Older children and adults: 6-8 Gm./100 ml.
b. **Albumin.** (S)
Premature: 2.8-3.9 Gm./100 ml.
Full term: 2.3-5.1 Gm./100 ml.
Children: 3.2-5.5 Gm./100 ml.
Adults: 3.5-5.5 Gm./100 ml.
c. **Alpha₁ fetoprotein.** (S)
Premature: 20-60 mg./100 ml.
Full-term: 0-25 mg./100 ml.
d. **Globulin.**
(1) **Total.** (3)
Premature: 0.5-2.4 Gm./100 ml.
Full term: 1.8-2.6 Gm./100 ml.
1-3 months: 1.2-2.3 Gm./100 ml.
Older infants: 1.7-3.5 Gm./100 ml.
Older children: 1.5-3.5 Gm./100 ml.
Adults: 1.3-3.3 Gm./100 ml.
(2) **Alpha₁ globulin.** (S)
Premature: 0.13-0.5 Gm./100 ml.
Full-term: 0.12-0.3 Gm./100 ml.
Children: 0.12-0.35 Gm./100 ml.
Adults: 0.2-0.4 Gm./100 ml.
(3) **Alpha₂ globulin.** (S)
Premature: 0.25-0.65 Gm./100 ml.
Full-term: 0.25-0.5 Gm./100 ml.
Infants: 0.4-0.9 Gm./100 ml.

Proteins.
d. **Globulin.**
(3) **Alpha₂ globulin.** (Cont'd.)
Older children: 0.35-0.95 Gm./100 ml.
Adults: 0.5-0.9 Gm./100 ml.
(4) **Beta globulin.** (S)
Premature: 0.3-1.2 Gm./100 ml.
Full term: 0.17-0.6 Gm./100 ml.
1-4 months: 0.27-0.55 Gm./100 ml.
Older children: 0.5-1.3 Gm./100 ml.
Adults: 0.6-1.1 Gm./100 ml.
(5) **Gamma globulin.** See Table 2.
Birth: 0.73-1.6 Gm./100 ml.
1 month: 0.5-0.95 Gm./100 ml.
2½ months: 0.21-0.7 Gm./100 ml.
Adults: 0.7-1.7 Gm./100 ml.
(6) **Gamma M globulins.** (S)
Cord: 2.4-19.5 mg./100 ml.
4 days: 3.6-32.1 mg./100 ml.
2 months: 20-100 mg./100 ml.
1 year: 3-200 mg./100 ml.
Adult males: 70-350 mg./100 ml.
Adult females: 10-430 mg./100 ml.

Protein-bound iodine (PBI). (S)
Premature (< 2000 Gm.): 3.7-6.9 μg./100 ml.
Newborn: 5-9 μg./100 ml.
2-5 days: 9-14 μg./100 ml. (in cool environment)
Older children and adults: 4-8 μg./100 ml.
Adolescent males: 3.5-7 μg./100 ml.
Pregnancy: 7.8 ± 1.8 μg./100 ml.

Prothrombin (Factor II). (P)
Children: 102 ± 21 units/100 ml. plasma

Prothrombin time. (P)
Children: 13 ± 2 sec.

Protoporphyrin, erythrocytic. (RBC)
15-100 μg./100 ml.

Pyrophosphatase. (Hgb.) (Kaplan)
Newborn: 0.69-1.01 units

Pyruvate. (S)
Children and adults: 0.05-0.14 mEq./L. (0.4-1.2 mg./100 ml.)

Pyruvate. (B)
Adult males: 55.3 ± 2.4 μM./L. (arterial sample).

TABLE 2. Serum gamma globulins*: Normal values for children.

	Total (Gm./100 ml.)	IgG (Gamma G) (mg./100 ml.)	IgA (Gamma A) (mg./100 ml.)	IgM (Gamma M) (mg./100 ml.)
Cord blood				
Mean	1.28	850	< 4	12
Range	0.81-1.61	400-1650	0-15	0-23
1-6 months				
Mean	0.63	400	19-25	32
Range	0.24-1.05	230-950	4-60	11-86
1 year				
Mean	0.84	725	50	75
Range	0.32-1.18	281-1280	15-170	36-176
2-3 years				
Mean	1.08	700	90	100†
Range	0.73-1.46	495-1562	21-250	43-230
4-7 years				
Mean	1.22	850	120	120†
Range	0.54-1.95	350-1760	30-330	26-325
8-9 years				
Mean	1.38	900	200	130†
Range	0.70-2.03	500-1719	50-650	27-280
10-16 years				
Mean	1.38	1220	200	130†
Range	0.70-2.03	600-1720	44-670	27-205
Adult				
Mean		995	200	187
Range		620-1700	46-650	70-384

*Synonyms: Gamma G = IgG, gamma$_2$, gamma$_{ss}$ globulin; gamma A = IgA, gamma$_{1A}$, beta$_{2A}$ globulin; gamma M = IgM, gamma$_{1M}$, beta$_{2M}$, a 19S globulin.
†Significantly lower levels have been reported by some investigators.

Pyruvate kinase. (RBC)
11.0 ± 3.7 units/Gm. Hgb.

Pyruvic acid, fasting. (B)
1.3-2.3 mg./100 ml.

Renin activity. (P)
Children: 19 ± 16 ng.(ng.)/L./min.
Adults: 9 ± 7.6 ng./L./min.

Sedimentation rate. (B)
Wintrobe or Landau-Adams: 0-20 mm./hour. (5% of normal children have higher rates; micromethods may be used.)
Cutler: 0-15 mm./hour
Low birth weight (first week): < 10 mm./hour

Serotonin. (B)
Adults: 0.05-0.2 μg./ml.

Sodium. (S)
Premature: 130-140 mEq./L. (300-323 mg./100 ml.)
Children: 134-146 mEq./L. (310-339 mg./100 ml.)
Adults: 136-150 mEq./L. (315-345 mg./100 ml.)

Specific gravity. (B)
1.048-1.05

Specific gravity. (P)
1.025-1.03

Sugar: See Glucose.

Sulfates, inorganic, as $SO_4^=$. (S)
0.5-1 mEq./L.
(2.5-5 mg./100 ml.)
Adults: 0.8-1.2 mg./100 ml. as sulfur

Sulfation factor (for growth hormone). (S)
< 6 years: 0.3-1 unit
> 6 years: 0.7-1.4 units

Sulfur, neutral. (S)
1.7-3.5 mg./100 ml.

T$_3$: See Triiodothyronine (T$_3$).

T$_4$: See Thyroxine (T$_4$).

Testosterone. (P)
Prepuberal males: 0.0085-0.11 μg./100 ml.
Young adult males: 0.72 ± 0.49 μg./100 ml. (range, 0.32-1.8 μg./100 ml.)

Testosterone. (Cont'd.)
Adult males: 0.31-1.1 µg./100 ml.
Females: 0.05-0.3 µg./100 ml.

Thiamine. (B)
5.5-9.5 µg./100 ml.

Threonine. (P)
1 day: 1.3-4.0 mg./100 ml.
1 month: 1.7-3.2 mg./100 ml.

Thrombin time. (P)
Children: 14 ± 2 sec.

Thymol turbidity. (S)
Children: 0-5 units

Thyroid-stim. hormone (TSH). (S)
First day: 50 µU./ml. (mean)
Children: 4.73 ± 2.47 µU./ml.
Adults: < 8 µU./ml.

Thyroxine-binding activity of TBG.
(S)
Children: 16-30 µg./100 ml.
Adults: 10-27 µg./100 ml.

Thyroxine-binding globulin capacity.
(S)
Children and adults: 15.9-25.5
µg./100 ml.

Thyroxine, "free." (S)
Cord: 2.9 ng./100 ml. (mean)
Second, third day: 7 ng./100
ml. (mean)
Adults: 1.6-2.4 ng /100 ml.
(mean)

Thyroxine (T₄) by column.
Cord: 11.2 µg./100 ml. (mean)
Second, third day: 16.2 µg./100
ml. (mean)
Children: 2.9-6.4 µg./100 ml.
Adult: 8.3 µg./100 ml. (mean)

Tocopherol (vitamin E). (S) (Hopkins)
Premature: 0.05-0.35 mg./100 ml.
Full-term: 0.1-0.35 mg./100 ml.
2-5 months: 0.2-0.6 mg./100 ml.
6-24 months: 0.35-0.8 mg./100 ml.
2-12 years: 0.55-0.9 mg./100 ml.
Breast-fed infants: 0.6-1.1 mg./
100 ml. (adult values)

Transaminase (SGOT). (S)
Infants: Up to 67 I.U./L.; occasionally up to 118 I.U./L.
Children: 3-27 I.U./L.
Adults: 12-30 I.U./L. (Females
about 25% lower.)
(1 I.U. at 30°C. = 0.67 Karmen
unit at 25° C.)

Transaminase (SGPT). (S)
Infants: Up to 54 I.U./L.
Children: 1-30 I.U./L.
Adults: 5-26 I.U./L.

Triglycerides. (P)
Cord blood: 14-61
Children: 10-175 mg./100 ml.
Adults: 30-135 mg./100 ml.

Triiodothyronine (T₃), free. (S)
Cord: 146 pg./100 ml. (mean)
Second day: 1260 pg./100 ml.
(mean)
Adult: 378 pg./100 ml. (mean)

Triiodothyronine (T₃), total. (S)
Cord: < 30-50 ng./100 ml.
Second day: 419 ng./100 ml.
(mean)
Children: 96-170 ng./100 ml.
Adult: 122 ng./100 ml. (mean)

Tyrosine. (B)
1-2 days (full-term): 1-4 mg./
100 ml.
2-10 days (full-term): 1-9
mg./100 ml.
0-5 days (premature): 1-6 mg./
100 ml.
5-21 days (premature): 3-27
mg./100 ml.
Adult: 0.5-1.7 mg./100 ml.

Urea nitrogen. (B)
Infants: 5-15 mg./100 ml.
Older children and adults: 10-20
mg./100 ml.

Uric acid. (S)
First day: Full-term, 5.6 ± 0.8
mg./100 ml.; low birth weight,
6.8 ± 1.8 mg./100 ml.
Children: 2-5.5 mg./100 ml.
Men: 3-6.5 mg./100 ml.
Women: 1.5-5.5 mg./100 ml.

Venous pressure.
3-5 years: 29-63 mm. water
5-10 years: 42-74 mm. water

Vitamin A. (P)
Newborn: 15-46 µg./100 ml.
Infants: 15-140 µg./100 ml.
Older children: 15-110 µg./100 ml.

Vitamin B₁₂. (S)
Children and adults: 100-900
pg./ml.

Vitamin C. (P)
Children: 0.4-1.5 mg./100 ml.
Adults: 0.2-2 mg./100 ml.

Volume. (B)
Premature: 98 ml./Kg. (mean)
Full-term: 75-100 ml./Kg.
One year: 69-112 (mean, 86)
ml./Kg.
Older children: 51-86 (mean,
70) ml./Kg.

Volume. (P)
Full-term: 39-77 ml./Kg.
Infants: 40-50 ml./Kg.
Older children: 30-54 ml./Kg.

Water.
Whole blood: 79-81 Gm./100 ml.
Serum: 91-92 Gm./100 ml.
RBC: 64-65 Gm./100 ml.

Water, body.
0-11 days: 69-84% of body weight
11 days-6 months: 63-83%
6 months-2 years: 52-72%

Water, body. (Cont'd.)
2-7 years: 55-73%
7-16 years: 50-64%

Zinc. (B) (Concentration in packed
RBC is about 15% of amount
in whole blood.)
Newborn: about 25% of adult value
1 year: about 50% of adult value
Adults: 80-165 µg./100 ml.

Zinc sulfate turbidity. (S)
2-8 Maclagen units

NORMAL VALUES: URINE, BONE MARROW, DUODENAL FLUID, FECES, SWEAT, AND MISCELLANEOUS

URINE

Acetyl kynurenine: 1.6-22.5 (mean, 9) µM./Kg./7 hours after a tryptophan load

Acidity, titratable: 20-50 mEq./day

Addis count (per 12-hour specimen):
Red cells: < 1 million
White cells: < 2 million
Casts: < 10,000
Protein: < 55 mg.

Aldosterone: Adults: 4-32 µg./day

Aldosterone:
Children: 3-13 µg./sq. M./day
Adults: 1-15 µg./day

Aldosterone secretion rate:
First week: 9-41 µg./day (mean = 23)
1 week - 1 year: 25-138 µg./day
(mean = 72)
1-15 years: 57-162 µg./day (mean = 91)
Adults: 39-138 µg./day (mean = 80)

Amino acid N₂: 2.2-4.4 mg./Kg./day
(about 2% of total NPN)
Adults: 50-200 mg./day

5-Amino-4-imidazolecarboxamide:
Children: 0.92 ± 0.33 µg./mg.
creatinine/day

Amino nitrogen:
Older children: 129 µM./Kg./day
Premature: 6 times as high
Full-term: 3 times as high

δ-Aminolevulinic acid: See Porphyrins.

Ammonia:
2-12 months: 4-20 µEq./min./
sq. M.
1-16 years: 6-16 µEq./min./sq.M.

Amount: (ml./day)
1-2 days: 30-60 ml.
4-5 days: 70-250 ml.
6-10 days: 200-300 ml.
10 days-2 months: 250-450 ml.
2 months-1 year: 400-500 ml.
1-2 years: 500-700 ml.
3-5 years: 600-1200 ml.
6-8 years: 700-1300 ml.
8-14 years: 800-1500 ml.

Amylase (diastase):
Adult males: 38-263 units/hour
Adult females: 47-310 units/hour

Ascorbic acid:
> 5% of an oral 20 mg./Kg.
loading dose/day

Calcium:
First week: < 2 mg./day
Children: 40-80 mg./day
Adults: 50-400 mg./day

Catecholamines: 0.4-2.0 µg./Kg./day

Chloride: Adults: 6-9 Gm. (170-254 mEq.)/day

Copper: 0-30 µg./day

Coproporphyrin: See Porphyrins.

Corticoids (Porter-Silber chromogens): 0.05-0.15 mg./Kg./day
(from Bongiovanni). (See also
17-Hydroxycorticosteroids.)

Cortisol production: 19.4-26.4
mg./sq. M.

Cortisol urinary excretion ratio:
$$\text{Ratio} = \frac{\text{Secretion rate}}{\text{Urinary 17-OHCS}}$$
Newborn: 5-60
Older individuals: 2-4

Creatine:
  Under 1 year: May equal creatinine
  Older children: Up to 30% of
    creatinine
  Adult males: < 150 mg./day
  Adult females: < 250 mg./day

Creatinine:
  Newborn: 7-10 mg./Kg./day
  Children: 20-30 mg./Kg./day
  Adult males: 21-26 mg./Kg./day
  Adult females: 16-22 mg./Kg./
    day

Creatinine clearance, endogenous:
  Newborn: 40-65 ml./min./1.73
    sq. M.
  Over 1.5 years, males: 98-150
    ml./min./1.73 sq. M.
  Over 1.5 years, females: 95-
    123 ml./min./1.73 sq. M.
  Adults: 72-140 ml./min./1.73 sq.M.

Cystine: Adults: 10-100 mg./day

Cystine (free): Children: 45-485
  μM./day

Dehydroepiandrosterone: 10-40%
  of total 17-ketosteroids

Dopamine: < 200 μg./day

Epinephrine:
  < 5 years: 0-15 μg./day
  > 5 years: 4-26 μg./day

Estradiol:
  Prepuberal girls: 0.5 μg./day

Estriol:
  Under 5 years: 0-3 μg./day
  6 years-puberty: 1-8 μg./day
  After puberty, males: 5-15 μg./day
  After puberty, females: 5-30
    μg./day (cyclic)

Estrogens:
  Children: < 2 mouse units/day
  After puberty, males: 8-26
    mouse units/day
  After puberty, females: 13-133
    mouse units/day (cyclic)
  Adult males: 4-25 μg./day
  Adult females: 4-60 μg./day

Estrone:
  Prepuberal girls: 0.9 μg./day

Galactose: < 5 mg./100 ml.

Glomerular filtration rate:
  Newborn: Approximately half of
    older child
  Children and adults: 45-95 ml./
    min./sq. M.

Glucose: < 5 mg./100 ml.
  Adults: 0-0.25 Gm./day

Gonadotropins:
  FSH:
    Children: < 5 mouse units/
      day; 0-3 I.U./day
    After puberty: 5-52 mouse
      units/day
  LH:
    Prepuberal children: 0-1
      I.U./day
  1 mg. NIH-FSH-S_1 = 25.6 I.U.
    FSH
  1 mg. NIH-LH-S_1 = 475.0 I.U. LH

Homovanillic acid:
  Adults: < 15 mg./day
  Children: 3-16 μg./Gm.
    creatinine
  Adults: 2-4 μg./Gm. creatinine

Hydroxyanthranilic acid:
  After tryptophan load: 1.2-4.9
    μM./Kg./7 hours

17-Hydroxycorticosteroids (children):
  Newborn: < 1.0 mg./day (Ulstrom)
  0-2 years: 1.1-6.8 mg./day
    (Clayton)
  2-10 years: 0.6-10.9 mg./day
    (Clayton)
  10-14 years: 4.1-14.2 mg./day
    (Clayton)
  Children: 3.1 ± 1.1 mg./sq. M./
    day (Aceto)

17-Hydroxycorticosteroids (17-keto-
  genic steroidal procedure):
  Adult males: 5-23 mg./day
  Adult females: 3-15 mg./day

17-Hydroxycorticosteroids (Glenn-
  Nelson procedure):
  Adult males: 3-10 mg./day
  Adult females: 2-6 mg./day

5-Hydroxyindoleacetic acid:
  After tryptophan load: 0.11-0.61
    μM./Kg./7 hours

Hydroxykynurenine:
  After tryptophan load: < 0.5-9.2
    μM./Kg./7 hours

Hydroxyproline, free:
  5-9 years: 59-80 mg./sq. M./day
  10-14 years: 52-131 mg./sq. M./
    day
  Adults: Up to 2 mg./day

Hydroxyproline, total:
  0-1 year: 21-75 mg./day
  1-10 years: 24-102 mg./day
  10-14 years: 68-169 mg./day
  Adults: 16-46 mg./day

Indole-3-acetic acid:
  Adults: 5-18 mg./day

Ketone bodies: 1.7-42 mg./100 ml. (as acetone)

17-Ketosteroids: (From Talbot and Butler, J. Clin. Endocrinol. 2: 724, 1942; and Hamburger, Acta endocrinol. 1:19, 1948.)
0-14 days: 0.5-2.5 mg./day
14 days-3 years: 0-0.5 mg./day
3-6 years: 0-2 mg./day
6-8 years: 0-2.5 mg./day
8-10 years: 0.7-4 mg./day
10-12 years: Boys, 0.7-6 mg./day
Girls, 0.7-5 mg./day
12-14 years: Boys, 1.3-10 mg./day
Girls, 1.3-8.5 mg./day
14-16 years: Boys, 2.5-13 mg./day
Girls, 2.5-11 mg./day
Adults: Men, 9-22 mg./day
Women, 6-15 mg./day
Ratio of beta to alpha < 0.2

Kynurenic acid:
After tryptophan load: 3.4-20.6 μM./Kg./7 hours

Kynurenine:
After tryptophan load: 3.8-50.5 μM./Kg./7 hours

Lactic dehydrogenase: Adults: Up to 8300 units/8 hours

Lead: < 400 μg./day

Leucine aminopeptidase:
Adult males: 50-175 units
Adult females: 20-70 units

Luteinizing hormone:
Prepuberal children: 0-1 I.U./day (Albert)
Boys 5-11 years: 1.3-6.5 I.U./day (Sciarra)

Magnesium:
Children: 0.1 mEq./Kg./day (fluorometric) (O'Brien)
Adults: 1.2-24 mEq./day

Mercury: < 50 μg. Hg/day

Metacatecholamines:
Full-term:
First day: 58 ± 28 μg./day
15th day: 40 ± 9 μg./day
Premature:
First day: 24 ± 9 μg./day
15th day: 30 ± 15 μg./day

Metanephrines, total:
Children: 0.02-0.16 μg./mg. creatinine
Adults: 0.3-0.9 mg./day

Milliosmols:
Infants: 50-700 mOsm./L.
Children: 50-1400 mOsm./L.

Mucopolysaccharides:
< 6 mg. hexuronic acid/day at age 4 years
< 12 mg. hexuronic acid/day by age 14 years

Myoglobin: Adults: < 1.6 mg./day

Norepinephrine: 0.4-1.6 μg./Kg./day (O'Brien)
< 5 years: 1-20 μg./day
> 5 years: 10-70 μg./day

Normetanephrine:
Children: 0.05-0.6 μg./mg. creatinine

Osmolality:
Infants: 50-700 mOsm./L. urine
Older children and adults: 50-1400 mOsm./L. urine

Phenylalanine:
< 6 weeks: 0-1.3 mg./100 ml.
> 6 weeks: 0-1.7 mg./100 ml.

Phosphorus:
First day: None
End of first week: 150 mg./day
Adults: 340-1000 mg./day

Porphyrins:
δ-Aminolevulinic acid:
Children: < 0.49 mg./100 ml.
Adults: 1.3-7 mg./day
Coproporphyrin:
Adults: < 160 μg./day
Porphobilinogen:
Children: < 0.11 mg./100 ml.
Adults: < 2 mg./day
Uroporphyrin:
Children: trace
Adults: up to 20 μg./L.

Potassium: Adults: 1-5 Gm./day (25-123 mEq.)

Pregnanediol:
First 5 days: 0.6-2.2 μg./mg. creatinine (as glucuronide)
Children: < 1.2 mg./day
Adult males: < 1.5 mg./day

Pregnanetriol:
First week: 2-5 mg./day
< 2 years: Barely present
Infants: < 0.8 mg./day (Wilkins)
2-15 years: 0.3-1.1 mg./day (mean = 0.6 mg.)
Adults: < 4 mg./day

Protein:
First month: 240 mg./sq. M.
Children: 140 mg./sq. M.
Children: 30-50 mg./day
Adults: 25-70 mg./day

Serotonin: Children: 1.3-7.7 µg. free base/100 mg. creatinine

Serotonin (as 5-HIAA): Adults: 1-5 mg./day

Sodium: Adults: 1-5 Gm./day (43-217 mEq.)

Testosterone:
Prepuberal females: 19 ± 8 ng./100 ml. (Fraser)
Adult males: 20-200 µg./day
Adult females: 5-10 µg./day

Testosterone glucuronide: Adults: 65 ± 26 µg./day

Tetrahydro compound S: Adults: < 1 mg./day

Tryptamine:
Children: 4-22 µg. free base/ 100 mg. creatinine
Adults: 36-120 µg./day

Urea: 215-500 mg./Kg./day

Urea clearance:
Premature: 3-10 ml./sq.M./min.
Full-term: 15-25 ml./sq.M./min.
Over 2 years: 30-50 ml./sq.M./ min.

Urea nitrogen: Adults: 6-7 Gm./day

Uric acid: 5-12 mg./Kg./day
Adults: 250-750 mg./day

Urobilinogen: < 3 mg./day

Uroporphyrin: See Porphyrins.

Vanillylmandelic acid (VMA):
First day:
Full-term: 606 ± 429 µg./day
Premature: 187 ± 111 µg./day
15th day:
Full-term: 471 ± 196 µg./day
Premature: 2506 ± 1319 µg./ day
< 2 years: 0.1-8.6 mg./L.
2-14 years: 0-10.2 mg./L.
Children:
83 ± 26 µg./Kg./day
2-12 µg./mg. creatinine
Adults: 0.7-6.8 mg./day

Xanthurenic acid:
0.8-5.6 µM./Kg./7 hours after tryptophan load

Xylose:
Up to 3 mg./100 ml.

Zinc:
Children: 0.4 mg./day
Adults: 0.35-0.6 mg./day

BONE MARROW CYTOLOGY

Myeloblasts	0-4%
Promyelocytes	0-6%
Myelocytes	7-25%
Metamyelocytes	7-30%
P. M. N.'s	5-30%
Eosinophils (all stages)	1-10%
Lymphocytes	5-45%
Monocytes	0-7%
Pronormoblasts	0-8%
Normoblasts	4-35%
Other cells	Occasional

DUODENAL FLUID VALUES

pH: 6.0-8.4

Viscosity: < 3 min. (Shwachman)

Enzymes: (Anderson or as noted)
Trypsin:
0-2 months: 110-160 units/ml.
2-6 months: 115-160 units/ml.
6-12 months: 120-290 units/ml.
(3-10 units, Nothman et al.)
1-2 years: 200-300 units/ml.
2-5 years: 200-275 units/ml.
Amylase:
0-2 months: 0-10 units/ml.
2-6 months: 10-20 units/ml.
6-12 months: 40-150 units/ml.
1-2 years: 100-225 units/ml.
2-5 years: 125-275 units/ml.
Chymotrypsin: 11-65 units (Ravin)
Carboxypeptidase: 0.4-1 units (Ravin)
Protease: 18-70 units (Free-Meyers)

FECES

Fecal chymotrypsin: 3-14 mg./ 72 hours/Kg.

Fecal urobilinogen:
2-12 months: 0.03-14 mg./day
5-10 years: 2.7-39 mg./day
10-14 years: 7.3-99 mg./day

Fecal fat, total:
2-6 months: 0.3-1.3 Gm./day
< 1 year: < 4 Gm./day
Children: < 3 Gm.
Adolescents: < 5 Gm./day
Adults: < 7 Gm./day

Fecal fat, percentage of dry weight:
2-6 months: 5-43%
0.5-6 years: 6-26%

Lipids, split fat:
Adults: > 40% of total lipids

Lipids, total:
Adults: Up to 7 Gm./day on normal diet; 10-27% of dry weight

Nitrogen:
Infants: < 1 Gm./day
Children: < 1.2 Gm./day
Adults: < 3 Gm./day

SWEAT

Sweat electrolytes: (Sodium and chloride concentrations, mEq./L.)
Normal: < 100 (Barbero), < 45 (Gochberg and Cooke)
Fibrocystic disease: > 100 (Barbero), > 50 (Gochberg and Cooke)

MISCELLANEOUS

Amniotic fluid testosterone:
3.2-67 ng./100 ml.

Chromosome number: 46

Circulation time (for Decholin®):
3-6 years: 8-12 seconds
6-12 years: 7.5-15 seconds
12-15 years: 10-16 seconds

Duodenal biopsy:
Enzyme activity (in units/Gm. protein/min.):
Lactase: 38.0 ± 13.4
Hetero-beta-galactosidase: 1.43 ± 0.35
Beta-glucuronidase: 1.90 ± 0.45

Exophthalmometric measurements:
Children, 10-14 years: 13.5-21 mm.

Heart rate:
First day: 75-155
Under 3 years: 100-200
3-8 years: 70-150
Over 8 years: 50-125

Radioactive iodine (RAI) uptake:
4 hours: 5-15%
24 hours: 12-45%

Spinal fluid: See Table 5.

Synovial fluid: Cell count, < 180 w.b.c./cu. mm., with less than 25% polymorphonuclear neutrophils.

TABLE 3. Normal peripheral blood values at various age levels.

	1st Day	2nd Day	6th Day	2 Wks.	1 Month	2 Months	3 Months	6 Months	1 Year	2 Years	5 Years	8-12 Years	Adults Males	Females
Red Blood Cells† (Millions)	5.9 (4.1-7.5)	6.0 (4.0-7.3)	5.4 (3.9-6.8)	5.0 (4.5-5.5)	4.7 (4.2-5.2)	4.1 (3.6-4.6)	4.0 (3.5-4.5)	4.5 (4.0-5.0)	4.6 (4.1-5.1)	4.7 (4.2-5.2)	4.7 (4.2-5.2)	5.0 (4.5-5.4)	5.4 (4.6-6.2)	4.8 (4.2-5.4)
Hemoglobin (Gm.)	19 (14-24)	19 (15-23)	18 (13-23)	16.5 (15-20)	14 (11-17)	12 (11-14)	11 (10-13)	11.5 (10.5-14.5)	12.0 (11-15)	13.0 (12.0-15)	13.5 (12.5-15)	14.0 (13-15.5)	16.0 (13-18)	14.0 (11-16)
White Blood† Cells	17,000 (8-38)		13,500 (6-17)	12,000	11,500	11,000	10,500	10,500	10,000	9,500	8,000	8,000	7,000 (5-10)	
P.M.N.'s (%)	57	55	50	34	34	33	33	36	39	42	55	60	57-68	
Eosinophils† (Total)	20-1000				150-1150		70-550	70-550					100-400	
Lymphocytes (%)	20	20	37	55	56	56	57	55	53	49	36	31	25-33	
Monocytes (%)	10	15	9	8	7	7	7	6	6	7	7	7	3-7	
Immature w.b.c.'s (%)	10	5	0-1	0	0	0	0	0	0	0	0	0	0	
Platelets*	350,000		325,000	300,000			260,000		260,000	260,000		260,000	260,000	
Nucleated r.b.c.'s /100 w.b.c.'s†	0-10		0-0.3	0	0	0	0	0	0	0	0	0	0	
Reticulocytes (%)	3.0 (2-8)	3.0 (2-10)	1.0 (0.5-5.0)	0.4 (0.0-2.0)	0.2 (0.0-0.5)	0.5 (0.2-2.0)	2.0 (0.5-4.0)	0.8 (0.5-1.5)	1.0 (0.4-1.8)	1.0 (0.4-1.8)	1.0 (0.4-1.8)	1.0 (0.4-1.8)	1.0 (0.5-2)	
Mean Diameter r.b.c.'s (μ)	8.6				8.1		7.7		7.4		7.4		7.5	
M.C.V. ‡(cu)	85-125		89-101	94-102	90		80	78	78	80	80	82	82-92	
M.C.H.C. ‡(%)	36		35	34	30		27	33	25	32	34	34	34	
M.C. Hgb. †($\gamma\gamma$)	35-40		36	31	30		27	26	25	26	27	28	27-31	
Hematocrit (%)	54±10		51	50	35-50		35	30-40	36	37	31-43	40	40-54	37-47

*Per cu. mm.

†Total nucleated r.b.c.'s: First day, <1000.

‡M.C.V. = Mean Corpuscular Volume. M.C.H.C. = Mean Corpuscular Hemoglobin Concentration.
M.C.Hgb. = Mean Corpuscular Hemoglobin.

TABLE 4. Schedule and check list for performance of pediatric screening procedures.

Assessment Of:	3-7 days	2-6 weeks	4-5 months	6-7 months	8-10 months	11-14 months	16-19 months	22-25 months	3-4 years	5-7 years	8-10 years	11-12 years	13-15 years	16-21 years
									Age of Child					
Medical status (by general and developmental history)	▓	▓		▓		▓	▓		▓		▓	▓		▓
Physical status (by physical examination)			▓											
Immunization status (1)		▓	▓		▓		▓	▓	▓		▓	▓		▓
Dental care status (2)				▓	▓	▓	▓	▓	▓	▓	▓	▓	▓	▓
Visual acuity (by observation and report)	▓	▓	▓	▓	▓	▓	▓	▓						
Visual acuity (by test)		▓	▓	▓	▓	▓		▓	▓	▓	▓	▓	▓	▓
Hearing acuity (by observation and report)	▓	▓	▓	▓	▓	▓	▓	▓						
Hearing acuity (by audiometry) (3)					▓	▓	▓	▓	▓	▓	▓	▓	▓	▓
Height, weight, and head circumference	▓	▓	▓	▓	▓	▓	▓	▓						
Psychomotor development by screening test (4)	▓	▓	▓	▓		▓	▓	▓	▓	▓	▓	▓	▓	▓
School progress									▓	▓	▓	▓	▓	▓

Tuberculin sensitivity (5)

Bacteriuria (girls only)

Anemia

Sickle cell disease

Sickle cell and hemoglobin C traits

Lead absorption (6)

Phenylketonuria and galactosemia (7)

Footnotes:

(1) A visit at approximately two months of age is necessary to begin the normal immunization schedule.

(2) Visual inspection of the mouth and teeth is part of the medical examination at all ages.

(3) Test hearing yearly from age three to six.

(4) Test development earlier and more frequently in known high-risk groups.

(5) Test tuberculin less frequently or omit in known low-risk groups.

(6) Test only exposed children. Test every six months from age one to three years.

(7) Preferably at four to seven days.

Adapted from: Frankenberg, W.K. & North, A.F.: A Guide to Screening. U.S. Dept. of Health, Education, and Welfare, SRS 74-24516, U.S. Government Printing Office, 1974.

Key:

Empty boxes mean that the procedure should be done at the age indicated at the top of the column. The procedure should be done at the next scheduled visit if not done at the recommended time.

TABLE 5. Cerebrospinal fluid in pathologic conditions.*

KEY: N = Normal   Decr. = Decreased   P.M.N. = Polymorphonuclear neutrophils   r.b.c. = Red blood cells
Mono. = Mononuclear cells   Incr. = Increased   w.b.c. = White blood cells

	Pressure (mm. H₂O)	Appearance	White Blood Cells (per cu. mm.)		Pandy	Protein (mg./100 ml.)	Sugar (mg./100 ml.)	Chloride†
			Number	Type				
Normal	40-200	Clear	0-5‡	Mono.	0	15-40	40-80	110-128 mEq./L.
Newborn	N	Clear or xanthochromic	Variable 0-25	Mono. (r.b.c. 0-700)		40-120		N
One month	N	Clear	0-15	Mostly P.M.N.		20-70		N
Meningismus	Incr.	Clear	N	Mono.	0 to ±		N	N
Acute purulent bacterial meningitis	Up to 300 or more	Turbid	500-15,000	P.M.N.	++ to +++	Up to 500 or more	Low or absent	103-116 mEq./L.
Tuberculous meningitis	Up to 300 or more	Clear or opalescent	30-500	Early mixed, Later Mono.	++ to +++	Up to 300 or more	0-45	Early N. Later 94-110 mEq./L.
Poliomyelitis	N to incr.	Clear or opalescent	15-400 (avg. 90)	P.M.N. early, Mono. later	0 to +	30-60; later 100-600	N	N
Lead encephalitis	N to very high	Clear	Up to 100	Mono.	0 to ++++	100-600 or more	N	N
Guillain-Barré syndrome	Incr.	Clear	N	Mono.	+ to ++++	Sl. to marked incr.	N	N
Encephalomyelitis, equine and St. Louis	Usually incr. May be N	Clear or opalescent	Up to 1000	P.M.N. early, Mono. later	0 to +++	N early; later 60-200	N to sl. incr.	N
Mumps	Usually incr. May be N	Clear or opalescent	150-2000. (avg. 400)	Mono.	0 to +++	N early; 60-200 later	N	N
Other encephalitides (rubeola, varicella)	Usually incr. May be N	Clear or opalescent	15-1000	P.M.N. early, Mono. later	0 to +	60-200	Usually N. May be decr.	N
Lymphocytic choriomeningitis	Incr. to greatly incr.	Clear or opalescent	100-2000	Lymph., P.M.N. early	++ to ++++	60-200	N	N
Rabies	N to incr.	Clear or opalescent	30-1000	P.M.N.	0 to ++	N to ++	N	N

Neurosyphilis§	N to incr.	Clear or opalescent	N to 200	Mono.	0 to ++	N to 200	N	N
Toxoplasma encephalitis	N to incr.	Clear or opalescent	30-2000	Mono.	0 to +++	N or greatly incr.	N	N
"Bloody tap"	N	Pink or red; clearer in successive tubes	Negative on benzidine on supernatant blood	r.b.c. and w.b.c. as in peripheral blood	0 to +	N to sl. elevated	N	N
Subarachnoid hemorrhage	Incr.	Grossly bloody; supernatant xanthochromic	See (**) below	r.b.c. and w.b.c. as in peripheral blood	0 to ++	N to sl. incr.	N to sl. incr.	N to sl. incr.
Subdural hematoma	N to incr.	Clear or xanthochromic	N to 30	May have P.M.N.	0 to -+	N to mod. incr.	N	N
Brain abscess, unruptured	Incr.	Clear	10-60	Mono.	0 to -	20-80	N	N
Brain tumor	Usually incr. May be N	Clear	Occasionally up to 500	P.M.N. or lymphocytes	0 to -+	N to sl. to marked incr.	N	N
Intracranial carcinomatosis	Incr.	Clear	Up to 1000	Mono.	0 to -+	60-100	Decr.	N
Uremia	Incr.	Clear	N	N	+ to ++	N to sl. incr.	N	N to sl. incr.
Diabetic coma	N	Clear	N	N	0	N	High	N

*Cerebrospinal fluid lactic dehydrogenase activity is 50 units (range, 22-73) in infants less than one week of age and 14 units (range, 0-40) in older children. The range is 50-2000 units in children with bacterial meningitis and 3-48 units in those with aseptic meningoencephalitis.

†Reported as NaCl in mg./100 ml. and as Cl⁻ in mEq./L.

‡Up to 10 cells/cu. mm. in infants and up to 8 cells/cu. mm. in children under five years of age.

§If a patient has a positive serologic test for syphilis, even small amounts of blood in the spinal fluid may give a false-positive test on the fluid. If a traumatic bloody tap is obtained, it should be repeated in two to three weeks.

**Many r.b.c. for eight to 12 days. Crenated after 12 hours.

Additional Normal Findings: Calcium, 4 to 6 mg./100 mL. magnesium, 2.5 to 3.3 mEq./L.; potassium, 2.8 to 4.2 mEq./L.; sodium, 130 to 165 mEq./L.; phosphorus, 1.5-3.0 mg./100 ml.; specific gravity, 1.005-1.009; pH, 7.33-7.42; carbon dioxide-combining power, 18-31 mEq./L.

LABORATORY TESTS

TESTS OF LIVER FUNCTION

Bilirubin. See p. 635 for normal values.

Phosphatase, Alkaline. See p. 640 for normal values.

Transaminase (SGOT and SGPT). See p. 643 for normal values.

Sulfobromophthalein (Bromsulphalein®, BSP) Test.
- A. Specimen and Test Material: Serum 45 minutes after test dose. Sulfobromophthalein (Bromsulphalein®), 5 mg./Kg. (0.1 ml./ Kg. of 5% sol.) I.V. within 60 seconds.
- B. Normal Value: First two weeks, < 25%; over five months, < 6%. Concentrations over 10% are definitely abnormal in children over five months of age.
- C. Interpretation: Test of glutathione-conjugating ability of the liver and of the biliary excretion of conjugates. After infancy a positive BSP test is a sign of impaired excretory function of the liver.

Serum Protein (Chromatography) Electrophoresis.
- A. Specimen: Serum.
- B. Normal Value: See p. 641
- C. Interpretation:
  1. Acute hepatitis - Alpha$_2$ globulin increased; gamma globulin markedly increased by second week. These changes become marked in chronic cases where the albumin also is diminished.
  2. Massive hepatic necrosis - Marked diminution of alpha and sometimes of beta globulins.
  3. Cirrhosis - Alpha globulins sometimes increased, but characteristically a large diffuse increase of gamma globulin.
  4. Nephrosis - See Chapter 18.

TESTS OF CHO METABOLISM

One-dose (Oral) Glucose Tolerance Test.
- A. Specimen and Test Material: Fasting blood and blood drawn in 30, 60, 90, 120, and 180 minutes; in suspected cases of carbohydrate reactive hypoglycemia, samples should also be taken at four and five hours. Collect urine prior to test and after one and two hours and test for glycosuria. Glucose: Up to 18 months, 2.5 Gm./Kg.; 1 1/2 to 3 years, 2 Gm./Kg.; over 12 years, 1.75 Gm./Kg. as an approximate 20% aqueous solution, with flavoring added.
- B. Normal Value: Rise of 30 to 80 mg.; peak in 30 to 60 minutes after ingestion; return to fasting level in 120 to 180 minutes. Capillary blood may be slightly higher than venous.
- C. Interpretation: Child should have been on a diet of average CHO for 2 weeks prior to the test. Abnormal responses consist of (1) fasting sample > 110 mg./100 ml.; (2) elevation > 170 mg./

100 ml.; (3) three-hour sample > 110 mg./100 ml. or above baseline level. Combination of above suggests carbohydrate intolerance. Same response in newborn, but fasting point is lower than in older infants. High, prolonged curves are found in hepatic disorders, septicemia, pneumonia, tuberculous meningitis, acute nutritional disturbances, diabetes mellitus, exogenous obesity, and glycogen storage disease. Flat curves are found in encephalitis, hypothyroidism, celiac disease, and with delayed gastric emptying. In hyperinsulinism the immediate response may be normal, but an abrupt fall to hypoglycemic levels may occur.

Disaccharide (Lactose, Sucrose) Tolerance Tests.

These tests are performed in the same manner as the one-dose (oral) glucose tolerance test except that the loading dose of the disaccharide should be twice the dose of glucose.

I. V. Glucose Tolerance Test.

A. Specimen and Test Material: Fasting blood and specimens taken at 5, 15, 30, 45, and 60 minutes after 0.5 Gm./Kg. of glucose in a 20 to 50% solution given over a period of two to four minutes.

B. Normal Value: Peak value is reached at five or ten minutes and normal at 45 to 60 minutes.

Glucagon Tolerance Test.

A. Specimen and Test Material: Fasting blood and specimens taken at 20, 40, and 60 minutes after 20 to 40 mcg./Kg. of glucagon I. M.

B. Normal Value: Abrupt increase of 40 to 60% or more of fasting blood glucose level by 20 minutes.

C. Interpretation: Flat curves found in cases of glycogen storage disease, in severe liver disease, during hypoglycemic period in ketotic hypoglycemia, and in small-for-dates neonates.

Laevo-leucine Tolerance Test.

A. Specimen and Test Material: Fasting blood and specimens taken at 15, 30, 45, and 60 minutes after ingestion of laevo-leucine, 150 mg./Kg. orally or 75 to 100 mg./Kg. I. V.; or after ingestion of casein in the following dosages: up to 18 months, 2.5 Gm./Kg.; 1 1/2 to 3 years, 2 Gm./Kg.; 3 to 12 years, 1.75 Gm./Kg.; over 12 years, 1.25 Gm./Kg. (minimum, 10 Gm.; maximum, 50 Gm.) as an approximate 20% aqueous solution.

B. Normal Value: No significant fall in blood glucose level.

C. Interpretation: Fall in blood glucose level to 50% of control levels occurs in 30 to 45 minutes in cases of sensitivity to leucine.

Insulin Tolerance Test.

A. Specimen and Test Material: Fasting blood and blood drawn 10, 30, 45, 60, 90, and 120 minutes after injection. Insulin: 0.1 unit/Kg. I. V. (preferred) or 0.25 unit/Kg. subcut. Use only one-half to one-third of calculated dose in children with potentially enhanced insulin sensitivity. **Caution:** Safety precautions are as for the insulin-glucose tolerance test, which is preferred.

B. Normal Value: After I.V. administration, blood glucose drops to 50% of fasting level in 15 to 30 minutes. A fall of the blood glucose value to greater than 50% of the fasting level and a delay of over 90 minutes in the return to fasting levels is considered abnormal by some.

C. Interpretation: Normal newborns have a low tolerance. Slow or blunted insulin responsiveness with exogenous obesity, some stages of diabetes mellitus, and excessive production of hyperglycemic hormones. Rapid drop is found in adrenal or pituitary insufficiency, starvation, organic intracranial lesions, and in cases with inadequate epinephrine response.

Insulin-Glucose Tolerance Test.

A. Specimen and Test Material: Fasting blood and specimens taken at 10, 20, 30, 60, 90, 120, and 180 minutes after administration of insulin. Insulin: 0.1 unit/Kg. I.V. At 30 minutes give glucose, 0.8 Gm./Kg. orally. In children with potential insulin sensitivity, be ready to terminate the test at any time by giving glucagon or I.V. glucose.

B. Normal Value: Fall to 20% of fasting level of blood glucose in 30 minutes; then prompt rise to 100 to 200 mg./100 ml. at 90 minutes with subsequent fall to normal by 180 minutes.

C. Interpretation: In idiopathic hypoglycemia, adrenal deficiency, and hypopituitarism, there is a normal response to insulin and a diminished response to glucose.

ᴅ-Xylose Absorption Test.

A. Specimen and Test Material: Fasting blood and blood drawn 30, 60, and 120 minutes after ingestion of test dose. Urine collected for five hours after test dose. (Nothing by mouth during this time.) ᴅ-Xylose: 10 ml./Kg. of a 5% solution orally.

B. Normal Value: Rise of blood xylose to 30 to 40 mg./100 ml. should be reached in 30 to 60 minutes and maintained for a further 60 minutes. Mean five-hour urine excretion is 26% (range: 16 to 33%) of ingested xylose.

C. Interpretation: Test is abnormal in certain malabsorption syndromes such as fibrocystic disease. Test is normal in colitis, liver disease, and primary pancreatic deficiencies. In malabsorption, mean urinary xylose excretion for five-hour urine is 5.2% (range: 3.2 to 10.4%).

Epinephrine Test.

A. Specimen and Test Material: Fasting blood and blood drawn 15, 30, 60, and 120 minutes after injection. Urine for hour before and four consecutive two-hour periods after injection. Epinephrine: 0.1 ml. of 1:1000 solution subcut.

B. Normal Value: Blood glucose rises 30 to 75 mg./100 ml. in one hour.

C. Interpretation: Subnormal rise: organic liver disease, glycogen storage disease, and malnutrition states.

Tolbutamide Tolerance Test.

A. Specimen and Test Material: Fasting blood and specimens taken at 15, 30, 60, 80, 120, and 180 minutes after administration of sodium tolbutamide, 25 mg./Kg. (maximum, 1 Gm.), in 10 ml. distilled water I.V. over a period of two minutes. The patient should have been on a high-CHO diet for at least three days. Terminate test with 50% glucose if severe hypoglycemic symptoms develop.

B. Normal Response: Decrease of blood glucose of 25 to 40% in 30 minutes. The return of blood sugar to fasting levels is slow in children. False-positive results are relatively common in children.

C. Interpretation: In hyperinsulin states there may be a rapid decrease in blood glucose to levels below 40 mg./100 ml. from 30 to 120 minutes after administration of tolbutamide, and failure to return to normal in three hours.

Chromatography of Urine Sugars.

A. Specimen: Clean specimen of urine.

B. Normal Values: Glucose, < 5 mg./100 ml.; xylose, < 3 mg./ 100 ml.; arabinose, < 15 mg./100 ml. after eating plums or cherries; lactose and galactose, small amounts may be detected in formula-fed infants.

C. Interpretation: In galactosemia, galactose elevated to 2 Gm./ 100 ml. In some congenital renal tubular defects glucose may be elevated up to 300 mg./100 ml. and fructose to 50 mg./100 ml. Fructose is excreted to an excessive degree in essential fructosuria and occasionally in liver disease.

TEST OF CREATINE AND CREATININE METABOLISM

Creatine and Creatinine Output.

A. Specimen: 24-hour urine specimen with 5 to 10 ml. of 5% thymol in chloroform as a preservative.

B. Normal Values Per 24 Hours:
1. Creatine - Children normally excrete creatine. One month, 2 mg./Kg.; gradual decrease to 1 mg./Kg. by 14 years.
2. Creatinine - A normal constituent of both blood and urine throughout life. Two weeks, 5 to 9 mg./Kg. Gradual increase to 20 to 30 mg. by 14 years. Creatinine excretion shows considerable variation between specimens and from day to day.

C. Interpretation:
1. Creatine output is decreased in prematurity, hypothyroidism, and amyotonia congenita; increased in hyperthyroidism, starvation, myasthenia gravis, and progressive muscular dystrophy.
2. Creatinine output is decreased in progressive muscular dystrophy; may be lowered in myasthenia gravis but is normal in thyroid disturbances, starvation, and myotonia congenita.

VITAMIN ABSORPTION TESTS

Vitamin A Absorption.

A. First Stage:
1. Specimen and test material - Fasting blood and blood drawn four hours after ingestion of 12,500 units of vitamin A palmi-

tate/Kg. orally. No extra vitamins are allowed during the previous week.
2. Normal value -
   a. Fasting, 70 to 200 I. U./100 ml. (mean, 130 I. U.).
   b. Four-hour level, 200 to 1250 I. U./100 ml. (mean, 650 I. U.).
3. Interpretation - Rise of less than 50 units/ml. of serum occurs in celiac disease, fibrocystic disease, obstructive and parenchymatous jaundice, cretinism, ulcerative colitis, allergic conditions, and some acute or chronic infections. In idiopathic hypercalcemia the results range from 120 to 365 I. U./100 ml. (mean, 275 I. U.), with a four-hour level of 600 to 3200 I. U./100 ml. (mean, 1800).

B. Second Stage:
1. After demonstration of abnormally poor absorption of vitamins by the above test, repeat the whole procedure after an interval of four days, giving 10 Gm. of enteric-coated pancreatin orally at the time the vitamin A is fed.
2. Interpretation - The child who absorbs vitamin A poorly without pancreatin and absorbs it well with pancreatin lacks pancreatic enzyme (e.g., fibrocystic disease). Children who show no improvement with pancreatin have an intestinal mucosal defect and have one of the other conditions listed above.

C. Test for Lipase Deficiency: In lipase deficiency the absorption of vitamin A palmitate will be impaired but the absorption of vitamin A alcohol will remain normal.

TESTS OF RENAL FUNCTION

Creatinine Clearance Test.
A. Specimen: Timed collection of urine made between 7:00 p. m. and 7:00 a. m. and assayed for creatinine. Blood specimens drawn at beginning and end of period.

$$Ccr = \frac{UV}{P} \times \frac{1.73}{S.A.}$$

where Ccr = creatinine clearance; U = urinary concentration of creatinine; V = total volume of urine divided by number of minutes in the collection period; P = average of the two plasma creatinine levels; and S. A. = surface area in square meters.

B. Normal Values:
   Newborn and premature: 40 to 65 ml./minute/1.73 sq. M.
   Males over $1\frac{1}{2}$ years: 124 ± 25.8 ml./minute/1.73 sq. M.
   Females over $1\frac{1}{2}$ years: 109 ± 13.5 ml./minute/1.73 sq. M.
   Adult males: 105 ± 13.9 ml./minute/1.73 sq. M.
   Adult females: 95.4 ± 18 ml./minute/1.73 sq. M.

Urinary Amino Acid Chromatography.
A. Specimen: Single or 24-hour (preferred) urine.
B. Interpretation: Characteristic abnormal amino acid patterns are found in many conditions, including liver disease, nephro-

sis, congenital renal tubular defects, phenylketonuria, scurvy, rickets, hypophosphatasia, galactosemia, and cystinuria.

Addis Sediment Count.

A. Specimen: All urine passed from 7:00 p. m. to 7:00 a. m. No fluids after 4:00 p. m.

B. Normal Value: Four to 12 years: casts, < 10,000; RBC < 1,000,000; WBC, < 1,000,000; protein, < 150 mg.

C. Interpretation: Not definitely established whether abnormal Addis counts in children are evidence of anatomic pathology only or of functional impairment as well.

TESTS OF ENDOCRINE FUNCTION

Growth Hormone.

A. Specimen and Test Material: Fasting blood and specimens taken at 15 minutes (for glucose concentration) and 30 and 60 minutes (for glucose concentration and assay of human growth hormone) after administration of 0.1 unit/Kg. I. V. of crystalline insulin. Be ready to terminate the test at any time by giving glucose orally or I. V. or glucagon orally.

B. Normal Value: Rise of serum growth hormone of greater than 7 pg./ml. from fasting to 30- or 60-minute sample in children whose blood glucose falls below 55 mg./100 ml. or below 66% of the fasting concentration.

C. Interpretation: Fasting sample may have undetectable amounts of human growth hormone. In the presence of a fall in blood sugar of one-third to one-half below fasting level, an increase of less than 7 pg./ml. suggests an impaired growth hormone response to hypoglycemia and a possible deficiency of growth hormone. Further clinical evaluation of growth hormone and repeat testing should be carried out before a definitive diagnosis is made. Response is decreased in hypothyroidism and may be abnormal in deprivation dwarfism.

The administration of arginine monohydrochloride, 0.5 Gm./ Kg. as 5 to 10% solution over a 30-minute interval (adult dose, 30 Gm.), will produce a significant rise in plasma concentration of human growth hormone 30 to 90 minutes postinfusion. Growth hormone level also rises without artificial stimulation 60 to 90 minutes after the onset of natural sleep.

Corticotropin (ACTH) Test (Thorn Test).

A. Specimen and Test Material: Fasting blood and blood drawn after four hours. Corticotropin (ACTH): 5 to 25 mg. subcut. or I. M.

B. Normal Value: Fall in eosinophil count of > 50% in four hours. Normal fall indicates normal function of adrenal cortex. Test most reliable in nonallergic patients. Failure to cause fall in eosinophil count in adrenal insufficiency.

Corticotropin (ACTH) 17-Hydroxycorticoid Test.

A. Specimen and Test Material: 24-hour urine specimen before, on last day of injection, and on day after injection. Corticotropin (ACTH): 0.5 unit/Kg. I.V. in isotonic saline or glucose solution over a period of eight hours on two or more successive days.

B. Normal Value: Increased output of 17-hydroxycorticoids to two to three times baseline value. A twofold or greater rise of urinary 17-hydroxycorticosteroids following corticotropin gel, 20 units, I. M. every 12 hours for a three-day period, is a normal response.

C. Interpretation: Normal response rules out primary hypoadrenocorticism; normal response occurs with hypoadrenocorticism secondary to hypopituitarism except in some cases of long-standing ACTH deficiency.

Metyrapone (Metopirone®; SU-4885) Test.

A. Specimen and Test Material: 24-hour urine specimen for 17-hydroxycorticoids on the day before and the day after giving metyrapone, 300 mg./sq. M. orally (never < 250 or > 750 mg.) every four hours for 6 doses.

B. Normal Value: Two- to fourfold rise in 17-hydroxycorticoids over control values, usually occurring on the day following the administration of the drug.

C. Interpretation: Metyrapone inhibits 11-beta-hydroxylation and blocks the conversion of compound S (11-deoxycortisol) to compound F (cortisol). Lowered serum F produces compensatory increased secretion of ACTH from the normal pituitary gland with resultant elevated production of compound S and raised urinary 17-hydroxycorticoids and/or 17-ketogenic steroids. Failure to respond occurs with primary adrenocortical failure and in conditions characterized by decreased corticotropin production.

17-Hydroxycorticoids. See p. 645.

17-Ketosteroids. See p. 646.

Protein-bound Iodine. See pp. 412-414.

Radioactive Iodine Uptake. See pp. 410, 412-414.

L-Triiodothyronine (T₃) Suppression Test.

A. Specimen and Test Material: Radioactive iodine uptake determination before and on the seventh day after the administration of 75 to 125 μg. of L-triiodothyronine daily for eight days.

B. Normal Value: Suppression of uptake to 60% or less of the initial amount.

C. Interpretation: Lack of normal suppression with hyperthyroidism.

Water Load Test of Adrenal Function.

A. Specimen and Test Material: Nothing by mouth after 6:00 p. m. At 10:30 p. m. the patient voids and discards urine. Collect and measure urine to 7:30 a. m. At 7:30 a. m., give 20 ml. water/Kg. orally within 30 minutes. Collect and measure urine at 9:00 a. m., 10:00 a. m., 11:00 a. m., and 12:00 noon.

B. Normal Values and Interpretation: A normal individual excretes > 70% of the water load within four hours, with the greatest volume being excreted during the second hour (9:00 a. m. to 10:00

a. m.). One of the hourly volumes should exceed the night volume. With adrenal insufficiency, < 65% is excreted.

The test may not be valid in diabetes insipidus, renal disease, and liver disease.

Water Deprivation Test for Diabetes Insipidus. See p. 405.

FLUORESCEIN STRING TEST IN UPPER GASTROINTESTINAL HEMORRHAGE

A white string or umbilical tape four to five feet long, weighted at the end with lead shot, is marked lengthwise with radiopaque thread taken from surgical sponges. Interval markers of similar thread are placed horizontally at one-inch intervals. The string is swallowed and allowed to progress through the gastrointestinal tract overnight while feedings are withheld. An x-ray of the abdomen is obtained to determine whether the string has passed through the pylorus.

While the patient is on the x-ray table, sodium fluorescein (Fluorescite®) processed with sodium bicarbonate* is given I.V. (infants, 1 to 2 ml.; children, 5 ml.; adults, 20 ml.), and after four minutes the string is removed and promptly examined for gross blood and under Wood's light or ultraviolet light for fluorescence. The presence of blood and fluorescence indicates an actively bleeding site. The presence of blood without fluorescence indicates that there is a bleeding point which was not active at the time of the test. By comparing a measured bloody or fluorescent segment of the string with its location on the x-ray, the site of bleeding can be determined.

Note: Fluorescein is not stable, and so the string must be examined promptly. Fluorescein is excreted by the biliary system and ultimately enters the duodenum.

---

*Supplied by C. F. Kirk Co., New York, N.Y.

TABLE 6. Chromosomal disorders.

Chromosomal Disorder	Chromosome Abnormality		Possible Mechanism	Usual Age of Mother	Prominent Characteristics
	Number	Abnormality			
I. Autosomal anomalies					
1. Down's syndrome (mongolism; trisomy 21 syndrome; G group trisomy)					
a. Standard or regular type (1:700 births)	47	Trisomy of chromosome 21	Nondisjunction during meiosis	Older mother	See p. 393. Other findings include abnormal dermatoglyphics with high axial triradius, arch tibial on foot, ulnar loops on all fingers and simian creases, abnormal tryptophan metabolism. Parents may
b. Translocation type (5-10% of patients with Down's syndrome)	46	Trisomy of 21 with one 21 attached to chromosome 14, 21, or 22	Translocation	No relation to maternal age	have increased incidence of taste abnormalities (insensitivity to quinine and certain thiourea-type compounds). Translocation type may be familial; standard and mosaic types usually are not. Parents of translocation type may have 45 chromosomes including translocation with a normal phenotype.
c. Mosaic type	46 and 47	One set normal; other with trisomy 21	Error in early mitotic division		See p. 393. Abnormalities may be less severe.
2. Trisomy 18 syndrome (E₁ group trisomy) (1:4000 births)	47	Trisomy 18	Nondisjunction during meiosis	More frequent with advanced maternal age	Flexion deformity of fingers with index finger over third; "rocker bottom" deformity of feet; prominent occiput; retrognathia; mental retardation; intrauterine growth retardation, failure to thrive; short sternum, small pelvis, dorsiflexed ("hammer") big toe; renal, cardiac, skeletal anomalies.
3. Partial deletion of short arm of 18	46	Partial deletion of short arm of 18	Chromosomal break	Unknown	Microcephaly, epicanthic folds, rounded facies, hypotonia, severe psychomotor retardation, short stature.
4. Partial deletion of long arm of 18	46	Partial deletion of long arm of 18	Chromosomal break	Unknown	Atresia of ear canals, high-arched palate, microcephaly, retraction of midface, receding chin, prominent antihelix, spindle-shaped fingers, psychomotor retardation, short stature. Absence of γA immunoglobulin has been noted.

5. Trisomy 13 syndrome (D group trisomy, D₁ group trisomy)	47	Trisomy 13	Nodisjunction during meiosis	More frequent with advanced maternal age	Cleft lip and palate; hyperconvex narrow fingernails; over-riding index finger, retroflexible thumbs; simian line; posterior prominence of heels; cryptorchism; polydactyly; apparent deafness; cardiac anomalies; large fleshy nose; arhinencephaly; hypoplasia of frontal lobes; microphthalmos; coloboma; failure to thrive, mental retardation.
6. Cat-cry syndrome (cri-du-chat syndrome)	46	Deletion of short arm of chromosome No. 5	Deletion	More frequent with advanced maternal age	"Cat-like" cry in infancy; deformed larynx in some; microcephaly; micro-retrognathia; "moon-like" facies; failure to thrive; severe mental retardation. Chromosome abnormalities in some relatives, especially parents. Abnormal dermatoglyphics.
7. Syndrome of congenital asymmetry and short stature (Silver's syndrome)	46 in most; occ. 46/69	Most with normal karyotype; mosaicism (46-69) in small percentage			Asymmetry; short stature; variations in sexual development (including early development); intrauterine growth retardation; downturned mouth; incurved fifth fingers; elevated urinary gonadotropins in some.
8. Chronic myelogenous leukemia	46	Abnormally small acrocentric chromosome No. 22 (Ph¹)	Balanced translocation - long arm of 22 to long arm of 9.		Chronic myelogenous leukemia. Low phosphatase of neutrophils. Chromosomal abnormality in bone marrow (90% of cases) and sometimes in peripheral blood.
9. Bloom's dwarfism	46	Multiple chromosome breaks, quadriradial figures, occasionally "pulverization"			Dwarfism, chronic erythematous rash, tendency to malignancy (esp. leukemia). Probably inherited as single gene autosomal recessive. Increased chromosomal breaks occasionally in close relatives.
10. Congenital aplastic anemia (Fanconi's anemia)	46	Increased number of chromosomal breaks			Skeletal (especially thumbs and upper extremity) and hematopoietic abnormalities. Pigmentation of skin, hypoplasia of gonads, defects of kidneys.
11. Trisomy 8 mosaicism	46 and 47	One set normal, one with trisomy 8	Possibly due to viral infection / Error in early mitotic division	No relation to maternal age	Short stature; unusual facies; abnormal pinnas; absent patellas; GU anomalies; mental retardation.
II. Sex chromosome abnormalities*					
1. Klinefelter's syndrome (1:700 births)	47	Usually XXY. Also XXYY, XXXY, XXXYY, XXXXY, and mosaicism	Nondisjunction		See p. 409. Rarely fertile. Increased risk of mental retardation and of behavioral and emotional problems.

TABLE 6. (cont'd.) Chromosomal disorders.

Chromosomal Disorder	Chromosome Number	Chromosome Abnormality	Possible Mechanism	Usual Age of Mother	Prominent Characteristics
2. XX male	46	XX	Interchange of X and Y chromosome during meiosis or loss of Y in mitosis		Normal, similar to Klinefelter's syndrome, or partial feminization.
3. XYY syndrome (1:1000 births)	47	XYY	Meiotic nondisjunction		Tall stature, very aggressive behavior.
4. XXXXY sex chromosome abnormality	49	XXXXY, sometimes XXXXY/ XXXY	Nondisjunction		Similar to Klinefelter's syndrome (see p. 409); synostosis of proximal radius and ulna; in some cases microcephaly, short stature, long lower extremities, incurved phalanges, elongation of the radii, abnormal ossification centers, scoliosis, and hypertelorism; nuclear chromatin with three Barr bodies.
5. Turner's syndrome (Bonnevie-Ullrich-Turner; gonadal dysgenesis) (1:3000 births)	45 or 46	Usually 45,X; often mosaicism; may have 45,X, fragment or 46,XX; isochromosome	Meiotic or mitotic nondisjunction, chromosome lag or breakage		See p. 367.
6. Male pseudohermaphrodite (45,X/46,XY); mixed gonadal dysgenesis	46,XY 45,X mosaicism	Missing Y chromosome in some cells	Mitotic nondisjunction or chromosome lag		Some of findings present in Turner's syndrome, with infantile female secondary sexual characteristics but with a variable degree of masculinization of the genitalia. Tendency to develop gonadoblastomas.
7. Male pseudohermaphrodite; testicular feminizing syndrome	46,XY				Tall, well-feminized, sterile female with testes. Probably a single gene defect which inhibits end-organ response to testosterone.
8. True hermaphrodite	46	46,XX; 46,XY 46,XX/46,XY	46,XX/46,XY; ovum fertilized by two sperm.		Ovum on one side, testis on other or ovotestis on one or both sides. Varying degrees of abnormal phenotypic sexual determinacy.
9. Triple-X syndrome (1:1000 births)	47	47,XXX. Rarely, XXXX or XXXXX	Nondisjunction		Increased risk of mental retardation, sterility, and emotional disturbances.

*A few cases with other karyotypes, including several types of mosaicism, have also been described. Sterility is common to most.

DIFFERENTIAL DIAGNOSIS OF CERTAIN COMMON SYMPTOMS AND SIGNS*

(See p. 609 for contents.)

ABDOMINAL ENLARGEMENT

Ascites.
Cardiac failure, congestive
Chylous ascites
Cirrhosis, biliary
Cirrhosis, portal
Glomerulonephritis
Hepatitis, viral
Hypoproteinemia
Nephrotic syndrome
Obstruction, hepatic vein
Obstruction, vena cava
Pericarditis, constrictive
Peritonitis
Polyserositis, idiopathic

Tympanites (Meteorism).
Adynamic ileus
Air swallowing
Cystic fibrosis
Fecal impaction
Gastroenteritis
Malabsorption syndrome
Megacolon
Obstruction, intestinal
Peritonitis
Pneumoperitoneum
Septicemia
Tracheo-esophageal fistula
Ulcerative colitis

Neoplasms and Cysts.
Adrenal tumor
Bowel, duplication of
Choledochal cyst
Dermoid cyst
Hepatic cyst
Mesenteric cyst and tumor
Neuroblastoma
Omental cyst
Ovarian cyst or tumor
Pancreatic cyst
Polycystic kidney
Sarcoma, retroperitoneal

Neoplasms and Cysts. (Cont'd.)
Teratoma, retroperitoneal
Urachal cyst
Vitelline duct cyst
Wilms's tumor
Other intra-abdominal tumors

Abdominal Wall Defects.
Inguinal hernia
Musculature, absent
Neoplasms
Omphalocele
Umbilical hernia

Miscellaneous.
Abscess, peritoneal
Adrenal hemorrhage
Bladder distention
Enteritis, regional
Fecal impaction
Gastric dilatation
Hepatomegaly
Hydrocolpos
Hydronephrosis
Hydrops of the gallbladder
Intussusception
Megacolon
Obstruction, intestinal
Pregnancy
Splenomegaly
Volvulus

CONVULSIONS AND/OR COMA

Hypoxia.
Anesthesia
Asphyxia
Breath-holding spells
Cardiac disease
Pulmonary hypertension
Respiratory diseases
Respiratory failure

---

*Adapted from Green and Richmond, Berkowitz, Douthwaite, MacBryde, Matousek, Nellhaus, and other sources.

CNS Degenerative Diseases.

Cerebromacular degenerative disease

Encephalopathies, demyelinizing

Gaucher's disease, infantile

Leukodystrophy (Krabbe)

Leukodystrophy, metachromatic

Niemann-Pick disease

Schilder's disease

Sclerosis, diffuse

Spinocerebellar degenerative diseases (Friedreich's ataxia, etc.)

Tay-Sachs disease

CNS Tumors.

Epilepsy.

Akinetic (drop) seizure

Cataplexy

Convulsive equivalent

Focal

Grand mal

Infantile spasm

Motor and sensory seizure

Myoclonic seizure

Narcolepsy

Petit mal

Psychomotor seizure

Cerebrovascular Disease.

Aneurysm, ruptured cerebral artery

Embolus, cerebral

Embolus, fat

Encephalopathy, hypertensive

Glomerulonephritis with encephalopathy

Hematoma, extradural

Hematoma, subdural

Hemiplegia, acute infantile

Hemorrhage with intracranial tumor

Hemorrhage with pertussis

Hemorrhage, parenchymal

Hemorrhage, subarachnoid

Hemorrhage, other intracranial

Thrombosis of cerebral vessels

Heart disease, congenital

Occlusion, cerebral vein

Sickle cell anemia

Cerebrovascular Disease.

(Cont'd.)

Thrombosis, platelet

Thrombus, cerebral

Vasospasm

Venous occlusion with severe dehydration

Hyperpyrexia. (See Fever, Chapter 2.)

Febrile convulsion

Heat stroke

Infections.

Abscess, intracranial

Botulism

Encephalitis

Encephalopathy, pertussis

Infectious disease, other acute

Infectious mononucleosis

Meningitis

Panencephalitis, subacute sclerosing

Pertussis

Poliomyelitis

Rabies

Shigellosis

Syphilis

Tetanus

Toxoplasmosis

Metabolic.

Acidosis

Adrenal insufficiency

Aminoacidurias, other

Antidiuretic hormone, inappropriate

Diabetic ketoacidosis

Histidinemia

Homocystinuria

Hypercalcemia

Hypernatremia

Hyperosmolarity

Hyperuricemia

Hyperventilation

Hypocalcemia

Hypoparathyroidism

Rickets

Steatorrhea, chronic

Tetany of newborn

Tetany, postacidotic

Hypoglycemia

Hypomagnesemia

Metabolic. (Cont'd.)
Hyponatremia
Liver insufficiency
Maple syrup urine disease
Phenylketonuria
Pyridoxine deficiency and
dependency
Renal insufficiency
Water intoxication

Poisons and Drugs.
Alcohol
Anticonvulsants
Antihistamines
Boric acid
Camphor
Carbon monoxide
Carbon tetrachloride and
other hydrocarbons
Diamthazole (Asterol®)
Drug addiction
Drug withdrawal
Encephalopathy, toxic
Ether anesthesia
Gasoline
Glue sniffing
Insecticides
Kerosene
Metals, heavy (lead, mercury,
arsenic, thallium)
Plants, poisonous
Pyrethrum
Renal insufficiency
Salicylates
Sedatives
Sodium fluoride
Strychnine
Sympathomimetic drugs
"Tranquilizers"
Water intoxication

**Postinfectious and Post-
immunization.**
Ataxia, acute cerebellar
Encephalopathy, after small-
pox vaccine
Myelitis, postinfectious
Postpertussis vaccine en-
cephalopathy

Trauma to Brain.
Concussion or contusion
Hematoma, epidural
Hematoma, parenchymal
Hematoma, subdural

Narcolepsy.

Miscellaneous.
Anaphylaxis
Ataxia telangiectasia
Bloch-Sulzberger's disease
Cerebral palsy
Cyst, intracranial
Effusions, subdural
Encephalopathy, hemorrhagic
Encephalopathy, toxic, with
systemic disease
Hemiplegia, acute infantile
Hydrocephalus
Kernicterus
Landry-Guillain-Barré
syndrome
Lupus erythematosus
Myelitis, transverse
Shock
Sturge-Weber disease
Von Recklinghausen's dis-
ease

DIARRHEA OF INFANCY
(SEVERE)

Infectious Diseases.
Enteric infestations
Infections adjacent to intes-
tine
Monilial enteritis
Other bacterial infections
Staphylococcal enteritis
Viral infections

Anatomic Abnormalities.
Blind loops
Fistula
Hirschsprung's disease
Stenosis of bowel
Vagotomy

Allergy and Intolerance.
Celiac disease
Cystic fibrosis
Disaccharide intolerance
Galactose intolerance
Glucose intolerance
Milk protein sensitivity

Endocrine.
Addison's disease
Adrenogenital syndrome
Neural crest tumors
Thyrotoxicosis

Deficiencies.
Abetalipoproteinemia
Agammaglobulinemia
Copper deficiency
Kwashiorkor
Magnesium deficiency
Vitamin deficiencies

Miscellaneous.
Acrodermatitis enteropathica
Altered intestinal flora
Darrow-Gamble syndrome
Exudative enteropathy
Hyperacidity
Sprue
Ulcerative colitis

FAILURE TO THRIVE
AND/OR SHORT STATURE

Skeletal Abnormalities.
Chondrodystrophia calcifi-
cans congenita
Chondrodystrophy
Congenital defects, other
Diaphysial dysplasia
Hunter's syndrome
Hurler's syndrome
Morquio's syndrome
Osteochondritis
Osteogenesis imperfecta
Osteopetrosis
Rickets, all types
Spinal diseases

Nutritional Disturbances.
Diabetes, poorly controlled
Disaccharidase deficiency
Fructose intolerance
Gastrointestinal disease,
chronic (regional enter-
itis, megacolon, etc.)
Intrauterine malnutrition
Malabsorption syndrome
Postnatal malnutrition
Psychologic anorexia

**Central Nervous System
Abnormalities.**
Cerebral abnormalities
Cerebral damage
Diencephalic syndrome
Down's syndrome
Hydranencephaly

**Central Nervous System
Abnormalities.** (Cont'd.)
Hypothalamic lesions
Laurence-Moon-Biedl
syndrome
Schilder's disease
Subdural hematoma

Endocrine Disturbances.
Adrenal insufficiency
Cushing's syndrome
Diabetes mellitus
Gonadal dysgenesis
Hypopituitarism
Hypothalamic lesions
Hypothyroidism
Pseudohypoparathyroidism

Metabolic Diseases.
Aminoacidurias
De Toni-Fanconi-Debre
syndrome
Galactosemia
Gaucher's disease, infantile
Glycogen storage disease
Hypercalcemia, idiopathic
Hypophosphatasia
Poisonings (vitamin A poi-
soning, acrodynia)
Renal tubular acidosis

Variations of Normal.
Delayed growth, normal
Dwarfism, familial
Dwarfism, racial
Genetic ("primordial")
Prematurity
Prenatal (intrauterine dis-
orders; low birth
weight infant)

**Other Unclassified Types of
Dwarfism.**
"Bird-headed dwarf"
Bloom's syndrome
Cornelia de Lange syndrome
Leprechaunism
Progeria
Progeroid syndrome
Rubinstein-Taybi syndrome
Silver's syndrome
Trisomy 13-15 syndrome
Trisomy 18 syndrome

Diseases of Other Systems.
Acidosis, chronic
Allergies, chronic
Anemia, chronic
Circulatory disorders
Deprivation dwarfism
Hepatic and biliary tract
disease
Infection or infestation,
chronic
Malignant disease
Parental neglect
Pulmonary disease, chronic
Renal disease, chronic
Reticuloendotheliosis

FEVER OF OBSCURE ORIGIN

Infectious Diseases.
Bacterial, mycotic, parasitic,
spirochetal, and viral infec-
tions of various tissues, or-
gans, and systems, including:
Abscess
Alveolar
Appendiceal
Intracranial
Pulmonary
Retropharyngeal
Subphrenic
Acute infectious lympho-
cytosis
Acute yellow atrophy
Amebiasis
Appendicitis
Ascariasis
Bacterial endocarditis
Bronchiectasis
Brucellosis
Cat-scratch fever
Cholangitis
Coccidioidomycosis
Empyema
Encephalitis
Exanthems
Haverhill fever
Hepatitis
Histoplasmosis
Infectious mononucleosis
Influenza
Leptospirosis
Lymphocytosis, acute
Malaria
Mastoiditis

Infectious Diseases. (Cont'd.)
Mediastinitis
Meningitis
Myalgia, epidemic
Myocarditis
Osteomyelitis
Otitis media
Pancreatitis
Perinephric abscess
Poliomyelitis
Psittacosis
Salmonellosis
Septicemia
Shigellosis
Sinusitis
Spinal epidural infections
Spirillum fever
Streptococcal disease
Syphilis
Torulosis
Toxoplasmosis
Trichinosis
Tuberculosis
Tularemia
Urinary tract infections

**Central Nervous System
Disorders.**
Brain tumors
Convulsive states
Hemorrhage, intracranial
Hypothalamic lesions
Medullary lesions
Third ventricle lesions

Diseases of "Hypersensitization."
Dermatomyositis
Lupus erythematosus
Polyarteritis nodosa
Rheumatic fever
Rheumatoid arthritis
Serum sickness

**Blood Diseases and Neoplastic
Diseases.**
Agranulocytosis
Cervical cord tumors
Ewing's tumor
Hemolytic anemia
Hodgkin's disease
Leukemia
Sickle cell anemia
Transfusion reaction
Other tumors

Dehydration.

Drug Reactions.

Immunizing Reactions.

Hemorrhage, External and Internal.

High Environmental Temperature.

Miscellaneous.
Acute yellow atrophy of liver
Agammaglobulinemia
Bacterial product reaction
Cardiac failure, congestive
Degenerative diseases
Dysautonomia, familial
Ectodermal dysplasia
Etiocholanolone fever
Factitious fevers
Hyperthyroidism
Infantile cortical hyperostosis
Myeloproliferative disorders
Paroxysmal atrial tachycardia
Periodic disease
Psychogenic fever
Regional enteritis
Sarcoidosis
Thyroiditis
Ulcerative colitis
Unknown cause

HEPATOMEGALY

Infectious Diseases.
Amebiasis or amebic abscess
Ascariasis
Brucellosis
Cholangitis due to various organisms
Coxsackievirus infection
Cytomegalic inclusion disease
Echinococcus (hydatid) cyst
Hepatic abscess, pyogenic
Hepatitis, viral (infectious and serum type)
Histoplasmosis
Infectious mononucleosis
Leptospirosis
Rubella syndrome
Septicemia
Syphilis

Infectious Diseases. (Cont'd.)
Toxoplasmosis
Tuberculosis
Visceral larva migrans

Blood Disorders and Neoplastic Diseases.
Erythroblastosis fetalis
Hemolytic anemias
Hepatic tumors, malignant and benign; primary and metastatic
Leukemia
Lymphomas
Myelofibrosis
Neuroblastoma
Sickle cell disease
Other tumors

Vascular Congestion.
Cardiac failure, congestive
Pericarditis, constrictive
Thrombosis of the hepatic vein (Chiari's disease)

Metabolic and Storage Diseases.
Amyloidosis
Cirrhosis of liver
Cystic fibrosis of pancreas
Cystinosis
Diabetes (poorly controlled)
Galactosemia
Gaucher's disease
Glycogen storage disease
Hemochromatosis
Hemosiderosis
Hurler's syndrome
Hyperlipidemia, idiopathic
Infiltration (fatty) due to malnutrition
Letterer-Siwe disease
Lipogranulomatosis
Niemann-Pick disease
Osteoporosis
Porphyria
Vitamin A poisoning
Xanthomatosis

Miscellaneous.
Biliary duct atresia
Choledochal cyst
Cirrhosis, biliary
Cirrhosis, portal
Cysts, congenital

Miscellaneous. (Cont'd.)
Diabetic mothers' offspring
Drugs and toxins
Hemangioma
Hemorrhage
Hepatoma, traumatic
Lupus erythematosus
Macroglobulinemia
Sarcoidosis
Wilson's disease

HYPERTENSION

Renal.
Aneurysm, renal artery
Congenital abnormality
Glomerulonephritis, acute
and chronic
Hemolytic-uremic syndrome
Horseshoe kidney
Hydronephrosis
Hypoplastic kidney
Nephrosis, lower nephron
Obstruction, renal artery
Perinephritis
Polycystic kidney
Pyelonephritis
Tuberculosis
Tumors (e.g., Wilms's)

Cardiovascular.
Aortic insufficiency
Arteriosclerosis
Coarctation of aorta
Ductus arteriosus
Mitral stenosis
Polycythemia vera

Central Nervous System.
Diencephalic disorders
Encephalitis
Increased intracranial
pressure
Poliomyelitis, bulbar
Tumors, hypothalamic or
pontine

Hormonal.
Adrenal tumors
Adrenocortical steroid
therapy
Adrenogenital syndrome

Hormonal. (Cont'd.)
Cushing's syndrome
Diabetes mellitus
Gonadal dysgenesis
Hyperaldosteronism
Hyperthyroidism
Neuroblastoma
Pheochromocytoma

Poisoning.
Acrodynia
Arachnidism
Carbon monoxide
Corticosteroids
Hypercalcemia, idiopathic
Lead poisoning, chronic
Mercury poisoning
Sodium chloride
Sympathomimetic drugs
Thallium
Vitamin D

Miscellaneous.
Angiitis
Dysautonomia
Emotional stress
Hypersensitization diseases
Hypertension, essential or
idiopathic
Licorice ingestion
Polyarteritis nodosa
Porphyria
Post-traumatic

JAUNDICE

Excess Hemolysis.
Erythroblastosis fetalis*
Hemoglobinopathy*
(Bart's, Zurich, etc.)
Hemolytic anemias, congenital*
Hemolytic anemias, acquired*
Pyknocytosis*

Enzyme Deficiency.
Glucose-6-phosphate dehydro-
genase*
Glucuronyl transferase
Cretinism*
Crigler-Najjar disease*
Gilbert's disease*
"Physiologic," of newborn*
Uridine diphosphopyridine*
Wilson's disease

---

*Items that should be considered in infants with jaundice.

Hepatocellular Damage.
Infection
Amebiasis
Ascaris
Cholangitis
Cytomegalic inclusion
disease*
Echinococcus
Hepatitis, congenital*
Hepatitis, infectious
Hepatitis, plasma-cell
Hepatitis, serum
Herpes simplex*
Infectious mononucleosis
Leptospiral infection
Sepsis*
Syphilis*
Toxoplasmosis*
Tuberculosis
Yellow fever
Poisons and drugs
Hydrocarbons (chloroform,
carbon tetrachloride,
etc.)
Metals, heavy
Novobiocin*
Vegetable toxins
Other drugs with competi-
tion with albumin
Heme pigments
Intravenous fat
Salicylates
Sodium glucuronate
Sulfonamides
Other drugs with competi-
tion for conjugating
mechanisms
Adrenocortical steroids*
Caffeine with sodium
benzoate*
Chloramphenicol*
Salicylates*
Sulfonamides*
Vitamin K, water-
soluble*
Other drugs with increased
hemolysis
Synthetic vitamin K*

Biliary Obstruction.
Atresia, biliary*
Cholangitis*
Choledochal cyst*
Cholelithiasis

Biliary Obstruction. (Cont'd.)
Cystic disease of liver*
Extrinsic pressure
Inspissated bile syndrome*
Peritoneal adhesions
Pyloric stenosis*
Tumors of bile ducts
Tumors of liver

Tumors.
Hemangiomas
Hodgkin's disease
Neoplasms, metastatic
Tumors of bile ducts
Tumors of liver

Miscellaneous.
Breast feeding*
Cirrhosis (Laennec's biliary)
Cretinism*
Cystic fibrosis of pancreas
Dubin-Johnson syndrome
Hypoxia in the neonate*
Leukemia, congenital*

LYMPHADENOPATHY

Infection.
Bacterial, mycotic, parasitic,
spirochetal, or viral
infection, including:
Brucellosis
Candidiasis (moniliasis)
Cat-scratch fever
Chickenpox
Coccidioidomycosis
Granulomas, other
Histoplasmosis
Infectious mononucleosis
Leptotrichosis
Measles
Mumps
Mycobacteria, atypical
Rubella
Salmonella infection
Scarlet fever
Septicemia
Sinusitis, chronic
Toxoplasmosis
Tuberculosis
Tularemia
Vaccinia

---

*Items that should be considered in infants with jaundice.

Neoplastic Disorders.
Hodgkin's disease
Leukemia
Lymphosarcoma
Metastases
Neuroblastoma
Tumors, other

Blood Diseases.
Hemolytic anemias
Mediterranean anemia
Sickle cell anemia

Metabolic and Storage Diseases.
Cystinosis
Gaucher's disease
Lipidosis, secondary
Niemann-Pick disease
Reticuloendothelioses

Drug-Induced.
Antithyroids
Hydantoins
Iodides
Mercurials
PAS
Sulfonamides

Miscellaneous.
Eczema
Oculoglandular syndrome
Sarcoidosis
Silicosis

PURPURA

Vascular Abnormality.
Anaphylactoid purpura
Ehlers-Danlos syndrome
Infections
    Congenital syphilis*
    Cytomegalic inclusion
        disease*
    Diphtheria
    Exanthems
    Meningococcus
    Rickettsial disease
    Sepsis*
    Toxoplasmosis*
    Typhoid fever
Letterer-Siwe disease

Vascular Abnormality. (Cont'd.)
Metabolic disease
    Cushing's disease
    Diabetes
    Uremia
Osteogenesis imperfecta
Poisons and drugs*
Scurvy
Steroids
Telangiectasia, hereditary*
Trauma
Von Willebrand's syndrome

Thrombocytopenia.
After exchange transfusion
Aldrich's syndrome
Allergy
Aplastic anemia
Coagulation, intravascular*
Cytomegalic inclusion disease*
Drug-induced*
Gaucher's disease
Hemangiomatosis*
Hypersplenism
Infections*
Irradiation
Isoimmunization of newborn*
Leukemia
Lipid storage disease
Neonatal*
Neuroblastoma
Niemann-Pick disease
Poisons and toxins*
Postinfection
Systemic disease
Thrombocytopenic purpura,
    congenital*
Thrombocytopenic purpura,
    idiopathic
Thrombotic thrombocyto-
    penic purpura
Tumors, other
Xanthomatosis

Qualitative Platelet Abnormalities.

**Congenital Hereditary Plasma
    Coagulation Defects.**
    (See Table 17-1.)

**Acquired Plasma Coagulation
    Defects.** (See Table 17-1.)

Fibrinogen Deficiency.

*Should be considered in neonatal period.

SEXUAL PRECOCITY

Complete ("True") Precocious Puberty.

Constitutional (functional or
 idiopathic)
Cerebral
 Cystic arachnoiditis
 Encephalopathy, degenera-
 tive
 Hydrocephalus, internal
 Hypothalamic lesions
 (hamartomas, hyper-
 plasia, congenital mal-
 formations, tumors)
 McCune-Albright syndrome
 Pineal or corpora quadri-
 gemina tumors
 Postencephalitis
 Postmeningitis
 Toxoplasmosis
 Tuberculoma, C.N.S.
 Tuberous sclerosis
 Tumors near third ventricle
 Von Recklinghausen's disease
Drug-induced

Incomplete ("Pseudo") Precocious Puberty.

Adrenogenital syndrome
 Adrenocortical hyperplasia
 Adrenocortical tumors
Drug-induced sexual pre-
 cocity (heterosexual
 and isosexual)
Gonadal tumors
 Tumors of the ovaries
 Chorio-epithelioma
 Dysgerminoma
 Follicle cysts
 Granulosa cell tumor
 Luteoma
 Teratoma
 Theca cell tumor
 Tumors of the testes
 Ectopic adrenal tissue
 Interstitial cell
 Teratoma
Premature pubarche (pre-
 mature adrenarche)
Premature thelarche (pre-
 mature gynarche)

Miscellaneous.

Down's syndrome (rare)
Hypothyroidism
Laurence-Moon-Biedl
 syndrome
Presacral teratoma
Primary liver cell tumors
 With disturbed androgen
 metabolism
 With elevated gonado-
 tropins
Silver's syndrome

SPLENOMEGALY

Infectious Diseases.

Brucellosis
Common communicable
 diseases
Coxsackieviruses
Cytomegalic inclusion
 disease
Hepatitis (infectious and
 serum)
Histoplasmosis
Infectious mononucleosis
Rubella syndrome
Salmonella infections
Syphilis
Toxoplasmosis, congenital
Tuberculosis
Tularemia

Vascular Congestion.

Cardiac failure, congestive
Cirrhosis of the liver
Pericarditis, constrictive
Thrombosis, hepatic vein
 (Chiari's disease)
Thrombosis, splenic or
 portal vein

Blood Disorders and Neoplastic Diseases.

Erythroblastosis fetalis
Hemoglobinopathies, other
Hemolytic anemia, congenital
 and acquired
Hodgkin's disease
Hypersplenism
Iron deficiency anemia
Leukemia
Lymphosarcoma
Mediterranean anemia

Blood Disorders and Neoplastic Diseases. (Cont'd.)
Myeloproliferative disorders
Sickle cell anemia
Thrombocytopenic purpura

Metabolic and Storage Diseases.
Amyloidosis
Cystinosis
Galactosemia
Gaucher's disease
Hemosiderosis
Hurler's syndrome
Hyperlipidemia, idiopathic familial
Letterer-Siwe disease
Niemann-Pick disease
Porphyria
Xanthomatosis

Miscellaneous.
Cystic fibrosis
Cysts
Hemangioma
Hemorrhage, subcapsular
Lupus erythematosus
Osteopetrosis
Rheumatoid arthritis
Sarcoidosis
Serum sickness
Splenic abscess
Waldenström's macroglobulinemia

VOMITING

Central Nervous System Disorders.
Abscess, intracranial
Cerebral edema
Concussion
Effusion, subdural
Encephalitis
Epilepsy
Hematoma, subdural
Hemorrhage, intracranial
Hydrocephalus
Meningitis
Migraine
Pseudotumor cerebri
Tumors, intracranial

Infections.
Gastrointestinal
Bacterial
Fungal
Granulomatous
Parasitic
Viral
Systemic

Obstructive Mechanical Gastrointestinal Disorders.
Adhesive bands
Atresia, esophageal
Atresia, intestinal
Bowel, duplication of
Bowel, malrotation of
Hernia, diaphragmatic
Hernia, incarcerated or strangulated
Hirschsprung's disease
Imperforate anus
Intussusception
Meconium ileus
Meconium plug
Pancreas, annular
Pyloric stenosis
Stenosis, intestinal
Volvulus

Metabolic.
Acidosis
Hypercalcemia
Hypoadrenalism
Hypocalcemia
Hypoglycemia
Hypopotassemia
Renal insufficiency

Diseases of Other Systems.

Poisons and Drugs.
Ammonia
Bleaches
Boric acid
Digitalis
Iron
Lead poisoning
Lye
Petroleum distillates
Salicylates
Theophylline

Miscellaneous.
Celiac disease
Cyclic vomiting

Miscellaneous. (Cont'd.)
Equilibrium disturbances
Foreign bodies
Gastrointestinal allergy
Hemorrhagic diseases
Hyperpyrexia

Mesenteric vascular
  occlusion
Motion sickness
Psychogenic vomiting
Rumination
Shock

Index*

*See Appendix (p. 609) for alphabetical listing of drugs, normal blood chemistry values, and miscellaneous normal values not listed in the Index.